BOTTICELLI REIMAGINED

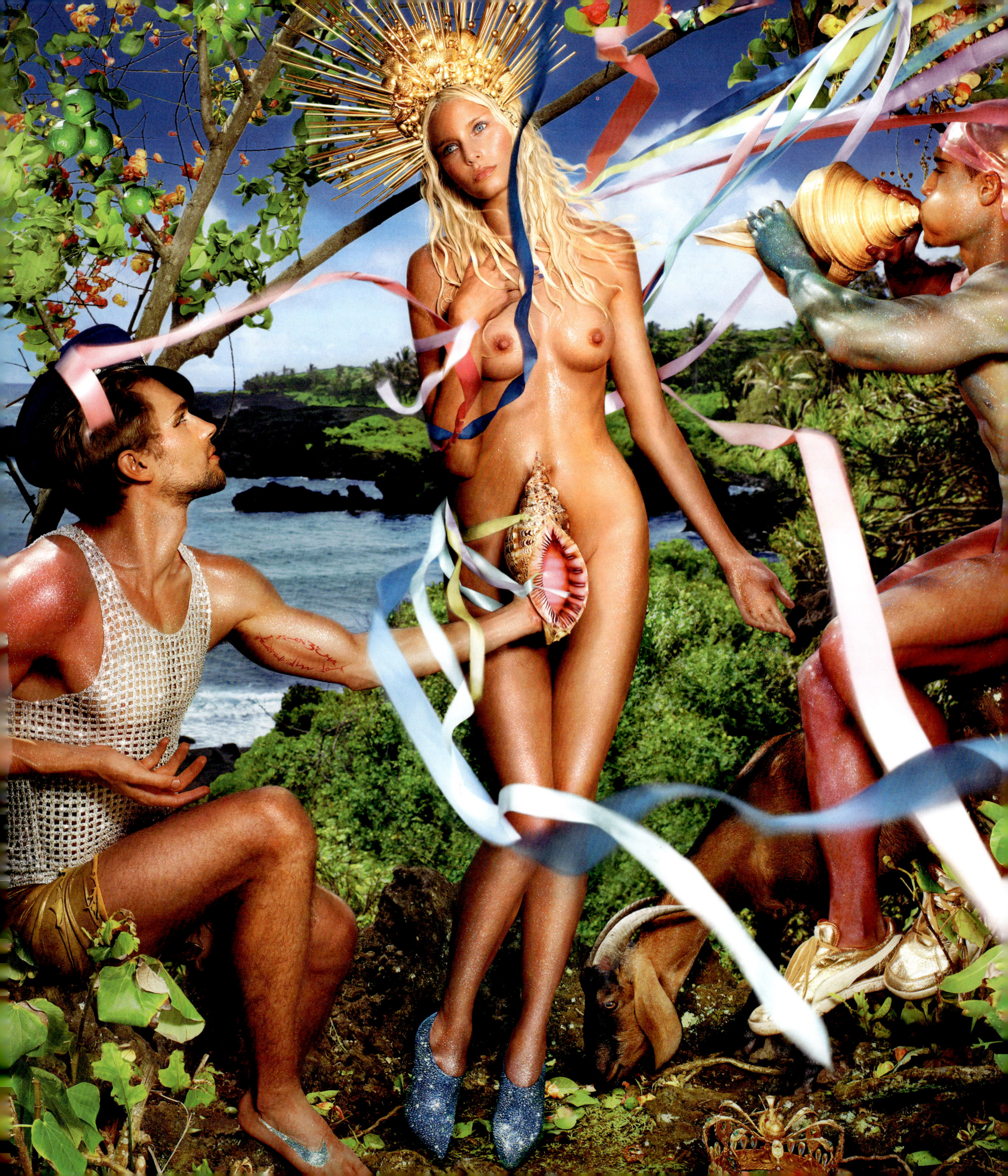

V&A Publishing

Mark Evans and Stefan Weppelmann

with Ana Debenedetti and Ruben Rebmann
and Mary McMahon and Gabriel Montua

BOTTICELLI REIMAGINED

Contents

Sponsor's Foreword

Botticelli Reimagined is essentially a story of impact and innovation. From his early days to modern times, this landmark exhibition explores how 'Sandro' Botticelli has been a source of inspiration for many, influencing the arts, business and even manufacturing.

It was this sense of innovation, one of the four core values of Societe Generale Group, that inspired us to be lead sponsor of this exhibition. Our sponsorship goes hand-in-hand with our long-term support for the arts, dating back 150 years, and with our commitment to championing contemporary art. Also, of course, our support is part of a decade-long relationship with the V&A, which itself was founded as a platform for contemporary art and design, and is an innovator through exhibitions of this type.

We at Societe Generale sincerely hope you will take as much as we have away from this wonderful exhibition, namely that tradition alongside innovation can truly inspire great things.

IAN FISHER
UK Country Head

SOCIETE GENERALE

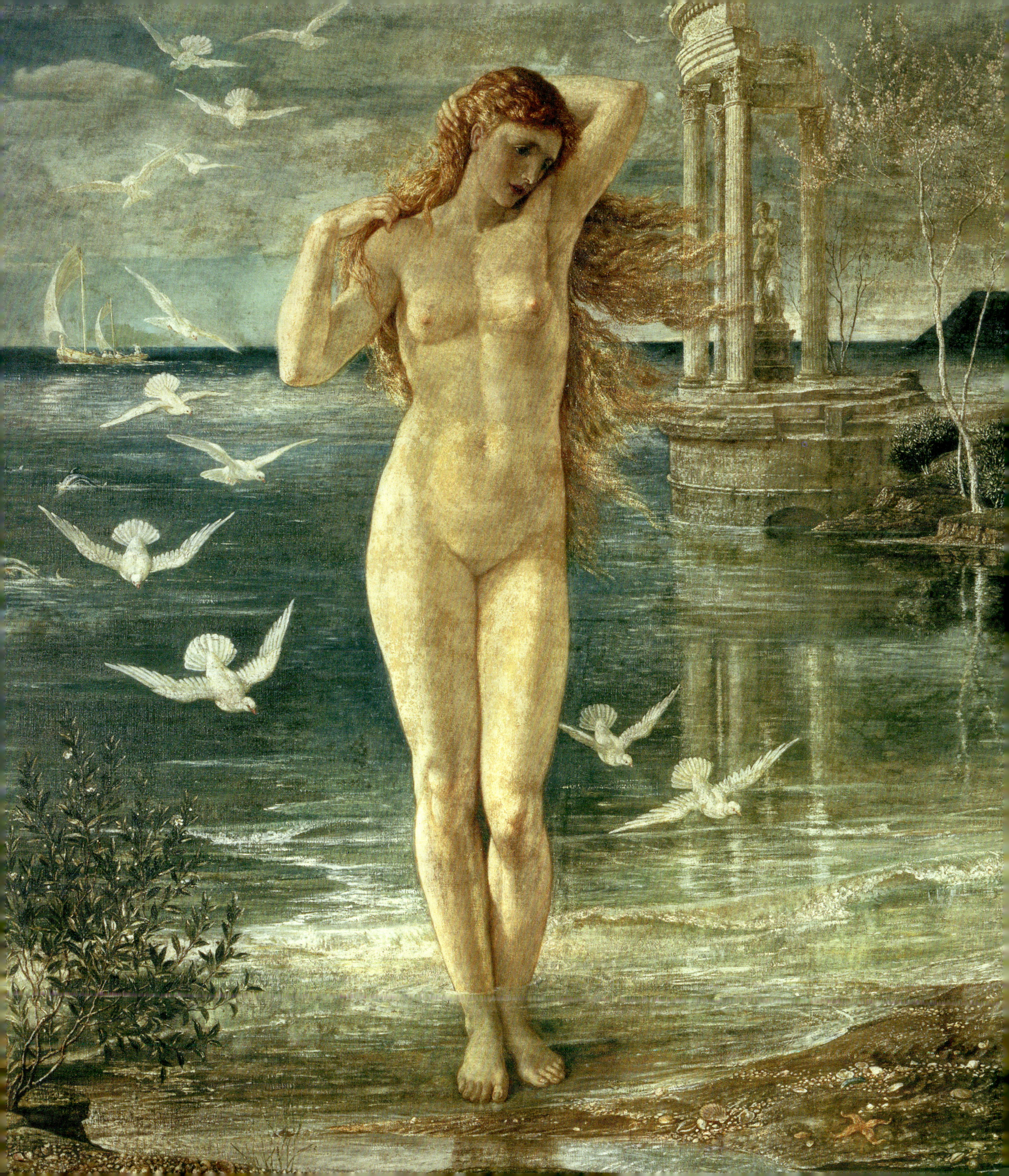

Foreword

Botticelli is unique among the Old Masters. While Leonardo and Michelangelo, Raphael and Dürer have been canonical figures since their own day, he was long lost to posterity. The artist's rediscovery – one hesitates to say 'reinvention' – may be likened to a protracted archaeological excavation by an enthusiastic international fellowship.

The systematic redisplay of the Uffizi was inaugurated during the Enlightenment by its director, Giuseppe Pelli Bencivenni, and a host of early paintings appeared on the market in consequence of the Napoleonic dispersals of pictures. Collected by William Young Ottley, Edward Solly and a few contemporaries, these entered the newly founded public art galleries in Berlin and London, under the guidance of the close friends G.F. Waagen and Sir Charles Eastlake. The Aesthetes Walter Pater and Dante Gabriel Rossetti conjured a 'Botticelli craze' from which the artist was redeemed by the expatriate scholars Herbert Horne, Aby Warburg and Jacques Mesnil. These 'three Florentines' initiated a process of critical reappraisal which was developed by such scholars as Bernard Berenson and his Japanese 'disciple' Yukio Yashiro and has been continued to the present by art historians and curators including Ronald Lightbown at the V&A.

Botticelli was remarkably gifted and versatile; his literally iconic images of the Virgin and Child defined the subject for a generation, while his mythological paintings reintegrated classical form and subject matter. Late in life he negotiated the abrupt change in the political and spiritual climate of Florence ushered in by Savonarola's notorious 'bonfire of the vanities'. In his lifetime, Botticelli's goddess of love in the *Birth of Venus* (1482–5) had already acquired the autonomous life as a replicable image, which in our own day makes it an endlessly quotable metaphor for youth and beauty, the chic and exclusive, or even art itself.

How we understand a work of art is determined by what we know and what we see. As the art critic John Berger memorably observed: 'Today we see the art of the past as nobody saw it before … all paintings are contemporary. Hence the immediacy of their testimony.'

Loan exhibitions would be impossible without the generosity of lenders. We are correspondingly grateful to the artists, private individuals and institutions from

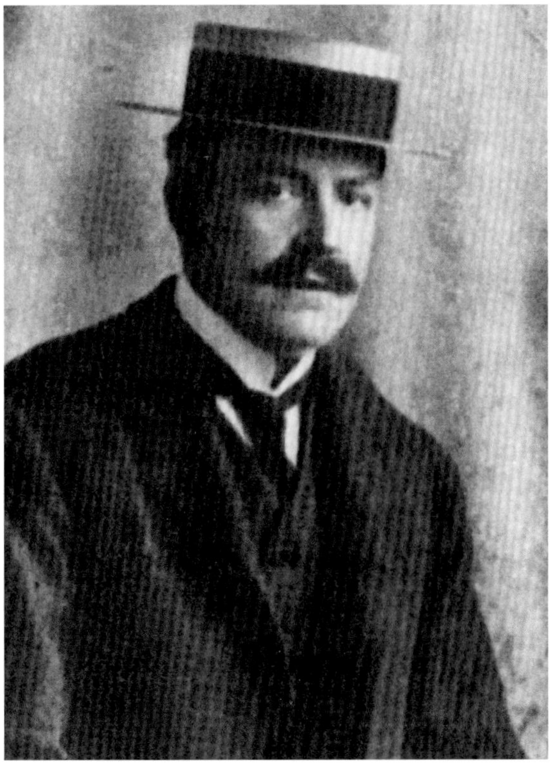

Herbert Horne (1864–1916)

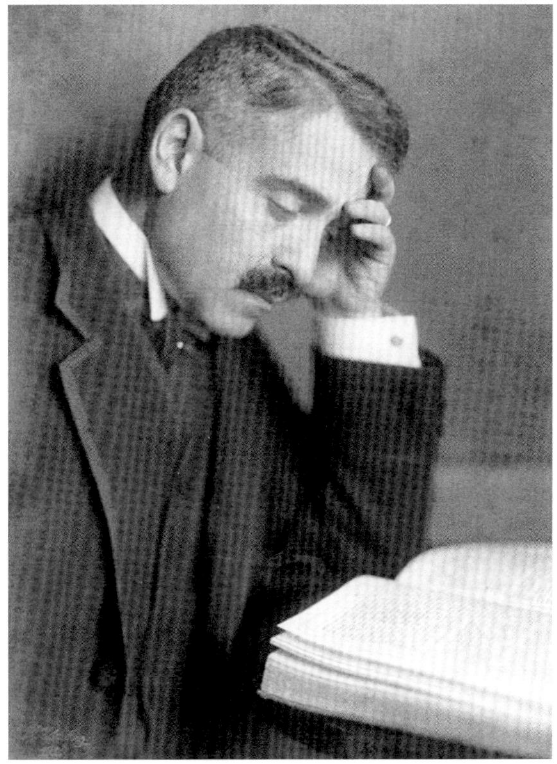

Aby Warburg (1866–1929)

three continents whose loans have made possible this re-interpretation of Botticelli's work and legacy. We sincerely hope they will feel that *Botticelli Reimagined* fully justifies the faith they have shown in lending their treasures to us.

This project began life with a conversation early in 2011 between Mark Evans, Senior Curator of Paintings at the V&A, and Stefan Weppelmann, formerly a Curator at the Staatliche Museen zu Berlin, and now Director of the Gemäldegalerie at the Kunsthistorisches Museum in Vienna. They have led this joint project for five years with their co-curators Ana Debenedetti and Ruben Rebmann, in collaboration with Stephen Calloway, Mary McMahon and Gabriel Montua. Our thanks are also due to the international team of scholars that has provided advice, and contributed essays to the supporting publication, which is dedicated to the memory of two great art historians Herbert Horne and Aby Warburg.

Exhibitions on Botticelli are rare, and we hope *Botticelli Reimagined* will challenge preconceptions and demonstrate that the art of the past is a vital force for the present.

MARTIN ROTH
Director of the
Victoria and Albert Museum,
London

MICHAEL EISSENHAUER
Director General of the
Staatliche Museen zu Berlin
– Preußischer Kulturbesitz

Introduction

ANA DEBENEDETTI
MARK EVANS
RUBEN REBMANN
STEFAN WEPPELMANN

Botticelli is one of a mere handful of artists whose works are instantly recognizable to a very wide and increasingly global public, and are reproduced in every medium from high fashion to street art. This unwonted celebrity contrasts startlingly with the obscurity from which Botticelli began to emerge around 1815. Since E.H. Gombrich remarked 70 years ago that 'The history of Botticelli's fame has still to be written', scholars have considered the artist's critical fortune in Victorian England, but his wider reception, until now, awaited investigation.[1] Our approach to this subject acknowledges a maxim of the poet T.S. Eliot:

> No … artist of any art, has his complete meaning alone … when a new work of art is created … something … happens simultaneously to all the works of art which preceded … it [is not] preposterous that the past should be altered by the present as much as the present is directed by the past.[2]

Eliot's insight that our perception of the art of the past is conditioned by that of the present is especially pertinent to an artist whose work has been the subject of a complex process of rediscovery and reinvention that mirrors the changing values of posterity. The use, re-use and even abuse of Botticelli's imagery obscure the fact that his persona remains, in large part, an artificial construct.

We lack Botticelli's own views on art, but his near-contemporary, the humanist Leon Battista Alberti, recommended that artists should associate with literary men who could suggest subjects for compositions.[3] The art historian Aby Warburg showed how the representation of beauty and movement in Botticelli's *Primavera* and the *Birth of Venus* relates closely to passages from the poems of the scholar Angelo Poliziano and proposed that Florentine 'festive performances set the characters before the artist's eyes as living, moving beings'.[4] Botticelli's figures typically seem to embody the Renaissance concept of *leggiadria*: 'a certain way of carrying the body, so light and agile that the figure appears to move but to have no weight, bearing itself with the greatest possible lightness.'[5]

Michael Baxandall suggested that the 'period eye' of the artist's contemporaries may have been schooled by the codified movements and gestures of dance to experience Botticelli's work as 'a danced sort of painting'.[6] The relationship between figures in a painting was theorized by Alberti, who defined beauty as 'that reasoned harmony of all the parts within a body, so that nothing may be added, taken away, or altered, but for the worse', and devised rules to achieve it, such as: 'the face in which the surfaces are so joined together that pleasing lights pass gradually into agreeable shadows and there are no sharp angles, we may rightly call … handsome and beautiful.'[7]

Alberti believed pictures should be 'so charming and attractive as to hold the eye … for a long while with a sense of pleasure and emotion'.[8] This could be taken to extremes, as in a 'divine subject' by Leonardo da Vinci, whose owner wished to 'kiss her without misgivings' until 'his conscience prevailed over his lust'.[9]

Giorgio Vasari remarked of one of Botticelli's paintings: 'it is not possible to describe the beauty that Sandro depicted … that reveal[s] to us the perfection of his skills. … This is truly a most admirable work, and executed so beautifully, whether in colouring, drawing, or composition, that every craftsman at the present day stands in a marvel thereat.'[10] However, the priority which Vasari accorded to the 'perfection' of Michelangelo and Raphael in his *Lives of the Artists* (1st ed. 1550, 2nd ed. 1568) stigmatized Botticelli and his contemporaries as outmoded. For over two centuries the artist was dimly remembered, mainly as an illustrator of Dante's *Divine Comedy* (cats 144–53).[11] Only the rejection by the generation of 1789 of the inherited culture of the *Ancien Régime* for its perceived lack of freshness and sincerity enabled a positive reappraisal of the so-called 'primitives' of the fifteenth century. This was underpinned by the insistence of the German historians J.G. von Herder, Carl Friedrich von Rumohr and Karl Schnaase that the art of the past should be understood in light of the values of its own time rather than judged by the standards of the present.[12]

The Napoleonic secularization of religious houses dispersed countless works of art throughout Europe, and numerous fifteenth-century pictures by Botticelli and others were assembled by the English merchant resident in Berlin, Edward Solly, who sold them in 1821–8 to the Prussian state.[13] Early paintings remained inexpensive and became popular with a few middle-class collectors, including William Roscoe in Liverpool, Sulpiz and Melchior Boisserée in Cologne, and the German expatriate in London, Carl Aders. The subsequent arrival of such 'primitives' in the newly-founded public art galleries in Berlin and London did not signal a revolution in taste, as they were initially admitted to help visitors 'still better to appreciate the great masters' of the High Renaissance, as the Prussian curator G.F. Waagen explained in 1836.[14]

In 1848 the first early Italian panels to enter the National Gallery in London, Lorenzo Monaco's *Adoring Saints*, influenced the inaugural Pre-Raphaelite painting, *Isabella* by Sir John Everett Millais.[15] A reviewer thought this subject from Boccaccio 'a very clever copy of that ancient style' whose 'absence of perspective and aerial distance … carries us back to the period of aspiring but imperfect art'.[16]

Commentators from John Flaxman in 1787 to Jacob Burckhardt in 1855 especially admired Botticelli's *Madonna del Magnificat* (see cat. 117), and Walter Pater shocked many in 1870 by equating the artist's characterization of the Mother of God with his depiction of the goddess of love.[17] John Ruskin agreed that Botticelli 'understood the thoughts of Heathens and Christians equally, and could in a measure paint both Aphrodite and the Madonna'.[18] Nevertheless, he regretted purchasing in 1877 a *Virgin and Child* attributed to Botticelli (cat. 127), which he found 'so ugly that I've not dared to show it to a human soul'.[19]

More seminal was the purchase a decade earlier by Ruskin's protégé and Millais's fellow Pre-Raphaelite, Dante Gabriel Rossetti, of Botticelli's *Portrait of a Lady known as Smeralda Bandinelli* (cat. 162).[20] Rossetti believed the sitter was also the model for the figure of Venus in *Primavera*, which he celebrated in the sonnet 'For Spring, by Sandro Botticelli', published in 1881.[21] The Florentine artist beguiled a generation of British artists, from Edward Burne-Jones to Aubrey Beardsley, while his flowing draperies encouraged the growing fashion among feminists, hygienists and devotees of the Aesthetic movement for 'Pre-Raphaelitism in Dress', as it was characterized in 1878 by the influential arbiter of taste Mary Haweis.[22] Botticelli's impact on Arts and Crafts décor is manifest in the tapestry after *Primavera* woven by Morris and Co. in 1893–6 for the poet Wilfrid Blunt and the large lead-glazed earthenware 'Angel Panel' after the *Mystic Nativity* modelled in 1900 by Edmund Rathbone for the Birkenhead Della Robbia Pottery.[23]

The Botticelli craze was also apparent at the French Academy in Rome, where Claude Debussy was inspired in 1887 by a reproduction of *Primavera* and a picture based on it by his fellow pensioner Marcel Baschet to compose the musical suite *Printemps*.[24] A full-size tapestry of *Primavera* was woven by the Gobelins manufactory, Paris, in 1902–6 as a gift for King Edward VII.[25] Around 1900 the 'spiritist' artist Fernand Desmoulin claimed to have made drawings while possessed by a spirit which proclaimed 'I am Botticelli', while the allusions to the Florentine in Marcel Proust's *In Search of Lost Time* were mediated through a copy of the *Birth of Venus* by Gustave Moreau and the writings of John Ruskin.[26]

At the turn of the nineteenth and twentieth centuries art historians became increasingly conscious of the pitfalls of projecting their own concerns onto the art of the past, and sought instead to retrieve its historic values. Warburg and his friend Herbert Horne both quoted Rossetti's sonnet 'For Spring, by Sandro Botticelli' in their books on the artist as if it were a talisman, and the former wryly observed in 1898 that 'The minority of Sandro's admirers … who would rather understand and follow him than sentimentally admire him … gather in front of *The Realm of Venus*'.[27]

Warburg hoped his research would 'have value for psychological aesthetics' by showing 'an emerging sense of the aesthetic act of "empathy" as a determinant of style'.[28] This concept, coined by the German philosopher Robert Vischer, also fascinated an English bluestocking resident in Florence, Violet Paget known as Vernon Lee, who tried in a purely empirical way to measure her physiological response to paintings.[29] Lee's research approached the influential concept of 'tactile values' advanced by her neighbour, the American art historian Bernard Berenson, who exhorted his readers:

> Look, for instance, at Botticelli's 'Venus Rising from the Sea' … the tactile imagination is roused to a keen activity … almost as life heightening as music … in the goddess' mane-like tresses of hair fluttering to the wind … the quintessence of all that is pleasurable to our imagination of touch and of movement.[30]

Burckhardt's student Heinrich Wölfflin also emphasized the formal values of *Primavera*.[31]

This preoccupation with empathy, rhythm and movement extended far beyond art history. In 1902 the pioneer of modern dance Isadora Duncan performed 'La Primavera' at Munich, wearing a dress with a floral print like that of Botticelli's 'Flora'. A critic admired how:

> … with wreathing arms and undulating body and bare, twinkling feet, she endeavours to present … the vibrant atmosphere, the pulsing ecstatic quickening of all of life, the langubrous [*sic*], delicious dolce far niente of this marvelous season as she reads it in Botticelli's masterpiece.[32]

Duncan's performance was attended by the German dancer, Rita Sacchetto, whose 'Tanzbilder' (Dance Pictures), performed at New York in 1910, included 'Der Tanz der Simonetta' narrating the death and mourning of Simonetta Vespucci.[33] Her 'Botticelli pantomime' may have incorporated recent research on *Primavera* by Warburg and Emil Jacobsen.[34] The 'concert tableaux' performed by the Irish-American society beauty Hazel, Lady Lavery, also included one in 1913 when she dressed as Botticelli's 'Flora' (cat. 45).[35]

Primavera yielded its primacy following the international exposure of the *Birth of Venus* as the centrepiece to the spectacular loan exhibitions of Italian Old Masters orchestrated by the Fascist dictator Benito Mussolini.[36] The *Birth of Venus* was more

FIG. 1
Spanish artist Adriàn Pino Olivera in front of the *Birth of Venus*, Galleria degli Uffizi
Photograph by Susanna Mantovani, 22 March 2014

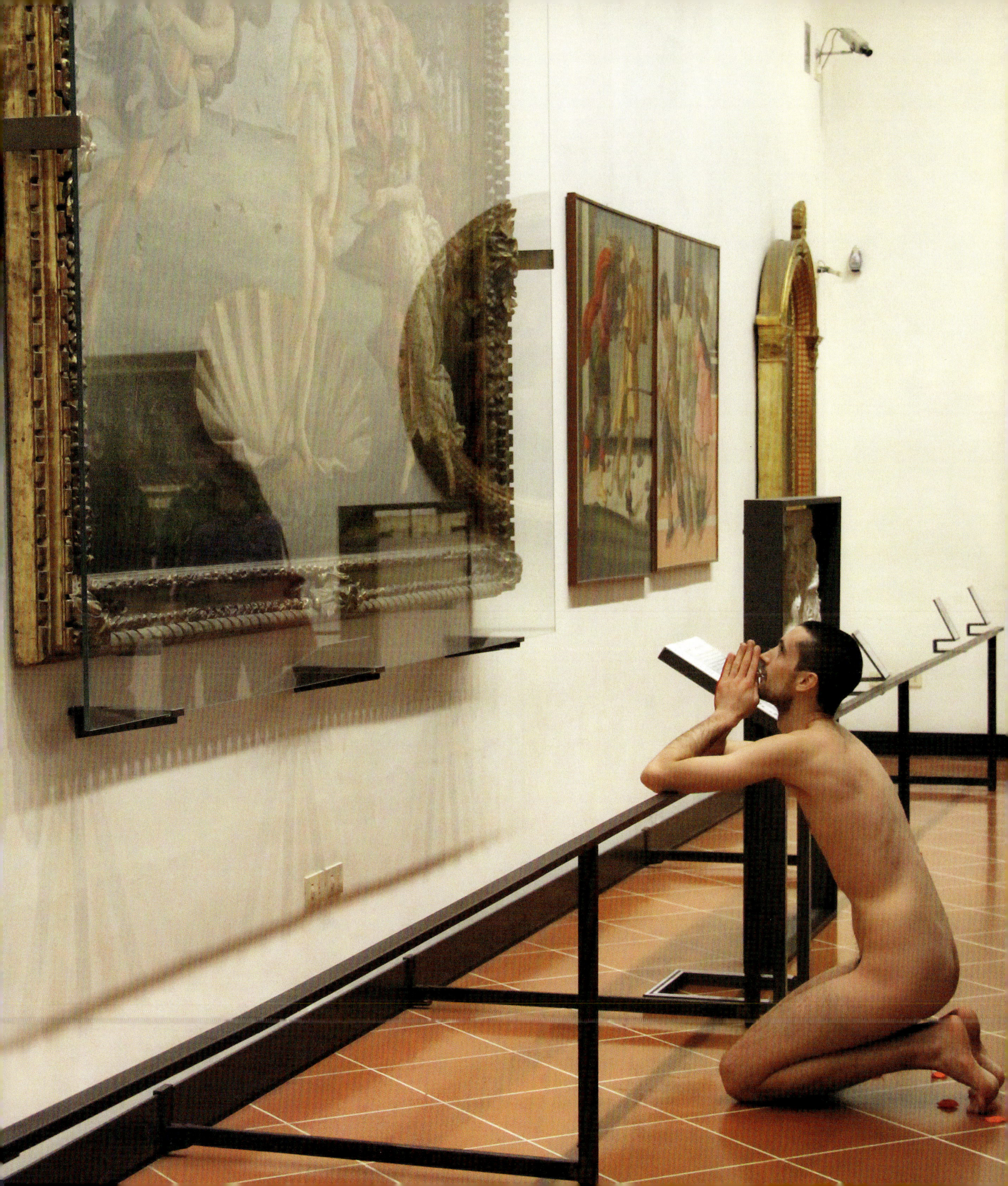

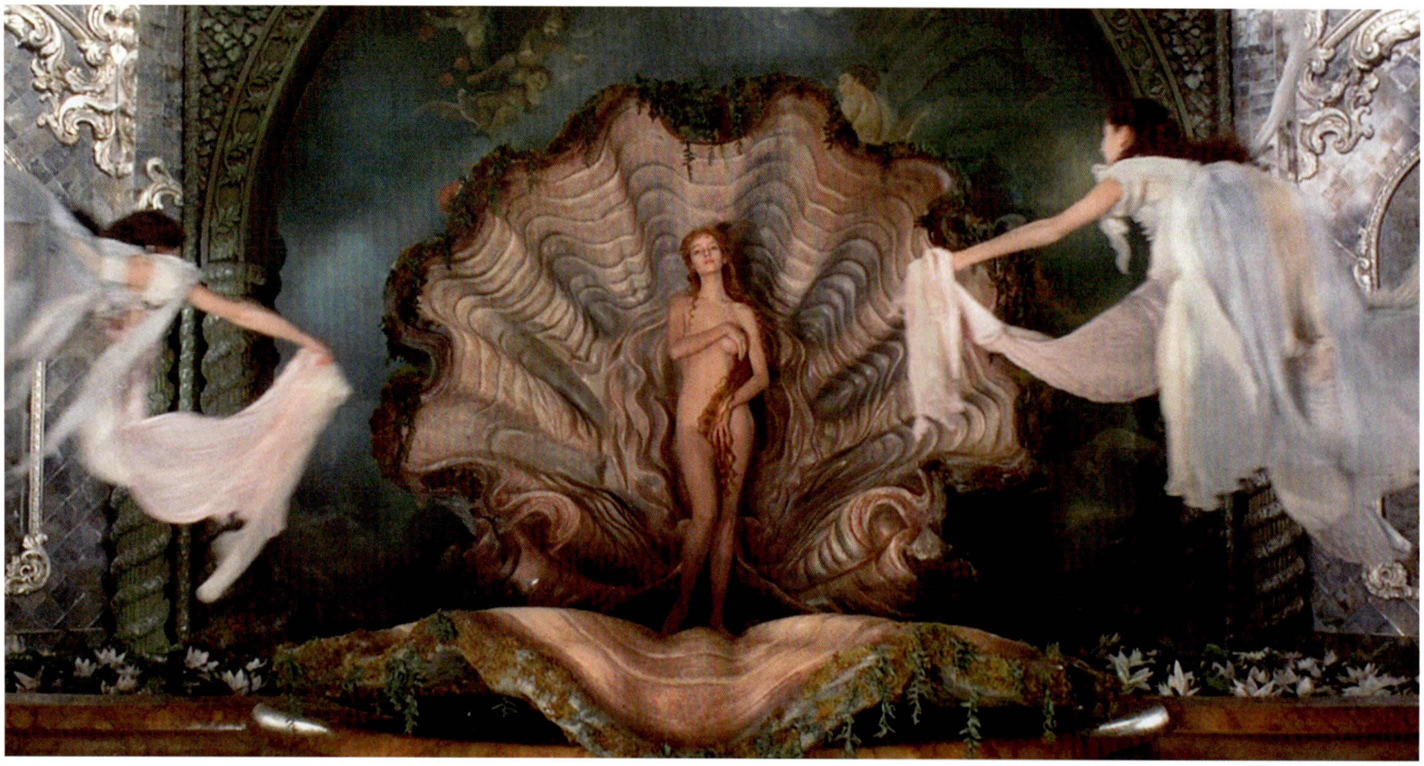

suited to the rigours of transport because its canvas was much lighter and less prone to warp than the thick poplar support of *Primavera*. At the Royal Academy, London, in 1930 the exhibition *Italian Art 1200–1900* was a huge success, with almost 540,000 visitors, a figure nevertheless exceeded by the 650,000 who flocked to see *L'Art Italien de Cimabue à Tiepolo* at the Petit Palais, Paris, in 1935.[37] Cartoonists were alert to the propagandist nature of these shows, although the *Punch* cartoon of a benign 'Benito' introducing a fetching Botticellian allegory of 'L'Arte Italiana' to a grateful John Bull lacks the critical satire of a photomontage in *La Bête noire* depicting the French foreign minister Pierre Laval wearing uniform and jackboots in place of Botticelli's Venus.[38] The *Birth of Venus* was also the principal exhibit in the smaller touring exhibition *Italian Masters Lent by the Royal Italian Government* at San Francisco, Chicago and New York during 1939–40.[39]

This painting's dreamlike quality lent itself to reinterpretation by the Surrealists, including René Magritte, Edward Baird and Salvador Dalí, and it inspired the fashion designer Elsa Schiaparelli (cats 34, 35) as well as the avant-garde film-maker Luciano Emmer.[40] In 1950 the *Birth of Venus* received the imprimatur of inclusion as Botticelli's representative work in what became the best-selling art book of all time, Gombrich's *The Story of Art*, which has appeared in over seven million copies in thirty languages.

Testimony to the picture's hold on the popular imagination ranges from the film sequence in the first James Bond movie, *Dr. No* (1962 fig. 3), in which the bikini-clad actress Ursula Andress emerges from the sea, conch shell in hand, to the cult science-fiction novel by the American fantasy author Philip José Farmer, under the pseudonym Kilgore Trout, *Venus on the Half-Shell* (1975). The latter title was parodied in the large 'Neo-Pop' acrylic painting *Venice on the Half-Shell* (1978) by the Californian muralist Rip Cronk, who recast Venus wearing a tank top, hot pants and thigh-high leg warmers, roller-skating down the boardwalk of Venice Beach, a hip counter-cultural neighbourhood of Los Angeles.[41] The screenwriter and director Terry Gilliam exploited the cinematographic potential of Botticelli's figure in a short animation in a 1969 episode of the TV comedy series *Monty Python's Flying Circus*.[42] It was further developed in the entrance of Venus sequence in Gilliam's movie *The Adventures of Baron Munchausen* (1988), in which the actress Uma Thurman adopts a trio of Botticellian poses resembling, in sequence, the *Birth of Venus* (fig. 2), the draped figure in *Venus and Mars* (fig. 4) and the ideal profile portrait known as 'Simonetta' (cat. 157).[43]

Since Venus re-entered the world of gallery art in 1984 as one of the *Details of Renaissance Paintings* by Andy Warhol (cats 19, 20), Botticelli has provided a mainstay of postmodern appropriation or quotational art, which turns upon the re-use of easily recognizable imagery from the art of the past.[44] In particular, photographic and video artists have explored the archetypal status of his work as embodying a paradigm of beauty and its performative quality.[45] By themselves posing as Botticellian creatures, ORLAN, Ulrike Rosenbach and Cindy Sherman have questioned the sexualization of 'the body beautiful' as a focus for mass-consumption (cats 10, 15, 17, 22, 24). Artists from Asia and the Middle East have similarly engaged with this canonical representative of European high art (cats 4, 8).[46] Over 40 years after the student movement of the 1960s ushered in an array of innovative approaches to art history, the study of Botticelli remains dominated by iconographic and documentary research in the tradition pioneered by Warburg and Horne, mitigated by a growing interest in historiography and material culture.[47] This has prompted a fundamental reconsideration of Botticelli's role as the designer of his studio productions.[48]

Recently, the *Birth of Venus* was one of ten paintings perceived as 'beautiful' used in recent brain-scanning experiments by the neurobiologists Tomohiro Ishizu and Semir Zeki, which demonstrated a distinct response from the part of the brain associated with 'the experience of pleasure and reward, whether real or imagined, and its expectation', leading them to formulate a 'brain-based theory of beauty'.[49] Over five centuries after they were painted, the subtle messages of life, love and lightness encoded into Botticelli's masterpieces continue to address our urgent concerns.

FIG. 2
Uma Thurman as Venus in *The Adventures of Baron Munchausen*, 1988
Directed by Terry Gilliam

FIG. 3
Ursula Andress as Honey Ryder in *Dr. No*, 1962
Directed by Terence Young

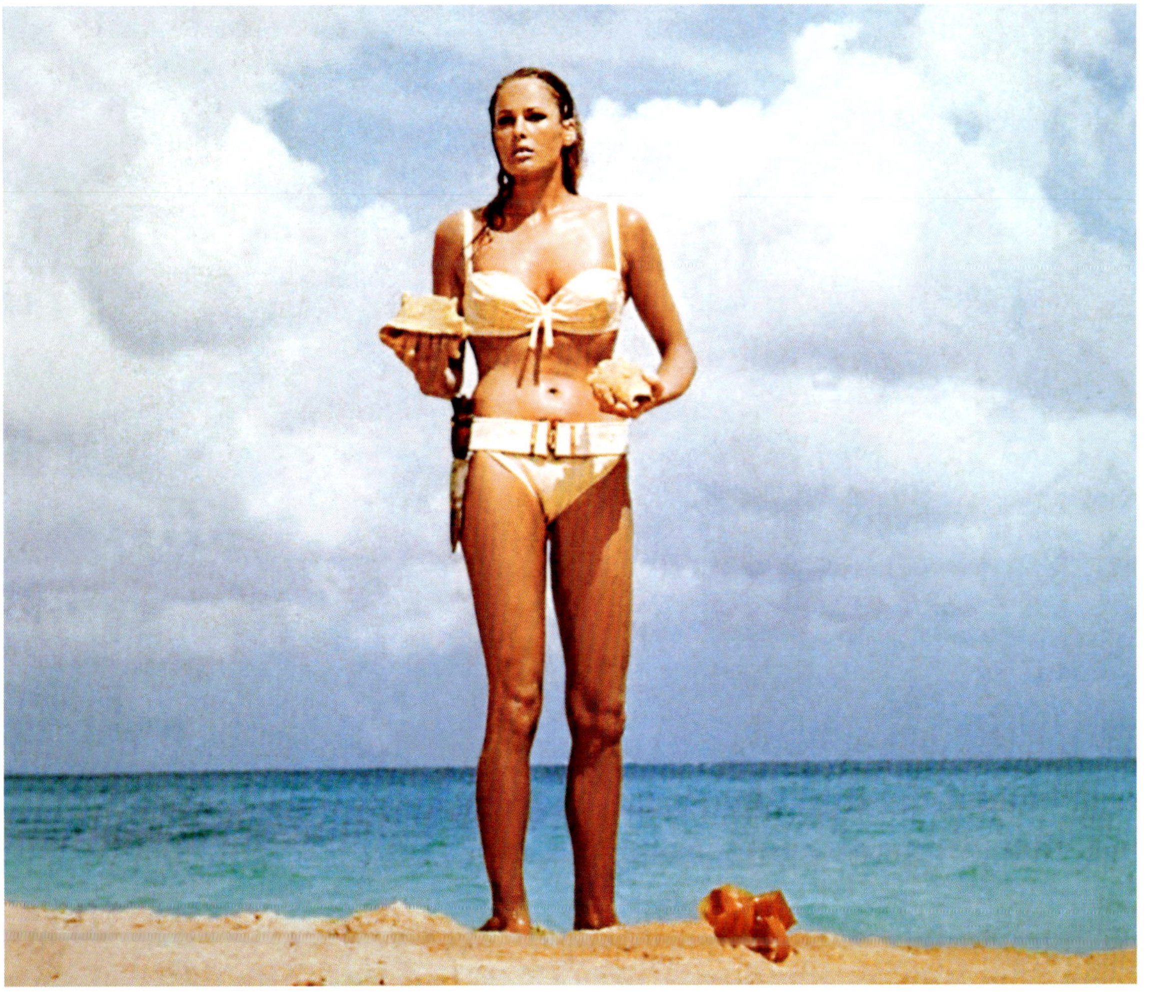

SANDRO BOTTICELLI

LIFE OF SANDRO BOTTICELLI
PAINTER OF FLORENCE (1568)

GIORGIO VASARI (1511–1574)

TRANSLATED BY
GASTON DU C. DE VERE (1912)

AT THE SAME TIME WITH THE ELDER LORENZO DE' MEDICI, THE MAGNIFICENT, WHICH WAS TRULY A GOLDEN AGE FOR MEN OF INTELLECT, THERE ALSO FLOURISHED ONE ALESSANDRO, CALLED SANDRO AFTER OUR CUSTOM, AND SURNAMED DI BOTTICELLO FOR A REASON THAT WE SHALL SEE BELOW. THIS MAN WAS THE SON OF MARIANO FILIPEPI, A CITIZEN OF FLORENCE, WHO BROUGHT HIM UP WITH CARE, AND HAD HIM INSTRUCTED IN ALL THOSE THINGS THAT ARE USUALLY TAUGHT TO CHILDREN BEFORE THEY ARE OLD ENOUGH TO BE APPRENTICED TO SOME CALLING. BUT ALTHOUGH HE FOUND IT EASY TO LEARN WHATEVER HE WISHED, NEVERTHELESS HE WAS EVER RESTLESS, NOR WAS HE CONTENTED WITH ANY FORM OF LEARNING, WHETHER READING, WRITING, OR ARITHMETIC, INSOMUCH THAT HIS FATHER, WEARY OF THE VAGARIES OF HIS SON'S BRAIN, IN DESPAIR APPRENTICED HIM AS A GOLDSMITH WITH A BOON-COMPANION OF HIS OWN, CALLED BOTTICELLO, NO MEAN MASTER OF THAT ART IN HIS DAY.

Now in that age there was a very close connection – nay, almost a constant intercourse – between the goldsmiths and the painters; wherefore Sandro, who was a ready fellow and had devoted himself wholly to design, became enamoured of painting, and determined to devote himself to that. For this reason he spoke out his mind freely to his father, who, recognizing the inclination of his brain, took him to Fra Filippo of the Carmine, a most excellent painter of that time, with whom he placed him to learn the art, according to Sandro's own desire. Thereupon, devoting himself heart and soul to that art, Sandro followed and imitated his master so well that Fra Filippo, growing to love him, taught him very thoroughly, so that he soon rose to such a rank as none would have expected for him.

While still quite young, he painted a figure of Fortitude in the Mercatanzia of Florence, among the pictures of Virtues that were wrought by Antonio and Piero del Pollaiuolo. For the Chapel of the Bardi in S. Spirito at Florence he painted a panel, wrought with diligence and brought to a fine completion, which contains certain olive-trees and palms executed with consummate lovingness. He painted a panel for the Convertite Nuns, and another for those of S. Barnaba. In the tramezzo of the Ognissanti, by the door that leads into the choir, he painted for the Vespucci a S. Augustine in fresco, with which he took very great pains, seeking to surpass all the painters of his time, and particularly Domenico Ghirlandajo, who had made a S. Jerome on the other side; and this work won very great praise, for in the head of that Saint he depicted the profound meditation and acute subtlety that are found in men of wisdom who are ever concentrated on the investigation of the highest and most difficult matters. This picture, as was said in the Life of Ghirlandajo, has this year (1564) been removed safe and sound from its original position.

Having thus come into credit and reputation, he was commissioned by the Guild of Porta Santa Maria to paint in S. Marco a panel with the Coronation of Our Lady and a choir of angels, which he designed and executed very well. He made many works in the house of the Medici for the elder Lorenzo, particularly a Pallas on a device of great branches, which spouted forth fire: this he painted of the size of life, as he did a S. Sebastian. In S. Maria Maggiore in Florence, beside the Chapel of the Panciatichi, there is a very beautiful Pietà with little figures. For various houses throughout the city he painted round pictures, and many female nudes, of which there are still two at Castello, a villa of Duke Cosimo's; one representing the birth of Venus, with those Winds and Zephyrs that bring her to the earth, with the Cupids; and likewise another Venus, whom the Graces are covering with flowers, as a symbol of spring; and all this he is seen to have expressed very gracefully. Round an apartment of the house of Giovanni Vespucci, now belonging to Piero Salviati, in the Via de' Servi, he made many pictures which were enclosed by frames of walnut-wood, by way of ornament and panelling, with many most lively and beautiful figures. In the house of the Pucci, likewise, he painted with little figures Boccaccio's tale of Nastagio degli Onesti in four square pictures of most charming and beautiful workmanship, and the Epiphany in a round picture. For a chapel in the Monastery of Cestello he painted an Annunciation on a panel. Near the side-door of S. Pietro Maggiore, for Matteo Palmieri, he painted a panel with an infinite number of figures– namely, the Assumption of Our Lady, with the zones of Heaven as they are represented, and the Patriarchs, the Prophets, the Apostles, the Evangelists, the Martyrs, the Confessors, the Doctors, the Virgins, and the Hierarchies; all from the design given to him by Matteo, who was a learned and able man. This work he painted with mastery and consummate diligence; and at the foot is a portrait of Matteo on his knees, with that of his wife. But for all that the work is most beautiful, and should have silenced envy, nevertheless there were certain malignant slanderers who, not being able to do it any other damage, said that both Matteo and Sandro had committed therein the grievous sin of heresy. As to whether this be true or false, I cannot be expected to judge; it is enough that the figures painted therein by Sandro are truly worthy of praise, by reason of the pains that he took in drawing the zones of Heaven and in the distribution of figures, angels, foreshortenings, and views, all varied in diverse ways, the whole being executed with good design.

At this time Sandro was commissioned to paint a little panel with figures three-quarters of a braccio in length, which was placed between two doors in the principal faade of S. Maria Novella, on the left as one enters the church by the door in the centre. It contains the Adoration of the Magi, and wonderful feeling is seen in the first old man, who, kissing the foot of Our Lord, and melting with tenderness, shows very clearly that he has achieved the end of his long journey. The figure of this King is an actual portrait of the elder Cosimo de' Medici, the most lifelike and most natural that is to be found of him in our own day. The second, who is Giuliano de' Medici, father of Pope Clement VII, is seen devoutly doing reverence to the Child with a most intent expression, and presenting Him with his offering. The third, also on his knees, appears to be adoring Him and giving Him thanks, while confessing that He is the true Messiah; this is Giovanni, son of Cosimo.

It is not possible to describe the beauty that Sandro depicted in the heads that are therein seen, which are drawn in various attitudes, some in full face, some in profile, some in three-quarter face, others bending down, and others, again, in various manners; with different expressions for the young and the old, and with all the bizarre effects that reveal to us the perfection of his skill; and he distinguished the Courts of the three Kings one from another, insomuch that one can see which are the retainers of each. This is truly a most admirable work, and executed so beautifully, whether in colouring, drawing, or composition, that every craftsman at the present day stands in a marvel thereat. And at that time it brought him such great fame, both in Florence and abroad, that Pope Sixtus IV, having accomplished the building of the chapel of his palace in Rome, and wishing to have it painted, ordained that he should be made head of that work; whereupon he painted therein with his own hand the following scenes–namely, the Temptation of Christ by the Devil, Moses slaying the Egyptian, Moses receiving drink from the daughters of Jethro the Midianite, and likewise fire descending from Heaven on the sacrifice of the sons of Aaron, with certain Sanctified Popes in the niches above the scenes. Having therefore acquired still greater fame and reputation among the great number of competitors who worked with him, both Florentines and men of other cities, he received from the Pope a good sum of money, the whole of which he consumed and squandered in a moment during his residence in Rome, where he lived in haphazard fashion, as was his wont.

Having at the same time finished and unveiled the part that had been assigned to him, he returned immediately to Florence, where, being a man of inquiring mind, he made a commentary on part of Dante, illustrated the Inferno, and printed it; on which he wasted much of his time, bringing infinite disorder into his life by neglecting his work. He also printed many of the drawings that he had made, but in a bad manner, for the engraving was poorly done. The best of these that is to be seen by his hand is the Triumph of the Faith effected by Fra Girolamo Savonarola of Ferrara, of whose sect he was so ardent a partisan that he was thereby induced to desert his painting, and, having no income to live on, fell into very great distress. For this reason, persisting in his attachment to that party, and becoming a Piagnone (as the members of the sect were then called), he abandoned his work; wherefore he ended in his old age by finding himself so poor, that, if Lorenzo de' Medici, for whom, besides many other things, he had done some work at the little hospital in the district of Volterra, had not succoured him the while that he lived, as did afterwards his friends and many excellent men who loved him for his talent, he would have almost died of hunger.

In S. Francesco, without the Porta a San Miniato, there is a Madonna in a round picture by the hand of Sandro, with some angels of the size of life, which was held a very beautiful work. Sandro was a man of very pleasant humour, often playing tricks on his disciples and his friends; wherefore it is related that once, when a pupil of his who was called Biagio had made a round picture exactly like the one mentioned above, in order to sell it, Sandro sold it for six florins of gold to a citizen; then, finding Biagio, he said to him, 'At last I have sold this thy picture; so this evening it must be hung on high, where it will be seen better, and in the morning thou must go to the house of the citizen who has bought it, and bring him here, that he may see it in a good light in its proper place; and then he will pay thee the money.' 'O, my master,' said Biagio, 'how well you have done.' Then, going into the shop, he hung the picture at a good height, and went off. Meanwhile Sandro and Jacopo, who was another of his disciples, made eight caps of paper, like those worn by citizens, and fixed them with white wax on the heads of the eight angels that surrounded the Madonna in the said picture. Now, in the morning, up comes Biagio with his citizen, who had bought the picture and was in the secret. They entered the shop, and Biagio, looking up, saw his Madonna seated, not among his angels, but among the Signoria of Florence, with all those caps. Thereupon he was just about to begin to make an outcry and to excuse himself to the man who had bought it, when, seeing that the other, instead of complaining, was actually praising the picture, he kept silent himself. Finally, going with the citizen to his house, Biagio received his payment of six florins, the price for which his master had sold the picture; and then, returning to the shop just as Sandro and Jacopo had removed the paper caps, he saw his angels as true angels, and not as citizens in their caps. All in a maze, and not knowing what to say, he turned at last to Sandro and said: 'Master, I know not whether I am dreaming, or whether this is true. When I came here before, these angels had red caps on their heads, and now they have not; what does it mean?' 'Thou art out of thy wits, Biagio,' said Sandro; 'this money has turned thy head. If it were so, thinkest thou that the citizen would have bought the picture?' 'It is true,' replied Biagio, 'that he said nothing to me about it, but for all that it seemed to me strange.' Finally, all the other lads gathered round him and wrought on him to believe that it had been a fit of giddiness.

Another time a cloth-weaver came to live in a house next to Sandro's, and erected no less than eight looms, which, when at work, not only deafened poor Sandro with the noise of the treadles and the movement of the frames, but shook his whole house, the walls of which were no stronger than they should be, so that what with the one thing and the other he could not work or even stay at home. Time after time he besought his neighbour to put an end to this annoyance, but the other said that he both would and could do what he pleased in his own house; whereupon Sandro, in disdain, balanced on the top of his own wall, which was higher than his neighbour's and not very strong, an enormous stone, more than enough to fill a wagon, which threatened to fall at the slightest shaking of the wall and to shatter the roof, ceilings, webs, and looms of his neighbour, who, terrified by this danger, ran to Sandro, but was answered in his very own words – namely, that he both could and would do whatever he pleased in his own house. Nor could he get any other answer out of him, so that he was forced to come to a reasonable agreement and to be a good neighbour to Sandro.

It is also related that Sandro, for a jest, accused a friend of his own of heresy before his vicar, and the friend, on appearing, asked who the accuser was and what the accusation; and having been told that it was Sandro, who had charged him with holding the opinion of the Epicureans, and believing that the soul dies with the body, he insisted on being confronted with the accuser before the judge. Sandro therefore appeared, and the other said: 'It is true that I hold this opinion with regard to this man's soul, for he is an animal. Nay, does it not seem to you that he is the heretic, since without a scrap of learning, and scarcely knowing how to read, he plays the commentator to Dante and takes his name in vain?'

It is also said that he had a surpassing love for all whom he saw to be zealous students of art; and that he earned much, but wasted everything through negligence and lack of management. Finally, having grown old and useless, and being forced to walk with crutches, without which he could not stand upright, he died, infirm and decrepit, at the age of seventy-eight, and was buried in Ognissanti at Florence in the year 1515.

In the guardaroba of the Lord Duke Cosimo there are two very beautiful heads of women in profile by his hand, one of which is said to be the mistress of Giuliano de' Medici, brother of Lorenzo, and the other Madonna Lucrezia de' Tornabuoni, wife of the said Lorenzo. In the same place, likewise by the hand of Sandro, is a Bacchus who is raising a cask with both his hands, and putting it to his mouth – a very graceful figure. And in the Duomo of Pisa he began an Assumption, with a choir of angels, in the Chapel of the Impagliata; but afterwards, being displeased with it, he left it unfinished. In S. Francesco at Montevarchi he painted the panel of the high-altar; and in the Pieve of Empoli, on the same side as the S. Sebastian of Rossellino, he made two angels. He was among the first to discover the method of decorating standards and other sorts of hangings with the so-called inlaid work, to the end that the colours might not fade and might show the tint of the cloth on either side. By his hand, and made thus, is the baldacchino of Orsanmichele, covered with beautiful and varied figures of Our Lady; which proves how much better such a method preserves the cloth than does the use of mordants, which eat it away and make its life but short, although, being less costly, mordants are now used more than anything else.

Sandro's drawings were extraordinarily good, and so many, that for some time after his death all the craftsmen strove to obtain some of them; and we have some in our book, made with great mastery and judgment. His scenes abounded with figures, as may be seen from the embroidered border of the Cross that the Friars of S. Maria Novella carry in processions, all made from his design. Great was the praise, then, that Sandro deserved for all the pictures that he chose to make with diligence and love, as he did the aforesaid panel of the Magi in S. Maria Novella, which is marvellous. Very beautiful, too, is a little round picture by his hand that is seen in the apartment of the Prior of the Angeli in Florence, in which the figures are small but very graceful and wrought with beautiful consideration. Of the same size as the aforesaid panel of the Magi, and by the same man's hand, is a picture in the possession of Messer Fabio Segni, a gentlemen of Florence, in which there is painted the Calumny of Apelles, as beautiful as any picture could be. Under this panel, which Sandro himself presented to Antonio Segni, who was much his friend, there may now be read the following verses, written by the said Messer Fabio:

INDICIO QUEMQUAM NE
FALSO LAEDERE TENTENT
TERRARUM REGES, PARVA
TABELLA MONET. HUIC SIMILEM
AEGYPTI REGI DONAVIT
APELLES; REX FUIT ET DIGNUS
MUNERE, MUNUS EO.

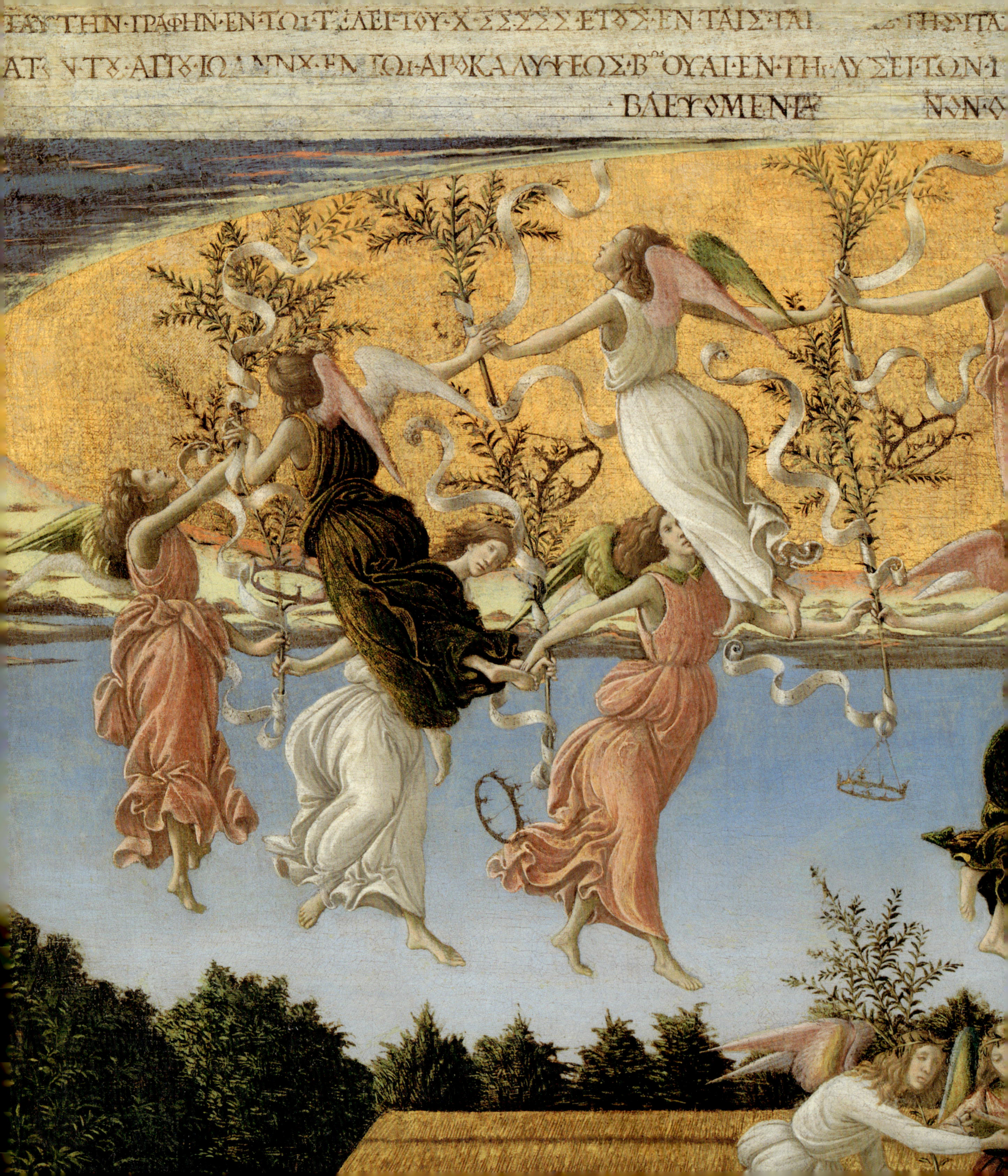

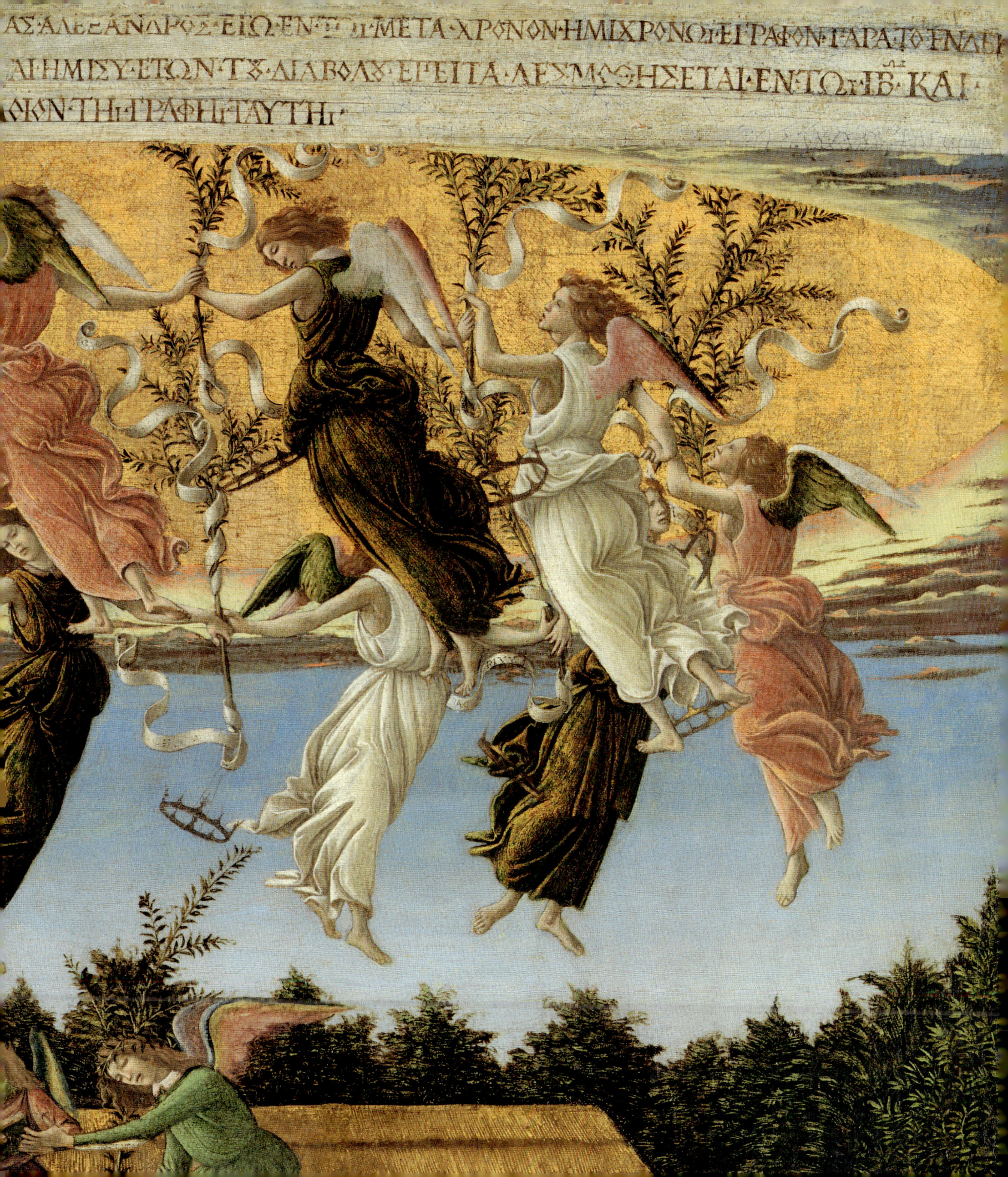

ΑΣ·ΑΛΕΞΑΝΔΡΟΣ·ΕΓΩ·ΕΝ·ΜΕΤΑ·ΧΡΟΝΟΝ·ΗΜΙΧΡΟΝ·ΕΓΡΑΦΟΝ·ΠΑΡΑ·ΤΟ
ΑΙ·ΗΜΙΣΥ·ΕΤΩΝ·ΤΟΥ·ΔΙΑΒΟΛΟΥ·ΕΠΕΙΤΑ·ΔΕΣΜΩΘΗΣΕΤΑΙ·ΕΝ·ΤΩ·ΙΒ·ΚΑΙ
ΟΝ·ΤΗΙ·ΓΡΑΦΗΙ·ΤΑΥΤΗΙ

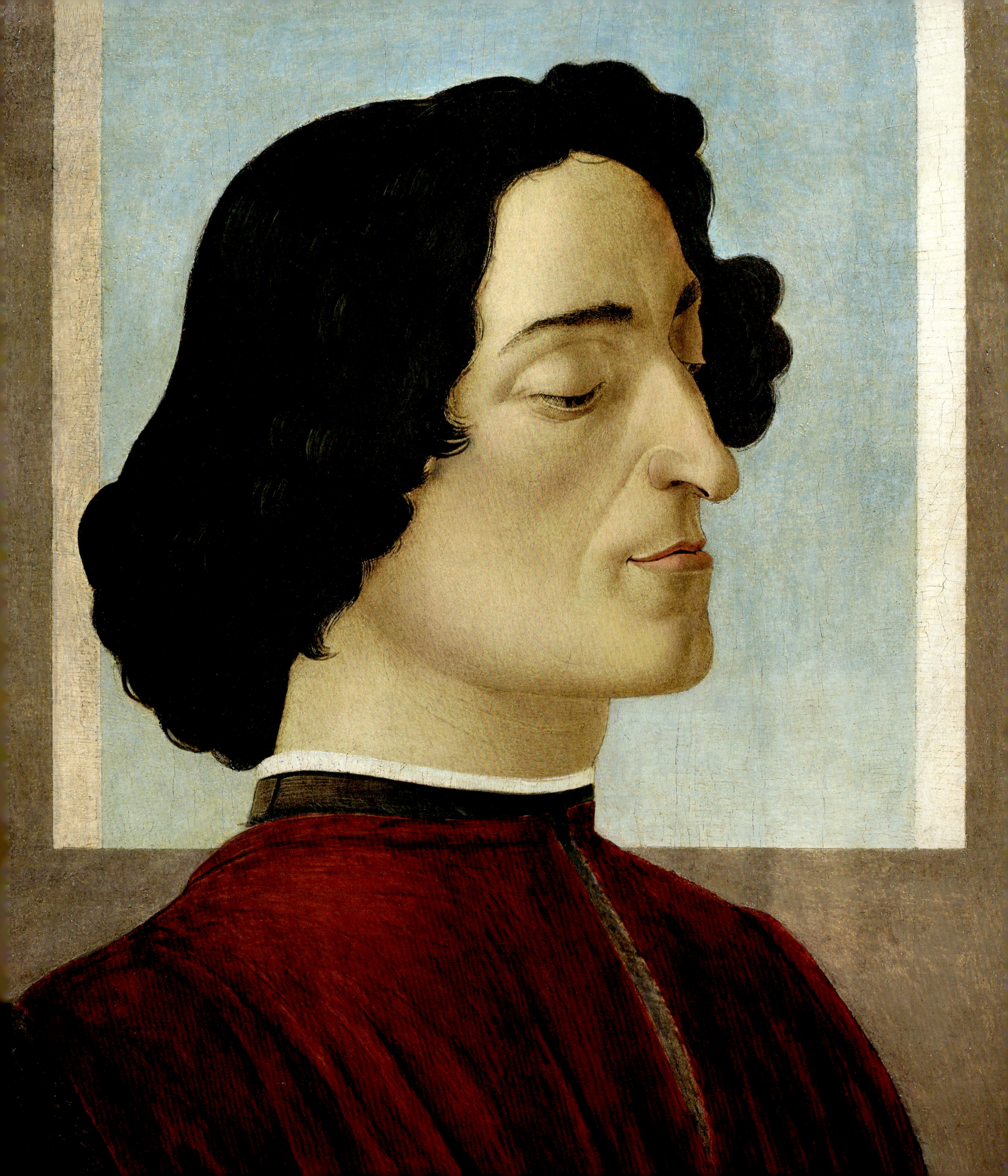

Botticelli in his Time

Sons of a modest tanner, Botticelli and his elder brother Simone, who prospered as a merchant banker, both pursued careers that exemplify the social and professional mobility encouraged by the dynamic economy of Renaissance Florence. The painter never married and from 1470 maintained a workshop at his family home near the convent of Ognissanti, engaging pupils and assistants but eschewing close involvement with the artists' guild. His celebrated commissions for the Medici family and their adherents include portraits, secular frescoes, mythological compositions and drawings of Dante's *Divine Comedy* (cats 147–53). Following the resumption of peace between Florence and Rome in 1480, Botticelli received his most prestigious commission from Pope Sixtus IV when he and a consortium of mainly Florentine artists painted frescoes of Old and New Testament subjects in the Sistine Chapel.

The poet Ugolino Verino compared the classical painters Zeuxis and Apelles to Botticelli, who gave his own picture of *The Calumny of Apelles* to a friend of Leonardo da Vinci, Antonio Senga Guidi. The latter composed a quatrain likening it to Apelles's original. Such opinions, and the artist's remarkable visualizations of poetic myths and Christian allegories, accord with Vasari's characterization of him as 'a sophisticated person'. Botticelli possessed an exceptional sense of linear design and his workshop propagated what might today be termed a highly recognizable 'corporate brand'.

During his last decade Botticelli painted expressive devotional images for clients ranging from Queen Isabel the Catholic to followers of Savonarola. An abrupt change in the ideological climate of Florence necessitated a considerable revision of his subject matter. Modern connoisseurs later disparaged the productions of his studio on account of their indifferent quality in comparison with the artist's presumably autograph works. ME

CAT. 155 (detail)

Botticelli and the Bottega

CAROLINE CAMPBELL

Botticelli's style is, today, perhaps the most recognizable of any early Renaissance painter. His crisply delineated female figures translate well into easily reproduced and manipulated images, and Botticelli's inventions appear in contexts wholly alien to their original use, from fridge magnets and aprons to advertising copy. Perhaps the reason for their continuing adaptability to other forms is that these designs were always meant to be used in many contexts. The Botticelli visual brand was intentionally compelling and clear. Based on strong outlines, it was devised to survive transformation into the work of other artists: painters of Botticelli's own day, both inside the master's studio (cat. 118) and further afield (fig. 7).[1] In an unsigned and undated vernacular text of around 1490–3 addressed to Ludovico Sforza, the Duke of Milan, Botticelli's works are described as having an *aria virile* ('a virile air') and being 'made with the best method and complete proportion'.[2] This phrase has often perplexed historians, but the most plausible way of interpreting it is that Botticelli's *cose* or things were easy to identify, and could not be confused stylistically with the works of other painters. In addition, they were well planned, symmetrical and coherently designed. Such comments suggest not just a talented master painter, but also an efficiently run and productive workshop.

Like every successful Florentine painter of the fifteenth and sixteenth centuries, Alessandro di Mariano di Vanni Filipepi was steeped in the life of the communal workshop, a place of shared endeavour within strict hierarchies.[3] The label, 'by Botticelli', implies a product of sufficient quality convincingly to represent both his pictorial manner and artistic style. It does not – and indeed it cannot for practically any Renaissance painter – predicate that any single work was produced by one individual artist. It is impossible to grasp the development of Botticelli's stylistic manner without reaching an understanding of his work within these structures.[4] By the fifteenth century, painters' workshops in Florence could be relatively flexible in their organization: in contrast to the twelve-year apprenticeship recorded by Cennino Cennini in *The Craftsman's Handbook* (*c.*1390–1400), the record book of the mid-century painter Neri di Bicci records the movement of around 20 employees, many of whom left before the end of their agreed period of employment.[5] According to Giorgio Vasari, the author of the *Lives of the Artists* published in the middle of the sixteenth century, Botticelli was a difficult and unsettled child who received his first artistic training with a goldsmith, where he learnt to draw, but as he wished to paint, his father subsequently moved him to the tutelage of Fra Filippo Lippi.[6]

Vasari, and others, have credited the pre-eminence of line in Botticelli's work to his early years with a metalworker, but this was also a definable element of Filippo Lippi's artistic style, seen particularly in small devotional works like the *Madonna and Child with Two Angels* (Uffizi, Florence, *c.*1465).[7] The latter's influence had a lasting impact on the younger painter's career. Botticelli's workshop, like that of Lippi, specialized in the production of graceful Madonnas, whose strong linear qualities favoured their effective transfer and copying, even by artists of significantly less talent.[8] Formally, too, Botticelli's shop shared features with that of his principal master. Just as Fra Filippo depended on the support of his (sometimes independent) associate, Fra Diamante, so Botticelli was indebted to Jacopo di Domenico di Papi da San Giorgio (also called Jacopo Foschi), who worked on and off with him from around 1480, possibly until Botticelli's death.[9] Other figures passed more quickly out of Botticelli's ambit,[10] some of whom developed their own individual stylistic manners. The most notable of these artists was Fra Filippo's son, Filippino ('little Filippo'), who may have spent much of the 1470s working with Botticelli. *The Adoration of the Kings* (National Gallery, London) is one of a number of paintings on which the two artists collaborated. In this picture, and in several others, two distinctive artistic manners are evident: Filippino was Botticelli's creative equal rather than his amanuensis.[11]

By the early 1470s, around the time that Filippino Lippi joined him as a *compagno*, Botticelli was already a painter greatly in demand. Although it is too simplistic to call Botticelli a 'Medicean' painter, the favour he was accorded by the Medici family and members of their circle provided the core of the success he enjoyed in his lifetime. It was within the milieu of these educated Florentine bankers and their intellectual associates, particularly Angelo Poliziano, that Botticelli was able to develop the mythological paintings for which he is most celebrated today (including fig. 4).[12] Botticelli's reputation in the fifteenth century, however, was somewhat different. It was based on a variety of commissions, including the frescoes he – together with Domenico Ghirlandaio, Perugino and Cosimo Rosselli – undertook for Pope Sixtus IV's chapel in the Vatican,[13] and large-scale altarpieces,[14] as well as secular works. Yet the mainstay of his commercial operation was provided by smaller panel paintings, most of which were made for private devotional purposes. These pictures give us the clearest sense of the variety of ways in which a painting can be 'by' Botticelli.

Several hundred of these pictures survive today.[15] Until recent years they have been largely ignored by scholars, but they provide the primary evidence for reconstructing the workings

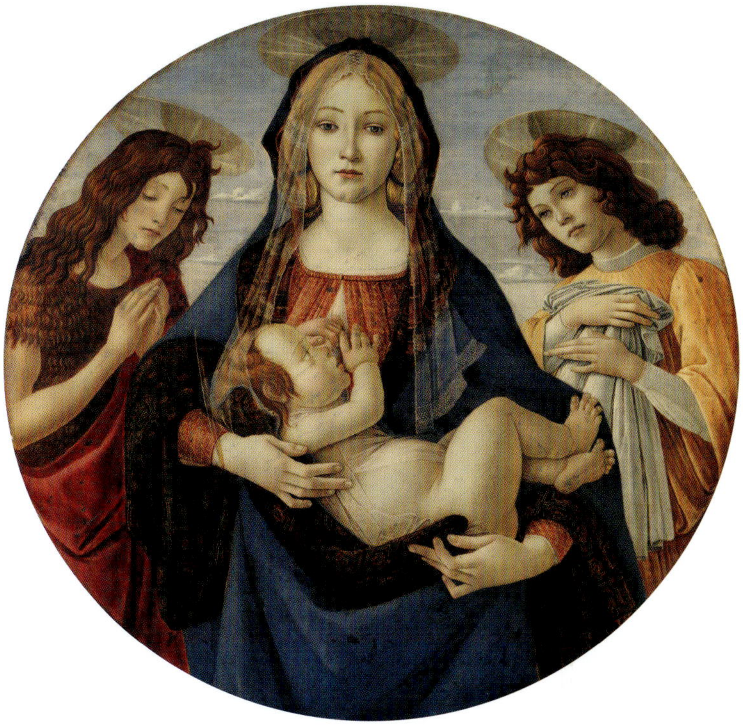

CAT. 118
WORKSHOP OF
SANDRO BOTTICELLI
The Virgin and Child with St John and an Angel, *c.*1490

of Botticelli's studio, and the discussion below is focused on a small sub-section of these paintings, in the National Gallery's collection.[16] There is no such thing as a straightforward 'Botticelli workshop' production, but we can use these so-called 'shop' paintings to begin to quantify, categorize and understand the different levels of quality (defined here as proximity to Botticelli's own stylistic manner) and production operating in Botticelli's *bottega*. The smallest category of paintings contains those which were produced with such high pictorial and design standards that they must have been intended to be considered as the work of Botticelli himself (even if they were not wholly by him), such as *Venus and Mars* (fig. 4).[17] There is no precedent for this composition, nor are there closely comparable works from the studio that derive from it.[18] It is likely – if unprovable – that workshop assistants would have been involved in the painting of elements with less narrative significance, such as the sky and the grass.

Other compositions developed in the painter's workshop do not derive from a so-called 'prime' version, attributed to Botticelli himself. A tondo of the *Virgin and Child with St John and an Angel* (cat. 118) dating from around 1490, is not by Botticelli, but was probably sold as by the master's hand.[19] This picture seems to be the finest example of this composition, known in at least two other versions, both larger than the National Gallery painting.[20] The fifteenth- or early sixteenth-century inscription on the back, *M.[?] Giuljano da san Ghallo*, has led to the suggestion that it was either owned by the celebrated Renaissance architect, Giuliano da Sangallo, or that he designed the frame.[21] If the latter, the frame and the painting were intended to harmonize together as a finely-crafted, complete work of art. In this context, it is interesting to note that some of the materials are of unusually high quality for a painting off the production line: the Virgin's robe and the sky contain particles of costly ultramarine. And, although the haloes are painted in lead-tin yellow, the gold in Mary's blonde hair seems original.[22]

A further category of work encompasses those paintings in Botticelli's manner, but which combine features from different compositions, invented as much as 20 years apart. *The Virgin and Child* (fig. 5) made by a member of Botticelli's workshop, probably in the 1480s, is based on the *Madonna del Roseto* of about 1465–70 (Louvre, Paris),[23] but with other elements, such as the Virgin's three-quarter profile, appropriated paintings of the following decade.[24] The figure of St John the Baptist has

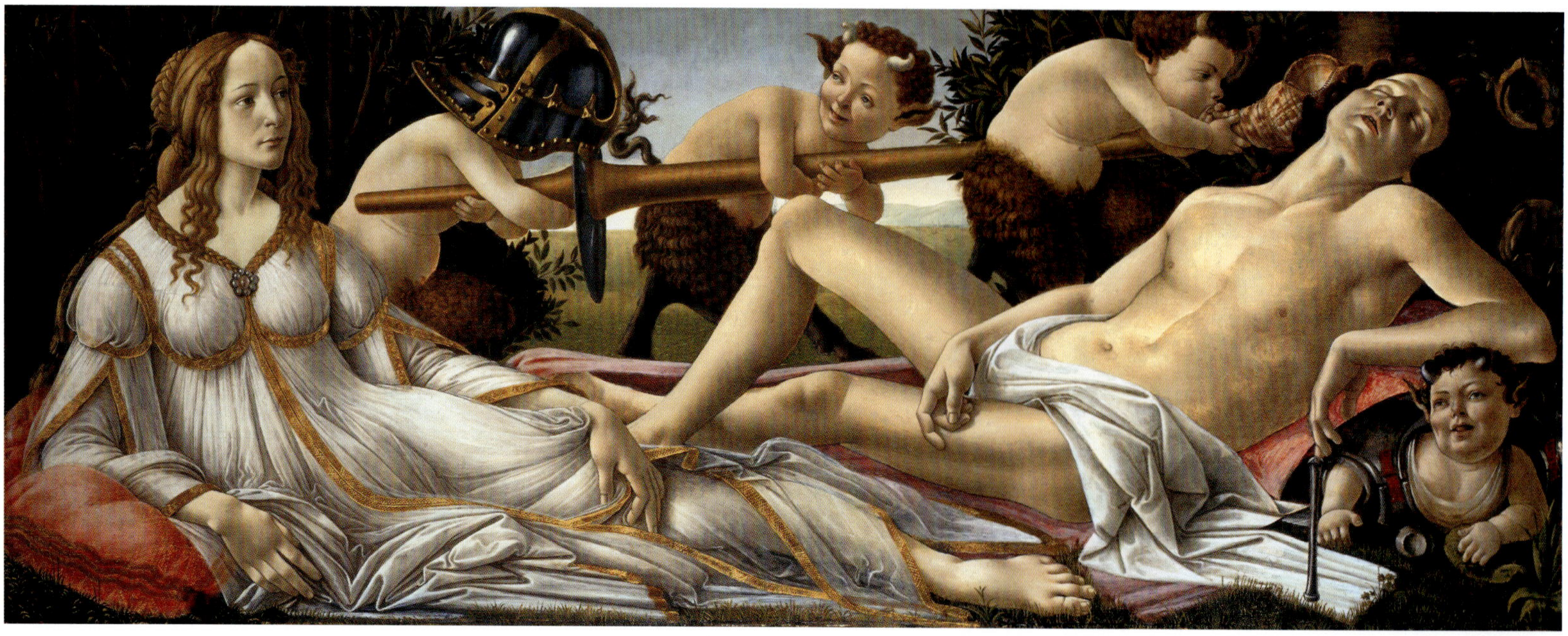

FIG. 4
SANDRO BOTTICELLI
(c.1445–1510)
Venus and Mars, *c.*1485
Tempera and oil on poplar,
69.2 × 173.4 cm
The National Gallery, London
(NG915)

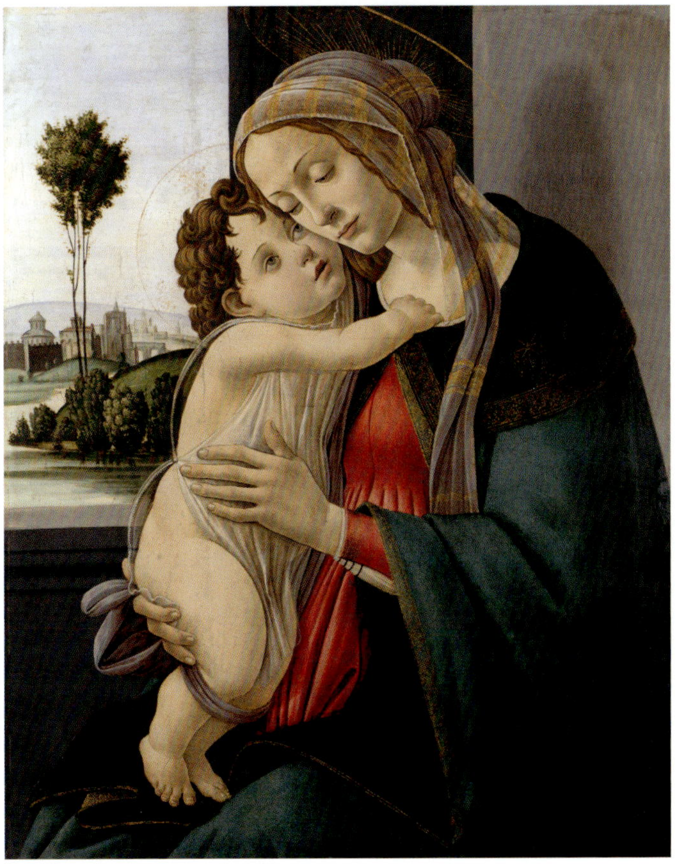

FIG. 5
WORKSHOP OF
SANDRO BOTTICELLI (c.1445–1510)
The Virgin and Child, *c.*1475–1500
Tempera on wood, 83.2 × 64.8 cm
The National Gallery, London
(NG782)

been omitted, as well as the roses, and the Virgin is now seated before an open window. Her headdress and drapery have less complex forms, and the figures have become far larger in relation to their surroundings. The composition has been greatly simplified, and it relies on large, easily traced outlines, which are hard and mechanical. This painting suggests not only a well-organized but also a lucrative – and adaptable – shop.[25]

Both of these pictures were produced under Botticelli's tutelage, but other Botticellian works have a more tenuous connection to his studio. One such painting is the *Allegory* (fig. 6), purchased by the National Gallery in 1874 as a work by Botticelli, along with *Venus and Mars* (fig. 4).[26] Within 25 years the attribution of the *Allegory* to Botticelli was questioned; for much of the latter part of the twentieth century it was speculated that it could be a later forgery. However, study of its materials has demonstrated that they are wholly compatible with a date around 1500. The underdrawing, in a liquid medium, probably derives from a cartoon, but there is no technical evidence to suggest that the painting was made in Botticelli's workshop.[27] Yet it cannot be denied that this Venus, reclining awkwardly on a cushion, shares the same basic pose as Botticelli's goddess, and her diaphanous white garments also derive from the same source. It is possible that the immediate inspiration for the *Allegory* is not *Venus and Mars*, but a further picture made under Botticelli's supervision, representing *Venus and Three Putti* (Louvre, Paris).[28] As the *Allegory* suggests, Botticelli's inventions continued to be valued – and emulated – after the fall of the Medici.

But perhaps the clearest understanding of how Botticelli's work cannot be separated from that of his workshop can be gleaned from an altarpiece painted around 1491–4 for the nuns of Sant' Elisabetta delle Convertite (fig. 7), a convent for reformed prostitutes. This picture was mentioned by Vasari, probably because it was one of the works by Botticelli then on public display,[29] but by the early twentieth century it was thought to be lost.[30] The central panel shows a vision of the Trinity floating above a barren landscape and flanked by the penitential saints John the Baptist and Mary Magdalene, whose life story, choosing austerity over sensuality, is depicted in the surviving panels of the predella (Philadelphia Museum of Art, figs 51–4).[31]

Scholars have been struck by the divergent quality of parts of this painting.[32] The putti surrounding the Trinity are schematically painted, and derive from the same cartoon, manipulated in different directions. If the central sections of the painting are lacking in inspiration, the same cannot be said of the small figures representing Tobias and the Archangel Raphael, placed to the left of the Trinity. They are on a different scale – figuratively and qualitatively – to the rest of the altarpiece, and have been attributed to Botticelli himself.[33] Further complexity is added by the fact that these were a late addition to the composition; examination of the painting with infrared reflectography has demonstrated that Tobias and Raphael were earlier included, as even smaller figures, in the middle distance between the Trinity and St John the Baptist.[34] These were arguably Botticelli's own invention; in both iterations they demonstrate a tremendous freedom in compositional drawing, absent from the rest of the altarpiece.

How can we explain such evidence? Why would Botticelli have added these figures to a perfectly competent workshop production, and made apparent these issues of stylistic discrepancy? The answer lies, perhaps, in coming to terms with how differently a twenty-first-century audience looks at Renaissance paintings, in comparison with men of the fifteenth century, such as the Duke of Milan's anonymous agent. The involvement of many hands in an artist's enterprise was not a cause for concern, or even a matter of note. Rather, it was Botticelli's ability to conjure a convincing whole out of many parts that made him, at least for this critic, 'the most excellent of painters'.[35]

FIG. 6
FLORENTINE SCHOOL
An Allegory, *c.*1500
Tempera and oil on wood, 92.1 × 172.7 cm
The National Gallery, London (NG916)

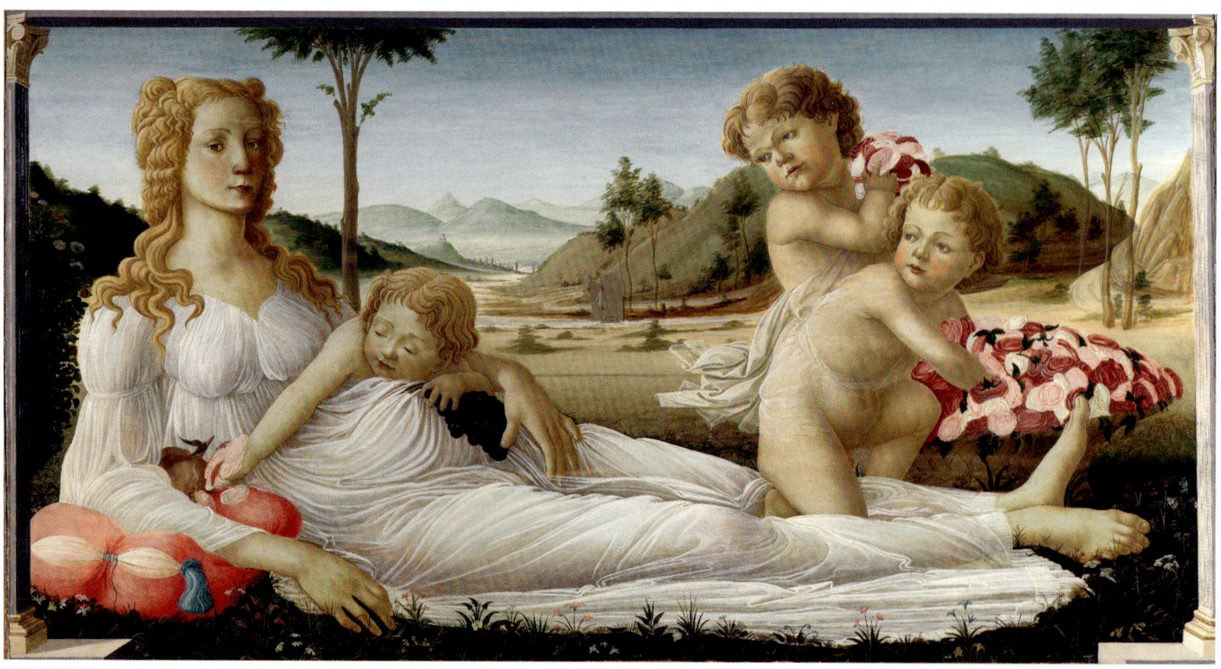

FIG. 7
SANDRO BOTTICELLI (*c.*1445–1510) AND WORKSHOP
The Trinity with St Mary Magdalene and St John the Baptist, the Archangel Raphael and Tobias, 1491–4
Tempera on wood, 214 × 192.4 cm
Bequeathed by Viscount Arthur Hamilton Lee of Fareham
The Courtauld Gallery, London (P.1947.LF.38)

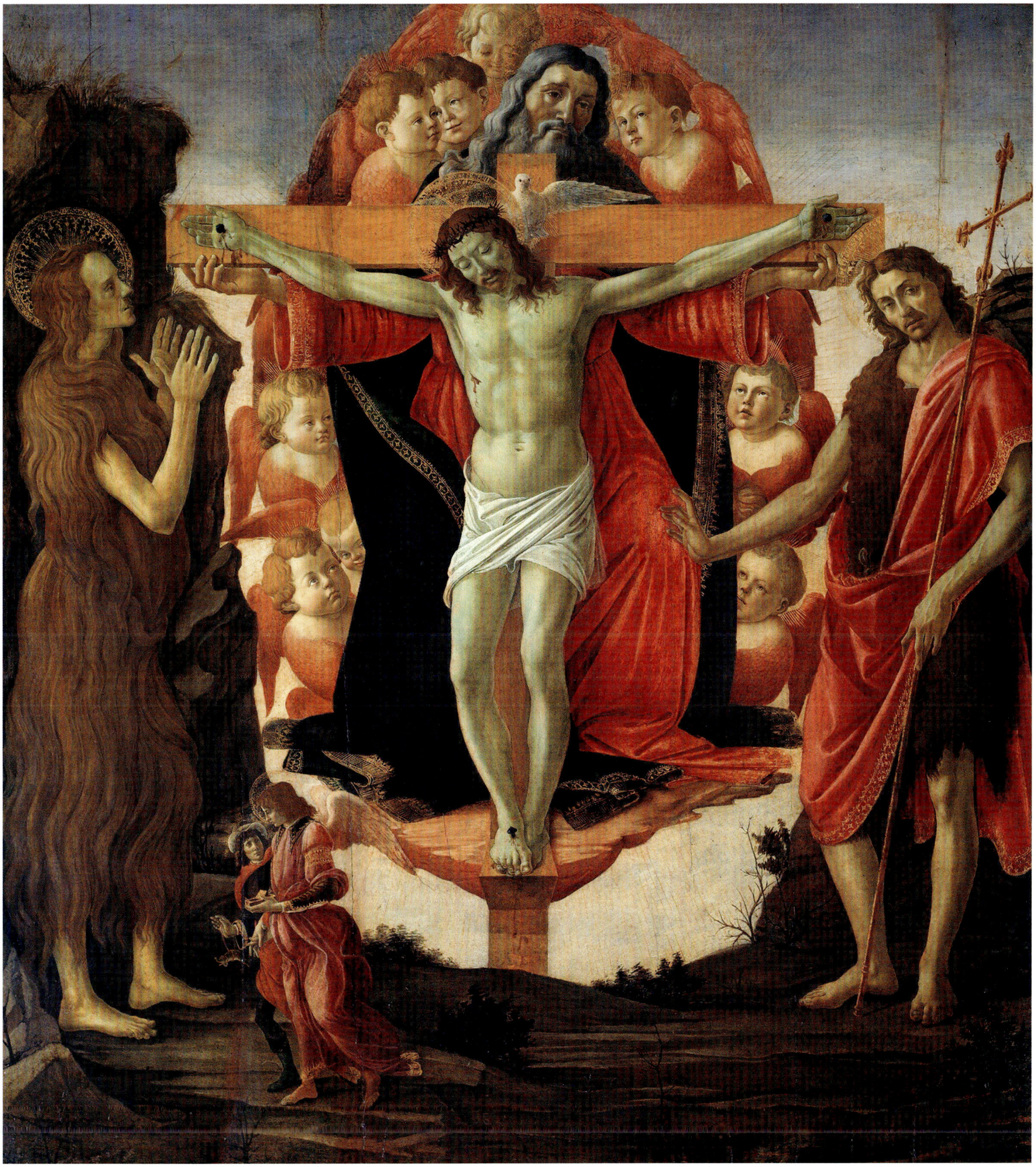

Botticelli: Between Neoplatonism and Savonarola

ANA DEBENEDETTI

At first glance, few movements seem more dissimilar than the revival of the antique philosophical tradition called Neoplatonism and the outbreak of religious fervour led by the Dominican friar Girolamo Savonarola, both prominent features of the cultural landscape of Florence during the later fifteenth century; and yet the Tuscan city provided the theatre where these movements were acted out, almost contemporaneously with a remarkable development in the visual arts, and both had a specific impact on the modern critical interpretation of Botticelli's stylistic development.

Neoplatonism was promoted around the 1450s by Cosimo de' Medici the elder, the greatest patron of early fifteenth-century Florence and the grandfather of Lorenzo the Magnificent. Cosimo entrusted the son of his personal physician, Marsilio Ficino, with the translation of Plato's works, which had been unavailable since antiquity apart from a partial version in Latin. Ficino translated not only Plato's original works but also those of the so-called Neoplatonist philosophers of the third century AD, namely Plotinus and his followers, who provided a new interpretation of Plato's teaching. As a result, these later interpreters heavily coloured Ficino's own understanding of Plato's philosophy.

The concept of divine love lies at the heart of Neoplatonist doctrines. Plato and Plotinus explained that beauty is a response to the love and desire humanity feels for the Divine. In this light, terrestrial beauty provides a way to consider the Divine, which could be described in quite ecstatic terms, for example, by Plotinus: 'This is the spirit that Beauty must ever induce: wonderment and a delicious trouble, longing and love and a trembling that is all delight.'[1] This is how, in mid-fifteenth-century Florence, the new school of thought called Neoplatonism appeared and a new Academy, modelled on its antique Athenian prototype, was founded.[2] Ficino assembled numerous friends and followers who helped to spread his ideas in the city and beyond. He became one of the most celebrated philosophers of the Italian Renaissance, and while his philosophy drew from various sources, his main concern was to combine and harmonize ancient wisdom with the Christian creed. Beauty became the path on which one could seek the classical notion of the Divine, which was likened to the Christian God. The mythological gods and goddesses of the pagan world were thus seen as precursors of Christianity, who foretold the coming of Christ.[3]

The movement coincided with a renewed interest in the visual arts of antiquity. The Florentine architect Filippo Brunelleschi as well as the sculptors Donatello and Lorenzo Ghiberti, for instance, went to Rome to study ancient remains and devised a new style based on their own observations, while a new category of men of letters, such as the papal secretary and self-taught architect Leon Battista Alberti, combined direct observation of antique monuments with the study of classical texts on the visual arts[4] to develop a new theory of artistic practice.[5] The classical conception of beauty was that it lay in the arrangement of parts into a coherent whole governed by a sense of proportion, harmony and symmetry. Alberti expanded on this, proclaiming that beauty was the primary goal of visual art, and provided artists with a number of rules to follow – arguing that their application would allow artists to achieve perfection in their works.

It was tempting, with this context and following his rediscovery, for some pioneering nineteenth-century art historians to address Botticelli's artistic persona through the lens of fifteenth-century Florence's cultural milieu. Viewed in this way, Botticelli's mythological paintings appeared to them to have been informed by Neoplatonist interpretations of classical Gods. This concept found its starting point from the correspondence between Ficino and the young patron of Botticelli, Lorenzo di Pierfrancesco de' Medici, which coincided (during the late 1470s) with the creation of *Primavera* and the *Birth of Venus* (figs 8, 10).[6] The ethereal beauty of such female figures, both classical goddesses and representations of the Madonna, reinforced a reading of Botticelli as a Neoplatonist artist. The Chigi Madonna (cat. 109) for instance was seen as a representation of the Neoplatonic doctrine that earthly beauty is but an image of heavenly beauty, 'while the sober infant who represents the Holy Child will grow into an Academician'.[7]

The enthusiasm for such iconographic interpretation gave rise to texts by Aby Warburg, Erwin Panofsky, Edgar Wind, E.H. Gombrich and others, which remain authoritative.[8] These authors accorded particular significance to another important figure of the Medici circle, Angelo Poliziano, a poet and a professor at the Florentine Studio (university), who may have played a formative role in the translation of Neoplatonist ideas into iconographic programmes.[9] We know that Botticelli lived for a time in a house near the church of San Paolino, where Poliziano was a rector. However, this period of pictorial abundance proved short-lived and the political situation in Florence changed dramatically after the arrival of Girolamo Savonarola, followed by the death of Lorenzo in 1492, and that of Poliziano just two years later.[10]

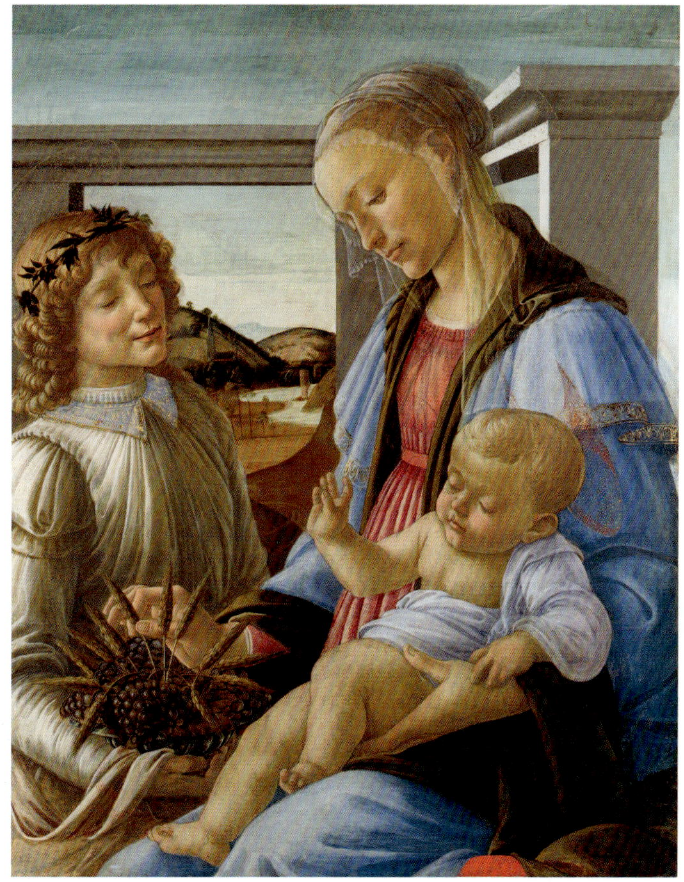

CAT. 109
SANDRO BOTTICELLI
(c.1445–1510)
The Virgin and Child with an Angel (Chigi Madonna), 1470s

Savonarola began to preach in the city in 1489, foretelling that a scourge would soon afflict Italy, Florence in particular, and exhorting his listeners to repent. He rapidly gained a reputation as a prophet, as his eschatological sermons coincided with the invasion of northern and central Italy by the French troops of King Charles VIII in 1494, and with scandals in Rome associated with the new pope, Alexander VI Borgia. Savonarola advocated a return to austerity in many aspects of civil and religious life, and especially in the arts, making a series of polemical attacks on non-religious paintings, which could be interpreted as direct assaults on Botticelli – then the leading painter of mythological subjects in Florence. A recurrent rhetorical reproach was that even in religious paintings, the beauty of the figures provided a cause of distraction, so that 'the people no longer think of God, but only of the art in the images' (Sermon on the Psalms).

During these years, Botticelli's style shifted quite dramatically and seemed to return to a 'medieval manner' utilizing more vivid colours and disproportioned figures, in which later scholars found what they took to be a mystical enthusiasm on the artist's behalf. Vasari's testimony, made only 40 years after Botticelli's death, that he 'became a Piagnone' (as the followers of Savonarola were then called),[11] caused art historians from Walter Pater and Eugène Müntz to Herbert Horne and

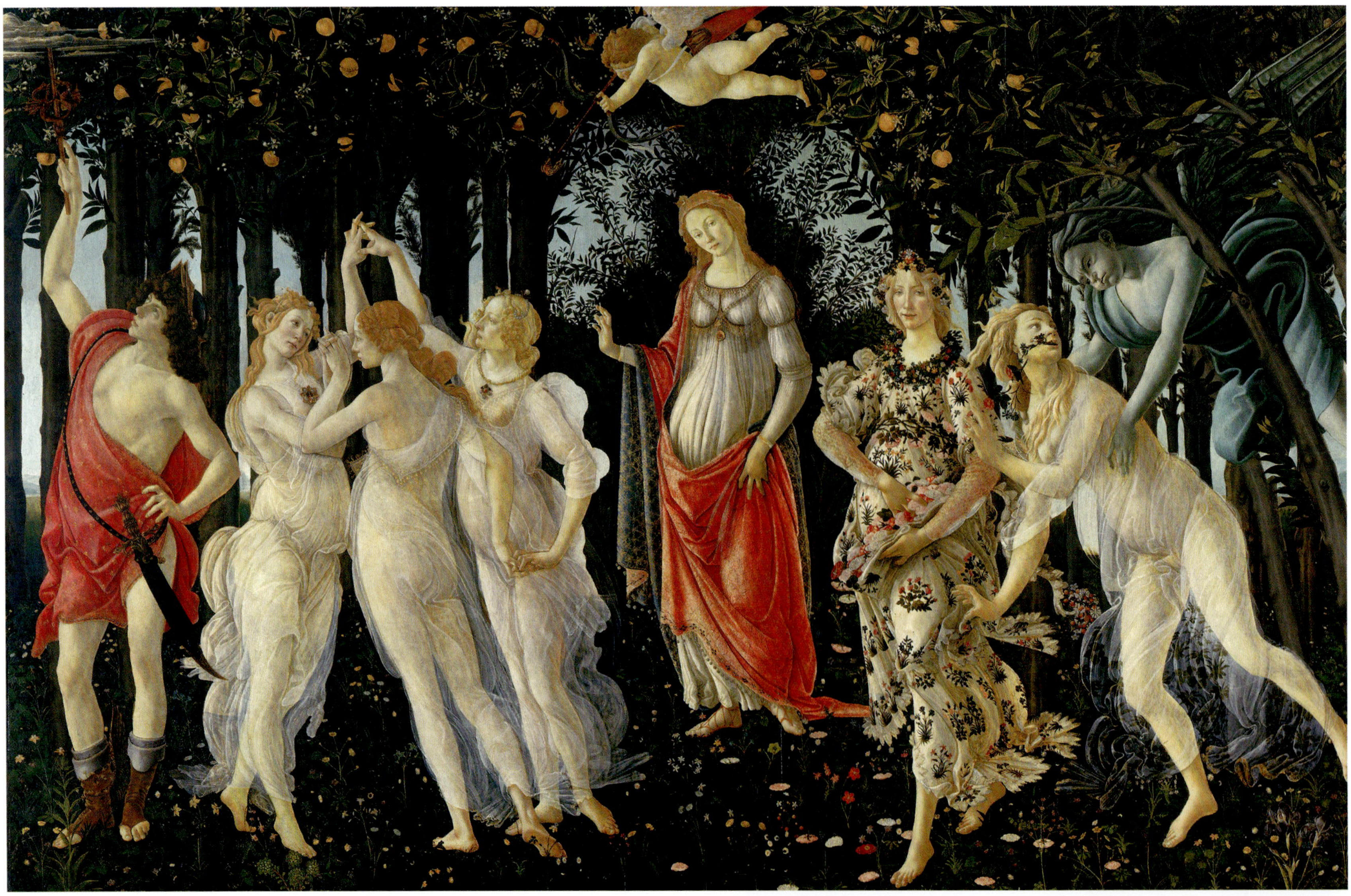

FIG. 8
SANDRO BOTTICELLI
(c.1445–1510)
Primavera, 1477–82
Tempera on wood,
203 × 314 cm
Galleria degli Uffizi, Florence (8360)

FIG. 9
ATTRIBUTED TO FRANCESCO ROSSELLI (1445–c.1513)
The Execution of Girolamo Savonarola, c.1498
Tempera on wood, 101 × 117 cm
Museo di San Marco, Florence
(1890 n.477)

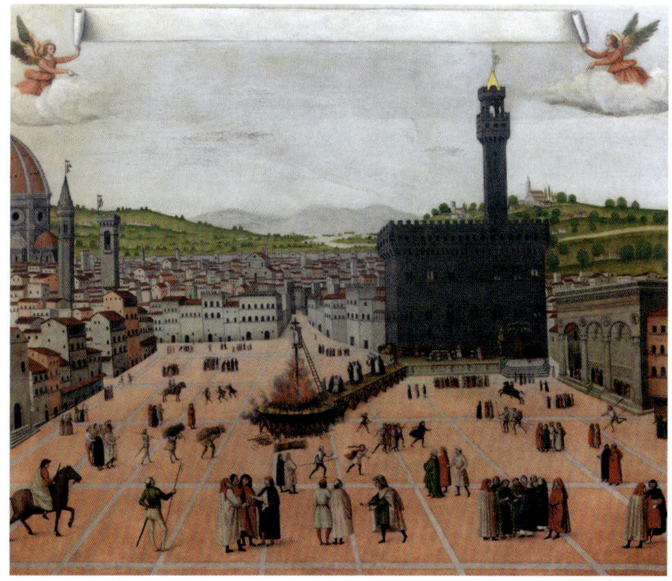

Wilhelm von Bode to assume that he became an adherent of the Dominican reformer.[12] The *Mystic Nativity* (cat. 101), Botticelli's only signed and dated work, was seen as a turning point in the artist's career, inaugurating the so-called archaic style of his late period through its complex eschatological iconography and enigmatic Greek inscription.[13]

The influence of Savonarola on Botticelli's late style was alleged in the wake of a religious revival that occurred during the middle of the nineteenth century, centred on the Dominican convent of San Marco in Florence, which became the meeting place for a group of devotees called the 'New Piagnoni', after the friar's original followers. This group was composed chiefly of scholars, who assembled a great quantity of documents relating to Savonarola as well as his letters and treatises, which fed the publication of a series of biographies.[14] The Renaissance historian and philosopher Eugenio Garin made good use of such material, but suggested that the Dominican friar had initially been received enthusiastically by the humanists and philosophers of Ficino's circle, and that his ultimate rejection by them had followed the *Bruciamenti delle Vanità* (Bonfires of the Vanities), on 7 February 1497 and 27 February 1498, which caused the destruction of many fancy goods – including paintings. The vandalism of the *Portrait of a Lady known as Smeralda Bandinelli* (cat. 162) may have resulted from such an event.

Garin's work argues that Savonarola's aspirations were not so dissimilar from those of the Florentine Neoplatonists, who also looked for a return to a so-called Golden Age, albeit of a rather different sort, aiming 'despite all differences, [towards] a common work of human reconstruction'.[15] A similar approach, also nuancing the mutual antagonism previously believed to have separated the exponents of Neoplatonism in Florence from Savonarola and his followers, was adopted by the art historian André Chastel, who interpreted Botticelli's late stylistic shift as reflecting a change of taste and commissions rather than a shift in the artist's personal beliefs as a Piagnone. Indeed, the *Mystic Nativity* was painted two years after Savonarola was burned at stake on 23 May 1498 in the Piazza della Signoria (fig. 9), for a member of the powerful Florentine family of the Aldobrandini, who were devotees of the friar. Botticelli's austere and archaic style seems therefore to go beyond Savonarola's influence to renew with a long lasting sensibility for the transcendent, which is manifest in the revivalist styles of other Florentine painters during the second half of the Quattrocento.[16] Marsilio Ficino himself, 'Prince of the Platonists', shows in his writings that he was particularly attracted by the 'pure colours, lights, the one voice, the shine of gold and the brightness of silver … which are all pure beauty'.[17]

FIG. 10
SANDRO BOTTICELLI
(*c*.1445–1510)
Birth of Venus, 1482–5
Tempera on canvas, 172.5 × 278.5 cm
Galleria degli Uffizi, Florence (878)

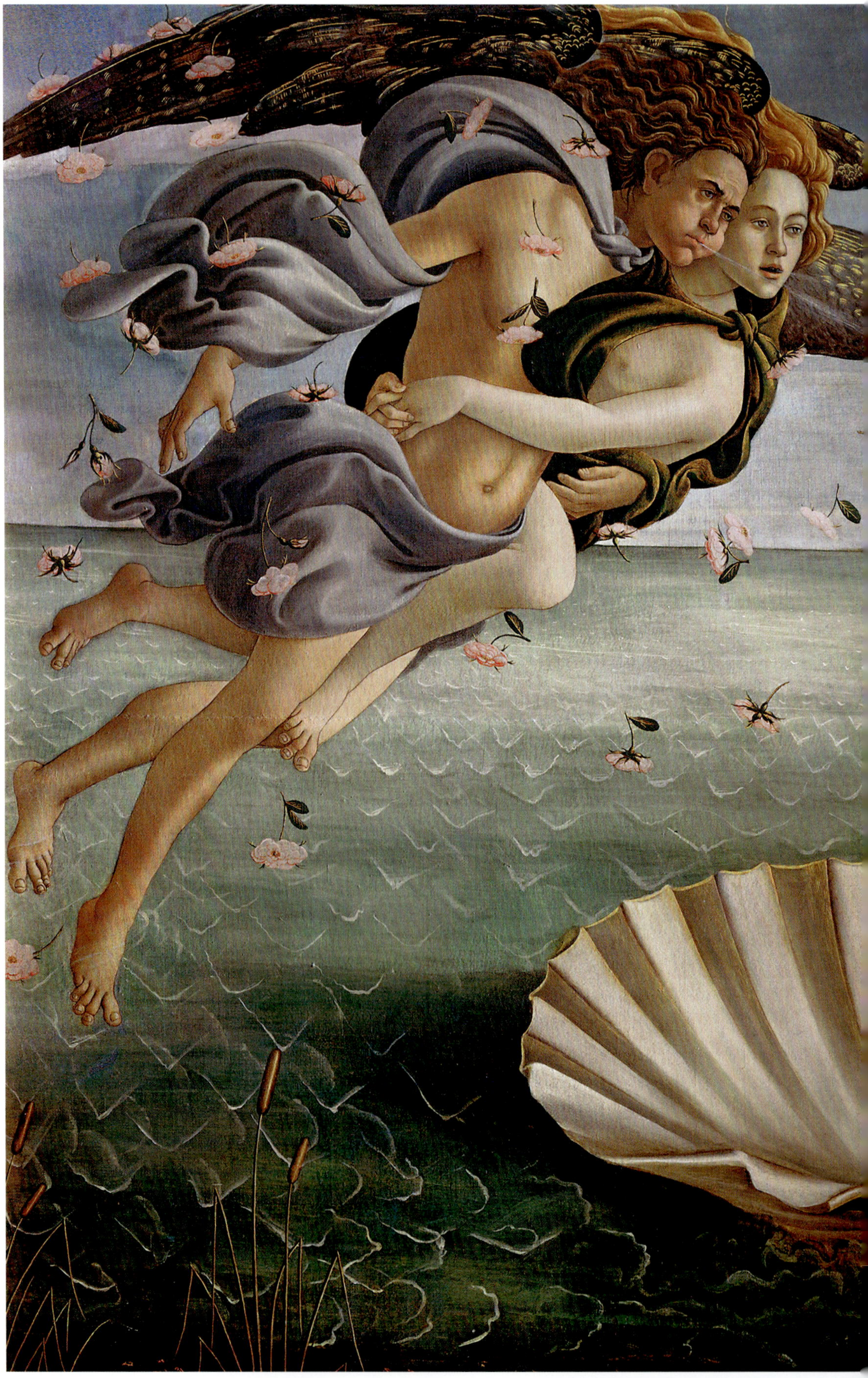

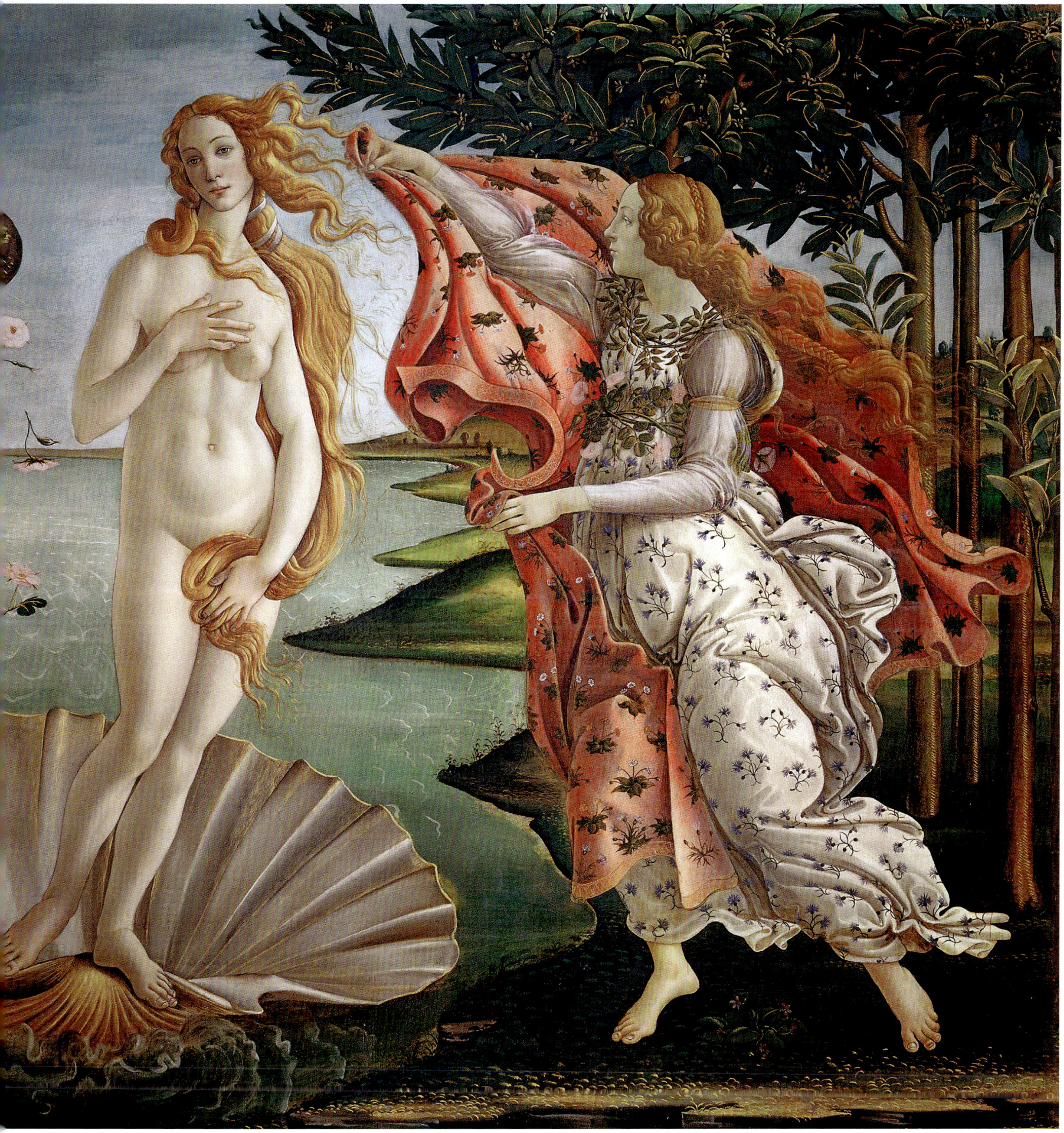

The Portrait of a Lady known as *Smeralda Bandinelli*

MARK EVANS

The critical fortunes of the painting known as *Smeralda Bandinelli* (cat. 162), with long periods of obscurity punctuated by picaresque, bohemian and opulent episodes, culminating in a recent rehabilitation, may serve as a paradigm for those of Botticelli.[1] This work was already attributed to the artist in 1841, when it re-entered the historical record, and was described thus:

> This lady is viewed at three-quarters and standing before an open window which shows the interior of her house. Her golden blonde hair is gathered and worn up at the back of her head. Her costume consists of a red undergarment, covered by a gown of transparent muslin trimmed with gold embroidery. Her right hand rests lightly on one side of the window, and her other hand, which is before her, holds a handkerchief ... At the bottom of the portrait is painted a partly erased inscription, in which one can still discern the name of this lady, who perhaps belonged to the ancient Bandinelli Family of Siena.[2]

The picture was demoted by Bernard Berenson to the composite artistic personality he called 'Amico di Sandro' (1899); an attribution supported in the monographs on Botticelli by Count Plunkett (1900), Herbert Horne (1908) and Adolfo Venturi (1925).[3] However, it was considered autograph by H.T. Kroeber (1911), Wilhelm von Bode (1921), August Schmarsow (1923) and Raymond van Marle (1931) and eventually readmitted to the artist's oeuvre by Berenson himself (1932). This view was supported by later scholars, including Carlo Gamba (1936) Lionello Venturi (1937), Jacques Mesnil (1938), Roberto Salvini (1958), C.M. Kauffmann (1973) and Ronald Lightbown (1978). Recently, in a critical climate conditioned by late twentieth-century feminism, the picture was hailed as 'one of the boldest inventions in Florentine fifteenth-century portraiture' (1999).[4]

The sitter's coiffure and summer at-home attire are found in other Florentine portraits of the 1470s: a white silk or linen *camisa* or chemise generously cut at the neck and sleeves; a costly *gamurra* or gown of red silk, slit and laced at the forearms; and, overall, a loose-fitting *guarnello* of sheer fabric with hanging cuffs, open to show the silk beneath. Her hair is demurely confined by a cap and her only jewellery is a simple necklace. The horizontal sill in the foreground indicates she is standing at a window embrasure on an upper storey, shown by the window with a central column at the left. A hand resting on the vertical framing element suggests she has just opened the panelled shutter at the right to look out at the viewer.

Technical examination of the picture reveals materials and techniques consistent with those described in *The Craftsman's Handbook* of Cennino Cennini: a single poplar panel faced with horizontal strips of fabric and a thick off-white gesso ground with two distinct types of underdrawing and incising with a blind stylus, painted in tempera.[5] Liquid drawing was used to plan the costume, and to delineate the originally lower position of her left forearm and the end of the sleeve, which formerly overlapped the sill. Higher up, this was drawn puffing out at the shoulder in front of the window frame, and a reserve left for the end of the handkerchief, which was draped over the sill. The architectural elements were crisply incised in perspective with a rule. A broad wash was used to shade the forms, particularly around the sitter's breast and down the outer contour of her left arm, adjusted after the red draperies were added. These were painted in full beneath the semi-transparent overgarment and the handkerchief in the sitter's left hand. An intense and well-preserved lake pigment was used lavishly – even in the grey architectural features. The decorative edging of the *guarnello* was once green. Only remnants of the original paint of the white cap survive at its lower edge, while other draperies are in excellent condition. Face and neck are abraded, with numerous scratches and deliberate scoring through of the mouth and right eye. The paint layer ends neatly at the top and sides, but the bottom edge of the panel has been crudely trimmed, probably by 7–17 mm. An engaged frame originally covered its unpainted borders.

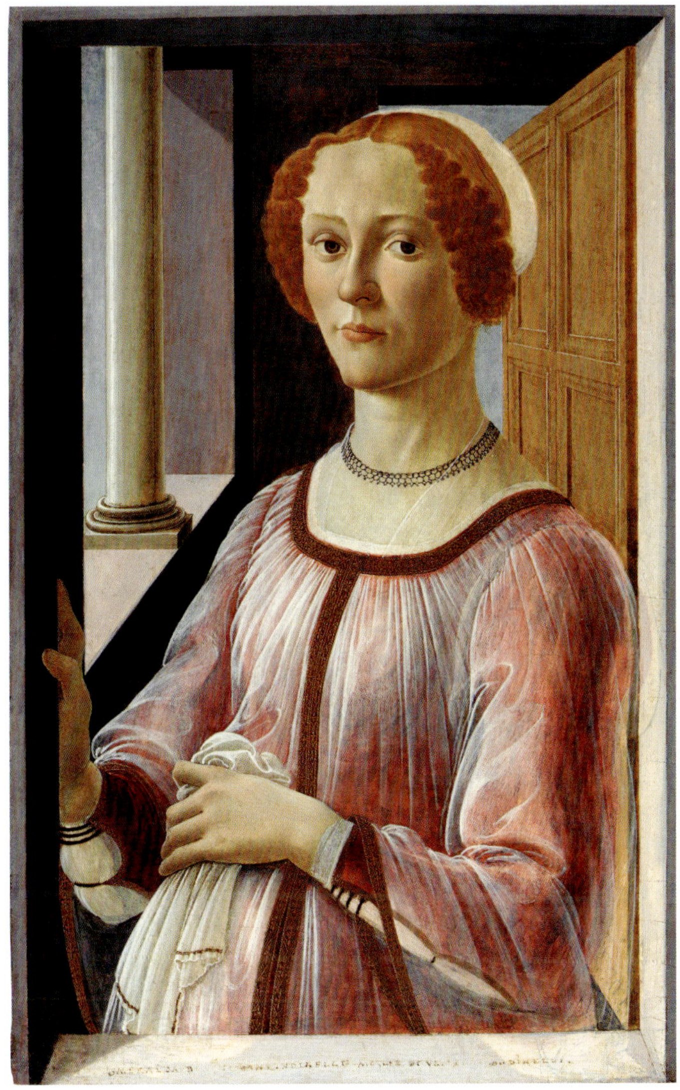

CAT. 162
SANDRO BOTTICELLI
(c.1445–1510)
Portrait of a Lady known as Smeralda Bandinelli, c.1470–5

Changes between underdrawing and painting are frequently encountered in Botticelli's pictures. Those in the present work show indecision over whether the drapery should overhang or be contained by the sill, and the illusion of looking through a window may have been enhanced by the original integral frame, now lost. To emphasize the sitter's glance, the diagonals of the window ledge at the left, cast shadow by the column and upper edge of the shutter all converge on her face, while her right pupil is located near the vertical centre-line. Her stare seems to challenge the conventions of female deportment then current. Lowered eyes signified modesty and obedience, while later moralists, including Savonarola, echoed the exhortation of the Franciscan San Bernardino of Siena that women should 'bury [their] eyes'. Such anxieties may have elicited the vandalism of the figure's right eye.

The literary theme of the 'woman at the window' can be traced back to Dante's vernacular poetry and prose collection of 1295, *La Vita Nova*:

> I paused thinking deeply, and with sad thoughts ... Then I saw a gentle and very lovely young lady, who was looking at me so pitifully from a window, showing so much in her face that all pity seemed concentrated in her ... And so I decided to write a *sonetto*, in which I would speak of her...[6]

The relationship of such imagery to actual life is suggested by a woodcut of around 1500 in the *Canzone per andare in maschera per carnesciale* by Lorenzo di Pierfrancesco de' Medici and others, which depicts young women looking down from the upper windows of a Florentine palace at masked carnival singers in the street below.[7] As late as 1610 a French visitor observed that in Florence 'women are more enclosed than in any other part of Italy: they see the world only from the small openings in their windows'.[8]

A similar setting but without a foreground sill appears in a half-length profile portrait of a lady confronted by an admirer, painted as early as 1438–44 and attributed to Fra Filippo Lippi.[9] A panel of a woman in profile later over-painted with the attributes of St Catherine, datable to the 1470s or 1480s and ascribed to Botticelli (cat. 161), has a similar setting within an illusionistic painted window frame.[10] Early Netherlandish portraits, which were imported to Florence, typically depicted their sitters turned at three-quarters to the viewer, sometimes with hands seeming to extend before a foreground parapet. A half-length of a man, attributed to Botticelli and dated around the 1470s, but destroyed in 1943, depicted its subject in an attitude very like the present composition.[11]

The abraded inscription on the sill identifies the sitter as Smeralda Bandinelli, born around 1439 and the wife of Viviano de' Brandini, whose grandson was the well-known Florentine sculptor Baccio Bandinelli. This compromises the spatial illusion, giving the impression of a vertical rather than a horizontal surface. Evidently an addition, it was probably added early in the seventeenth century by Bandinelli's grandson, who falsified many documents to exaggerate his family's supposedly noble genealogy.[12]

Thereafter, the picture disappears until 1841, by which time it belonged to the wealthy financier James-Alexandre de Pourtalès-Gorgier, a member of a Protestant banking family from Neuchâtel, then a Prussian principality.[13] In 1806 he settled in Paris and was later created a count and a royal chamberlain by the King of Prussia. Pourtalès's fortune was reckoned in 1817 at around £82,000 and he visited Italy, Greece and the Near East, making excursions to London, the Netherlands and Vienna to purchase paintings and antiquities. He was a guest of the King of France, Lord Lansdowne and the Baring Brothers and visitors to his collection included the King of Prussia, Alexander von Humboldt and the Duke and Duchess of Berry.[14] In 1826 Pourtalès sold his 147 'most choice and estimable' Dutch and Flemish seventeenth-century cabinet pictures for over £13,500 and reshaped his collection of ultimately 320 paintings, mainly comprising Italian works of the fifteenth and sixteenth centuries, pictures by Paul Delaroche (fig. 13), François-Marius Granet, Jean-Auguste-Dominique Ingres and other modern French artists, with a

FIG. 11
Photograph from an album of the collection of C.A. Ionides, c.1900
V&A: PH.2–1980

FIG. 12
FRANS HALS
(1582/3–1666)
The Laughing Cavalier, 1624
Oil on canvas, 83 × 67.3 cm
Wallace Collection, London (P84)

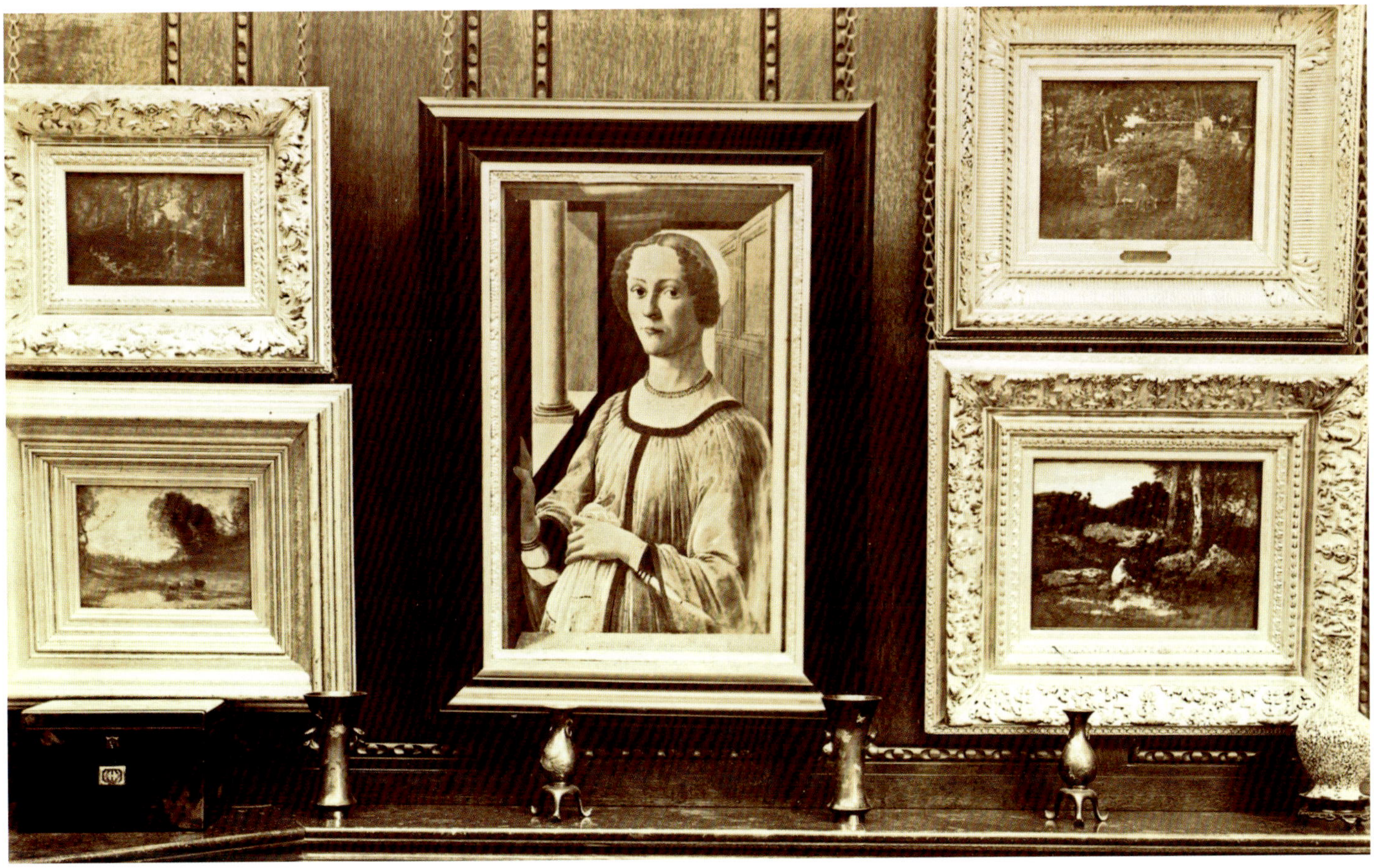

few northern primitives and seventeenth-century paintings.[15] These were catalogued by his adviser Léon-Jean-Joseph Dubois, a lithographer who had accompanied him to Italy in 1802 and in 1832 became curator of Egyptian antiquities at the Louvre.[16] The paintings were displayed in a top-lit gallery at the collector's sumptuous neo-Renaissance mansion on the rue Tronchet, built in 1837–9 by Félix Duban.[17]

After his death Pourtalès's collection remained accessible, and Napoleon III sought to purchase it for the French state.[18] Its eventual sale by his heirs in 1865 was energetically promoted and realized the colossal sum of £111,336.[19] Highlights included Frans Hals's *Laughing Cavalier* (fig. 12), acquired in 1822 for about £57 and bought by the 4th Marquess of Hertford for £2,024, and Antonello da Messina's portrait known as *Il Condottiere*, reputedly purchased in Venice around 1835 for under £30, for which the Louvre paid over £4,500 (fig. 14).[20] The Baron de Triqueti bought a panel then misidentified as a self-portrait of

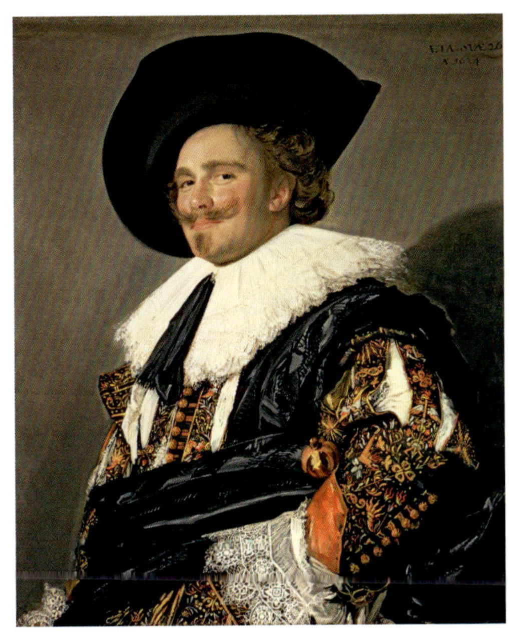

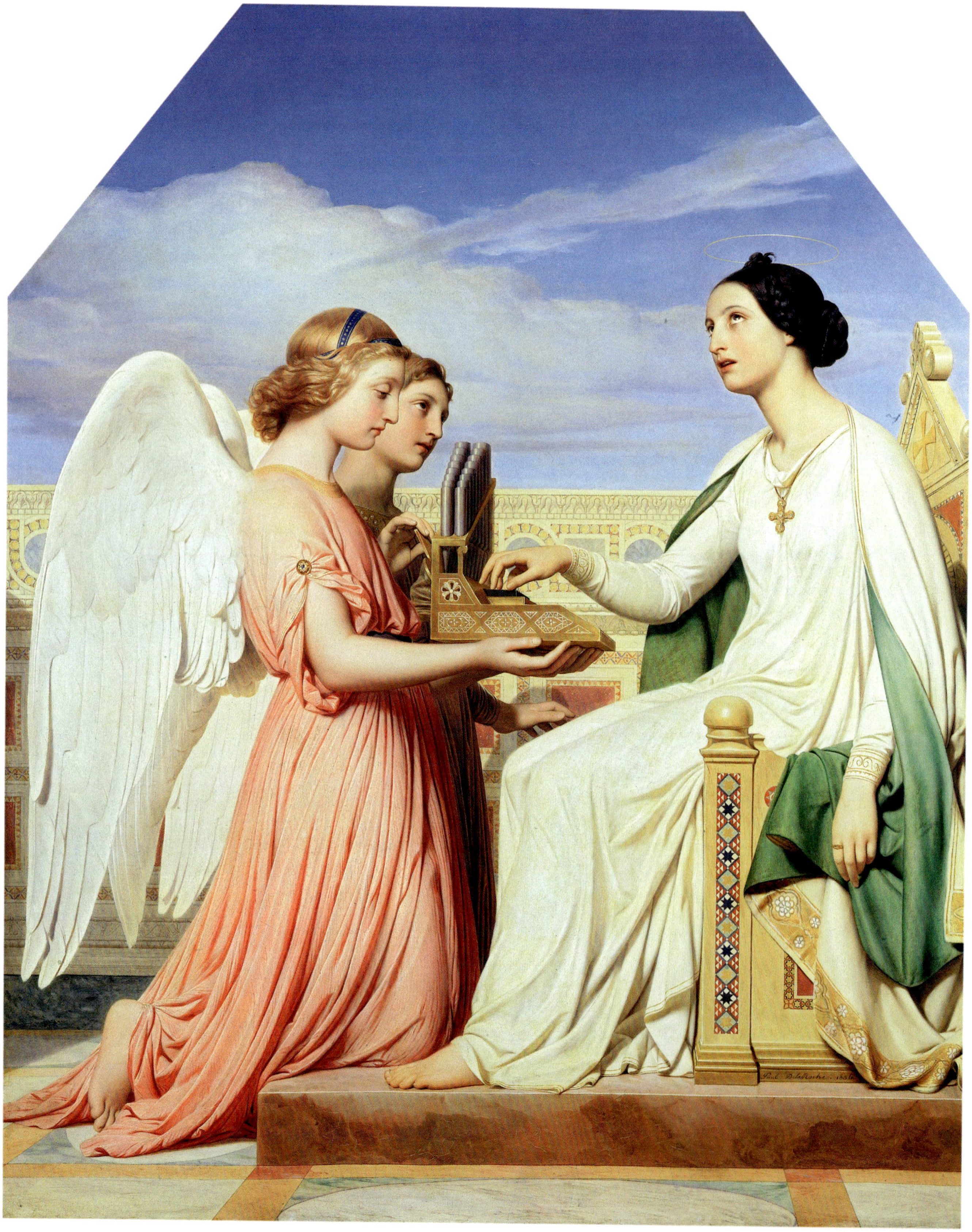

FIG. 13
PAUL DELAROCHE
(1797–1856)
St Cecilia and the Angels, 1836
Oil on canvas, 205.7 × 162.5 cm
Given by Mrs Henry Jephson
V&A: 553–1903

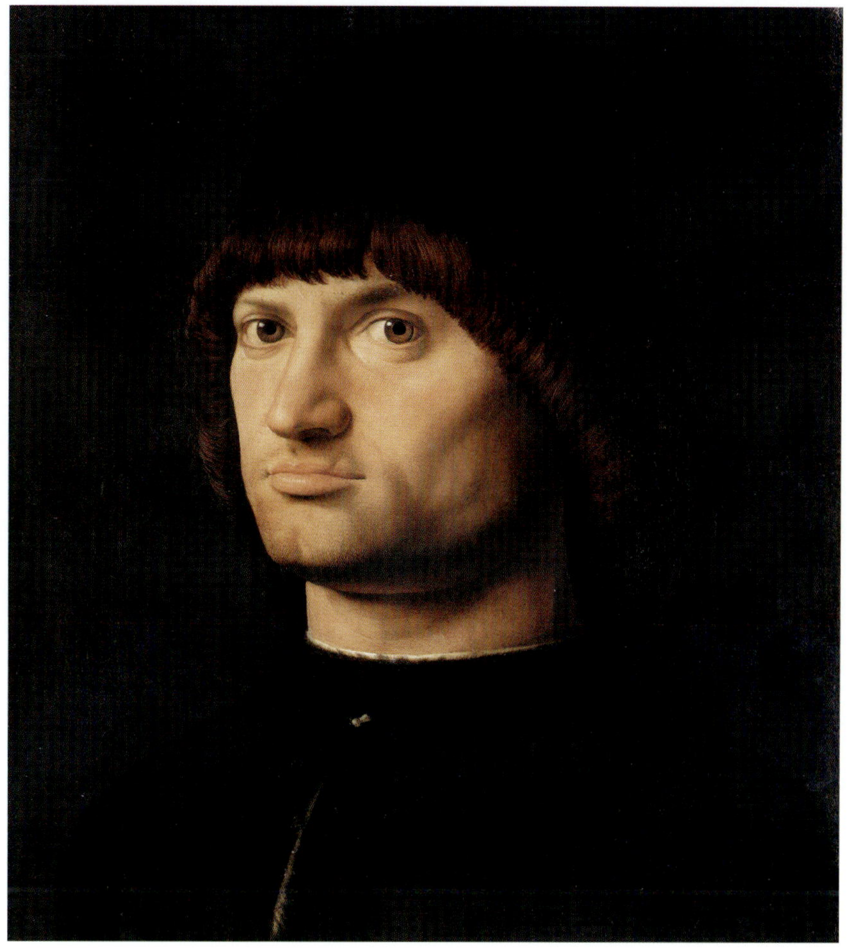

FIG. 14
ANTONELLO DA MESSINA
(c.1430–1479)
Portrait of a Man called Il Condottiere, 1475
Oil on wood, 36 × 30 cm
Musée du Louvre, Paris
(M I 693)

Masaccio but now also attributed to Botticelli for a more modest £103 (cat. 163); a sum comparable with the £135 paid by the dealer Goupil for the present work.[21]

On 11 March 1867 this painting was noticed in a sale of Colnaghi's stock at Christie's by the Pre-Raphaelite artist Dante Gabriel Rossetti, who at Paris in 1849 had been impressed by works by Botticelli.[22] Fancying 'The portrait evidently represents the same head which appears in the central personage of Botticelli's "Spring" at Florence', he purchased it for a trifling £20, paid £4 to have it cleaned, and may himself have repainted the cap.[23] In 1870 Rossetti began a half-length young woman at a window titled *La Donna della Finestra* (fig. 37), evidently inspired by the portrait and the poem of that title in Dante's *Vita Nova*.[24] In January 1872 Rossetti lent the present work to an exhibition at the Royal Academy, and later that year a partner of his roguish agent Charles Augustus Howell sent it without its owner's knowledge on approval to the King of Italy.[25] Rossetti eventually sold it in May 1880 for 300 guineas to the Anglo-Greek stockbroker Constantine Ionides, who had commissioned his large painting of *The Day Dream* for 700 guineas.[26] The artist exulted to his friend and model Jane Morris: 'I have turned dealer! … The idea of selling pictures you don't have to paint is certainly a very great one. If M Angelo had once smelt blood in that way, we should never have had the Sixtine [*sic*] Chapel!'[27]

Ionides included the present work in a display of Old Masters and nineteenth-century French cabinet paintings (fig. 11) in the gallery added in 1889–91 to his house at 23 Second Avenue, Hove, by the Arts and Crafts architect Philip Webb.[28] He lent it in 1893–4 to the exhibition *Early Italian Art, from 1300 to 1550* at the New Gallery in London (no. 110) and in 1901 bequeathed his 1,138 pictures, drawings and prints 'for the benefit of the nation to be kept … as one separate collection' in the recently renamed Victoria and Albert Museum. It was joined there by Delaroche's *St Cecilia and the Angels*, also formerly owned by Pourtalès (fig. 13).

The Story of Botticelli's Drawings for Dante's *Divine Comedy*

DAGMAR KORBACHER

Drawings, even those from the hands of the greatest artists, rarely have an exciting historical reception or significant influence. This is to be expected, given that – whether used as working materials in an artist's workshop or hidden away in collectors' albums – they are on the whole relatively small and intimate in nature. Drawings by the great masters have nonetheless always been coveted, including those by Botticelli, who according to Vasari drew 'extraordinarily prolifically and well', 'which is why later artists tried to acquire his drawings'.[1] Indeed, Vasari claimed that he himself owned works by Botticelli, among them probably his *Allegory of Abundance* (cat. 165).[2] Loose drawings that were thought to bear the hand of Botticelli were always considered of high quality and desirable for collectors, as the presence of a number of works attributed to him in the Richardson collection attests.[3] The Dante cycle, however, originally comprising 102 drawings, cannot be compared with such individual works, nor – despite being similar in scope – with other collections of drawings, such as the volumes by Jacopo Bellini, which belong to the model-book tradition and were intended for circulation among other artists.[4]

Dante's *Divine Comedy* was composed around 1307–21. Manuscript copies continued to be made through the fourteenth and fifteenth centuries, supplemented by a Florentine tradition of composing spoken and written commentaries on this celebrated text. Over 600 early manuscripts of Dante's *Divine Comedy* have survived, but only a few are illustrated. The first printed edition of the *Divine Comedy* was published in Foligno by Johann Neumeister and Evangelista Angelini di Trevi in 1472, followed closely by Venetian and Mantuan editions of the text. In 1481, the definitive edition was published in Florence, with a commentary by the humanist Cristoforo Landino and engraved illustrations by Baccio Baldini after designs by Botticelli.

Botticelli's distinctly singular drawings for the *Divine Comedy* are not indebted to any of these traditions and their original function remains an open question.[5] They offer a vision of Dante's universe, and were intended for an educated patron, probably Lorenzo di Pierfrancesco de' Medici, as the Anonimo Gaddiano, Vincenzo Borghini, asserted.[6] He provides the most concrete piece of evidence available to us in connection with this cycle of drawings:

Botticelli 'painted and devised a Dante on vellum for Lorenzo di Pierfrancesco de' Medici, which was a thing of wonder'.[7] Whether Lorenzo's death in 1503 was the reason why Botticelli only added colour to a few of the drawings is impossible to determine, as is the question of their later history. We do not know whether the cycle was still in Florence in the 1540s, when Borghini was writing; it disappeared without trace immediately after its creation. Formal similarities with individual works suggest that at least a few artists in sixteenth-century Florence – among them perhaps Michelangelo,[8] Giovanni Stradano and Federico Zuccaro, whose drawings for the *Divine Comedy* (1585–8) exhibit certain parallels with Botticelli's pictorial solutions[9] – had the opportunity to study the series of images, or single sheets from it. However, the possibility that contemporary copies were made and used to disseminate the drawings cannot be ruled out. We know of a few examples that are drawn on vellum like the originals, but differ from them slightly in terms of size and significantly in terms of the stiffness of their execution and use of red chalk underdrawing (the originals used metal-point).[10] All things considered, it seems entirely plausible that they functioned as *ricordi* (workshop copies after finished pieces) in the early sixteenth or late fifteenth century.

Tracing the subsequent transmission of Botticelli's Dante drawings leads us to Paris, where they may have been presented as a diplomatic gift as early as the beginning of the sixteenth century. This would preclude the possibility of their reappearance in Florence, supporting the notion that at least a few *ricordi* remained there. At first the sheets were probably unbound, which made it easier to split them into two groups. The smaller group, consisting of seven drawings, was in 1632 in the library of Alexandre Pétau in Paris, then from 1658 it was in the possession of Queen Christina of Sweden.[11] After passing through the hands of the cardinals Decio and Pompeo Azzolino, as well as Pope Alexander VIII, the drawings eventually found their way into the Vatican Library, where they were only rediscovered in 1885 after the greater part of the cycle had already come to light.[12] In 1803 this latter group of 88 sheets surfaced in Paris in the possession of the book dealer Giovanni Claudio Molini. They were attributed to 'Botticelli or another artist from this golden age of the art of drawing' and were bound together into an album around the same time. This volume was sold to Alexander, Marquis of Douglas and Clydesdale, later the 10th Duke of Hamilton, and mentioned as part of his library in 1819.[13] It was still in his collection in 1851, when the then director of the Berlin Gemäldegalerie, G.F. Waagen, was permitted to admire it.[14] The Hamilton collection, which also included numerous valuable and very fine manuscripts, remained in his family's possession until financial difficulties obliged the 12th Duke of Hamilton to put them up for sale.

When this became public in 1882, representatives from museums in Berlin – above all Friedrich Lippmann, director of the Kupferstichkabinett (engravings collection) – went to great lengths to acquire the Dante drawings. It was only when word of the impending sale got out that their extraordinary significance became apparent. In a few short years Botticelli had ascended from being a 'secondary painter'[15] to an 'artist of the highest rank'.[16] In 1868 the poet Algernon Charles Swinburne wrote an essay celebrating his drawings.[17] John Ruskin similarly praised the unusual graphic qualities of Botticelli's art, calling him 'the greatest Florentine master of engraving' and noting that 'of Delineators, the chief is Botticelli'.[18] The association with Dante helped Botticelli to gain acceptance. Walter Pater[19] and Ruskin,[20] both great admirers of Dante, saw in Botticelli a profoundly Dante-esque artist – one in an aesthetic, poetic sense and the other in a theological, moral sense.[21] In their eyes Dante was key to understanding the art of Botticelli,[22] while Botticelli was an artist who, more than any other, possessed an understanding of and feeling for Dante and his poetry.[23] Pater concluded from a comment made by Vasari[24] that Botticelli had written a commentary on Dante, but this has never been found; the nineteen copperplate engravings for the *Inferno* in Landino's edition of the *Divine Comedy* (1481), however, which were attributed to Baldini after sketches by Botticelli, are well known.[25] Botticelli came to be styled as the Dante illustrator *par excellence*, so when the *Divine Comedy* drawings from the Hamilton collection were rediscovered they must have seemed like the crowning achievement of his artistic career.[26] The loss they represented for Great Britain – perceived as a tragedy, even a national scandal[27] – which coincided so closely with their rediscovery, contributed to the Botticelli myth, carried on a wave of British national sentiment and contemporary artistic taste. Despite intervention by Ruskin and by the British royal family, the Dante illustrations were sold to Berlin as part of the Hamilton collection.[28]

Here their story really begins. Under the auspices of the museum they were made accessible, removed from the album, mounted and published (as full-size collotype facsimiles in 1887,[29] among other versions), giving the illustrations the kind of publicity that drawings, as previously observed, are generally denied. After the Berlin group of drawings was split up during the division of Germany and then reunited, in 2000 an exhibition took place in Berlin, Rome and London that brought together all 92 images known today, representing the peak of their art-historical reception so far.[30] Their reputation among artists, too, continued to thrive. In his digital images Andreas Siekmann[31] confronts Botticelli's Dante and Virgil with the problems of the modern world, while other artists such as Jorinde Voigt[32] and Nick Fox also draw inspiration for their work from the Dante drawings.

The creation of Botticelli's *Divine Comedy* was shaped by the cult of Dante in late fifteenth-century Florence, and its rediscovery by the cult of Dante in nineteenth-century England. For his preoccupation with Dante Botticelli was chided by Vasari, and praised by Pater and Ruskin. His posthumous reputation is indissolubly linked to these drawings. It therefore seems prescient that Botticelli should have immortalized himself in one of the images with a plea for intercession, placing his future, his fate as a draughtsman, in the hands of an angel bearing a tablet inscribed with his name (cat. 153).

CAT. 153 (detail)
SANDRO BOTTICELLI
(c.1445–1510)
Dante Sees God as a Brightly Shining Point of Light Surrounded by Choirs of Angels in the Ninth Sphere of Paradise (Crystal Heaven or Primum Mobile) (The Divine Comedy, Paradise, canto XXVIII), *c.*1492–5

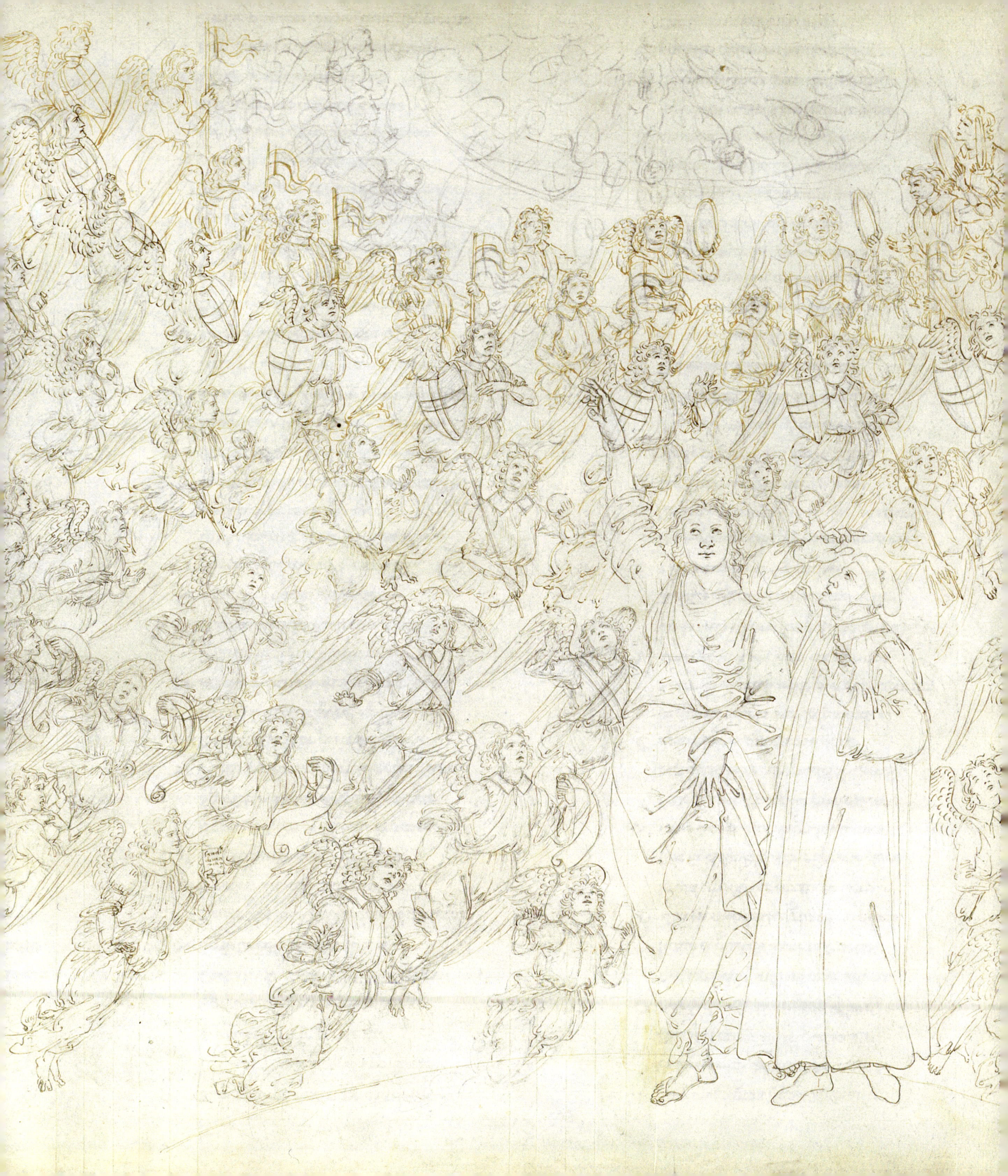

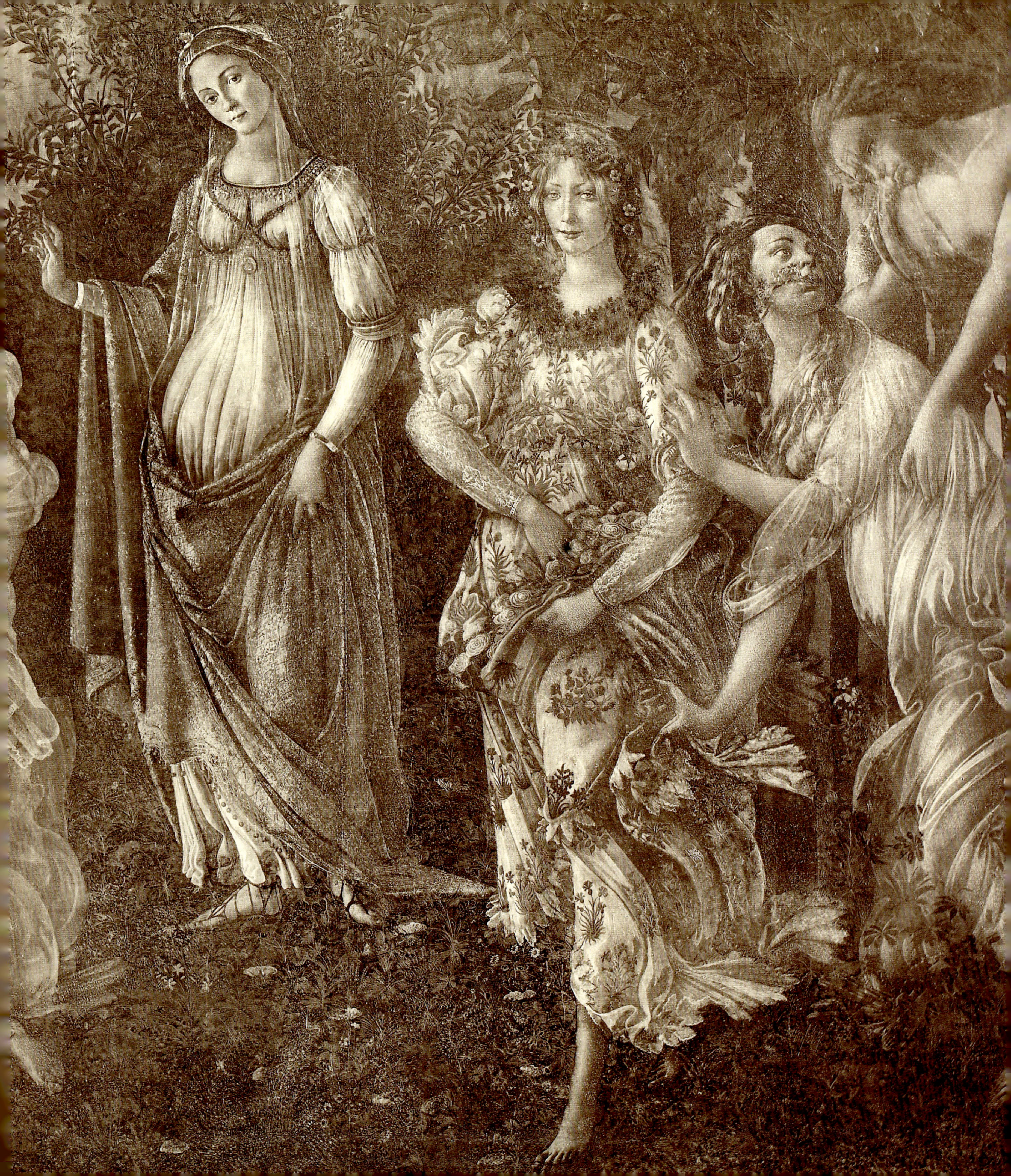

The Rediscovery of Botticelli in the Nineteenth Century

During the nineteenth century, a host of Old Master painters were rediscovered, from Fra Angelico to El Greco and from Vermeer to Watteau. The pioneering generation of art historians such as Luigi Lanzi, Johann Dominico Fiorillo and Carl Friedrich von Rumohr reconsidered the works of the Italian painters of the century before Raphael, whose style had been condemned as obsolete over two centuries earlier by Giorgio Vasari. The professor of art history in Berlin, Franz Kugler, felt that Botticelli was best represented by his *Madonna del Magnificat* (see under cat. 117), while the *Birth of Venus* (fig. 10) exemplified a 'fanciful bias' which 'often degenerates into mannerism'.

In 1870 appeared Walter Pater's influential 'Fragment on Sandro Botticelli', and Dante Gabriel Rossetti's first version of *La Donna della Finestra*, inspired by a Botticelli portrait (cat. 162). Pater felt the *Birth of Venus* 'reminds you of the faultless nude studies of Ingres' although 'the sorrow in her face was at the thought of the whole long day of love yet to come'. Inspired by such examples, the Pre-Raphaelites developed a languid and historicist style, whose aesthetic proved hugely influential during the last decades of the nineteenth century.

For the art historian Aby Warburg, Botticelli was the creator of complex allegories whereas his friend Herbert Horne analysed the artist's wide-ranging oeuvre to show its stylistic development. Building on the 'scientific connoisseurship' of Giovanni Morelli, the American Bernard Berenson clarified Botticelli's place among the most important Renaissance painters, both as the creator of remarkable inventions and the designer of numerous works made with the help of collaborators and assistants.

Around 1910 Berenson's method of classification itself became the stuff of fiction when the decadent writer Frederick William Rolfe, styled Baron Corvo, began his unfinished homoerotic novel *Amico di Sandro*, which imagined an encounter with the youthful Botticelli, inspired by his *Portrait of a Young Man* (fig. 33). Thus it was that Botticelli's work elicited the erotic response that has co-existed with its spiritual aspect and intellectual dimension until the present day.
AD/ME/RR

CAT. 53 (detail)

The Critical Fortunes of 'Vasari's Botticelli' in the Nineteenth Century

ULRICH REHM

Almost everything earlier scholars thought they knew about the life of Botticelli came from the pen of Giorgio Vasari. In his *Lives* of Italian artists, first published in 1550, 40 years after Botticelli's death, the painter was attributed a rather ignoble end.[1] During the power vacuum in Florence in 1494 Botticelli became – according to Vasari – so in thrall to the Dominican friar Girolamo Savonarola that he abandoned painting, thereby losing his source of income and getting into terrible difficulties.

Savonarola's followers, referred to by Vasari as cult members, were known as 'whiners' (*piagnoni*) and opposed the hedonistic excesses of the powerful and the vogue for 'pagan' antiquity. Naturally Vasari also had something to say about the symptoms of Botticelli's alleged decline: after his return from Rome in 1482 – being a 'sophisticated person' (*persona sofistica*) – he began to waste time studying the poetry of Dante Alighieri.

Vasari's caricature has little basis in recorded fact,[2] and was doubtless part of the reason why Botticelli was largely forgotten until around 1800. In the nineteenth century, however, it was precisely the story of the whiners and the 'sophisticated person' that captured attention. Various influential authors, motivated by different interests, transformed Vasari's eccentric late Botticelli into a positive individual with considerable religious, cultural and social impact on an essentially medieval culture. This was portrayed either as a kind of internal cultural and spiritual renewal or as the first signs of an epochal turn towards the early modern era.

This new assessment of the painter was given significant impetus by the French author Alexis-François Rio, whose large-scale survey of Christian art (*poésie chrétienne*), in which he credited Girolamo Savonarola with a decisive role as a religious reformer, was first published in 1836. Its author reached this reassessment in the context of the nineteenth-century revival of Catholicism in France and Germany. Rio saw the arts as the quintessential realization and agent of the Christian mysticism that had emerged under Savonarola's influence. Botticelli, he believed, had become a Christian mystic,[3] and as a follower of Savonarola had deliberately renounced painting, distancing himself from the 'pagan' images so popular with his former patrons in Florence. Rio echoed Vasari's claim that Botticelli had executed one final work, a print inspired by Savonarola's teachings titled *The Triumph of Faith*. This, he said, had surpassed all his previous endeavours, and after the Dominican friar's death he remained so resolutely loyal that he would rather starve than pick up a paintbrush again. Rio's conception of a pre-Renaissance religious style, whose exponents included such painters as Fra Angelico and Botticelli, had important consequences for the English Pre-Raphaelites.

A few decades later, in 1870, the English art critic Walter Pater wrote an essay on Botticelli that approached him from a very different perspective, and which was explicitly critical of the Church. What interested Pater was how an artistic genius could thrive despite the religious and ecclesiastical shackles of his day, and the restrictions that 'the religious system of the Middle Ages imposed on the heart and imagination'.[4] Botticelli was, for him, the epitome of the poetic painter[5] and, in terms of artistic development, a shining example of the 'outbreak of the human spirit'.[6] He embodied 'the freshness, the uncertain and diffident promise, which belong to the earlier Renaissance itself, and make it perhaps the most interesting period in the history of the mind'.[7]

Like Rio, Pater based his argument on 'Vasari's Botticelli', but took a thoroughly critical stance. He called into question the notion that Botticelli had been a 'sophisticated person', and played down the painter's alleged interest in literature and theory. Instead he emphasized the aesthetic aspirations of his engagement with Dante's *Divine Comedy*, claiming that in them Botticelli had achieved 'a true painter's vision'.[8] He explained Botticelli's apparent religious conversion and its disastrous consequences described by Vasari as 'a sort of religious melancholy'. He was also – rightly – sceptical of Vasari's claim that he remained artistically inactive for so long.[9]

Just as Rio believed that Botticelli had reinvigorated Catholicism in France, the English critic of art and society John Ruskin declared him to be a historical forerunner of the Reformation, much like Dante and Savonarola, whom he called the 'southern reformers' and likened to the northerners Hans Holbein the younger, Martin Luther, King Henry VIII and Oliver Cromwell.[10] Indeed, many Anglicans identified Savonarola as a proto-Protestant, and he was commemorated as such in 1881–3 beside the English Lollard John Wycliffe and the Czech reformer Jan Hus among the alabaster roundels at St Stephen's, Hampstead, a Gothic Revival church endowed by a friend of Ruskin.[11] In his lectures of the 1870s Ruskin drew on some important aspects of Rio's 'epoch' model, in particular his idealized notion of a fundamentally religious pre-Renaissance. Botticelli represented 'the most learned theologian, the most perfect artist, and the most kind gentleman whom Florence produced';[12] he was the universal painter *par excellence*, possessing an understanding of both pagan and Christian thought.[13] In a letter dated 1872, Ruskin quoted some key passages from 'Vasari's Botticelli', lending the painter an added socio-political dimension: his alleged membership of the 'whiners' is adduced as evidence of a charitable commitment, to which the author is clearly sympathetic.[14]

In the 1890s the newly established academic discipline of art history started to discover Botticelli for itself. The positive reinterpretations of 'Vasari's Botticelli' now gave way to an attempt to fully comprehend the various phases of Botticelli's artistic career. While in 1878 the National Gallery's acquisition of Botticelli's so-called *Mystic Nativity* (cat. 101) was widely applauded, by the start of the twentieth century this same religious painting, a dated late work of 1500 (after the Florentine calendar), was generally viewed as a retrograde withdrawal from the achievements of the Renaissance into pious irrationality. The ageing painter's purported religious radicalism was identified – again echoing Vasari – as the cause of this retreat.[15] This rejection of Botticelli's later works often went hand in hand with growing disapproval of the increasingly unfashionable Pre-Raphaelites. Wilhelm von Bode's verdict on the *Mystic Nativity* was typical: 'to a decadent art movement like that of the English Pre-Raphaelites, this picture … must have seemed like a revelation.'[16]

Botticelli Enters the Museum: The Rediscovery of a Painter and the Invention of the Public Art Museum

RUBEN REBMANN

Art museums have the power both to remember and to forget. Their history was shaped well into the twentieth century by a crucial contradiction, which quickly proved to be a productive one. In the Enlightenment, armed with the conviction that recognizing beauty in art made it easier for people to recognize moral virtues, public museums focused on bringing art sanctioned by the acknowledged classical canon to a wide audience, for their ethical development and edification. This canon emphasized classical sculpture and the painting of the Italian High Renaissance. The parallel objective of teaching people about the history of art would soon, however, enable new aesthetic discoveries that caused that very canon to be eroded. Unknown artists from eras previously seen as 'primitive' or 'decadent' might find themselves the focus of attention, threatening traditional authorities such as Raphael. This journey from the periphery to the centre of museums' concerns – which can in part be traced across the space of the buildings themselves – is also the story of Botticelli's rediscovery in the nineteenth century. While hardly any eighteenth-century collections of paintings featured his work, today they are found almost exclusively in public museums and a few private collections. Almost none of them has remained in its original context – even frescoes were transplanted into the narrative of the museum.

For educated tourists travelling to Florence around 1900, the highlight of their trip would have been seeing *Primavera* in the Botticelli room of the Galleria dell'Accademia and the *Birth of Venus* in the Uffizi. Two hundred years earlier, however, Botticelli would have meant nothing to visiting art lovers, and they would most likely have left the city without even having heard him mentioned. Guidebooks like Francesco Bocchi's *Bellezze della Città di Fiorenza* (1591), which was considerably expanded by Giovanni Cinelli in 1677, did nonetheless point visitors in the direction of a few works.[1] Botticelli's great altarpieces had already been removed from their original locations. His San Marco altarpiece, for instance, had been transferred to the monastery's chapter house,[2] and the San Barnaba altarpiece was moved from its original position to 'behind the main altar'.[3] After the dissolution of the monasteries from which they take their names, both works found their way to the Accademia in 1808, and finally to the Uffizi in the twentieth century. The Bardi altarpiece, originally located in a chapel at Santo Spirito but now in Berlin, was replaced with another in the Baroque style as early as 1677.[4] An old altarpiece was more

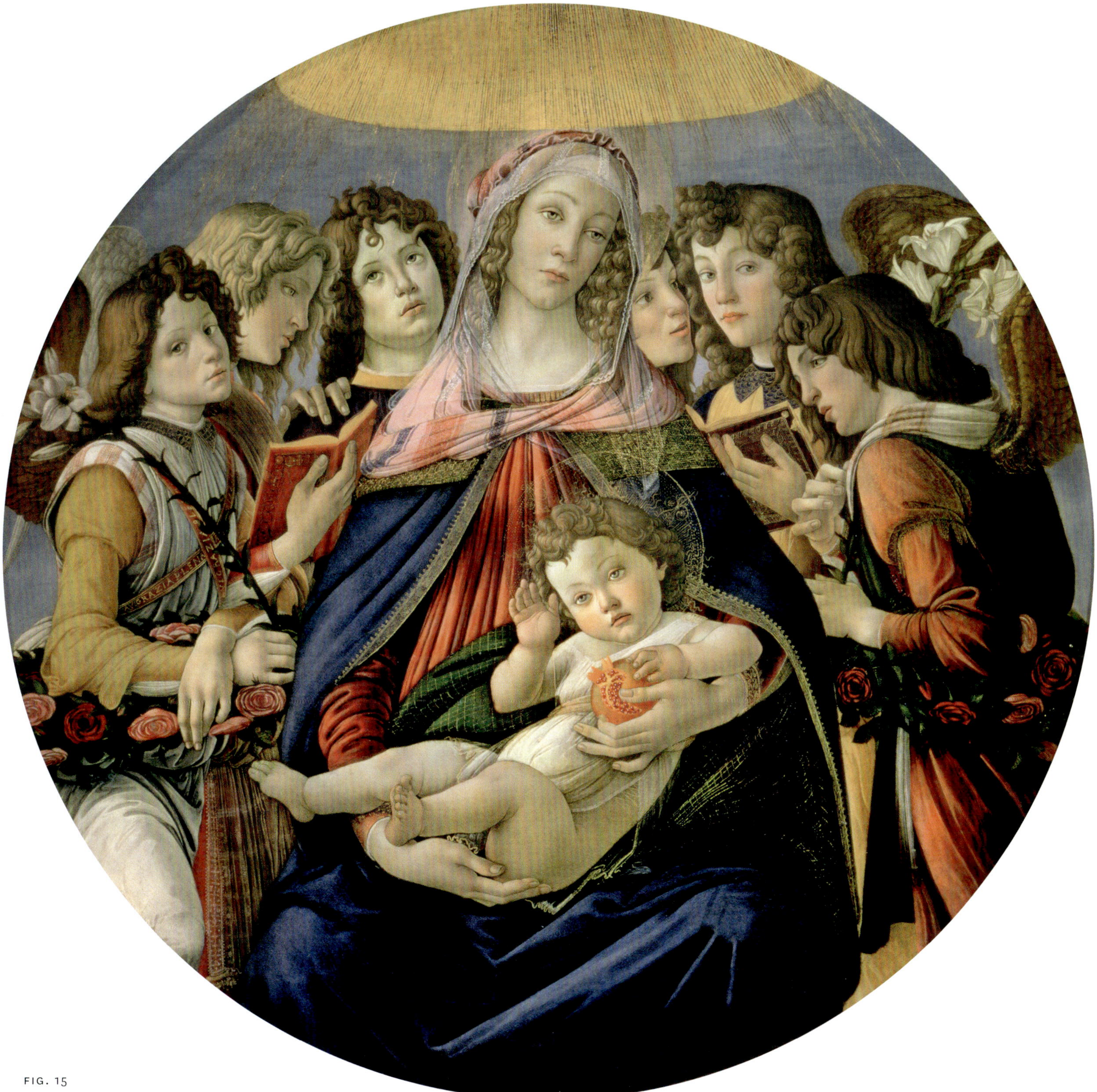

FIG. 15
SANDRO BOTTICELLI
(c.1445–1510)
Madonna of the Pomegranate, c.1487
Tempera on wood, 143.5 × 143.5 cm
Galleria degli Uffizi, Florence (1607)

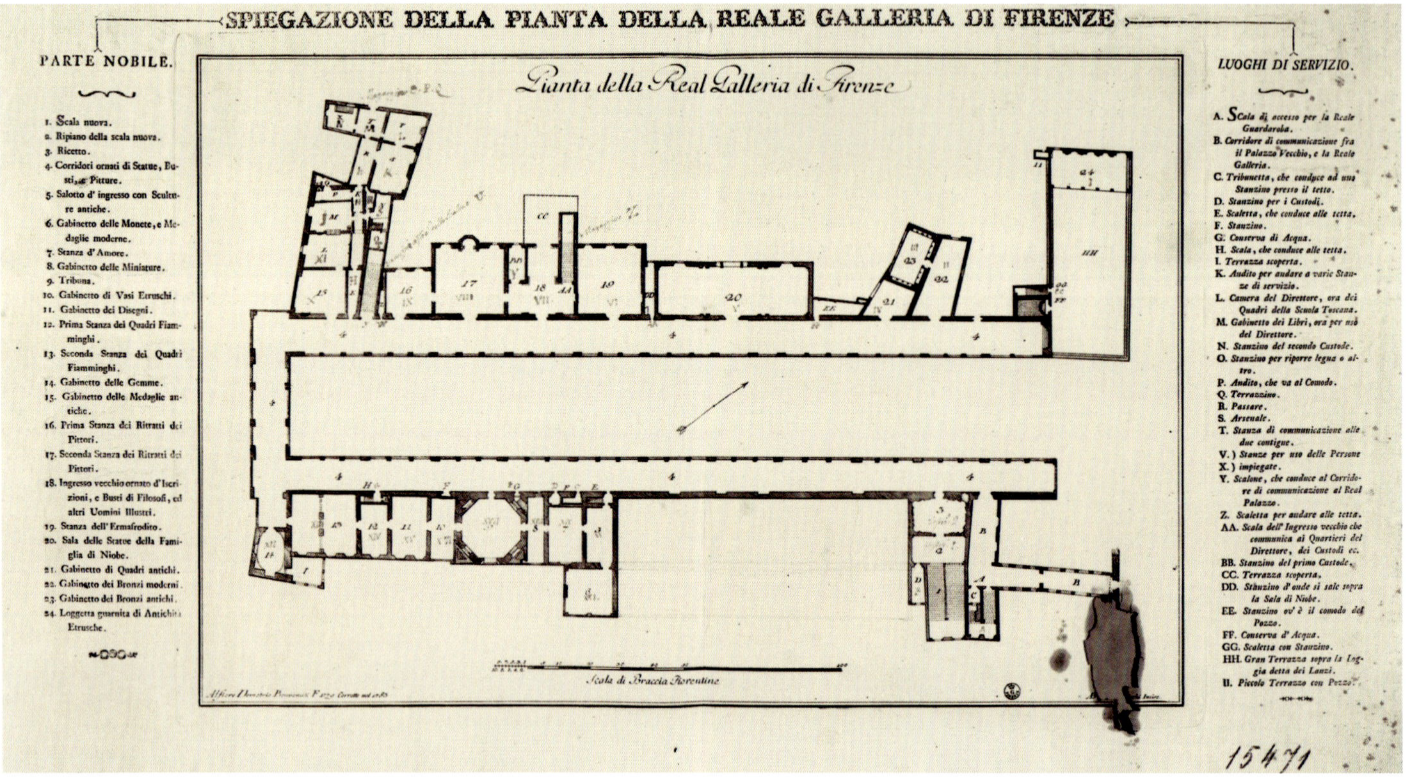

FIG. 16
DEMETRIO BENVENUTI and
GIOVAN BATTISTA CANOCCHI
Floor plan of the Galleria degli Uffizi in Florence, 1779, 1783 (updated in 1790)
Galleria degli Uffizi, Florence (n.15471)

likely to be replaced with a new one in seventeenth-century Florence if a prominent collector was interested in acquiring the original painting for his gallery. Whether this was the fate of the Botticelli altarpieces is unknown. It is more likely in this case that the removal was due to changes in contemporary taste.

Probably the only Baroque collector who deliberately acquired paintings by Botticelli was Cardinal Leopoldo de' Medici. The 1675 inventory of his collection includes a *Madonna of the Pomegranate*, which by that time was already attributed to Botticelli (fig. 15).[5] The painting would later be transferred to the Uffizi in 1780,[6] so it could be shown alongside other recently acquired paintings by Botticelli in a newly created 'Old Paintings' Gallery'.[7] The establishment of this room was one of the most successful steps in the process of restructuring the 'Imperial and Royal Gallery' into a public museum, that did not merely restrict itself – in a 'gesture of purification'[8] – to classical sculpture and post-classical painting, but went a step further and widened the latter category to include the whole 'renaissance de la peinture en Italie'.[9] Above all, this expansion meant including painting before Raphael, a decision that culminated in a new rehang in the east corridor, completed in 1799. Beginning with Byzantine painting and ordered chronologically, it was the visual realization of a 'progressive', linear conception of art history.[10] Leopoldo's *Madonna of the Pomegranate* was relocated here too, and assigned its place in 'stylistic single file'.[11]

The rehang was overshadowed by Napoleon's military campaigns, which occasioned the extensive seizure of artworks from Italian collections. In 1811 Dominique-Vivant Denon, director of the Musée Napoléon, came to Florence to appropriate paintings for a new wing dedicated to early Italian painting before Raphael. From the Accademia's collection he chose, among other works, a piece by Botticelli. Upon its arrival in Paris in 1812, Denon protested vehemently that instead of the work he had chosen in Florence – he must have been referring to the San Marco or San Barnaba altarpiece – he had been sent a round painting of the Virgin Mary with four angels.[12] The tondo foisted on Denon was a version of Botticelli's *Madonna del Magnificat*, today in Montpellier,[13] and was exhibited shortly afterwards in 1814 at the great Paris

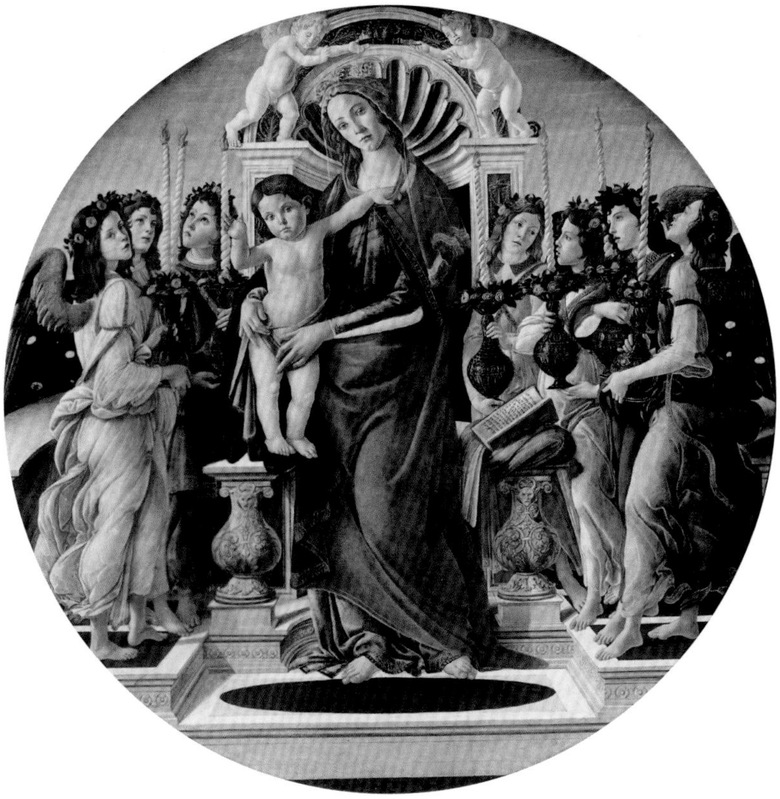

exhibition of the 'Écoles Primitives'.[14] Not least because of the subterfuge involved in his painting's transfer from Italy, Botticelli would remain a mere footnote in the narrative of what was then the most comprehensive display of the history of painting before Raphael. The Musée Napoléon also had another of Botticelli's Madonnas (today in Lille), though until 1840 it was attributed to Cimabue.[15] The *Madonna del Magnificat* (see cat. 117) in the Uffizi was also not attributed to Botticelli, but to the 'German school'.[16] Though the version of the *Magnificat* tondo in Paris was never returned to Florence, it evidently helped the director of the Uffizi to reattribute the gallery's own copy.[17]

It was not only French museums that benefited from the exodus of artworks from Italian collections and churches. In the Prussian capital of Berlin there had been plans dating as far back as the late eighteenth century to make the royal collections, scattered across numerous locations in Potsdam and Berlin, accessible to a wider audience by amalgamating them into a single public art museum.[18] From 1815 these plans were pursued more intently, due in no small part to the example of the Musée Napoléon. What was new, however, was the idea that the royal collections should be significantly expanded to include examples from hitherto unrepresented schools and eras, in order to depict the history of European painting more broadly. As in Florence, this notion was closely connected to the development of art history as an academic discipline. In 1815 the King of Prussia, Friedrich Wilhelm III, bought the Giustiniani collection from Rome, then in 1821 the collection belonging to the English businessman Edward Solly, who lived in Berlin and was advised in his purchases by German art experts.[19] Significantly for the museum, which had long been planning this acquisition, the latter collection featured works that had previously only rarely appeared in major galleries, including Italian, German and Netherlandish panels from the centuries before Raphael, among them the wings of Jan van Eyck's celebrated Ghent altarpiece. It contained eight paintings by Botticelli and his workshop alone, including the *Venus*, a tondo almost two metres across of a *Madonna with Angels Carrying Candles* (lost in 1945; fig. 17), an *Annunciation* (lost in 1945; fig. 18), a *Madonna with Young St John the Baptist* (lost in 1945) and a *St Sebastian*, which at that time was attributed to Antonio Pollaiuolo. The large tondo was mentioned in a list drawn up by Karl Friedrich Schinkel, a member of the museum's committee, of the 77 most important works from a total of 3,000 paintings in the Solly collection, and was valued by

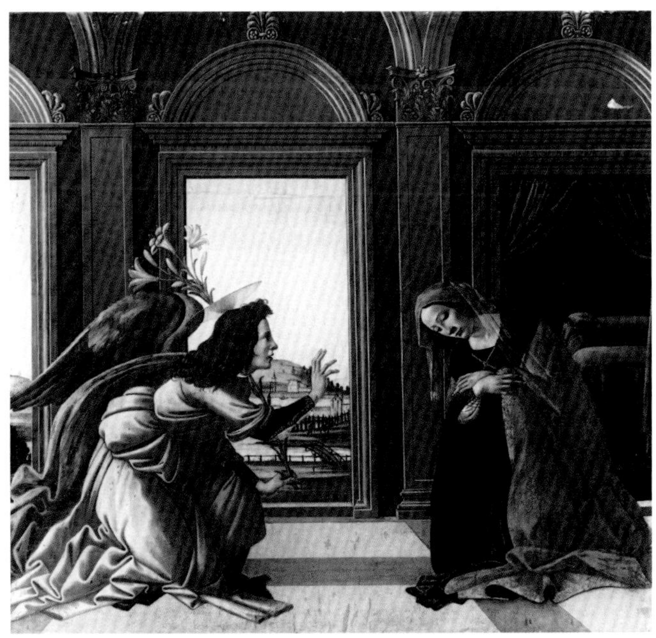

FIG. 17
SANDRO BOTTICELLI
(c.1445–1510)
Madonna with Angels Carrying Candles, c.1485–90s
Tempera on wood, 192 × 192 cm
Formerly Gemäldegalerie, Berlin
(no.102)

FIG. 18
SANDRO BOTTICELLI
(c.1445–1510)
Annunciation, c.1490
Tempera on wood, 106 × 113 cm
Formerly Gemäldegalerie, Berlin
(no.1117)

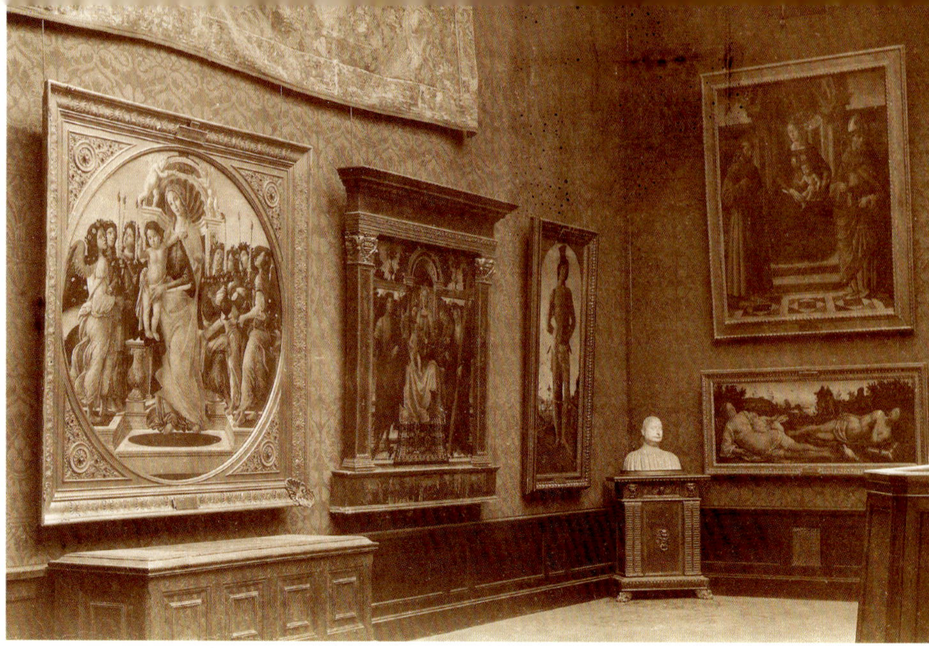

FIG. 19
Botticelli Room, part of the picture gallery and sculpture collection in the Kaiser Friedrich Museum (Room 38), Berlin, 1910
Gemäldegalerie, Staatliche Museen zu Berlin

FIG. 20
Botticelli Room, part of the picture gallery in the Kaiser Friedrich Museum (Room 37), Berlin, 1935
Gemäldegalerie, Staatliche Museen zu Berlin

him at 3,000 thalers.[20] The acquisition of these Botticelli paintings was not simply part of a bulk purchase, but was motivated by a specific interest in the artist's work, as evidenced by the additional works Carl Friedrich von Rumohr bought in Italy in 1828–9 on behalf of the museum in Berlin, which opened a year later. He was able to acquire the Bardi altarpiece (cat. 106) and a painting of a woman (today in Houston, cat. 159), which he believed was a portrait of Simonetta Vespucci. This identification (and similar ones for portraits of women in Frankfurt and the Palazzo Pitti; cats 157, 160) was clearly influenced by Vasari, who was still considered an authority in terms of reconstructing Botticelli's oeuvre.

Even before the museum opened, its collection of Botticellis seems to have sparked greater interest in the artist. Two prominent Berlin collectors, Count Ingenheim[21] and Count Raczyński, purchased other paintings by the early Renaissance master. The Botticelli tondo (cat. 113) took pride of place among the Old Master paintings in the latter's collection, which was open to the public in his palace on the future site of the Reichstag (the German parliament building). Raczyński was also particularly interested in works by contemporary German painters.[22] Among them, however (and particularly among the Nazarenes), there seems to have been little enthusiasm for Botticelli. The continental rediscovery of Botticelli by artists, rather than art historians, originated mainly among French writers and painters, who were fascinated by his mythologies.

The most important of these – *Primavera* and the *Birth of Venus* – were initially largely ignored by the Florentine museum directors, though they had been in their storage since 1815. Although *Primavera* was shortly afterwards hung in the second of the rooms dedicated to Tuscan art in the Uffizi, it was relegated to storage after the room was renovated in 1821,[23] before re-emerging in 1853 and being transferred to the Accademia.[24] The *Venus*'s first documented appearance was in 1844, when it was hung in the Uffizi's east corridor next to the tondos of the *Madonna of the Pomegranate* and *Madonna del Magnificat*,[25] the location originally envisaged for it in 1815.[26] It was here that Edmond and Jules de Goncourt saw the painting on their travels around Italy in 1855–6. They celebrated its depiction of a blonde, Nordic Venus who 'seems to have been born on Walpurgis Night', contrasting her with the moribund heathenism of the ancient Medicean Venus.[27] Three years later the picture captured the imaginations of Gustave Moreau and Edgar Degas, who made copies of it (cats 82, 88). When Moreau temporarily left Florence, Degas remained, and wrote to his fellow artist about a new discovery he had made – the *Primavera* in the Accademia.[28] In France, where in 1824 another Botticelli Madonna (cat. 110) had been added to the Louvre's collection, the discovery of the *Venus* was also celebrated as a rediscovery of its creator. In 1862 Léon Lagrange directed anybody who thought Botticelli was merely a painter of 'Madonnas and nothing but Madonnas' to Florence, to gaze in silent wonder at the *Venus*. 'Alas!' he added, however, 'the Florentines themselves have abandoned Botticelli in a corridor, and reserved pride of place in the Tribuna for paintings by Reni and Guercino.'[29]

It was in the Accademia, then, that this new interest in Botticelli first resulted in his work being presented more prominently. When part of the building was renovated, reopening in 1882, two rooms named after him were created, in which *Primavera* and other important works by the artist and his contemporaries were housed.[30] The Uffizi followed suit shortly afterwards. The *Birth of Venus*, having already been removed from its corridor around 1880 into what was then known as the 'Sala di Lorenzo Monaco',[31] was given its own 'Room of the *Birth of Venus*' around 1900, which also brought together the other Botticellis in the Uffizi's collection.[32] When almost all the Accademia's Botticelli paintings were transferred to the Uffizi after 1919, the collection was hung together, finally setting the seal on the early Renaissance painter's now assured status and capable even of surpassing the Tribuna, traditionally the glory of the collection.

A similar pattern can be observed in other large museums, where the re-evaluation of Botticelli's work was echoed in the way it was presented, generally with the creation of dedicated 'Botticelli Rooms'. In Berlin, Botticelli's paintings were split across two rooms in 1830 as part of the chronology of the central Italian school leading up to Raphael.[33] In 1904 the collection of post-classical paintings and sculptures was removed from the building by the Lustgarten (pleasure garden), by now called the Altes Museum (Old Museum), into a new one, which was explicitly intended as a museum of the Renaissance. Three decades previously the collection had been enriched by the acquisition of portraits of Giuliano de' Medici and Simonetta Vespucci, and in 1884 it had been given the Raczyński tondo on loan, reason enough to dedicate a room – which was also named after him – to the Florentine master in the new Kaiser Friedrich Museum (today the Bode Museum).[34] Works by other early Renaissance masters were shown alongside Botticelli – densely hung, as was typical of the day – as well as the occasional tapestry and bust (fig. 19). Thanks to a new extension, which relieved some of the pressure on space, museum officials were able to plan a new Botticelli Room in 1930 that would focus exclusively on his work. From 1933 Berlin's rich collection of Botticellis could be seen here against a neutral background, before it was significantly depleted in May 1945 (fig. 20).

Botticelli's progress to the heart of museums' permanent collections was facilitated by the ambitions of the public museums established around 1800 to offer an overview of the history of painting from Cimabue to Carracci. This expansion of their remit to include the eras of historic rather than aesthetic interest – as they were referred to in those days – primarily affected the centuries before Raphael. A comprehensive assessment of Botticelli's work on its own terms did not take place until around 1850, through the efforts of enthusiastic museum-going writers and painters. But Botticelli had already achieved what every nineteenth-century painter dreamed of: he had become an artist of the museum.

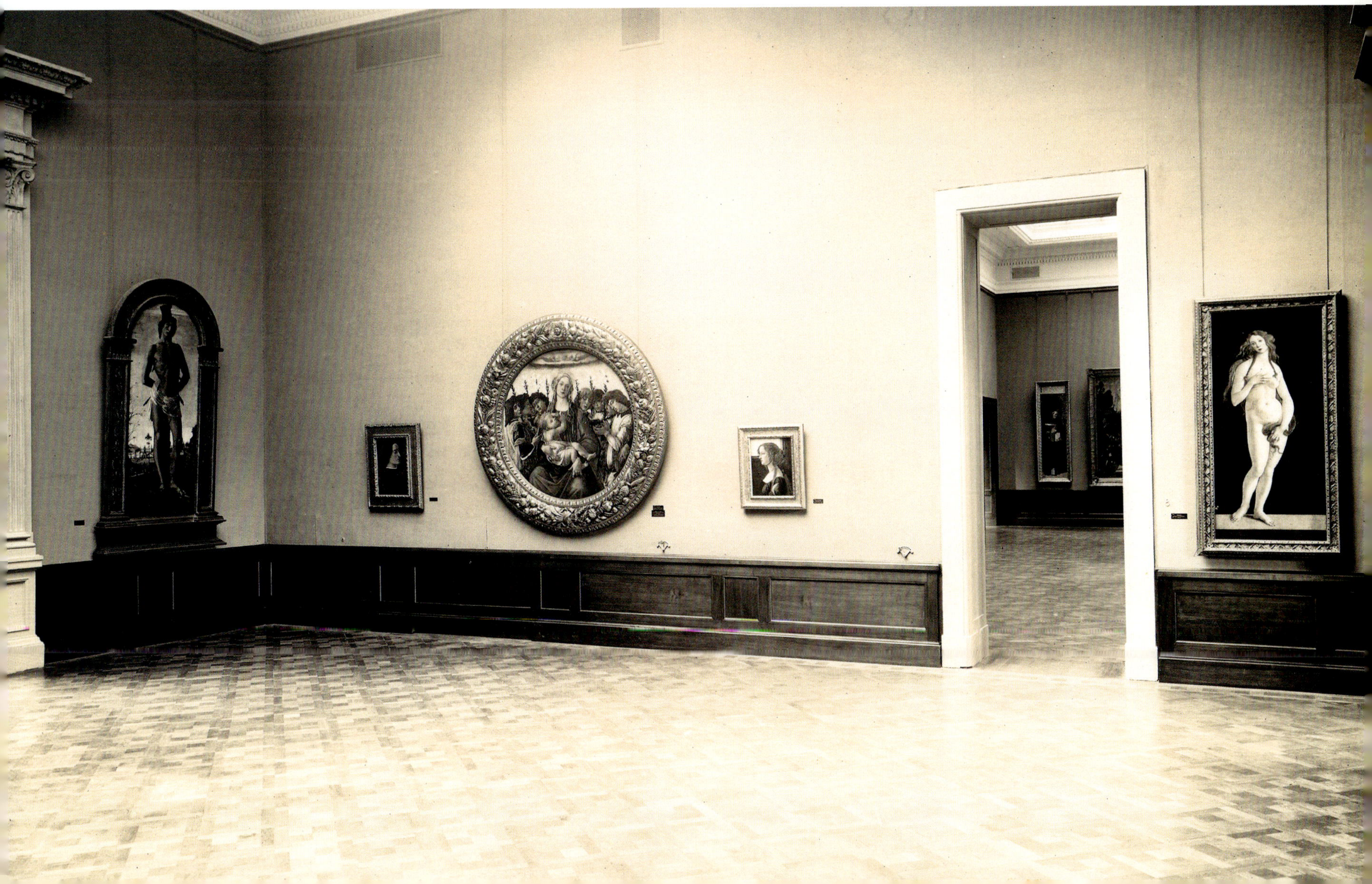

Botticelli and the Georgians

MARK EVANS

In 1877 the historian of the Renaissance, John Addington Symonds, reflected:

> In the last century and the beginning of this, our present preoccupation with Botticelli would have passed for mild lunacy, because he has none of the qualities then most in vogue and most enthusiastically studied, and because the moment in the history of culture he so faithfully represents, was then but little understood.[1]

However, major works by the Florentine master found their way to Britain during the Georgian age, including his only signed painting, the *Mystic Nativity* (cat. 101), and the remarkable ink drawings of Dante's *Divine Comedy* (cats 147–53). We may therefore legitimately question Symonds's generalization that Botticelli's aesthetic qualities were unappreciated by the Georgians.

Prior to the twentieth century, almost the entirety of received knowledge on Botticelli was that provided by Vasari's *Lives of the Artists*, which was still interpreted uncritically, as though it was a primary source. The earliest documented copies of the *Lives* in England were those catalogued in 1583 in the extensive library of the antiquary and astrologer Dr John Dee, and given in 1601 to the Bodleian Library in Oxford by the physician Dr Richard Haydock, a friend of the portrait miniaturist Nicholas Hilliard and translator of Giampaolo Lomazzo's *Trattato de la pittura.*[2] Henry Peacham recommended Vasari to readers of his *Complete Gentleman* (1st ed. 1622) although it was 'hard to come by', and mentioned further copies 'in the Libraries of two my especiall and worthy friends', the celebrated architect and Surveyor of the King's Works, Inigo Jones, and a former Prebendary of St Paul's Cathedral, Dr John Mountford.[3] Peacham's own 17-page account of 'the lives of the famous Italian painters', based largely on Vasari, dealt at some length with early painters from Cimabue to Orcagna, and closed with Raphael; its author apologizing: 'I overpasse for brevity sake, many other excellent and famous Artists of Italy … as *Bellino, Pollaiuoli, Botticello, Verrocchio, Andreas Mantegna … Francesco Francia, Michael Angelo…*'[4]

The first partial translation of Vasari into English was that by the physician and diplomat William Aglionby published in 1685.[5] This moved smartly from Giotto to Leonardo, merely listing among the 'great *Painters* of this Second AGE … Dominico, Ghirlandaio, Sandro, Botticello, Francesco, Francia,

Andrea Mantegna; *and many others*'.[6] Aglionby believed 'These were all *Florentines* ... or at least, bred in the *Florentine* Schoole' and compounded his error by separating the first names of Ghirlandaio, Botticelli and Francia from their surnames, thus effectively turning three artists into six.

When the essayist Jonathan Richardson the younger visited the Uffizi in Florence in 1720 or 1721, he saw a painting attributed to Botticelli, which he described as an 'Adoration of the *Magi*; the Angels, and several other things, heighten'd with Gold'.[7] Uffizi inventories of 1753 and 1769 also mention such a work with dimensions of 1.33 × 1.6 braccia (77.5 × 93.3 cm), but this was probably Mantegna's *Adoration of the Magi*, which was repeatedly confused with Botticelli's *Del Lama Adoration* in Medici inventories of the seventeenth and eighteenth centuries.[8] Richardson's father, of the same name, assembled a fine drawings collection with over 100 early sheets, and ascribed several to Botticelli.[9]

Another early collector of primitives was the painter Ignazio Hugford, the son of an English Catholic clockmaker, who was born in Pisa and elected to the Florentine Accademia del Disegno in 1729.[10] He edited the sixth edition of Vasari's *Lives of the Artists* and was highly regarded as a connoisseur. Hugford lent several fifteenth-century paintings to the exhibition organized in 1767 by the Accademia at SS. Annunziata for the feast of St Luke, which he later sold to the Grand Duke of Tuscany.[11] These included a supposed *Self-Portrait* of Masaccio, since reattributed to Filippino Lippi but perhaps a fake, and a *St Augustine Writing in his Cell*, then given to Fra Filippo Lippi and now recognized as by Botticelli, purchased in 1779 for 24 scudi, or around 6 guineas.[12]

A convivial member of the thriving British community in Florence, presided over by the 'intelligent, conscientious, kind-hearted and busy' Sir Horace Mann, was the painter and caricaturist Thomas Patch.[13] He published between 1770 and 1774 illustrated volumes on Masaccio, Giotto, Fra Bartolomeo and Ghiberti's Baptistery doors.[14] Patch's engravings of the frescoes in the Brancacci Chapel at Santa Maria del Carmine – after Filippino Lippi, but misattributed to Masaccio – and

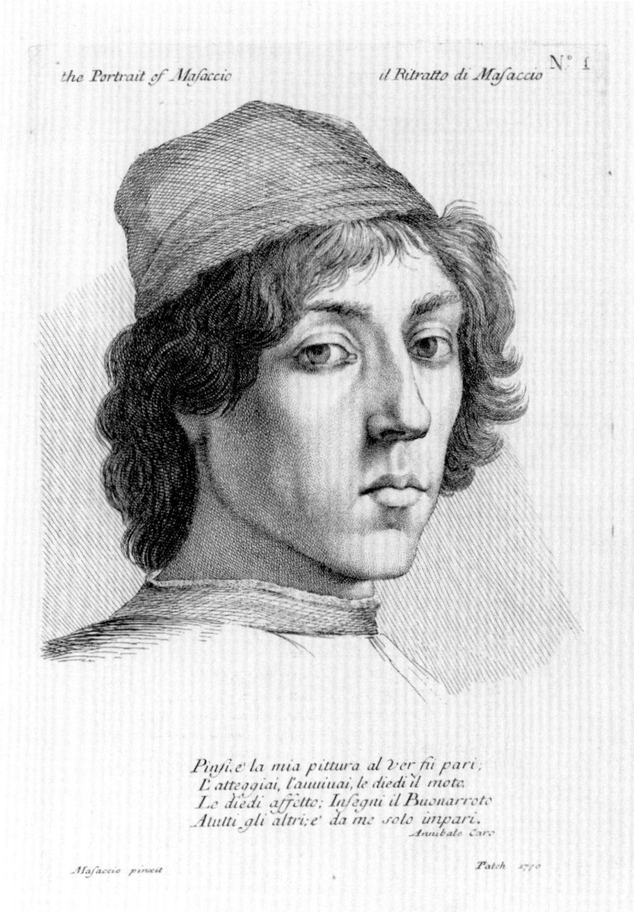

FIG. 21
THOMAS PATCH (1725–1782) after
FILIPPINO LIPPI (c.1457–1504)
'The Portrait of Masaccio' from *The Life of Masaccio*, 1770
Engraving, 45.6 × 36 cm (sheet)
V&A: NAL

were lavishly praised by Mann's friend Sir Horace Walpole: 'I am transported by them! They are nature itself, and evidently the precursors of Raphael. He plainly availed himself of their dignity but scarce reached the infinite truth of their expression.'[15] These include a reputed *Self-Portrait* of the painter (fig. 21), very like that sold by Hugford to the Grand Duke, which probably caused the later misattribution to Masaccio of two bust portraits of young men in berets, both since recognized as by Botticelli.[16] One of these, catalogued as 'Masaccio, His own Portrait – curious and rare' (fig. 33), was among the Italian primitives owned by Colonel Matthew Smith, a Fellow of the Society of Antiquaries and Major of the Tower of London, sold on 12 May 1804 at Christie's and bought for £15 by Lord Northwick.[17] The other had by 1841 entered the Parisian collection of Comte James-Alexandre de Pourtalès-Gorgier, and was catalogued as '[Masaccio] Par le même … Portrait présumé de ce peintre' (cat. 163).[18]

Inspired by Vasari's *Lives* and encouraged by Peter Leopold, the enlightened Grand Duke of Tuscany, between 1775 and 1793 the Uffizi was transformed from a princely cabinet into a public art museum by its reforming director Giuseppe Pelli Bencivenni and his deputy and rival Luigi Lanzi.[19] Bencivenni's *Catalogo delle pitture*, compiled in 1775–84, lists five works by Botticelli, including *Fortitude* and *The Calumny of Apelles*, mostly authenticated by Vasari or Raffaello Borghini.[20] Lanzi drew on this in his pioneering history of Florentine art, published in 1792, which remarked on the difficulty of distinguishing Botticelli's work from that of Mantegna and drew attention to the former's leading role in the frescoes on the side walls of the Sistine Chapel.[21] These were disparaged by the Anglo-Swiss painter Henry Fuseli, who was enthralled by Michelangelo's Sistine frescoes, and complained of the earlier cycle:

> The superintendence of the whole the Pope, with the usual vanity and ignorance of princes, gave to Sandro, the least qualified of the group, whose barbarous taste and dry minuteness palsied … his associates, and rendered the whole a monument of puerile ostentation, and conceits unworthy of its place.[22]

Despite Fuseli's distaste for 'the culinary abominations of Sandro Botticelli', he had no qualms in 1774 about borrowing motifs from the latter's ink drawings of the *Divine Comedy* (figs 22, 23).[23] These may have been at Rome since at least the time of Pope Alexander VIII (r.1610–91), who gave seven illuminated leaves from the series (see cats 147, 148, 149) to the Vatican Library, but are first documented, attributed to Botticelli, in April 1803 in the hands of the Parisian bookseller Giovanni Claudio Molini, an Italian who collaborated with his brothers in Florence and London.[24]

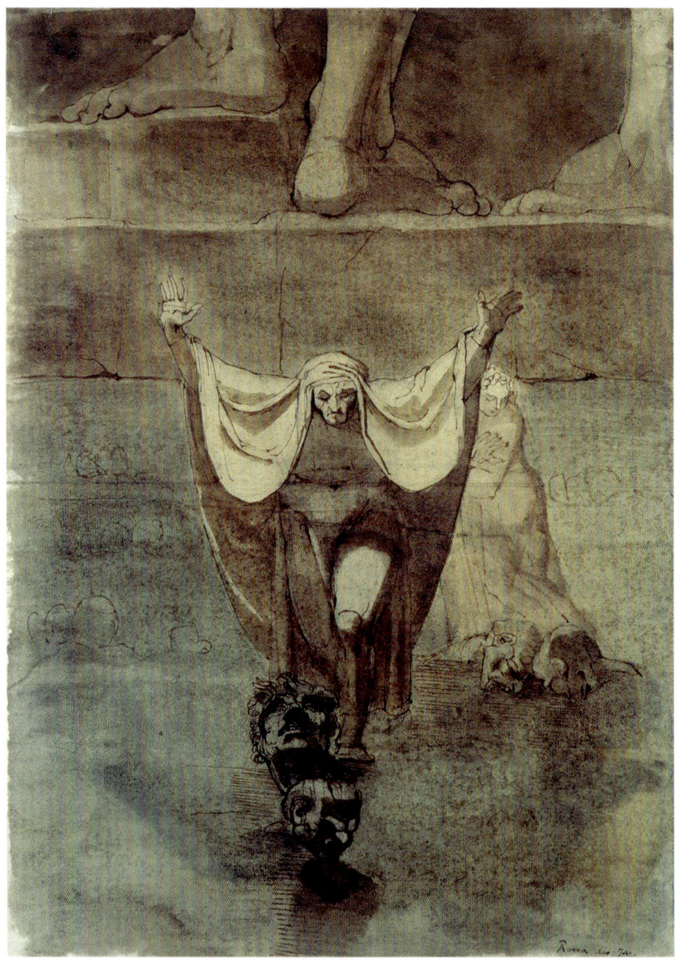

FIG. 22
HENRY FUSELI
(1741–1825)
'The Ninth Circle of Hell', The Divine Comedy, Inferno XXXII, 1774
Ink, sepia and watercolour on paper
39 × 27.4 cm
Kunsthaus, Zurich (1916/13)

FIG. 23
SANDRO BOTTICELLI
(*c.*1445–1510)
'The Ninth Circle of Hell', The Divine Comedy, Inferno XXXII, *c.*1488–92
Metalpoint and ink on vellum
32.5 × 47.5 cm
Kupferstichkabinett, Staatliche Museen zu Berlin

In Liverpool, Fuseli's friend and patron, William Roscoe, earned an international reputation as a historian with his biographies of Lorenzo de' Medici (1796) and Leo X (1805).[25] 'Chiefly for the purpose of illustrating ... the rise and progress of the arts', he also assembled a notable collection of primitives, several acquired from the amateur William Young Ottley.[26] In 1816 bankruptcy obliged Roscoe to sell his library and art collection. These included a first edition copy of Dante's *Divine Comedy* (1481), described as: 'with the commentary of Landino ... ornamented with two of the prints designed by Sandro Botticelli, and engraved by Baldini, and with Drawings in Indian ink at the head of many of the cantos. An original Folio Drawing by Botticelli of the Inferno, Purgatorio, and Paradiso, is also prefixed to the work', as well as two further drawings attributed to Botticelli: a 'very fine' *Man's Head*, formerly owned by Richardson, and *A Figure of a Man in Profile,* which Roscoe believed had belonged to Vasari.[27] The illustrated *Divine Comedy* made a creditable 15 guineas, while the loose drawings realized modest sums of £1 and 15/- respectively, and the latter was afterwards bound into a grangerized copy of Roscoe's son's English translation of Lanzi's *History of Painting in Italy* (1828).[28] It also bears the collector's marks of Richardson and the watercolourist Paul Sandby, and was later reattributed by Berenson to Davide Ghirlandaio.[29]

Ottley had spent 1791–9 in Italy, working first as a copyist for the French antiquarian Jean-Baptiste Séroux d'Agincourt on his illustrated history of art from the fourteenth to seventeenth centuries.[30] He took advantage of the instability caused by the French invasion of Italy to assemble a large collection, including drawings attributed to Botticelli, fragments of a cartoon by the artist (cats 104, 105), and his only signed painting, the *Mystic Nativity* (cat. 101), acquired from the Villa Aldobrandini.[31] Ottley offered this for sale in 1811 as 'A very

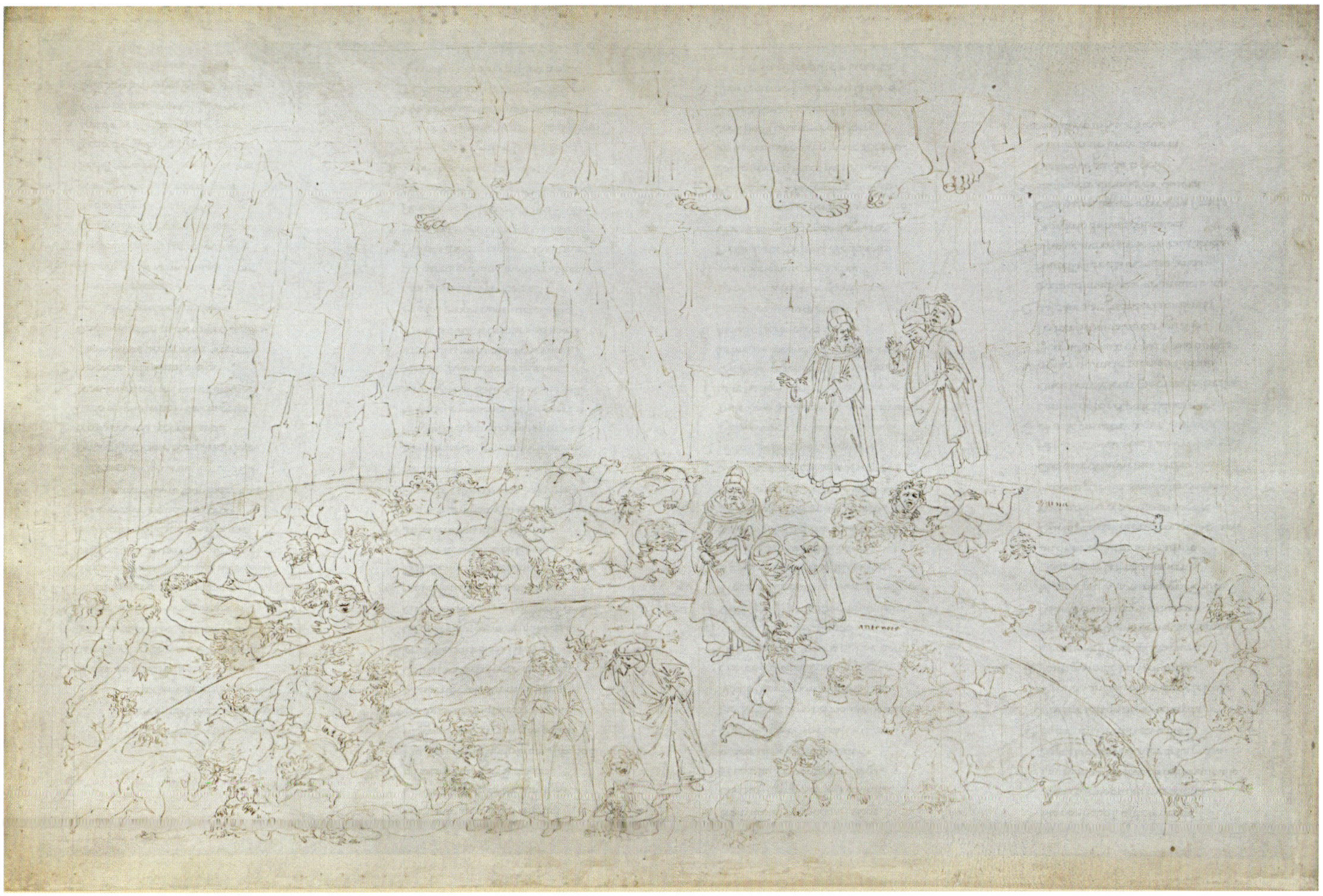

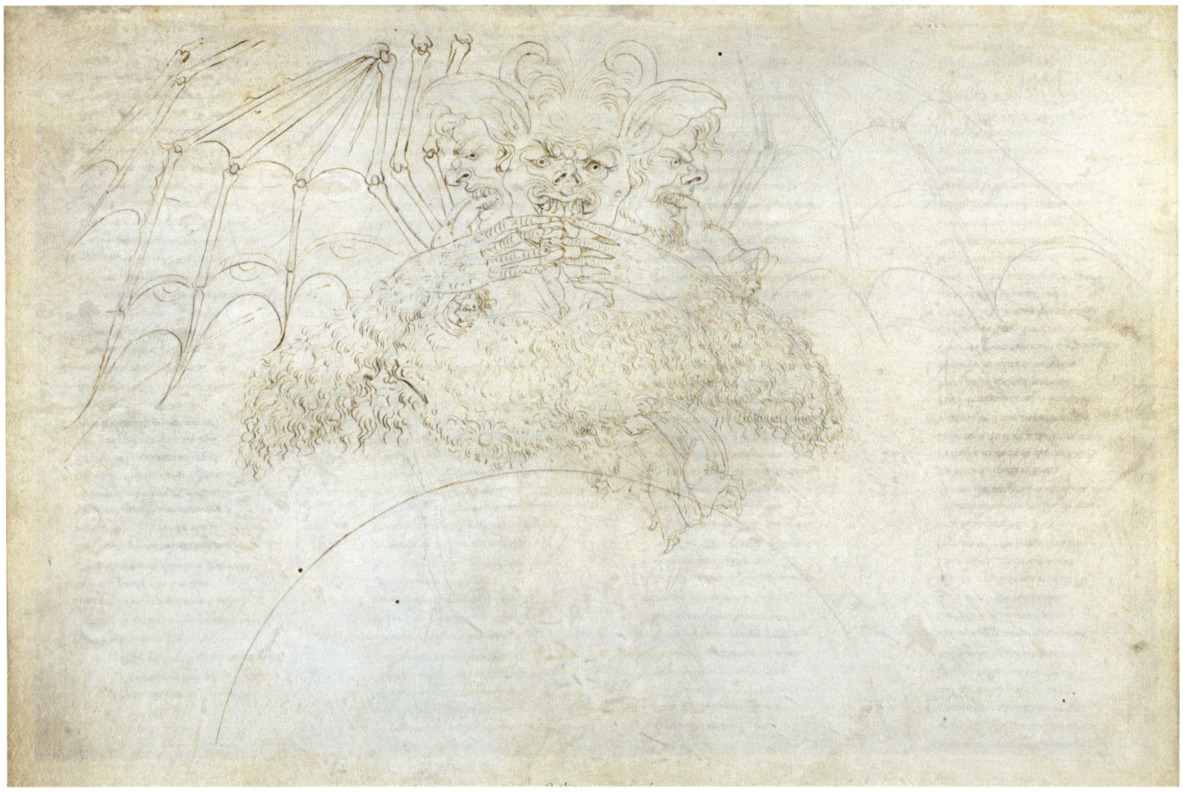

FIG. 24
SANDRO BOTTICELLI
(*c*.1445–1510)
'The Centre of Hell: Lucifer', The Divine Comedy, Inferno XXXIV, *c*.1488–92
Metalpoint and ink on vellum, 32.5 × 47.5 cm
Kupferstichkabinett, Staatliche Museen zu Berlin

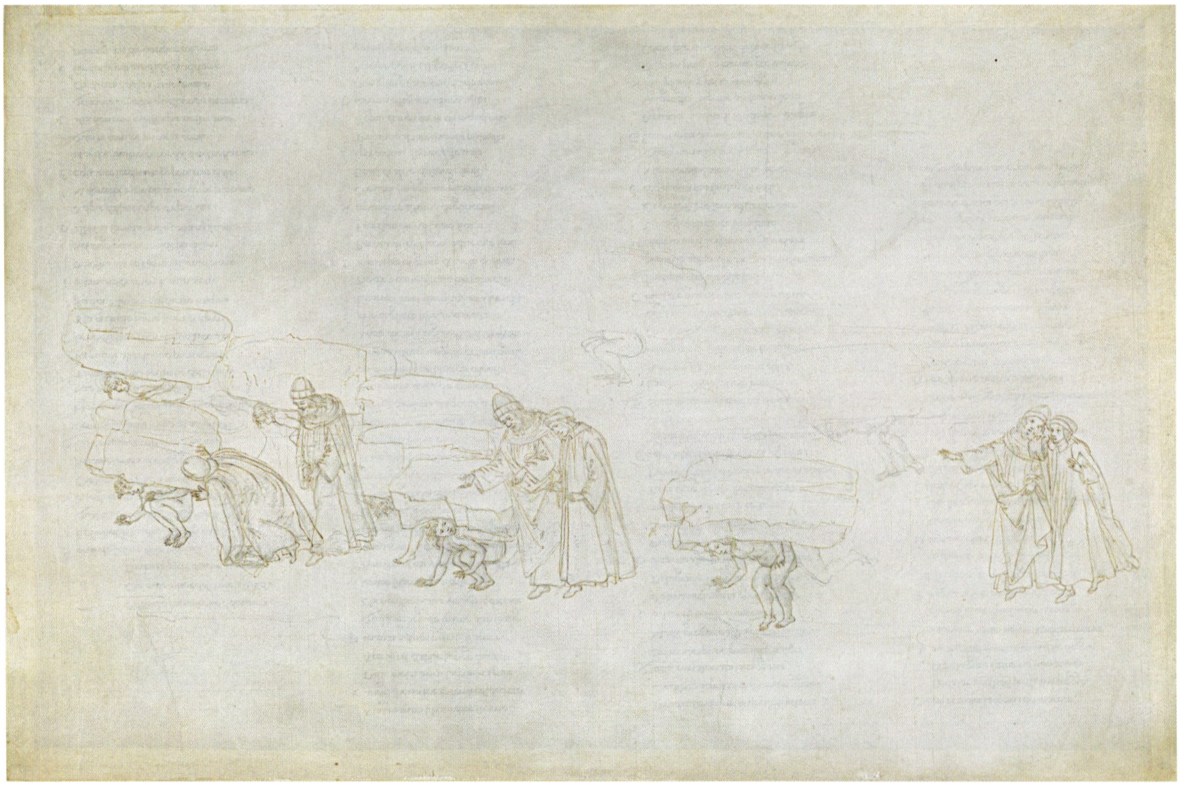

FIG. 25
SANDRO BOTTICELLI
(*c*.1445–1510)
'The First Terrace: Penance of the Proud', The Divine Comedy, Purgatorio XI, *c*.1488–92
Metalpoint and ink on vellum, 32.5 × 47.5 cm
Kupferstichkabinett, Staatliche Museen zu Berlin

interesting specimen of the fancy of its author … and of the state of Italian art, about the year 1480', but it was bought in for 40 guineas.[32]

At Rome Ottley became friendly with the sculptor John Flaxman, who the wealthy architect and collector Thomas Hope paid one guinea a drawing to illustrate an edition of Dante's *Divine Comedy*, which was published privately in 1793 and in a large unauthorized edition in 1802 (cat. 100).[33] Flaxman was impressed by the Italian primitives and on his arrival at Florence in 1787 he called Botticelli's *Madonna del Magnificat*, recently acquired by the Uffizi: 'A beautiful picture of the Infant Jesus sitting in the Virgin's lap with Angels', but misattributed it to Taddeo Gaddi.[34] Although J.W. von Goethe had remarked in 1799 on Flaxman's 'gift of adopting the innocence of the older Italian school', it seems not to have been previously noticed that his Dante illustrations are directly related to Botticelli's drawings of *The Divine Comedy*, which had been studied years earlier by Fuseli at Rome.[35] While Flaxman borrowed little from the previous illustrated edition of *The Divine Comedy*, published by Antonio Zatta at Venice in 1757–8, his citations from Botticelli's *Inferno* and *Purgatorio* are numerous (figs 24, 25, 26).[36]

By 1819 the *Divine Comedy* drawings had entered the library of Alexander Douglas, Duke of Hamilton, whose taste for lavish Renaissance manuscripts was shared by his cousin and father-in-law, the legendary collector William Beckford.[37] The latter lived in Paris in 1801–3, purchased books and manuscripts there, and was in the habit of suggesting purchases for Hamilton, so he may have facilitated his acquisition of *The Divine Comedy*.[38] Beckford also knew Ottley, of whom he complained decades later that 'Nothing fair or genuine can be expected … I know him of old', but grudgingly conceded 'As far as connoisseurship goes … [he] … is not defficient [*sic*]'.[39] In 1826 Ottley included in his volume of illustrations, *The Early Florentine School*, which he dedicated to his friend Flaxman, an engraving of the lower half of the *Mystic Nativity*, one of the first reproductions after Botticelli to be published.[40]

The Georgian outlook on Botticelli was based on Vasari, who characterized him as a haphazard eccentric who squandered time illustrating Dante and eventually abandoned art to become an impoverished follower of Savonarola. He lacked Masaccio's status as a seminal pioneer, the glory reflected on Giovanni Bellini, Domenico Ghirlandaio and Perugino by their canonical students Titian, Michelangelo and Raphael, the notoriety of Filippo Lippi who eloped with a nun, or the local reputation of Mantegna, famous in England for his *Triumphs of Caesar* in the Royal Collection.[41] However, the nucleus of autograph works assembled at the Uffizi by 1784 provided a touchstone for Botticelli's style, augmented by the discovery of the signed *Mystic Nativity*, and his identification as the draughtsman of the *Divine Comedy* sheets acquired by Hamilton. These lyrical outline drawings on a blank field, as well as classical reliefs and vase paintings, inspired Flaxman's 'primitive' Dante illustrations, which proved immensely influential, especially in Germany.[42] The wheel came full circle when his Outline Style was utilized in 1808 by Franz and Johannes Riepenhausen to copy Botticelli's *The Calumny of Apelles* (cat. 95), and in 1819 by Julius Schnorr von Carolsfeld in a drawing after his *Life of St Zenobius* (cat. 96).[43] Between 1775 and 1803 the curator Lanzi, the bookseller Molini and the dealer Ottley provided the key to Botticelli's artistic personality while the artist Flaxman propagated his linear style; a later generation would fetishize both.

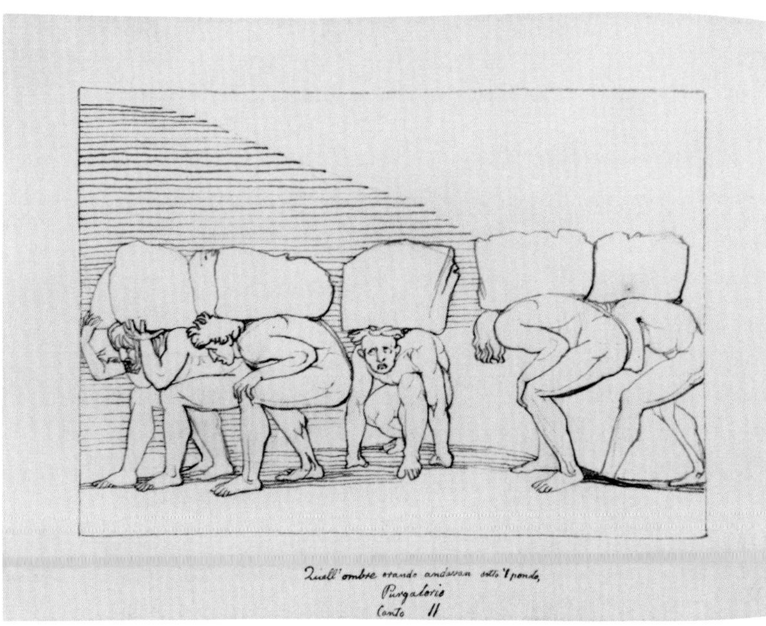

FIG. 26
JOHN FLAXMAN (1755–1826)
'The First Terrace: Penance of the Proud', The Divine Comedy, Purgatorio XI, 1793–4
Ink on paper,
14 × 19.3 cm
Houghton Library, Harvard University, Cambridge MA

The Love Affair with Florence

Florence is everything and all the rest is nothing

Edward Burne-Jones[1]

STEPHEN CALLOWAY

The rediscovery of Botticelli should properly be viewed in the larger context of what was, effectively, a 'rediscovery' of Florence itself and a widespread reimagining of the historic city. The elevation of the previously shadowy figure of Botticelli to totemic status is paralleled by an equally remarkable re-evaluation of Florence's own place in the broader narrative of Italian art and culture.

Florence, as the chief city of Tuscany and the seat of its Grand Dukes, was always considered a principal stopping point on the canonical circuit of the Grand Tour (fig. 27). But for eighteenth-century visitors and especially for the English *milordi* sent abroad to see life and form their artistic tastes, Florence lacked the picturesque decay (and exciting possibilities of dalliance) of Venice, the antiquity and grandeur of Rome or the frisson of danger that added spice to Naples. By comparison Florence seemed safe, provincial and rather a backwater.

It requires a leap of the imagination to form a sense of what Florence was like in the eighteenth and early nineteenth centuries, and how very different were the expectations and perceptions of Grand Tour visitors in that period as compared to those of travellers for whom the coming of the railways in the middle years of the century unlocked new possibilities of access (fig. 28). By 1880 the streets, churches and galleries of Florence were filled with a new breed of tourists armed with their popular guidebooks, causing Violet Paget, the precocious 24-year-old Aesthetic disciple of Walter Pater (writing under her pen-name of 'Vernon Lee'), to look back to an earlier, quite different era: an Italy of 'quiet medieval towns, – where crumbling monuments overshadow grass-grown streets, and only a few heavy gilt coaches rumble across the time-worn pavement'.[2]

As Mrs Oliphant put it in her *Makers of Florence*, a popular guide first published in 1876, it had been the city's earlier days of turmoil that had also seen its greatest artistic achievements. This vigorous era was long passed:

> The sight of Florence … is proof enough of the prosperity which accompanied her struggles; for none of those glorious churches and decorations with which she is adorned like a bride, and few of the pictures that fill her galleries, have come into being during the years of deadly quiet in which she has languished …[3]

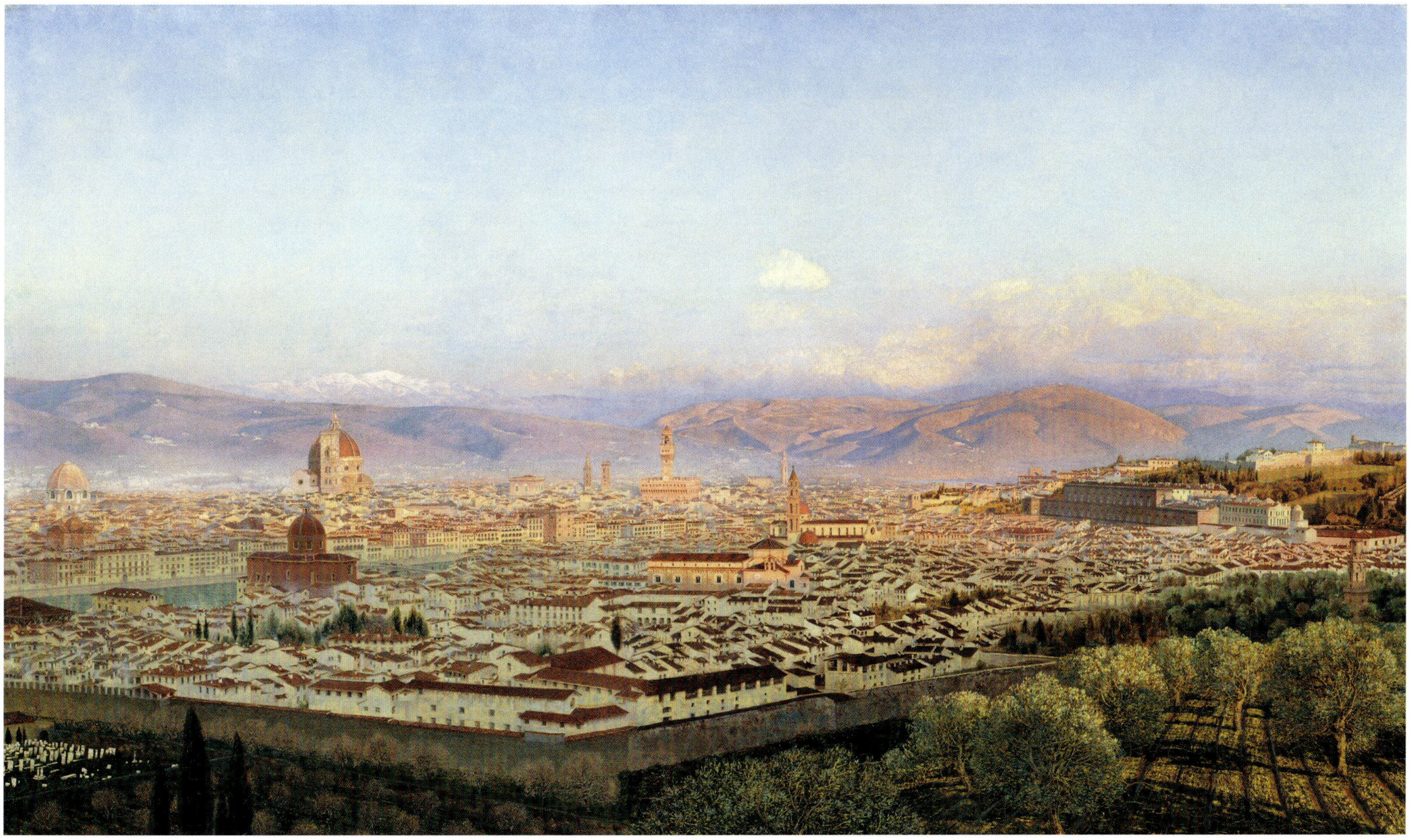

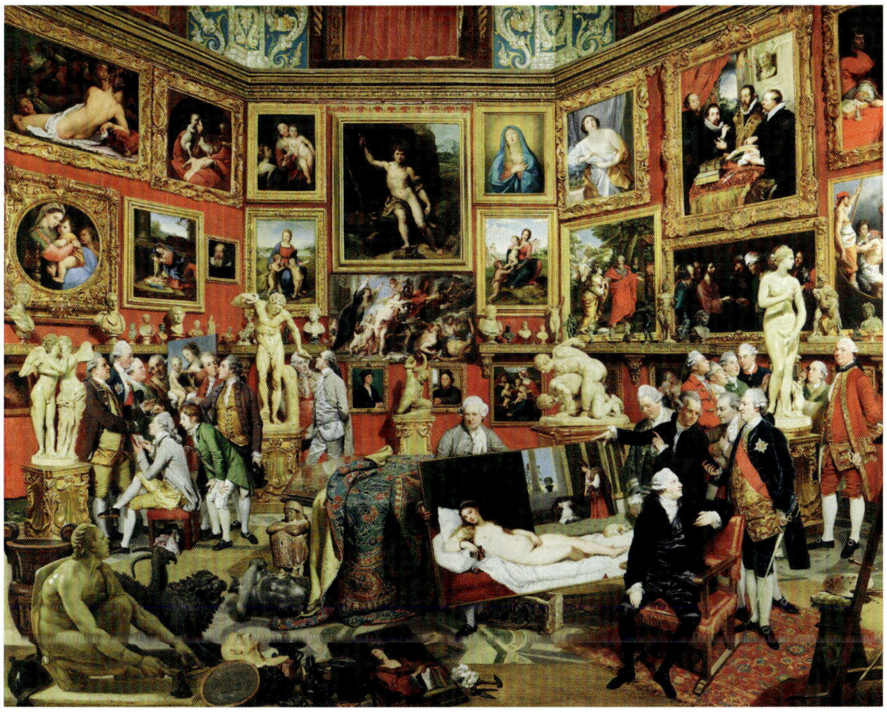

FIG. 27
JOHN BRETT
(1831–1902)
Florence from Bellesguado, 1863
Oil on canvas, 60 × 101.3 cm
Tate, London
Presented by Thomas Stainton in memory of Charles and Lavinia Handley-Read 1972 (T 01560)

FIG. 28
JOHAN JOSEPH ZOFFANY
(1733–1810)
The Tribuna of the Uffizi, 1772–7
Oil on canvas, 123.5 × 155 cm
Royal Collection Trust, London
(RCIN 406983)

Herbert Horne and subsequent writers have drawn attention to the near total eclipse of Botticelli's reputation even shortly after his death, citing as evidence that after his mention in the *Memoriale* of 1510,[4] the earliest Florentine 'guidebook', and Vasari's short 'life', his name all but disappears from the record. Even the rediscovery and public display from 1815 of *Primavera* and the *Birth of Venus* (figs 8, 10), seems to have been less noticed than might have been expected. Both the painters Charles Eastlake, who reached Florence in 1816, and William Dyce, who arrived in 1825 to study fresco techniques, failed to respond to these now celebrated works.

With the arrival of the ever-growing numbers of new tourists, the city changed to welcome and exploit them; hotels and restaurants became more numerous and improved their premises and service. To accommodate those who wished to stay longer in the spring or autumn the *pensione* became institutionalized. Travellers' expectations inevitably altered and with them the image and sense of identity of the city evolved too, as a result of a shift that occurred affecting notions of which buildings were most to be admired and which of the 'sights' were most worth visiting. Unlike earlier Grand Tourists, for whom social position and connections opened the doors of palaces and private collections, the middle-class tourist and his family frequented only the galleries that were open to all, churches and other publicly accessible buildings. Where previously, young gentlemen had been guided by tutors, the new tourists went from one monument or chapel to the next, instructed by their guidebooks what to look at and what to think.

Those who benefited from the greater ease of travel and the improvement in Florence's facilities also included serious scholars with specific interests in the city's literary and cultural history and its older art. Among these, Lord Lindsay and the young John Ruskin both came to study the depiction of Christian subject matter in early Renaissance art, a preoccupation which chimed with the search for a new purity and earnestness in painting that would lead Dante Gabriel Rossetti, John Everett Millais and William Holman Hunt (fig. 29) to found their Pre-Raphaelite Brotherhood in 1848.

In that same year Ruskin and Lindsay (alongside other luminaries including Eastlake) established the Arundel Society with the idea of making high-quality colour reproductions of early paintings available to scholars, collectors and clergymen.[5] Florentine painters figured significantly in the works chosen and the society's preferences had a distinct effect upon taste. It has been remarked that these 'advocates of the Early Masters' were, 'already mining away at the fortified authority of the Renaissance'.[6]

Lindsay had first arrived in 1839, in the early stages of research for his *Sketches of the History of Christian Art*, published in 1847.[7] Both Ruskin and Lindsay perceived Florence as the cradle of the Renaissance and would use the qualities they

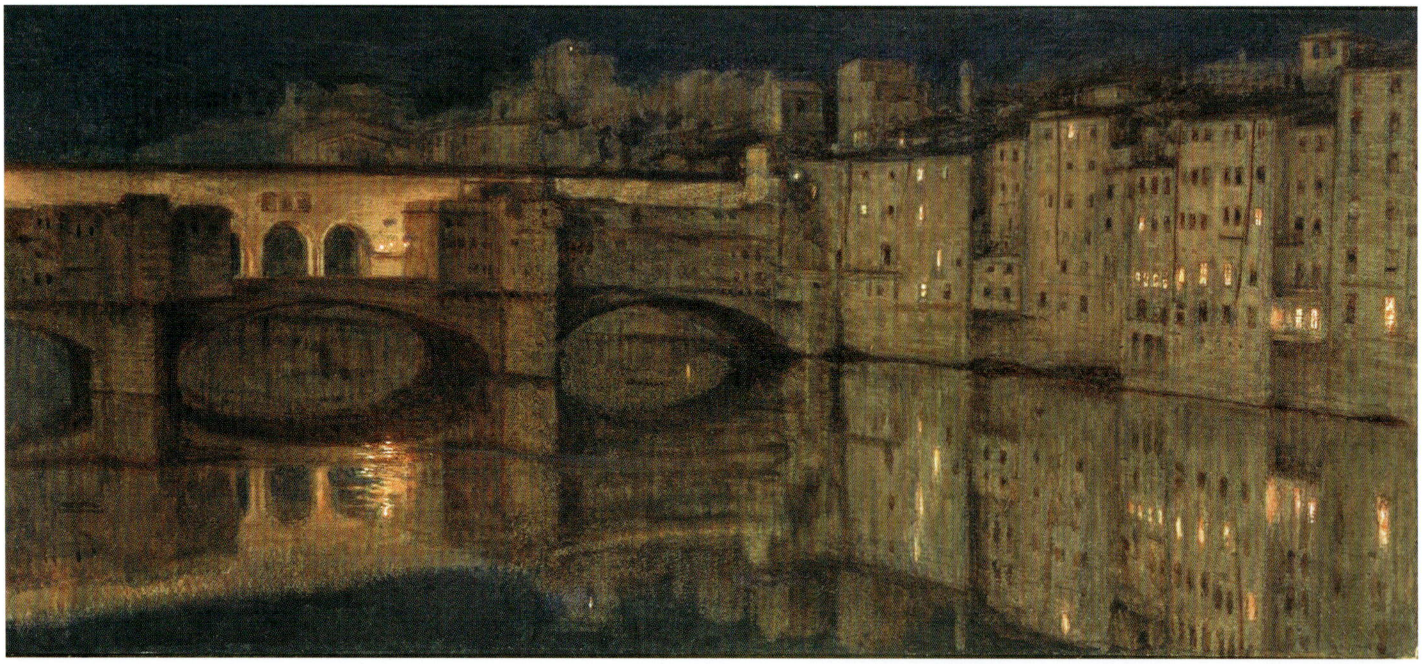

perceived in the art of the Trecento and Quattrocento as a stick to beat the works of later and, as they saw it, overblown High Renaissance painters. In his autobiographical recollections *Praeterita*, Ruskin transcribed from an early journal his initial reactions upon arrival: '*Nov. 15th.* [1840] – I still cannot make up my mind about this place, though my present feelings are of grievous disappointment.' Even his mature reflections still echoed the reactions of eighteenth-century travellers:

> At Florence then … the Newgate-like palaces were rightly hateful to me; the old shop and market-streets rightly pleasant; the inside of the Duomo a horror, the outside a Chinese puzzle. All sacred art,—frescoes, tempera, what not, mere zero, as they were to the Italians themselves … the whole, a provocation and weariness …[8]

Later, he strikes a new, sensitive note:

> When first I saw Florence, in 1840, the great street leading into the Baptistery square from the south had not been rebuilt, but consisted of irregular ancient houses … I mourned over their loss bitterly in 1845; but for the rest, Florence was still, then, what no one who sees her now could conceive.[9]

Ruskin's adaptation here of a traditional topos of romantic nostalgia more usually associated with Venice marks a significant transformation. It is a shift in attitude confirmed by Henry James, who as early as 1873 could, it seems, rely on his readers to see the joke undoubtedly intended as a teasing riposte to such elegiac posing:

> I first knew Florence early enough … to have heard the change for the worse, the taint of the modern order, bitterly lamented by old haunters, admirers, lovers—those qualified to present a picture of the conditions prevailing under the good old Grand-Dukes … for its blest reflection of sweetness … and cheapness.[10]

No such nostalgia can be detected in Ruskin's memory of the Florentine public galleries as he first encountered them:

> … the Uffizi collection in general, an unbecoming medley, got together by people who knew nothing, and cared less than nothing, about the arts.… It was not to be expected of me at that time to like either Angelico or Botticelli; and if I had, the upper corridor of the Uffizi was an entirely vile and contemptible place wherein to see the great Madonna of the one, or the Venus Marina of the other. Both were then in the outer passage from the entrance to the Tribune … In the Accademia I studied the Angelicos only, Lippi and Botticelli being still far beyond me.[11]

Herbert Horne drew attention to this passage to point up the error of the notion that Ruskin's championing of Botticelli dated from his early sojourns in Florence.[12] In fact it developed only later in the 1870s; after Algernon Charles Swinburne's ecstatic response to Renaissance drawings in the Uffizi expressed in his *Fortnightly Review* essay of July 1868 and later, too, than Walter Pater's poetic evocation, which did so much to fix the Aesthetic movement's attitude to Botticelli.[13] Pater, attempting to anatomize the curious appeal that Botticelli held for aesthetes of his time, speaks of: 'the freshness, the uncertain and diffident promise, which belong to the early Renaissance itself.'[14] For Pater, Botticelli was the earliest proponent of 'Art for Art's Sake': 'He thus sets for himself the limits within which Art, undisturbed by moral ambition, does its most sincere and surest work.'[15]

Horne, himself an Aesthete, had grown cynical about the movement's unscholarly espousal of Botticelli. Ostensibly criticizing Ruskin for his discredited ideas about Botticelli and printmaking in *Ariadne Florentina* (1873), Horne widens his attack:

> Both this book and 'Mornings in Florence' … were widely read, and contributed not a little … to bring about that peculiarly English cult of Botticelli, which now became a distinctive trait of a phase of thought and taste … as odd and extravagant as any of our odd and extravagant time. With the 'Aesthetic Movement' and

FIG. 29
WILLIAM HOLMAN HUNT
(1827 1910)
The Ponte Vecchio, Florence, 1867
Watercolour, 25.4 × 54.6 cm
V&A: 196–1894

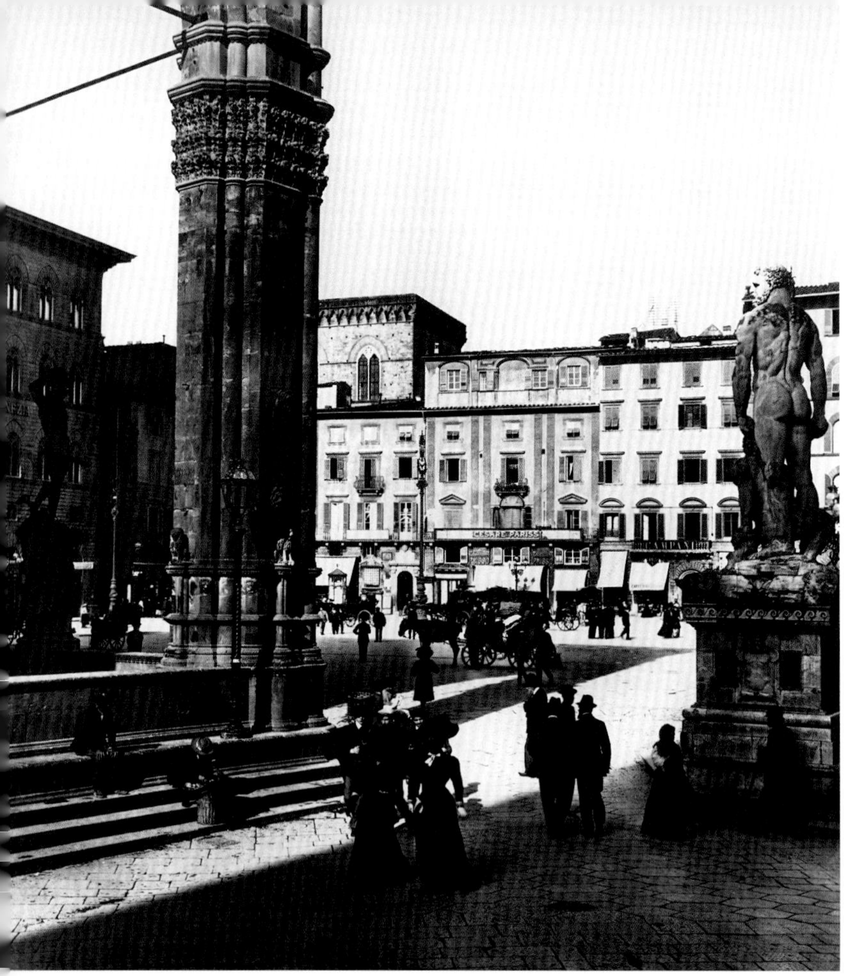

FIG. 30
View of the Piazza della Signoria, with the Loggia dei Lanzi, from the Loggiato of the Galleria degli Uffizi, Florence, c.1885
Alinari Archives, Florence

FIG. 31
Still from the film *A Room with a View*, 1985
Directed by JAMES IVORY

> the classic epoch of '1880', the name of Botticelli grew to be a catch-word among persons for whom early Italian art could never possess any real significance.[16]

By the 1880s Botticelli and Florence had become inseparably linked in the imagination of the devotees of the new Cult of Beauty. For the 'artistically-minded' the city was now one of the most important destinations for 'sight-seeing', for in Florence it seemed possible to get closest to the beauty of earlier ages and to imbibe the spirit of the Renaissance (fig. 30).

Very different from these tourists were those who chose to live in Florence in pursuit of art and also, as they would claim, the beauty of everyday existence. They followed in a tradition that had been established since the days of the Romantics, when figures such as the Shelleys or the writer Leigh Hunt had sought to escape the confines of English life in a place where limited funds stretched much further than at home.[17] By 1848, the poets Robert and Elizabeth Barrett Browning at their palazzo Casa Guidi commanded a central position in literary and artistic circles. Browning found in Florence much material for his dramatic, if perplexingly versified historic tales, while his wife wrote passionately of her feelings for the city in her volume *Casa Guidi Windows* (1851). In their time the popularity of the Brownings' writings was challenged only by George Eliot's novel *Romola*, also based on Florentine history.

The extraordinary events of the 1490s, when Savonarola advocated a return to religious purity with so great an effect, led many to regard him as a sort of protestant reformer and martyr. Ruskin even interpreted Botticelli in the same light, claiming that 'Botticelli was – what Luther wished to be but could not be – a reformer still believing in the church'.[18] Others, such as Mrs Oliphant, took up the theme, identifying with Savonarola's followers the 'Piagnone'. As a result of this curious mental leap, the English were comfortable in Florence in a way that they could never be at ease faced with the counter-reformation pomp of Rome or the darker Catholic atmosphere of Naples.

Even in the later decades of the century, it was still possible to live both grandly and cheaply in Florence. 'The villas', wrote Henry James, 'are innumerable ... Most of them are offered to rent ... at prices unnaturally low; you may have a tower and a garden, a chapel and an expanse of thirty windows, for five hundred dollars a year.'[19] The novelist E.M. Forster's description of the English artistic community captures the essence of their existence: 'Living in delicate seclusion, some in furnished flats, others in Renaissance villas on Fiesole's slope, they read, wrote, studied, and exchanged ideas.'[20]

Questions concerning the vexed and divisive issues of taste and class lie at the heart of E.M. Forster's *A Room with a View* (1908) in which Florence and its permanent and transient populations figure significantly. But he also addresses a fundamental divergence of attitudes to art and life that was, because of the Aesthetes' espousal of the city, made manifest in Florence. Mr Eager, as resident Anglican chaplain, is a pillar of the British community. Sociable and welcoming, he is nevertheless anxious to maintain the proprieties and is greatly aware of social distinctions. He promotes Renaissance culture as an appropriate, respectably improving interest for young women such as the heroine of the story Lucy Honeychurch. The plot of Forster's book turns on the contrast between Eager's narrow views and the 'dangerous' ideas of Miss Lavish. A self-styled free spirit in search of the 'true' Florence, she

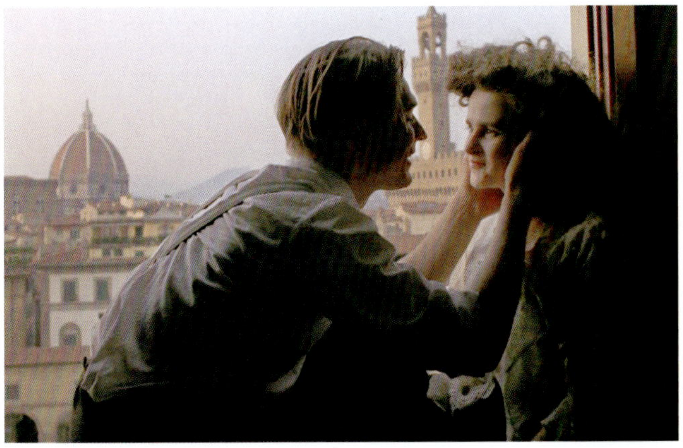

suggests that one should experience every aspect of the city's art and life sensuously, directly and unmediated by received ideas, which Forster symbolizes by Baedeker's popular travel guide, first published in 1860.

This 'art or life' scenario is prefigured in one of Henry James's pieces on Florence in *Italian Hours*, which describes how: 'Seeing one morning, in a shop-window, the series of *Mornings in Florence* (fig. 32) … by Mr. Ruskin, I made haste to enter and purchase these amusing little books …'[21] James is affronted when he reads on.

> The wreck of Florence, says Mr. Ruskin, 'is now too ghastly and heart-breaking to any human soul that remembers the days of old'… I had really been enjoying the good old city of Florence, but I now learned from Mr. Ruskin that this was a scandalous waste of charity.

James then uses the device of a critical friend to deliver his verdict:

> We see Florence wherever and whenever we enjoy it, and … find a great many more pretexts than Mr. Ruskin seems inclined to allow … he will never bear the test of being read in this rich old Italy, where art … was spontaneous, joyous, irresponsible … 'One may read a hundred pages of this sort of thing,' said my friend, 'without ever dreaming that he is talking about *art*. You can say nothing worse about him than that.' Which is perfectly true.[22]

The James–Forster view of the importance of 'lived life' gained the ascendancy, as can be seen in the enduring popularity of the Merchant Ivory film version of *A Room with a View* (1985, fig. 31), which emphasized the contrast between the warmth and passion of the lower-middle-class autodidact George Emerson and the acidulated aestheticism of Lucy's fiancé Cecil Vyse. This played well to a new generation of visitors and 'ex-pats' whose presence led to Tuscany being christened 'Chiantishire'. This latest in a series of ever-changing reactions to this fairly unchanging city, suggests that it is, paradoxically, Florence's capacity to be continually reimagined that has made it the subject for the English of such a passionate and extended love affair.

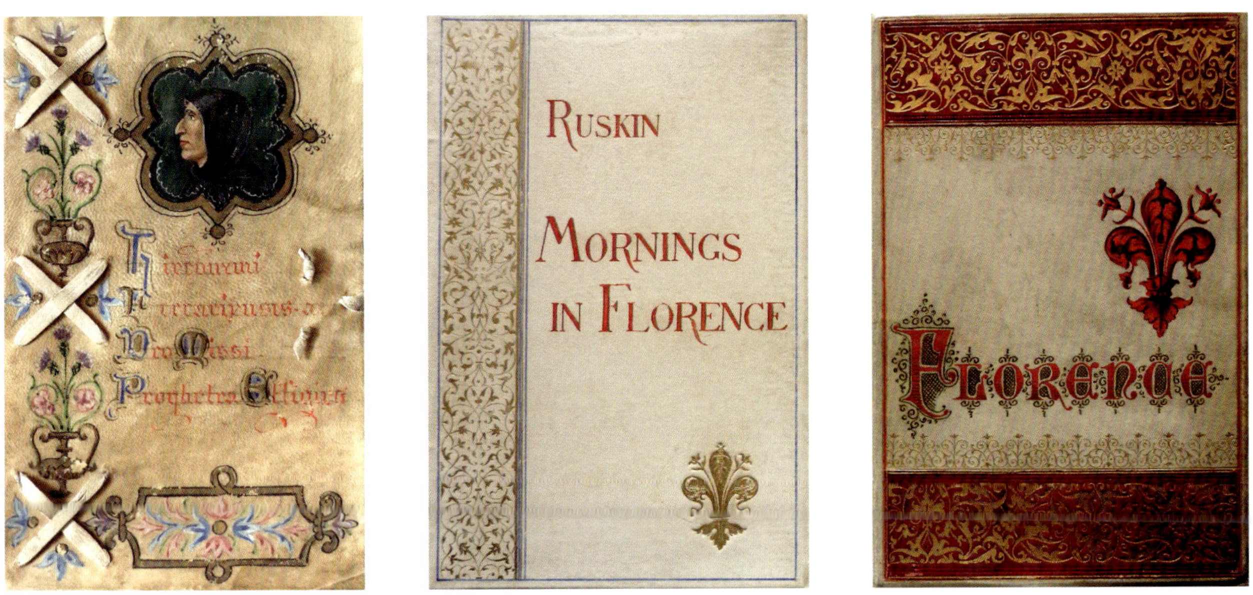

FIG. 32
Florentine souvenir bookbindings,
c.1890–1905
Vellum, with gilt-tooled and painted decoration, Private collection

Botticelli and Victorian Art Collecting

SUSANNA AVERY-QUASH

By the turn of the twentieth century, Botticelli's art had become big business. Isabella Stewart Gardner's expensive acquisition of the Chigi Madonna (cat. 109), in 1899, involved an agent from Colnaghi's giving a false address on the Italian export application before disappearing with it, and a two-year concealment of the picture in Paris.[1] Such smuggling was not unique, as Ronald Lightbown's catalogue raisonné of 1978 makes clear, but it did not reflect a longstanding demand for Botticelli; when William Young Ottley put up for auction the artist's signed *Mystic Nativity* in 1811 (cat. 101), the picture was bought in for 40 guineas. We will here trace the reception of Botticelli's art in Britain, as reflected by its acquisition for private and public collections, from the early nineteenth century until the First World War.

It is generally considered that Botticelli was one of the last of the great Florentines to be rediscovered. Indeed, scholars usually date his art-historical rediscovery in Britain to the 1870s,[2] coinciding with the publication of Walter Pater's *The Renaissance*, but in terms of the interest in collecting his art a significant shift had already occurred by the 1840s. Another disputable norm is that public acquisition of the artist's work preceded private collecting, as was claimed by Charles Dempsey, who noted: '[I]mportant paintings by Botticelli were gradually entering the great museums of Europe ... Museum acquisition and display were slightly in advance of public and critical response and in an important way laid the foundations for it.'[3] However, the fundamental display of the artist's work in the Uffizi was founded on the Medici collection, bequeathed to the Tuscan state in 1743, and that in the Altes Museum in Berlin, inaugurated in 1830, was based upon the huge collection of the English merchant Edward Solly, purchased by the Prussian state in 1821. Similarly, in Britain the evidence firmly points to private purchasing preceding museum acquisition.

Indeed, Ottley obtained Botticelli's *Mystic Nativity* around 1799 from the Villa Aldobrandini, Rome. Within this first wave of Botticelli enthusiasts we can place Colonel Matthew Smith, who, before 1804, owned Botticelli's *Portrait of a Young Man* (fig. 33, then thought to be a self-portrait by Masaccio), as well as better known, more systematic collectors of early Italian art, including the diplomat W.T.H. Fox-Strangways, whose major gift of paintings to Christ Church Oxford in 1828 included two Botticelli-style panels depicting seated Sibyls, obtained in Italy, and the Revd John Sanford, whose

FIG. 33
SANDRO BOTTICELLI
(c.1445–1510)
Portrait of a Young Man, *c.*1480–5
Tempera and oil on wood,
37.5 × 28.3 cm
The National Gallery, London
(NG626)

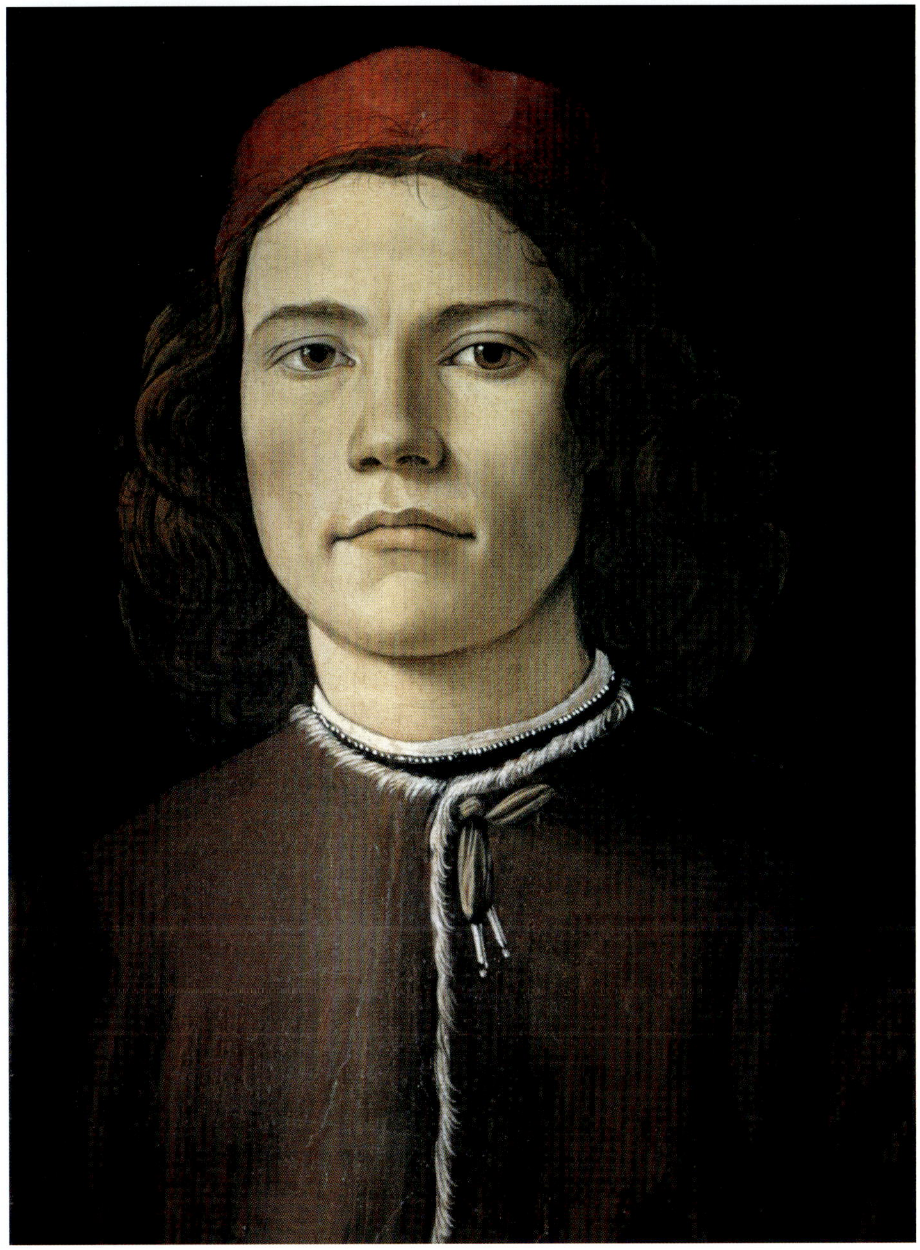

acquisitions at Florence between 1811 and 1837, included an *Annunciation* attributed to Botticelli (Kelvingrove Art Gallery and Museum, Glasgow).

A new bout of purchasing Botticellis and works by other early Italian painters, which occurred during the second quarter of the nineteenth century, can be mapped from the survey volumes of two German visitors, the art historians Johann David Passavant and G.F. Waagen.[4] The latter records that Smith's previously mentioned portrait had found a new home in Lord Northwick's celebrated collection at Thirlestane House, Cheltenham, from where it was lent to the 1857 Manchester Art Treasures exhibition.[5] The keenest British collectors of Botticelli's art were then Alexander Barker, who owned by 1857 *An Allegory* and *A Lady in Profile*, both by followers of Botticelli, and went on to acquire such major works as the *Venus and Mars* (fig. 4) and the *Nastagio degli Onesti* series (fig. 34), and the Revd Walter Davenport Bromley, who owned five or six paintings by, or from the circle of, Botticelli.

A third group of private British collectors of Botticelli's art appeared from the 1860s, all artists in the Pre-Raphaelite Brotherhood or their patrons and promoters. When John

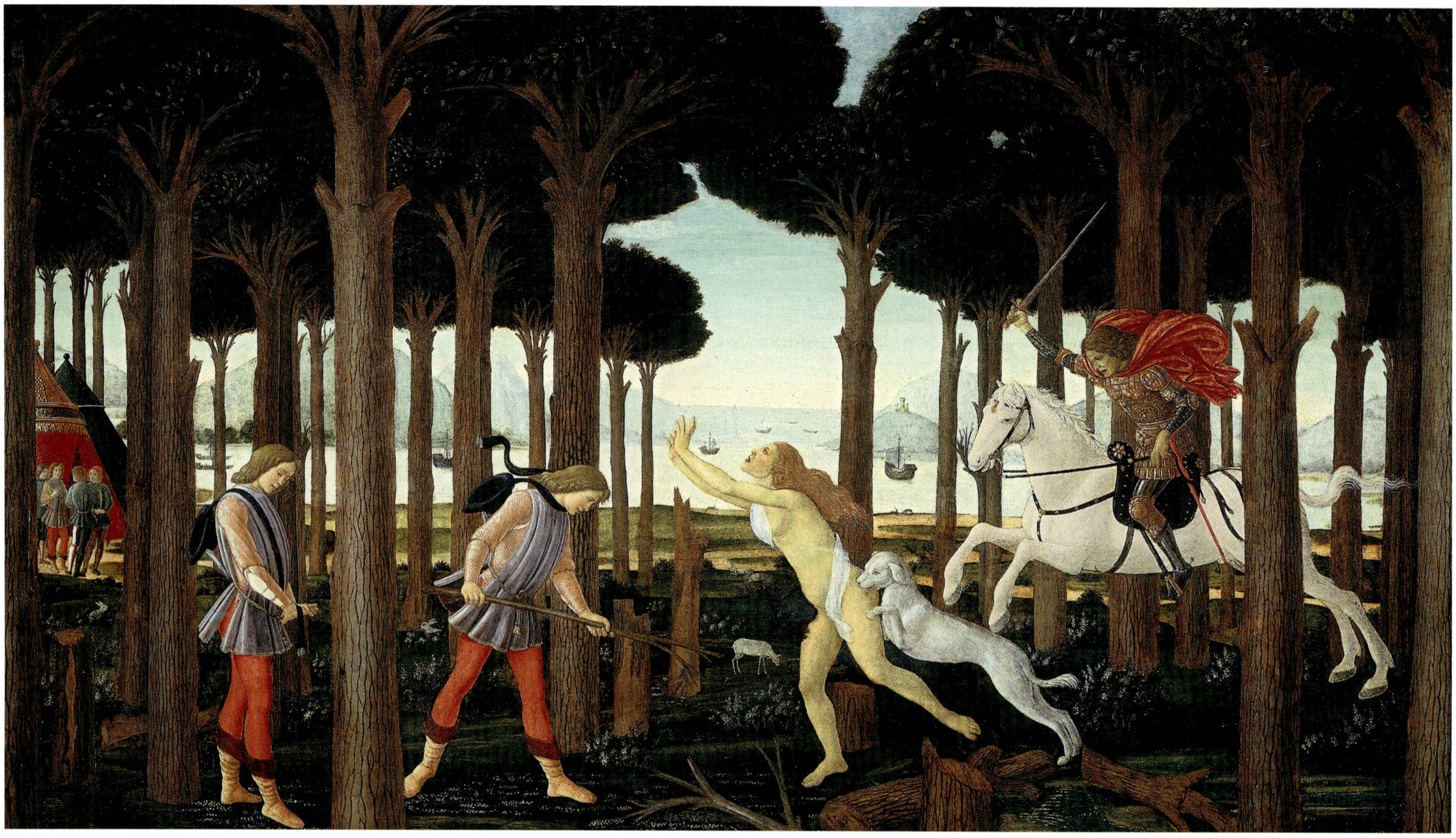

Everett Millais saw *Primavera* at the Accademia, Florence, in 1865, he was enraptured.[6] Dante Gabriel Rossetti and William Holman Hunt had seen in 1849 works by Botticelli in the Louvre, while in 1860 Rossetti's brother, the art critic William Michael Rossetti, was struck by the painter's *Birth of Venus* in Florence. On his return home, he 'spoke about these works to [his] brother', which 'refreshed his interest in Botticelli'.[7] In March 1867 Gabriel bought the *Portrait of a Lady known as Smeralda Bandinelli* (cat. 162). William Michael later observed: 'Botticelli was little or not at all in demand at that now remote date. If my brother had not something to do with the vogue which soon after began to attach to that fascinating master, I am under a misapprehension.'[8] Edward Burne-Jones came to own two works attributed to Botticelli: *The Annunciation, with Raphael and Tobias* (untraced), which was a gift from his patron, William Graham, and *The Coronation of the Virgin* (now Metropolitan Museum, New York; cat. 137). Burne-Jones's friend and protégé J.R. Spencer Stanhope, bought a *Virgin and Child* (untraced) in 1879, from the Medici Castello del Trebbio and the champion of the Pre-Raphaelites, John Ruskin, purchased a *Virgin and Child with St John and an Angel* by Botticelli that had been brought to his attention by the dealer Charles Fairfax Murray in Florence in 1877 (cat. 127). The Liverpool shipowner Frederick Richards Leyland, a patron of Rossetti and Burne-Jones, who famously quarrelled with James Abbott McNeill Whistler, acquired all four *Nastagio degli Onesti* panels, and lent them to the Royal Academy in 1880 (fig. 34).

From the mid-1850s, such private – but never royal – interest in Botticelli's art started to be reflected in the public sphere. The earliest painting by Botticelli to enter a British public collection was the *Annunciation*, formerly owned by Sanford, which formed part of the bequest made in 1854 by the wealthy carriage builder Archibald McLellan to found an art gallery in Glasgow. The National Gallery in London was reorganized under Sir Charles Eastlake in 1855 with the principal aim of assembling a survey collection of Western European painting, funded by a new £10,000 annual purchase

FIG. 34
SANDRO BOTTICELLI (c.1445–1510)
The Story of Nastagio degli Onesti (I), c.1483
Tempera on wood, 83 × 138 cm
Museo Nacional del Prado, Madrid (P02838)

grant. It was agreed that the Gallery required 'a few specimens of the earlier masters ... in order to understand and still better appreciate the great masters'.[9] Lady Eastlake, the first director's wife, remarked of fifteenth-century Florentine painting: 'I shall be truly proud if we succeed both in rescuing some examples, and in introducing them into England, where already there are a chosen few who adore them.'[10]

In fact Eastlake's acquisition of works attributed to Botticelli was patchy, starting in 1855 with the purchase in Florence and Bologna of two versions of the *Virgin and Child* (NG 226 and 275; cat. 118) now considered workshop pieces. The three other Botticellis that Eastlake went on to acquire were all bought as by other painters. Thus, among the 22 works acquired in 1857 from the Lombardi-Baldi collection in Florence was an *Adoration of the Kings* (NG 592), then thought to be a Filippino Lippi, as well as a *Virgin and Child with an Angel* (NG 589), considered to be by a follower of Filippo Lippi. The *St Francis* (NG 598), purchased the following year from the Costabili collection in Ferrara, was then also attributed to Filippo Lippi. Finally, in 1859, Eastlake purchased from the Northwick collection the *Portrait of a Young Man* formerly owned by Smith. By then, Eastlake clearly felt that the Gallery had enough early Italian art. So, when Sir Austen Henry Layard, with Baron Luigi Hombert and Millais, urged him in 1865 to purchase the four *Nastagio degli Onesti* panels from the Pucci Palace he did not do so. Layard perhaps anticipated Eastlake's refusal when he noted 'the somewhat unpleasant nature of one of the subjects – the lady being cut up!'[11] It was also largely on account of its disagreeable subject that Eastlake declined another Botticelli that he had seen in 1863, in the collection of William Currie on Lake Como – in this instance because 'the centre of the picture [was] occupied by corpses'.[12] Eastlake was reluctant to buy pictures that were likely to offend public taste by their subject matter, especially images that were deemed ugly or violent.

The exclusion of Botticelli's seemingly more idiosyncratic works from the national collection continued under Eastlake's successor. William Boxall again refused the Pucci Palace Botticellis as 'not adapted to find favour in modern eyes'.[13] Nor did he buy in 1867, from the Quandt collection, Botticelli's *Miracle Performed by St Zenobius* (Gemäldegalerie, Dresden), thinking it 'less desirable than the Moretto Madonna for which [he was] in treaty'.[14] However, that year he did purchase, in Milan, an attractive *Virgin and Child* (fig. 5). Later, in 1871, he tried unsuccessfully to acquire *The History of Virginia* (now Accademia Carrara, Bergamo), a celebration of female virtue, which had been discovered by the connoisseur Giovanni Morelli. It was under the Gallery's third director, Frederic Burton, that some more adventurous examples of the artist's work were purchased. In 1874, from the Alexander Barker sale, the Gallery acquired Botticelli's celebrated *Venus and Mars* (NG 915; fig. 4) as well as a more problematic *Allegory* (NG 916; fig. 6).[15] Four years later, from the sale of William Fuller Maitland, Burton bought the *Mystic Nativity* (cat. 101) and also the tondo of the *Adoration of the Kings* (NG 1033). The acquisition of these four pictures from English collections is indicative of increasing difficulty in exporting the artist's work from Italy. After protracted negotiations, the huge *Assumption of the Virgin* (NG 1126) was acquired as a Botticelli at the 1882 Hamilton Palace sale, but soon downgraded to Francesco Botticini. Since then, and despite occasions when pictures by Botticelli became available for purchase,[16] the National Gallery's Botticelli acquisitions have come about via bequests, as did four (workshop) pictures during Charles Holroyd's directorship (1906–16). The last to have reached the National Gallery are the panels of *Four Scenes from the Early Life of St Zenobius* (fig. 35), which were accepted as part of the collection assembled by the chemist Ludwig Mond with the assistance of the scholarly dealer Jean-Paul Richter, bequeathed in 1924.

Although the National Gallery dominates the story of public collecting of Botticelli's art in Britain, two other national institutions also helped familiarize the public with his oeuvre. In the wake of two blockbuster exhibitions – at Manchester in 1857 and Leeds in 1868 – the South Kensington Museum (now V&A) also displayed works by Botticelli, as part

FIG. 35
SANDRO BOTTICELLI (*c*.1445–1510)
Four Scenes from the Early Life of St Zenobius, *c*.1500
Tempera on wood, 66.7 × 149.2 cm
The National Gallery, London
(NG3918)

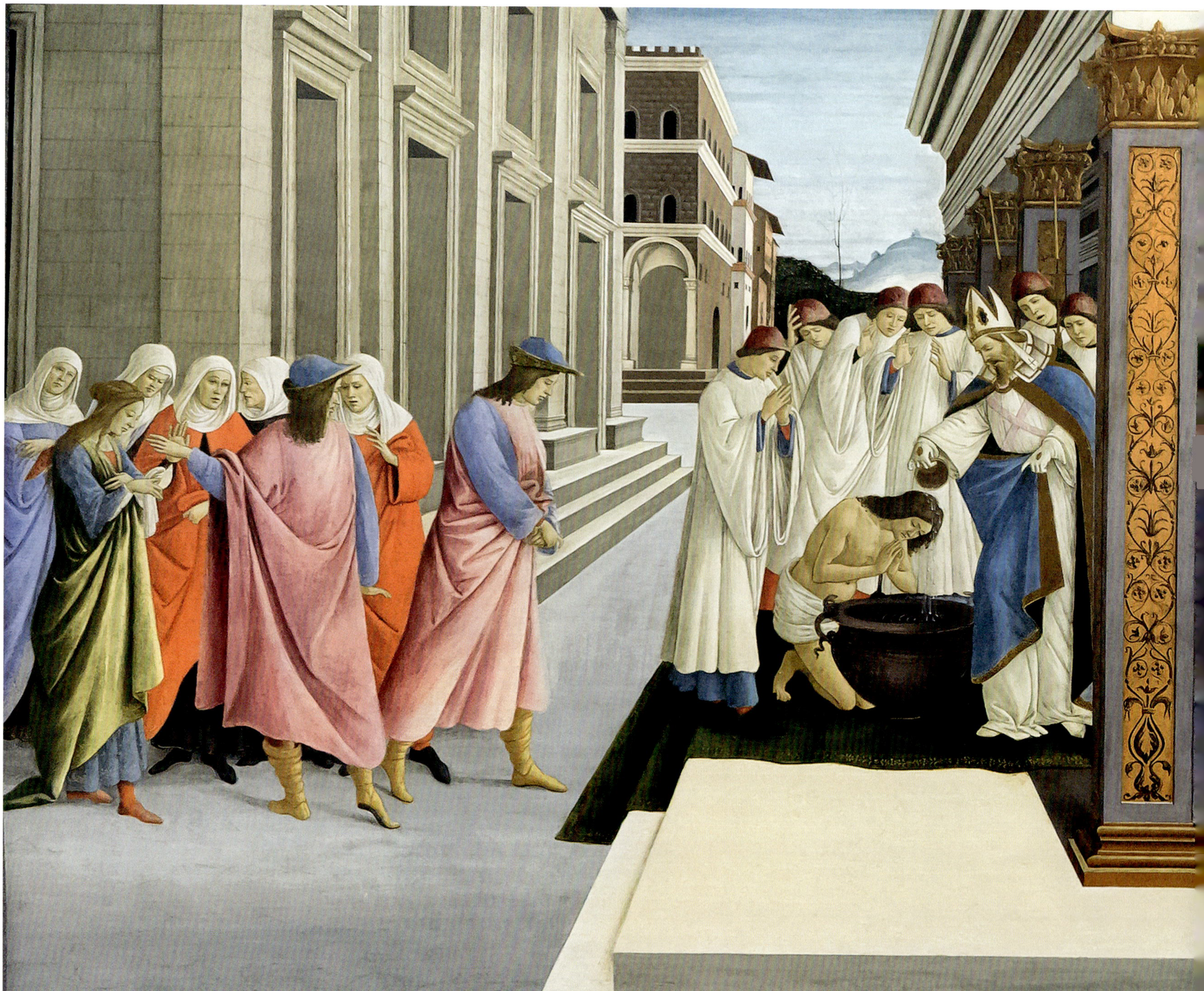

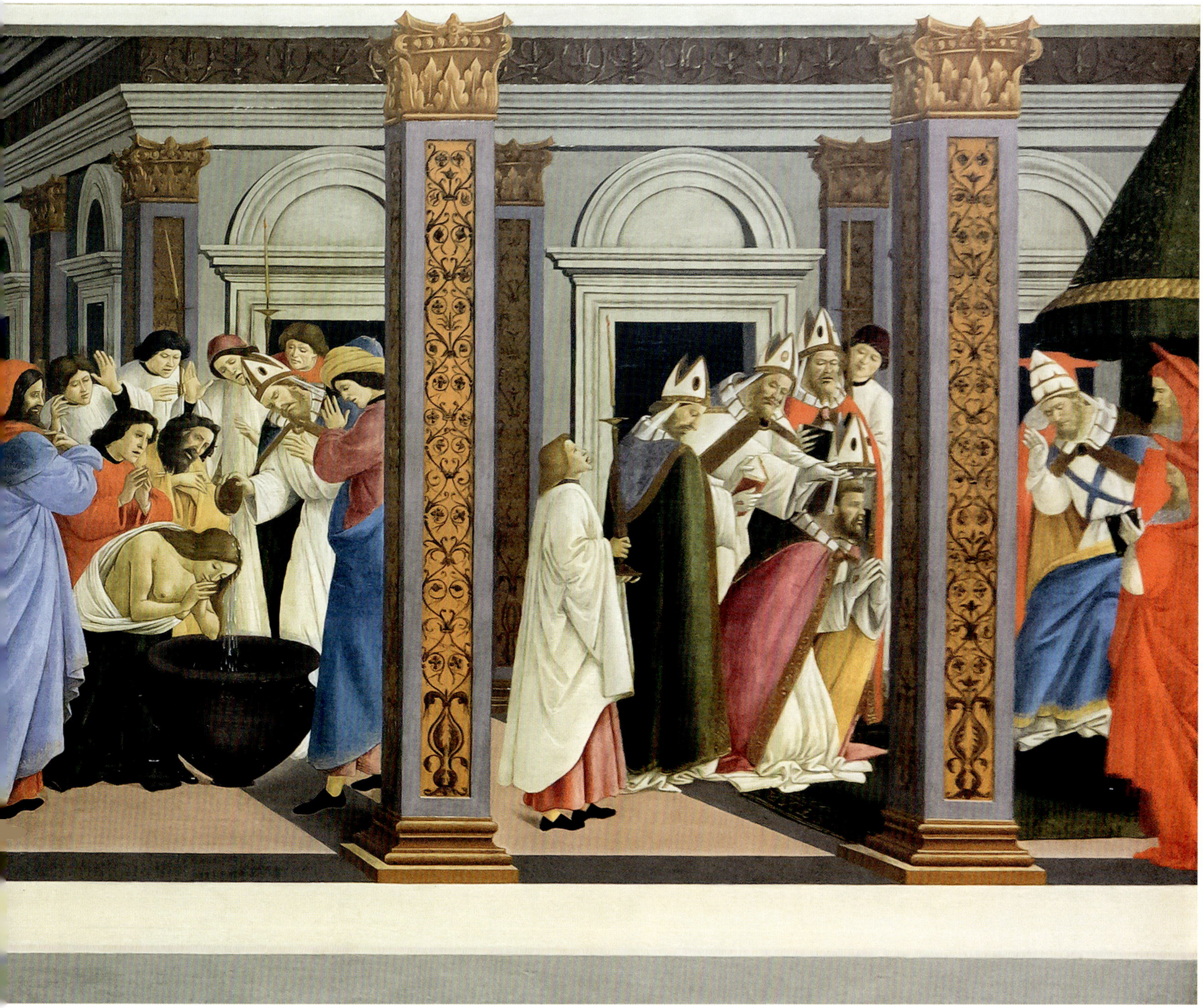

of a large loan of items from the Barker collection in 1869.[17] Perhaps as a response, Fuller Maitland lent his Botticellis to the same institution in the 1870s. But it was only in 1900 that the V&A acquired its Botticelli, the *Portrait of a Lady known as Smeralda Bandinelli* (cat. 162), as part of the Ionides Bequest.[18] In 1895 the British Museum acquired three drawings by Botticelli, together with a fourth since demoted, with the collection of John Malcolm of Poltalloch, who had been advised by John Charles Robinson of the South Kensington Museum (cats 138, 165, 167).[19]

Few British regional museums were able to acquire significant works by Botticelli. The tondo at the Fitzwilliam Museum, Cambridge, came as part of the 1912 Marlay Bequest, while two fragments, formerly owned by Ottley and from the same cartoon of the *Adoration of the Magi*, were given to the Fitzwilliam in 1913 and 1918 (cats 104, 105, 122). In 1921, the National Gallery of Scotland purchased Botticelli's *Virgin and St John the Baptist Adoring the Child* (from Fuller Maitland's collection). Few works by Botticelli remain in private ownership, although one is at Buscot Park, Berkshire (cat. 121).

In Britain Botticelli was initially the preserve of a few private collectors, before being sought after by the National Gallery from the mid-century, but barely any examples of his work had entered regional galleries by the time of the First World War. During the nineteenth century, the nature of Botticelli's artistic personality and the extent of his oeuvre was constantly under review, and it is therefore unremarkable that a number of his works in the National Gallery – now believed to comprise seven autograph works, five workshop productions and four by followers – were acquired as by other painters, including Masaccio and Filippino Lippi. While private collectors were at liberty to enjoy the artist's more difficult subjects, official decisions to acquire his work were influenced by issues of public taste and propriety. Consequently, his charming religious images were favoured, a preference apparent in the National Gallery's collection: six are images of the Virgin and Child, three depict Adoration scenes, one St Francis; two are portraits while two represent Venus, but fully clothed! Indeed, the only example of Botticelli's more expressive narrative style – the panel depicting *Three Miracles of St Zenobius* – was not bought with public funds, and entered the collection in 1924, the gift of a German patron with a German adviser. But this type of circumspection was not unique to British public collections. For instance, panels from the *Nastagio degli Onesti* series did not easily find a home in any European public gallery: the Museum of Lyons refused them in 1892, and the Prado in Madrid accepted them in 1941 as part of a larger gift.

CAT. 122 (detail)
WORKSHOP OF
SANDRO BOTTICELLI
(c.1445–1510)
The Virgin and Child, 1490s

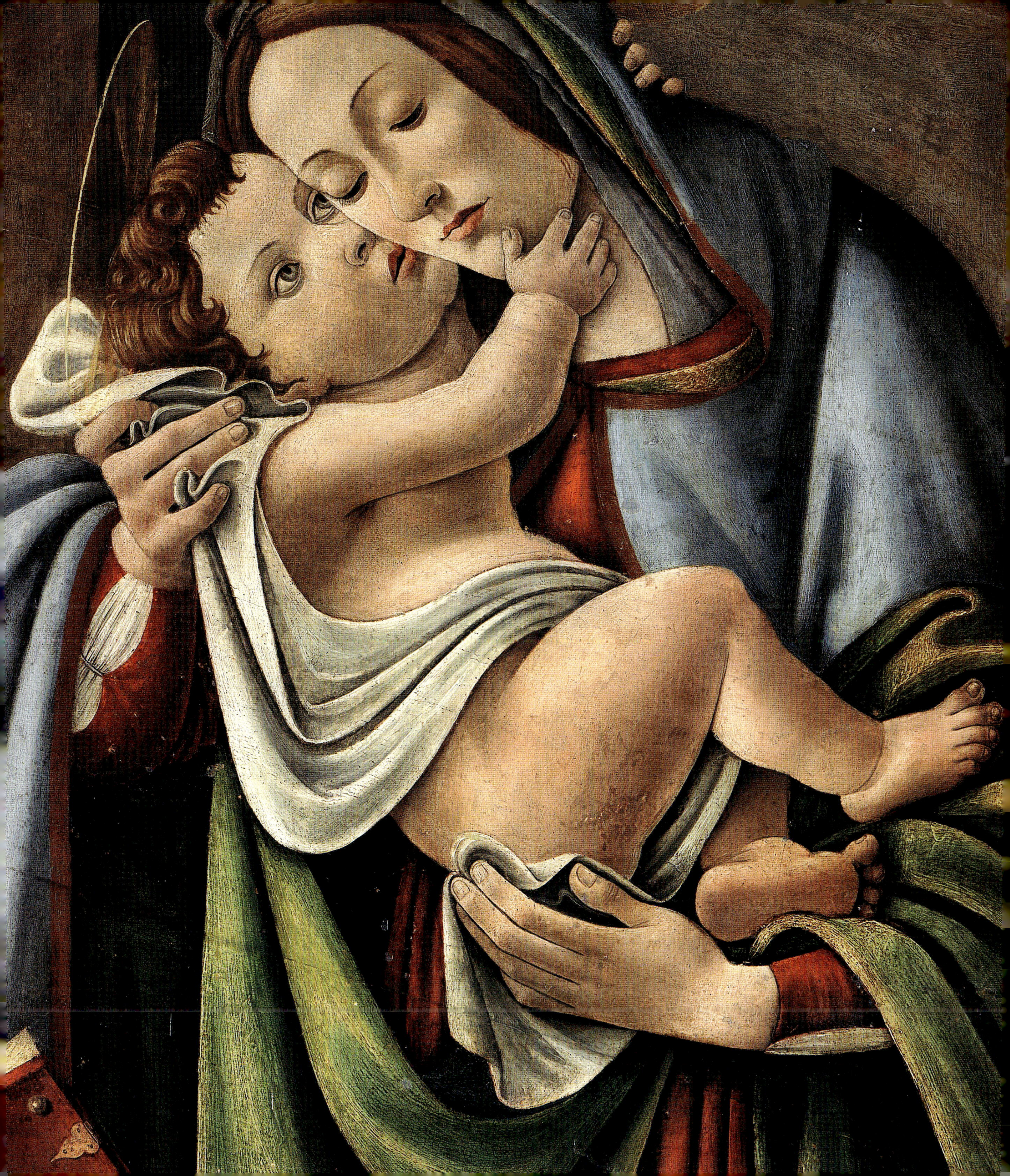

Botticelli and the Pre-Raphaelites

ELIZABETH PRETTEJOHN

It is difficult to imagine a more enviable bargain than Dante Gabriel Rossetti's in 1867, when he secured a female portrait by Botticelli in a Christie's auction for a mere £20.[1] Moreover, the attribution, unlike those of many putative Botticellis, has survived scrutiny, although the identity of the sitter remains mysterious; after a recent conservation treatment the *Portrait of a Lady known as Smeralda Bandinelli* (cat. 162) fully justifies Rossetti's connoisseurial judgement of 1867. Perhaps the low price reflects the slightly austere character of the presentation, a single figure, forthright and sober rather than alluring in her gaze, in a rather plain interior. Yet it is not difficult to see why the painting appealed to Rossetti at this date, when it must have seemed almost uncannily to chime with his own experimentation, over the eight years since 1859, with the half-length, single female figure. Over the next few years Rossetti assimilated the Botticelli still more closely into his artistic practice, retouching a passage he thought ineptly restored, and imitating it repeatedly, perhaps even compulsively, in his own pictures. Indeed the presence of the Botticelli portrait can be felt throughout Rossetti's work in the remaining years of his life. Elements such as the diaphanous overgown, the long-fingered hands and the direct gaze recur

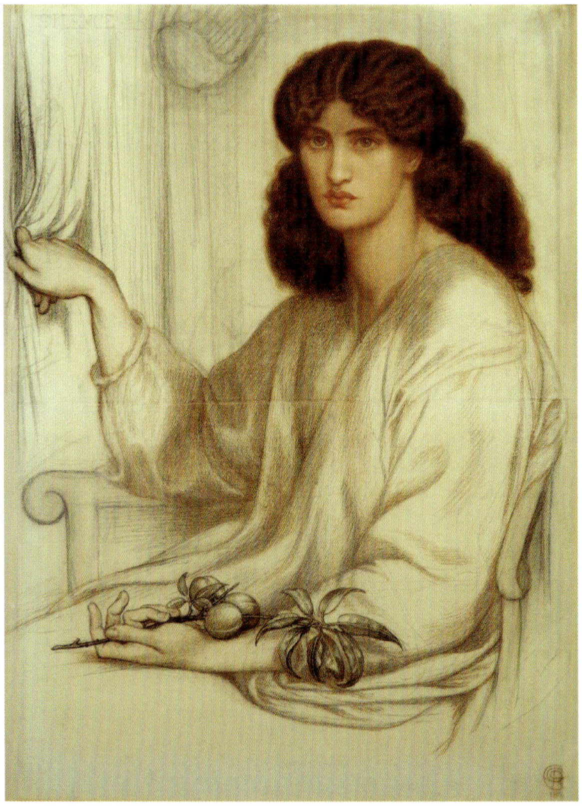

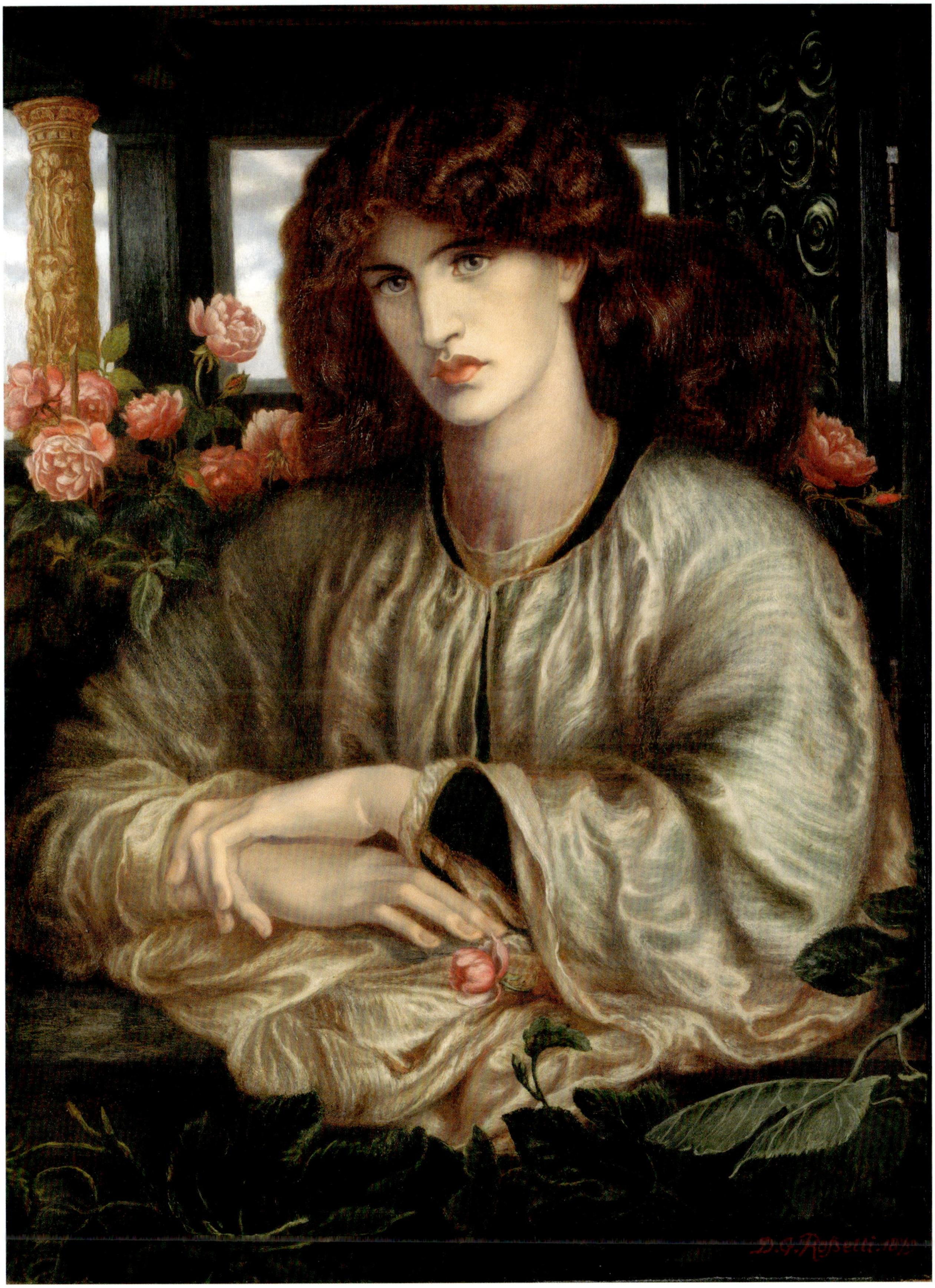

FIG. 36
DANTE GABRIEL ROSSETTI
(1828–1882)
Silence, 1870
Black and red chalk on paper, 104.5 × 76 cm
Given by Mr Luke Vincent Lockwood
Brooklyn Museum of Art, New York (46.188)

FIG. 37
DANTE GABRIEL ROSSETTI
(1828–1882)
La Donna della Finestra, 1879
Oil on canvas, 100.7 × 74 cm
Bequeathed by Grenville L. Winthrop
Harvard Art Museums/ Fogg Museum, Cambridge MA
(1943.200)

with the force of quotation in the multiple versions of *La Pia de' Tolomei*, *La Donna della Finestra* and *Proserpine*.[2] In certain works the engagement with the Botticellian prototype is so close as to verge on copying, for example in the haunting chalk drawing of 1870, *Silence* (fig. 36). In making his drawing, Rossetti seems to be trying to discover what kind of artist Botticelli is, something not yet well established in 1870 (the year of Walter Pater's 'A Fragment on Sandro Botticelli', the first full article on the artist).[3] In the process he discovers what kind of artist he might himself become.

By imitating his own Botticelli so closely, Rossetti is adding the Italian painter to his circle of self-selected mentors, figures from the past with whom he identifies so closely that his style and theirs seem to merge. The first of those mentors, both in date and in importance, was the poet Dante: it was by making a translation of the *Vita Nova*, Dante's story of his early life, that Rossetti initiated his own career as a poet in the late 1840s.[4] In a painting such as *La Donna della Finestra* of 1879 (fig. 37), his imitation of his own Botticelli amounts to the visual equivalent of a translation, and it cannot be coincidental that the subject is from the *Vita Nova*.[5] Rossetti represents his beloved model, Jane Morris, with clear autobiographical significance, as Dante's *donna della finestra* ('woman at the window'); she looks with pity on Rossetti, bereaved by the death of Elizabeth Siddal, just as Dante's *donna* looks consolingly on Dante after the death of Beatrice. Rossetti persuaded himself that the sitter in his portrait was the same as the central figure of *Primavera*, casting her in his imagination as a significant figure in the Italian painter's life.[6] That creates a triple analogy among Jane Morris, Botticelli's model and Dante's woman at the window, which implicitly mirrors the affinity among Rossetti, Botticelli and Dante. Rossetti's painting makes this threefold affinity visible through a startlingly close imitation of the Botticelli portrait. He studies the portrait after the fashion of the art student who copies an Old Master painting, or the scholar who analyses its distinctive features: the spatial organization, the way the eyes rivet the viewer's attention, the mannered positioning of the hands with their overlong fingers, the ripples of hair and gown. He even copies what an art teacher might describe as its errors of perspective, the too-sharp angle of the window opening inwards on the right, and the sense that the figure of the woman is somehow too large for the interior space she inhabits. He follows Botticelli's visual style with the same fidelity as his translation had followed Dante's *Vita Nova*. At the same time, the painting is instantly recognizable as a Rossetti: he has joined Botticelli's style to his own.

When Rossetti sold his Botticelli in 1880, to his patron Constantine Ionides, it was priced at 300 guineas; as Rossetti remarked in a letter to Jane Morris, 'The idea of selling pictures you don't have to paint is certainly a very great one'.[7] Interestingly, *La Donna della Finestra* sold to another Rossetti patron in the previous year, 1879, for 400 guineas, one-third again as much as the Botticelli: the Victorian period, like our own, was one in which contemporary art was in the ascendant. Nonetheless, the appreciation in value of the Botticelli, in just 13 years, is remarkable, and (even though the auction price of 1867 was a fraction of that realized by the same painting when it was sold in Paris two years earlier)[8] gives some idea of the rise in Botticelli's reputation over those years. Credit for that rise has been given largely to the critics, art historians and museum professionals seen to have fostered what is often termed a 'revival' or 'rediscovery' of Botticelli.[9] Yet William Michael Rossetti was surely right to note the role of his brother, Dante Gabriel, in what he calls the 'vogue' for Botticelli that gathered pace after the 1860s,[10] and the point can be extended to the Pre-Raphaelite group as a whole. By the 1880s, the link between late Pre-Raphaelite chic and the Botticelli 'vogue' was matter for satire or parody, as in George Du Maurier's cartoons for *Punch* magazine or Gilbert and Sullivan's comic opera *Patience*, and later scholars have often wished to distance themselves from the Pre-Raphaelite 'cult of Botticelli'.[11] Yet a joke is funny only when its point is readily understood, and that suggests something distinctive about the fascination with Botticelli in the later nineteenth century. It is not a matter of the engaging anecdote, along the lines of Cimabue's discovery of the young Giotto or Fra Filippo Lippi's elopement with a nun (both frequent subjects for nineteenth-century historical genre paintings); nor is it even a matter of a salient visual motif, ready for imitation or caricature, such as Laocoön struggling with the sea serpents, or the pointing finger of God in Michelangelo's *Creation of Adam*. The Botticelli revival involves instead an entire visual style, one in which the special character of Botticelli and that of the Pre-Raphaelites blend so persuasively that the sight of one seems to conjure up the other, without the viewer's conscious volition.

Rossetti was predisposed to like Botticelli, known from the account in Vasari's *Lives of the Artists* (certainly familiar to Rossetti) to have illustrated Dante, the focus of his father's scholarship and of his own earliest practice as a poet, as we have already seen.[12] That may help to explain why, as early as 1849 and most unusually for that date, he noticed the works of Botticelli when he made his first trip abroad in the company of his Pre-Raphaelite Brother, William Holman Hunt. According to his real brother (also a PRB), William Michael Rossetti, 'he observed in the Louvre, with particular pleasure, one or two pictures by Botticelli, and talked about them on his return'.[13] Frustratingly, William provides no further detail. Nonetheless, the anecdote raises the intriguing possibility that the work of Botticelli was under discussion in the Pre-Raphaelite circle in the earliest days of the Brotherhood. Moreover, those associated with the Pre-Raphaelite circle continued to take note of Botticelli as they began, increasingly, to visit Florence: Edward Burne-Jones in 1859, William Michael Rossetti in 1860, Algernon Charles Swinburne in 1864, John Everett Millais in 1865, Simeon Solomon in 1866 (cat. 85), and Walter Crane in 1871 – all paid attention to Botticelli when it was still unusual to do so.[14] The gregarious Pre-Raphaelite artists and poets may, then, have played a larger role in spreading the word about Botticelli than the scholarly literature has yet acknowledged.

More important, however, is the way they took inspiration from Botticelli's art to create works of their own. Interestingly,

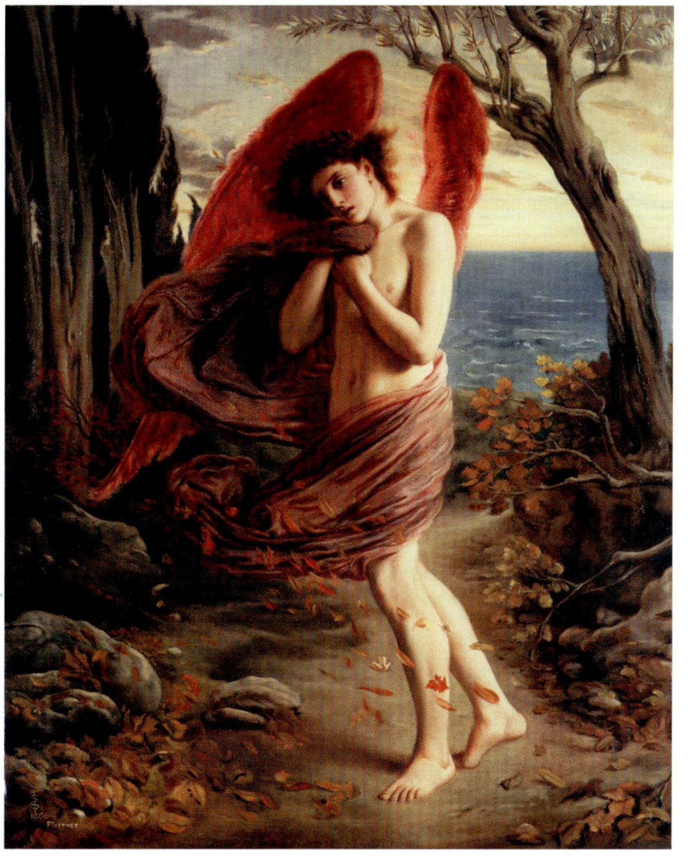

CAT. 85
SIMEON SOLOMON
(1840–1905)
Love in Autumn, 1866

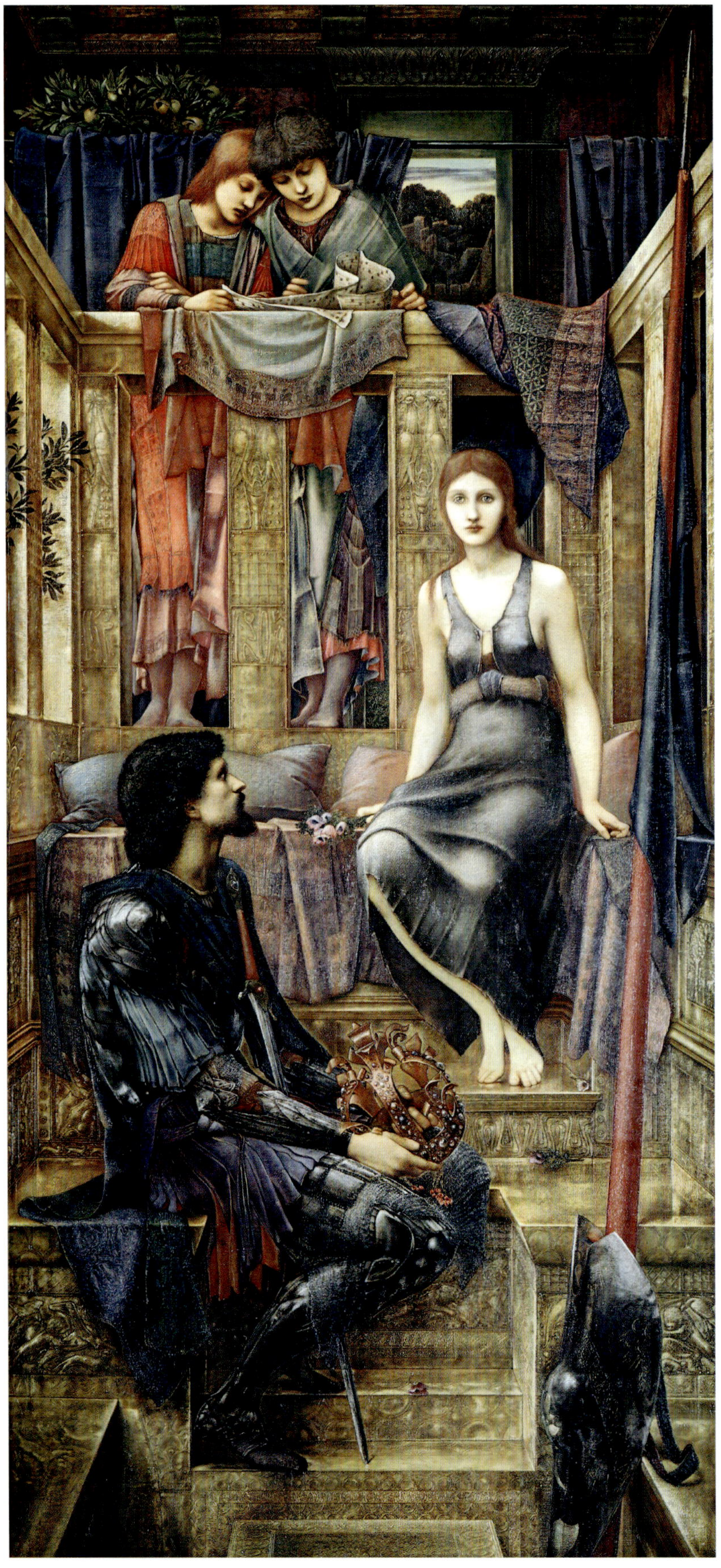

FIG. 38
EDWARD BURNE-JONES
(1833–1898)
King Cophetua and the Beggar Maid, 1880–4
Oil on canvas
293.4 × 135.9 cm
Presented by subscribers
Tate, London (N01771)

FIG. 39
EDWARD BURNE-JONES
(1833–1898)
Phyllis and Demophoön, 1870
Watercolour and bodycolour with gold medium and gum arabic on composite layers of paper on canvas,
93.8 × 47.5 cm
Birmingham Museums and Art Gallery (1916P37)

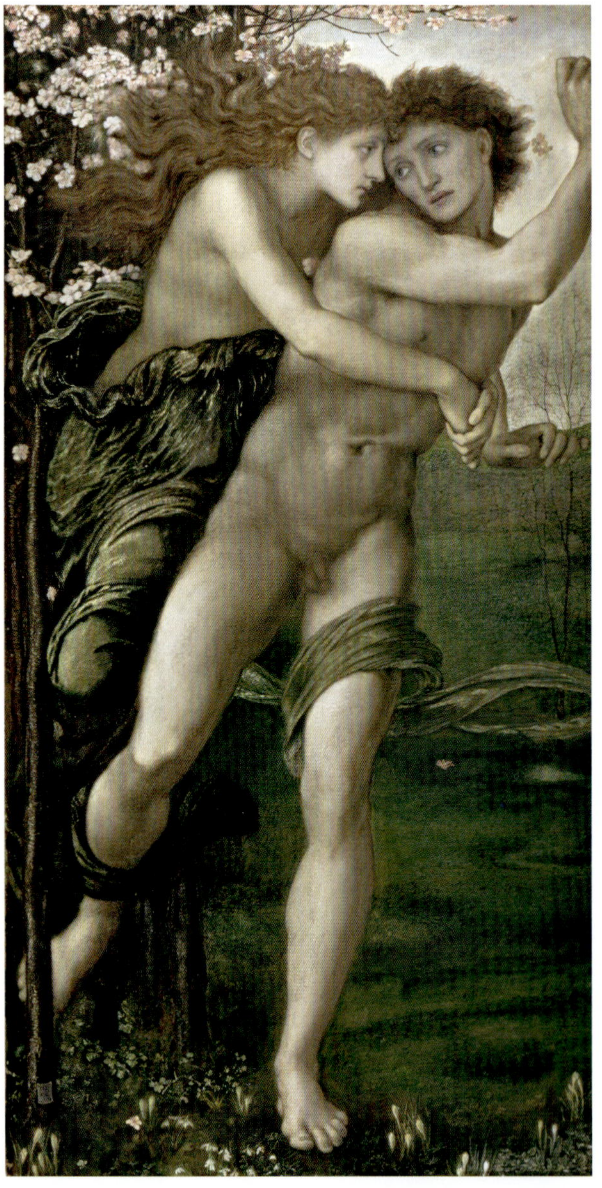

many of the Pre-Raphaelites were particularly struck by *Primavera*, the 'beautiful and battered picture' (in Swinburne's words), which had been difficult to see earlier in the century and remained relatively little known.[15] Burne-Jones, however, drew from the painting on his first Italian journey of 1859, and it made a powerful impression on Millais in 1865. Rossetti, who never visited Italy, seems to have discovered what the *Primavera* looked like only from a large photograph he received in 1879, when his response was a triumphant flash of recognition – as he writes to Jane Morris, 'Isn't Ned Jones's Phillis & Demophoon just about as plain as a pikestaff in one corner – isn't it just!'[16] This is perceptive: the two figures in Burne-Jones's watercolour of 1870, *Phyllis and Demophoön* (fig. 39), echo those to the right of Botticelli's painting, only in reverse; at the same time he reverses their genders. At the date of Burne-Jones's watercolour, the interpretation of the group in *Primavera* as a representation of Zephyr's rape of Chloris had not been established, yet Burne-Jones takes the visual cue to dramatize his own mythological subject, where Phyllis emerges from the almond tree to embrace her errant lover, Demophoön. This is blended with a reminiscence not merely of the pair of winds in Botticelli's *Birth of Venus*, but also of the haunting figure of Eros in Simeon Solomon's painting, *Love in Autumn*, made in Florence in 1866 (cat. 85).[17]

Thus the exploration of Botticelli's art became a shared project in the Pre-Raphaelite circle, sparked, perhaps, by Rossetti's initial interest in Botticelli as the illustrator of Dante, but extended and deepened as the artists studied Botticelli's paintings more closely. Whereas Rossetti concentrated on the few prototypes available to him in London,[18] characteristically assimilating them to his own personal history, Burne-Jones studied a far wider range of works. His paintings contain echoes of such Botticellis as *The Calumny of Apelles* and *The Coronation of the Virgin* (cat. 137), as well as sundry Madonnas and angels.[19] Equally characteristic is the way in which he combined them with his responses to other artists, both past and present. 'From Botticelli he took his type of female beauty', wrote the French critic Robert de La Sizeranne, while from 'Mantegna he copied his elegant types of knights in armour'.[20] Sizeranne was thinking of Burne-Jones's *King Cophetua and the Beggar Maid* (fig. 38), a painting that manages not only to combine its disparate references to early Renaissance art into a compelling compositional whole, but also to make the result appear utterly characteristic of its nineteenth-century painter. It is among the artist's grandest works; seen first in London at the Grosvenor Gallery in 1884 and then in Paris at the Exposition Universelle of 1889, it became a key work in the international dissemination of the Pre-Raphaelite cult of Botticelli.

The scholarship of the next generation, led by Aby Warburg's dissertation of 1893 and Herbert Horne's learned monograph of 1908, showed some disdain for what Horne called 'that peculiarly English cult of Botticelli', particularly in its more voguish or popularizing aspects.[21] This, though, would appear to reflect an anxiety of influence. Both Warburg and Horne find occasion to quote Rossetti's sonnet 'For Spring, by Sandro Botticelli', and between the lines of their texts one may sense the inspiration of the Pre-Raphaelite vision of Botticelli.[22] Horne's phraseology when describing the aesthetic effect of Botticelli's paintings often recalls that of Walter Pater's 'A Fragment on Sandro Botticelli', a key text for both the Aesthetic movement and the nineteenth-century 'rediscovery' of Botticelli. Published in 1870, this essay has often been credited with initiating the rediscovery, yet it closely follows the visual interpretations of Botticelli in the work of such artists as Rossetti, Solomon and Burne-Jones. Pater's 'Fragment' may, then, be better described as an unusually subtle response to a revival already well under way, not among critics or connoisseurs, but rather among practising artists.

Beardsley and Botticelli

SUSAN OWENS

Any discussion of Aubrey Beardsley's artistic sources must take into account his remarkable omnivorousness. As his friend, the literary editor C. Lewis Hind, remarked:

> But this matter of influences is rather idle talk. Beardsley was mentally so quick, his artistic antennae so supersensitive, that he could perhaps get all he needed from an artist by browsing in his luncheon hour among the rarer books in the establishment of Messrs. Jones and Evans, of Queen Street, Cheapside.[1]

The sheer range of Beardsley's influences may, at the risk of talking idly, quickly be established. In his short life he took inspiration from Japanese prints, Ancient Greek vase decoration, Regency chinoiserie, French Rococo book illustration, seventeenth-century ornament prints, Renaissance paintings and engravings, and – closer to home – the works of English artists of an older generation, Dante Gabriel Rossetti, William Morris and Edward Burne-Jones. It is an extraordinarily eclectic list – and, as Hind indicates, mostly comprised material that Beardsley knew through printed sources.

A reliable guide through this artistic thicket is Beardsley's close friend Robert Ross, who identified a specific 'Botticelli phase' in his early work.[2] The most overtly Botticellian of Beardsley's drawings are two designs, both tondi, for Christmas cards (figs 40, 41), and an imaginary portrait drawing of Botticelli himself (cat. 55). The card designs were commissioned by an important figure for Beardsley at this period of his life, Father Alfred Gurney, the vicar of St Barnabas, Pimlico, in London. Gurney was, as Ross put it, 'the earliest of his friends to realize that Beardsley possessed something more than cleverness or precocity'.[3] An enthusiast for the arts, Gurney encouraged Beardsley by buying drawings from him and showing the young artist his own collection. He owned drawings by Rossetti, described by Beardsley as 'very capital … sketches'.[4] Indeed, one of Beardsley's card designs, *Adoramus Te* (fig. 40), with its archaic musical instrument, is as Rossettian in tone as it is Botticellian, recalling such works by Rossetti as *Morning Music* (1864; Fitzwilliam Museum, Cambridge) and *A Christmas Carol* (1867; Walker Art Gallery, Liverpool).[5] Beardsley's design for his own *Christmas Carol* features angels loosely based on those in Botticelli's *Mystic Nativity* in the

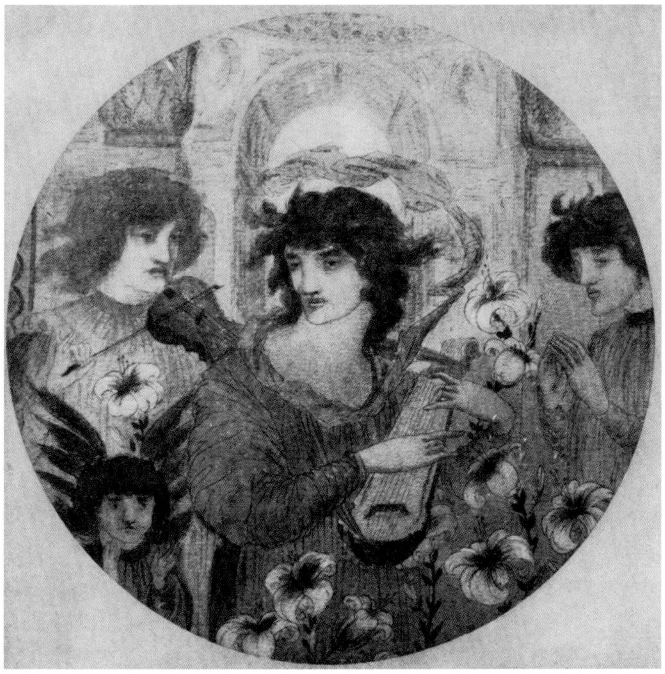

FIG. 40
AUBREY BEARDSLEY (1872–1898)
Adoramus Te, *c.*1890–2
Reproduction of drawing in graphite and coloured chalks, 29.5 × 22.8 cm
V&A: NAL

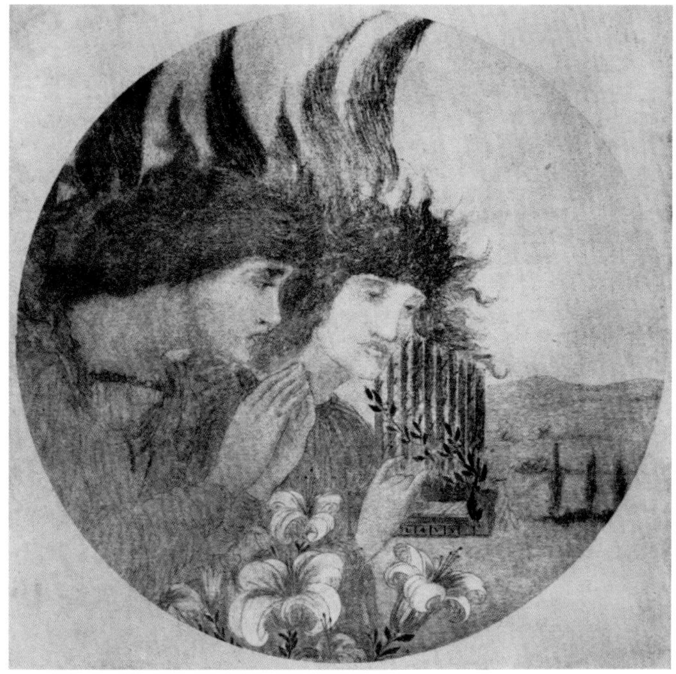

FIG. 41
AUBREY BEARDSLEY (1872–1898)
A Christmas Carol, *c.*1891–2
Reproduction of drawing in graphite and coloured chalks, 29.5 × 22.8 cm
V&A: NAL

National Gallery (cat. 101), London – the collection of which, Ross recalled, 'he knew with extraordinary thoroughness'.[6]

In both of these drawings Beardsley attempts a hazy *sfumato* by using soft graphite and chalks. Strangely, this was the opposite of the style with which Botticelli was associated, the severity of outline and cool light upon which Walter Pater had remarked in his chapter on the artist in *Studies in the History of the Renaissance*.[7] Two explanations for this suggest themselves, both of which concern the way in which Botticelli was, conceptually, framed for Beardsley. One is the quality of the reproductions he would have seen. While photogravures could produce crisp, high-quality images, this was an expensive process; more common was the half-tone line-block, which was cheaper but produced a fuzzier image.[8] Beardsley's impressions of paintings by Botticelli would have been acquired from misleadingly soupy reproductions. The other is to do with Beardsley's great art hero Burne-Jones, whose warm encouragement led the young artist to regard him as a mentor.[9] Burne-Jones himself was deeply influenced by Italian Quattrocento artists, in particular Botticelli and Andrea Mantegna, and he transmitted this interest to Beardsley; around September 1891 Beardsley told an old school friend that he was 'studying the life and works of Mantegna, who, as you know, has inspired Burne-Jones all along'.[10] The soft tones of *Adoramus Te* and *A Christmas Carol* are at least as characteristic of Burne-Jones and Rossetti as Botticelli, which suggests that, during his 'Botticelli phase', Beardsley's admiration for the newer masters coloured his understanding of the old.

Beardsley presented his graphite portrait of Botticelli to another key acquaintance of these early years, Aymer Vallance.[11] Vallance, who compiled one of the earliest catalogues of Beardsley's drawings, surely recorded conversations when he noted in his entry for the portrait that it was 'a reconstruction of the Florentine painter's physiognomy from his extant works, to illustrate Aubrey Beardsley's theory that every artist tends to reproduce his own physical type'.[12] As well as the evidence the drawing gives of a shared fascination with Botticelli's personality, this snippet also suggests that Beardsley was familiar with a wide enough range of his work to extrapolate a typical cast of features.[13]

In addition to those in the National Gallery, Beardsley was also able to see major paintings by Botticelli in the collection of Frederick Richards Leyland, whose house he visited in July

FIG. 42
AUBREY BEARDSLEY
(1872–1898)
Hamlet Patris Manem Sequitur, 1891
Graphite on paper, 30.7 × 13.5 cm
The British Museum, London
(1922,1209.8)

CAT. 55
AUBREY BEARDSLEY
(1872–1898)
Portrait of
Sandro Botticelli, 1893

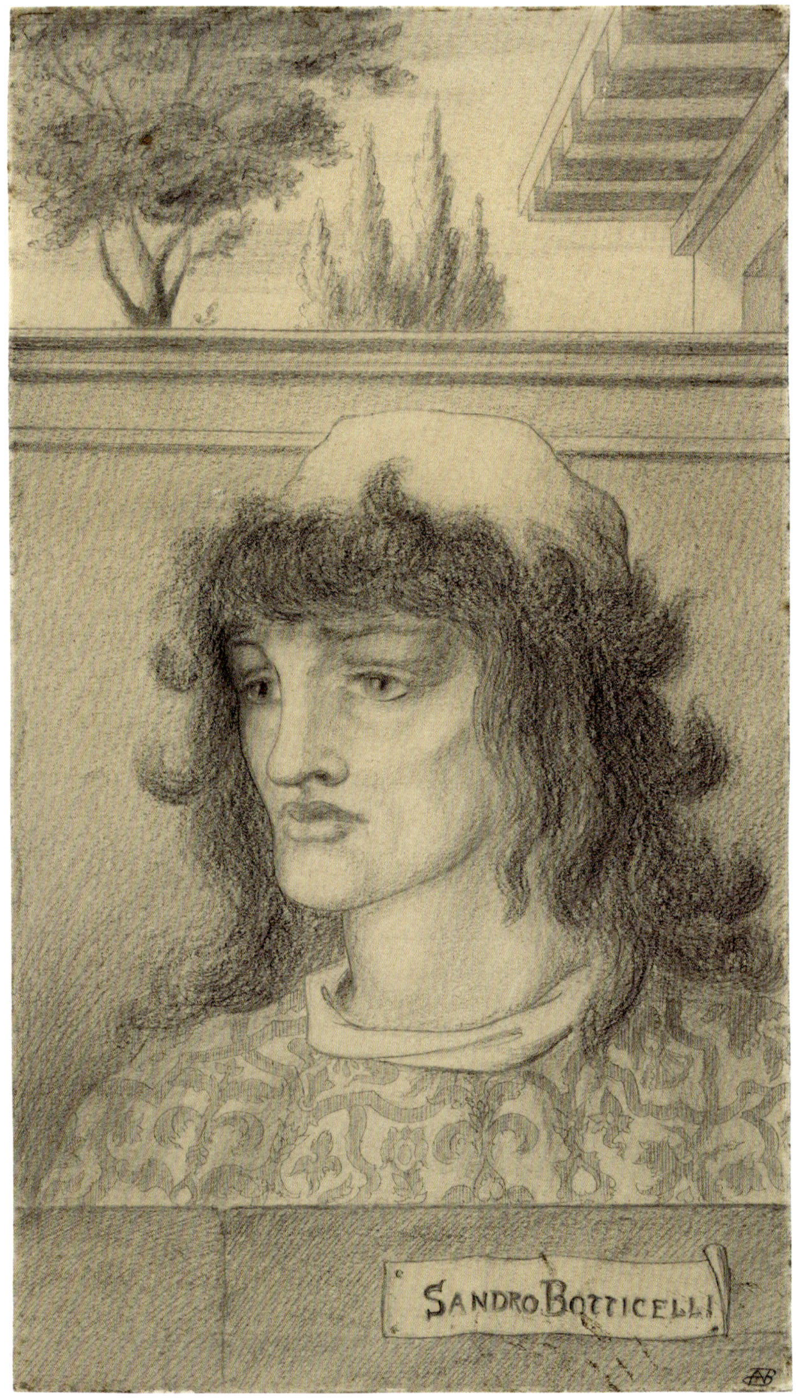

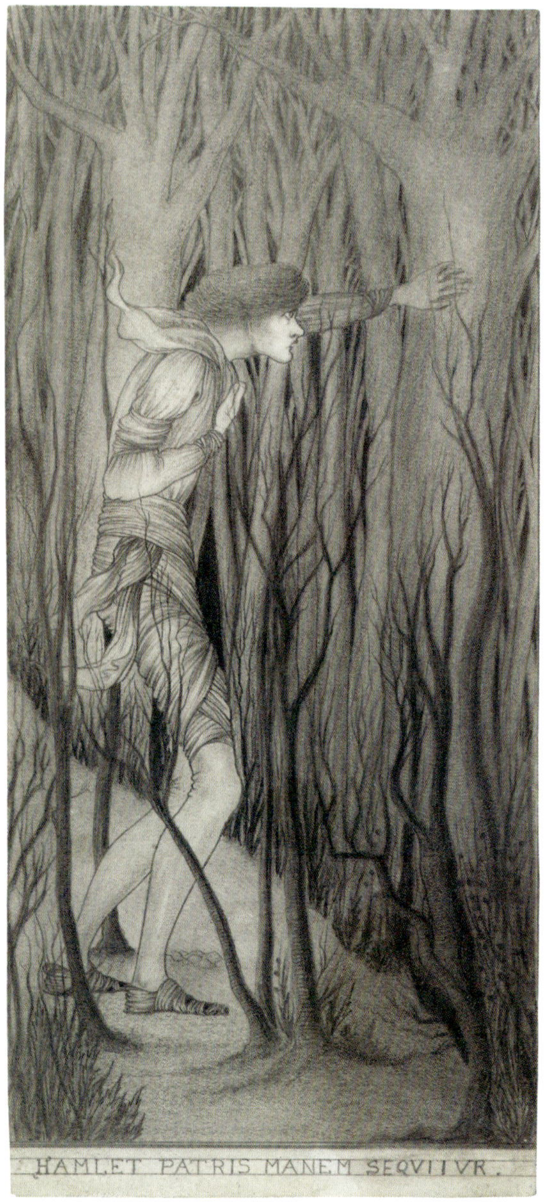

1891, exclaiming the next day in a letter to a friend: 'His collection is GLORIOUS'.[14] Beardsley listed the works that most struck him, with an exclamation mark by his favourites. A Botticelli Madonna received this accolade, and '4 pictures for Nastagio' are also mentioned.[15] A drawing Beardsley made shortly after this visit, representing Hamlet following his father through a dense wood (fig. 42), although Burne-Jonesian in mood, compositionally echoes the left-hand section of the *The Story of Nastagio degli Onesti* (*I*) (now Prado, Madrid; fig. 34).

Although Beardsley's 'Botticelli phase' and its associated soft tonal register are confined to his juvenilia, evidence of Botticelli's influence continues to emerge in his mature work. This is particularly marked in a drawing executed in 1894, *The Mysterious Rose Garden* (fig. 43), which quotes from *Primavera* with its flower-strewn ground, elongated figure-types and the right-hand figure's sprigged and lace-hemmed garment and the placing of his feet; moreover, it has a similarly pagan theme and enigmatic, highly-charged atmosphere.[16] This drawing represents Beardsley's most direct engagement with Botticelli – if in his early work he saw the Old Master through the misty prism of Rossetti and Burne-Jones, here he adapts Botticellian pictorial elements, incorporating them into his own stylistic framework.

The soft religious sweetness that Beardsley initially found in Botticelli matched the milieu in which he inhabited at that time, and corresponded with his early admiration for Burne-Jones and Rossetti. Later on, the mysterious and pagan elements of Botticelli's compositions chimed with the tenor of his work. But ultimately it was Mantegna who provided the more constant influence. As Ross recalled, 'Even ... when he devoted himself to eighteenth-century models and ideals, his love of Andrea Mantegna never deserted him. He always kept reproductions of Mantegna at his side, and declared that he never ceased to learn secrets from them.'[17] A poignant photograph of Beardsley in his Menton hotel room, taken shortly before his death in March 1898, shows his treasured facsimiles of Mantegna prints pinned up on the wall.[18]

FIG. 43
AUBREY BEARDSLEY
(1872–1898)
The Mysterious Rose Garden, 1895
Line block print from the drawing of 1894
19.7 × 15.6 cm
V&A: NAL

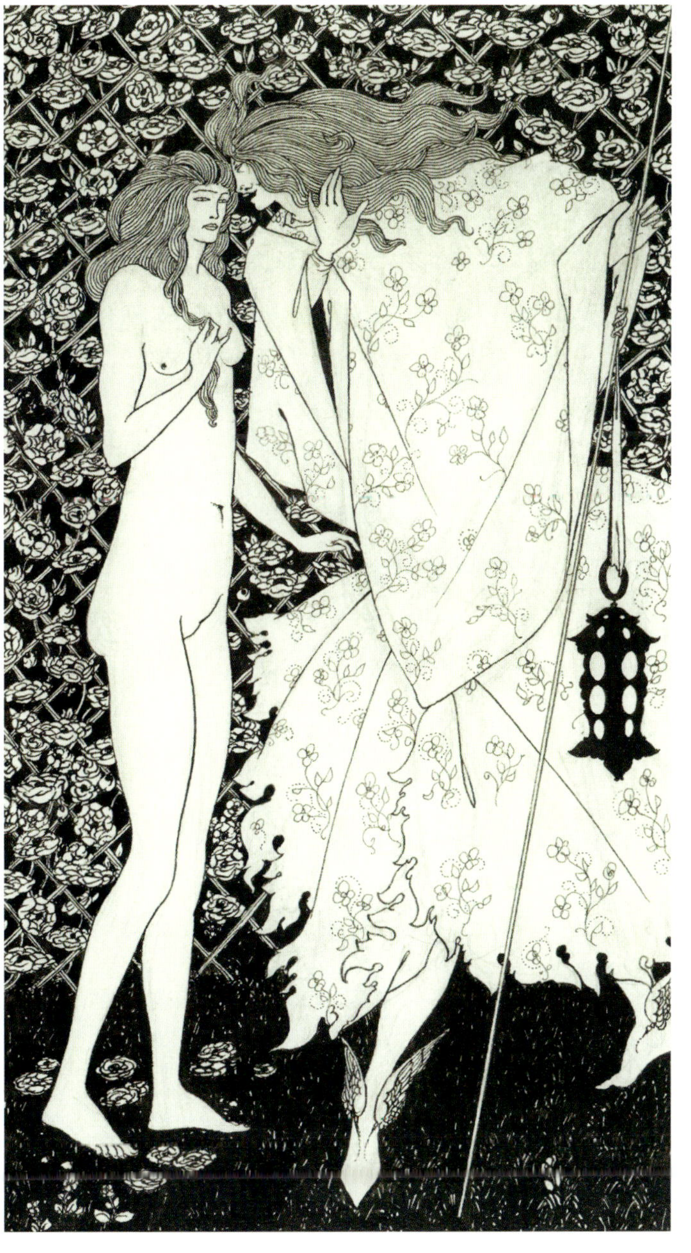

Botticelli's Path to Modernity: Continental Reception 1850–1930

GABRIEL MONTUA

The enthusiasm for Botticelli of the Pre-Raphaelites in England was paralleled in France until the mid-1890s when the link between this twin process of reception was severed, paving the way for an independent, modernist approach to the artist.

At the beginning of the nineteenth century, Jean-Auguste-Dominique Ingres referenced Botticelli's work in several drawings and paintings, although no written source exists to document his interest in the Florentine artist (cats 90, 91, 92). The French Roman Catholic author Alexis-François Rio's interpretation of Botticelli, which first appeared in print in 1836, viewed him as reinvigorating the Christian faith.[1] However, he remained an obscure 'primitif italien' in France, and was not included in the monumental panoramic mural (3.9 × 24.7 metres) depicting 75 of the most significant artists from antiquity to the seventeenth century, executed between 1837 and 1841 by Paul Delaroche, who was guided in his choices by Giorgio Vasari's *Lives of the Artists* for a semi-circular wall in the lecture theatre of the Ecole des Beaux-Arts in Paris.[2]

The first documented engagement of French artists with Botticelli occurred in 1858–9, soon after English Pre-Raphaelite paintings were first exhibited in Paris at the 1855 Exposition Universelle. Edgar Degas discovered him in Florence, promising in a letter to his friend Gustave Moreau, also travelling through Italy, to show him 'an allegory' by Botticelli in the Accademia – meaning *Primavera* – of which he would tell him nothing else, as he wanted 'to make his mouth water'.[3] However, Moreau had already discovered Botticelli for himself, and recorded his impressions in drawings made in Rome and at the Uffizi. Together, the two artists made further drawings from originals in Florence (cats 88, 89). Back in Paris, Moreau continued during the 1860s to make sketches from works by Botticelli – such as the paintings in the Campana collection (cat. 108), which had been purchased and exhibited by Napoleon III – and at least intended to incorporate elements of them directly into later works.[4] Around 1870 Moreau painted a free adaptation of the *Birth of Venus* (cat. 83), based on a colour copy he had done in oils and brought back with him from Florence (cat. 82). Botticelli had less residual influence on Degas. Only his *Scene of War in the Middle Ages* (Musée d'Orsay, Paris), exhibited in 1865, may have been inspired by the *Nastagio degli Onesti* panels (fig. 34), in the possession of the Pucci family in Florence until 1868.[5]

Admiration both for the Pre-Raphaelites and for Botticelli reached its apex in France during the mid-1880s, intensified by the acquisition of the latter's frescoes for the Villa Lemmi (fig. 45) by the Louvre, shortly after Wilhelm von Bode had failed to acquire them for Berlin.[6] In 1882 these were prominently displayed facing the *Nike of Samothrace* on the Daru staircase of the Louvre, and framing the entrance to the large gallery dedicated to French painting (today they are in the first room to the right of the *Nike*). Two contemporary paintings depict women absorbed in copying the frescoes in the Louvre (cat. 51; fig. 44). The museum's register of copyists demonstrates the extraordinary popularity of the frescoes at the time, particularly with female, British and American visitors (cats 61, 62). Henri Evenepoel, a pupil of Moreau who died young, copied them in 1893 under the guidance of his ageing teacher, who declared then and there that 'nothing more decorative' had ever been created.[7]

The interest prompted by the Lemmi frescoes raised Botticelli's profile significantly just as the Pre-Raphaelites' views and ideas found their way into literature, encouraging an affected fashion in language and dress that was widely imitated on the Parisian stage.[8] Mimicking the androgyny of the figures in Pre-Raphaelite paintings and their blend of shame and sensuality, disciples of this cult took every opportunity to use adjectives like 'lily-like', '*primavera*-esque' or 'Botticelli-esque', while the women referred to themselves as 'souls'.[9] In 1884 the French writer Joris-Karl Huysmans caused a sensation with his novel *À rebours*, in which the protagonist Des Esseintes is inspired to visit London by an exhibition of works by John Everett Millais and George Frederic Watts at Georges Petit's Parisian gallery – which had actually occurred the previous year.[10] Des Esseintes's compulsive aestheticization of life appears to surpass even the most extravagant Pre-Raphaelite fashions. Other symptoms of this art fever are amusingly depicted in critical satires. Like the English, the French projected the Pre-Raphaelites' sensibility onto their hero Botticelli to such an exaggerated extent that in 1895 the critic Jean Lorrain, responding to the general surfeit of flowery beauty and rapturous frailties of the soul, wrote: 'After Burne-Jones's fall from grace comes Botticelli's; yes, from now on Botticelli himself is out of fashion, suspect and compromised.'[11] Another art critic, Octave Mirbeau, similarly excoriated the art and the ostentatious lifestyle of the Pre-Raphaelites and their disciples in two articles of 1895 titled 'Lilies! Lilies!' and 'Even More Lilies!' The following year, he made yet another attempt to distance Botticelli from the English artists by publishing an article titled 'Botticelli Protests!' in which the narrator meets a mournful old man in an enchanted place. When asked his name and the reason for his sorrow, the man responds with suspicion, interrogating the narrator: 'Are Ruskin's writings your prayer book? … Have you got into bed with Maurice Denis? … Do your female friends dress up in wilting Liberty fabrics and have their portrait painted by Burne-Jones?' When the narrator denies these allegations the old man reveals that he is, in fact, Botticelli himself and protests: 'What madness inspires all these ignoramuses, these lunatics and charlatans, who can neither paint nor draw, who know nothing, to call upon me? … My painting, which is certainly the absolute negation of theirs, has become their bizarre religion … Why do the women flaunt ribbons upon their brows like my Madonnas, who are so pure and sad? Why have they chosen me to lead this carnival procession, and not Ghirlandaio … or the divine Piero della Francesca?'[12]

While such critics were profoundly sceptical of the emotional excesses of the Aesthetic attitude promoted by the new style of English painting, their regard for Botticelli endured, and once he was no longer viewed through the Pre-Raphaelite lens, his reception assumed more diverse forms. An independent assessment of the artist, quite separate from that of the Pre-Raphaelites, remarkably began with Maurice Denis, a symbolist painter and Catholic who was numbered among the 'mystico-larvists' in Mirbeau's essay, although in his diary in 1887 he praised Botticelli's work in similar terms to Mirbeau himself.[13] In formal terms his *Child in Blue Trousers* of 1897 (cat. 40) seems pre-Fauvist, but its theme of motherly love evokes Botticelli's *Virgin and Child with the*

Young St John the Baptist (cat. 110), acquired by the Louvre in 1824 and represented on the back wall of the room, thus echoing Alexis-François Rio's Catholic interpretation of Botticelli in 1836. During the Christmas of 1898 Huysmans, recently converted to Catholicism and writing as an art critic, turned his attention to early nativity scenes in the Louvre. Reserving his praise for Hans Memling's *Virgin and Child*, he condemned all the Italian representations of the Infant Jesus as 'pygmy notaries' and 'hydrocephalic consumptives', apart from the Botticelli *Virgin and Child* featured in Denis's painting, observing that the child 'is at least beautiful'.[14]

The high point of an early modernist appreciation of Botticelli was attained in the first volume of Marcel Proust's novel cycle *In Search of Lost Time*, published in 1913 as 'Swann's Way', in which the love affair between Charles Swann and Odette de Crécy represents an extraordinary intermingling of art and real life. Here the Pygmalion myth is reversed: the more Swann compares the living human being with Botticelli's image of Zipporah, daughter of Jethro, in the Moses fresco in the Sistine Chapel, the lovelier she appears. Proust's point of reference was Ruskin's copy of the fresco (cat. 69), reproduced in 1906 as the frontispiece to volume 23 of his collected works. Moreover, the character of Charles Swann was inspired by the art critic and collector Baron Charles Ephrussi, who acted as a middleman for the Louvre in its purchase of Botticelli's Lemmi frescoes.[15]

In Italy, appreciation of Botticelli was bolstered by the local version of art nouveau, termed 'Liberty' style after the shop of that name in London and similarly influenced by the Pre-Raphaelites, which was championed by writers, including the poet Gabriele D'Annunzio.[16] His wife and child posed in 1895 for the principal figures in *Madonna of the Angels (Magnificat)* (cat. 50) by Giulio Aristide Sartorio. One of the clearest examples of Botticelli's reception during the Italian *fin de siècle*, this tondo exhibits marked similarities in composition, colour and facial expressions to Botticelli's *Madonna del Magnificat* (see under cat. 117). However, Sartorio's portrayal of the Infant Jesus seems to anticipate the 'New Objectivity' of the 1920s,

FIG. 44
NORBERT GOENEUTTE
(1854–1894)
In the Louvre in front of a Botticelli, 1892
Oil on canvas, 69.3 × 89 cm
Musée départemental Anne-de-Beaujeu, Moulins (75.1.1)

FIG. 45
SANDRO BOTTICELLI
(*c.*1445–1510)
Giovanna degli Albizzi Receiving a Gift of Flowers, *c.*1483–5
Fresco, transferred to canvas, 211 × 283 cm
Musée du Louvre, Paris (RF321)

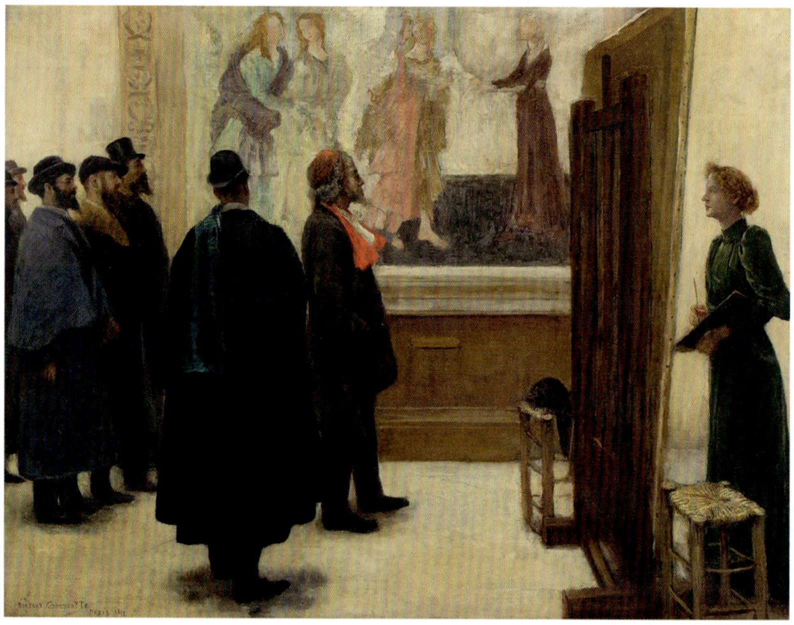

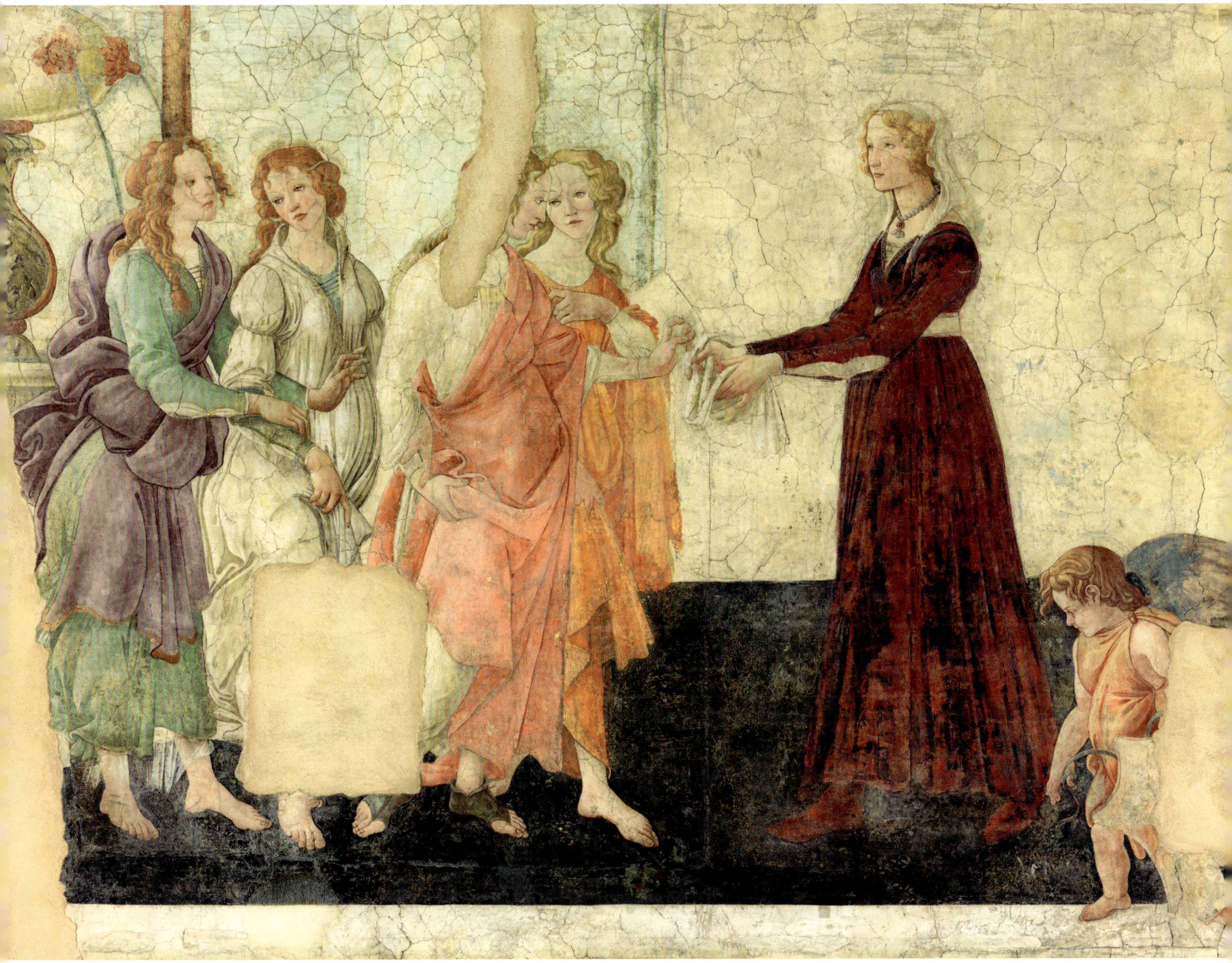

and would surely have appealed to Huysmans. Botticelli's rediscovery in Italy was manifest both in pure expressions of 'Liberty' style, such as the poster for the 1902 Turin Exhibition of Art (cat. 47) by Leonardo Bistolfi, as well as in the resurgence of representational objectivity later characterized by the French artist and poet Jean Cocteau as 'a return to order', which may be typified by the *Woman at the Café* of 1931 (cat. 37) by Antonio Donghi. This represents a woman reminiscent of Botticelli's ladies but wearing plain, contemporary dress before a sober background. The flowing garments and flowery backgrounds of the Pre-Raphaelites no longer provided a way of engaging with Botticelli, just as the French critics of the mid-1890s had predicted.

During the same period in Germany responses to Botticelli were even more sober. From the spring of 1933, museums began to be 'purged'. In Dresden, works by Wilhelm Lachnit were targeted, and the artist himself arrested and briefly detained. His *Neue Sachlichkeit* painting *The Sad Spring* (fig. 46) portrays a melancholy *Primavera* wearing a dark and heavy garland of flowers and thorns, completely subverting the connection between spring and rebirth celebrated in Botticelli's picture.[17] The withered dandelion resembles a botanical metaphor for the end of days; quite the opposite of that of the 'Semeuse' designed in 1890 by Eugène Grasset for the cover of Larousse dictionaries, where the gentle breath of knowledge scatters its feathery seeds to pollinate her surroundings. The delicate flowers of Lachnit's painting seem threatened by the *Sturmalarm* (call to arms) – the popular anthem of the Nazi Party, which trumpeted the coming storm with the Horst Wessel Song.

The Dadaists had unleashed a storm of their own just after the First World War, but one limited to the world of art. Francis Picabia, among the movement's leaders, announced the demise of Dadaistic anti-art in 1927, declaring a return to 'beautiful form and a beautiful consciousness',[18] so the public could rediscover the joy of life. It comes as no surprise, then, to find that his *Transparences*, begun in 1928, met this challenge by drawing on Botticelli (cat. 38). Picabia overlaid outlines of heads, bodies and body parts taken from earlier works of art with images and words from a wide variety of sources, from erotic postcards to scientific illustrations of butterflies. While his numerous borrowings from Botticelli were certainly 'beautiful forms', Picabia was somewhat indifferent as to their origin, and if he drew particularly on material from the fifteenth century, it was only because this was plentiful in the illustrated books he had to hand. The *Transparences*' dizzying array of simultaneous images raises the question of whether Old Masters like Botticelli elevate its content or are merely subsumed by other sources. 'The recurrence of particular motifs – such as faces by Botticelli or Piero della Francesca – does not define an aesthetic, but rather reveals a process of combination ... Painting is the result of bricolage out of the accumulated remnants of an indistinct and oversaturated memory, which can no longer be understood.'[19] Picabia heralded a genuine break – from the soulfulness of the Pre-Raphaelites to Lachnit's sad *Primavera*, artists had sought to respond directly to specific features encountered in the work of Botticelli. Whether as continuation or response, their contributions participated in a dialogue. Today, we encounter Botticelli in a different way: from an oversaturated cultural memory his motifs surface in contexts with no direct relationship to the commonly assumed meaning or intention of his work.[20] As with Picabia's use of Botticelli in his *Transparences*, whether this represents the end or a new beginning for the artist's cultural significance is entirely a question of perspective.

FIG. 46
WILHELM LACHNIT
(1899–1962)
Der Traurige Frühling 1933
(The Sad Spring)
Oil on wood, 35 × 29 cm
Nationalgalerie, Staatliche Museen zu Berlin
(INV. A IV 223)

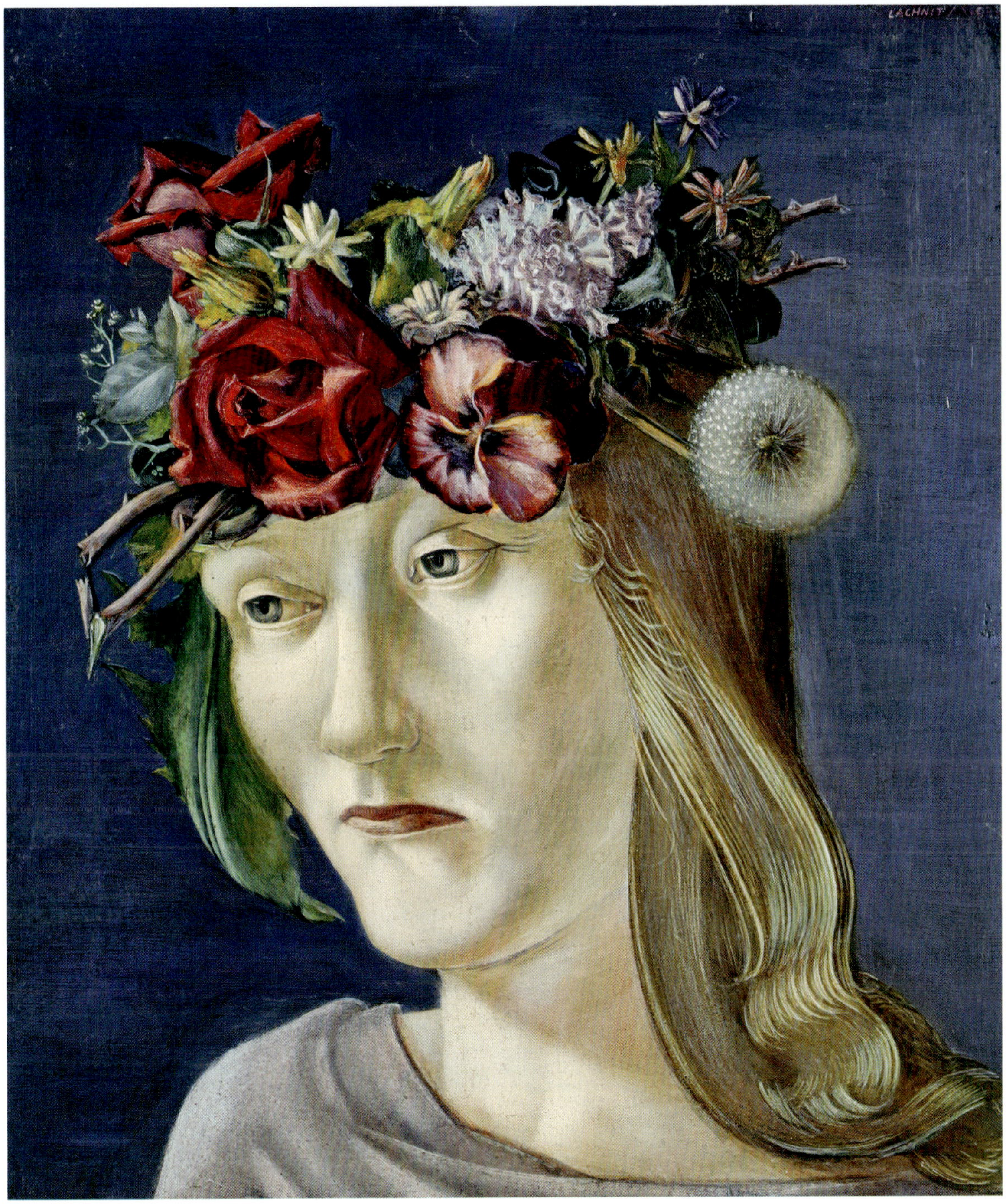
LACHNIT

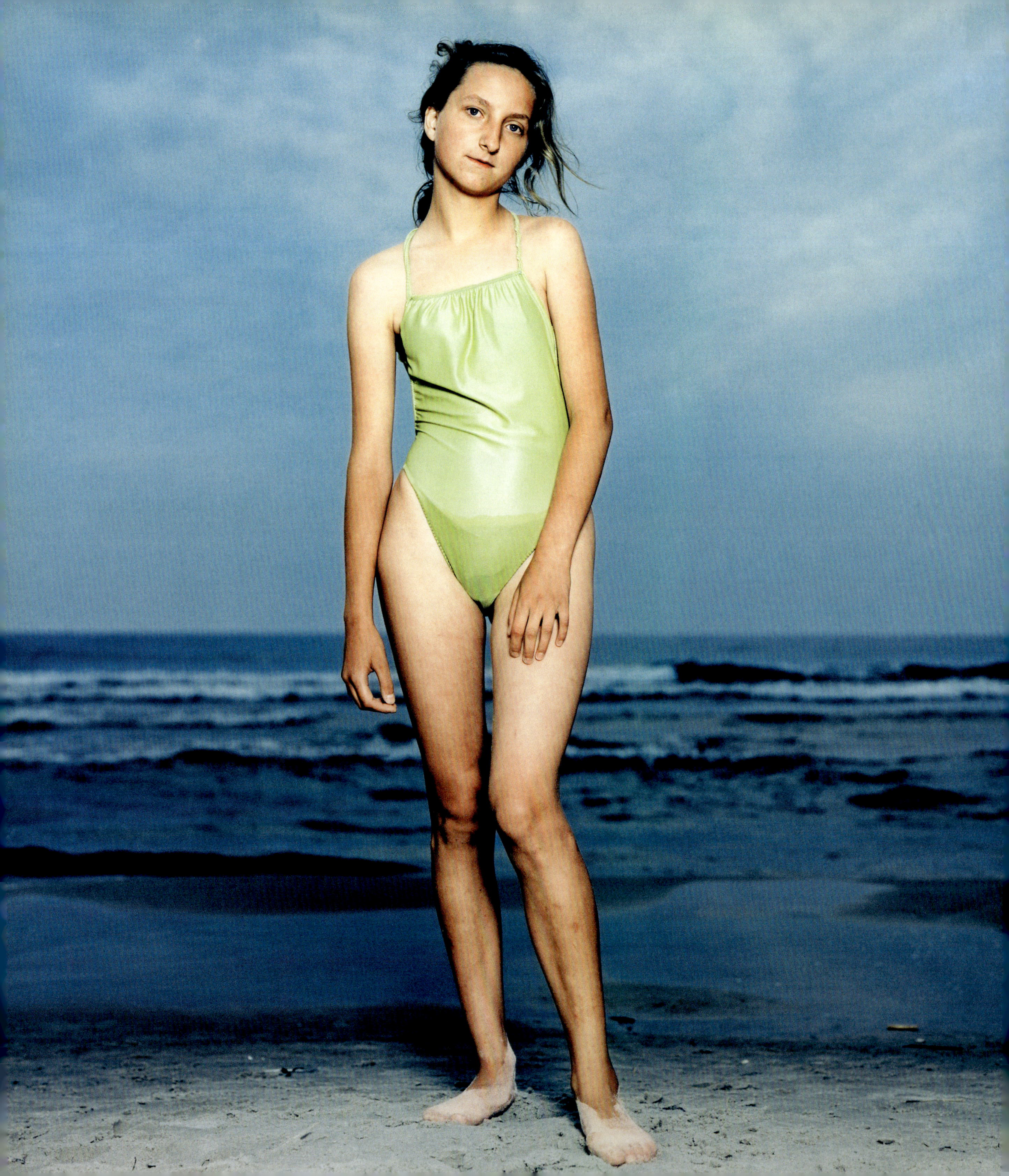

The Twentieth and Twenty-First Centuries: Botticelli as Brand

In the twentieth century, the United States became second only to Italy as the country with the greatest number of works attributed to Botticelli. While Herbert Horne had stressed the connection between the painter's compositions and the decorative arts, it was above all American art historians who recognized Botticelli's abstract qualities in terms of linearity, strong colours and flatness. It is no coincidence that the art-historical films of Luciano Emmer (1948) and Carlo Ludovico Ragghianti (1961) argue for an abstract reading of Botticelli's work.

More recently, mass media have narrowed the reception of the artist's corpus, focusing on the *Birth of Venus* and *Primavera*. This reduction to the celebrated mythologies in the Uffizi has coincided with a relentless promotion of archetypal blonde Botticellian nymphs through advertising. However this modern, stylized representation of women is no longer connected to specific sources in Botticelli's work. A similar phenomenon can be observed in the fashion industry: while sketches by Elsa Schiaparelli (1938–9) appear indebted to Renaissance garments both in cut and overall feel, Dolce & Gabbana or Alexander McQueen utilize Botticelli simply as a source of decorative motifs. Andy Warhol's selective quotations from the *Birth of Venus* (cats 19, 20) seem like a commentary on such appropriations. The original artworks, fragmented, disappear behind the products that draw on them. As a result, even the artist's name has become increasingly decoupled from actual works of art, itself becoming a brand that stands for the Italian Renaissance in the broadest sense (cat. 2).

The same is true of recent artists' engagement with Botticelli, although there are some works – particularly those with feminist connotations – where an interest in the painter's visual language is unmistakeable. Many more contemporary approaches, however, use quotations from the *Birth of Venus* and *Primavera* precisely because these popular icons have become so ambiguous in intention and meaning. SW

CAT. 12 (detail)

Herbert Horne's Botticelli

CAROLINE ELAM

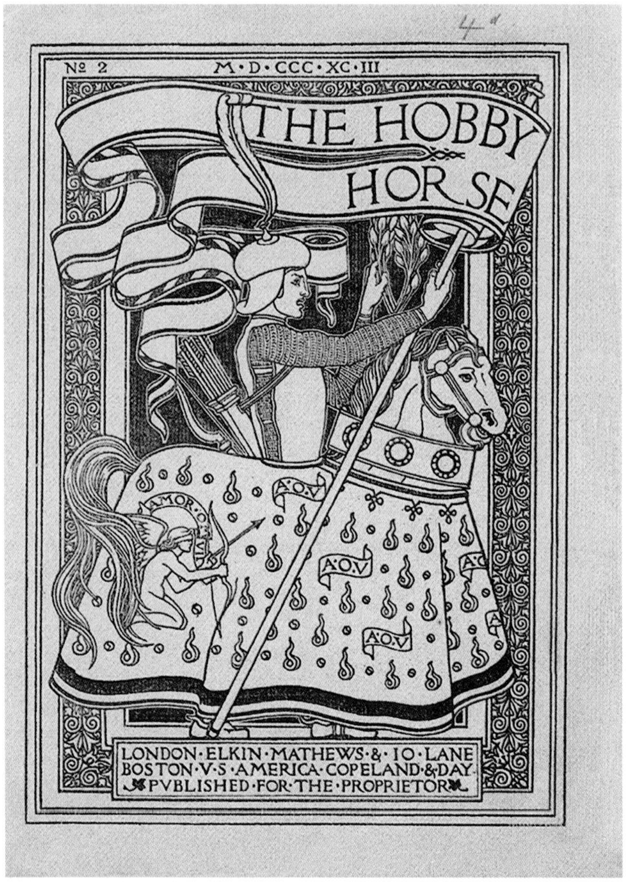

Unlike his friend Roger Fry, Herbert P. Horne remained a child of the Victorian era.[1] His work on Botticelli laid the foundations for serious twentieth-century art history, but it was rooted in English antiquarianism, and the aesthetic strand of the Arts and Crafts movement.[2] A practising architect and a founder member of the Century Guild, Horne was also editor of *The Hobby Horse*, at the centre of the London literary world in the 1890s (fig. 47). His amatory life was secretive, involving a string of mistresses.[3] He never married, and in his book recounts with empathy a contemporary anecdote about Botticelli: the artist dreamt he had a wife and was so upset that he roamed the Florentine streets all night.[4] Horne moved permanently to Florence in 1905 to complete his study of Botticelli, also impelled by increasingly poor health and the need for economy. A lifelong collector, he supported himself as a *marchand amateur*.[5] Despite a seemingly split persona – the 1890s man about town in London versus the ascetic scholar of the 1900s – there are strong continuities in his career.[6] His final achievement, the Museo Horne, with paintings, sculpture and decorative arts displayed as a unified ensemble in a Renaissance interior, was a summation of lifelong concerns: 'what the Italian part of the S[outh] K[ensington] M[useum] – ought to be and isn't.'[7]

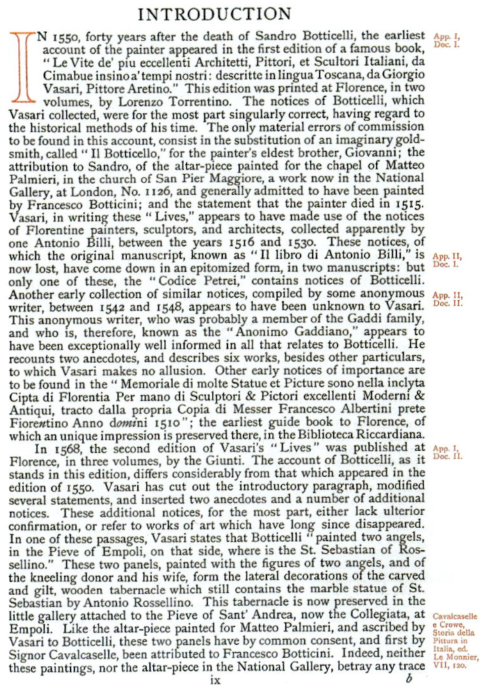

INTRODUCTION

IN 1550, forty years after the death of Sandro Botticelli, the earliest account of the painter appeared in the first edition of a famous book, "Le Vite de' piu eccellenti Architetti, Pittori, et Scultori Italiani, da Cimabue insino a' tempi nostri: descritte in lingua Toscana, da Giorgio Vasari, Pittore Aretino." This edition was printed at Florence, in two volumes, by Lorenzo Torrentino. The notices of Botticelli, which Vasari collected, were for the most part singularly correct, having regard to the historical methods of his time. The only material errors of commission to be found in this account, consist in the substitution of an imaginary goldsmith, called "Il Botticello," for the painter's eldest brother, Giovanni; the attribution to Sandro, of the altar-piece painted for the chapel of Matteo Palmieri, in the church of San Pier Maggiore, a work now in the National Gallery, at London, No. 1126, and generally admitted to have been painted by Francesco Botticini; and the statement that the painter died in 1515. Vasari, in writing these "Lives," appears to have made use of the notices of Florentine painters, sculptors, and architects, collected apparently by one Antonio Billi, between the years 1516 and 1530. These notices, of which the original manuscript, known as "Il libro di Antonio Billi," is now lost, have come down in an epitomized form, in two manuscripts: but only one of these, the "Codice Petrei," contains notices of Botticelli. Another early collection of similar notices, compiled by some anonymous writer, between 1542 and 1548, appears to have been unknown to Vasari. This anonymous writer, who was probably a member of the Gaddi family, and who is, therefore, known as the "Anonimo Gaddiano," appears to have been exceptionally well informed in all that relates to Botticelli. He recounts two anecdotes, and describes six works, besides other particulars, to which Vasari makes no allusion. Other early notices of importance are to be found in the "Memoriale di molte Statue et Picture sono nella inclyta Cipta di Florentia Per mano di Sculptori & Pictori excellenti Moderni & Antiqui, tracto dalla propria Copia di Messer Francesco Albertini prete Fiorentino Anno domini 1510"; the earliest guide book to Florence, of which an unique impression is preserved there, in the Biblioteca Riccardiana.

[App. I, Doc. I.] [App. II, Doc. I.] [App. II, Doc. II.]

In 1568, the second edition of Vasari's "Lives" was published at Florence, in three volumes, by the Giunti. The account of Botticelli, as it stands in this edition, differs considerably from that which appeared in the edition of 1550. Vasari has cut out the introductory paragraph, modified several statements, and inserted two anecdotes and a number of additional notices. These additional notices, for the most part, either lack ulterior confirmation, or refer to works of art which have long since disappeared. In one of these passages, Vasari states that Botticelli "painted two angels, in the Pieve of Empoli, on that side, where is the St. Sebastian of Rossellino." These two panels, painted with the figures of two angels, and of the kneeling donor and his wife, form the lateral decorations of the carved and gilt, wooden tabernacle which still contains the marble statue of St. Sebastian by Antonio Rossellino. This tabernacle is now preserved in the little gallery attached to the Pieve of Sant' Andrea, now the Collegiata, at Empoli. Like the altar-piece painted for Matteo Palmieri, and ascribed by Vasari to Botticelli, these two panels have by common consent, and first by Signor Cavalcaselle, been attributed to Francesco Botticini. Indeed, neither these paintings, nor the altar-piece in the National Gallery, betray any trace

[App. I, Doc. II.] [Cavalcaselle e Crowe, Storia della Pittura in Italia, ed. Le Monnier, VII, 120.]

ix b

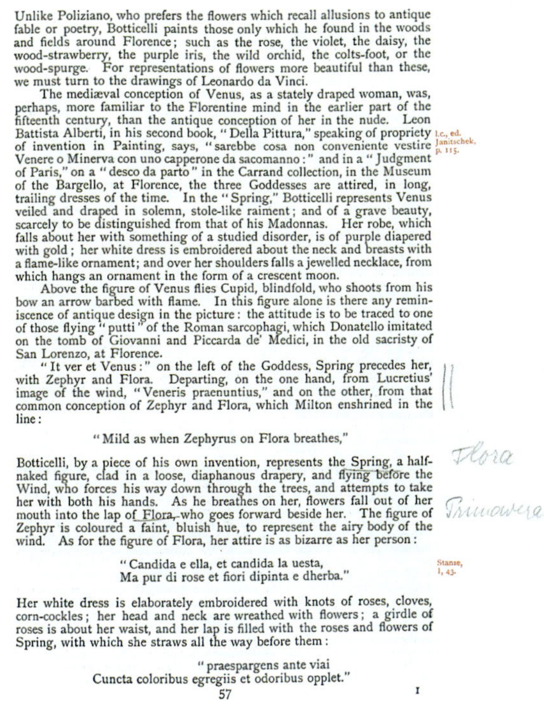

Unlike Poliziano, who prefers the flowers which recall allusions to antique fable or poetry, Botticelli paints those only which he found in the woods and fields around Florence; such as the rose, the violet, the daisy, the wood-strawberry, the purple iris, the wild orchid, the colts-foot, or the wood-spurge. For representations of flowers more beautiful than these, we must turn to the drawings of Leonardo da Vinci.

The mediæval conception of Venus, as a stately draped woman, was, perhaps, more familiar to the Florentine mind in the earlier part of the fifteenth century, than the antique conception of her in the nude. Leon Battista Alberti, in his second book, "Della Pittura," speaking of propriety of invention in Painting, says, "sarebbe cosa non conveniente vestire Venere o Minerva con uno capperone da sacomanno:" and in a "Judgment of Paris," on a "desco da parto" in the Carrand collection, in the Museum of the Bargello, at Florence, the three Goddesses are attired, in long, trailing dresses of the time. In the "Spring," Botticelli represents Venus veiled and draped in solemn, stole-like raiment; and of a grave beauty, scarcely to be distinguished from that of his Madonnas. Her robe, which falls about her with something of a studied disorder, is of purple diapered with gold; her white dress is embroidered about the neck and breasts with a flame-like ornament; and over her shoulders falls a jewelled necklace, from which hangs an ornament in the form of a crescent moon.

[l.c., ed. Janitschek, p. 115.]

Above the figure of Venus flies Cupid, blindfold, who shoots from his bow an arrow barbed with flame. In this figure alone is there any reminiscence of antique design in the picture: the attitude is to be traced to one of those flying "putti" of the Roman sarcophagi, which Donatello imitated on the tomb of Giovanni and Piccarda de' Medici, in the old sacristy of San Lorenzo, at Florence.

"It ver et Venus:" on the left of the Goddess, Spring precedes her, with Zephyr and Flora. Departing, on the one hand, from Lucretius' image of the wind, "Veneris praenuntius," and on the other, from that common conception of Zephyr and Flora, which Milton enshrined in the line:

"Mild as when Zephyrus on Flora breathes,"

Botticelli, by a piece of his own invention, represents the Spring, a half-naked figure, clad in a loose, diaphanous drapery, and flying before the Wind, who forces his way down through the trees, and attempts to take her with both his hands. As he breathes on her, flowers fall out of her mouth into the lap of Flora, who goes forward beside her. The figure of Zephyr is coloured a faint, bluish hue, to represent the airy body of the wind. As for the figure of Flora, her attire is as bizarre as her person:

Flora

Primavera

"Candida e ella, et candida la uesta,
Ma pur di rose et fiori dipinta e dherba."

[Stanze, I, 43.]

Her white dress is elaborately embroidered with knots of roses, cloves, corn-cockles; her head and neck are wreathed with flowers; a girdle of roses is about her waist, and her lap is filled with the roses and flowers of Spring, with which she straws all the way before them:

"praespargens ante viai
Cuncta coloribus egregiis et odoribus opplet."

57 I

FIG. 47
HERBERT P. HORNE
(1864–1916)
Cover of *The Hobby Horse*
Woodcut, 1893
31.5 × 23.5 cm
V&A: E.3259–1921

FIG. 48
HERBERT P. HORNE
(1864–1916)
Aby Warburg's copy of *Botticelli* (London 1908), p.ix, introduction
Warburg Institute, University of London

FIG. 49
HERBERT P. HORNE
(1864–1916)
Aby Warburg's copy of *Botticelli* (London 1908), p.57
Marginal annotations by Gertrude Bing
Warburg Institute, University of London

The Book

Horne's book on Botticelli, published in 1908, is best known today through a paperback edition of 1980.[8] In the preface, John Pope-Hennessy described it as 'the best monograph in English on an Italian painter'. This cheap reprint gives a shadowy glimpse of Horne's original luxurious, limited-edition folio, published on heavy paper, with its initial letters and marginal notes printed in red, and its fine photogravure plates. The most perceptive review of the book, by Roger Fry, appeared in *The Burlington Magazine*.[9]

As well as phenomenal erudition, Fry noted eccentricities, which he understood as part and parcel of Horne's achievement. There are 'no headings, no chapters, no index. All the knowledge that Mr. Horne has accumulated in years of patient study is here poured out in one continuous stream.' Horne wanted the monograph to resemble a book published in its subject's lifetime, an *incunabulum* like those he himself collected. He designed many books and typefaces, becoming ever more austere and closer to Florentine prototypes, and loved to publish little-known source materials.[10]

The principal achievement of Horne's book was its accurate and evocative account of Botticelli's life and art, based on intensive archival research and first-hand study of individual works, their facture and condition.[11] Horne paved the way for the positivistic strand of twentieth-century study of the Italian Renaissance arts and the interaction between them.

The book was planned to be around 30,000 words, because Horne was not sure there was 'sufficient material at hand, for a longer essay', but was estimated by 1899 at 350 pages, and took a further nine years to appear. Only 240 copies of the book were printed, sold at the then astronomical price of 10 guineas (£10 10s). Its important Appendix III – the catalogue of paintings by Botticelli, his school and followers – languished in the form of corrected proofs in Horne's library, appearing in print only 70 years after his death.[12]

Horne's introduction gives one of the clearest and most subtle accounts of Botticelli's critical fortunes.[13] As a collector and dealer he recognized how the breaking up of altarpieces after the suppression of the Florentine religious houses stimulated interest in early Italian art, while as an aesthete he points out Rossetti's poem on *Primavera*, as well as Walter Pater's hugely influential essay of 1870 – both his point of departure and the focus of disagreement.[14] Horne the antiquarian notes how Italian archivists had found documents to modify Vasari's 'legend', and Horne the connoisseur pays tribute to Giovanni Morelli's astringent contributions,[15] contrasted with the solid foundations laid by J.A. Crowe and G.B. Cavalcaselle in their *New History of Painting* of 1864–6, despite their general lack of enthusiasm for the artist.[16]

Horne's aims were historicizing – to use whatever contemporary evidence he could find to throw light on Botticelli's life and work – and connoisseurial – to 'distinguish the genuine productions' from 'those of his imitators', while noting 'the significant qualities of such genuine works'.

Horne, Berenson and Warburg

Horne and Berenson first met in London in 1888.[17] When Horne came to Florence to work on the Botticelli book, Berenson gave him much encouragement and for a time in 1898–9 the two were close. They even briefly became commercial partners, agreeing to sell pictures in London and share the profits.[18] In 1902, Horne still felt warmly enough towards Berenson to dedicate to him an annotated translation of Vasari's 'Life of Leonardo da Vinci'.[19] As so often with Berenson, intimacy was succeeded by suspicion, and their relationship cooled. However, Berenson was persuaded to visit Horne in his last illness, and wrote after his death: 'It is a very great loss to our studies & such a waste … for he was in his way a living spring.'[20]

In the years 1897 to 1904 that Aby Warburg spent in Florence, he saw much of Horne, describing him as 'the only truly cultivated contemporary'.[21] They first met when Horne was staying with Berenson, whom Warburg did not like at all.[22] Correspondence between Warburg and Horne shows the two men meeting in the archives, exchanging publications as well as hard-won sources. They believed fervently in the importance to history of original documents: 'God dwells in the detail' was one of Warburg's favourite maxims.[23]

While Horne's assessment of individual pictures often followed Berenson's, he was always his own man, and eventually overturned what Berenson considered his major contribution to the understanding of Botticelli, the creation in 1899 of the so-called 'Amico di Sandro' (Friend of Sandro).[24] Berenson saw the Amico as a minor but attractive figure, perhaps a fellow member of Fra Filippo Lippi's workshop, whose career ended in around 1485. He attributed to the Amico a number of works that turned out to be by Filippino Lippi, as well as others which continue to hover on the edge of Botticelli's oeuvre. These included several portraits: among them the *Smeralda Bandinelli* in the Victoria and Albert Museum (cat. 162), the woman in profile in the Palazzo Pitti, Florence (cat. 160), and the *Giuliano de' Medici* in Bergamo (cat. 155).[25]

Horne was initially convinced, and even produced from Vasari's *Lives of the Artists* a plausible name: a certain Berto Linaiuolo, several of whose paintings had been sent to Hungary.[26] But Horne's acquisition of a small picture in 1909 (*Queen Vashti Leaves the City*, Fondazione Horne, Florence, fig. 50) led him to the correct solution. Identifying it as a part of two marriage chests of the Story of Esther from the Torrigiani collection, of which the other panels are scattered but survive, Horne realized that much of their painting was by Filippino Lippi, enabling him to 'dissect the blooming Amico, as I have long wished to do'.[27] Characteristically, Horne never wrote the article on this subject, and it was not until 1932 that Berenson silently eliminated the Amico from his lists.[28]

Horne's most significant addition to Botticelli's oeuvre was made only after the publication of his monograph, when the dealer Grassi in Florence showed him four predella panels (figs 51–4) he immediately recognized as 'genuine and delightful', adding: 'It is the first time that I have ever come across quite unknown and undoubtedly genuine pictures by Sandro.'[29] Initially Berenson, who was firmly against the attribution, attempted to give them to his 'Amico', but he finally recognized them as early works.[30] Horne realized they were likely to come from a documented altarpiece (painted for the house of reformed prostitutes in Florence, the Convertite), but it remains puzzling that they are superior in quality and earlier in date than what is now often considered to be its main element, the *Trinity* panel in the Courtauld Gallery, identified as such after Horne's death by the Japanese art historian, Yukio Yashiro (see fig. 7).[31]

Aby Warburg and 'old slips of paper'

Horne shared with Warburg his discovery that *Primavera* had probably belonged not to Lorenzo the Magnificent but to his younger cousin Lorenzo di Pierfrancesco de' Medici, the owner in 1478 of the Villa Castello, where Vasari saw the picture.[32] The re-evaluation of this patron of Botticelli (who

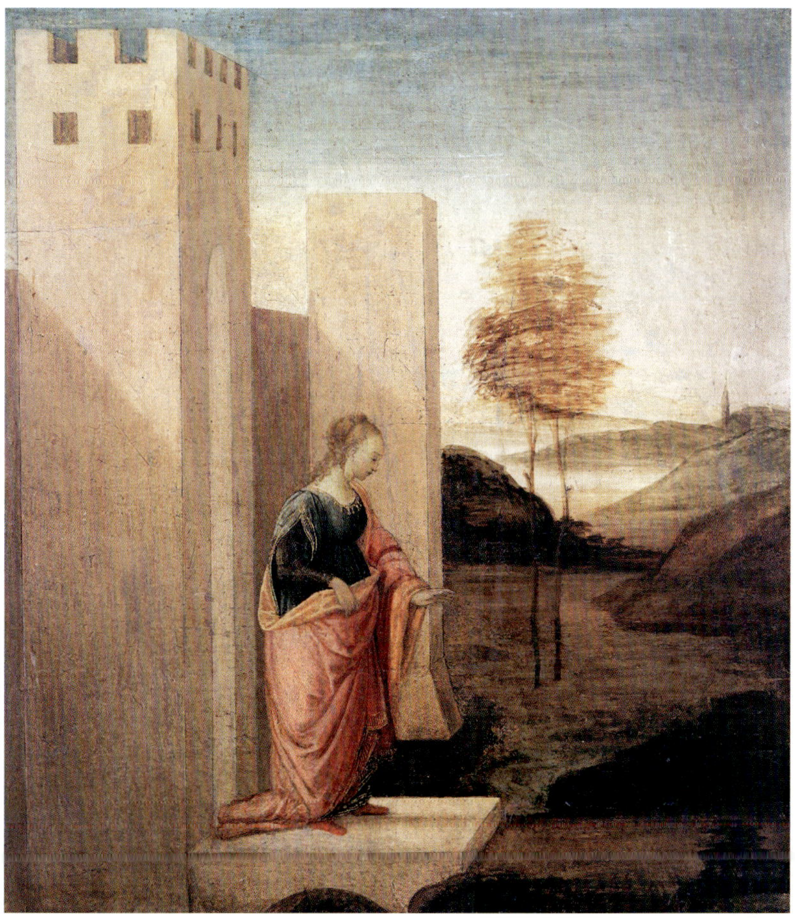

FIG. 50
FILIPPINO LIPPI (*c.*1457–1504) and SANDRO BOTTICELLI (*c.*1445–1510)
Queen Vashti Leaves the City, *c.*1475
Tempera on wood
45.4 × 40 cm
Museo Horne, Florence

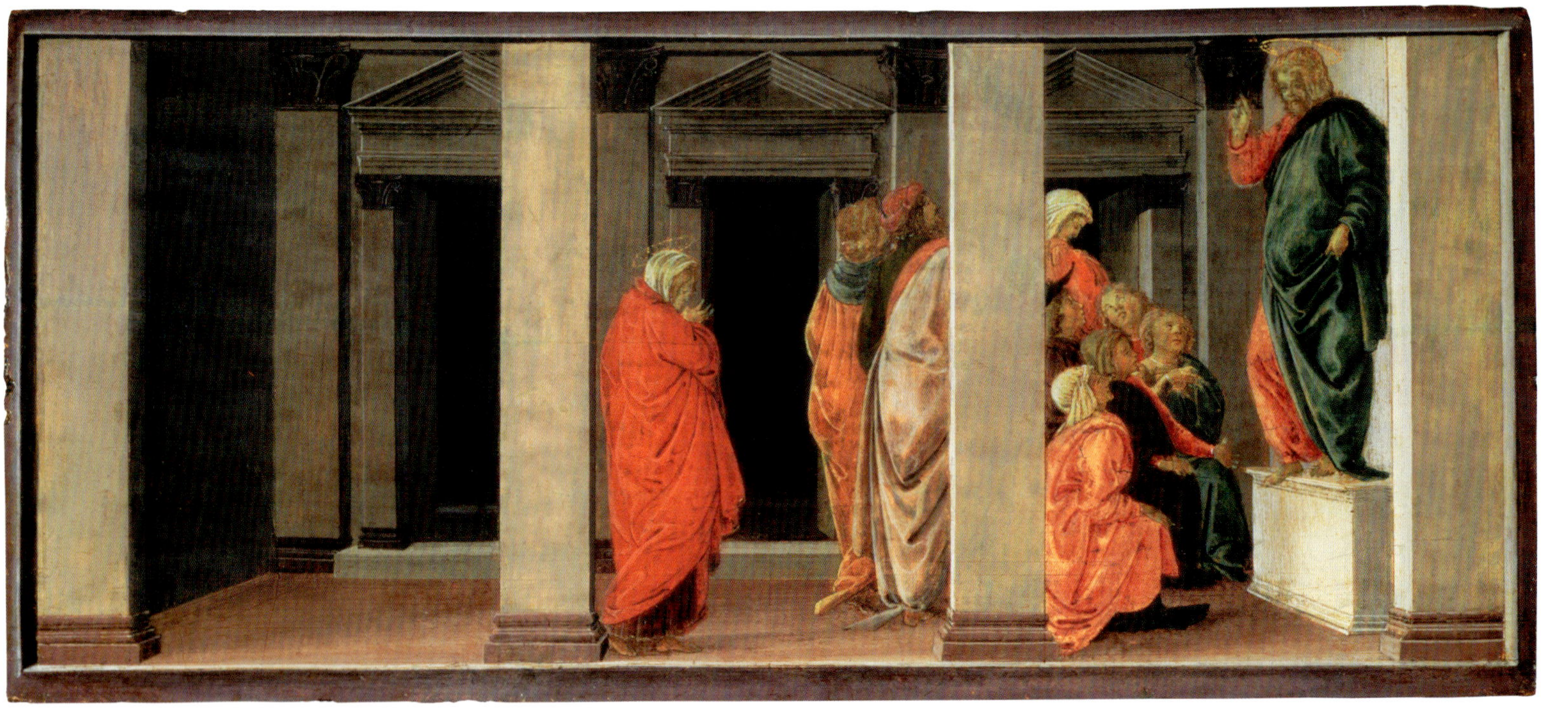

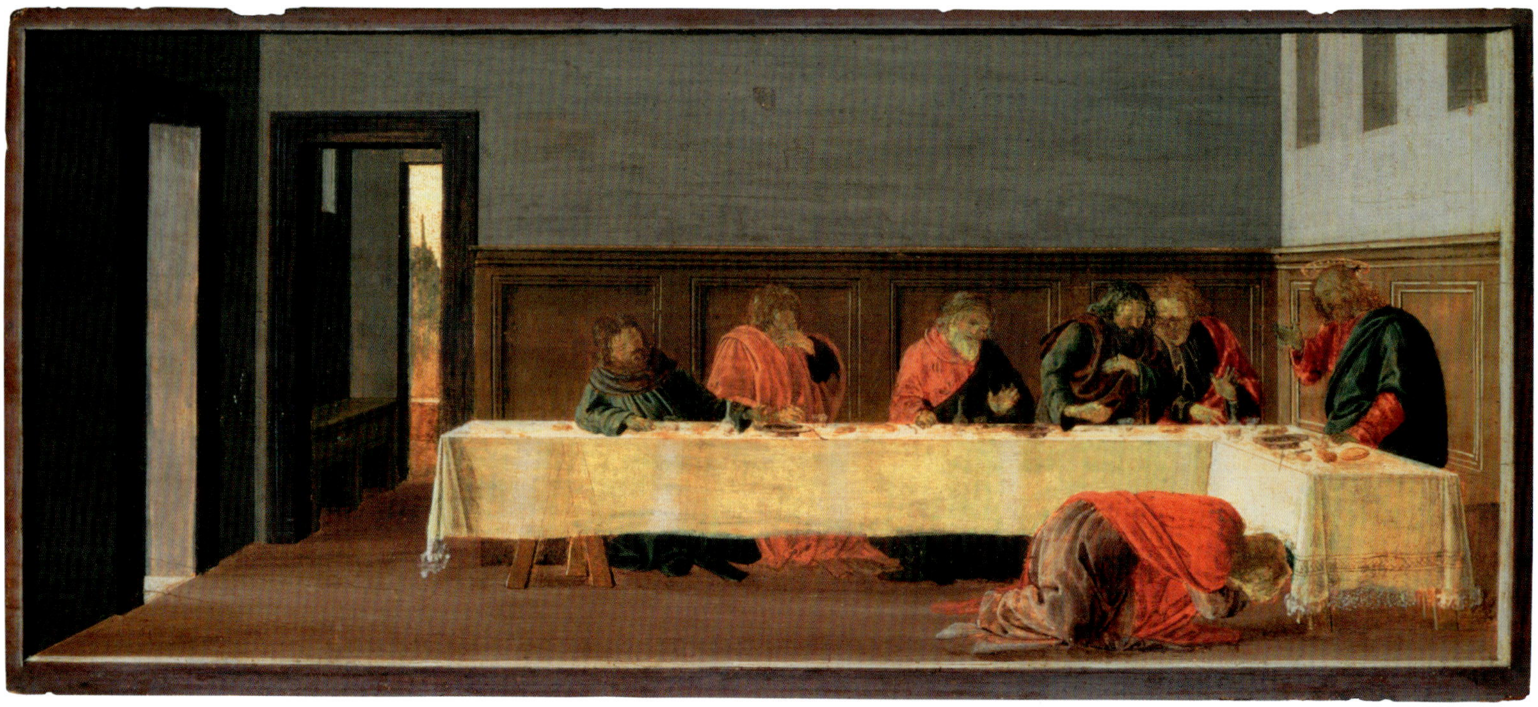

FIGS 51–4
SANDRO BOTTICELLI (c.1445–1510)

St Mary Magdalene Listening to Christ Preach, 1470s?
Tempera on wood, 18.8 × 42.5 cm
John G. Johnson Collection, 1917
Philadelphia Museum of Art (Cat.44)

The Feast in the House of Simon, 1470s?
Tempera on wood,
18.5 × 42.5 cm
John G. Johnson Collection, 1917
Philadelphia Museum of Art (Cat.45)

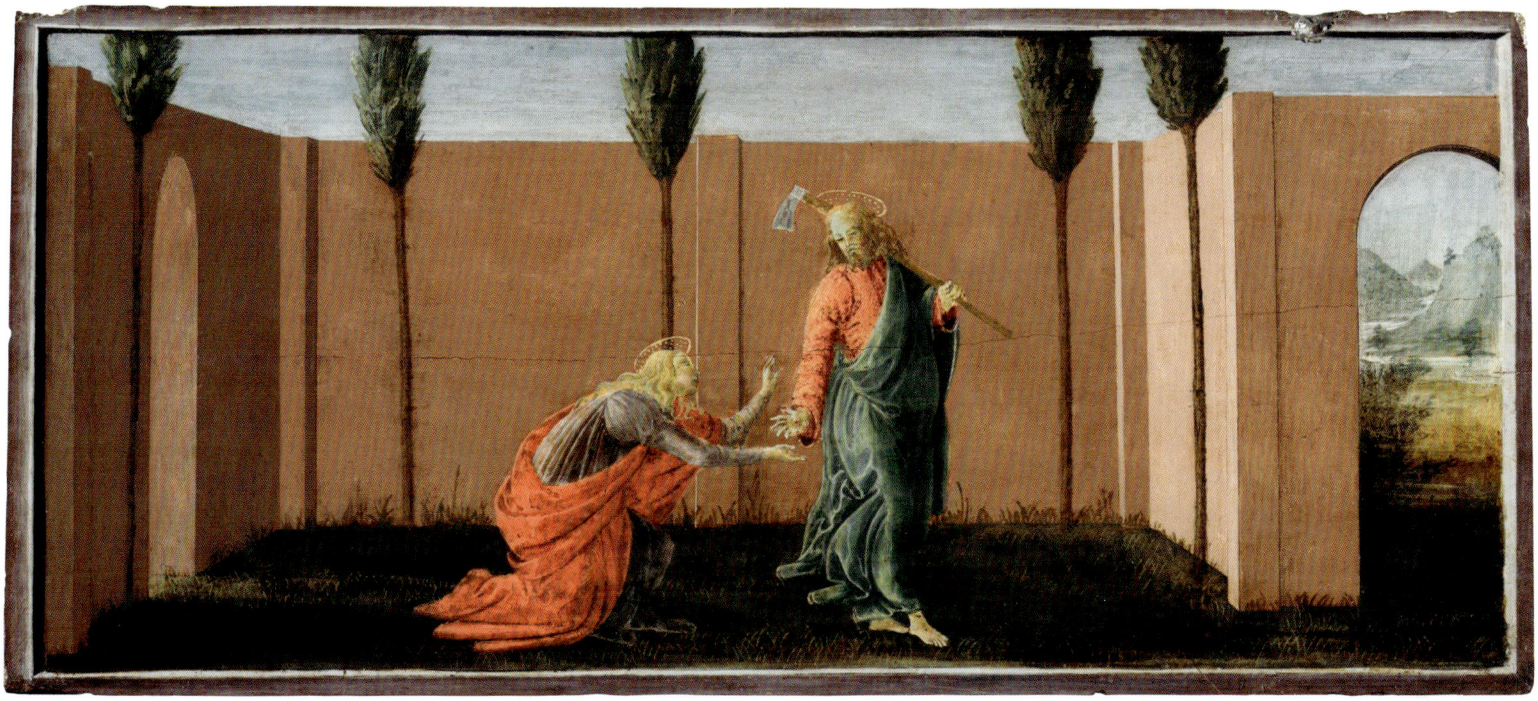

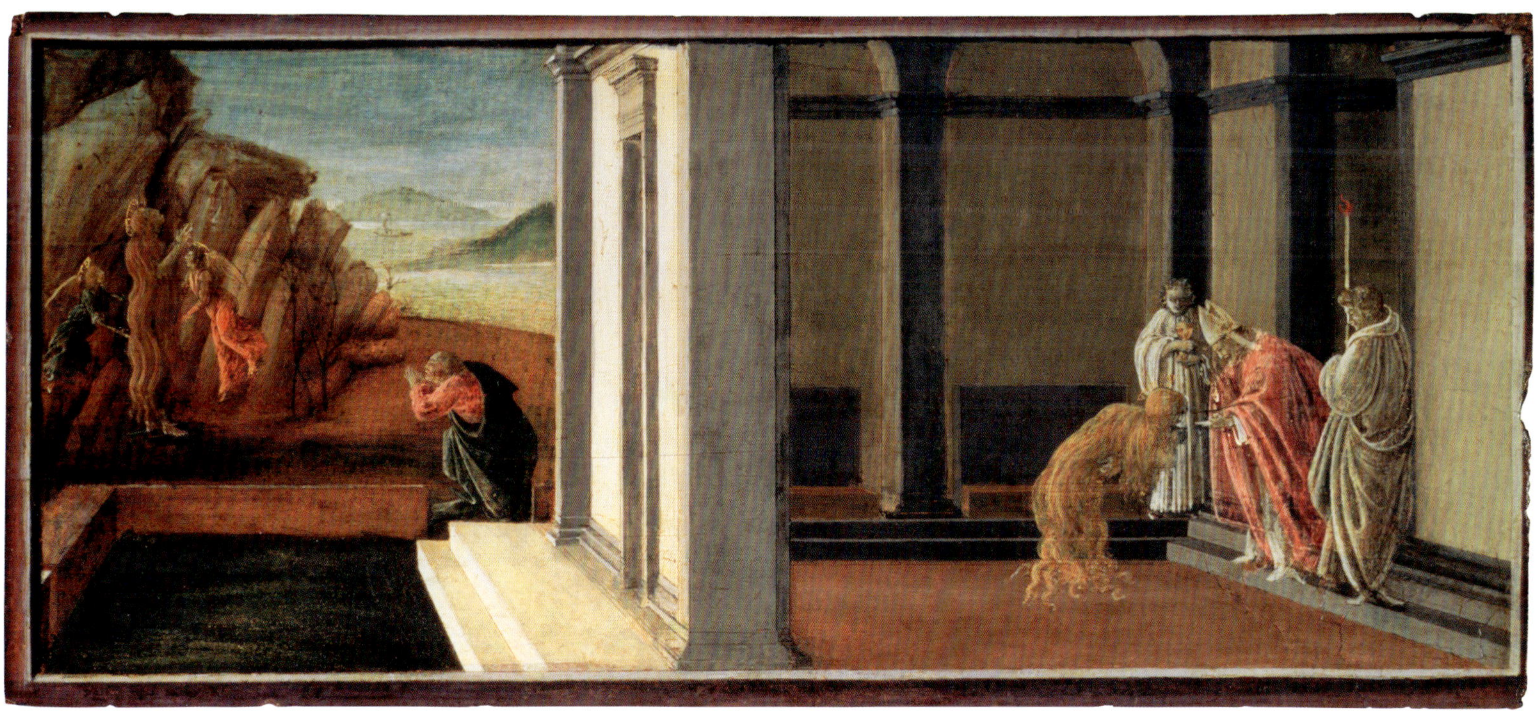

Noli me tangere, 1470s?
Tempera on panel, 18.5 × 42.3 cm
John G. Johnson Collection, 1917
Philadelphia Museum of Art (Cat.46)

The Last Moments of St Mary Magdalene, 1470s?
Tempera on panel, 18.5 × 42.5 cm
John G. Johnson Collection, 1917
Philadelphia Museum of Art (Cat.47)

commissioned the Dante drawings) was a cornerstone of Horne's research.[33] In 1902 Warburg commends Horne's approach in these terms:

> You are one of the few workers in the field who are inclined and able to appreciate the detail-work we have to do, and you have, I am sure, the conviction too that doing the next duty of reading old slips of paper is better than opening large views, without having anything real to point out.[34]

Despite mutual admiration, there remained unbridgeable gulfs between them. Both sought to reconstruct the cultural milieu of the fifteenth century; but for Warburg this was a world of ideas, masquerades and psychological struggles, for Horne one of workshop encounters, carpenters, picture frames and wainscoting.

Horne and Warburg both sought to escape the clichés of nineteenth-century Botticelli criticism, to judge the artist in the terms of his own era. Warburg set out this position clearly in a short article in 1898.[35] To understand Botticelli, it was important not to linger in 'the twilight of that delightful melancholy', but rather to 'follow him into the broad daylight of his work as a recorder of an intense and vigorous physical and mental life'.[36] A contemporary, comparing Botticelli to Filippino Lippi, Perugino and Ghirlandaio, commented that 'his works have a virile air and are made with the best method and complete proportion'.[37] It was precisely this assessment of Botticelli's *aria virile* and *optima ragione*, that Horne made the key to his revisionist, historicizing interpretation.[38]

Key to Warburg's interpretation of *Primavera* was his identification of the figure usually called Flora as an idealized portrait of Giuliano de' Medici's poetic *innamorata*, Simonetta Vespucci. He cannot have liked Horne's dismissal of this idea, along with other Botticellian portraits supposedly of her.[39] This still rankled in 1920, when Warburg was discussing Horne's book with Bode, then about to write his own Botticelli monograph. To Bode's negative comments on Horne's judgements Warburg replied:

> [Horne] was an architect originally, and despite his incredible, unremitting feeling for documentary evidence, he lacked an element of scholarly imagination (*phantasie*), unable to perceive, to understand the connection between the Simonetta cult and the *Realm of Venus* and the *Birth* [*of Venus*], which today is still unquestionable.[40]

Imagination – or fantasy? This remains the question. For Fry, Horne's demolition of the Simonetta myth exemplifies his 'valuable destructive criticism', but such debunking can close off promising avenues of enquiry.[41]

Horne assumed that 'nothing stands between the researcher and his documents, and that true valuations depend on the full understanding thus achieved', while Warburg was acutely conscious of the changing configurations of history.[42] But Horne was also aware of the impossibility of escaping one's own distinctive and time-bound culture. In his *Memorie autobiografiche*, he writes: 'I am a believer in the perpetual fluctuation and vicissitudes of taste. Raphael is not now admired from the same point of view as when Carracci and Guido Reni were uttered in the same breath.'[43] He was fully aware of his debt to Pater, the co-dedicatee of his monograph, often quoting phrases from the celebrated essay of 1870.

Despite Horne's feeling that his book had been a failure, every major publication on Botticelli since 1908 has taken his work as its starting point. This was handsomely admitted by Bode in 1925, although he took up Warburg's criticism of lack of imagination, claiming (wrongly) that Horne had failed to do 'full justice to the artist and poet in Botticelli'.[44] In an illuminating article of 1930, 'Connaissons-nous Botticelli?', prompted by Yashiro's monograph of 1926, the Belgian art historian Jacques Mesnil outlined the difficulties in constructing a truly historical view of Botticelli's life and work which would surpass Vasari's morality tale or the subjective impressions of recent critics.[45] The best modern writing about Botticelli continues to draw from Horne's 'living spring'.

CAT. 156 (detail)
SANDRO BOTTICELLI
(c.1445–1510)
Ideal Portrait of a Lady ('Simonetta Vespucci'),
c.1475–80?

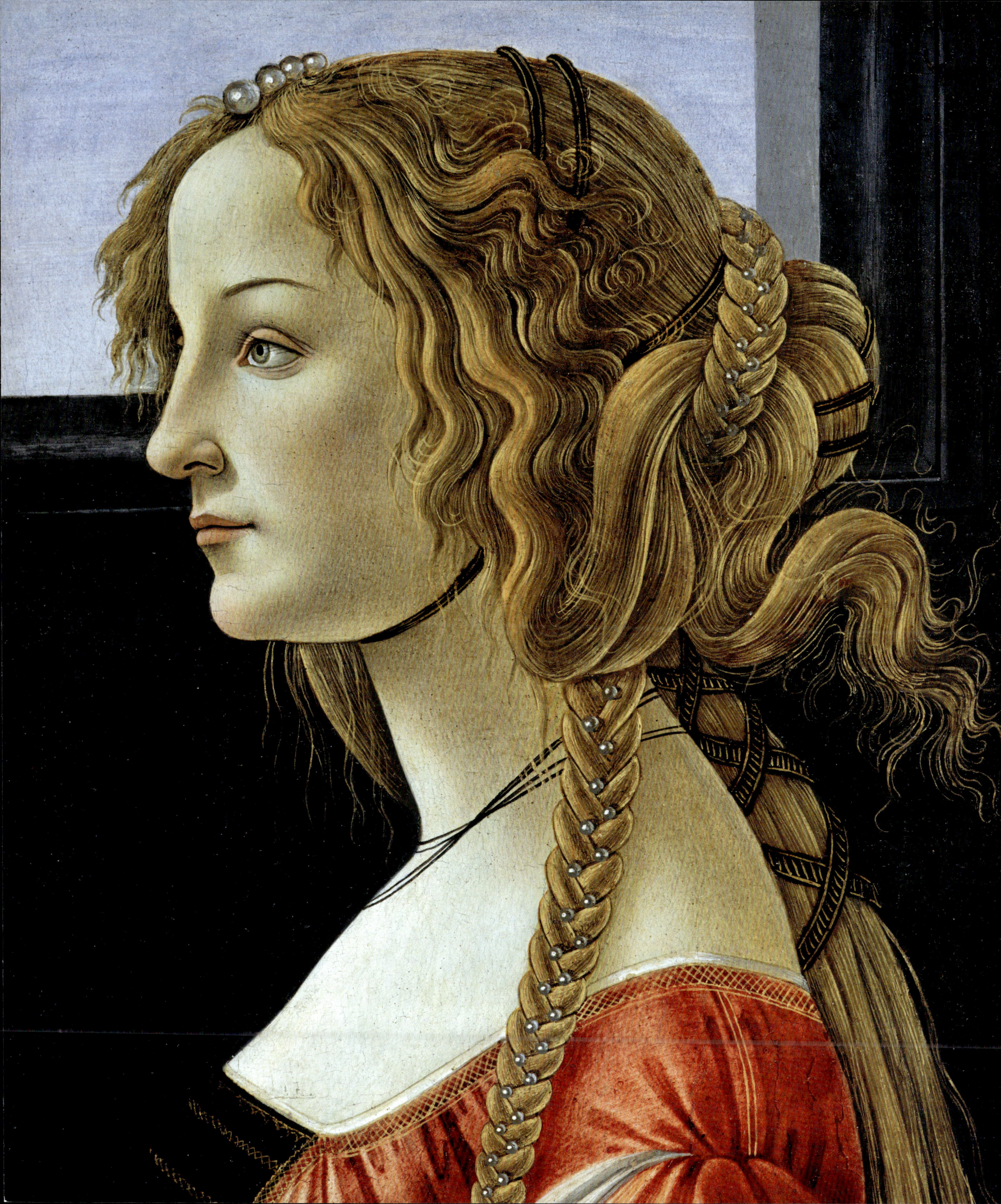

Warburg's Botticelli and Botticelli's Nymph

GERHARD WOLF

Botticelli was a central figure in Aby Warburg's life. He wrote his doctoral dissertation on the *Birth of Venus* and *Primavera*, his paper on the Palazzo Schifanoia ended with Sandro, and Botticelli's work figures prominently in the picture atlas *Mnemosyne*. Yet, unlike Herbert Horne, with whom he shared an interest in archival work and philological detail, Warburg never wrote a monograph on the artist. Like Horne, Warburg was opposed to aestheticism and the cult of Botticelli, though at the same time he drew inspiration from it. He wanted to 'understand the artist psychologically', so it was all the more important to set himself apart from Botticelli's 'sentimental admirers'.[1]

Warburg's dissertation (1891–3), which consists of a selection of literary quotations interspersed with commentary, is a foundation work of iconological research: at the core of his interpretation there is an artist – advised by a poet (Angelo Poliziano) – who according to Warburg had to work out his own artistic position step by step.[2] The dissertation had three objectives: first, to contextualize Botticelli's images in terms of literature and art theory; second, to explore 'the way in which [artists] and their advisers recognized the antique as a model that demanded an intensification of outward movement, … whenever accessory forms – those of garments and of hair – were to be represented in motion'; and finally – enabling a 'psychological aesthetic' – 'to observe … an emerging sense of the aesthetic act of "empathy" as a determinant of style'.[3] Warburg focused especially on 'accessory forms in motion' (*bewegtes Beiwerk*). Fluttering hair and clothing reappear throughout the work. In his dissertation they enable a psycho-historical reassessment of artistic creation through a reception of and response to classical antiquity. The dissertation's appeal lies in this approach, distinguishing it from subsequent attempts to reconstruct the Neoplatonic implications and conventions of the *Birth of Venus* and *Primavera*.[4] For Warburg, the artists of the fifteenth century turned both 'to the artwork of antiquity, whenever they wanted to embody life in motion', and to Florentine festival culture, which 'brought those figures to life before [them] in physical form'.[5]

Beginning with Leon Battista Alberti's treatise on painting, Warburg in his dissertation traced the transformations of 'accessory forms in motion', an approach inspired by his study of Gottfried Semper's theory of ornament.[6] When captured in a fixed image, such accessory forms express a certain dynamic, and Warburg's central question was whether this dynamic was rooted in external movement or internal emotion. Reflecting on Botticelli's time, he stated that antiquity had drawn attention to the most difficult problem of the visual arts: 'using a motionless image to capture life in motion.'[7] Warburg's analysis of *Primavera* must be read in this context – in its tension between the circular dance of the Three Graces and Zephyr's erotic pursuit of Chloris. He makes no reference to the limits of the wind's effect; it catches at the latter figures' clothes and hair, but does not reach beyond them. There is a clear separation in Warburg's text between his discussion of the pursuit scene and that of the figure partially overlapping with Chloris, into whom she is transformed: Flora. The reason Warburg did not recognize this pictorial metamorphosis[8] is because he saw the woman strewing flowers in isolation, identifying her as Simonetta Vespucci in the guise of a goddess of spring. In doing so Warburg was following a tradition of Botticelli-worship. He even tried to support his assertion by making a comparison of proportions between pictures of Simonetta and 'Flora', again taking his cue from antiquity.[9] Warburg therefore saw the two figures from different points of view: the movement of Zephyr and Chloris's bodies, hair and clothing represented the universal dynamic of erotic pursuit, while the goddess of spring captured an image of individuality.

How did Warburg depict the artist in his dissertation, and how did he develop this interpretation further? 'Botticelli was one of those [artists] who were all too pliable,' he wrote, stating that he wanted to show how Botticelli 'engaged with contemporary perceptions of antiquity as if with a force that demanded resistance or submission.'[10] He ascribed to Botticelli a 'particular penchant for peaceful states of the soul … that lent the faces of his human figures that dreamy, passive beauty which today is still admired as the special quality of his creations.' When called upon to depict scenes of passion and excitement, continued Warburg, Botticelli was able to draw on his capacity for 'detailed description'. The accessory forms in motion, having 'no will of their own', were an 'easily manipulated outward sign'.[11] The 'goldsmith-painter' was essentially presented as a kind of engraver, more given to fossilizing movement than simulating it as it played around a figure (as with the marble-like Venus, for instance). This, however, was only one aspect of Warburg's conception of Botticelli. Making reference to a late fifteenth-century text, he also claimed that Botticelli had an *aria virile* ('a virile air'), painting with 'care and proportion'.[12] It was left to 'sentimental modern idealizations of Botticelli to present … his fundamental essence as "lovely naivety" or "charming melancholy"'. The artist himself 'does not make a spectacle of his temperament, like a delicate garment worn for show, but inhabits it like a restrictive mantle, the enlargement of which – with the inadequate means available to a thinking artist – was the conscious goal of his life's work.'[13] In his paper on the Palazzo Schifanoia, Warburg called Botticelli a transitional artist 'between Cossa and Raphael', writing that he 'first had to free his goddess of beauty from the medieval realism of banal genre art *alla franzese*, from illustrative subservience and from astrological practice'. He continued, 'from the Burgundian caterpillar's narrow cocoon emerged a Florentine butterfly, a "Nynfa" with the winged headdress and fluttering garments of the Greek maenads or Roman Victoria.'[14] The artist and his 'distinctive and ideal human creation'[15] were given a positive re-evaluation, and yet it is clear how Warburg struggled to conceptualize artistic work in active terms.

In his famous text on the *ninfa fiorentina*, Warburg worked out his ideas with regard to the frescoes of Domenico Ghirlandaio, another artist from the 'world of goldsmiths', but he found Botticelli the more psycho-historically interesting figure. The prototype of the *ninfa* originated with him: it is in one of his frescoes in the Sistine Chapel that 'the figure of the running woman acquires that lively, self-confident beauty' from which other painters learned 'to establish her role in art as the decorative symbol of the Florentine nymph'.[16] For Warburg the Florentine patrons were the true protagonists, while the dynamism of the ancient figures and motifs also possessed their formative power, with which the artist had to engage. Botticelli was for Warburg the prime artist of the transitional period of the late fifteenth century, one who strove for the ideal human form and sought a balance of ecstatic energies, and who '[was able to] express the whole gamut of human emotion, from silent melancholy to intense passion'.[17]

Warburg, then, was as fascinated with Botticelli's women as John Ruskin, though ultimately their preferences were very different. This is evident in Warburg's complete lack of interest in the figure that Ruskin had made his heroine, and which Proust's *In Search of Lost Time* made famous: Zipporah, Jethro's daughter from the Moses fresco in the Sistine Chapel, the shepherdess lost in thought by the well. Zipporah would certainly have been too 'Botticellian' for Warburg. Yet just as Warburg recognized a nymph in the woman carrying wood in the *Temptations of Christ*, so Ruskin saw in Zipporah, Moses' future wife, a figure from antiquity – an 'Etruscan Athena'.[18]

The priest's daughter Zipporah and the serving-girl nymph, both featuring in Botticelli's Sistine Chapel frescoes, are two utterly different iconizations of clothed female figures, and each has played a significant formative role in the visual memory of modernity. Whether with accessories like the shepherdess's bag and fur cloak or moving embellishments like flowing hair, ribbons and gauzy scarves, in contemplative poses or with a 'self-confident' catwalk stride, they have experienced a rich afterlife, from Mariano Fortuny to the world of contemporary fashion.

FIG. 8 (detail)
SANDRO BOTTICELLI
(*c*.1445–1510)
Primavera, 1477–82

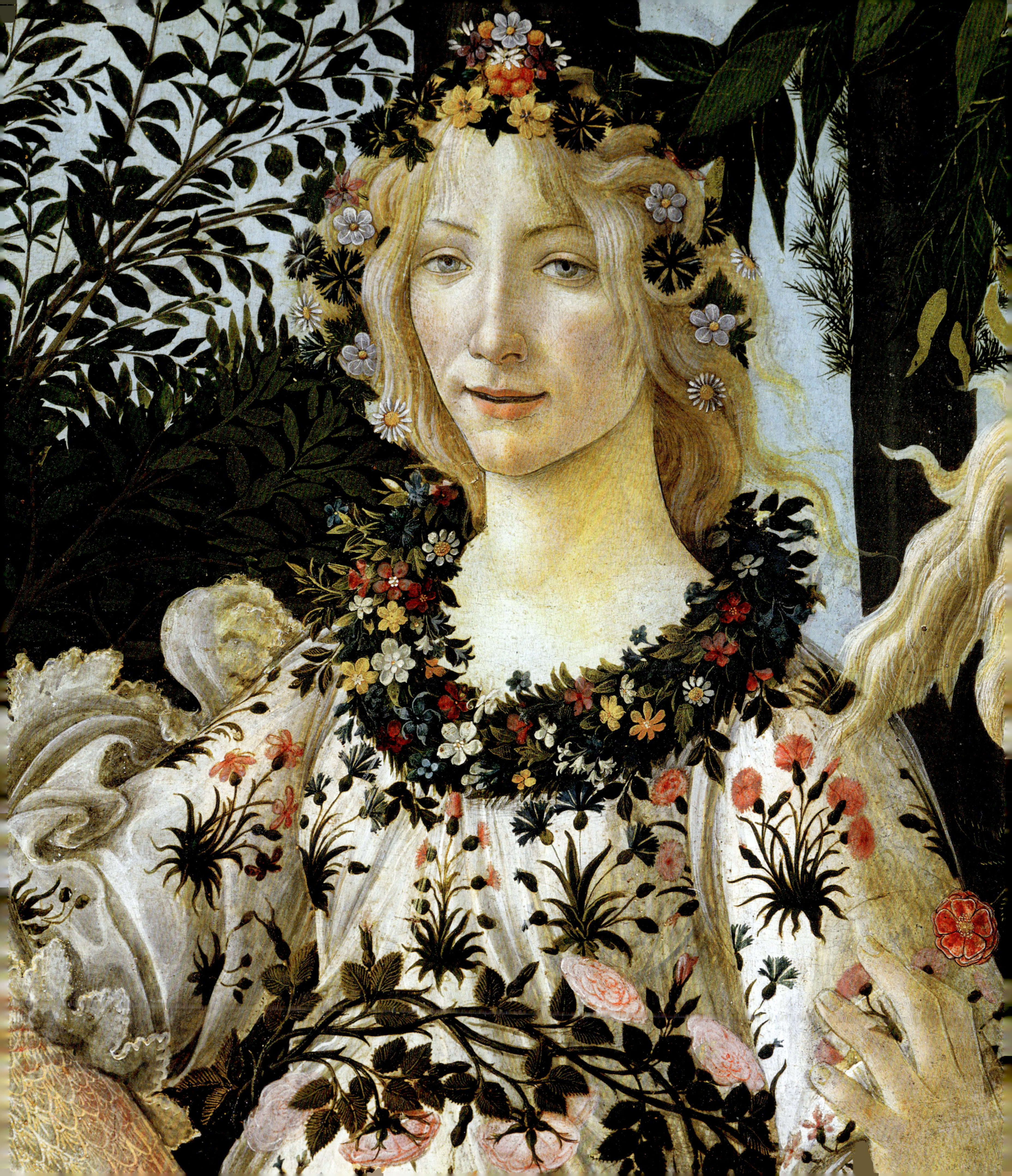

Bernard Berenson and America's Discovery of Sandro Botticelli

OLIVER TOSTMANN

Like many other Italian artists of the Renaissance, Sandro Botticelli was not discovered by the United States of America until the late nineteenth century.[1] In 1865, the year Bernard Berenson was born, there were no paintings by Botticelli in American collections. Within a few decades this would change dramatically, and by 1959, the year of Berenson's death almost a hundred years later, there were more paintings by Botticelli in the USA than any other country apart from Italy.[2] The National Gallery of Art in Washington, founded in 1937, holds no fewer than seven of his works.[3] By the mid-twentieth century, Botticelli was no longer an obscure Renaissance painter, familiar only to a few connoisseurs, but one of the best-known and most popular artists in the country. Berenson played a key role in this radical transformation of taste, making significant contributions towards Botticelli's inclusion in the national cultural canon.

Born in Lithuania, Berenson grew up in Boston, studied at Harvard University and subsequently worked as an independent art historian, agent and teacher.[4] His publications on Italian – and particularly Florentine – art, such as *The Florentine Painters of the Renaissance* (1896) and *The Drawings of the Florentine Painters* (1903), broke new ground,[5] and within a few years Berenson had become one of the leading art historians of the age. Influenced by Giovanni Morelli's methodology of connoisseurship, he compiled lists of famous Renaissance artists, to which he added monographic sketches. At the same time he published influential articles on Botticelli and his school, praising in particular the artist's use of elegant lines as a fundamental element of his visual language. In his characteristic, occasionally esoteric style, he described Botticelli's work as timeless and 'irresistible', and even – in terms of its effect on the viewer – as 'life-enhancing'.[6] When it came to the public, such fulsome words fell on sympathetic ears, and from then on many American tourists would only visit famous collections in Florence, Paris or London armed with one of Berenson's widely circulated publications.

His expertise also made him an ideal adviser for wealthy American art collectors, who after the turn of the twentieth century became increasingly interested in the art of the Italian Renaissance. As the collectors themselves were usually not particularly knowledgeable on the subject, they needed well-connected art experts who were in a position to track down masterpieces in European hands. Berenson made a crucial contribution to building up several significant

FIG. 55
Bernard Berenson, 1903
Image courtesy of Villa I Tatti

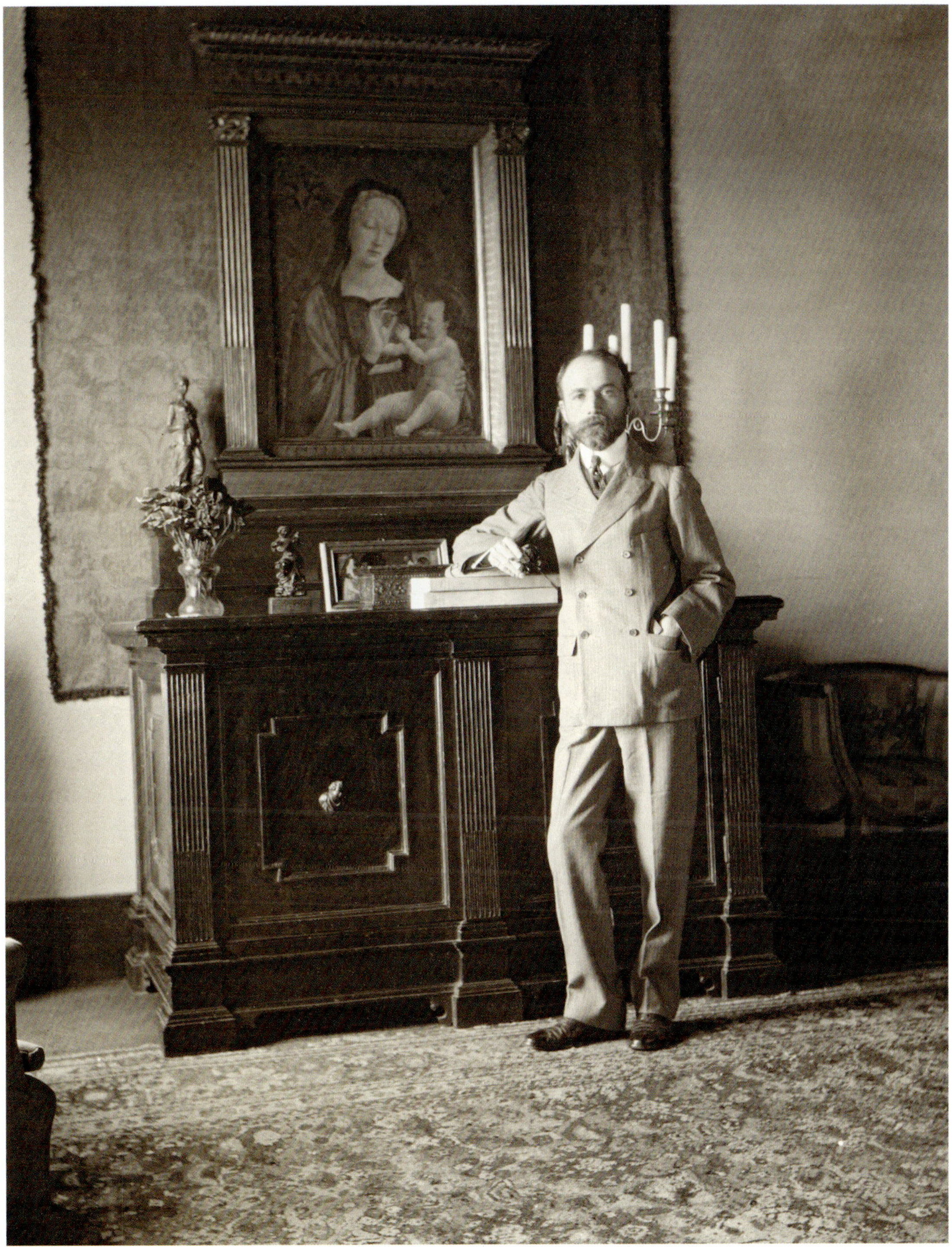

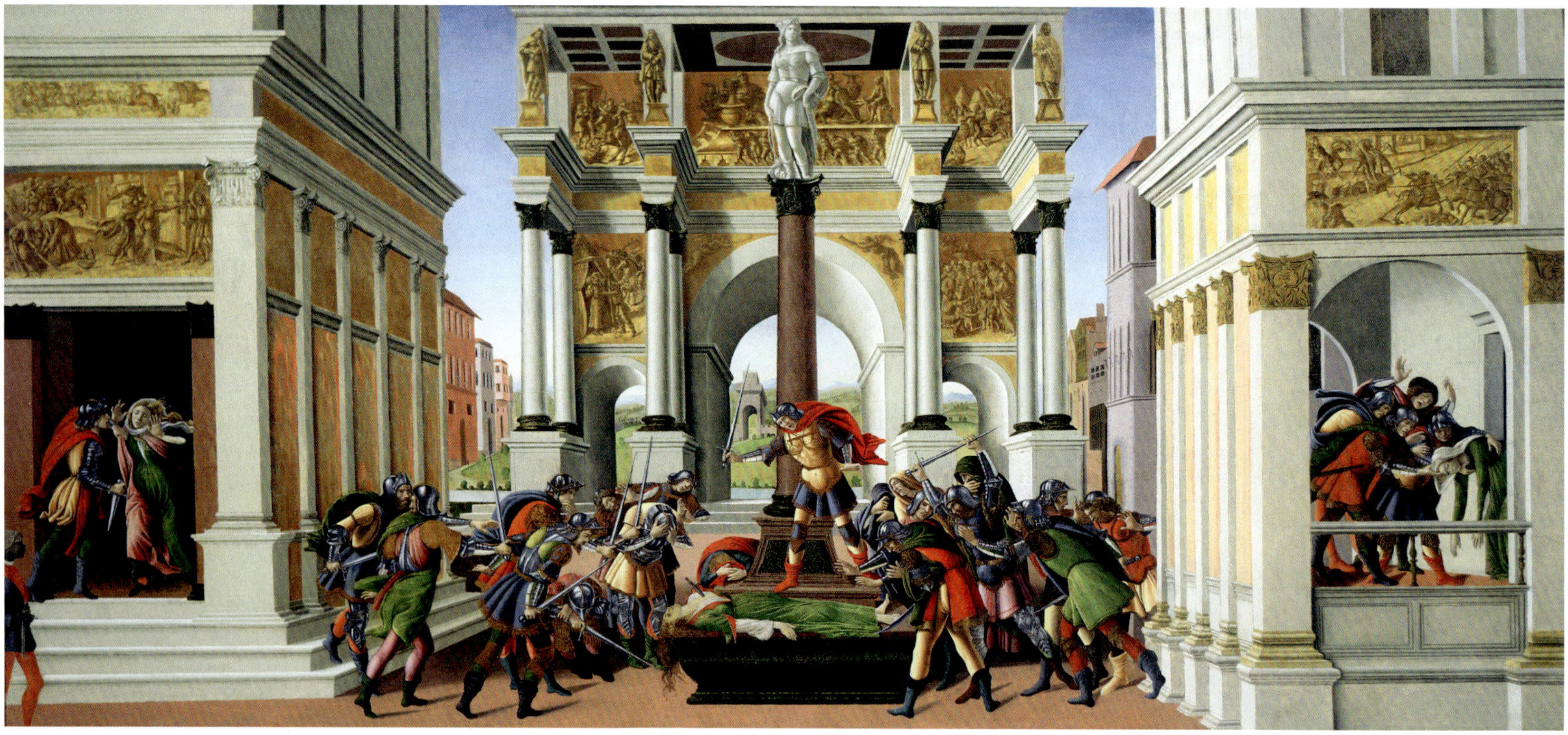

American collections that were opened to the public during his lifetime, shaping American taste more broadly. He also worked on cataloguing these collections, including those of John G. Johnson and Peter A.B. Widener.[7]

While Berenson spent much of his life working for billionaires across the country, the beginnings of his career are to be found in Boston. His first benefactor was Isabella Stewart Gardner, who got to know him as a student at Harvard.[8] From the early 1890s onwards, with considerable assistance from Berenson, Gardner established an extraordinary collection with an emphasis on Italian Renaissance painting. One of the most significant works that she acquired through Berenson was Botticelli's *The Tragedy of Lucretia* (fig. 56) in 1894. This important painting was the very first Botticelli to be brought to the United States.[9] In 1899, just five years later, Gardner purchased – again, with Berenson's help – the Chigi Madonna (cat. 109). The sale provoked a scandal in Italy.[10] Another painting, now attributed to his workshop, was acquired in 1900, finally rounding off Gardner's assortment of Botticellis.[11] He now held a prominent place in her eclectic collection.

Formative for both Berenson and Gardner was the prevailing adulation for Botticelli in late nineteenth-century Boston, above all in literary circles.[12] Art enthusiasts took popular courses on the Italian Renaissance given by Charles Eliot Norton at Harvard and read Walter Pater and John Ruskin, whose works celebrated Botticelli as a key figure of the Renaissance.[13] After consulting with Norton, in 1887 Gardner acquired a valuable printed copy of Dante's *Divine*

FIG. 56
FILIPPINO LIPPI (c.1457–1504) and
SANDRO BOTTICELLI (c.1445–1510)
The Tragedy of Lucretia, c.1500–1
Oil on wood, 83.8 × 176.8 cm
Isabella Stewart Gardner Museum,
Boston (P16E20)

Comedy with numerous illustrations after Botticelli. In 1895, another of Botticelli's Madonnas arrived in Boston.[14] William Sturgis Bigelow purchased the picture for the Museum of Fine Arts probably with support from Gardner and Berenson, as Bigelow's unpublished correspondence makes clear.[15] At the turn of the twentieth century, Boston assumed a leading role as the centre of all things Botticelli in the United States.

Berenson played a central, if somewhat ambiguous, part in helping to build Gardner's art collection. In the case of the *Lucretia*, for instance, though he made Gardner aware of the picture and advocated eloquently for its purchase, he also allowed her to believe that he had discovered the painting himself in Lord Ashburnham's collection,[16] deliberately making no mention of the fact that it had already been unearthed by the London art dealer Colnaghi & Co., and that if it were sold he would receive a commission not only from Gardner, but also from them.[17] In many respects Berenson often walked a thin line, both between the opposing interests of collectors and dealers, and between scholarship and business. He later went on to develop his clandestine connections in the art world still further. From 1907 to 1938 he worked for an art dealership run by Joseph Duveen, who from 1927 paid him a fixed salary.[18] Berenson's research into Italian Renaissance paintings lent his name a certain authority, which in turn helped Duveen to sell pictures. Berenson authenticated various works of art offered for sale by Duveen, including numerous Botticellis, and wrote about them in scholarly publications. A 1941 catalogue raisonné of the collection formerly belonging to Duveen, which by then had been transferred to American museums, lists six paintings attributed to him.[19] In each case Berenson had guaranteed the authenticity of the work.

From 1900 onwards, Berenson lived in the Villa I Tatti in Fiesole, near Florence, which by the time of his death he had transformed into a major centre for research. It attracted not only illustrious guests like the Crown Prince of Sweden and the American president Harry S. Truman, but also young art historians, who could enjoy an exclusive apprenticeship there. This sort of personal teaching was perhaps Berenson's greatest achievement. He shaped a generation of art historians, who continued to propagate his views after his death. Several future directors of the National Galleries in London and Washington, including Sir Kenneth Clark, John Walker and J. Carter Brown, studied with Berenson,[20] and they communicated their enthusiasm for the art of the Italian Renaissance to a wide audience. All his life Berenson performed a number of simultaneous roles. His close dealings with the art-collecting elite as well as his influence on a wide, art-loving public made him a unique figure in art history. For American museums he was a godsend, and they benefited greatly from his influence. It was Berenson who brought Botticelli into the public eye in America.

Botticelli, Yukio Yashiro and Scholarship on Western Art in Japan

TOSHIO WATANABE

The Japanese art historian, Yukio Yashiro, published his magnum opus *Sandro Botticelli and the Florentine Renaissance* in 1925. This was a major and at the time most unusual achievement by a non-Western scholar. What is often not realized is that Japan has a long and venerable tradition of scholarship in the history of Western art. When the Tokyo School of Fine Arts was established in 1889 the curriculum included aesthetics and art history, taught by the American Ernest Fenollosa. After Fenollosa left Japan the following year, Kakuzo Okakura was appointed Principal of the School and taught art history, including the history of Western art, during the academic year of 1891–2.[1] Fenollosa had previously taught at Tokyo University from 1878, where there was no defined course on art history. His successor, the German Ludwig Busse, taught philosophy and aesthetics from 1887 until 1892, and his lectures apparently included the history of Western art. Busse was followed by the German-Russian Raphael von Koeber, who also taught this subject, and the first Japanese Chair of Aesthetics, Yasuji Otsuka, incorporated the history of Western art into his lectures. In 1914, a separate art history department was created. Its first formal course on the history of Western art was held in 1919 and taught by Yomokichi Sawaki, who had previously studied under Heinrich Wölfflin in Munich and translated his *Principles of Art History* into Japanese. Sawaki was followed by Ino Dan in 1923. Both scholars published books containing discussions of Renaissance art in Florence in 1917 and 1922 respectively. Since then, the subject has been taught continuously to this day, a situation that at this early date was lacking in many Western countries.[2]

Yukio Yashiro, who was born and bred in Yokohama, was fluent in English from an early age and became interested in the history of Western art in his youth. After studying at the University of Tokyo and graduating with a thesis titled 'Emotional Principles of Art', which focused on late nineteenth-century British poets and writers, he was appointed to teach art history at the Tokyo School of Fine Arts in 1918 before moving to Europe in 1921. After a short period in London he settled in Florence where he became an early disciple of Bernard Berenson. Yashiro was an admirer and a loyal pupil of Berenson and he benefited enormously from his tutelage, especially in a form of connoisseurship based on incisive attention to detail, which Berenson had himself learnt from Giovanni Morelli, the inventor of 'scientific' connoisseurship.

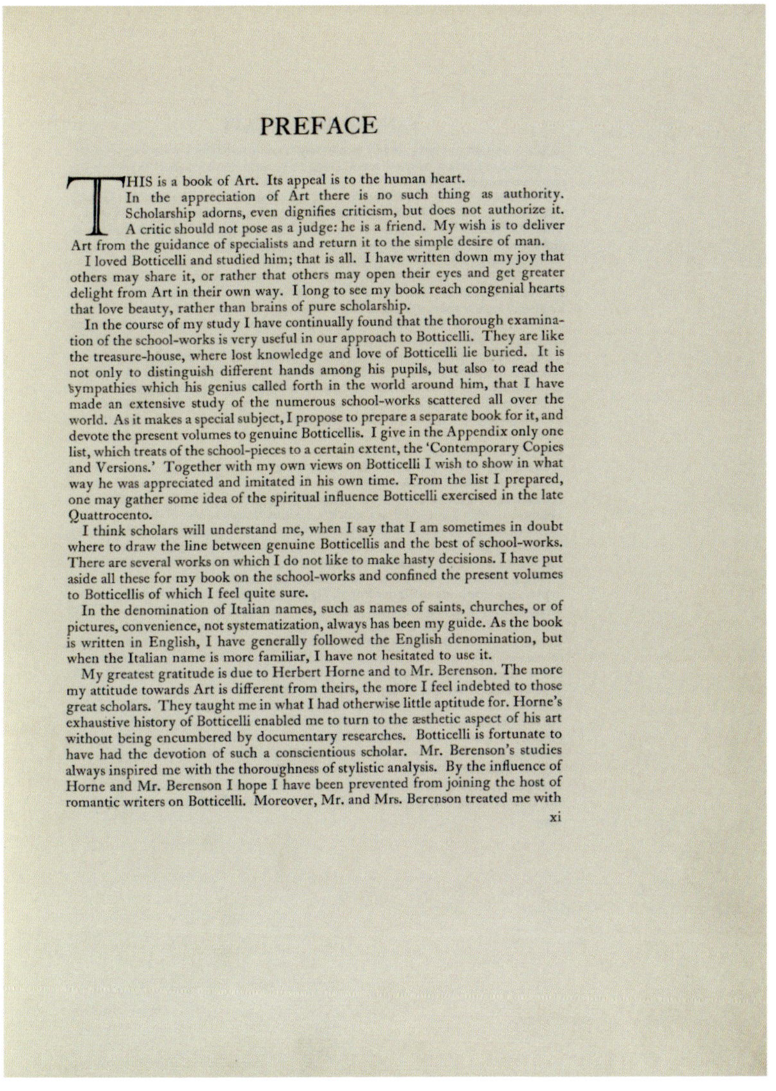

PREFACE

THIS is a book of Art. Its appeal is to the human heart.
In the appreciation of Art there is no such thing as authority. Scholarship adorns, even dignifies criticism, but does not authorize it. A critic should not pose as a judge: he is a friend. My wish is to deliver Art from the guidance of specialists and return it to the simple desire of man.

I loved Botticelli and studied him; that is all. I have written down my joy that others may share it, or rather that others may open their eyes and get greater delight from Art in their own way. I long to see my book reach congenial hearts that love beauty, rather than brains of pure scholarship.

In the course of my study I have continually found that the thorough examination of the school-works is very useful in our approach to Botticelli. They are like the treasure-house, where lost knowledge and love of Botticelli lie buried. It is not only to distinguish different hands among his pupils, but also to read the sympathies which his genius called forth in the world around him, that I have made an extensive study of the numerous school-works scattered all over the world. As it makes a special subject, I propose to prepare a separate book for it, and devote the present volumes to genuine Botticellis. I give in the Appendix only one list, which treats of the school-pieces to a certain extent, the 'Contemporary Copies and Versions.' Together with my own views on Botticelli I wish to show in what way he was appreciated and imitated in his own time. From the list I prepared, one may gather some idea of the spiritual influence Botticelli exercised in the late Quattrocento.

I think scholars will understand me, when I say that I am sometimes in doubt where to draw the line between genuine Botticellis and the best of school-works. There are several works on which I do not like to make hasty decisions. I have put aside all these for my book on the school-works and confined the present volumes to Botticellis of which I feel quite sure.

In the denomination of Italian names, such as names of saints, churches, or of pictures, convenience, not systematization, always has been my guide. As the book is written in English, I have generally followed the English denomination, but when the Italian name is more familiar, I have not hesitated to use it.

My greatest gratitude is due to Herbert Horne and to Mr. Berenson. The more my attitude towards Art is different from theirs, the more I feel indebted to those great scholars. They taught me in what I had otherwise little aptitude for. Horne's exhaustive history of Botticelli enabled me to turn to the æsthetic aspect of his art without being encumbered by documentary researches. Botticelli is fortunate to have had the devotion of such a conscientious scholar. Mr. Berenson's studies always inspired me with the thoroughness of stylistic analysis. By the influence of Horne and Mr. Berenson I hope I have been prevented from joining the host of romantic writers on Botticelli. Moreover, Mr. and Mrs. Berenson treated me with

xi

However, it is also clear that Yashiro was neither servile nor uncritical of Berenson. For example, he disagreed with Berenson's description of Botticelli's art as 'Oriental', and he was contemptuous when others claimed to see a direct Chinese influence on Botticelli or the Sienese school.[3]

Yashiro himself confessed that when he stood in front of *Primavera* or the *Birth of Venus*, he was overcome with a strange enchantment.[4] He valued a certain sensitivity in Botticelli's art and contrasted his own approach with that of the acknowledged authority on and aficionado of the artist, Herbert Horne.[5] In his publications Yashiro recognized Horne's achievement in documenting Botticelli's life and works and was very appreciative of this groundwork. However, he did not agree with Horne's interpretation of Botticelli's art, which he thought put too much emphasis on *aria virile*, or masculine virility. Yashiro believed there were two reasons why Horne reached this conclusion, based upon the archival reference of an agent of the Duke of Milan, first published by Paul Müller-Walde in 1897, which described Botticelli's art as possessing an *aria virile*.[6] First, although he agreed that this important document could be applied to certain works by

FIG. 57
YUKIO YASHIRO (1890–1975)
Sandro Botticelli (London 1925), p.xi
and title page
V&A: NAL

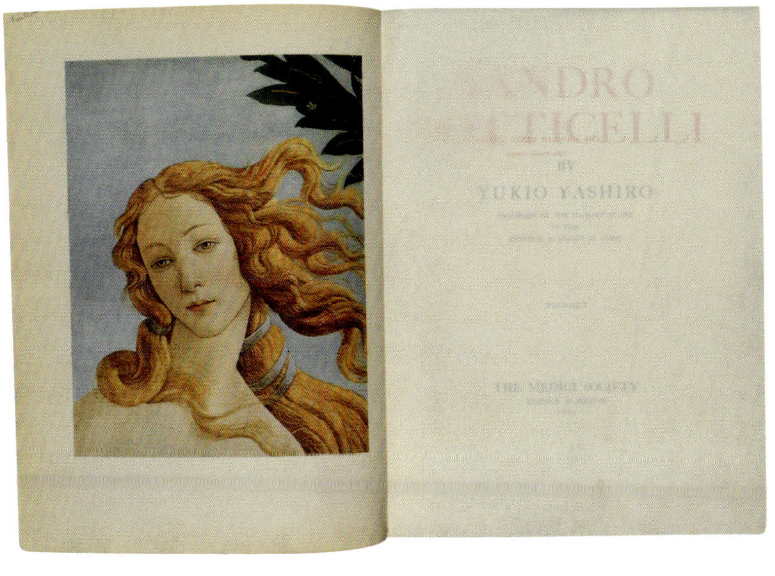

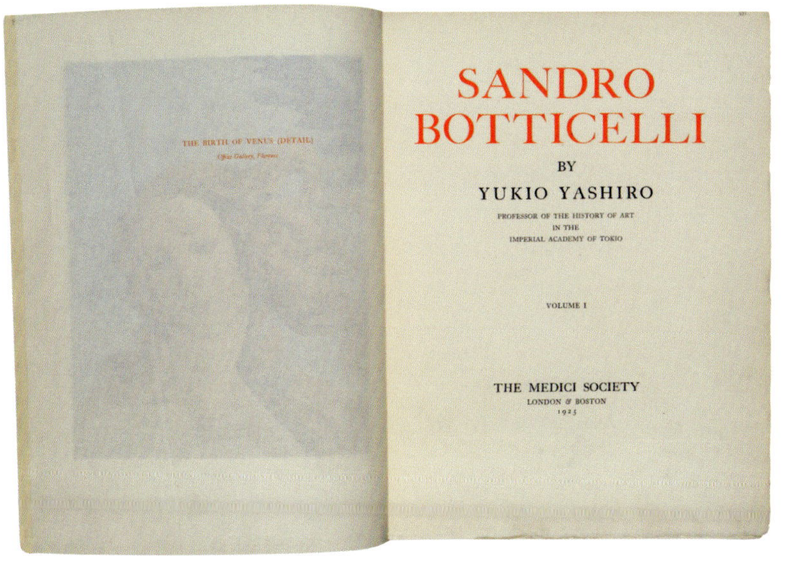

Botticelli, he thought it excessive to characterize the whole of Botticelli's oeuvre as a demonstration of *aria virile*. Second, Yashiro saw art history as operating like a pendulum and considered Horne's attitude to be a reaction to the poetic interpretations of Botticelli's art by writers such as Walter Pater. Late nineteenth-century views verging on sentimentality were countered by an early twentieth-century examination of stylistic analysis based on supposedly scientific criteria.[7]

Yashiro considered his own place within this cycle and his own interpretation of Botticelli's art as a return towards a Pater-like view, which valued poetic sentiment. However, he became highly irate when Horne's friend, Roger Fry, wrote a substantial critique of his own Botticelli book, which criticized Yashiro for going too far towards sentiment. In the preface to his second edition Yashiro reports: 'that incomparable work [by Horne] leaves me cold, and I doubt if Horne did not take more genuine interest in documentary research among archives than in the aesthetic contemplation of Botticelli's works.'[8] He also insisted that, contrary to what Fry insinuated, he did pay attention to the plastic value of Botticelli's works. Yashiro then mentioned that the reviewer of his book in the *Times Literary Supplement* had understood what he was trying to do, and 'noticed the essential importance I attached to the plastic value in the estimation of Art, and observed that it was somewhat contrary to his expectation from an Oriental mind'.[9] As the *TLS* then observed a policy of anonymous reviewing, Yashiro did not know that the author was none other than his friend, the poet, curator and expert on Oriental art, Laurence Binyon.

The assumption that an 'Oriental mind' would not normally understand Western 'cutting edge' scholarship, was something Yashiro had to fight continuously during his early career, and in this context he more or less accused Fry of racial discrimination. In his autobiography he related a number of such incidents, especially when he discovered hitherto unrecognized paintings by Domenico Veneziano and Botticelli, and was generally disbelieved. However, the publication of his major book on Botticelli in 1925 alleviated this situation substantially. Indeed its genesis was partly due to a well-meaning but incautious comment by his teacher Berenson. Apparently when Yashiro told him of his intention of writing a book on Botticelli, Berenson noted that it was a good idea but recommended that he publish a slim volume on the appreciation of the art of Botticelli from an Oriental perspective, as nobody would want to learn about Botticelli from a Japanese person. This fired up Yashiro to produce a substantial book in Europe.[10]

Apart from Yashiro's astute scholarship, two factors contributed greatly to the success of his book. First was the care taken in its publication by Harry Lawrence of the Medici Society, who seems to have been a truly remarkable editor. He sought to preserve the personal style of Yashiro. When he was unhappy with a passage Yashiro had written, Lawrence did not correct it himself, but explained why it was not acceptable and then let Yashiro compose a better one. Lawrence would not let it go until he was satisfied and Yashiro confessed that this was the most painful experience of his entire life. They worked together in this manner almost every day for three months. After this gruelling process the text was then given to Arthur Waley, the Orientalist and colleague of Binyon at the British Museum, later famous for his translation of the Japanese classic *Tale of Genji*. Once Waley had returned his comments, the whole exercise of editing was repeated. The revised manuscript was then read by a non-specialist young woman working at the Medici Society shop, after which author and editor went back to the grind with the marked manuscript. Yashiro acknowledged that it was thanks to the method adopted by Lawrence that the text remained his own and its personal character was preserved, even after so many revisions.

The second reason for the book's success was its illustrated matter. The Medici Society had been founded in 1908 to produce reproductions of works of art and consequently, the quality of Yashiro's illustrations was high and their quantity was numerous. However, the main point of departure from conventional publications of the time was the plentiful use of details. While researching Botticelli in Florence Yashiro wanted to get to the core characteristics of the artist's technique and decided to commission photographs of details taken according to his own precise specifications. He asked the Florentine photographic studio of Brogi to take these photographs and they were reportedly so intrigued and delighted by the result that they waived their fee for the roughly 200 photographs. As an impecunious student Yashiro was naturally grateful for this, but noted that Brogi also made a considerable profit by selling these photographic details, which became very popular. His teacher Berenson praised them and Yashiro's friend Sir Kenneth Clark was inspired to produce a series of three books with the title *One Hundred Details: From the National Gallery, London* between 1938 and 1946, in which he acknowledged his debt to Yashiro.

Yashiro's approach is expressed concisely in the first paragraph of his introduction:

> This is a book of Art. Its appeal is to the human heart. In the appreciation of Art there is no such thing as authority. Scholarship adorns, even dignifies criticism, but does not authorize it. A critic should not pose as a judge: he is a friend. My wish is to deliver Art from the guidance of specialists and return it to the simple desire of man.

When about 40 years later Yashiro visited the home of a family friend, his daughter recited this passage by heart and told him that her late mother had recommended it as a motto to the local art school.

As we have seen, Yashiro was singularly attracted to Botticelli, but this artist has also enchanted many other Japanese during the years since Yashiro published his magnum opus. It is not that they argue that Botticelli is the greatest of all Renaissance artists, a position usually reserved in the West for Leonardo da Vinci, but that he seems to be the artist many Japanese are most attracted to. This may be gauged by the frequency with which his paintings appearing on the covers of art books. For example, that of the revised edition of *The Handbook on History of Western and Japanese Art*, published by the Committee of Art Certification Test in 2014, is divided into two, with on the upper part a reproduction of the *Birth of Venus* by Botticelli representing Western art, and on the bottom half Hokusai's famous woodcut *The Wave off Kanagawa*, representing Japanese art. However, most of the Hokusai print is obscured by the book title and wraparound band, and one's attention is irresistibly drawn to the melancholic face of Botticelli's Venus. Another book for the general public published in 2014, *The Best 100 Western Paintings* by Yoshihiro Otomo, also has Botticelli's *Birth of Venus* on its cover, this time featured with even greater prominence. These are not isolated examples but just the most recent ones. As the task of a book cover is to attract the attention of a potential buyer, one must assume that the designers and the marketing departments of these Japanese publishers know the taste of their audience.

The taste for Botticelli in contemporary Japan can also be gauged by the many entries in the popular amateur illustrator's website Pixiv, which contains a number of Botticelli *Birth of Venus* parodies ranging from gay versions to Pokémon characters. Contemporary artists are also not far behind. A well-known appropriation artist, Yasumasa Morimura, created a series of photographs and montages of himself posed as protagonists in parodies of major paintings from world art. His *Hands* series includes a close-up of Venus's torso, in parody of Botticelli. However, this cult of Botticelli is not a monopoly of Japan and may also be encountered in other Asian countries. Korea has a female guitar quartet called 'Botticelli' and a Chinese artist based in Paris, Yin Xin, painted a version of Botticelli's Venus with a distinctly Chinese countenance (cat. 8). For many East Asians, Botticelli's art has become an integral part of the vocabulary of their visual imagination.

Botticelli and Fashion

SONNET STANFILL

When fashion designer Elsa Schiaparelli launched her Autumn/Winter 1938–9 designs in Paris, she titled them her *Pagan* collection. Fascinated by Botticelli's mythological themes, she referenced myths explored by the artist in this collection of some 70 models. Schiaparelli's designs, featuring three-dimensional leaves, blossoms, branches and insects stitched and woven onto the garments and accessories, imitated the botanical profusion of Botticelli's *Birth of Venus* and *Primavera*. Her gowns included a slim-skirted silk design with sprays of embroidered flowers encircling the waist and bodice, and an abundance of artificial flowers made from fabric, plastic and sequins, sewn around the neckline in a bristling wreath of colour and texture (cat. 34).

British *Vogue*, reporting on the popularity of three-dimensional flowers that season, described creations of Edward Molyneux, who 'balanced long sprays of sweet pea, mimosa, lily-of-the-valley, on the shoulders of a white piqué dress', as well as the more overtly referential designs by Schiaparelli, who 'strips the trees of their leaves … and sews them … in green silk over a waist length cape … curls ivy tendrils round your throat … takes a spray of green metal and twines it up your arm to cling like a convolvulus.'[1] The design from Schiaparelli's *Pagan* collection described by *Vogue* alludes to the myth of Daphne, the nymph who is transformed into a laurel tree while attempting to escape the pursuit of Apollo.

Schiaparelli was active as a fashion designer in Paris from 1928, when she showed her first collection, until the early 1950s. Her habit of appropriating motifs from fine art extended to much-documented collaborations with the Surrealists and embraced a range of unexpected themes from architectural details to the circus. In fact, Schiaparelli's interest in Botticelli's *Birth of Venus* was first expressed several years before her *Pagan* season. In 1935 she dressed the Vicomtesse Benoist d'Azy as Botticelli's Venus for the *Bal des tableaux célèbres* (Famous Paintings Ball) complete with long blonde wig and flesh-toned leotard (fig. 58).[2]

It should come as no surprise that Botticelli's paintings have served as a source of inspiration for fashion designers throughout the last century, since their harmonious and inimitable decorative system presents appealing portrayals of feminine beauty. For some, the imagery in these paintings became a kind of shorthand for the artistic supremacy associated with the Italian Renaissance. In the 1950s, the Florentine

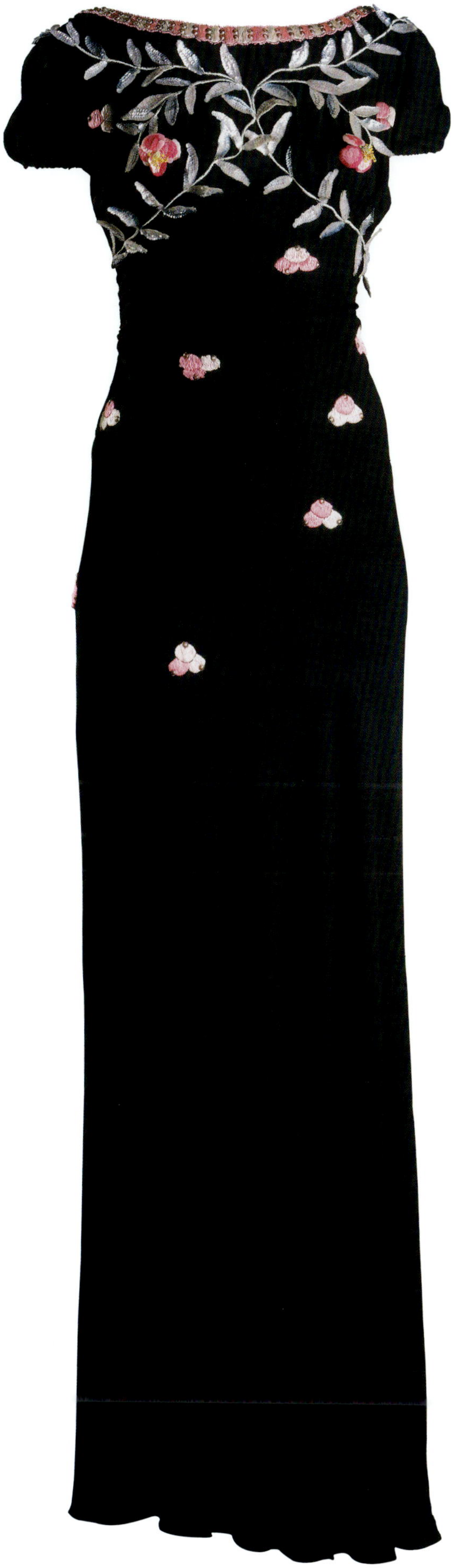

CAT. 34
ELSA SCHIAPARELLI
(1890–1973)
Evening Dress, 1938

FIG. 58
SIGNED 'MEERSON'
Viscomtesse Benoist d'Azy dressed as the 'Birth of Venus' at Comte Etienne de Beaumont's *Bal des tableaux célèbres*, Summer 1935
Courtesy of Anne Benoist d'Azy, France

buying agent Giovanni Battista Giorgini used reproduction Botticellis to promote Italy's nascent fashion industry. From 1952, Giorgini produced fashion show invitations, programmes and souvenirs emblazoned with Renaissance art, much of it by Botticelli, to distribute to the buyers and press attending the catwalk presentations he staged in the Palazzo Pitti. Botticelli's images, including his likeness of Giovanna degli Albizzi, featured prominently in these fashion show promotions (figs 59 and cat. 62). Ahead of its time, Giorgini's sophisticated marketing campaign aimed to associate Italy's burgeoning fashion industry with the artistic patrimony of Florence. Italy's fashion designers, little known outside the country before the

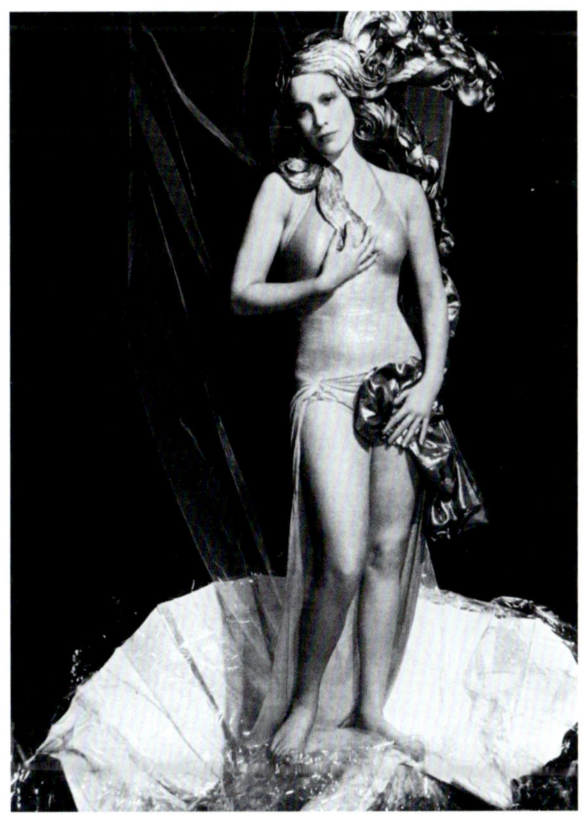

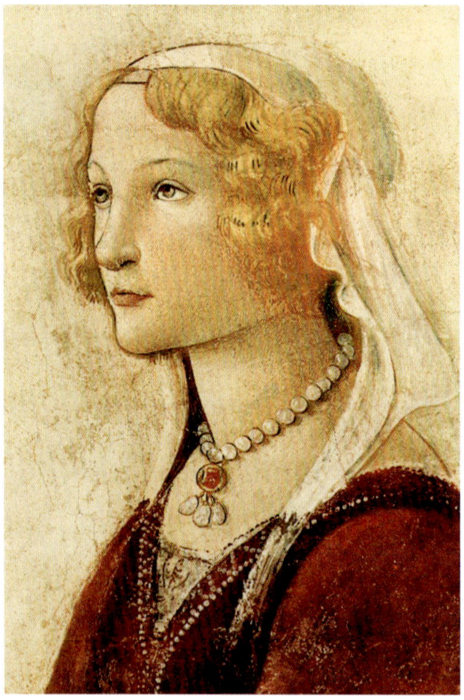

war, benefited from these astute, profile-raising efforts, which equated modern Italian couture houses with Botticelli's artistic legacy.

Another related sector influenced by Botticelli, particularly the lifelike botanical depictions within his masterworks, is that of fashion textiles. In the 1970s, abstract floral prints became fashion's currency, one that British fashion and textile designers used effectively. The printed textiles created by Celia Birtwell, David Hockney's muse, for the London designer Ossie Clark resulted in some of the most archetypical fashions of the period. Birtwell wound her flowers, vines and leaves around hems and scattered them across skirts and sleeves. Their sweetness and realistic clarity suggest a debt to Botticelli, which she later acknowledged, stating, 'I was inspired by Italian painting, by Piero della Francesca and Botticelli'.[3]

Fashion designers continue to cite Botticelli, employing a range of methods to make their point. The Milan-based designers Domenico Dolce and Stefano Gabbana used elements from Botticelli's paintings as a graphic device, which they applied directly onto garments. Known for mining their Italian heritage for inspiration, they created several looks for their Spring/Summer 1993 collection composed of a patchwork-like compilation of fragments from the *Birth of Venus*. A trouser suit included a full-length representation of Venus, as well as details of her face, hair and limbs montaged across the wearer.

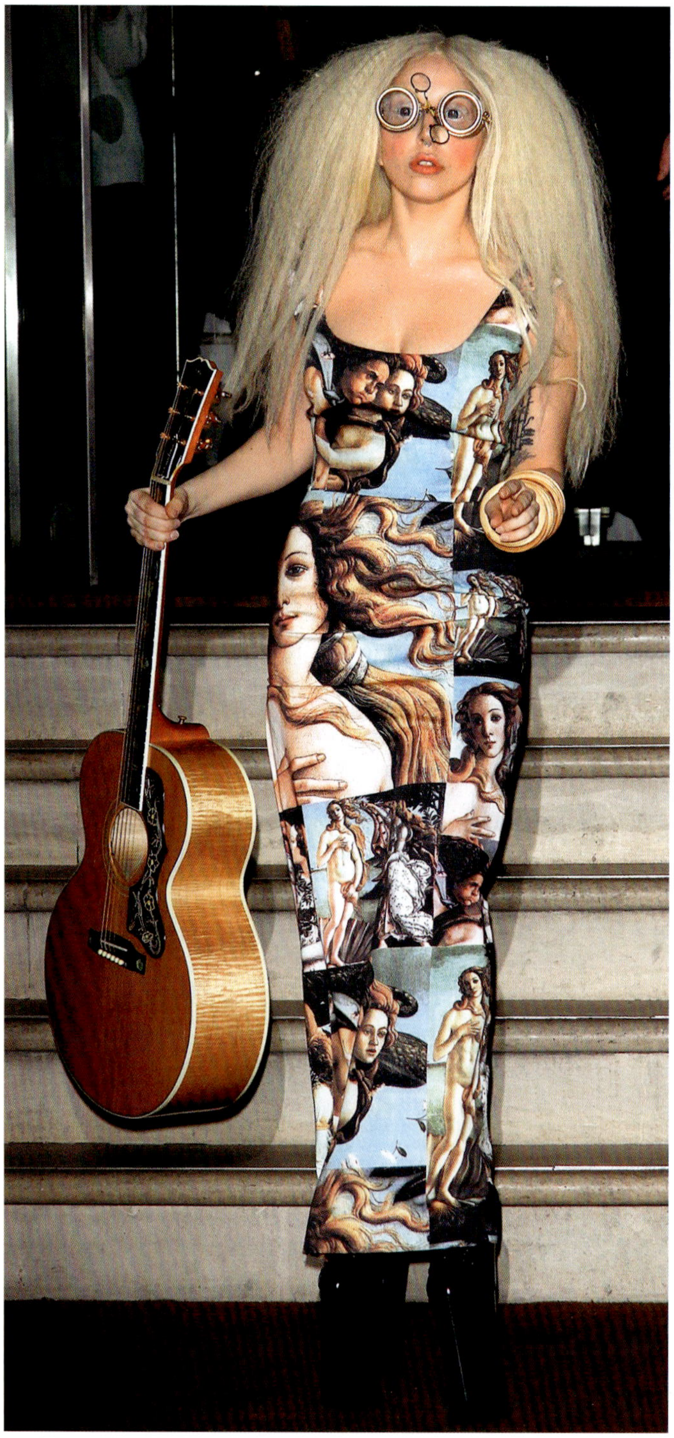

FIG. 59
Printed reproduction of Botticelli's portrait of Giovanna degli Albizzi on a fashion show invitation, 1951
Private collection

FIG. 60
Lady Gaga wearing a vintage Dolce & Gabbana dress, London, 2013
(See CAT. 13)

FIG. 61
ARTPOP by LADY GAGA, 2013
Cover design by JEFF KOONS

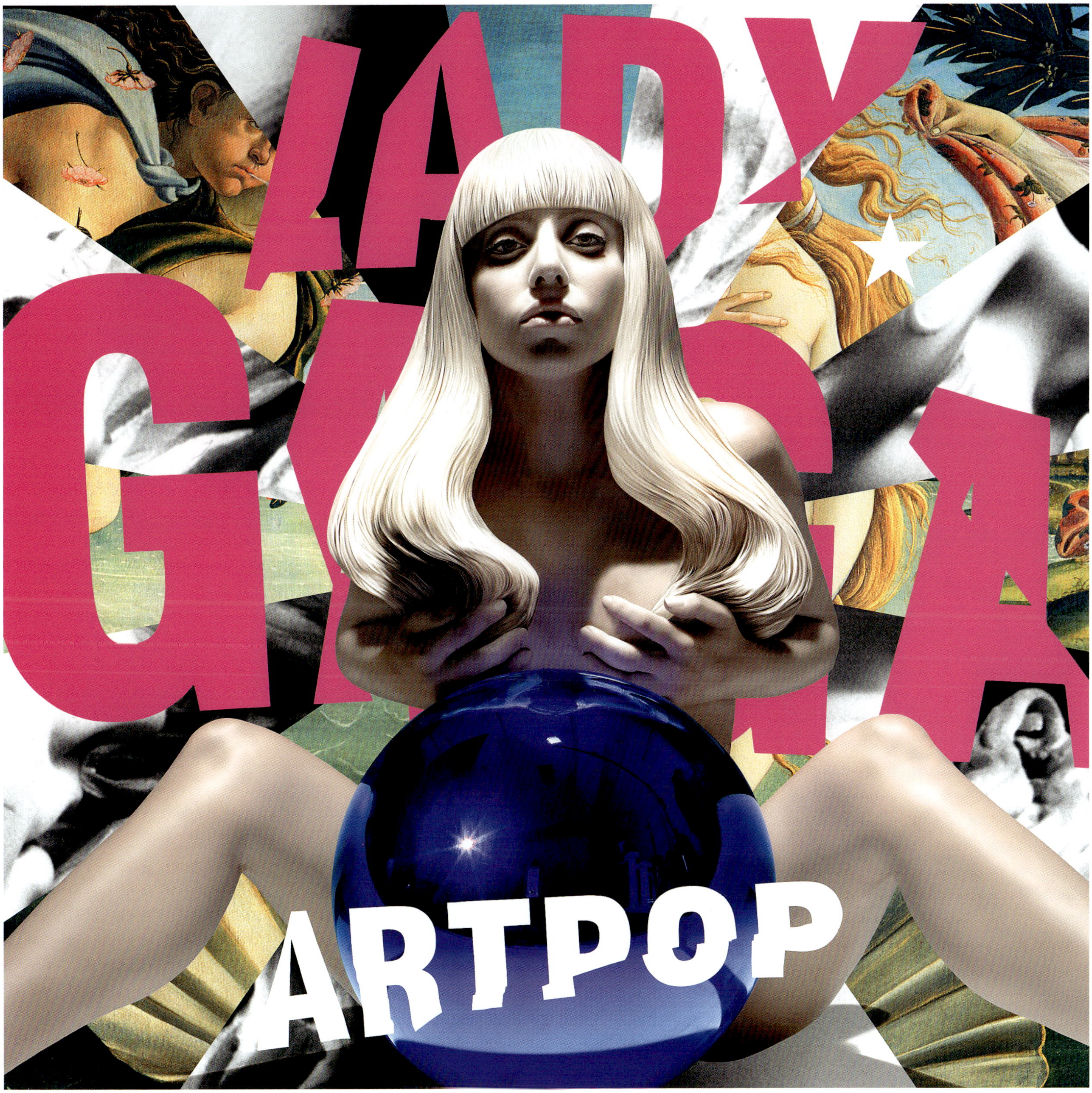
LADY
GAGA
ARTPOP

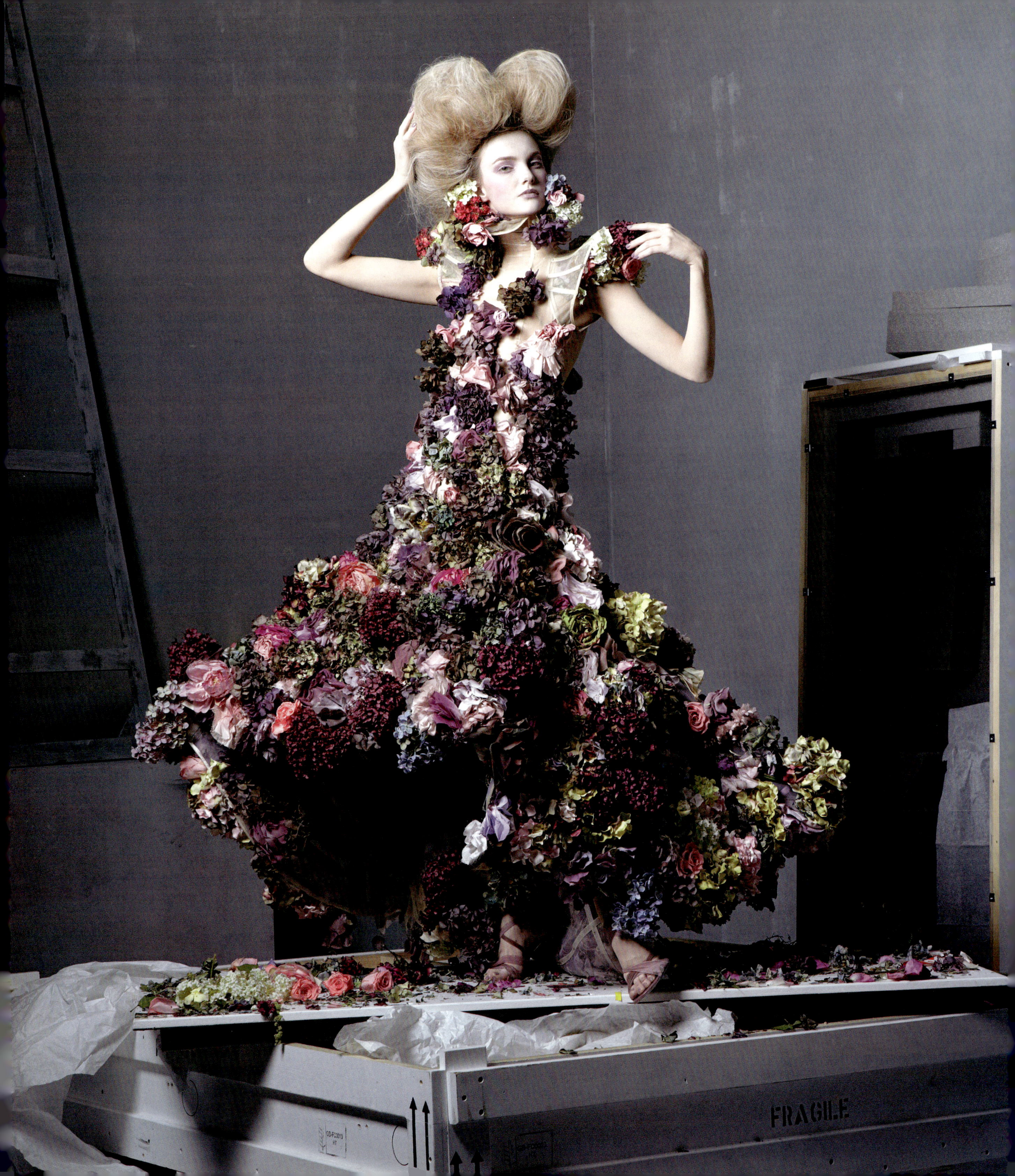
FRAGILE

A skirt and blouse ensemble and a dress were of similar design (cats 13, 14). In a remixing of Dolce & Gabbana's Botticelli quotation, in October 2013 the entertainer Lady Gaga was photographed wearing a 1993 dress (fig. 60). She was snapped by photographers in Dolce & Gabbana's design the day before the launch of her single 'Venus', a song she performed on British television wearing a scallop-shell bikini in front of supersized screens depicting the *Birth of Venus*.

Dolce & Gabbana's playful Botticelli pastiche contrasts with a more sinister interpretation by Alexander McQueen. His Spring/Summer 2007 *Sarabande* collection included an evening dress embroidered with silk as well as real roses, hydrangeas and peonies. Sarah Burton, creative director at Alexander McQueen, recalled: 'This dress had fresh flowers on it. We put them on just before she went out, and they started to fall off one by one as she walked.'[4] Fashion journalist Suzy Menkes described McQueen's vision of floral excess as, '… botanic beauty as flowers spilled out of hats, brimmed from a bodice or smothered a gown, leaving a floral trail across the stage'.[5] While McQueen credited the collection's inspiration to Handel's 'Sarabande', used in the soundtrack to Stanley Kubrick's 1975 film *Barry Lyndon*, the gown's floral profusion recalled spring's fecundity in Botticelli's *Primavera.* Yet in McQueen's hands, the theme takes on new meaning. The gown's encrusted floral carapace was so dense it appeared almost suffocating. While Botticelli's spring is a symbol of life, in McQueen's interpretation it signalled the beginning of decay. McQueen said of the dress: 'Remember Sam Taylor-Wood's dying fruit? Things rot … I used flowers because they die. My mood was darkly romantic at the time.'[6]

In its May 2011 issue American *Vogue* included a photograph of this gown which suggested a convergence of Botticelli's two masterpieces (fig. 62). The image formed part of a retrospective series of photographs of McQueen's designs taken by Steven Meisel. The model Caroline Trentini's demure stance, facing forward but with one knee delicately bent, recalls that of Botticelli's Venus. The scattering of petals and buds beneath her feet echoes the carpet of soft grasses and flowers in *Primavera.* Yet in Meisel's photograph, the model emerges, not from the sea, but from a packing crate placed within a windowless building site; the carpet of petals beneath her feet is formed not by growing verdure but from decaying flowers that have fallen from her dress.

McQueen's three-dimensional florals echo, 60 years on, Schiaparelli's lifelike homage to Botticelli. Such creations mimic nature and demonstrate, in the words of Caroline Evans, 'swapping between organic and inorganic, alive and dead, procreation and decay'.[7] In fashion designs created across decades and borders by the individuals discussed here, clothing imitates the natural world viewed through the prism of Botticelli's oeuvre. Botticelli's rarefied realism produced joyous depictions of nature and the human form. The designers' responses to these visions have provided fashion history with welcome moments of grace and whimsy.

FIG. 62
ALEXANDER McQUEEN
(1969–2010)
Silk evening dress embroidered with silk and flowers, 2007
Photograph by STEVEN MEISEL

Filming Botticelli in Post-War Italy

RICCARDO VENTURI

'One could view our relationship with painting in this way: these are not static images but rather stills charged with movement from a film that is missing. One has to get them back to the film (you will recognize this as Aby Warburg's project).'[1] This was how the philosopher Giorgio Agamben proposed to transform the relationship between painting and cinema – today still too limited – between the framed picture and the projection screen, between the arts of form and images in movement. Pictures would become stills of an absent film, which will inexorably withdraw from our gaze despite all our attempts to identify it. It is with this notion in mind that I discuss here the development of documentaries in which artists, art historians and film-makers have collaborated. In respect of Botticelli, the most important figures are Luciano Emmer and Carlo Ludovico Ragghianti.

'La fabula danzante'
(THE DANCING FABLE)

In September 1945 Luciano Emmer submitted to the Congrès international du cinéma in Basel what amounted to a manifesto for the art documentary, entitled *Pour une nouvelle avant-garde* (Towards a new avant-garde). Three years later, in 1948, in collaboration with the film director Enrico Gras and in consultation with Lauro Venturi, son of the famous art historian Lionello Venturi, whose own essays on Botticelli appeared in 1937 and 1961, he filmed *L'allegoria della Primavera (dalle pitture di Botticelli)* (The Allegory of *Primavera* by Botticelli), a documentary of nine minutes in black and white. In Emmer's view a commentary would have weakened the visual effect of the work, but music complemented it, and he commissioned a score from the composer Roman Vlad.

Already by 1949 one could talk of 'Emmerism' in terms of cinema.[2] However, his Botticelli film passed unnoticed; it is hard to find any mention of it in the contemporary press.[3] It is still one of the least known of his documentaries, and probably also one of his least sophisticated or innovative: ponderously the camera travels over the lineaments of the compositions to end up usually at the figures' faces; close-ups gradually give way to figure groups and vice versa (in *Primavera* and *Birth of Venus*). Care is taken not to dwell on the individual figures but to present the tableau in its entirety, with only occasional cuts to details (such as the feet or hands of the dancing Graces).

However, for Emmer painting and cinema remained two entirely distinct languages, there being no question of translating the one into the other, or of introducing movement into something inherently static. There was no point in making a film documentary unfilmically, because the camera 'eye' saw not better, but differently. Emmer was conscious of the existence of two distinct spheres, that of the articulated – which he identified in large part with Renaissance painting – and that of the articulating, in other words the process of making a film. It was in the sphere of active articulation that the future of the art documentary was to be found, so that it should not translate but transform – or, better still, transgress – pictorial composition.

Emmer was not cowed by the masterpieces with which he competed; he did not fear traducing the intentions of the artist or the conditions under which his work should be viewed or destroying its completeness or unity – a unity that had crystallized when the artist laid down his brush – a moment otherwise regarded as sacrosanct. He demonstrated a kind of *sprezzatura* (studied nonchalance) in this regard, for which he was criticized by the art-historical community – combining acute artistic sensibility with a rapacious cinematographic eye. Unsurprisingly, one critic wondered after seeing his Botticelli film whether Emmer was not prepared to risk destroying the artwork in his (more or less, according to your point of view) creative act.[4]

Emmer's camera, nevertheless, remained within the limits of the painting, without moving to its edges. The German film theorist Siegfried Kracauer has highlighted this conditionality: anatomizing a painting without ever showing its borders or the painting as a whole has the effect of evoking 'three-dimensional life more vividly than do the originals themselves,' as the images become 'free-floating entities'; 'by decomposing any such whole, the film-maker endows the imagery with a semblance of life as it evolves outside the aesthetic dimension'.[5] In his own work on Botticelli, Ragghianti would come to similar conclusions: '... if you look at a work of art, you do not look at the frame or outside it, precisely because the frame cuts it off from its environment. Therefore you have to work inside the image... You have to see everything inside.'[6]

For Ragghianti, however, the picture plane was a text to decipher, while for Emmer it offered rather a story told in images: 'My first documentaries had no intention of describing a pictorial reality. They were attempts to tell stories through images.'[7] The composer Roman Vlad remarked of Emmer's film on Bosch: 'Here, the painting was regarded as an infernal dance. The work was made not only to move, but in a sense to dance.'[8] This reference to dance is important: it marks the supersession of the static idea of sculpture inherent in Warburg's project. Emmer achieved this by finding an equilibrium between two opposing tendencies – the drama of the scenario or story and the cinematic close-up or zoom.

'Deconstructing' Botticelli

Fantasia di Botticelli. La Calunnia (Fantasia of Botticelli: *The Calumny* [*of Apelles*]; 1961) though the title recalls the Walt Disney film of 1940 (released in Italy in 1946) the film is actually one of the most exemplary of Carlo Ludovico Ragghianti's so-called 'crito-films', a series of 22 documentaries that he made between 1948 (Raphael's *Deposition*) and 1964 (Michelangelo). A crito-film is 'a critical film, or rather art criticism conducted through the language of cinema'.[9] The outcome of a theoretical position that he formulated in 1933 in his essay *Cinematografo rigoroso* (The rigorous cinema), a crito-film makes cinematography into a figurative medium or an 'art of vision' (*Arte della visione*, the title of a collection of writings by Ragghianti that was published in the 1970s and of which the first volume was dedicated to the cinema). The moving images are in fact observed with the methodology of the history of art. The movements of the camera make possible the exploration of the painting, revealing gradually its different components (points, lines, surfaces, colours), imitating the ductus (or path) of the brush over the canvas, the coordination of eye and hand. In conformity with an ultimately Neoplatonic aesthetic, film is a scientific instrument that exposes the essential content of the work. Through films about art one may better understand not cinematography but the creative process of artistic production, the act of creating form. In sum, while Emmer wanted to explore the possibilities offered to film by painting, Ragghianti was interested in the possibilities of exploring painting through film.

'I have sought to show by cinematic means the processes that actually took place in works of art.'[10] But this is to imply a transmission from painting to film that does not entail significant losses, and in this confrontation of the two media, cinema gains little in compensation. The result is in fact to make nothing of the medium's potential, because it cannot contribute usefully on the level of artistic expression or intuition – which reveals Ragghianti's fundamental debt to the approach to history of Benedetto Croce, one of the most influential philosophers of the first half of the twentieth century. Unlike Emmer, he had no use for accompanying music.

Nonetheless, during a period when attention was given almost exclusively to the formal dynamic of works of art rather than to the experience of the historic or contemporary viewer, cinema foregrounded pressingly the question of the gaze. To what degree did the shots taken by a camera correspond to the track of the gaze of the human viewer in front of the real painting? How did the two worlds, of the work itself and of the spectator's vision, intersect or diverge?

The 'eye' of the camera could bring to life the implicit world of a painting, determine its duration, lend a temporal dimension to the gaze. The problem was the risk of overlaying the film on the painting, of making the film the agent directing the phenomena of the gaze that in the painting was crystallized in a single moment. But for Ragghianti film shots made evident not only the viewer's time – the finite period that the viewer needed to digest the work, to run the gaze over the painted surface, a matter purely of reception – but rather the painting's own internal temporality. It could be a journey as much analytical as creative, as *Fantasia* shows.

Fantasia, which is devoted to Botticelli's *Calumny of Apelles* in the Uffizi (1495), opens with a slow sideways track of the camera from left to right, moving from an identifiable male figure to a contextless and largely featureless detail. Following this disorientating oscillation between figuration and abstraction, the camera pulls back to take in a female figure on the right and we understand at last that we have been looking at the background seen through the largest arch of the loggia in which the action takes place. The film then traces a series of white lines, making a diagram of the gaze within the painting. This is counterpointed by a vertiginous circular swoop: the eye of the camera breaks out of the viewer's view of the painting and upsets the picture's vertical axis.

The camera makes comparative raids into other pictures by Botticelli, follows the line of some drapery, an architectural moulding, lingers on a portion of anatomy, alternates between the contours of a figure and the tunnels of the arches looking into distance. The cross-cuts of the film play as much on the general as on the particular, establishing parallels between particular elements that recur in other paintings by Botticelli as well as the compositional and narrative relations between the various units of the *Calumny*.

In more experimental mode, between one zoom and another, there are flashes of light rather like the flickering of experimental cinema, and very distant from the contemplative position associated with Renaissance painting. The sheer variety of filmic devices employed made any commentary supernumerary, and any soundtrack would have seemed too lyrical.[11] The painting is analysed as if the viewer were walking around in a three-dimensional space.

In general, the visual experience of Ragghianti's films is like a kaleidoscope, which must have been rather irritating for the spectator, in so far as it baffled the didactic intent.[12] He chose a style of direction that mulitiplied and fragmented the space, to the point of excess in the case of the *Calumny*. A viewer who had never seen Botticelli's picture would have had difficulty in grasping its real dimensions; he or she might even

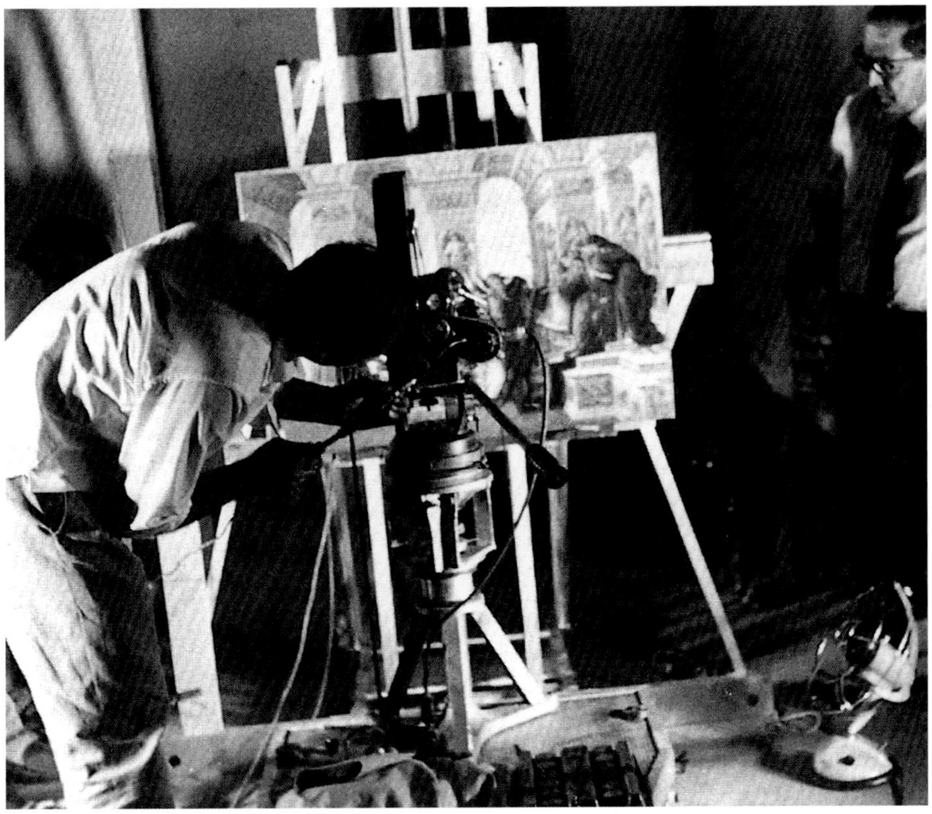

FIG. 63
C.L Ragghianti during the shooting of *Fantasia di Botticelli. La Calunnia*, 1961

gain an idea that it was enormous. It is rather surprising that this twelve minutes of close ups was centred on one of the artist's smaller paintings (62 × 91 cm).

Ragghianti knew Emmer's films, even if in his writing on cinematography he mentions him only fleetingly and in order to distance his own position. Emmer and Ragghianti are now seen as the proponents of two different approaches to the filming of art – on one side populist narrative or indeed mythmaking, on the other didactic criticism; on one side the path of expression and poeticizing interpretation (which Ragghianti linked explicitly with the inspired connoisseur Roberto Longhi), on the other scholarship and science. It is difficult, however, to separate the critical from the creatively interpretative without discounting or disregarding the cinematographic element in any supposed neutrality before the painting. It seems to me that Botticelli's painting constituted in both cases such an unusual territory to explore in film that any such a division becomes absurd.

Ragghianti, though often concerned to proffer a synthetic vision of the work of art in question that would balance the analysis of it by his lens, adopted in Botticelli's case a deconstruction of his pictorial language, which thus amounted to an emphasis on the dramatic element dear to Emmer. Radically dislocating the pictorial space of the *Calumny*, liberating it from its figurative purpose, and from the rules of composition and perspective – from a strict division between figure and ground, between figures and architectural setting – Ragghianti, whatever his intentions, turned it into a work of abstraction. Indeed his reading of Botticelli is redolent of the abstract aesthetics of the 1950s, especially in contrast to Emmer's work. It was no coincidence that while he was filming his Botticelli documentary Ragghianti was in the process of finishing his comprehensive monograph on Piet Mondrian, published in 1962.[13]

The dizzying anachronism of Ragghianti's Botticelli–Mondrian *Fantasia* makes it a unique product of its time. And, to conclude, I suggest, it is from this starting point that one has to view the reception of Botticelli in post-war Italy. Held the hostage, in the Fascist era, of a conservative conception of his art intent on deriving a national ideal of beauty from his figures, Botticelli was hereby liberated at last as a fertile subject for experimentation in an altogether reconciliatory meeting of painting and cinema.

Branding Venus: Botticelli as Mirrored in American Art Since 1940

STEFAN WEPPELMANN

At the beginning of the twentieth century, the United States of America shared Europe's interest in the Italian Renaissance;[1] this did not, however, result in greater attention being paid to Sandro Botticelli. For the most part only his small-scale works reached the States, though this was not due to a systematic acquisitions policy, nor any particular demand on the part of the public. Even the few significant pieces – Isabella Stewart Gardner's Chigi Madonna (cat. 109), for instance – did nothing to boost Botticelli's wider reception in America, since they were only accessible to the bourgeois elite.

It was therefore left to a European, the Surrealist Salvador Dalí, to confront the wider American public with Botticelli – not with the painter himself, but rather with a quotation from one of his works. At the 1939 New York World's Fair, Dalí hung a reproduction of Venus, extracted from Botticelli's painting in the Uffizi, above the entrance to his 'Dream of Venus' pavilion in the 'Amusement Area' (fig. 64). Inside, visitors encountered floating girls,[2] whose performance must have seemed like a dream. Dalí's mermaids duplicated and brought to life Botticelli's Venus, incarnating and celebrating the World's Fair as the birth of modernity, the goal and fulfilment of which seemed to be beauty itself.

Despite this preamble, the hysteria that Botticelli's *Birth of Venus* elicited just weeks later was astonishing. The original painting was brought over from Florence as part of an exhibition of Renaissance masterpieces organized by the Italian government, which between 1939 and 1940 travelled to San Francisco, Chicago and New York. By this point the work was not yet considered essential viewing in the way that it is today.

The fact that this sensational display of the Old Masters took place not in the Metropolitan Museum of Art, the most prominent site for exhibitions of pre-twentieth-century European art, but in the Museum of Modern Art – in other words, in the midst of work testifying to the production of contemporary art – suggests an interpretation of the Renaissance as a kind of proto-modernity. The museum's decision to schedule a simultaneous exhibition of 'Modern Masters', featuring 29 paintings from the late nineteenth and early twentieth centuries, is fully consistent with this. The concept underlying these parallel exhibitions is an unambiguous

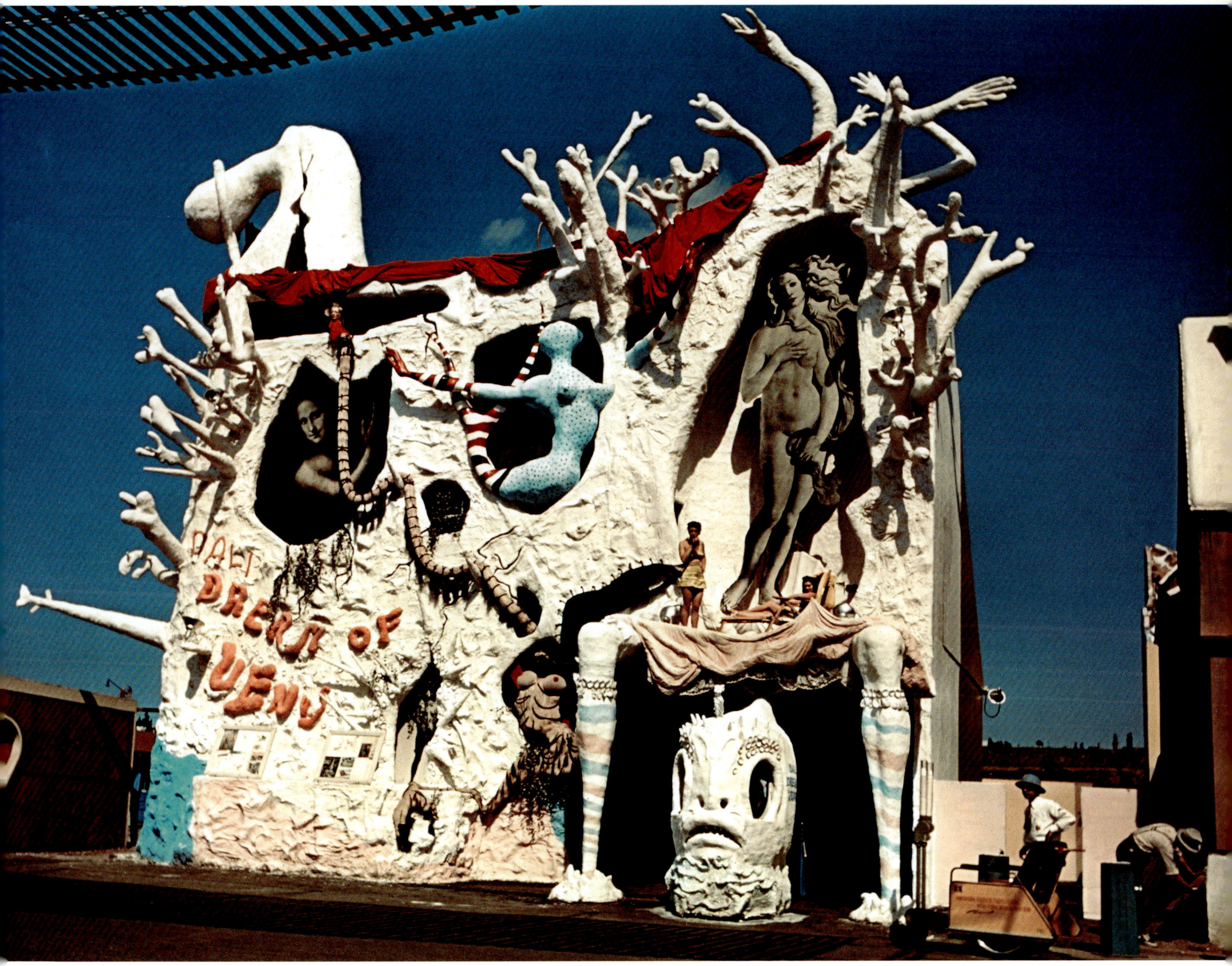

FIG. 64
ERIC SCHAAL (1905–1994)
View of the 'Dream of Venus' pavilion by Salvador Dali, realized for the World's Fair New York, 1939

declaration of the continuity and universality of modernity, and interprets the artistic products of the Renaissance as pioneering and still relevant.

The frontispiece of the exhibition catalogue was a full-page reproduction of the head of Venus. The director, Alfred Barr Jr, announced in the foreword, 'For the Renaissance and Baroque art of Italy stands at the very heart of the great tradition of European art and its American branches…',[3] giving the *Birth of Venus* a modernist reading that proved to be momentous for Botticelli.

The painting was hung by itself in a room 80 metres square, installed on a kind of stage. This setting enabled the museum to orchestrate the viewer's encounter with the picture by re-enacting – in keeping with its subject – the origin myth of modernity. The curtains were swept to the side, and Venus rose from the waves (fig. 65). To accompany the emptiness of the space and the theatricality of the presentation, the room was dimmed using a special installation of spotlights.[4]

In Chicago alone some 250,000 people had seen Botticelli's masterpiece,[5] and MoMA had to extend its opening hours to cope with the crowds – in 74 days, the New York exhibition drew in 290,000 visitors,[6] their enthusiasm only matched by the media's for Botticelli, who was played up as one of the main attractions.[7] The *Birth of Venus* appeared in all the publications accompanying the exhibition, and thousands of posters featuring the image were disseminated across New York and dispatched to schools, public libraries and cultural institutions.[8]

Before the 'Italian Masters' tour, Botticelli had occasionally been characterized as 'decorative', and – due to the much-emphasized importance of line in his compositions – as 'feminine'.[9] Bernard Berenson, by 1940 an international pundit on the Renaissance, picked up on precisely those traits, identifying in his linearity and decorativeness the fundamental guarantors of Botticelli's abstract qualities. He saw in Botticelli's paintings the pure values of movement, 'unconnected with any representation whatsoever'.[10]

Such analyses, fundamentally art-theoretical and literary rather than verifiable against Botticelli's work, are very much in the tradition of Walter Pater and his followers.[11] Working within this mindset, elements of the American art critical

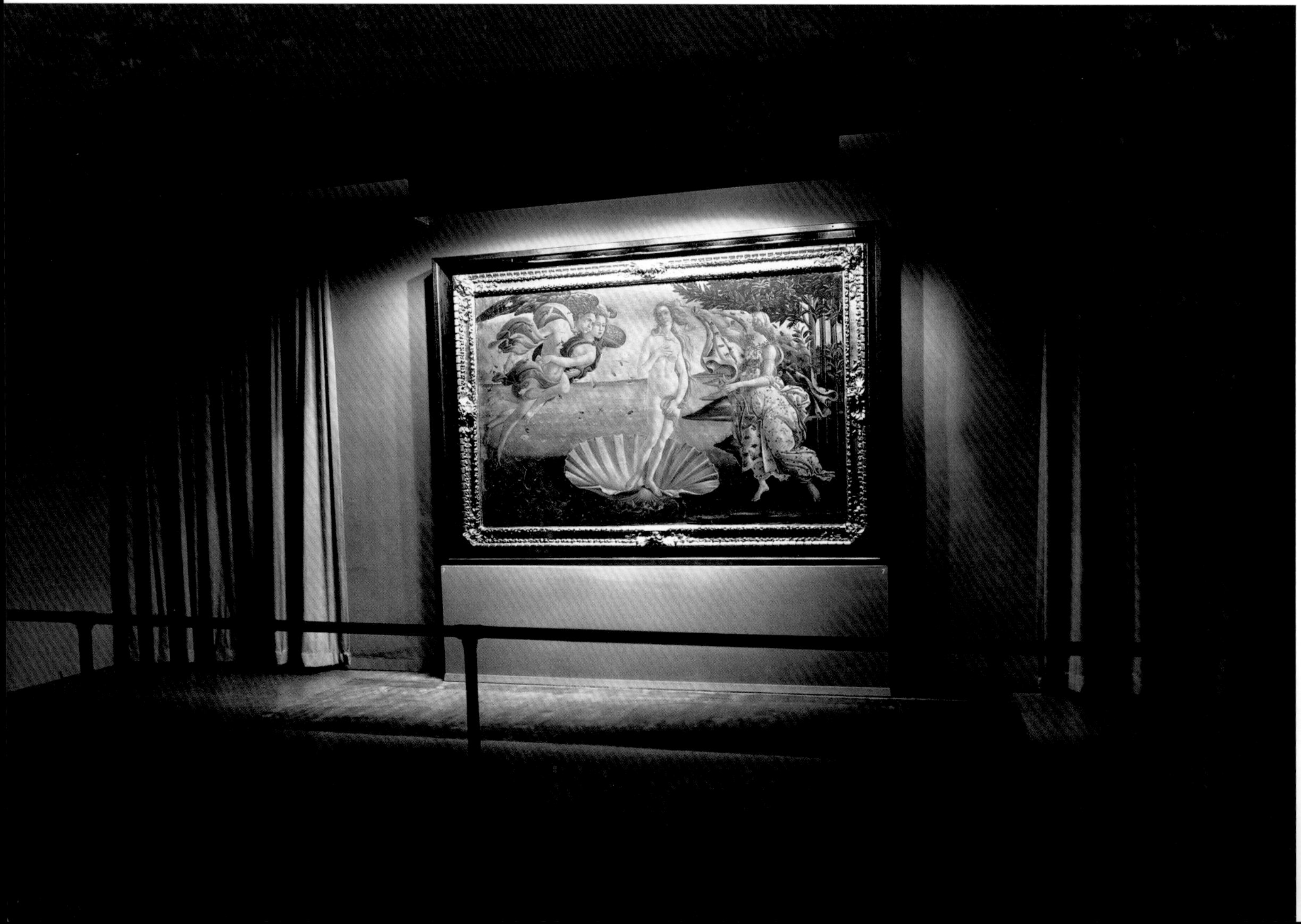

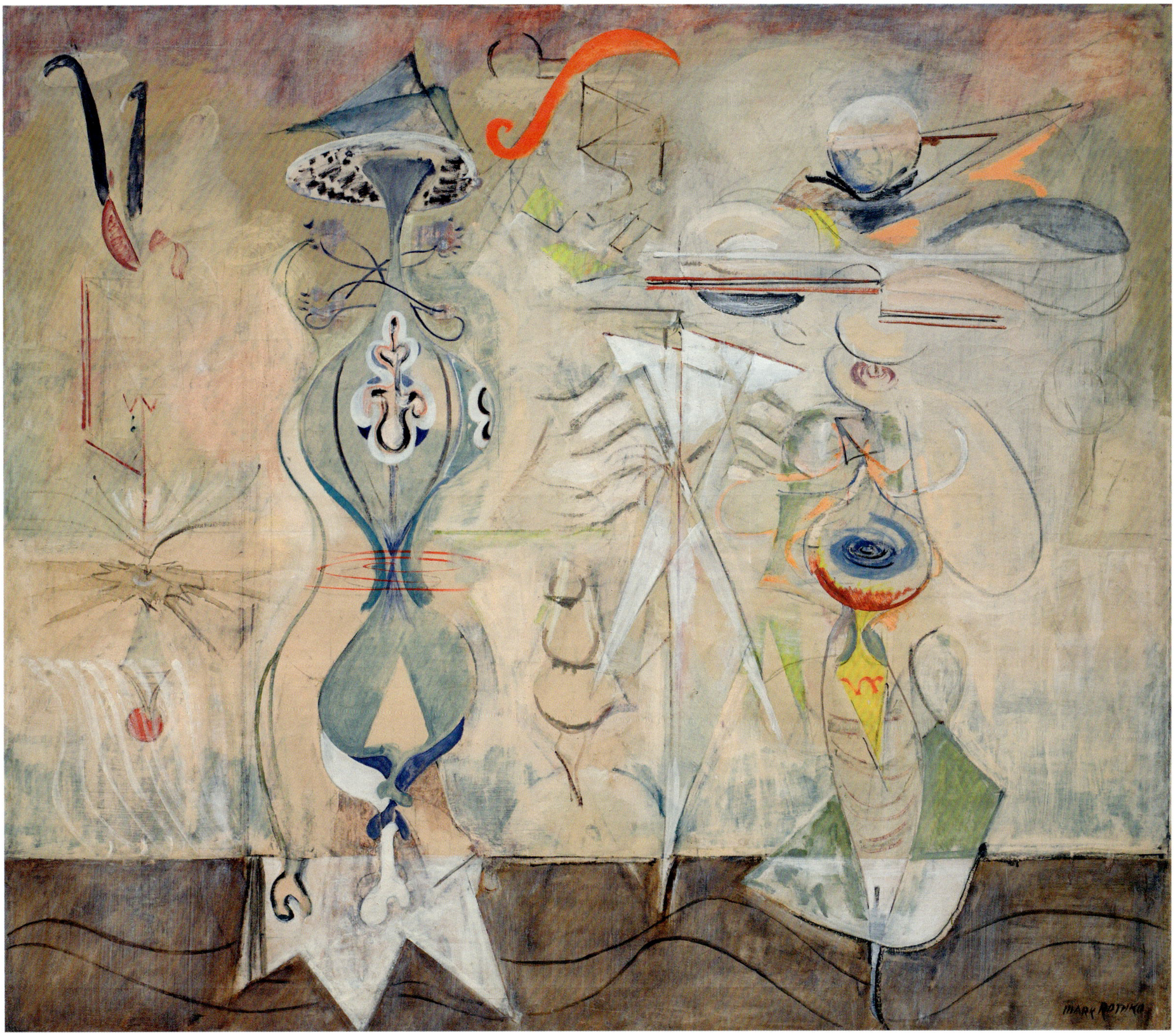

FIG. 65
Installation view of the *Italian Masters* exhibition at the Museum of Modern Art, New York (26 January–7 April 1940) with Botticelli's *Birth of Venus*, 1940
Silver gelatin print

FIG. 66
MARK ROTHKO (1903–1970)
Slow Swirl at the Edge of the Sea, 1944
Mixed media, 191.4 × 215.2 cm
The Museum of Modern Art, New York
(429.1981)

establishment stressed contemporary art's connectedness to tradition: Jackson Pollock and Mark Rothko found favour because their art was reminiscent of the Renaissance, and Botticelli, as well as other Renaissance artists, served as a rhetorical support for their historiographical constructs. During his early phase of creativity, preceding the 'all-over' paintings of the 1950s, Rothko may have made reference to Botticelli's *Birth of Venus* in his *Slow Swirl at the Edge of the Sea* (fig. 66),[12] while Duncan Phillips, founder of one of the first collections of contemporary art on the East Coast and commissioner of some of the key works of the postmodern period, including the famous Rothko Room,[13] identified Botticelli – along with some other fifteenth-century painters – as crucial to an understanding of contemporary art.[14]

From around 1940 in the USA, in conjunction with an appraisal of the American avant-garde, opinions were floated that declared abstraction and a lack of realistic perspectival space to be fundamental prerequisites of contemporary art. Such opinions can be seen, for instance, in the work of Clement Greenberg and other New York critics.[15] Greenberg explicitly differentiated between the decorative and ornamental, which was 'feminine' and kitsch, and high art, by which he meant abstract art.[16] Although he was not referring specifically to Botticelli, his value judgement assigned a role to the avant-garde that could not be reconciled with the argument made by Alfred Barr Jr's staging of Botticelli at MoMA. This context also explains the polemics flatly denying Barr's claims that the Old Masters were modern and progressive. In a scandalized letter about the 'Italian Masters' exhibition to the *New York Sun*, for instance, one writer complained, 'As a visitor of the Museum of Modern Art, I object very energetically to seeing this boring old stuff. I do not use a buggy either when I can ride with motor cars…'[17]

In the following decades the *Birth of Venus* was the only work that brought Botticelli true celebrity. Its subject – Venus, the goddess of beauty – assisted in the canonization of feminine beauty in the 1950s, though it is interesting to note that the 'Botticelli girl' of the post-war period initially radiated natural rather than idealized good looks. The realist photographs by Paul Himmel (cat. 30) or Maggie Diaz, who titled her images of children from socially marginalized groups on the streets of Chicago *Botticelli Girls* (fig. 67), was soon outshone by colourful fashion photography. At the same time the painter was discovered by the prêt-a-porter market. Beginning with Erwin Blumenfeld's cover for American *Vogue*, references to him in the fashion industry can be found well into the present day. Collections by Dolce & Gabbana (cats 13, 14) and Alexander McQueen (fig. 62) have been mentioned as more recent examples.[18]

The use of Botticelli's name as a synonym for ideal feminine beauty has led to its adoption in other contexts. Famous racehorses have been called 'Botticelli',[19] and it is hardly surprising that Barbie's blonde, curly-haired pony is still marketed under this name today, as are other consumer goods.

Early pop art was also interested in the way in which his name had been appropriated by the manufacturing industry, as illustrated in Alain Jacquet's 1963–4 *Camouflage Botticellis* (cats 25, 26). The artist clothed Botticelli's Venus in the garb of global oil commerce, depicting her emerging from the waves in the form of a Shell petrol pump. By appropriating Botticelli, he created a new artwork that plays both with the shifting meaning of the seashell (the logo of the company Shell) and with the visual interweaving of the two bodies – literal (Venus) and metaphorical (the petrol pump) – a juxtaposition that permits further ironic interpretations.

Botticelli's transformation in the 1970s into an internationally familiar trademark is evidenced less in artistic statements than in consumer products. One notable example is Philips' K9 'Botticelli' Delta TV, launched onto the market in 1974. The painter had now become a fully-fledged commercial symbol of modern life, though because such references lacked clarity of meaning or intent he himself was becoming increasingly unfamiliar.

This is witnessed not least by the fact that tourists visiting the Uffizi were interested almost exclusively in the *Birth of Venus* and *Primavera*. Even today, the general public still largely ignores other works, no less relevant within the context of his oeuvre, such as his altarpieces in the very same room. In 1977 the situation led to a reorganization of the exhibition room in order to cope with the crowds of visitors,[20] after which the *Birth of Venus* and *Primavera* advanced still further towards the status of a 'must see' for every visitor to Florence. Their reception accordingly became even more distinct from that of other works, bolstered not least by tourists' snapshots. When Andy Warhol, who had been experimenting on his home computer with 'alienated images' of Venus, produced his series *Details of Renaissance Paintings* in 1984, Botticelli could hardly be left out (cats 19, 20). The strategy, however, of critiquing the relevance of the original through the abbreviated cipher

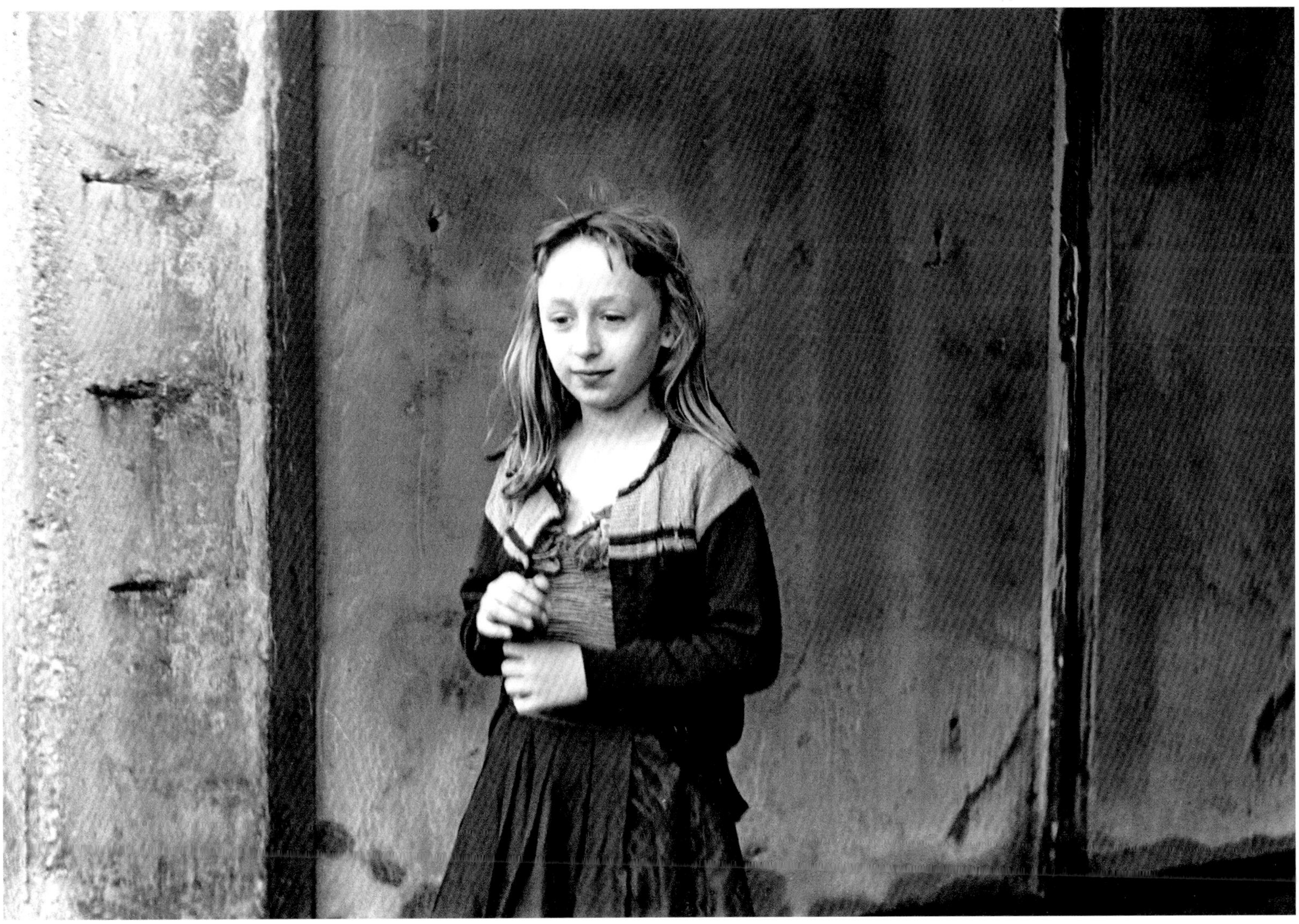

FIG. 67
MAGGIE DIAZ (B.1925)
Botticelli Girl, *c.*1954
Private collection

paradoxically only functions because anyone seeing the detail will immediately think of Botticelli's original, and not, for example, merely of a woman's face with flowing hair.

This reduction of Botticelli to the *Birth of Venus* has characterized our engagement with him more recently, too. Nonetheless, since the end of the 1970s, there has been a more systematic account of the scope of his work, and his religious pieces have drawn closer attention than previously. This broadening of appreciation has modified the rhetoric framing Botticelli as an exponent of proto-modernity, placing him instead within the Late-Gothic tradition and searching for mystical meaning in many of his works.

A powerful work by Bill Viola (cat. 9) may help to clarify this. For the 2002 video installation *The Path* (a sequence from the five-part work *Going Forth By Day*), Viola made a preparatory note that read, 'Forest – A scene in a forest – Stylized: After Botticelli's "Story of Nastagio degli Onesti" 1483'. Viola's composition does indeed resemble Botticelli's cycle of paintings (fig. 34). In both, tall tree trunks create a sense of rhythm within the space, forming compartments, like pillars in a sacred building, with figures moving between them. Botticelli has created a place where the earthly and the celestial can co-exist. Viola's scene, too, appears real – we have all wandered through a similar wood at some time in our lives – and yet his *Path* can equally be interpreted as a spiritual piece, the vision of a journeying soul.[21]

Botticelli's reception among successful artists such as Cindy Sherman (cat. 17), Brice Marden, David LaChapelle (cats 5, 6), Andy Warhol and Bill Viola has encouraged the imitation of Botticelli-esque motifs, further detaching the images from the originals. On the other hand, Botticelli's continued presence in the postmodern era has had an effect on the prices his work can command. Until the end of the 1990s, no Botticelli painting had crossed the million-dollar threshold, but the boost in popularity that Botticelli's *Birth of Venus* experienced in the 1990s and the early years of the new millennium was followed by a sudden jump in prices. In December 2006 a Madonna was sold at auction for 7.4 million US dollars,[22] then in January 2013 the Rockefeller Madonna fetched more than 10 million dollars, the current record for a Botticelli.[23] The artist's fame is inextricably bound up with the *Birth of Venus*, a work that is not for sale, even though virtual reproductions of its image have heavily influenced the market and its workings. Its perpetual international reiterations have ultimately led to its becoming a general shorthand for Western high art per se. Given this backdrop, it is clear that some contemporary artists have used Botticelli as a peg for their arguments for precisely this reason, making reference to him in order to formulate their critiques. The Chinese artist Yin Xin (cat. 8) presents an Asian Venus, problematizing the self-proclaimed hegemony of Eurocentric culture.[24] Nguyen Xuan Huy, on the other hand, evokes the traumatic wartime experiences of his home country Vietnam (fig. 68).[25] He makes use of the physical deformities caused by the defoliant Agent Orange, which were themselves much publicized by the media, in disturbing ways. Disfigurement, rather than beauty, is the result – Venus has become both a farce and a victim of war. Meanwhile the Japanese artist Tomoko Nagao (cat. 1) paraphrases Botticelli's composition using the visual language of the computer game. The seashell has become a console. What began with Botticelli as the creation of a single, unique image has today become the universally available, wordless content of a game. Everything has been transplanted into a garish world of consumer goods, in which Nagao has – not without humour – placed Botticelli's image on the same level as other Italian brands like Barilla, Baci Perugina and Esselunga, once again staging the topos of the interchangeability between culture and products.

Botticelli's multiplication across the globe is at odds with the narrow focus on a single work, the *Birth of Venus*. The cult of Botticelli has come full circle from the 1940s: the present has actually made this painting part of itself, thrusting the original body of work and its creator increasingly into the background.

FIG. 68
NGUYEN XUAN HUY (B.1976)
The Birth of Venus (after Botticelli), 2009
Oil on canvas, 177 × 269 cm
Private collection

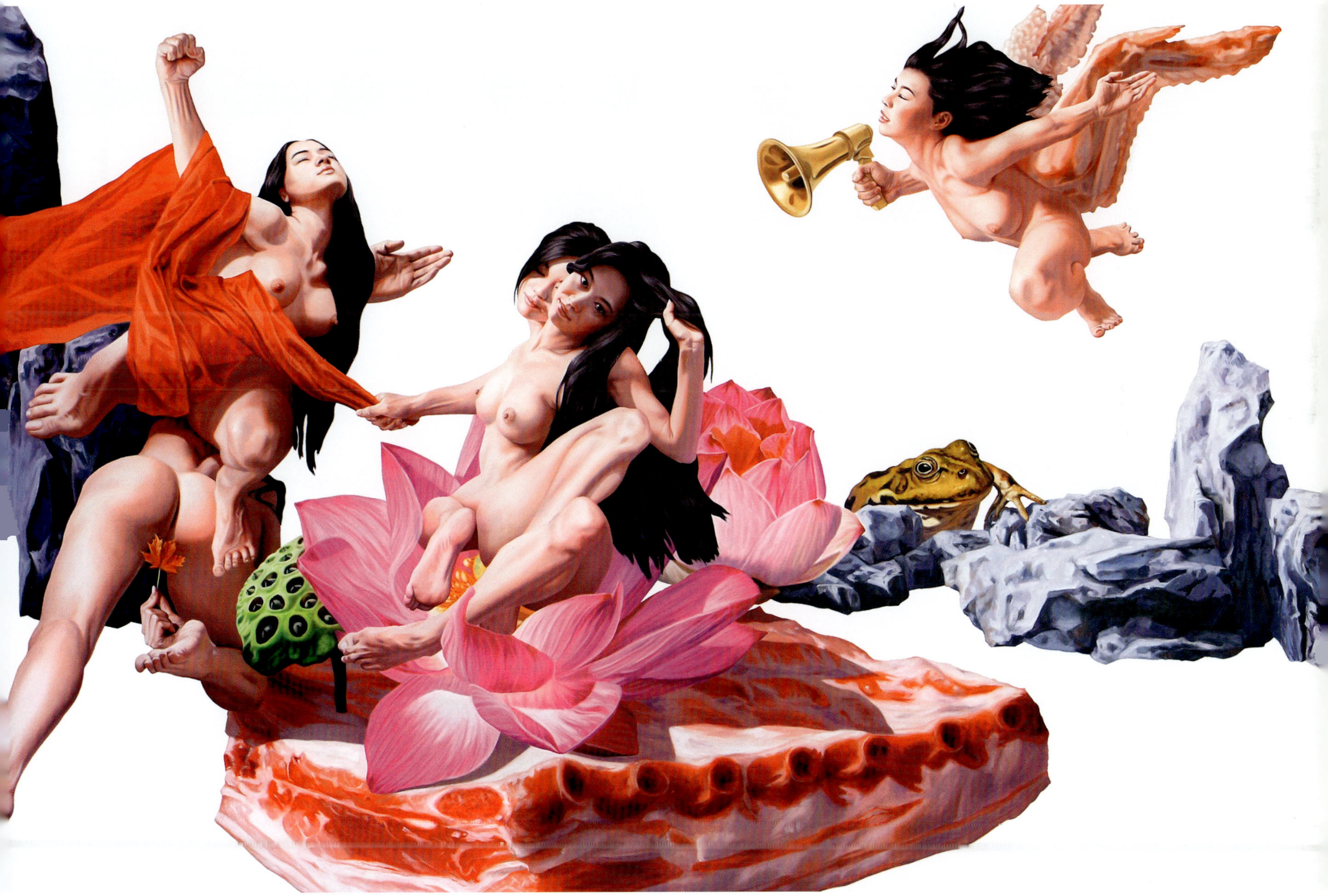

The Lessons of a New Picture Hang

ANTONIO NATALI

The Uffizi Gallery is perhaps the prime reason for making a visit to Florence. Though the city is blessed with many other great buildings and works of art which are enough in themselves to make it famous throughout the world, if there were no Uffizi a trip to Florence would lose a lot of its magic. This is one reason why the museum has remained open despite the huge and long-drawn-out programme of works it has undergone, that otherwise would have justified its closure, even for a number of years – as has happened elsewhere. To illustrate the point: since December 2011 the Gallery has doubled in size – from 50 rooms to 100 – necessitating a radical reordering of the entire collection, once presented on the second floor only, but now occupying the first floor as well. This followed, on the one hand, the restoration of the great rooms to their original appearance – the Sala della Niobe in 2006, the Ricetto Lorenese and its staircase in 2007, the Tribuna in 2012 – and, on the other, the repainting of the new rooms in vivid colours (for the first time in the Gallery's history), which mark out the different epochs and schools of the exhibits – green for the Early Renaissance, red for the High Renaissance and Mannerism, yellow for the Baroque and blue for non-Italian schools. All this required a seemingly endless relocation of works of art from room to room and from floor to floor, essential so the museum, one of the city's best loved destinations, could remain open with its exhibits on display.

The appeal of the Uffizi for most people is in large part due to the works by Botticelli, conspicuous both in their quantity and in their quality. The space in which the Botticelli paintings are hung is sought out by every visitor. This room, though large, indeed the largest in the Gallery, is always crowded, which undoubtedly affects the experience of viewing Sandro's sweet and striking poetry. If a painting may be regarded as a poem expressed in figures rather than in words, then, obviously, just as happens when confronting a written text, no one can fully enjoy the suffused lyricism of Botticelli's images in a crowd. No reader can concentrate on a novel when its pages are continually being jostled or entirely obscured by other people who press or scrimmage around. The same happens with figurative art. Visitors only tolerate the nuisance of packed museums because they are resigned to mass culture, and I fear that the majority of them do not even notice this disturbance since they have come to the museum less to appreciate its contents than to participate in a ritual expression of veneration inculcated by the media.

Anyone who comes to Florence and enters the Uffizi has to see Botticelli and probably indeed commemorate his or her visit with a selfie in front of *Primavera* or the *Birth of Venus*. For some, it is not even necessary to pause and look at those works of art but enough simply to obtain a souvenir snapshot. The Botticelli room is hence converted into a chapel of miraculous relics – what an ironic reversal of the original motivation to establish museums during the Age of Enlightenment.

Such attitudes are a consequence above all of contemporary education, which struggles to transmit the values that underpin cultural awareness in today's world and enable an appreciation of history. Most have not been taught to read a work of art like the text of a poem; simply that there is beauty in the surface appearance of a work of art without being encouraged to go beyond the superficial or the apparent. If the young were better grounded in the appreciation of a construct like a painting and in the investigation of its complexities, then surely, in due course, the desire to recognize and understand would grow and idolatry would diminish.

Museums themselves, however, must share responsibility for this as the presentation and the interpretation of works of art are themselves educational activities. It is not by exalting the greatness of the most celebrated masters that sensibility is nurtured. To fence off or raise on an isolated pedestal a work of art that everyone craves to see if only for a moment may be a justifiable security measure, but it also increases its fetish value. This is a vicious spiral. Museums should be laid out on quite different principles. If instead they emphasized lesser-known works that deserve wider recognition, few people would stop rushing to see the iconic masterpieces but more would be excited by discovering novelties.

The Botticelli room, which will soon be refurbished, should exemplify this principle. At present the large room in which the Botticelli paintings hang is preceded by a smaller space in which superb panels by the brothers Piero and Antonio del Pollaiuolo are installed. Most visitors pass rapidly through this room with their minds fixed on the Botticelli pictures that await, so that few pause to gaze on the sublime *Virtues* by Piero and Antonio or their altarpiece originally painted for the Chapel of the Cardinal of Portugal. To exit a room of modest size containing works by artists of less renown (even if also of lyrical quality, as the Pollaiuolo certainly are) and to enter a hall-like space housing a magnificent collection of masterpieces by one of the most celebrated artists in the world does nothing to emphasize the merits of the art of the Pollaiuolo nor to qualify the iconization of Botticelli.

This is the reasoning that has led to the division of the large room devoted to Botticelli into two more modest spaces of identical dimensions. In the first will be displayed not only all the works by the Pollaiuolo brothers, but also Botticelli's early paintings, which will therefore retrace the beginning of his career. In the second room will be installed Botticelli's later works including *Primavera* and the *Birth of Venus*. The presence of the three artists together will assist the viewer to perceive the development of Florentine art in the second half of the fifteenth century and so to understand that Botticelli was not an obelisk soaring from a flat plain but, rather, a peak protruding above a range of high mountains.

1

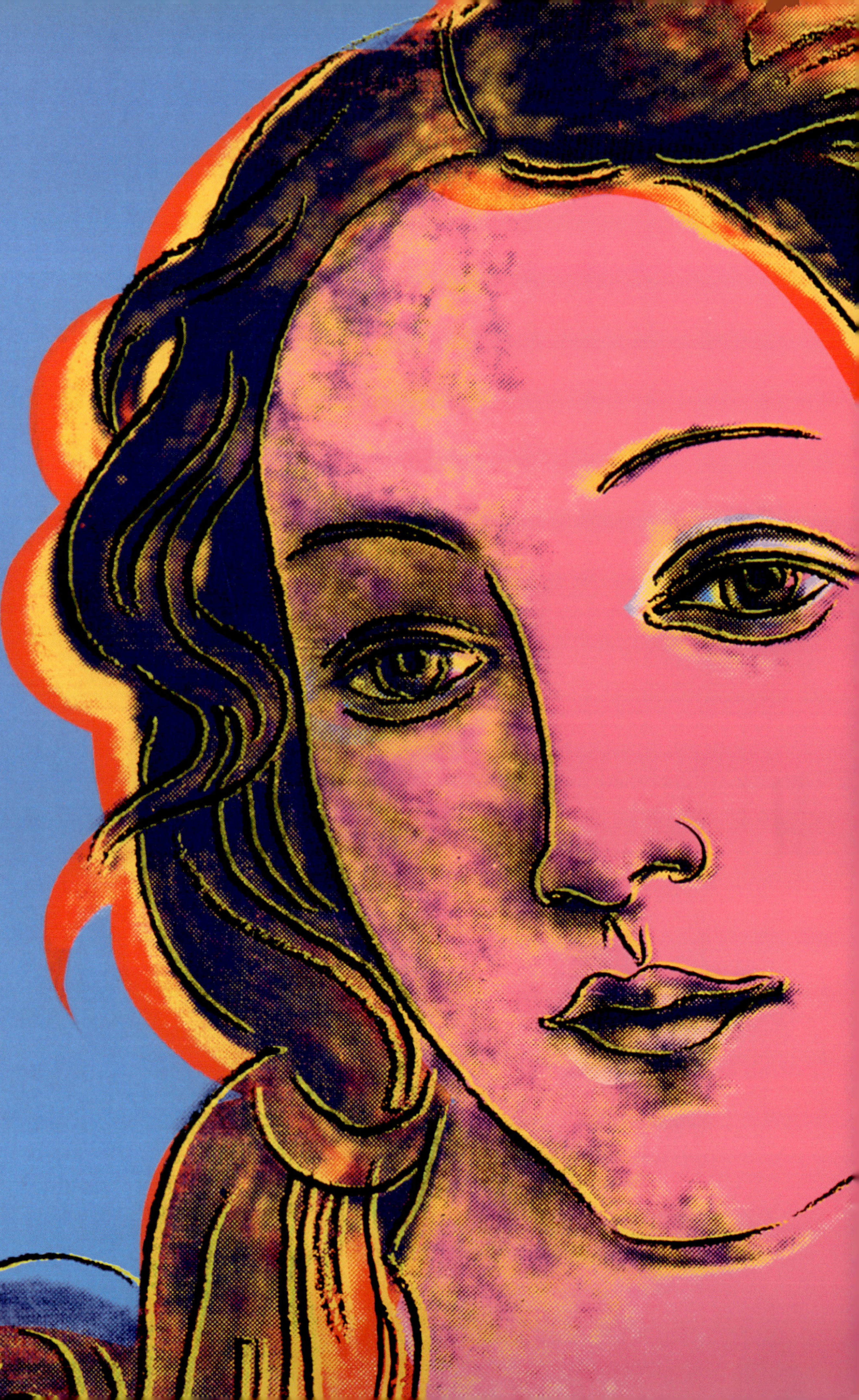

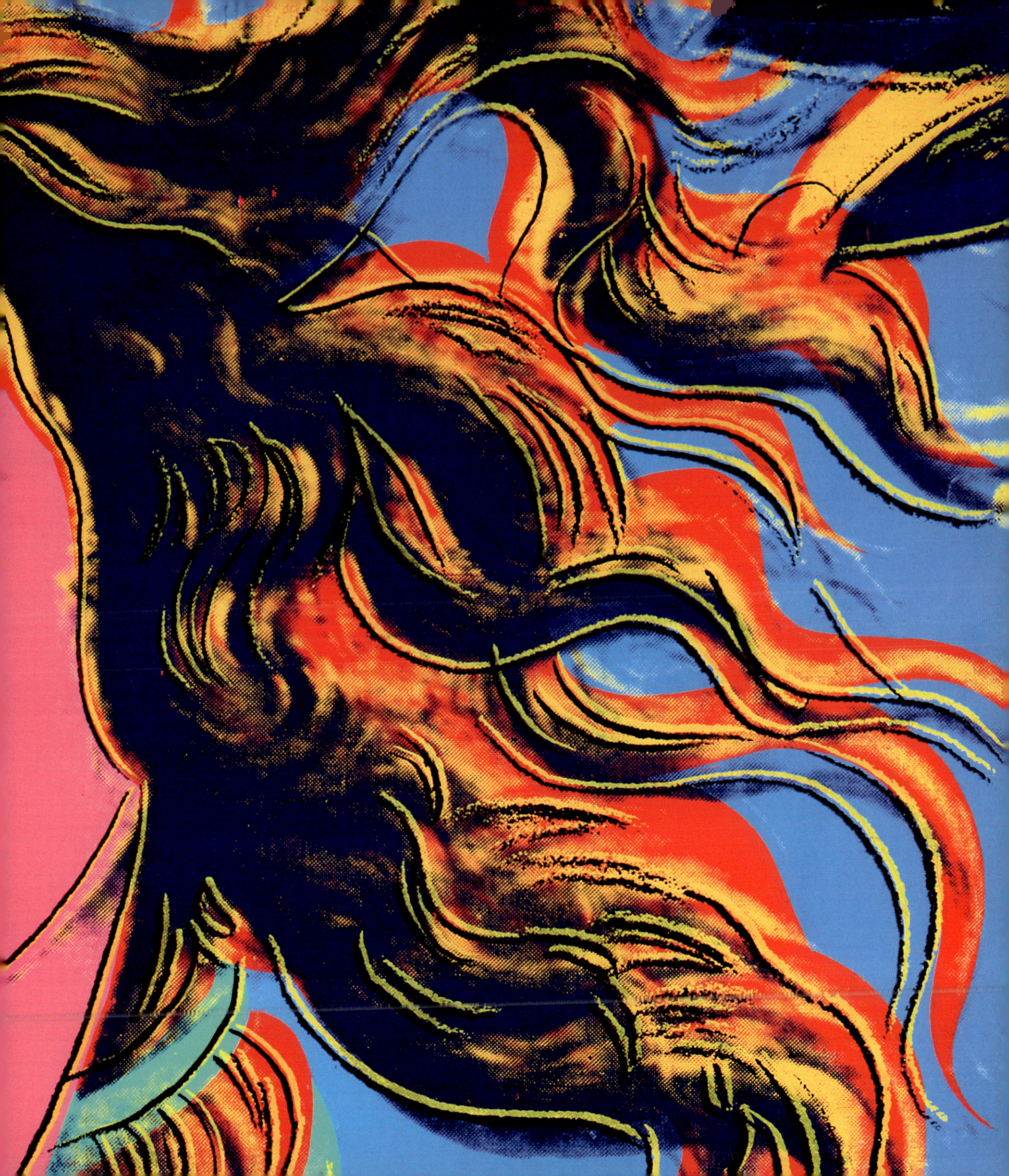

TOMOKO NAGAO (b.1976)

Botticelli – The Birth of Venus with Baci, Esselunga, Barilla, PSP and Easyjet, 2012 (2014)

Digital image, exhibition print, 3 panels,
150 × 105 cm each
Private collection

Tomoko Nagao's paraphrase of Botticelli's Venus stands on a gaming console floating in a sea of Italian consumer goods, while the sky is crowded with the planes of a budget airline that facilitates cheap access to Italian products and works of art. In the 2014 version of this print, there is a tablet to the left of the image showing a film uploaded to YouTube of the catastrophic tsunami off the eastern coast of Honshu in 2011.

The emphatic flatness of the image and its clearly defined outlines, derived from the visual language of the postmodern Japanese art movement Superflat, here seem like an extreme version of the style of the Renaissance master, which worked on similar principles. This affinity is unintentionally reminiscent of the way in which Japanese art of the Edo period was perceived in Europe during the second half of the nineteenth century, around the same time as Botticelli was rediscovered. Superflat routinely employs the aesthetic concept of 'kawaii', known in Europe primarily through Japanese animated films, using it to comment on Japanese consumer culture. Nagao's adaptations of Old Master paintings are intended as an ironic reference to the economic mechanisms of power in the production of images, where Renaissance patrons like the Medici have now been replaced by the creative directors of major brands. RR

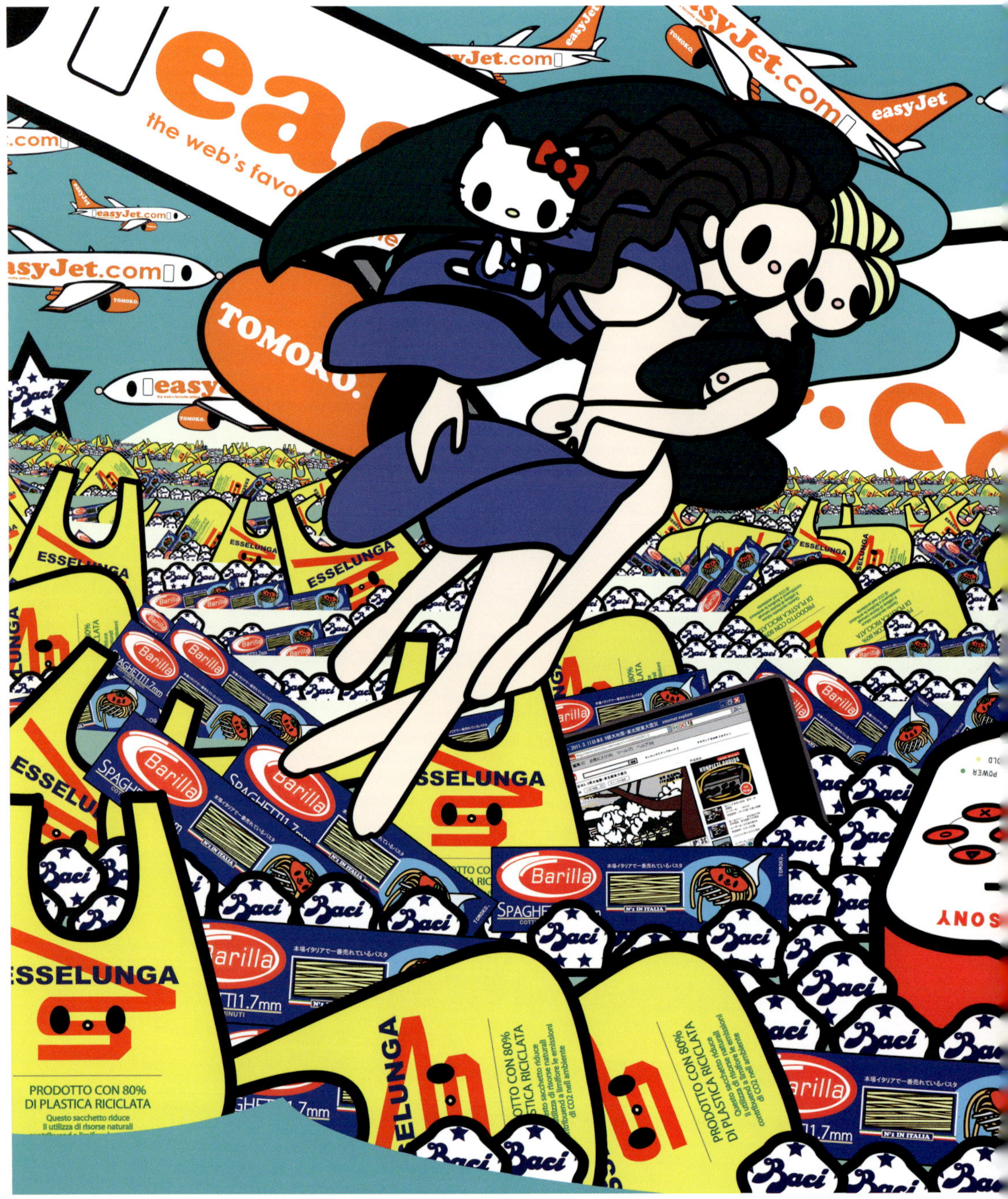

LITERATURE
Gancitano 2012

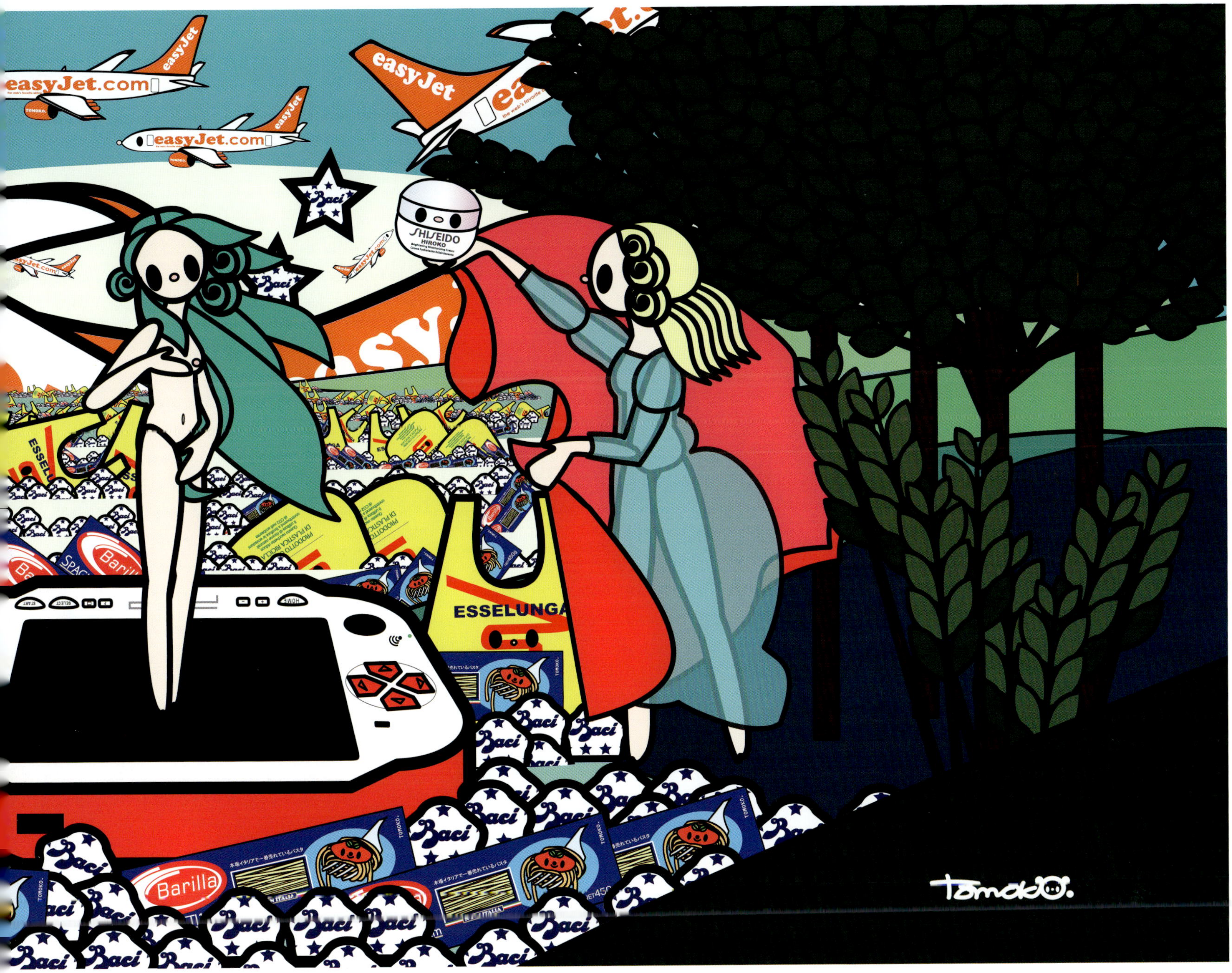
easyJet.com
easyJet
Baci
SHISEIDO
HIROKO
ESSELUNGA
Barilla
Tomoko.

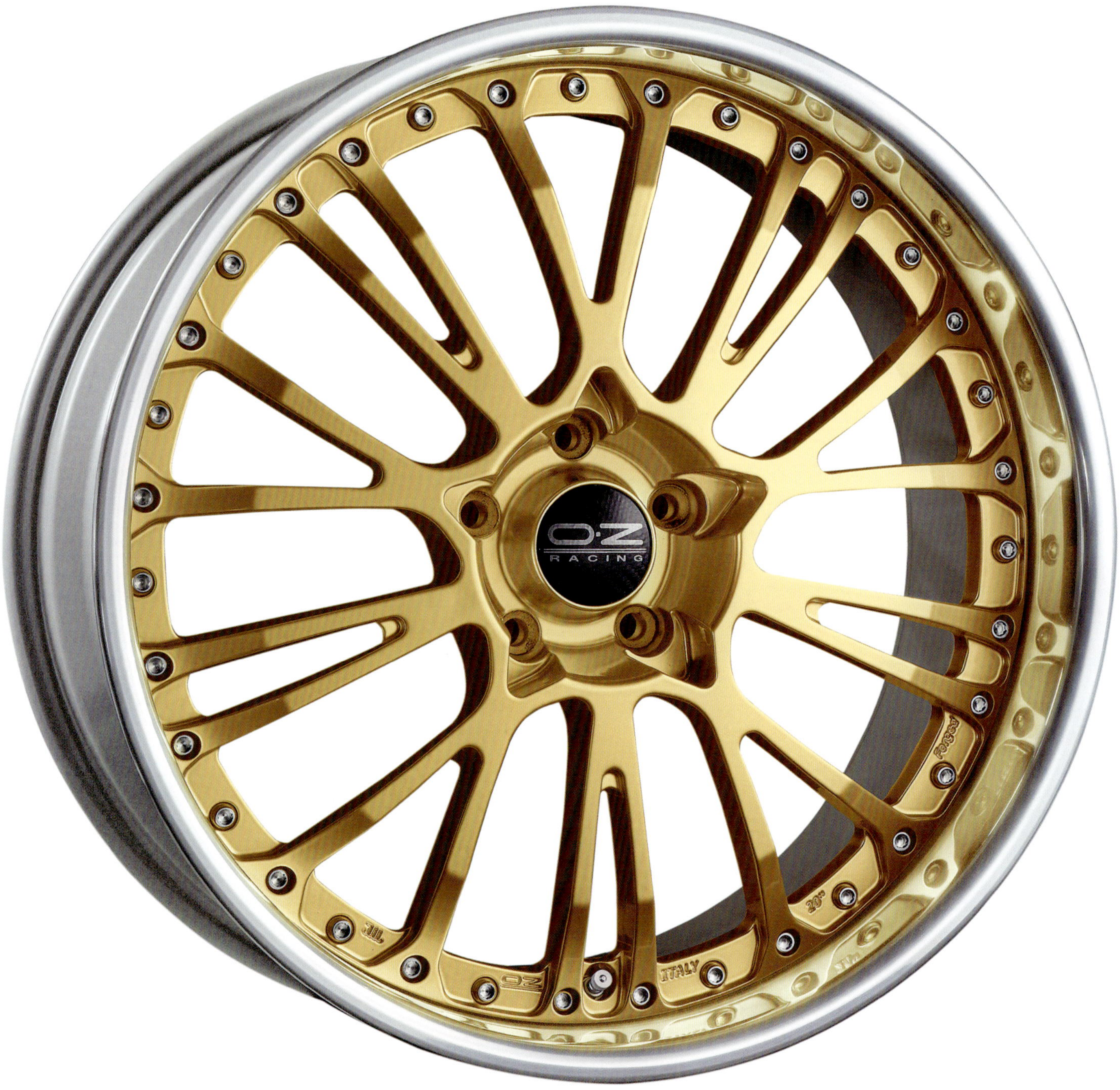
O·Z
RACING

2

OZ RACING S.p.A (Italy)

OZ Botticelli III Wheel, designed in 2006 and currently in production

Three-part light alloy multi-spoke wheel for motor vehicles, consisting of spokes, inner rim and outer rim; aluminium and stainless steel, carbon fibre hub cap, diameter 55 cm
Victoria and Albert Museum, London
(NCOL.518-2015)

This object is a star-spoke wheel from the 'Botticelli' product line, developed over several years by the Italian manufacturer OZ. It consists of ten main spokes that radiate outwards, each pair forming an alternately wider or narrower 'V' shape. The forged flange creates a star-like pattern around the centre, a motif reminiscent of the brooch worn by the leftmost of the Three Graces in Botticelli's *Primavera* (fig. 8). OZ runs a corporate museum that documents its different products and strives to furnish its wheel rims with the aura of original artworks (OZ also has a 'Raffaello' and a 'Michelangelo' line). This product exemplifies the distance possible between art-historical fact and image transfer, which the manufacturer is trying to capture with the name 'Botticelli'. It aims to combine fashionable elegance with sportiness; the reference to Botticelli hints at the Renaissance ideals of modernity and innovation, in an attempt to set itself apart from its competitors. SW

LITERATURE

Rose 2008

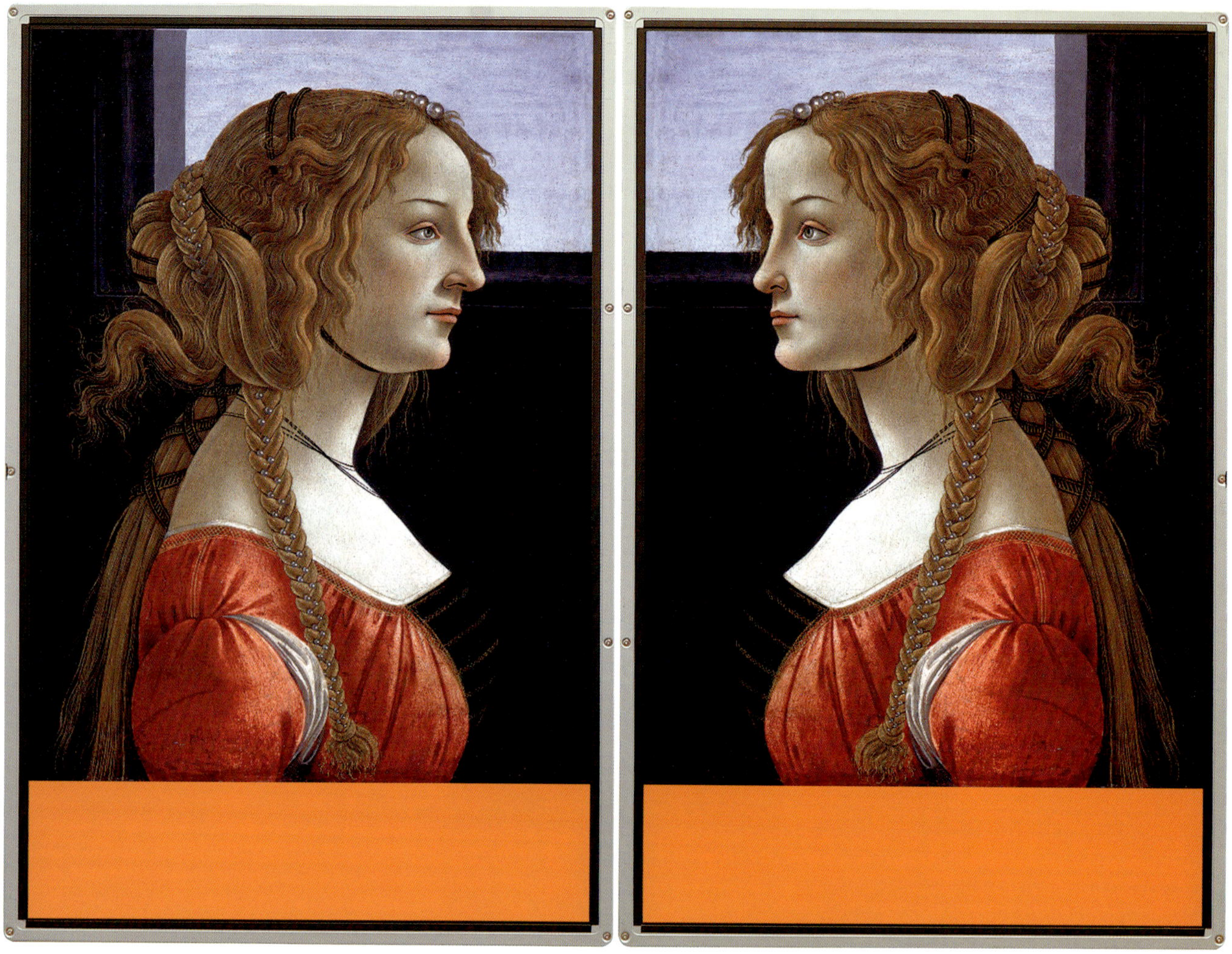

3

MICHAEL JOAQUIN GREY (b.1961)

Between Simonetta, 2011

Computer-generated animation,
two LCD monitors in a Plexiglas case,
68 × 89 cm (edition: 4)
Courtesy of the artist, Sherin Najjar and Carol Fletcher

Michael Joaquin Grey, who studied medicine and genetic engineering alongside his artistic training, often takes the process of perception as his theme. This is the case with *Between Simonetta*, which Grey refers to as a 'generative portrait'. The animation is based on Botticelli's *Ideal Portrait of a Lady* in the Gemäldegalerie, Berlin (cat. 156), known by scholars as the *Portrait of Simonetta Vespucci*. The reproduction is arranged on monitors so that the two profiles face each other. Digitalized algorithms have been placed at ten points – chin, eyes, nose, forehead, mouth and so on – that imperceptibly, slowly but continuously alter the portrait's physiognomic appearance. This reaches such a degree that the face has morphed into a twisted caricature, before it gradually resumes the appearance of Botticelli's original. The artist vividly dissects the topos of feminine beauty, celebrated in art and literature since antiquity, and typical of Botticelli's works in particular. The original emerges for an ephemeral split-second, making the conventions of classical beauty, canonized for centuries, appear improbable and fleeting. SW

LITERATURE

Weppelmann in Berlin 2011–12, pp. 12–23

4

YOUSSEF NABIL (b.1972)

Self-Portrait with Botticelli, Florence, 2009

Photograph, 50 × 75 cm
Courtesy of the artist and Galerie Nathalie Obadia, Paris

Youssef Nabil has written of his self-portrait:

The idea behind my portrait with Botticelli's *Primavera* (fig. 8) began with my personal experience with it; it was the first artwork I knew as a child in Cairo. We had a large, framed reproduction of it in my room in the mid-1970s, and I had this image in front of me as the last thing I saw before I went to sleep, and the first I saw every morning.

I had my own interpretation of it as a kid, but also many dreams about the painting. As the image was in our house for many years, it remained in my mind until I got older and knew more about Botticelli and the real painting. In 2009, I decided to make a self-portrait – sleeping again, after so many years – next to the real *Primavera*, so I wrote to the Uffizi Gallery and the curators there eventually gave me permission to make my work. It was 7:00 am on a Monday, when the museum is usually closed. I wore an Egyptian djellaba to remind me of my country, and slept on the bench next to the painting. It was a very personal moment, where I was once again sleeping in front of the first painting that I ever knew.

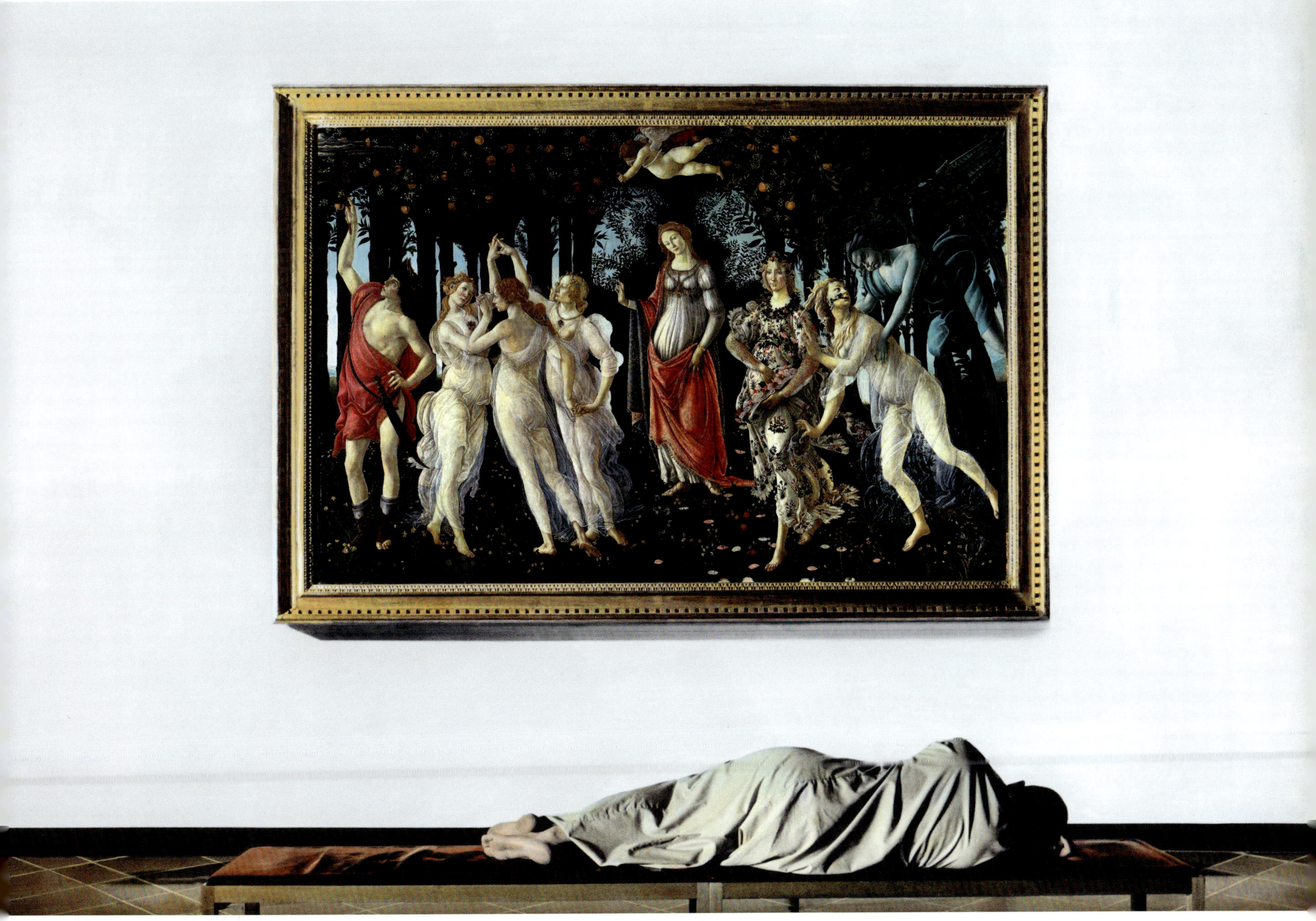

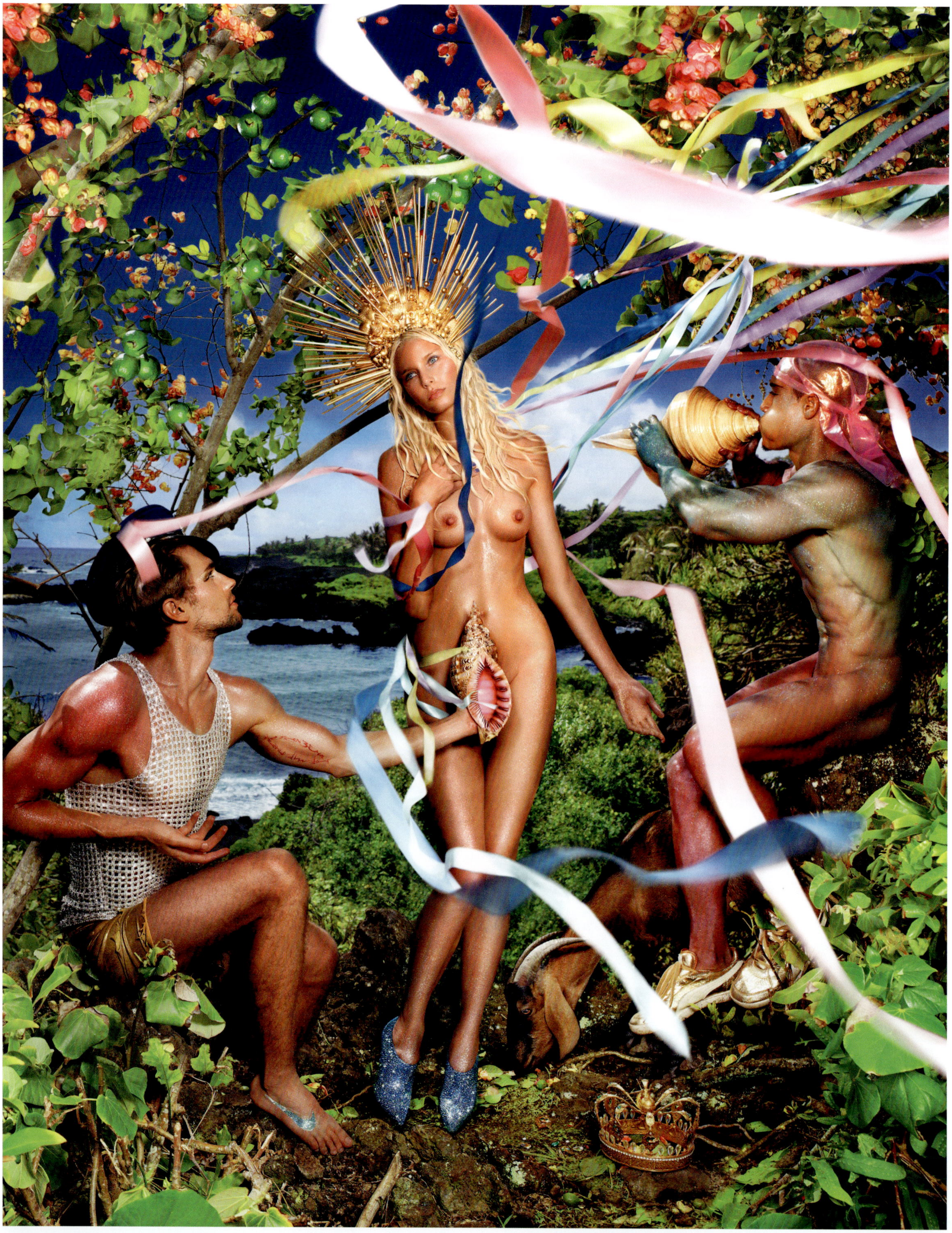

5, 6

DAVID LACHAPELLE (b.1963)

Rebirth of Venus, 2009

C-print, 241.3 × 182.88 cm (from an edition of three)
Private collection

Rape of Africa, 2009

C-print, 132.1 × 304.8 cm (from an edition of five)
Private collection
BERLIN ONLY

The American photographer, film-maker and video artist David LaChapelle is best known for his large-format C-print editions. His images, often conceived as series, play with photographic genres like documentary or fashion photography. LaChapelle's works often contain references to Old Master paintings and Renaissance sculptures; above all those of Michelangelo.

Twice he has turned to Botticelli. In his version of the *Birth of Venus* (fig. 10) the goddess has been transformed into a blonde model. Flanked by two muscular men, Venus's genitals are covered by a conch shell held by the figure on the left. Whereas Botticelli's goddess of love alights from her shell like some distant, unapproachable apparition, LaChapelle uses the shell ironically, as the locus of the physical connection between men and women.

Rape of Africa employs similarly glaring colours, drawing on the painting *Venus and Mars* in the National Gallery, London (fig. 4). In place of Venus is the supermodel Naomi Campbell, evidently identified as a personification of Africa. LaChapelle remarked of the idea behind this image, 'The use of Africa in my photograph is about it being the cradle of civilization, the idea of Mother Earth and Mother Africa. The production of gold in Africa is destroying both the society and the country itself'. SW

LITERATURE
Wiggins in Amsterdam and Los Angeles 2009, pp. 9–21; Oliver 2010; Toronto 2010, pp. 40–1; Prague 2011, p. 18

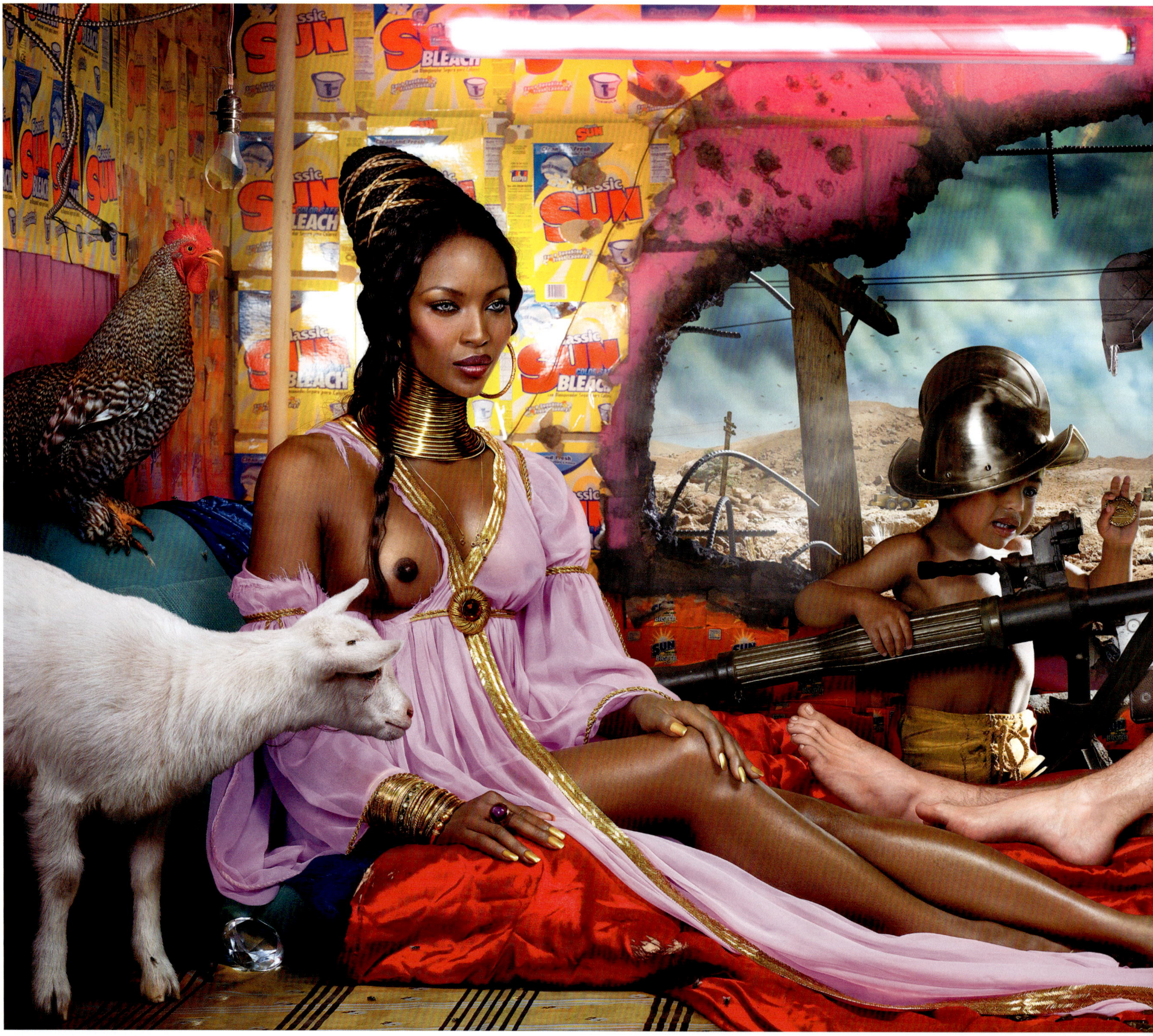
Classic
SUN
BLEACH

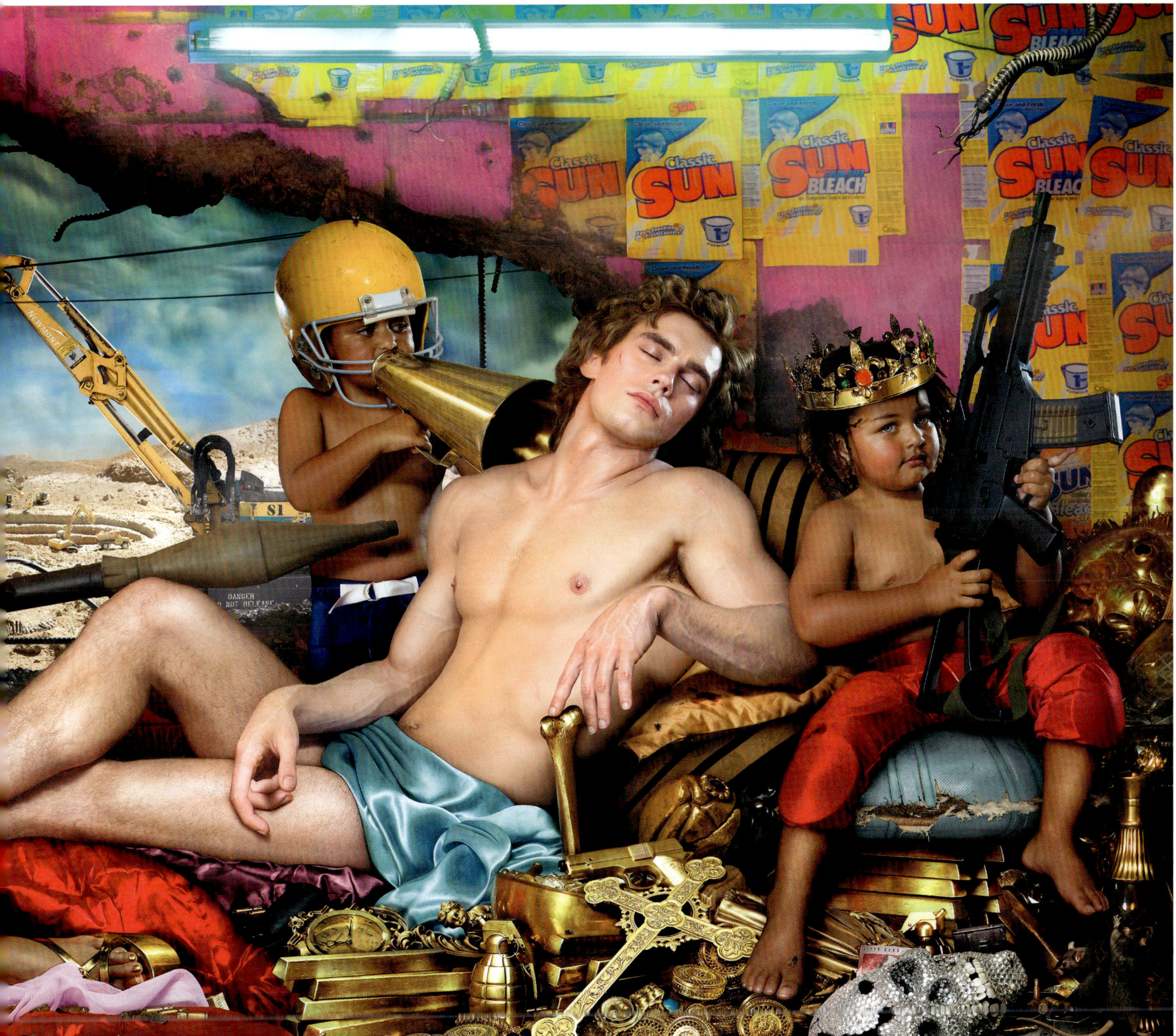
SUN
Classic
SUN
BLEACH

7

VIK MUNIZ (b.1961)

The Birth of Venus, after Botticelli (Pictures of Junk), 2007

C-print (triptych), 235 × 390 cm (multiple)
Courtesy of the artist and Pace Gallery, New York

LITERATURE
Bologna 2007, pp. 430–4; Roberts 2007, p. 161; Tel Aviv 2014

The Brazilian artist Vik Muniz incorporates a variety of materials into his work, ranging from food (*Pictures of Chocolate*) to soil (*Earthworks*) to diamonds. For the series *Pictures of Junk* he began with three-dimensional collections of industrial and domestic waste, which were arranged around a large-scale contour drawing. These assemblages were photographed from a distance, producing images where the three-dimensional elements create very specific sculptural perspective effects. Venus, the goddess of beauty, represents Western culture (the Renaissance) *par excellence*. Muniz depicts her standing in her shell, but the sea from which she emerges has become a carpet of discarded consumer goods, primarily technological junk and plastic containers. Muniz humorously takes as his theme the ironic ambivalence of collective waste production as, on the one hand, a cultural threat and, on the other, global common ground between different societies and political systems. SW

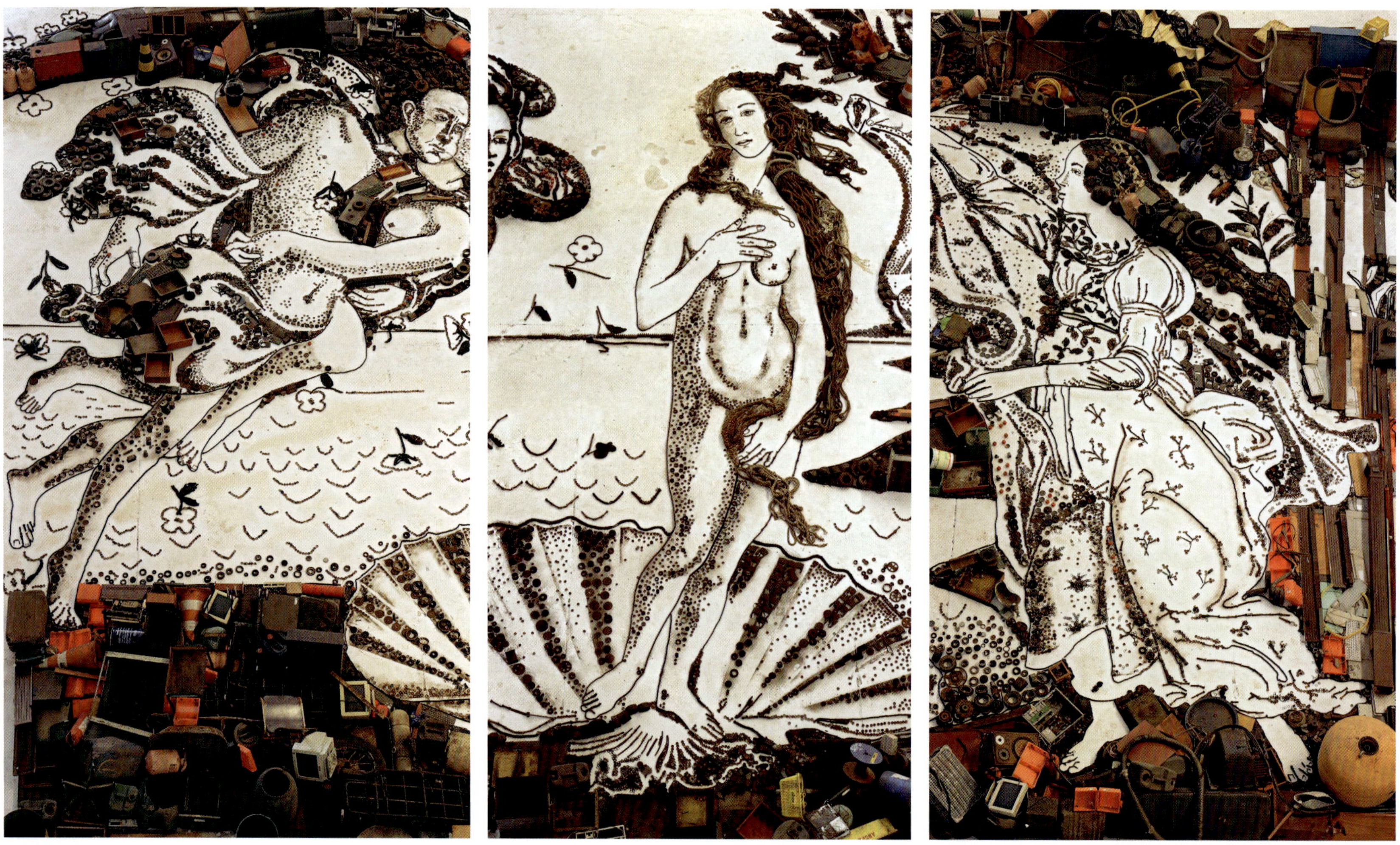

8

YIN XIN (b.1959)

Venus, after Botticelli, 2008

Oil and acrylic on canvas, 130 × 162 cm
Guillaume Duhamel, Duhamel Fine Art, Paris

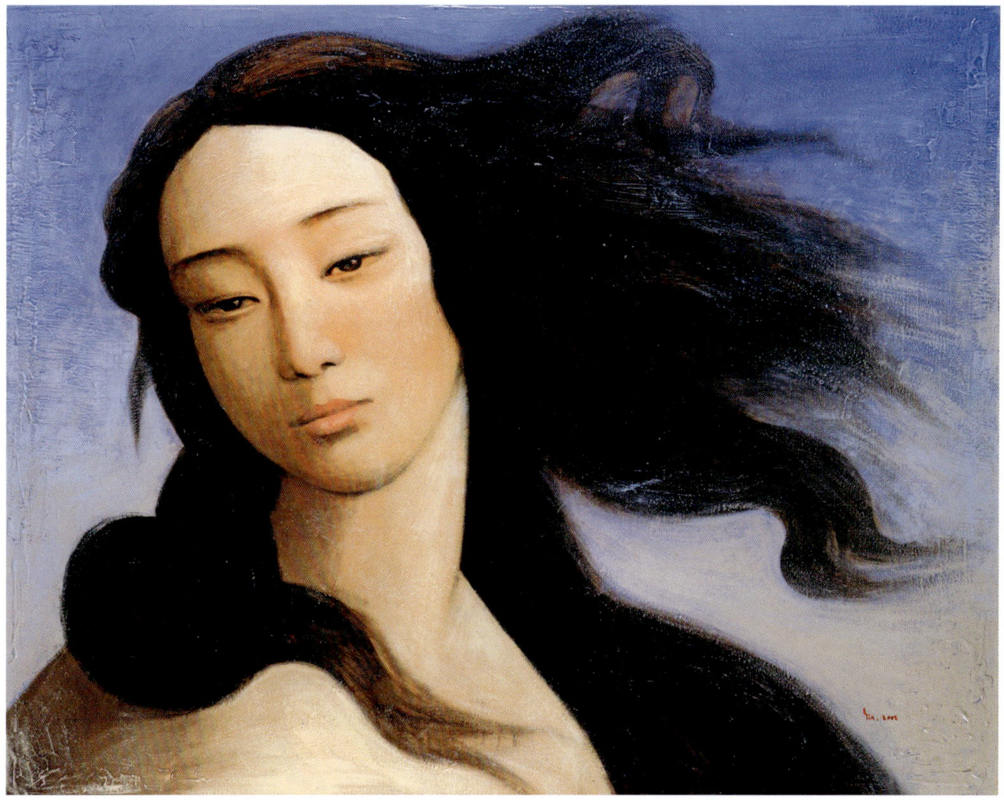

The hallmark of Chinese artist Yin Xin's work is the way in which he adds Chinese characteristics to traditional Western painting. He is especially interested in works by famous painters, such as Botticelli's *Birth of Venus* (fig. 10), which have attained the status of canonical, universally recognized masterpieces in the West.

The canvas exhibited here depicts the primary figure reduced to her head and shoulders, her black (instead of blonde) hair blowing in the wind. The shape of her eyes is also unmistakeably Asian. The artist has said that he reworks the Old Masters of European art largely out of a sense of wonder and fascination. Nonetheless, Yin Xin's work, in its combination of Western and Far Eastern elements, stresses how much our perception of a cultural artefact is dependent on and determined by the culture that produced it. At the same time, Yin Xin takes his prototypes – and ultimately the viewer – out of their self-reflexive loop, opening up new perspectives.
SW

LITERATURE
Shanghai 2005

9

BILL VIOLA (b.1951)

The Path, panel 2 from
Going Forth By Day, 2002

Five-part video and sound installation, colour video projection with four channels of sound, 36 minutes
Projected image size: 2.28 × 10.97 m, edition 1/2
Commissioned by Deutsche Bank AG in consultation with the Solomon R. Guggenheim Foundation for the Deutsche Guggenheim, Berlin (2005.116)

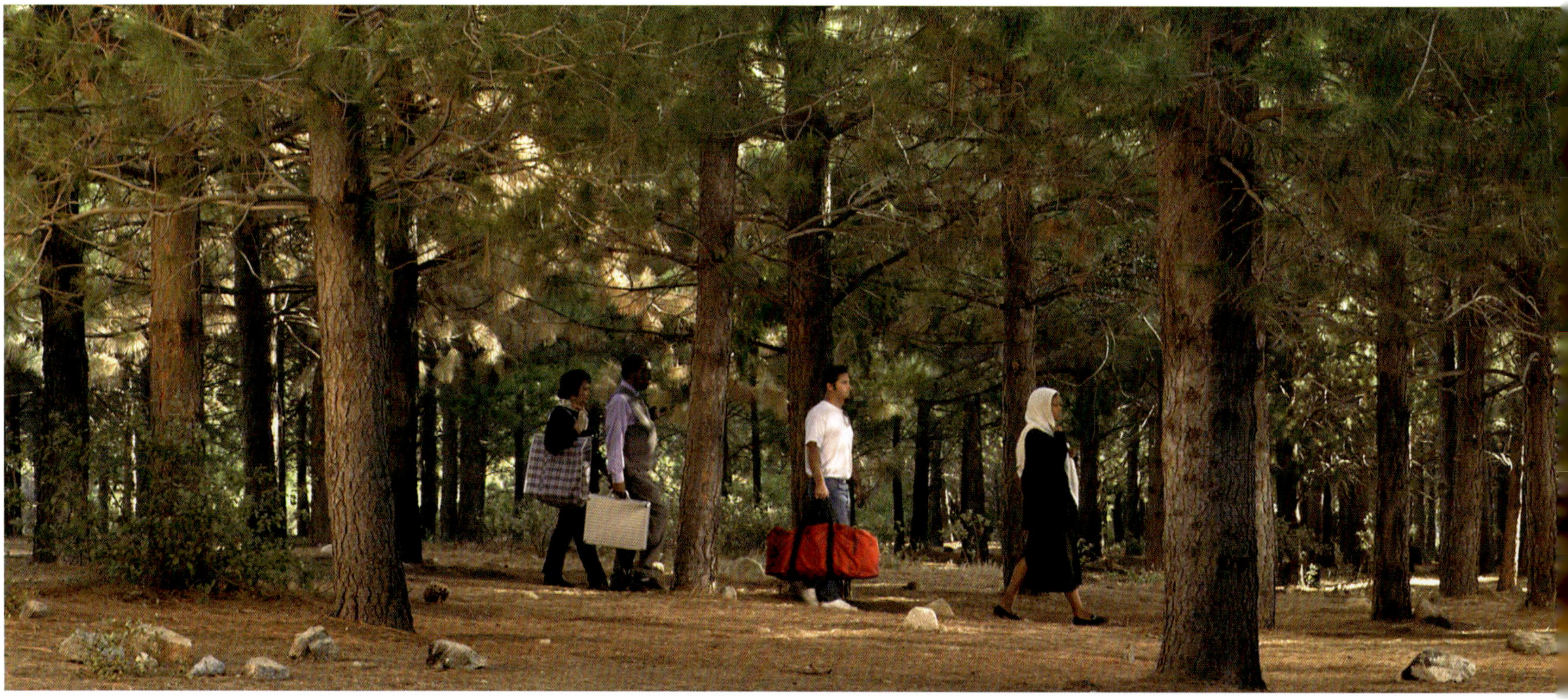

The American video and installation artist Bill Viola is a pioneer of video art, and one of the most significant contemporary artists. From 1970 to 1974 he lived in Florence, where he encountered the art of the Italian Renaissance. In his installation *Going Forth By Day* – the title borrowed from the ancient Egyptian Book of the Dead – Viola takes as his theme fundamental human experiences. The individual sequences function like the frescoes by Giotto and Signorelli he had studied in Assisi and Orvieto. In *The Deluge* a flood of water bursts forth from a house as panic-stricken figures flee to safety before it, contrasting ordinary human existence with the destructive power of nature. In *Fire Birth* a floating figure emerges from watery flames – existence is interpreted as perpetual creation and decay. *The Voyage* is a scene in which a house is set above a wide lake. A boat is slowly loaded with household furniture as a couple care for a dying man whose wife waits on the shore below. The need for stability and for escape or change becomes a metaphor for human existence. In *First Light*, rescue workers fall asleep on the edge of a small pond in the desert, thereby missing a celestial occurrence: a young man rises from the water towards the sky.

Religious metaphors and ideas are implicit in these compositions, playing on the subject of this world and the next. This is especially true for the largest, frieze-like scene *The Path*. According to an annotation in Viola's sketchbook, which contains preparatory ideas for this large-scale video piece, the artist was inspired by a scene from Botticelli's *Story of Nastagio degli Onesti* (fig. 34) for this sequence, which is presented as an endless loop. One striking formal parallel between the two works is the way in which visual space is structured, with the limbless trees positioned some distance apart, as well as the similar proportions of the figures and the tree trunks. Evidently, in his search for a landscape appropriate to the depiction of the eternal path of humanity, Viola turned again to an example from the Italian Renaissance. SW

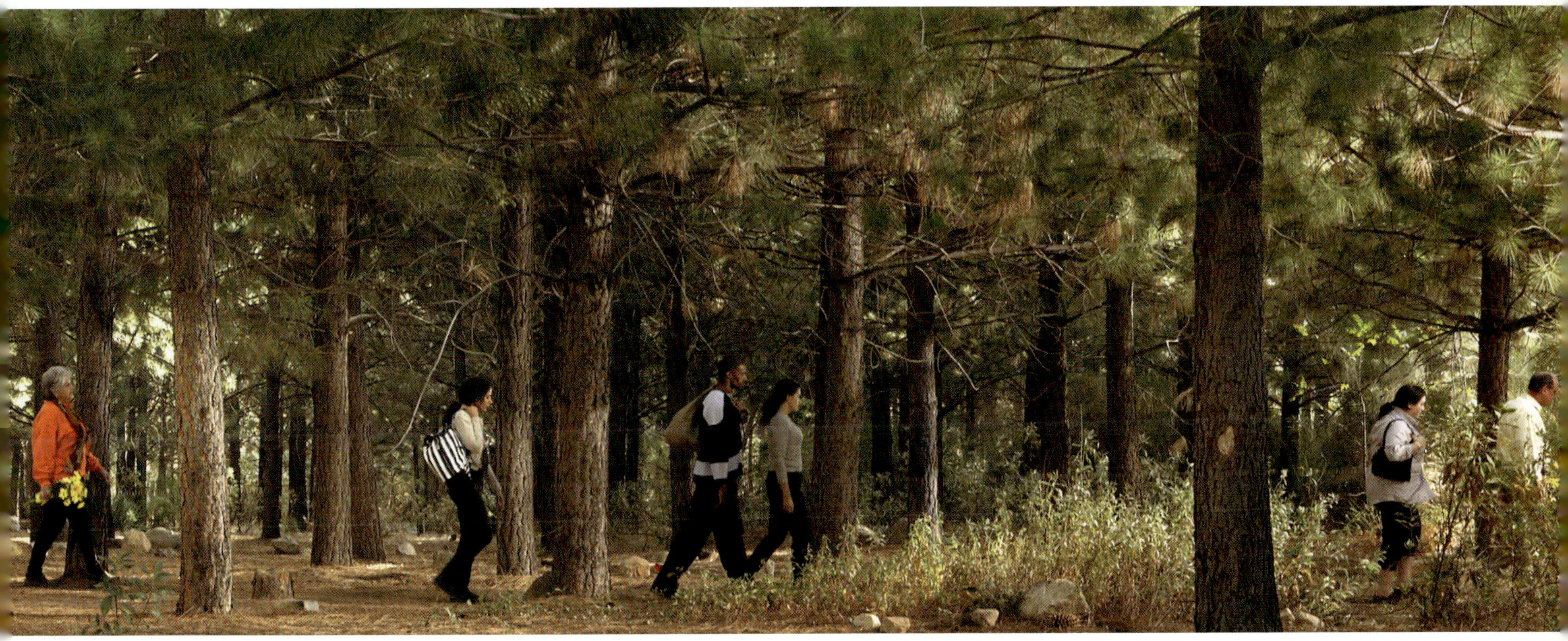

LITERATURE
Berlin 2002

10

ORLAN (b.1947)

I'm reading, he's operating on me, 5th Surgery Performance titled 'Operation Opera', 6 July 1991, 1991

Colour photographs, each 110 × 165 cm
Courtesy of the artist and Michel Rein, Paris/Brussels

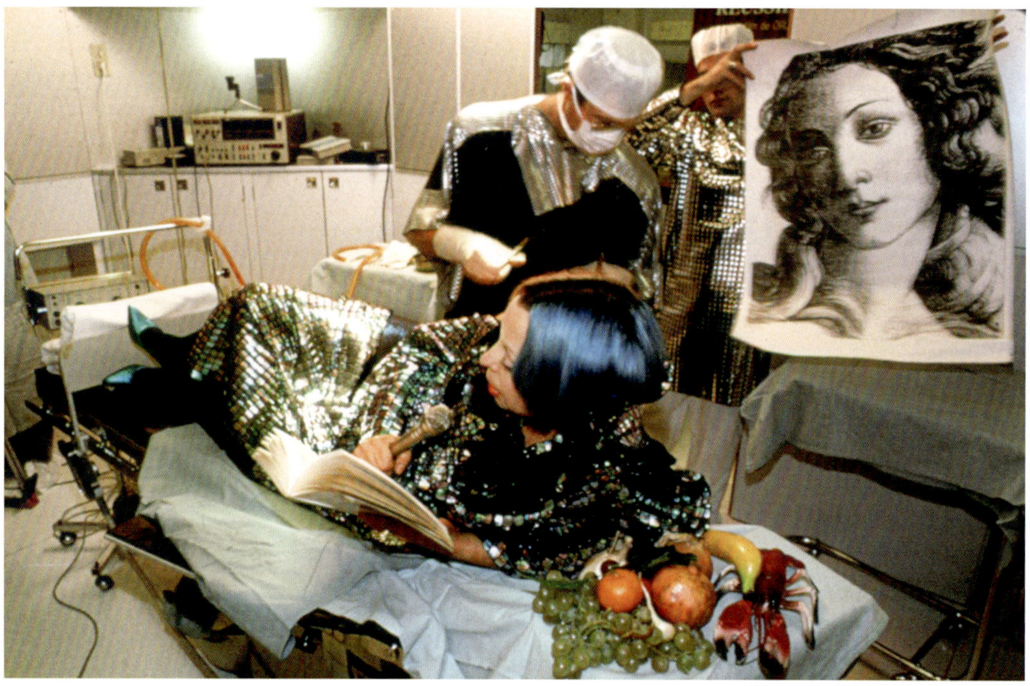

The French artist ORLAN, born Mireille Suzanne Francette Porte, is a primary exponent of body art. She caused an international furore with several performances in which she used her own body as a medium for her art, sometimes in extremely radical ways.

Between 1990 and 1993 ORLAN underwent a total of nine cosmetic procedures. In July 1990, the artist brought a large-scale piece of card with her into the operating theatre as a prop. It depicted a life-size, cut out, nude photograph of ORLAN at the age of 28. The image was taken from the performance *Occasional Strip-tease* (cat. 24). ORLAN's pose was a direct reference to Botticelli's painting of Venus, the goddess of love. On the one hand, most cosmetic procedures are carried out to reverse the ageing process – erasing wrinkles, for instance (hence the photograph of ORLAN as a slim young woman). The performance thus evokes an idealized lost youthful body. A collective, socially rooted ideal type is also referenced in the pose, which recalls that of Botticelli's Venus. These performative aspects lend the piece a sense of the surreal, theatrical and occasionally grotesque. Parts of the video in which ORLAN appears onscreen with bloodied features, or with areas of skin pierced by surgical implements, repel the viewer: here, ideals of beauty are framed as injuries. It is because these surgical performances are so far from Botticelli's model of divine beauty that their effect is so powerful and revelatory. SW

LITERATURE

Paris 2004, pp. 122–39

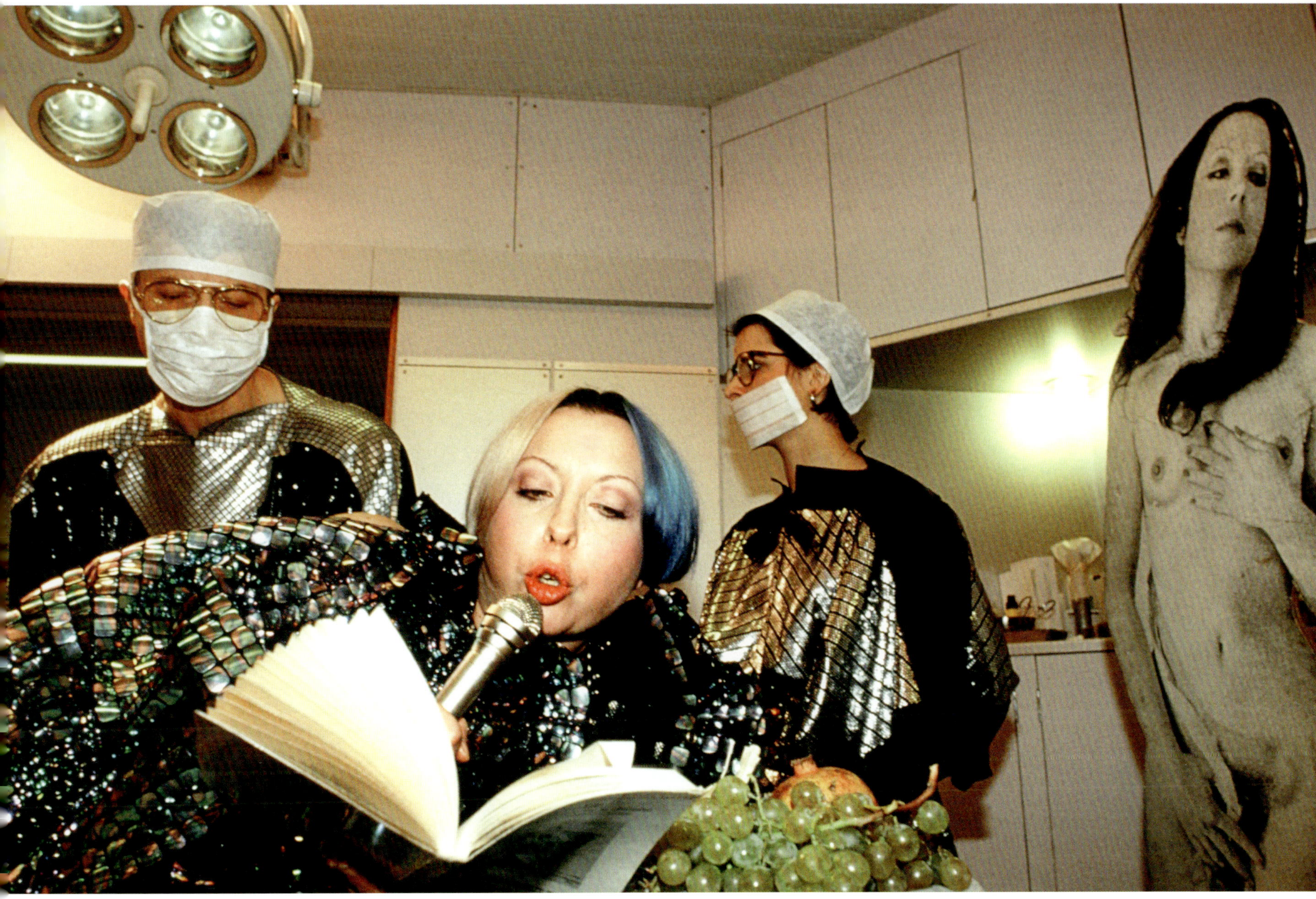

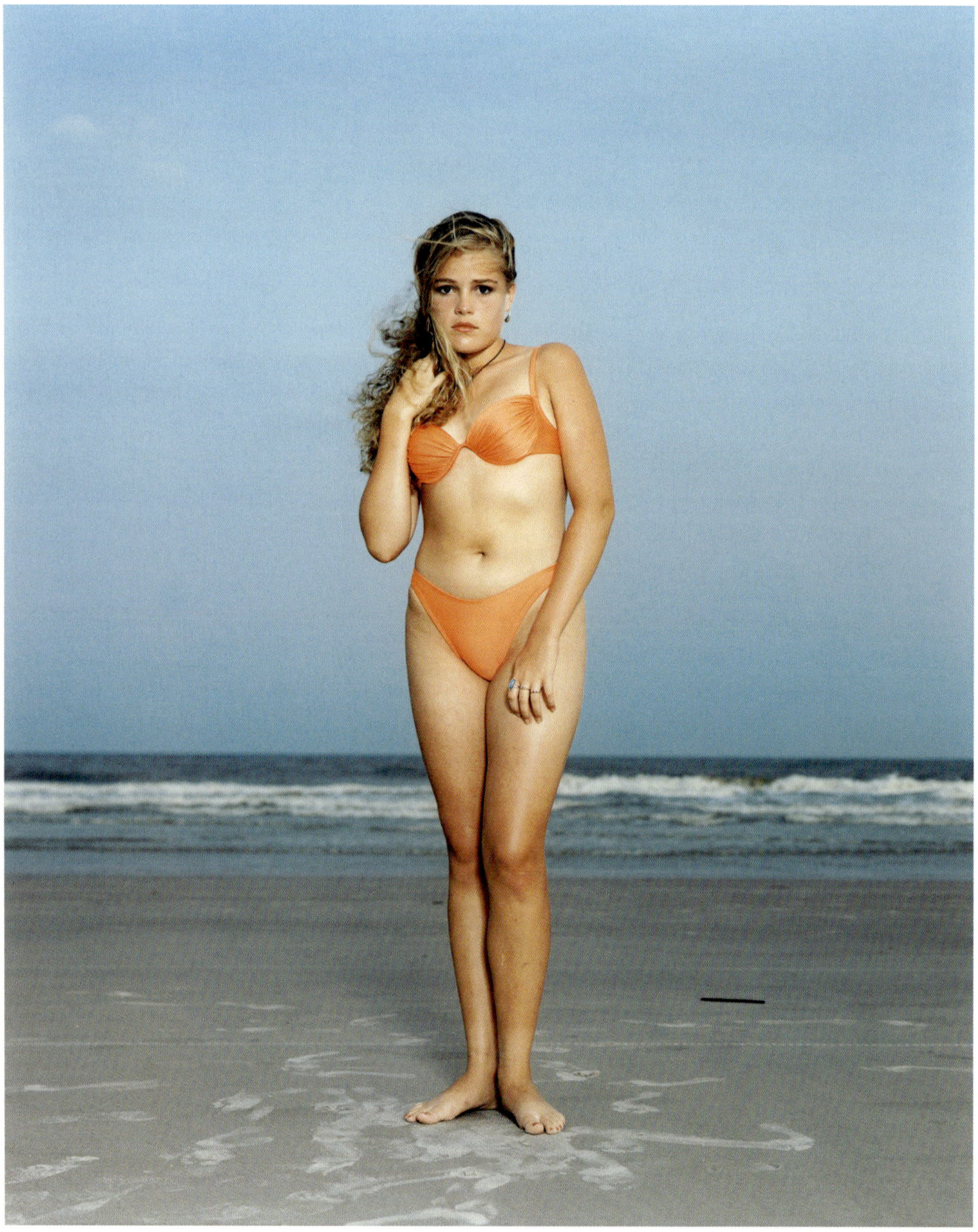

11, 12

RINEKE DIJKSTRA (b.1959)

Hilton Head Island, South Carolina, USA, June 24, 1992, 1992

C-print, 117 × 94 cm
Galerie Marian Goodman, Paris

Kolobrzeg, Poland, July 26, 1992, 1992

C-print, 137 × 107 cm
Tate, London (P78330)

Rineke Dijkstra lives in the Netherlands, and works with video and photography. The *Beach Portraits* are a thematic series in which the individual images are titled according to where they were photographed. The girl in the green swimsuit was taken in Kolobrzeg, a spa town on the Baltic coast in Poland. The blonde girl in a bikini, however, was taken at Hilton Head Island on the American Atlantic coast. The artist explores the significance of heritage and nationality for young people, and therefore necessarily the influence of personality and society. Dijkstra remarked that she didn't explicitly intend to reference Botticelli in the *Beach Portraits*, and Erin Kinney, who posed for the Hilton Head photograph at the age of fourteen, recently said of the shoot, 'It was very windy. My hair kept being blown into my face, until I held it back. The *Venus* pose that many people see in the image was accidental.' Nonetheless, the resemblance to Botticelli's famous depiction strikes almost everyone who comments on the series; it is clear just how deeply this visual model has become embedded in our collective memory. SW

LITERATURE

Phillips in San Francisco and New York 2012, pp. 13–28; Friedewald 2014, pp. 58–9

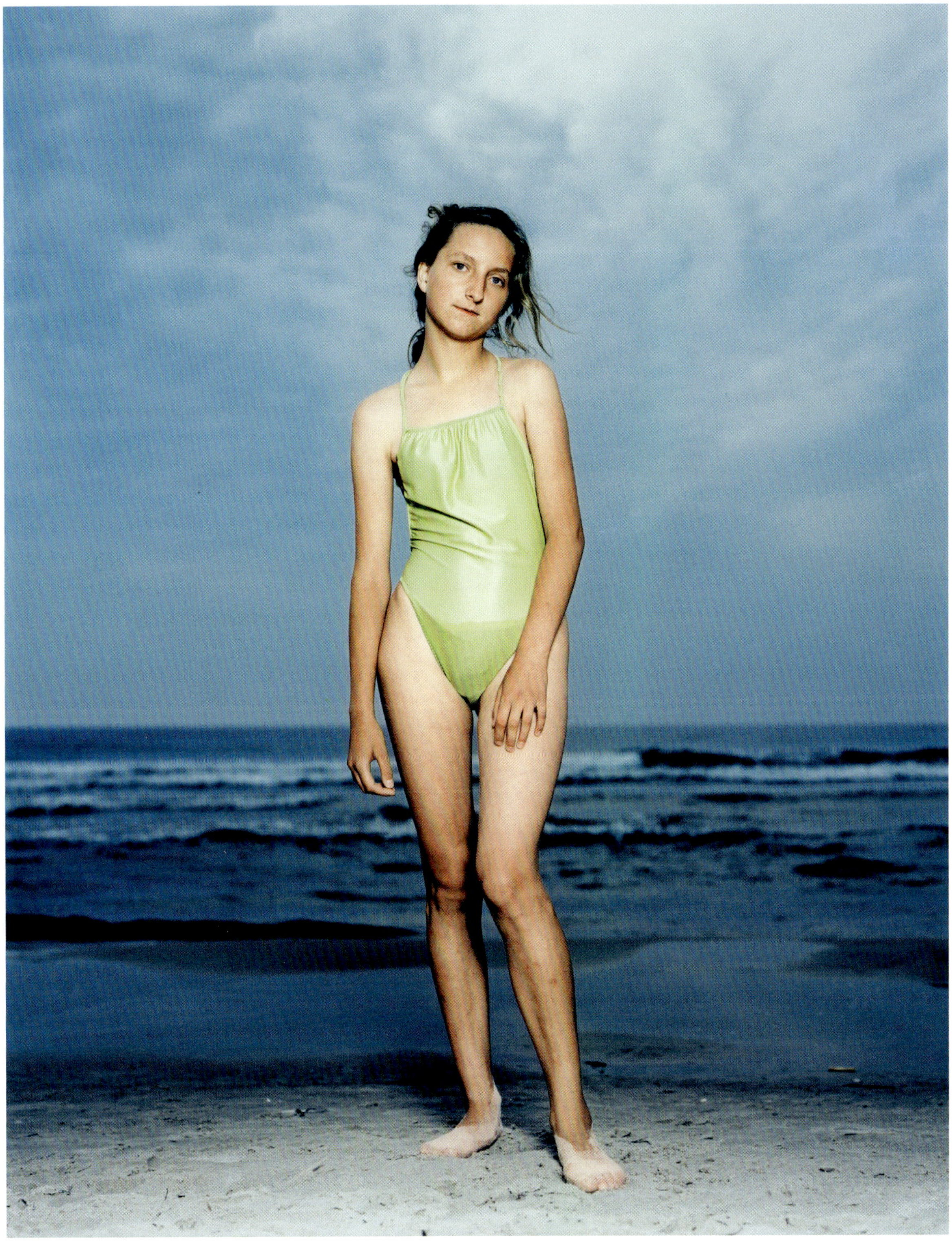

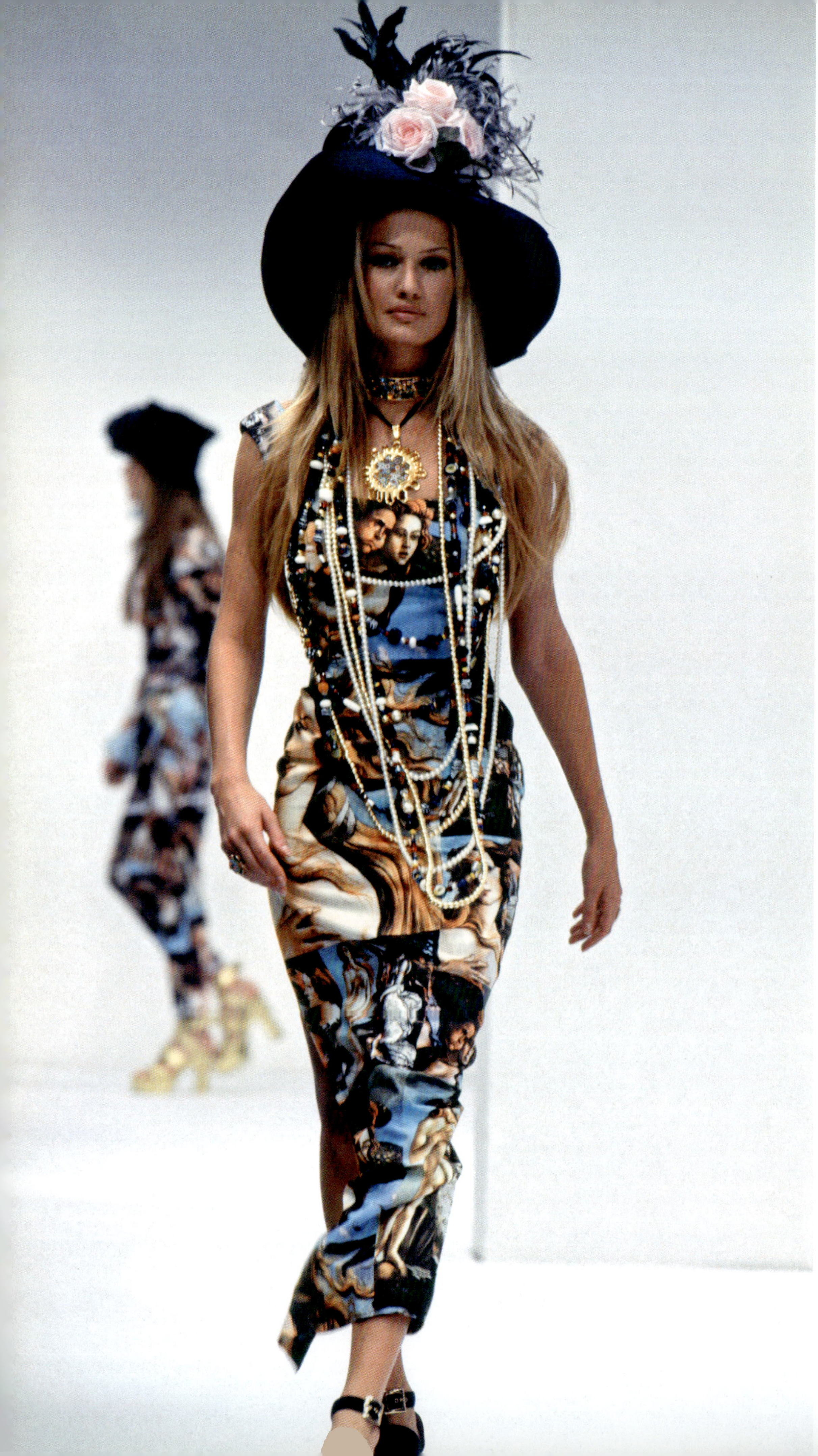

13, 14

DOLCE & GABBANA

(DOMENICO DOLCE, b.1958;
STEFANO GABANNA, b.1962)

Venus Dress: Look 15,
Spring/Summer 1993

Cotton and viscose,
145 cm (length) × 65 cm (waist)
Dolce & Gabbana Estate

Trouser Suit: Look 13,
Spring/Summer 1993

Cotton and viscose,
75 cm (blazer length), 50 cm (vest length),
110 cm (trouser length) × 70 cm (trouser waist)
Dolce & Gabbana Estate

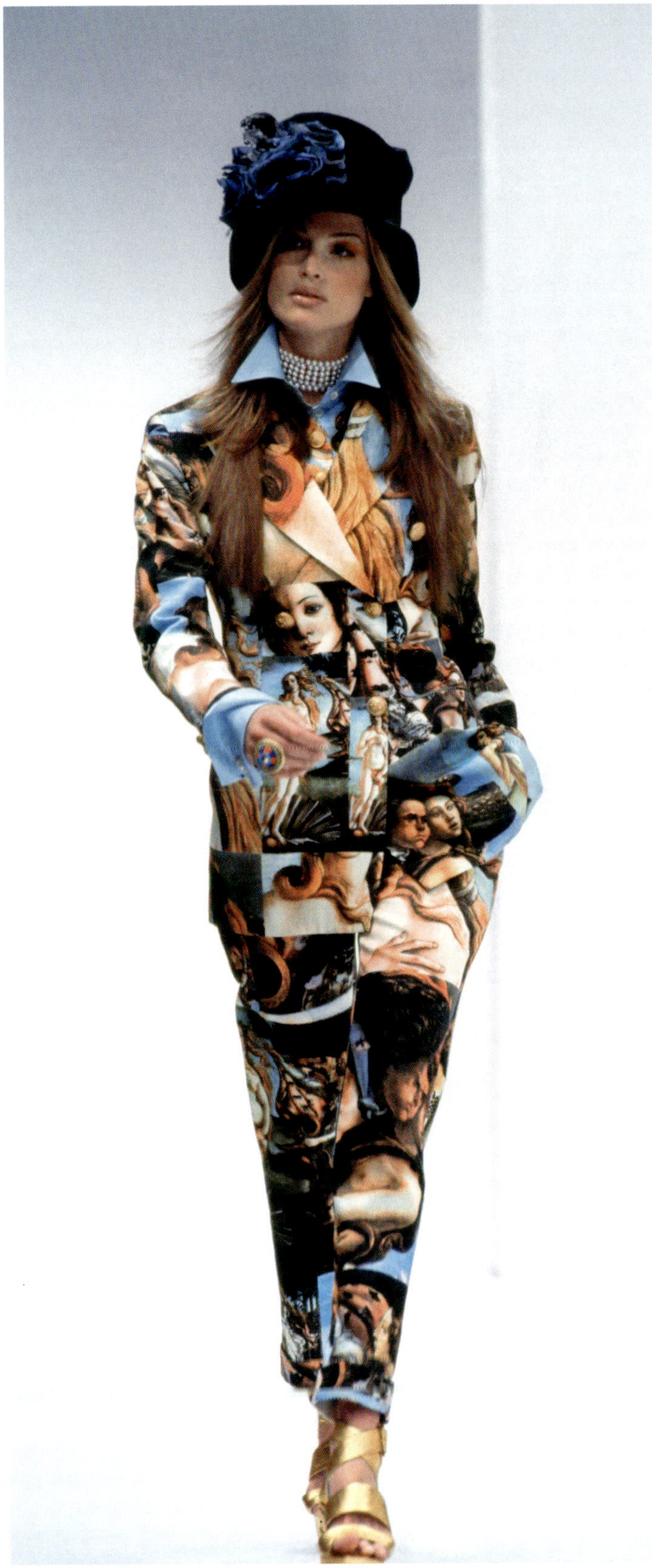

In a logical progression from previous seasons in which the designers had taken designs from the 1950s and 1960s as their source, Dolce & Gabbana's 1993 Spring/Summer collection was inspired by the 'hippy' or 'gypsy' look of the 1970s. The result was a dense layering of fabric, flowers, ribbons and exotic accessories.

These two outfits from that collection incorporate layers of photo-printed sections from the face and body of the goddess in Botticelli's *Birth of Venus* (fig. 10) as a pattern in the structured form of a trouser suit and in a loose and flowing dress. By fragmenting and reconstructing an image that has come to embody a universal ideal they addressed contemporary concerns of mass culture, femininity and the ongoing search for a new canon of beauty. A third look from the 1993 Spring/Summer collection used the wind-blown drapery of the Three Graces and the figures of Chloris and Zephyr in Botticelli's *Primavera* (fig. 8) in a way that echoed its freely falling fabric.

The enduring impact of this dress was underlined when the pop star Lady Gaga appeared wearing a now vintage Dolce & Gabbana *Venus Dress* during the promotion of her album *ARTPOP* in October 2013 (figs 60, 61). MM

PROVENANCE
Dolce & Gabbana Estate, Milan

LITERATURE
Sozzani 1999, pp. 6–8; Mower 2005, pp. 178, 188, 190

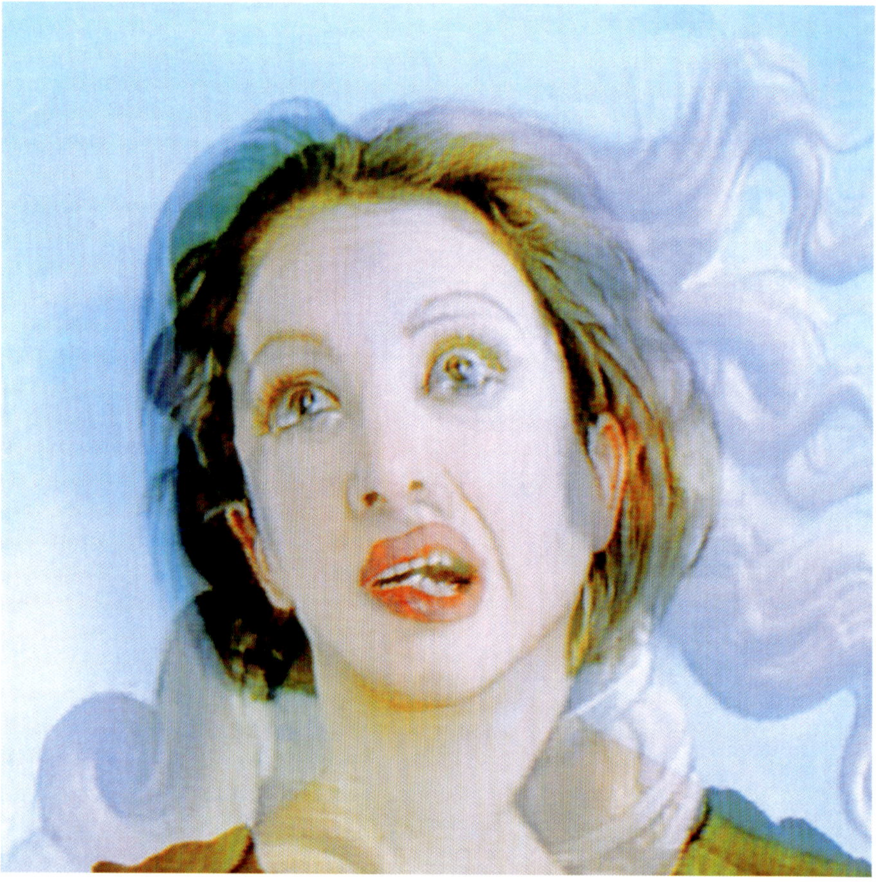

15

ORLAN (b.1947)

Hybridization of Botticelli's Venus and ORLAN's Face, in-between Hybridizations, 1990

Duratrans photograph in light-box with aluminium frame, 49 × 53 cm
Courtesy of the artist and Michel Rein, Paris/Brussels

A feminist approach is central to ORLAN's work, and the piece exhibited here can be seen in this context. It is an extract from a larger complex – titled *Omnipresence* – which the artist has placed in a light-box as an independent work. The larger series consists of 40 portrait-format rectangular metal plates organized in pairs (total size about 1.6 × 17 m), each laminated with a photograph. The bottom row shows ORLAN's face as it morphs into those of various classical beauties. Her features become volatile, dissolving and sometimes even distorting. Botticelli's *Venus* provides the matrix for no. 15. The artist superimposes her appearance on that of Venus, taking as her theme firmly entrenched roles in which processes that transform the body, particularly those to do with ideals of feminine beauty (make-up, clothing, digital manipulation), render the real *persona* unrecognizable by conforming to the conventions of fashion. SW

LITERATURE

Paris 2004, pp. 144–7

16

ROBERT RAUSCHENBERG
(1925–2008)
Swim / ROCI USA (Wax Fire Works), 1990

Silkscreen and wax mixed media on polished aluminium, 185.1 × 245.8 cm
(from an edition of 22)
National Gallery of Art, Washington DC
(1991.76.25)
Gift of Saff Tech Arts and the Artist

LITERATURE
Kotz 1990, pp. 18–22; Washington 1991; New York et al. 1997–9, pp. 581–5; Mattison 2003, pp. 220–59

Robert Rauschenberg's multifaceted oeuvre has eluded attempts to pin it down to any one aspect of postmodernism. 'ROCI' stands for 'Rauschenberg Overseas Cultural Interchange'. Fundamentally, this project is about the possibility of promoting an international understanding of culture.

Swim features a photograph of a sculpture that resembles the central figure in Botticelli's *Birth of Venus*. Alongside other artworks – plaster casts, perhaps – that recall classical antiquity, it appears to be part of an auction. On the left the tangled rigging of a ship can be discerned, and on the right a clothes horse, a towel hanging over it – accessories of daily life. The collage evokes America's European roots and its appropriation of European culture; at the same time its motifs and title refer to the geographical gulf between the continents, connected by the sea. The work transforms Botticelli's Venus into a metaphor for the birth of (American) culture from that of Europe. Rauschenberg had previously incorporated Botticelli's *Birth of Venus* into some of his early works – the collage *Rebus* (1955) for instance. SW

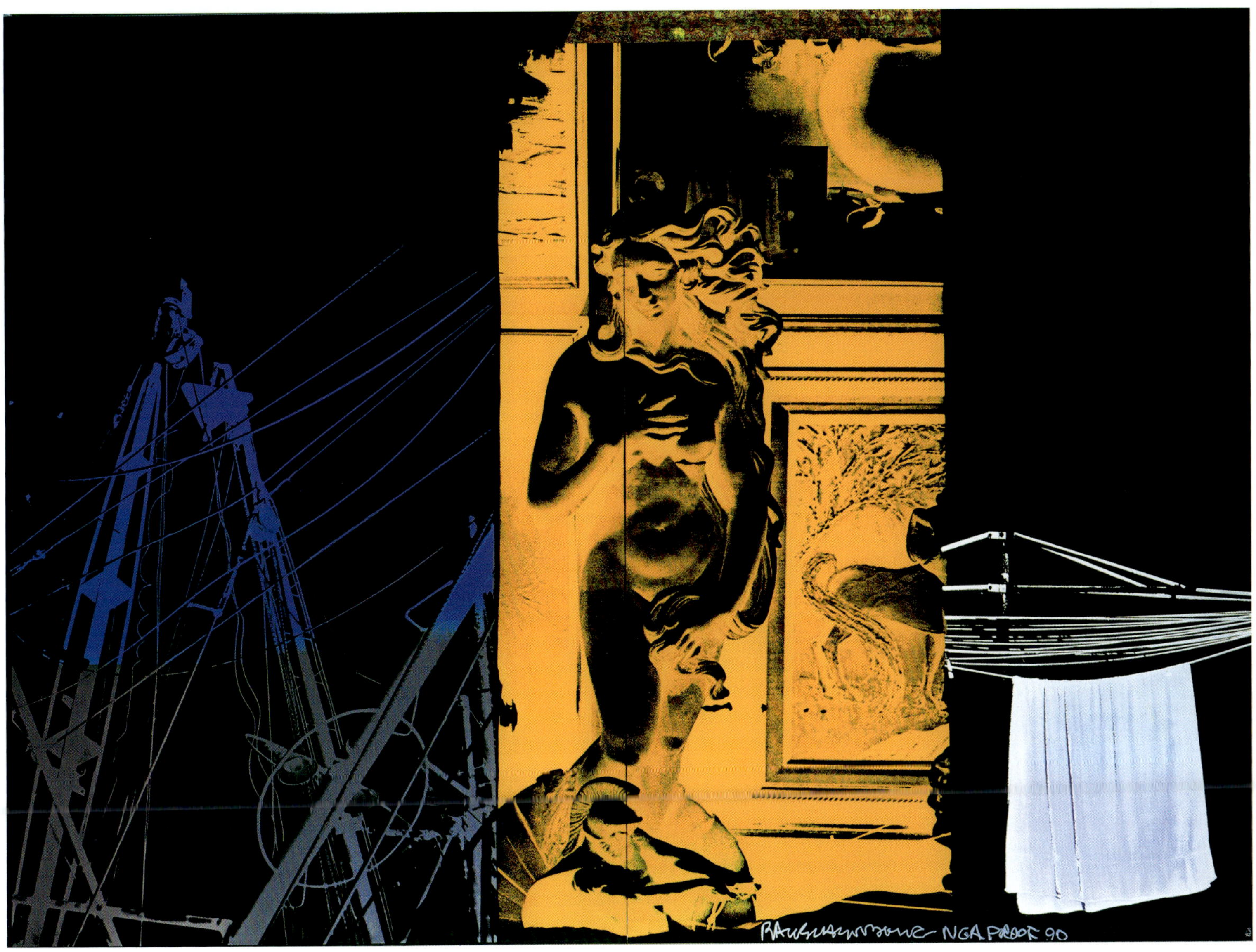

17

CINDY SHERMAN (b.1954)

untitled #225 (*History Portrait* after Botticelli's *Allegorical Portrait of a Lady*, private collection), 1990

C-print, 121.9 × 83.8 cm (from an edition of six)
The Collection of Nina and Frank Moore

Cindy Sherman is one of the most significant representatives of 'appropriation art', a movement that originated in America in the 1970s, in which works by other artists are deliberately and strategically incorporated – through copying or free adaptation – in new works of art. Sherman's *History Portraits* are central works in her oeuvre. She performs paintings by Old Masters as if they were theatre, staging her subjects in similar poses and with appropriate clothing and props, while being careful to emphasize the staged character of her images. This can be seen in her reinterpretations of Botticelli's Amsterdam *Judith* and *Allegorical Portrait of a Lady* (private collection; cat. 158). Sherman did not engage with the Florentine painter's most significant works, but with lesser-known pieces. Her reinterpretations disregard the scale of the originals, making no pretence of staying as close to them as possible. On the contrary, she overtly introduces inaccuracies in the form of prostheses added to the body: the chest and nose in #228, for instance. In this way, Sherman thematizes artistic representation, taking an ironic approach to the status of the originals and their reproduction in her theatrically artificial personification of the Renaissance image. SW

LITERATURE
Sherman 1991; Sherman 1993, pp. 173–91; Blass-Simmen in Berlin 2011–12, pp. 66–9; New York 2012–13, p. 184, no. 244

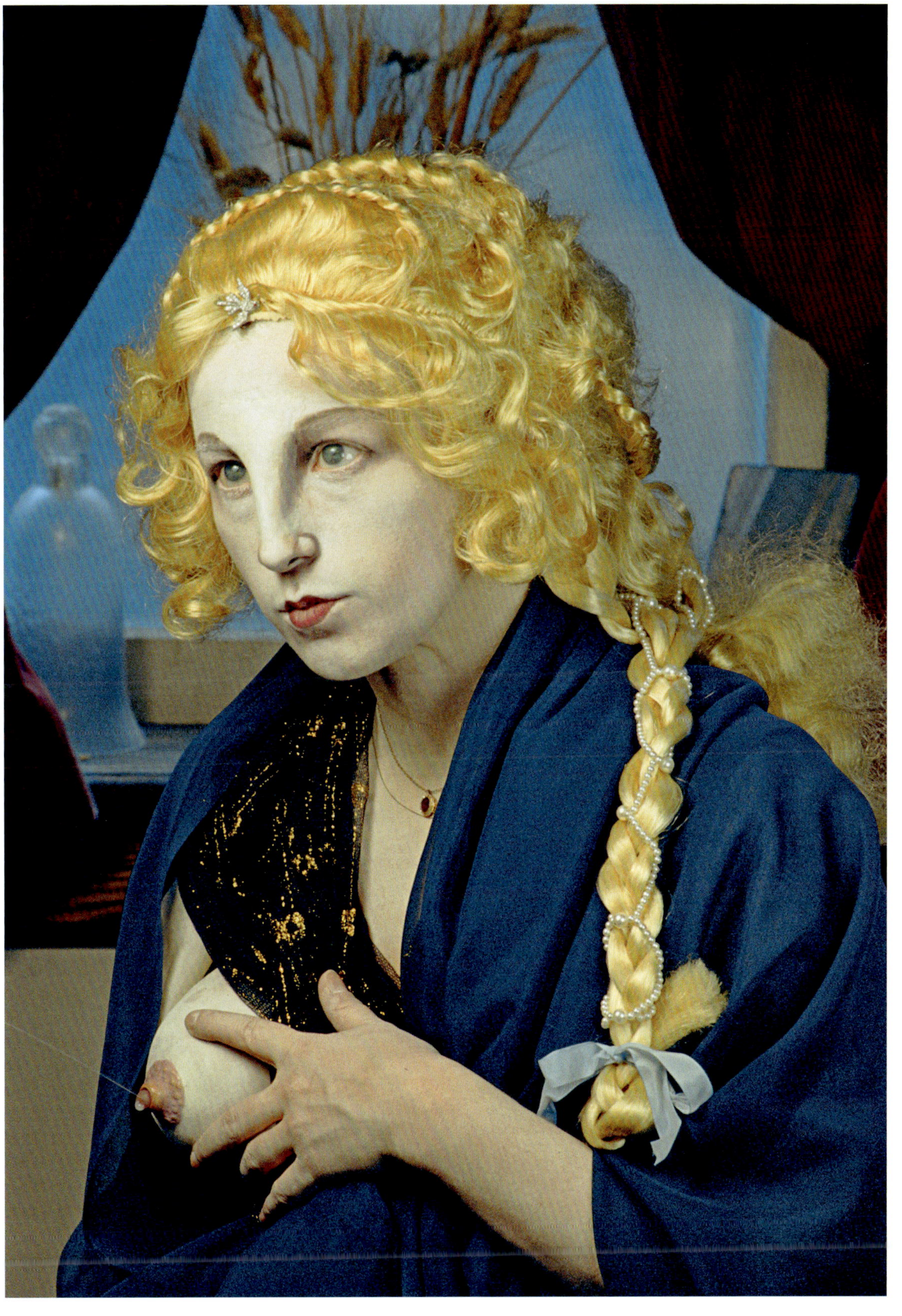

18

JOEL-PETER WITKIN (b.1939)

God of Earth and Heaven, Los Angeles, 1988

Silver gelatin print, 81.3 × 77.5 cm
Courtesy of the Artist and
Bruce Silverstein Gallery, New York

Human beings are central to Joel-Peter Witkin's work. However, it is the fragile and the fragmented, the side of human existence ignored by others, that the artist seeks to honour in his photographs. After a lengthy phase of getting to know his subjects, Witkin works out his compositions in minute detail, lending the individuals in the photograph a dignity often denied them by society. He is interested in people with physical disabilities as well as those who reject the constraints of gender. The first systematic series of portraits of transgender people, photographed by Diane Arbus, made a deep impression on him. Another of Witkin's techniques is the re-staging of historical photographs or famous works of art. Here he selected Botticelli's *Birth of Venus* (fig. 10), putting the central figure, with both male and female physical attributes, in place of the goddess of love, and staging the scene as theatrically as in Botticelli's original. GM

LITERATURE

Jena 2002, p. 78, no. I/32

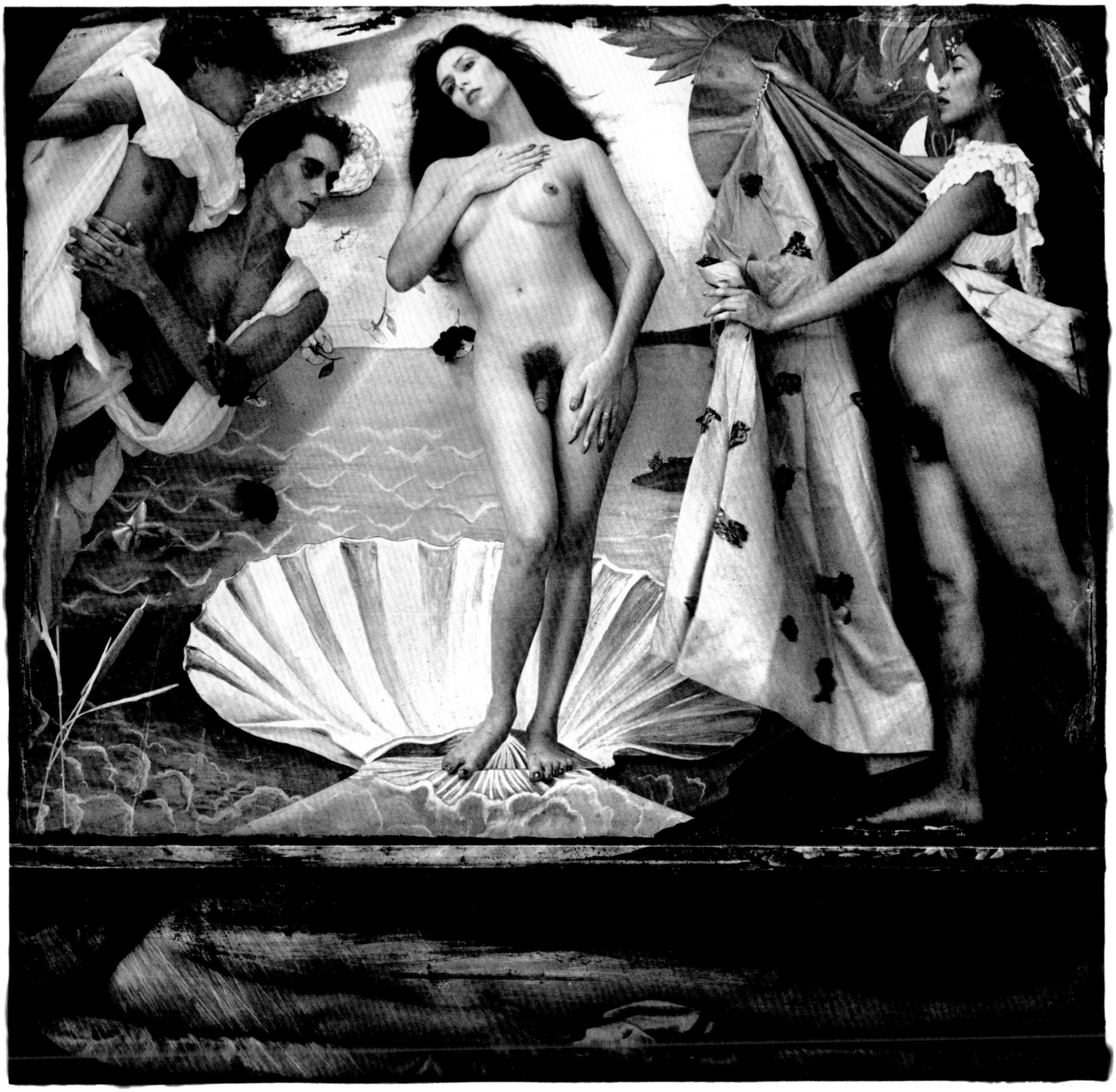

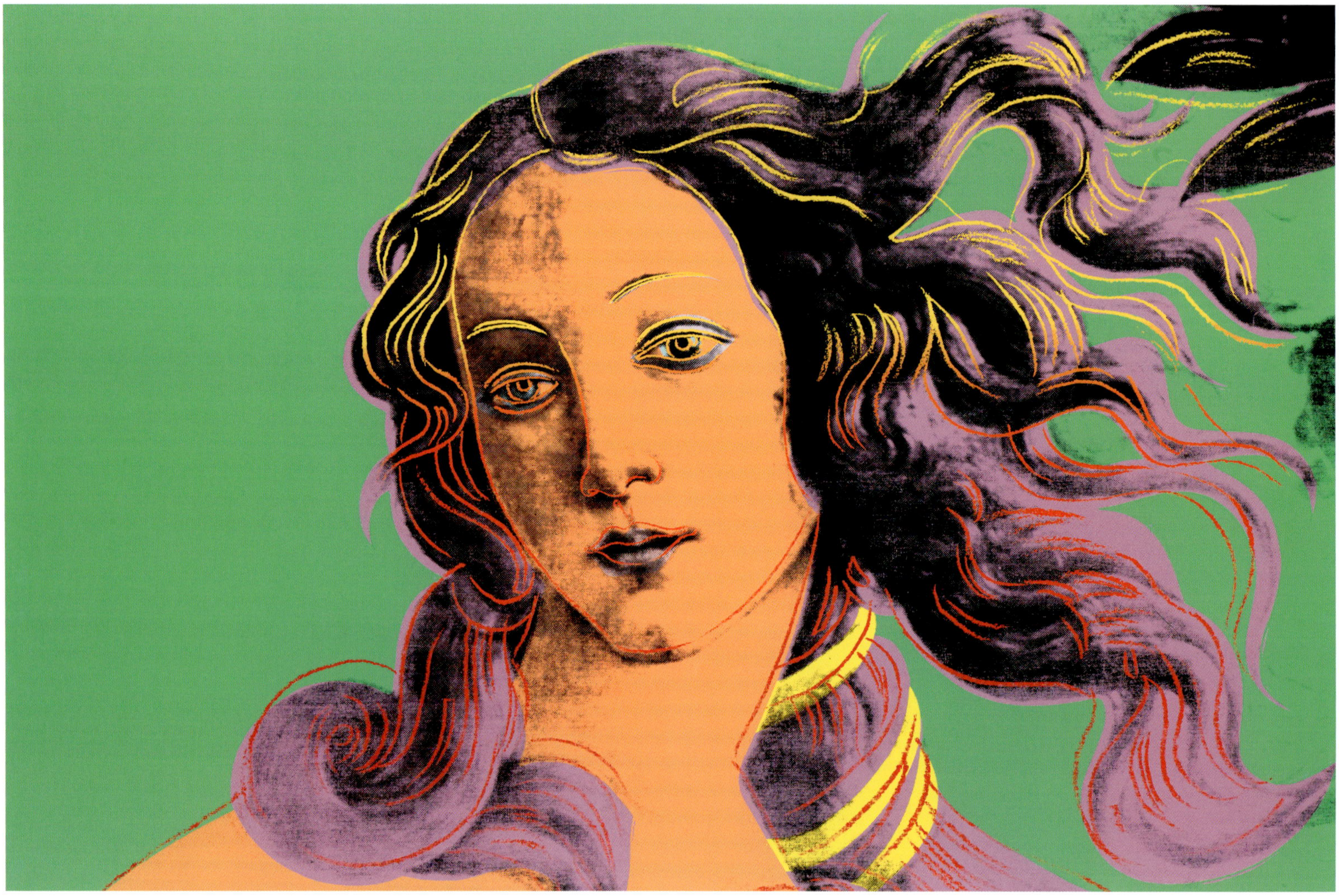

19, 20

ANDY WARHOL
(1928–1987)

Details of Renaissance Paintings (Sandro Botticelli, Birth of Venus, 1482), 1984

Acrylic and silkscreen ink on linen, 121.9 × 182.9 cm
Exeter Private Foundation

Details of Renaissance Paintings (Sandro Botticelli, Birth of Venus, 1482), 1984

Acrylic and silkscreen ink on linen, 121.9 × 182.9 cm
The Andy Warhol Museum, Pittsburgh; Founding Collection, Contribution The Andy Warhol Foundation for the Visual Arts, Inc (1981.1.307)

Andy Warhol is known as the founder and most significant exponent of Pop Art. In 1984 he produced a series of works that made reference to Renaissance paintings. As well as the head of Venus from Botticelli's painting in the Uffizi, he also used details from works by Leonardo da Vinci, Piero della Francesca and Paolo Uccello. The reference to Botticelli – as well as to Italian Renaissance artists less well known to the general public – suggests that this was coincidental. Warhol stylizes the head of Venus into a flat, clichéd decorative pattern of colours that, logo-like, create a memorable cypher. He produced two acrylic versions, both exhibited here. Four additional variants were made using silkscreen, each in an edition of seven.

Frequently reproduced, this glut of Venus icons promotes Warhol's popularity, as well as Botticelli's. At the same time, Warhol reduces Botticelli to the painter of a single iconic work – the Uffizi Venus. SW

LITERATURE

Dillenberger 1998, pp. 48–57; Sotheby's, New York, 14 November 2012 (lot 176), Contemporary Art Day Auction; Bock 2014, p. 18

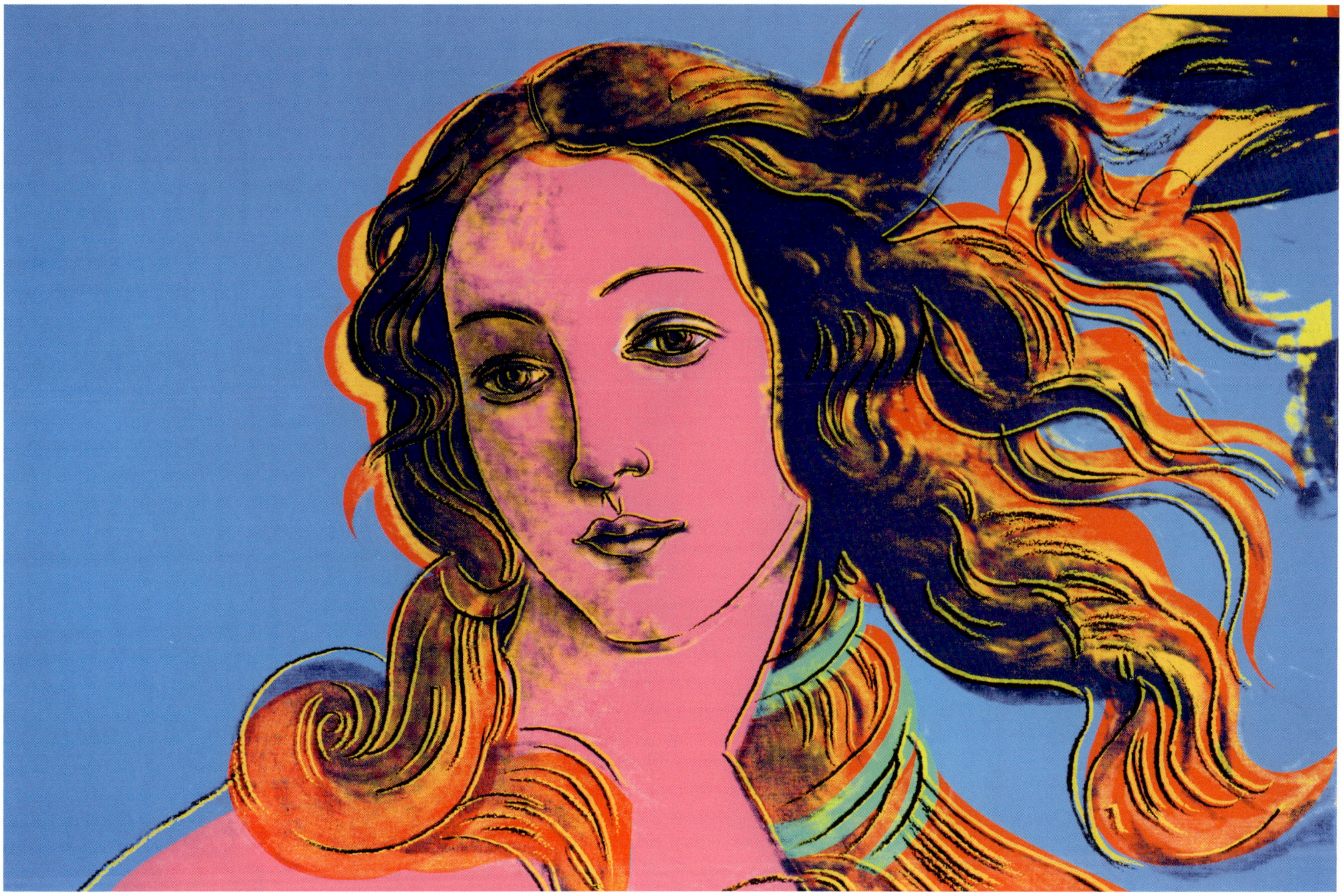

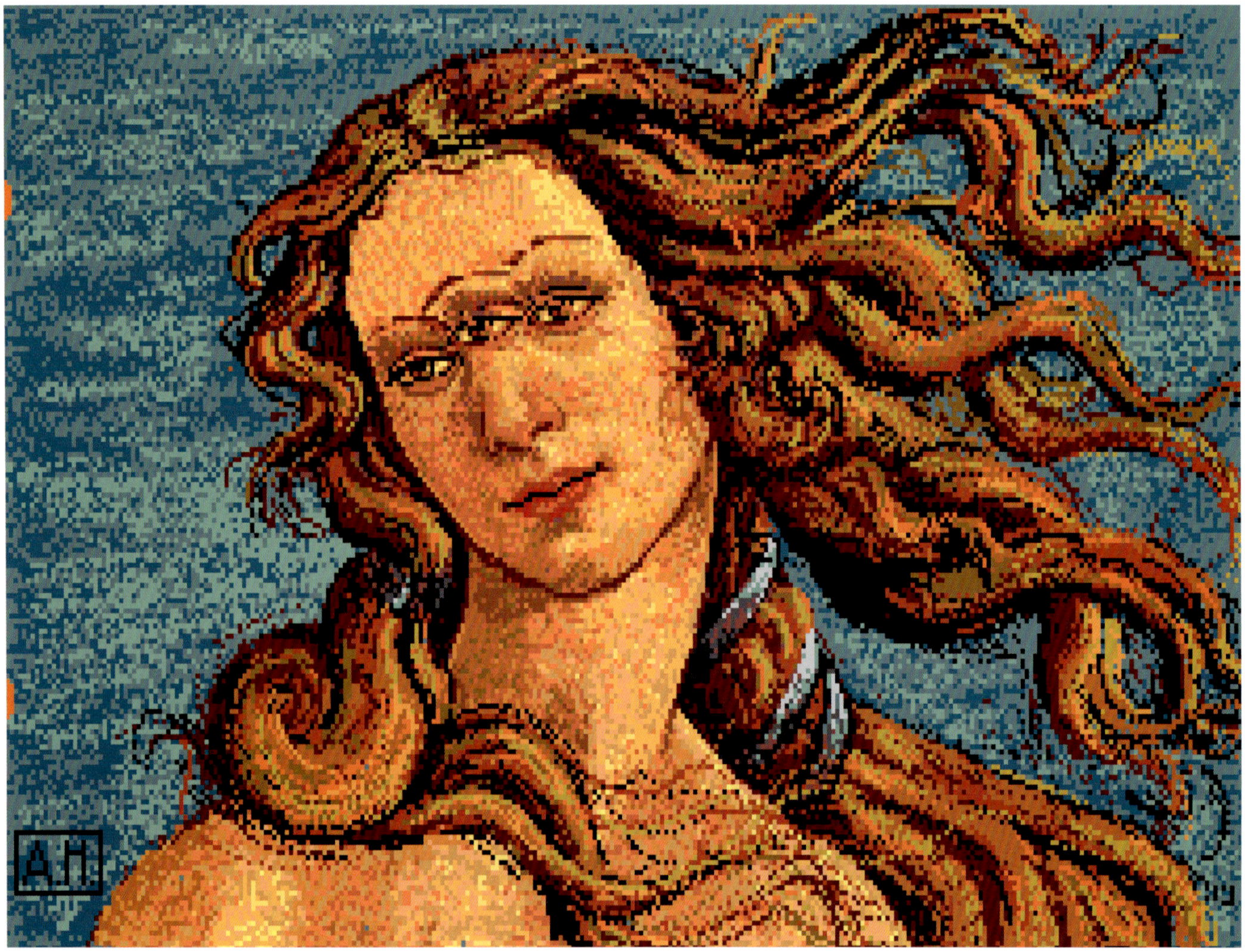

21

ANDY WARHOL
(1928–1987)

Digital Amiga 1000 Image after Sandro Botticelli, Birth of Venus, 1482, 1985

Amiga 1000 computer, screen
The Andy Warhol Museum, Pittsburgh

BERLIN ONLY

In the 1980s Warhol collaborated with Commodore International as part of a marketing campaign. He was given prototypes of graphics software as well as an Amiga 1000 personal computer, with which he created a series of digital works – video graphics, audio experiments and animation. Among them is a graphic in which Warhol reworked the head of Venus from Botticelli's painting in the Uffizi. It is untitled, and is not purely experimental in nature, as for a while Commodore used the image as an illustration on the cover of the user manual for its software 'Paint Deluxe', which was released in November 1985.

Warhol's approach here is comparatively minimalist, merely adding a third eye to Venus's forehead. Evidently he has not excluded other mythological contexts from his interest in the iconography of Venus; in the simplicity of his gesture there is an ironic and cryptic amalgamation of the goddess of love with the figure of the Cyclops. In any case, Warhol's experiment transformed Botticelli's Venus into one of the very earliest works of computer graphics. SW

LITERATURE

Wright and Suokko 1986; Maher 2012, pp. 79–81

22

ULRIKE ROSENBACH (b.1943)

Reflections on the Birth of Venus, 1976–8

Video tape, colour/PAL, sound, 20:34 minutes
Distributor: Inter media art institute, Düsseldorf
BERLIN ONLY

LIMA, Amsterdam
LONDON ONLY

This is part of a larger ensemble of works by the feminist performance and video artist Ulrike Rosenbach, who addresses female archetypes and myths, and their 'patriarchal' reframing and trivialization. Rosenbach has used her own body, turning in circles, as a projection screen for the iconic figure of Botticelli's Venus, challenging the viewer to take a critical approach to models of female identity and their cultural constructs. Her critique is not primarily aimed at the historical painting; in her opinion, Botticelli is 'the only painter … who actually interpreted Venus in a pre-patriarchal sense. She emerges onto the land from the sea, and in that moment flowers bloom. Only later did Venus become a symbol of eroticism.' Rather, the painting has been 'consumed' through its reduction to a one-dimensional cliché and commercial exploitation, ultimately falling victim to its own beauty. Bob Dylan's ballad *Sad-Eyed Lady of the Lowlands* (from the album *Blonde on Blonde*, 1966) accompanies the performance, an ironic swansong for the much-invoked melancholic gaze of the Renaissance painter's figure. SH

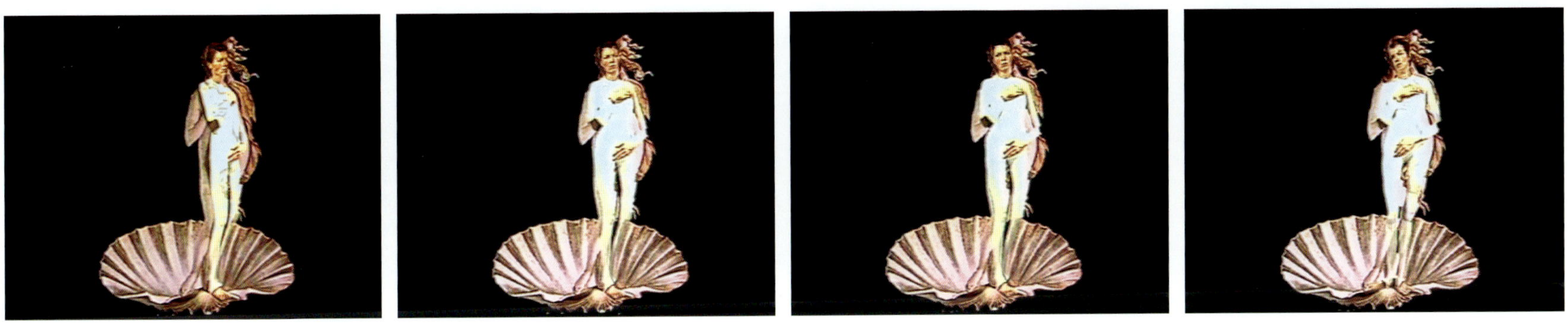

LITERATURE
Rosenbach 1982, pp. 11–20; Glüher 2005, pp. 64–71; Paul 2006; Rotermund 2012, pp. 91–102; Bonn 2014, p. 72

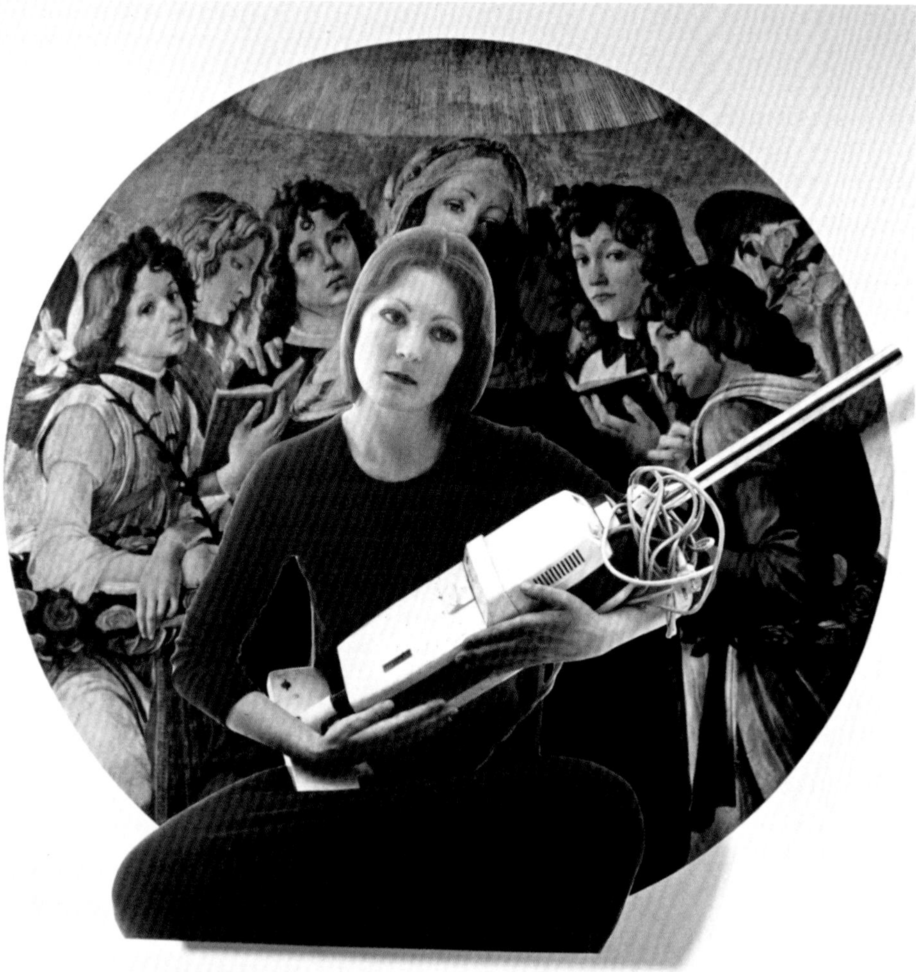

23

VALIE EXPORT (b.1940)

Expectation, 1976

Photograph, 59.8 × 50 cm
Charim Gallery, Vienna

VALIE EXPORT works extensively with the female body as her subject. In her series *Body Configurations* (1972–6) she posed in contorted positions on steps and kerbs in public spaces built by men. Her next series explored the social pressures on women by incorporating works of the Old Masters (1974–6): 'The oppression of women is visually apparent in the idealized images of them made by men.... By modelling or re-enacting these poses, then using materials from women's everyday lives to insert them into the context of contemporary social conditioning, I am trying to unmask their appearance of meekness.'

In this photomontage, EXPORT superimposes a photograph of herself with Botticelli's *Madonna of the Pomegranate* (fig. 15). Her pose mimics that of the Virgin but instead of the Christ Child she cradles a vacuum cleaner in her arms. The ambiguous title *Expectation* alludes to the role assigned to women by a patriarchal society, which reduces them to child-bearing domestic appliances. As in the Botticelli, EXPORT's gaze is melancholic, but she conveys a sense of danger as well as resignation: the vacuum cleaner and its tube resemble a machine gun, a gesture reminiscent of her earlier series *Action Pants: Genital Panic* (1968). GM

LITERATURE
Linz 1992, p. 85; Mueller 1994, p. 118; Vienna 1997, p. 130

24

ORLAN (b.1947)

Occasional Strip-tease, 1974–5

18 photographs (multiple), 135 × 170 cm
Centre national des arts plastiques (FNAC 2478)

These eighteen photographs document a private performance in which ORLAN draped herself in linen sheets from her trousseau, before systematically removing them, layer by layer, until she was completely naked. ORLAN used facial expressions and gestures, as well as the removal of the sheets, to perform her flamboyant self-transformation. With these limited means, she was able to reveal our perception of the body – and especially the female body – as a construct conditioned by preconceived ideas. At the beginning of the performance the artist had even wrapped the sheets around her head, like a nun's wimple. Gradually this clerical figure morphed into an ecstatic saint. ORLAN utilized the stylistic device of the baroque drapery to visualize the dissolution and expansion of the body's boundaries. During a further transformation she eventually completed the change in role from saint to nude goddess of beauty and love. ORLAN's pose was a direct reference to Botticelli's Venus in the Uffizi, which served as an archetype for the nude female body, and therefore as a metaphor for love and beauty. SW

LITERATURE

Paris 2004, pp. 28–9; Pape 2008, pp. 134–8

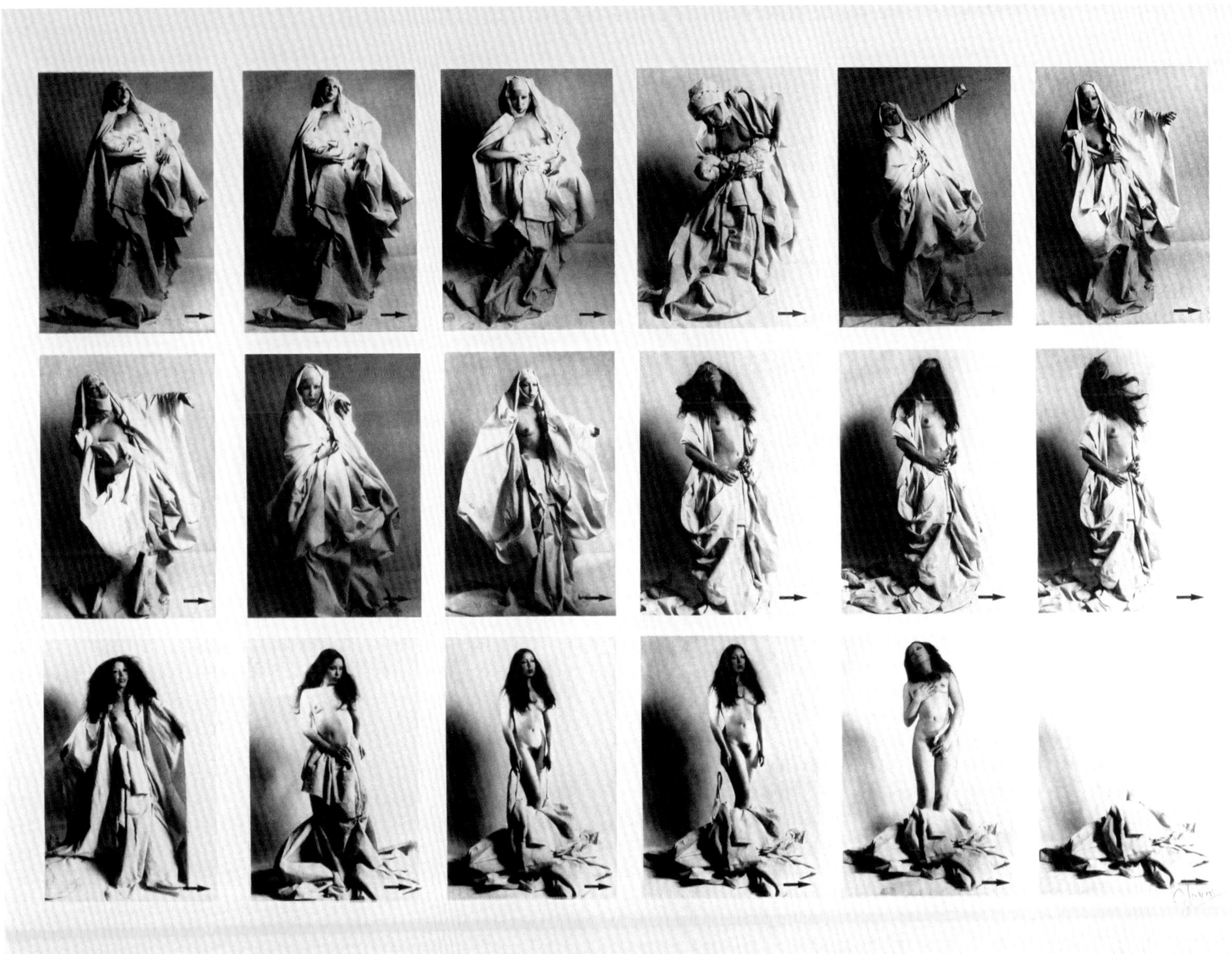

25, 26

ALAIN JACQUET
(1939–2008)

Camouflage Botticelli, Naissance de Venus I, 1963

Oil on canvas, 220.5 × 105 cm
Collection of Jean Coulon, Paris;
Courtesy Comité Jacquet &
Galerie G-P & N Vallois, Paris

Camouflage Botticelli, Naissance de Venus III, 1964

Oil on canvas, 220.5 × 105 cm
Collection of Jean Coulon, Paris;
Courtesy Comité Jacquet and Galerie
G-P & N Vallois, Paris

These are two of at least three variants based on Botticelli's *Birth of Venus* painted by the American Pop artist Alain Jacquet for his *Camouflage* series between 1961 and 1964. The paintings have extremely diverse sources, both two- and three-dimensional, including cartoons by Walt Disney, traffic signs, adverts and reproductions after works by Leonardo da Vinci, Michelangelo, Bronzino, Piet Mondrian, Henri Matisse, Giorgio de Chirico, Roy Lichtenstein and Jasper Johns. Like Warhol, Jacquet had little specific interest in Botticelli as a painter, but sought rather to connect his own work with the giants of art history. In *Camouflage Botticelli* the shell from the Renaissance painting and that of the Shell company logo are combined in a seemingly accidental way. This work should be viewed in the context of the entire series, in which Jacquet makes a topic of signs, meaning and their dissolution. The association of the word 'Shell' on the petrol pumps with the figure of Venus provides an additional layer of meaning.
SW

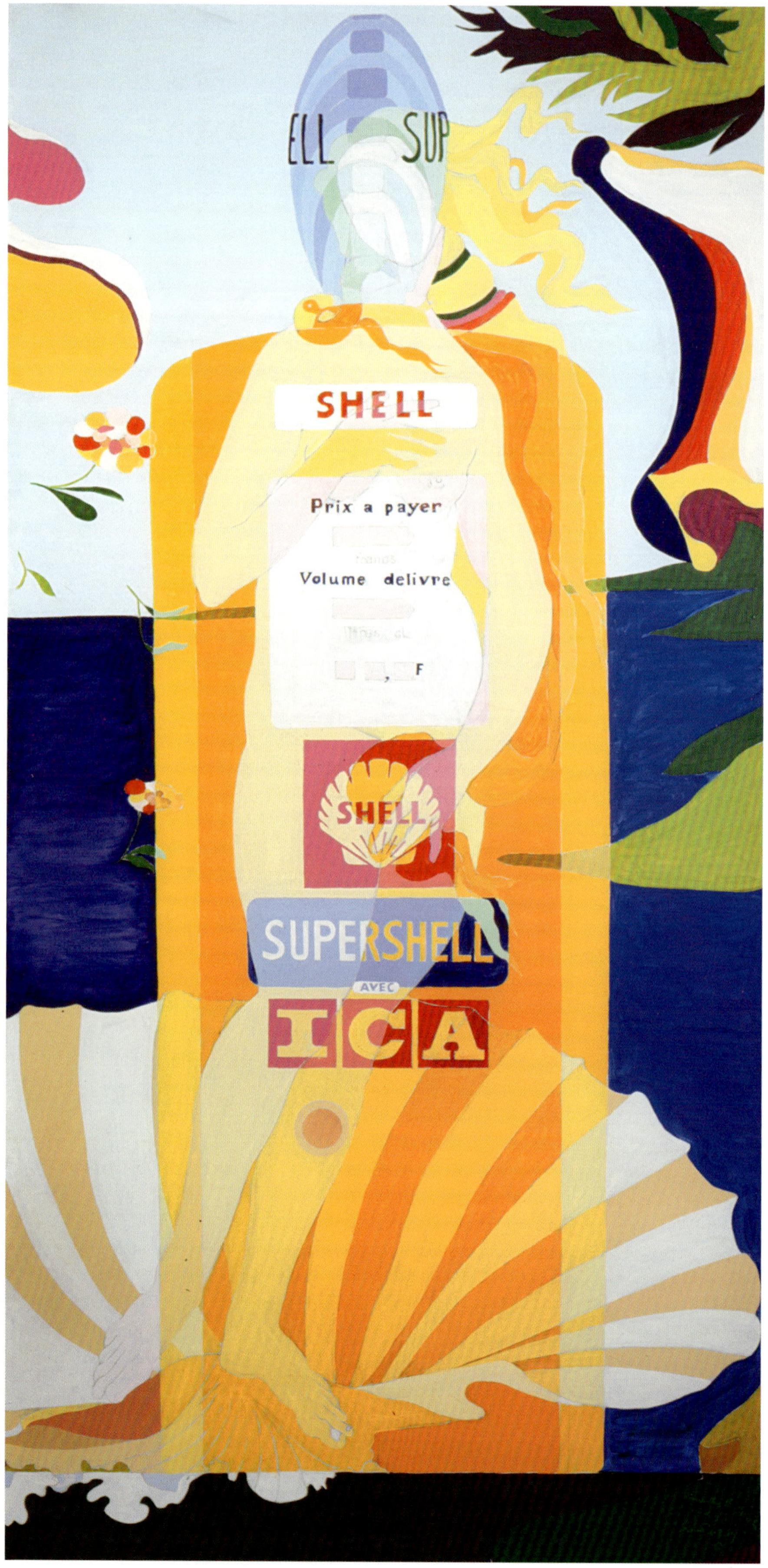

LITERATURE
Scarpetta 2002, pp. 115–16; Nice 2005; Shanes 2010, p. 141

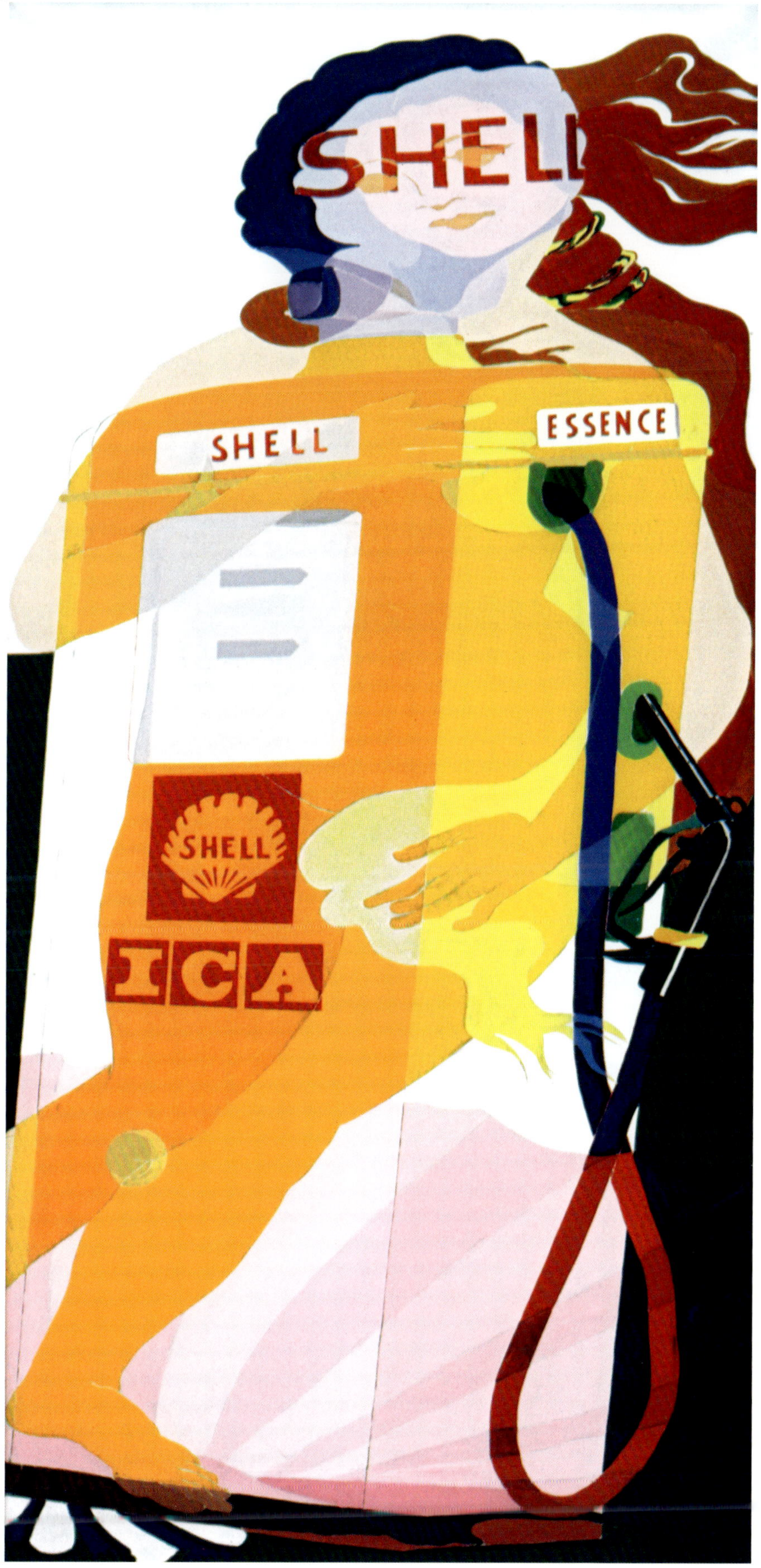

SHELL
SHELL
ESSENCE
SHELL
ICA

27, 28, 29

RENÉ MAGRITTE
(1898–1967)

Le bouquet tout fait
(*The Ready-made Bouquet*), 1957

Oil on canvas, 163 × 130.5 cm
Osaka City Museum of Modern Art
LONDON ONLY

Study for *Le bouquet tout fait*
(*The Ready-made Bouquet*), 1956

Graphite on paper with touches of blue, 41.6 × 26 cm
Collection of Charly Herscovici, Brussels

Le bouquet tout fait
(*The Ready-made Bouquet*), 1956

Oil on canvas, 60 × 50 cm
Private collection, Switzerland
BERLIN ONLY

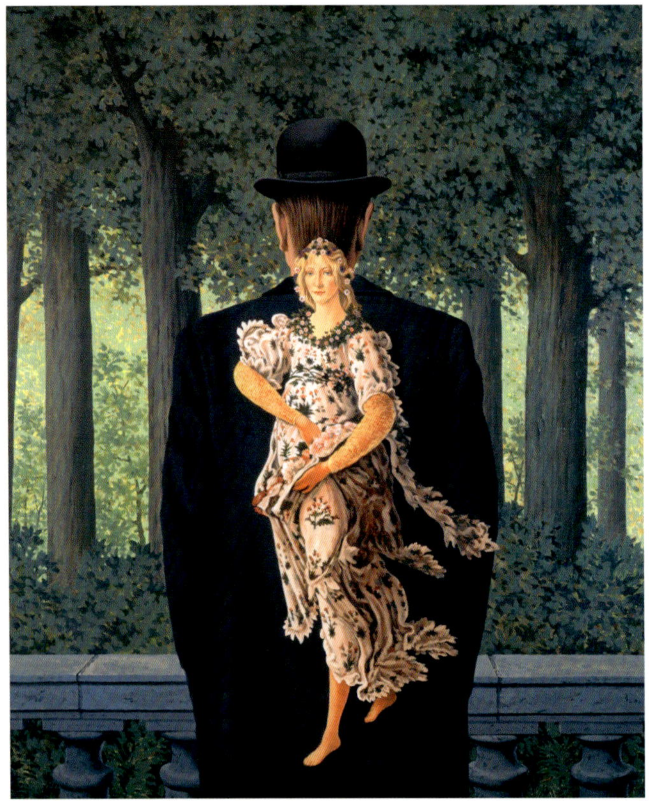

In early 1956 René Magritte planned a work consisting of six images titled *La place au soleil* (*The Place in the Sun*), intended to comprise two unrelated motifs, with the smaller superimposed above the larger. He only completed two paintings, including the one he described in a letter as the '*Primavera* by Botticelli on a man with a bowler hat seen from behind'. He prepared a sketch on paper for this figure, based on that of Flora in Botticelli's painting. His friend, the Belgian surrealist poet Louis Scutenaire, gave the painting its title. As was often the case, Magritte never attempted to explain the mystery of this image.

In his original painting the clear contrast between the autumnal forest the man is looking at and the figure borrowed from Botticelli's allegory of spring, provides a further level of ambiguity. However, a year later Magritte also blurred the contrast between the seasons in a larger version of the composition in which the man with an image of Flora on his back looks from a balustrade at a verdant summery forest. When Magritte, accompanied by Scutenaire, later saw Botticelli's original work in the Uffizi, he apparently said, 'It's not bad, but it's better on a postcard'. GM

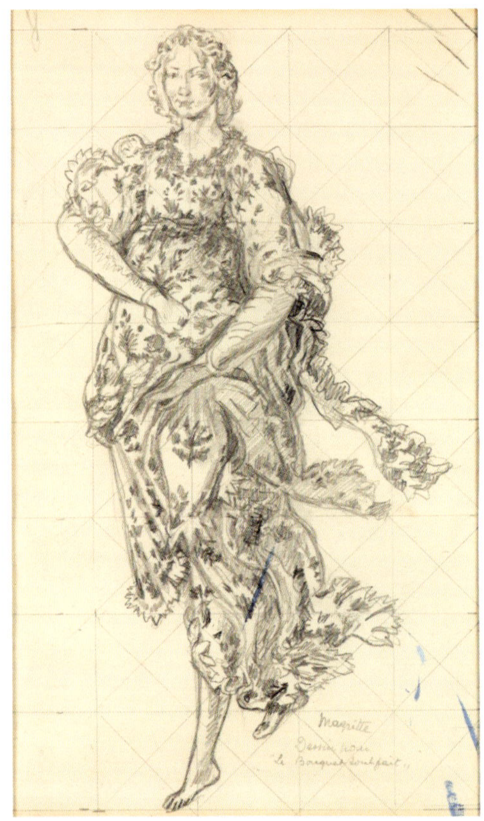

PROVENANCE

CAT. 27 Alexander Iolas Gallery; Barnet Hodes, Chicago; 1982 purchased at Christie's, New York, private collection, Japan; Osaka City Museum of Modern Art

CAT. 28 René Magritte; Robert Rauschenberg; Robert Rauschenberg Foundation; Gagosian Gallery; Charly Herscovici

CAT. 29 Purchased from the artist by Alexandre Iolas, New York, 1956; John and Sylvia de Cuevas, New York; Daniel Malingue, Paris, 1974; Pascal Sernet, Paris; Alabano Bochatay, Geneva; private collection, Switzerland, 1993

LITERATURE

Sylvester 1993, pp. 258, 274; Venice and Basel 2014, p. 169, no. 81

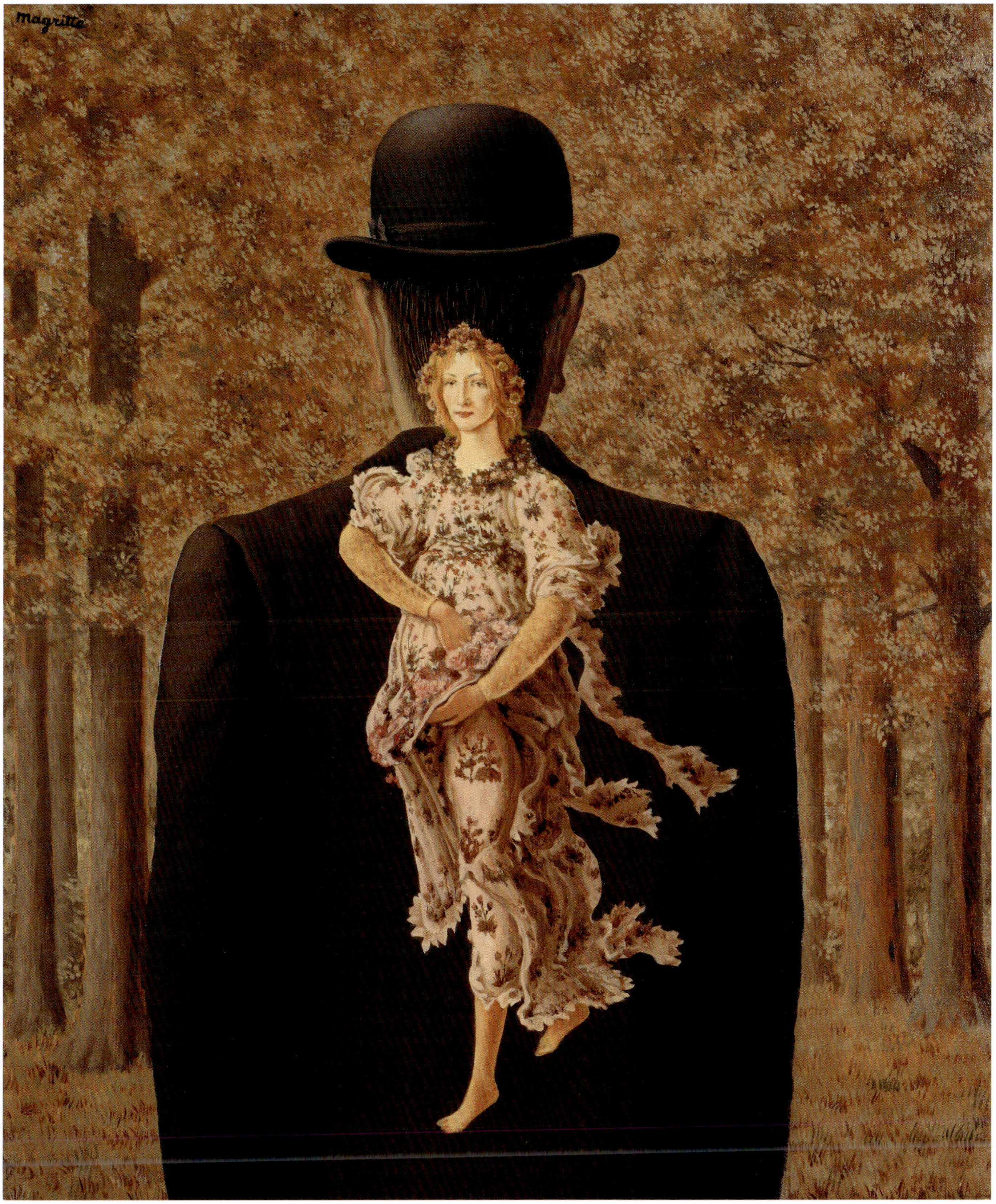
Magritte

30

PAUL HIMMEL
(1914–2009)
Botticelli Girl (Patricia McBride), Fire Island, c.1954–5

Silver gelatin print, 50.8 × 40.6 cm
Lizzie Himmel Collection

The influential American photographer Paul Himmel made his name with the exhibition *The Family of Man* (part of UNESCO's world documentary heritage), curated by Edward Steichen, a selection of over 500 images by 273 photographers. Himmel contributed to this mammoth undertaking with a portrait of the young dancer Patricia McBride, who in 1961 became the youngest ever prima ballerina in the New York City Ballet. The young woman seems lost in contemplation, gazing away from the camera. Her slightly parted lips, highlighted with reflected light, and hair that falls loosely over her shoulders, framing her face and contrasting with her peaceful features, lend a sensuous radiance to the image. Both the pensive expression and lowered gaze are typical of works by Botticelli, such as his Madonnas. However, the moving hair is specific to his depictions of Venus. It is no wonder, then, that Himmel was reminded of Botticelli's work when looking at the young dancer. SW

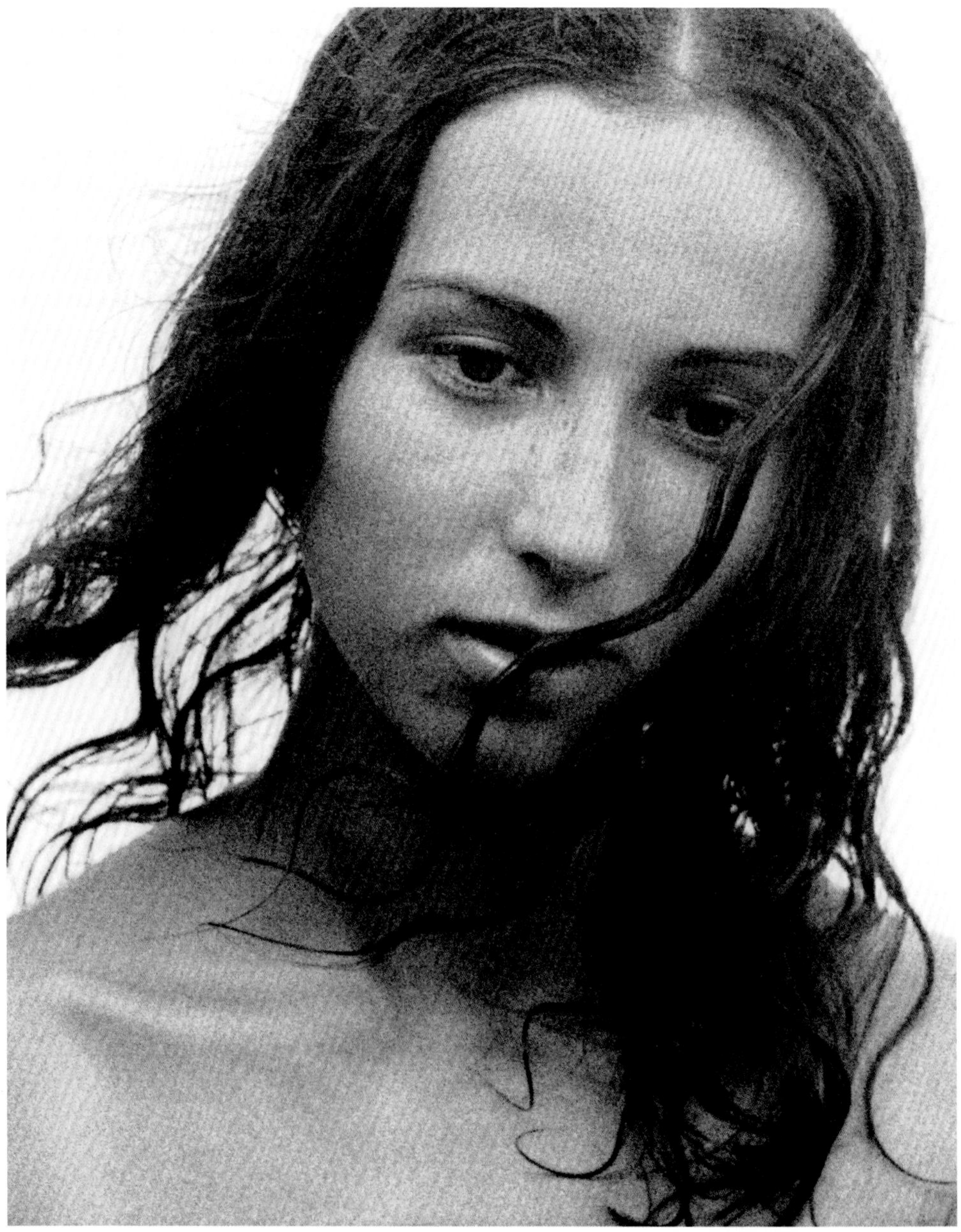

LITERATURE
Hamburg 2009–10; Jordanova 2012, p. 141

31

TAMARA DE LEMPICKA
(1898–1980)
Trompe-l'oeil Painting with a Botticelli, 1946

Oil on board, 40.5 × 30.5 cm
Private collection, London

In 1925 the Polish artist Tamara de Lempicka visited Florence to study the Renaissance masters. She made sketches and copies after several of Botticelli's paintings, including the *Madonna del Magnificat* (see under cat. 117). Many of her bold, hard-edged paintings of beautiful women in primary colours reveal the profound impact of his style.

This composition pays homage to *trompe-l'oeil* pictures, which were popular from the sixteenth to the eighteenth centuries. It presents the optical illusion of a reproduction of a Botticelli Madonna tacked to an unpainted wooden panel. The face of Botticelli's *Madonna of the Pomegranate* (fig. 15) which de Lempicka would have seen in the Uffizi, is reproduced as a tattered and well-worn print, suggesting that it has been used repeatedly for reference. Its juxtaposition with a key hanging from a ribbon to the right suggests that Botticelli's works provide the key to art. MM

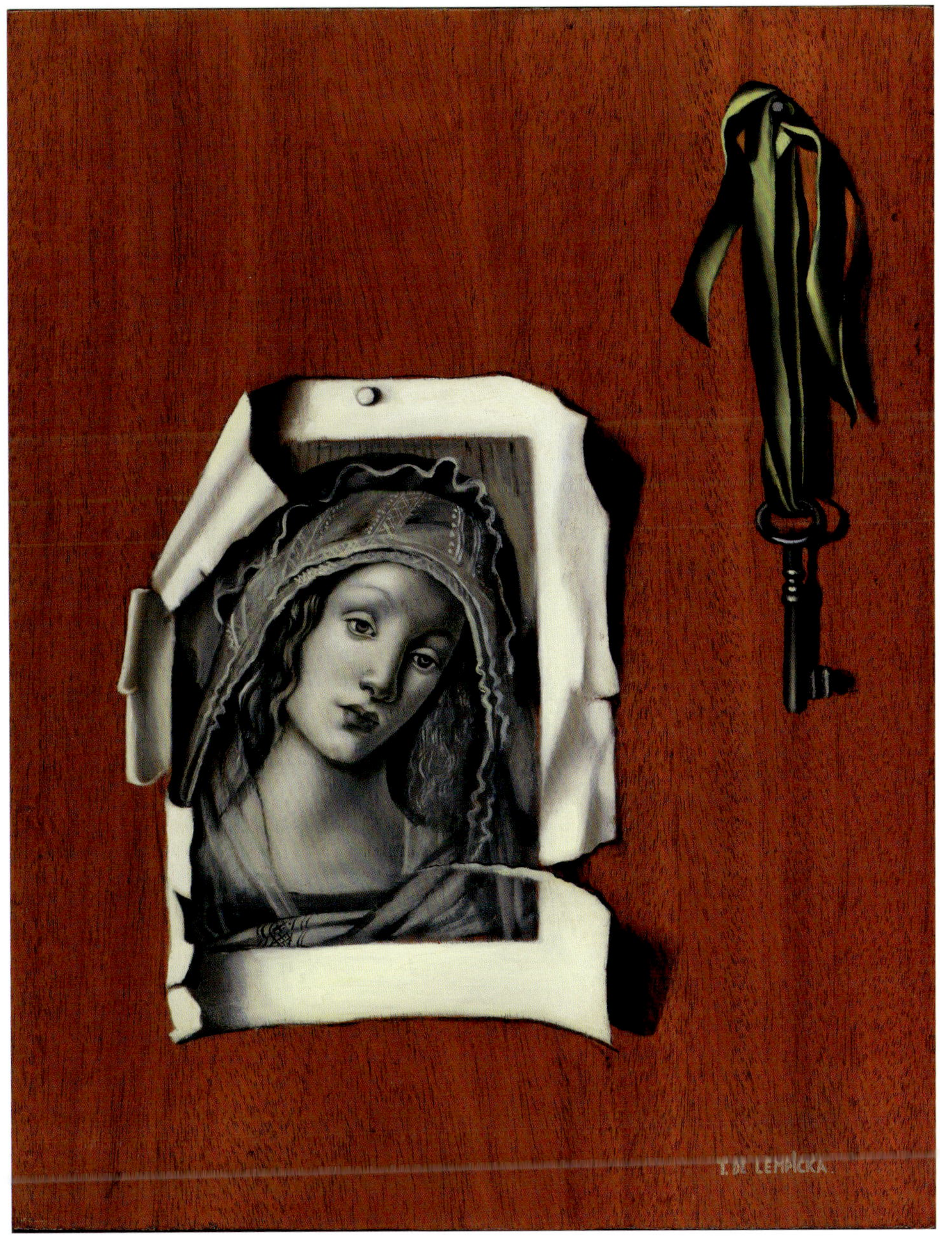

PROVENANCE
Douglas and Vibeke Bergeron; MacDougall's sale, 29 November 2007 (lot 78)

LITERATURE
Blondel 1999, p. 342; Mori 2011, p. 301, no. 71

32

RAOUL DUFY
(1877–1953)
Birth of Venus, after Botticelli,
c.1940

Oil on wood, 60 × 50 cm
Musée d'art moderne de la ville de Paris
(AMVP 2027)

From 1936 until well into the 1940s, Raoul Dufy produced over 20 variations of Botticelli's *Birth of Venus* (fig. 10). Under the title *Venus*, or sometimes *Amphitrite*, Dufy painted female nudes standing, half-reclining or sitting on a shell or shell-like wave in a contemporary harbour with steamships and sailing boats. Occasionally he took a step back from the original, painting an empty shell on the beach, flanked by female nudes. Once Dufy even relocated Venus and her shell away from the sea, to a grassy French landscape with a characteristic village church. Almost all these versions are small-scale and rapidly executed in quick brushstrokes, with a huge range of colours, including a Venus against a black background. The version exhibited here is one of the most faithful copies, and retains Botticelli's colours except for the red garment to the left (green in the original), and introduces no new elements, despite reducing the extent of the background. GM

PROVENANCE
Berthe Reysz collection, then a gift to the Musée d'art moderne de la ville de Paris

LITERATURE
Laffaille 1977, p. 171, no. 1610

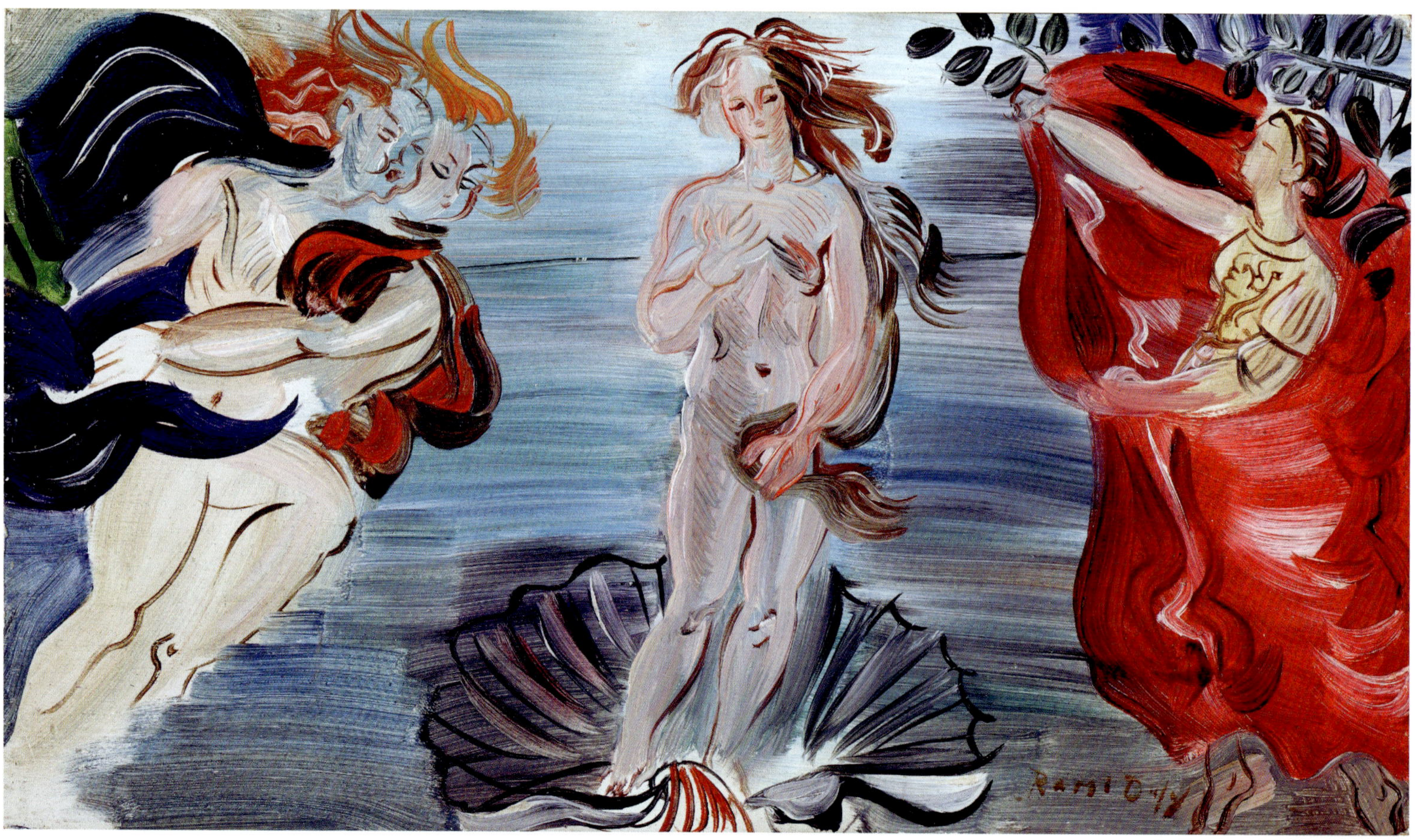

33

SALVADOR DALÍ
(1904–1989)

Declaration of the Independence of the Imagination and the Rights of Man to his own Madness, 1939

Ink on paper, 40.3 × 24.35 cm
National Art Library Victoria and Albert Museum, London (38041800859019)

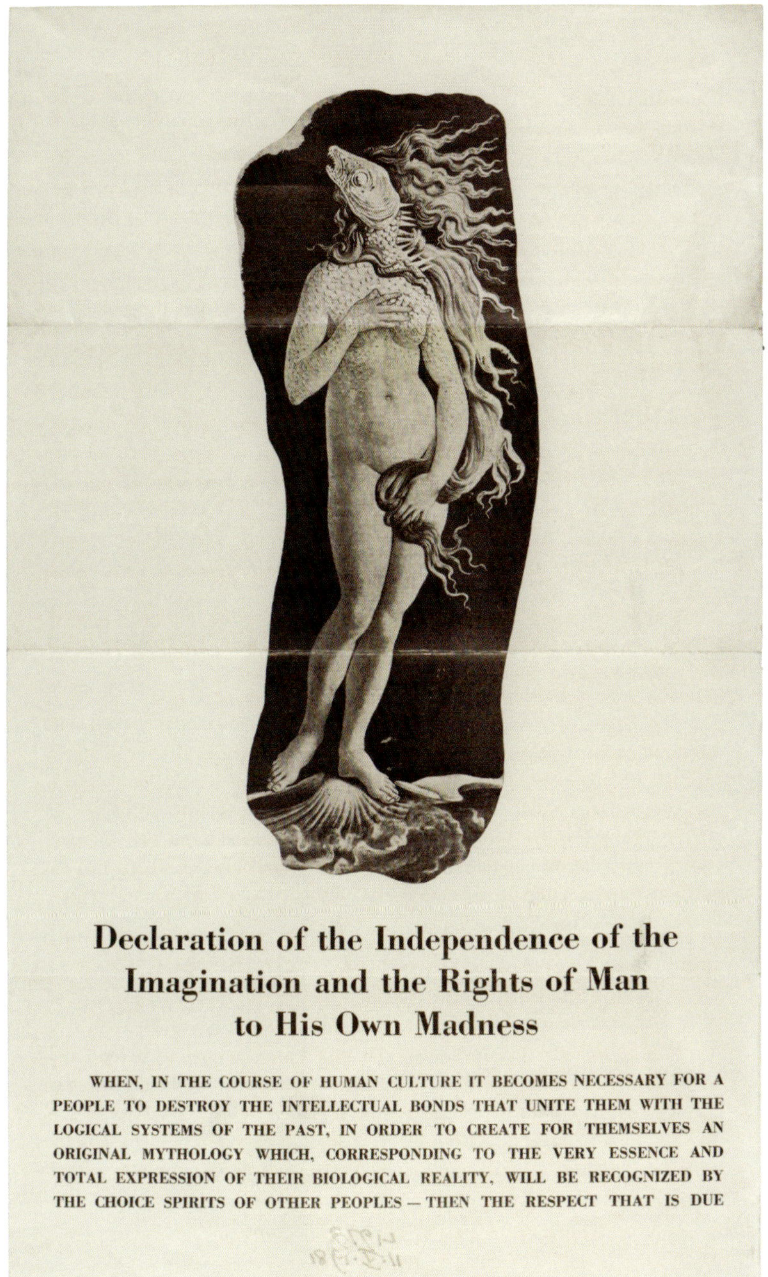

Declaration of the Independence of the Imagination and the Rights of Man to His Own Madness

WHEN, IN THE COURSE OF HUMAN CULTURE IT BECOMES NECESSARY FOR A PEOPLE TO DESTROY THE INTELLECTUAL BONDS THAT UNITE THEM WITH THE LOGICAL SYSTEMS OF THE PAST, IN ORDER TO CREATE FOR THEMSELVES AN ORIGINAL MYTHOLOGY WHICH, CORRESPONDING TO THE VERY ESSENCE AND TOTAL EXPRESSION OF THEIR BIOLOGICAL REALITY, WILL BE RECOGNIZED BY THE CHOICE SPIRITS OF OTHER PEOPLES – THEN THE RESPECT THAT IS DUE

Made famous by his spectacular window displays on Fifth Avenue, Salvador Dalí was commissioned to design a pavilion titled 'Dream of Venus' for the 'Amusement Area' of the 1939–40 New York World's Fair. Inside, reminiscent of the Surrealists' exhibition in Paris in 1938, Dalí staged his interpretation of the goddess's dreams. Perhaps alluding to her sea-birth, he choreographed female swimmers in pools of water, their bathing suits – decorated with the image of a piano keyboard – revealing plenty of flesh. What really provoked a scandal, however, was the five-metre-tall reproduction of Botticelli's *Birth of Venus* (fig. 10) that Dalí wished to display above the entrance, the goddess's face replaced with a less appetizing fish head. While the sirens had the lower bodies of fishes, from her navel her upper body gradually morphed into scales. Eventually it was decided that an unaltered depiction of Botticelli's Venus would greet visitors, and Dalí's creation was relegated to the title page of a pamphlet – copies of which were apparently dropped from an aeroplane – in which he bemoaned the exhibition committee's lack of imagination. 'Had there been similar committees in Immortal Greece… the Greeks would never have created their sensational and truculently Surrealist mythology.' Even if, to Dalí's knowledge, there were no women with the heads of fish in Greek mythology, there were sirens, and 'a Minotaur bearing the terribly realistic head of a bull'. GM

LITERATURE
Gibson 1997, pp. 390–2; Dalí 1998, pp. 331–4; Barcelona et al. 2004–5, pp. 118–39

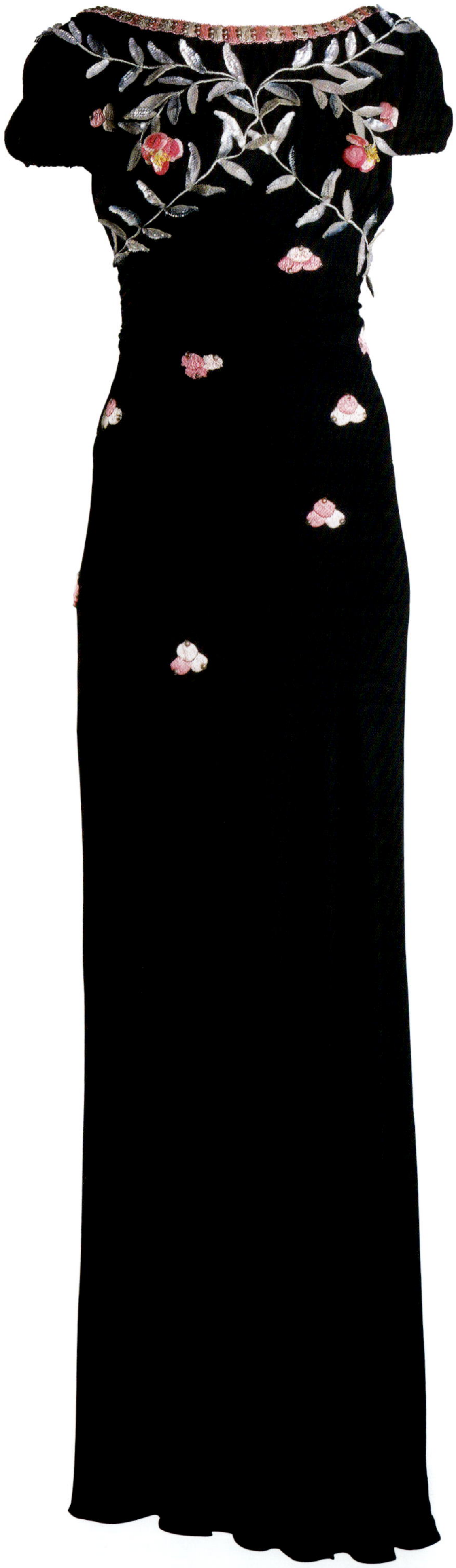

34, 35

ELSA SCHIAPARELLI (1890–1973)

Evening Dress, 1938

Silk crepe, plastic sequins and silk thread embroidery,
156.2 cm (centre front length) × 66 cm (waist)
Philadelphia Museum of Art (1969-232-40)
Gift of Mme Elsa Schiaparelli, 1969

Evening Dress, 1938

Silk crepe, plastic sequins and silk thread embroidery,
141 cm (centre front length) × 76 cm (waist)
Collection de l'Union Française des Arts du Costume
Musée de la Mode et du Textile
Les arts décoratifs, Paris (UF73-21-7)
Gift of Mme Elsa Schiaparelli, UFAC, 1973

Schiaparelli created these dresses for her *Pagan* collection of autumn 1938. The designer used a simple, slim-cut dress to set off the embroidered foliage and embellishments by Maison Lesage giving a three-dimensional effect, which marked a departure from the traditions of this decorative form.

The evening gowns take their inspiration from the long dress worn by the female figure in Botticelli's *Pallas and the Centaur* (cat. 164). Her painted gown is wreathed in sprigs of olive leaves and embroidered with patterns of interlinking diamond rings, a traditional symbol of the Medici, who commissioned the picture. Schiaparelli's design reinterprets this motif in the form of three large overlapping pink sequins scattered around the waist of the dress. The leaves and delicate blooms lift away from the figure to resemble living flowers, as represented in the painting, rather than flat decoration. When Schiaparelli's collection was first presented in April 1938 the models posed against reproductions of Botticelli's mythologies, from which they then appeared to step forth. MM

LITERATURE

White 1986, pp. 136, 170–2; Philadelphia 2003–4, pp. 180–5

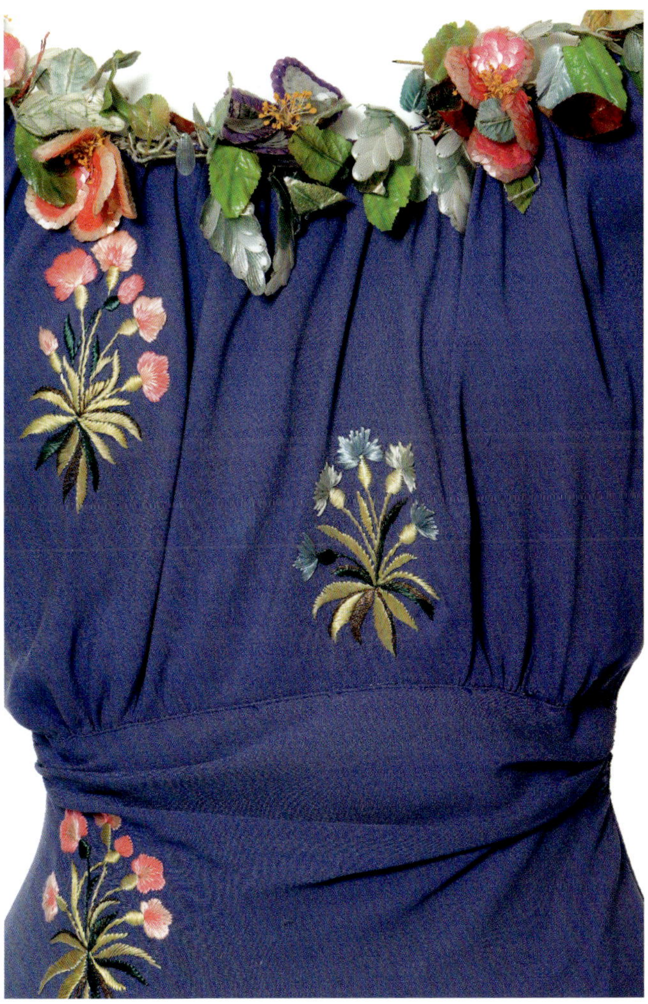

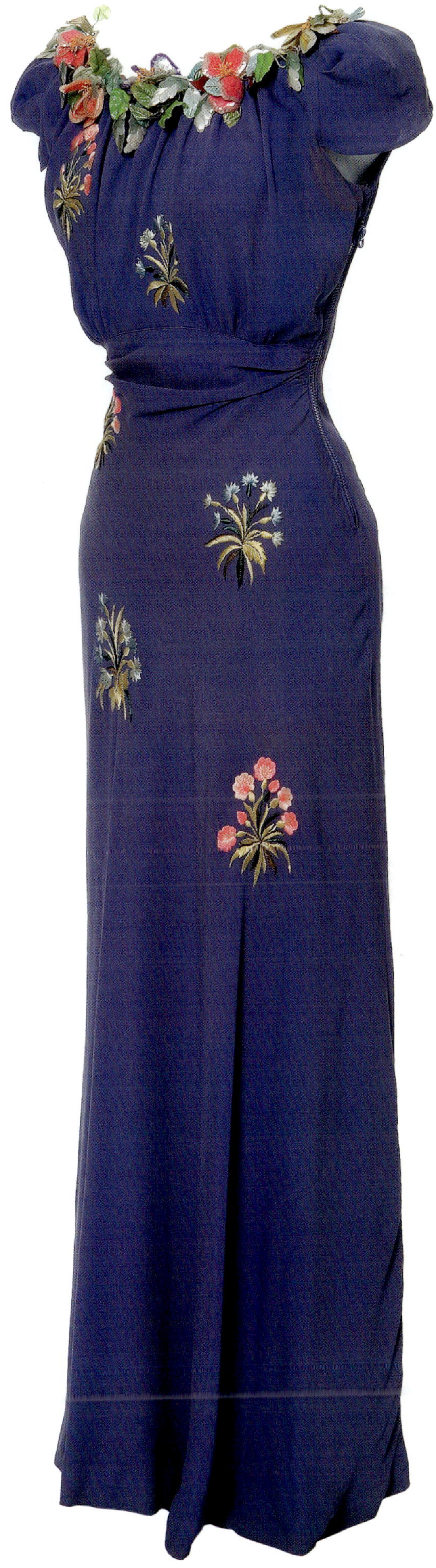

36

EDWARD BAIRD
(1904–1949)
The Birth of Venus, 1934

Oil on canvas, 51 × 69 cm
Scottish National Gallery of Modern Art, Edinburgh
National Galleries Scotland (GMA 4473)

The Scottish artist Edward Baird painted this surrealist composition as a wedding gift for his fellow artist James McIntosh Patrick, who explained that 'being a sentimental person, he chose Venus, the goddess of love, as the subject… the "Scottish Venus" as he called it, arose out of his associations with a wedding, his involvement with Scottish Nationalism, his love for messing about in boats, and his love of Botticelli.'

Baird visited Florence in 1929 to study 'the Primitives', in which he found 'a purer and deeper and more direct inspiration'. The title, subject and pale tonalities of this work derive from Botticelli's *Birth of Venus* (fig. 10), which he would have seen in the Uffizi and perhaps again in London at the Royal Academy in 1930. Baird's fiancée Ann Fairweather posed for the principal figure on the beach at his home town, Montrose. Around the periphery of the scene are a variety of objects including lenses, driftwood, seashells, a purple orchid, the head of an archaic Greek kouros and the rudder of a boat.
ME

PROVENANCE
The artist; by whom given in 1935 to James McIntosh Patrick; Accepted by HM Government in lieu of inheritance tax and allocated to the Scottish National Gallery of Modern Art 2002

LITERATURE
Elliot 1992, pp. 10, 23; Blackwood 2004, pp. 28–9, 40–3, 90, 95

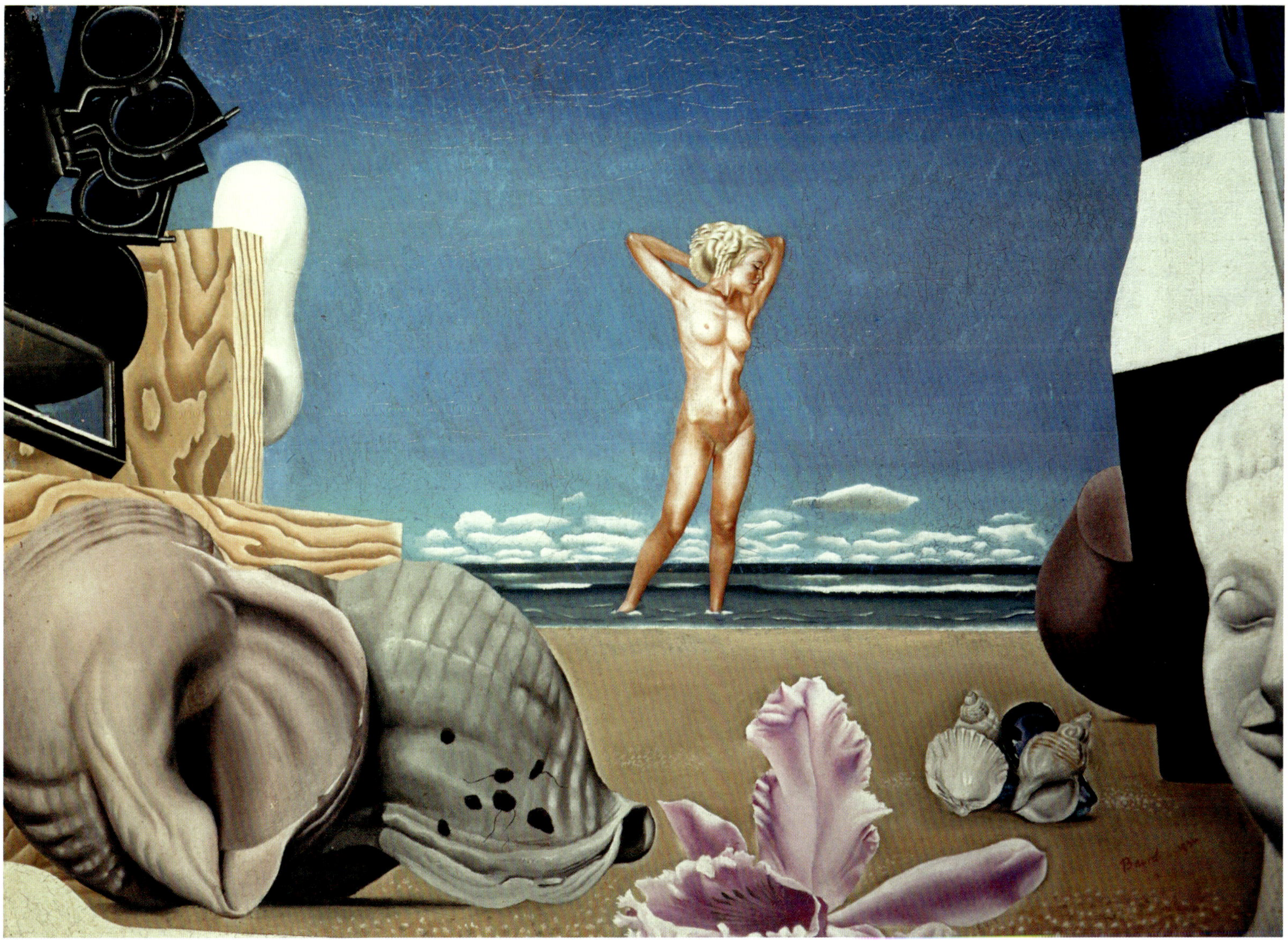

37

ANTONIO DONGHI
(1897–1963)
Woman at the Café (Donna al caffè), 1931

Oil on canvas, 80 × 60 cm
Fondazione Musei Civici di Venezia, Galleria Internazionale d'Arte Moderna di Ca' Pesaro, Venice (899)

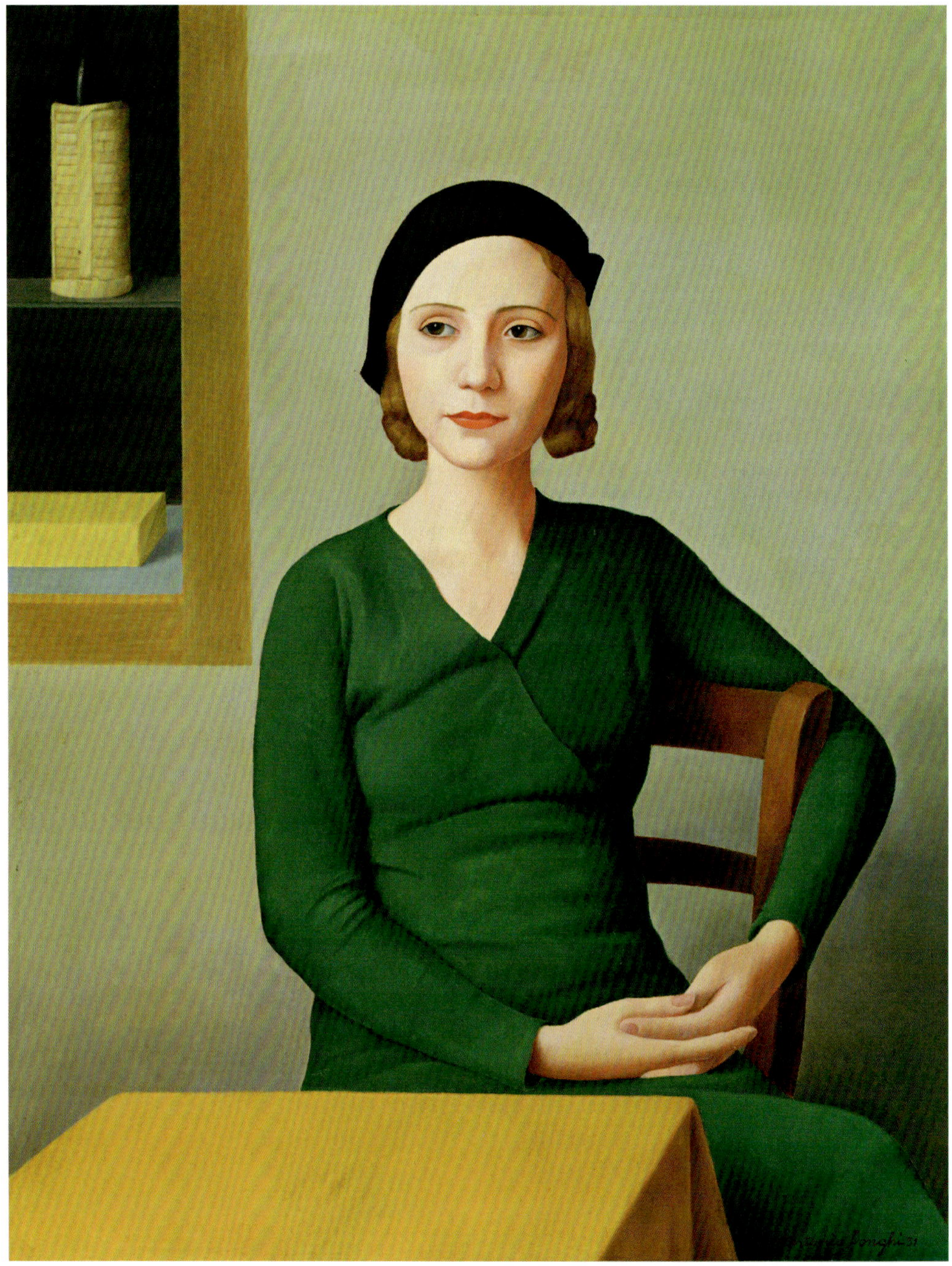

There was a significant movement in Italian inter-war painting towards rejecting the flat, abstract compositions of the international avant-garde in favour of promoting three-dimensionality in art. Indeed, *Valori Plastici* was the programmatic title of an influential art magazine that appeared between 1918 and 1922. Not least, the movement sought inspiration in earlier traditions of Italian painting, especially those of the fifteenth century. The Roman painter Antonio Donghi, a proponent of magic realism, has here used the austere structure of his picture to transport its subject – a fashionably dressed young woman at a plain table – into a world that transcends time. Donghi's reduction of his subject to clear outlines, as well as the sober interior with a still life on the recessed shelves to the left, evokes Florentine fifteenth-century portraits. SH

PROVENANCE
Bought at the 28th Venice Biennale in 1932

LITERATURE
Rome 1985, pp. 128–9; Florence 2012–13, p. 128, no. 1.17

38

FRANCIS PICABIA
(1879–1953)
Study for Ino, 1929

Watercolour on canvas, 62 × 47 cm
Courtesy of Galerie 1900–2000, Paris
BERLIN ONLY

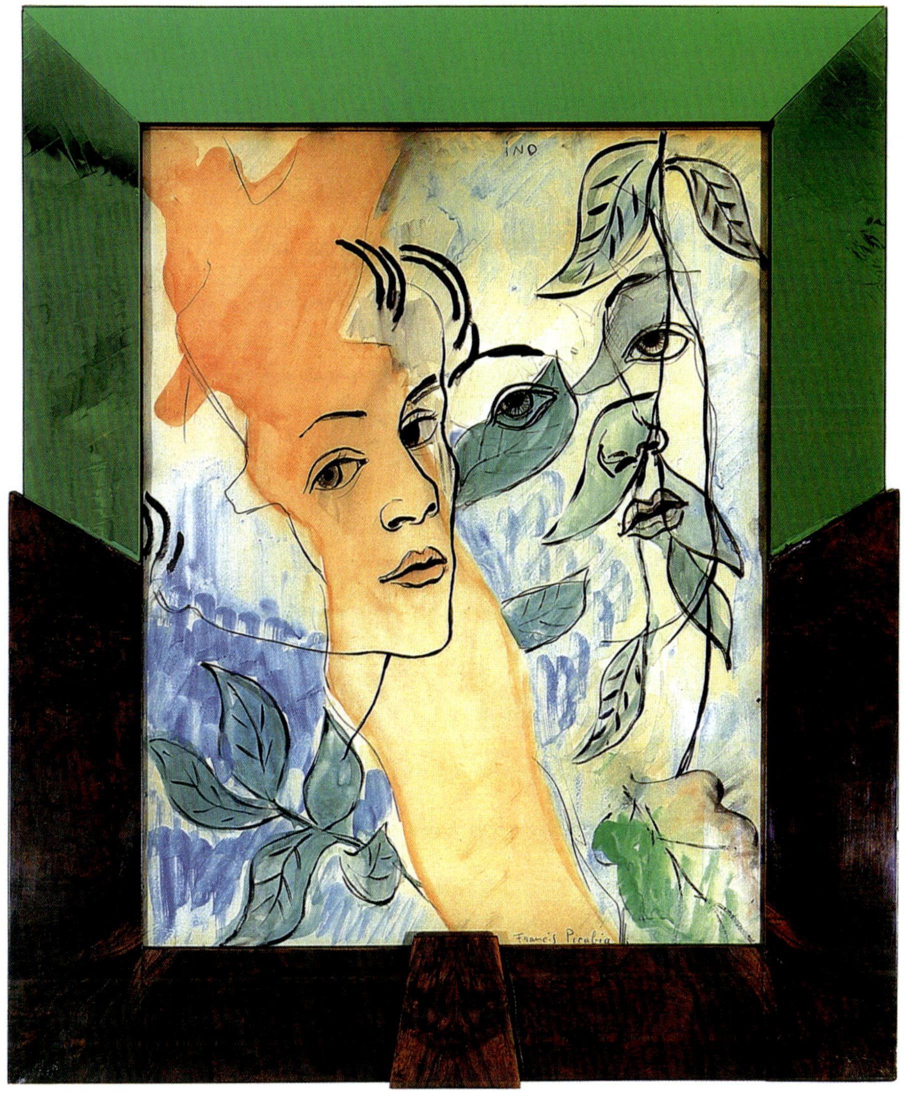

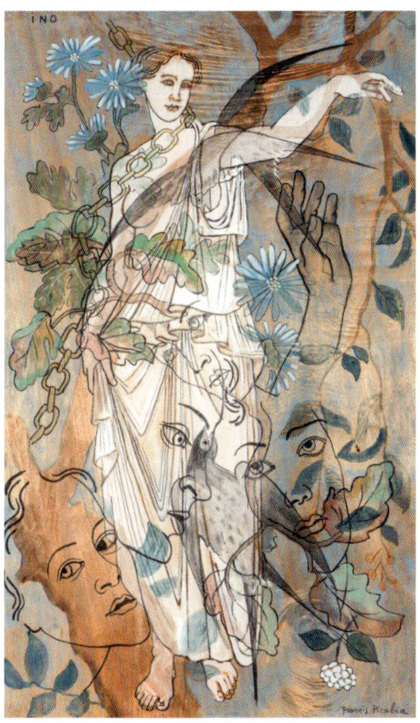

FIG. 69
FRANCIS PICABIA (1879–1953)
Ino, 1929–30
Oil on plywood, 161 × 96 cm
Private collection

One of the most active members of the Dadaist movement, Picabia made collages and paintings that resembled technical building plans, and depicted people with more than two eyes. He announced the demise of this kind of art in 1927, and began instead to superimpose different silhouettes within the same visual space. By the end of the 1920s he had fully developed these *Transparences*, as he called them, incorporating the outlines of works from antiquity and the Renaissance. He drew on Botticelli often, but his borrowings from the Florentine artist are themselves generally transformed in his finished paintings.

In the case of *Ino*, this process of appropriation is strikingly well documented by a preparatory study. On the left can be clearly discerned the face of the young St John the Baptist from *Virgin and Child with the Young St John the Baptist* (cat. 110); on the right-hand side of the same page this face has already undergone a transformation (with different eyes, lips and an altered profile). This changed face appears in the lower left-hand corner of the finished painting (see fig. 69). The other faces, like the one of the commanding Pompeian goddess, also appear to be free adaptations from Botticelli. GM

LITERATURE
Camfield 1979, p. 235f. and fig. 324

39

AUGUSTUS JOHN
(1878–1961)
Portrait of his Son, Pyramus, 1910

Oil on panel, 38.7 × 31.7 cm
Private collection

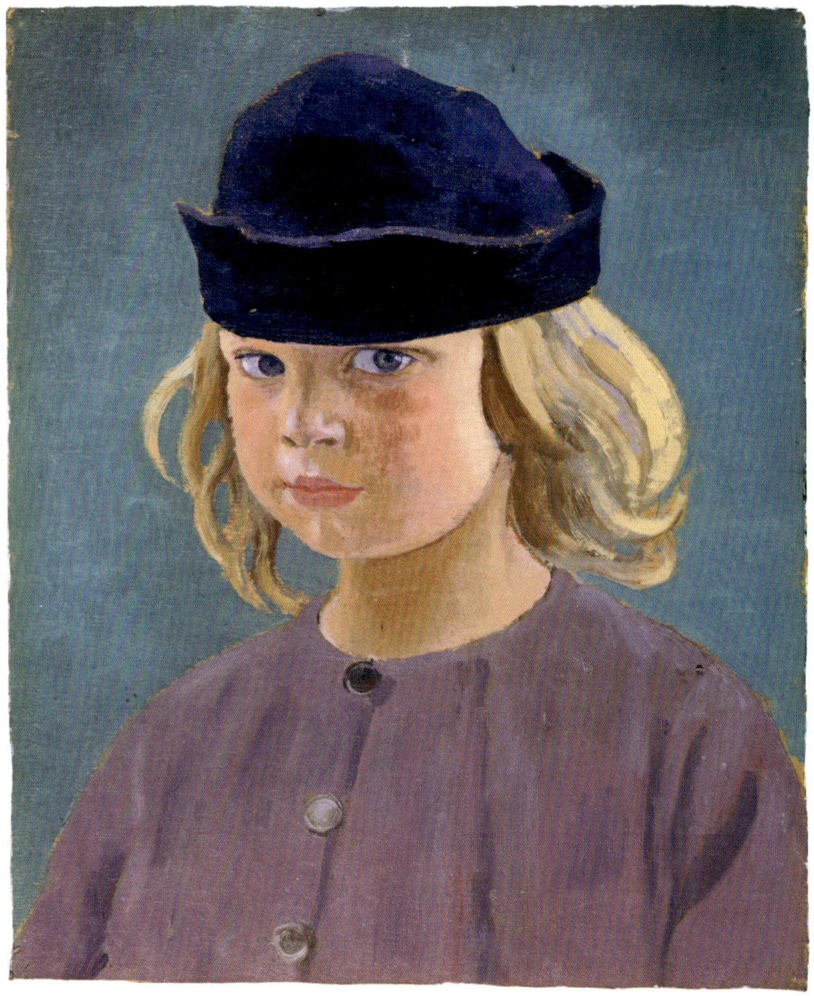

This portrait was painted the year Augustus John first visited Florence, which he found 'magnificent and uncomfortable ... too many masterpieces to digest at one meal', but where he was entranced by Botticelli's *Primavera* (fig. 8). As late as 1943 he remarked that in Botticelli 'is to be found the outline we are all in search of and may yet delimitate the "shape of all things"'.

The vibrant oil studies of his children, which Augustus John painted around 1909–12 in oils directly onto panel, are some of his most striking works. John's eldest child with Dorothy McNeill, Pyramus was born in a caravan on Dartmoor and died of meningitis a few days after the birth of his sister Poppet. The composition and attitude of the portrait of Pyramus and its flat primary colours are reminiscent of Botticelli's bust-length portraits of young men wearing red caps in London (fig. 33) and Washington (cat. 163). ME

PROVENANCE
The artist; by descent; private collection

LITERATURE
Easton and Holroyd 1974, pp. 68–9; Holroyd 1974, pp. 332–3; Evans 1996, pp. 13–16

40

MAURICE DENIS
(1870–1943)
Child in Blue Trousers, 1897

Oil on canvas, 52.5 × 39.2 cm
Musée d'Orsay, Paris (RF 1987 24)

As at the birth of his other two children, Maurice Denis celebrated the arrival of his first daughter Noëlle, on 30 June 1896, with a painting. The striking dominance of blue tones contrasts with the flesh tones of the faces, which are half covered with shades of grey, and with the matt gold of the mother's hair and the picture frame above her and the child, who together form the centre of the composition. The garish yellow light shines through the window in the background on the right, and is also visible from another source, reflecting off the inner edge of the picture frame. This directs the viewer's attention to the framed reproduction of Botticelli's *Virgin and Child with the Young St John the Baptist* in the Louvre (cat. 110). Denis used this painting-within-a-painting to lend the intimate scene an almost sacred feel, drawing a parallel between the love of a mother for her infant and that of the Virgin Mary for the Saviour. Denis, a pious Christian, thereby presented motherly love as the foundation of faith, extending this to the whole of humanity. This painting demonstrates both his profound religiosity and his admiration for Botticelli, already recorded in his diary as early as 1887. GM

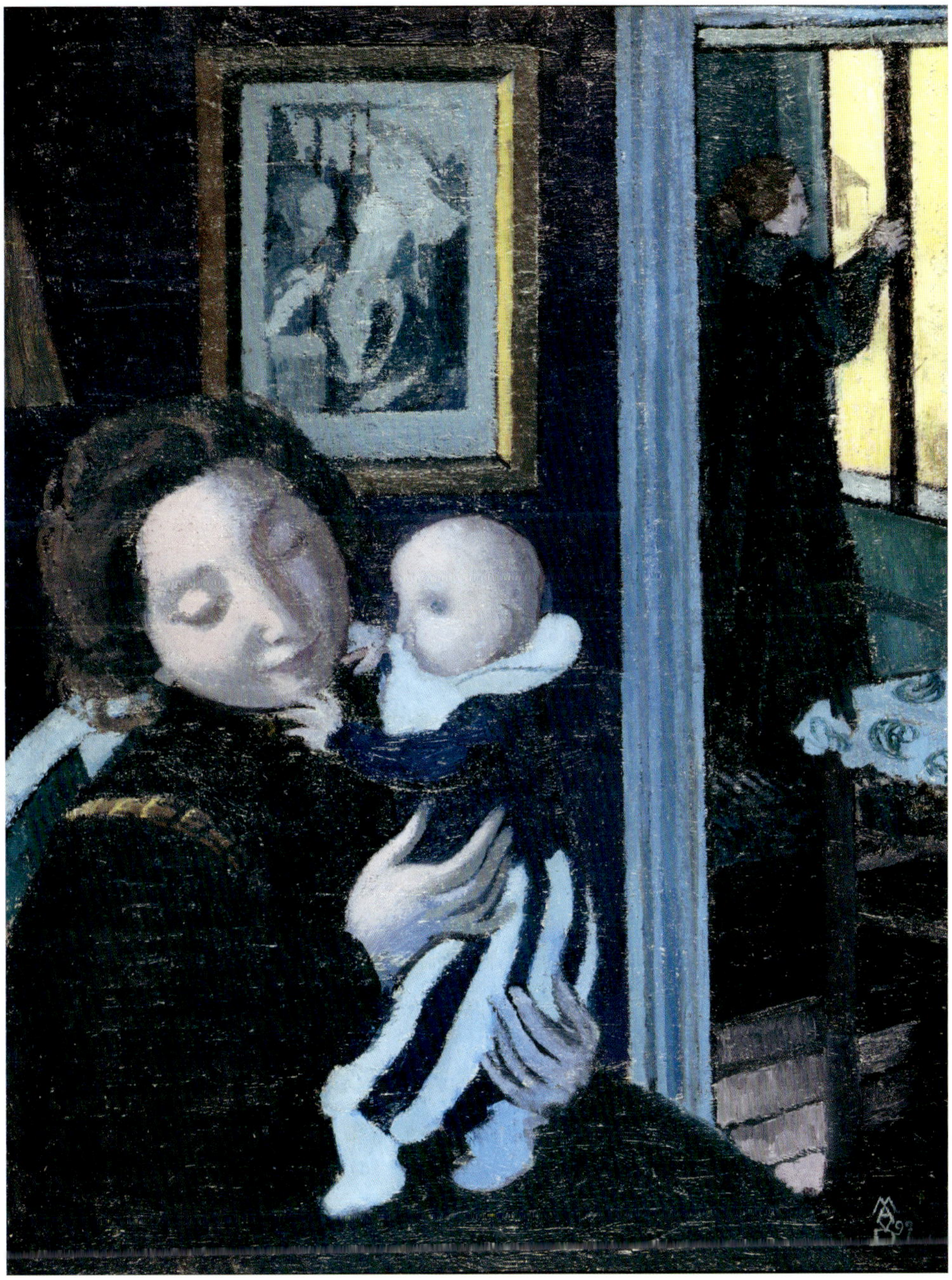

PROVENANCE
Acquired from the artist by Ambroise Vollard 1899; various owners; 1987 acquired by the Musée Nationaux for the Musée d'Orsay, Paris

LITERATURE
Vienna 2007–8, p. 144

2

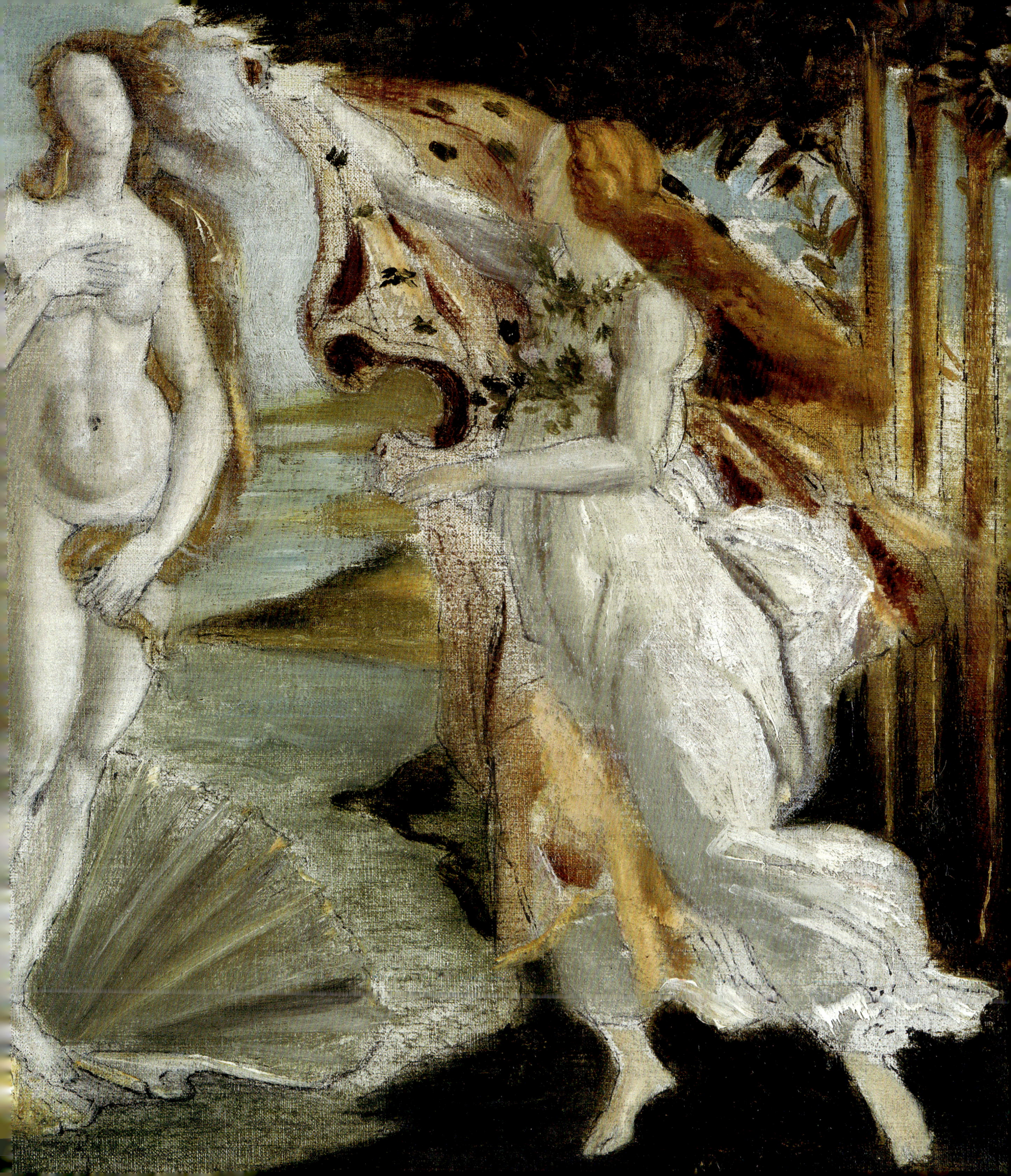

41

ELEANOR FORTESCUE-BRICKDALE (1871–1945)

Botticelli's Studio: The First Visit of Simonetta Presented by Giulio and Lorenzo de' Medici, 1922

Oil on canvas, 75 × 126.5 cm
Private collection

Brickdale was primarily a designer and illustrator, known as the 'last of the Pre-Raphaelites', a label she gladly accepted. In the early 1920s she painted two scenes of the lives of Renaissance artists, a genre that was popular in France in the first half of the nineteenth century. *The Forerunner*, executed in 1920, took Leonardo da Vinci as its subject. This sequel depicts a fictional encounter of Botticelli with 'la bella Simonetta', and was painted for Brickdale's patron Montague Rendell, headmaster of Winchester College.

Botticelli is portrayed at work on his most celebrated religious painting, the *Madonna del Magnificat* (see cat. 117). He is wearing a red cap and brown garb similar to those in his portraits of young men in London (fig. 33) and Washington (cat. 163). The other principal figures are based upon well-known paintings by or once attributed to Botticelli. Giuliano de' Medici (bowing) was the subject of several portraits (cats 154, 155) and 'la bella Simonetta' (in the green dress) is based upon an ideal head of a lady in Chantilly. The likeness of Lorenzo de' Medici (smiling) resembles a posthumous sixteenth-century portrait by Girolamo Macchietti in the Palazzo Pitti. A distant view of the Palazzo Vecchio through the window confirms Florence as the location.

This painting was exhibited in 1922 at the Royal Academy Exhibition (no. 246), and at the Walker Art Gallery Jubilee Autumn Exhibition (no. 443) in Liverpool. It attests to the survival of the Pre-Raphaelite aesthetic into the third decade of the twentieth century. MM

PROVENANCE

Montague Rendell, commissioned from the artist, 1922; Coolings Gallery, London; private collection, Maryland, c.1981; by descent to present owner

LITERATURE

Nunn 2012, pp. 29–30

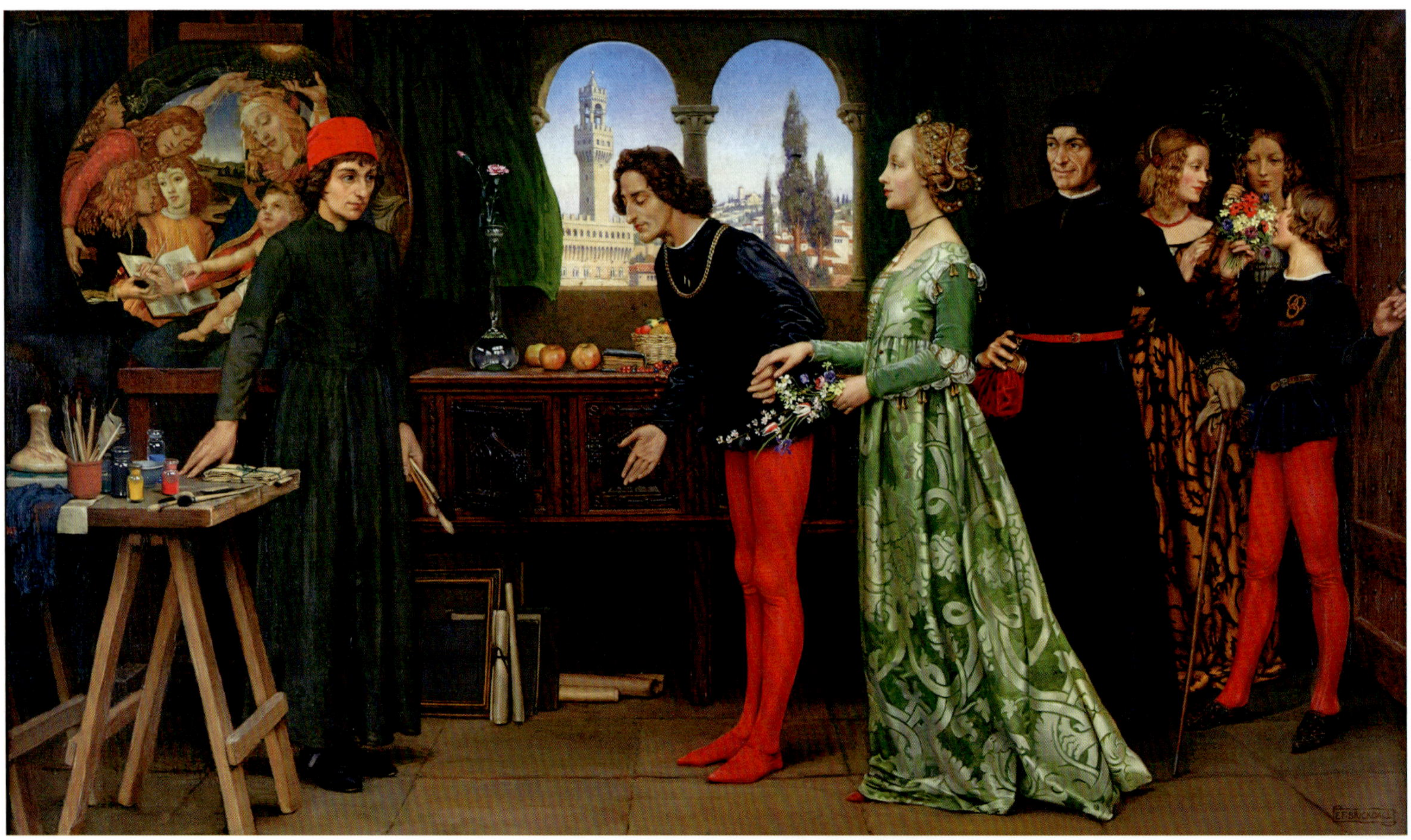

42

NOEL LAURA NISBET (1887–1956)

Dryads in Flight or *Startled Wood Nymphs*, c.1935

Oil on canvas, 62.3 × 62.3 cm
Private collection

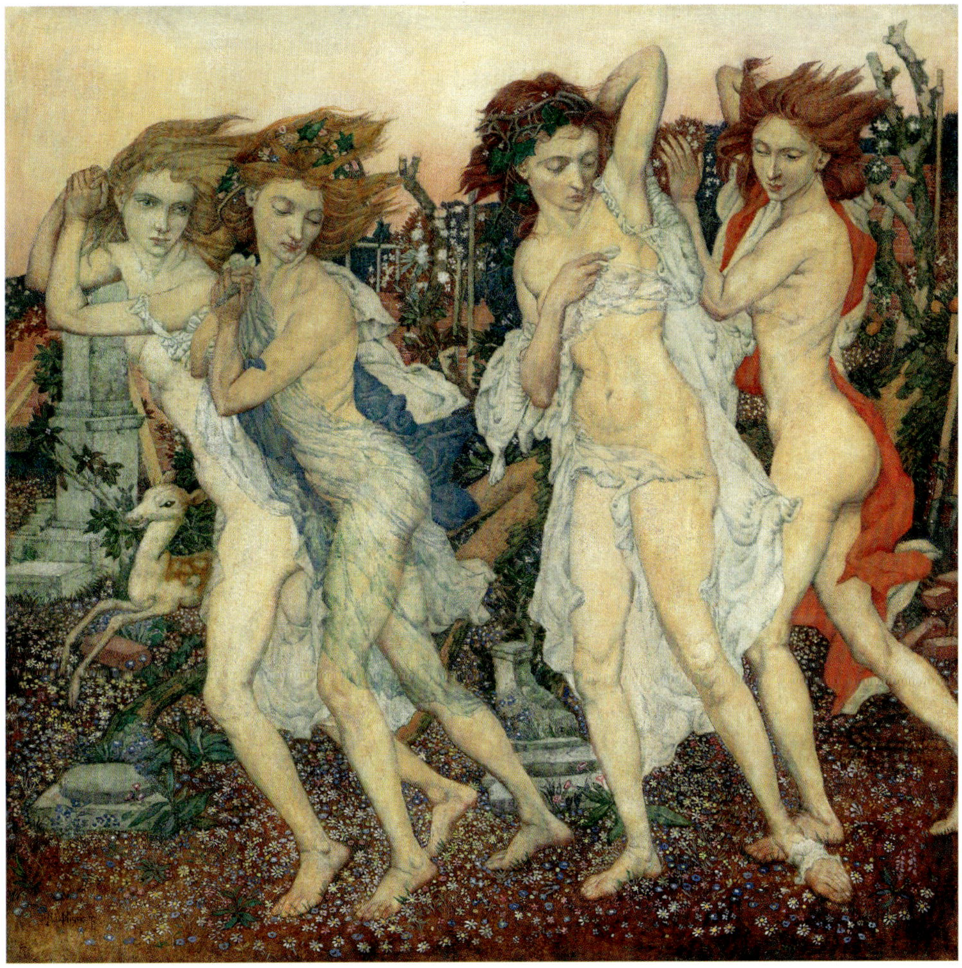

Nisbet was an illustrator who studied at the Clapham School of Art in London. Initially influenced by the Pre-Raphaelites, she later developed a more linear style with harder outlines. The artist regularly exhibited at the Royal Academy, and the present work is probably that shown there in 1934 under the title *Wood Nymphs in Flight* (no. 680). The following year she painted a similar picture titled *Startled*, (no. 137) minus one foreground figure and with additional background detail.

This painting indicates the persistent influence of Botticelli's *Primavera* well into the 1930s. In particular, Nisbet has responded to the dancing gait and fluttering transparent draperies of Botticelli's Three Graces, and the nymph Chloris at the right of his composition, which had also fascinated performers including the dancers Isadora Duncan (cat. 46) and Rita Sacchetto, as well as Hazel, Lady Lavery (cat. 45). MM

PROVENANCE
Private collection

LITERATURE
Catalogue 1984

43

ATTRIBUTED TO

UMBERTO GIUNTI (1886–1970)

Madonna of the Veil, c.1920–9

Tempera (and other media) on panel, 88.2 × 45.7 cm
The Samuel Courtauld Trust, The Courtauld Gallery, London (P.1947.LF.40)

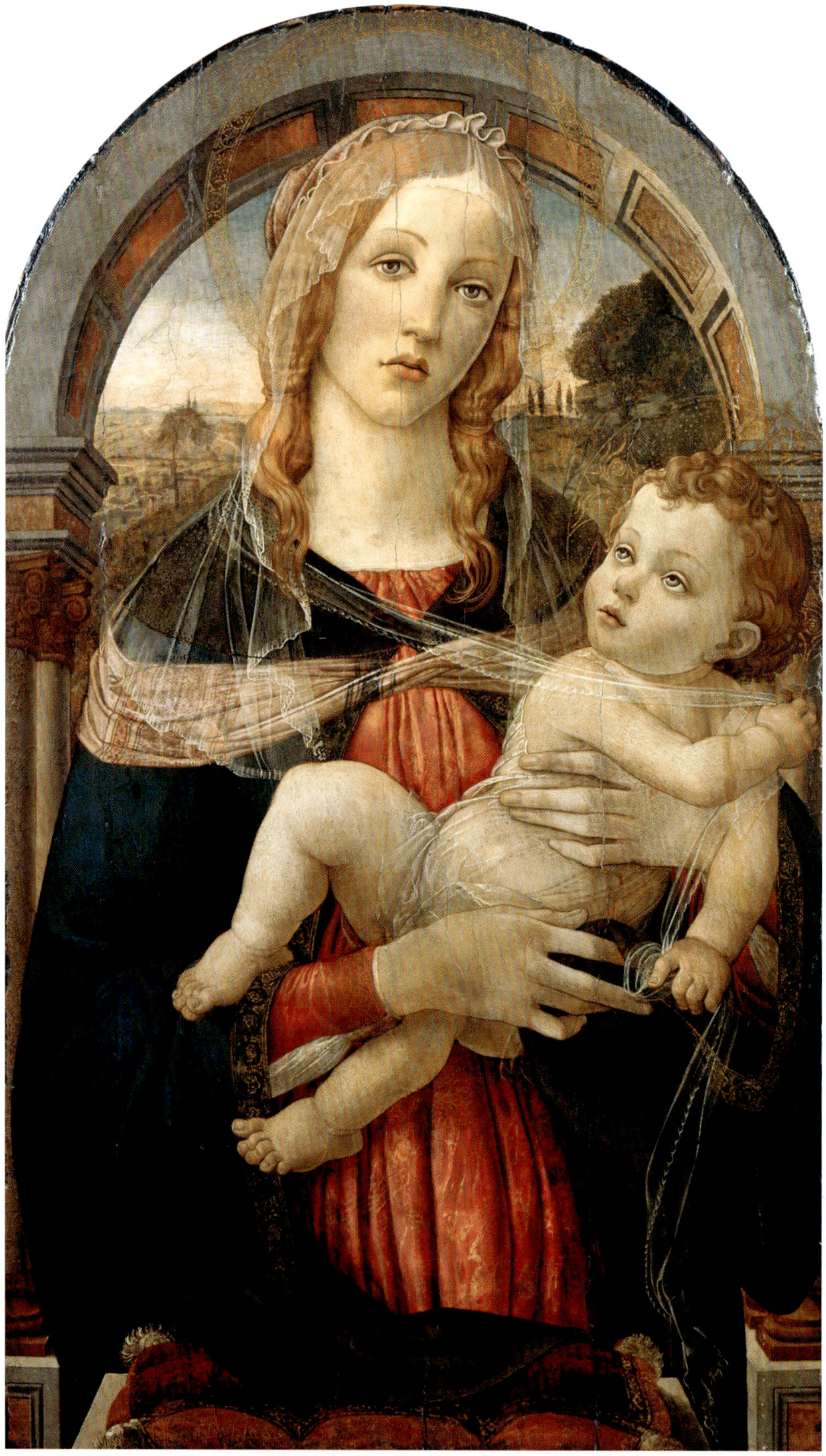

This painting was acquired for $25,000 in 1930 from a Milanese lawyer and art dealer by Arthur Hamilton, Lord Lee of Fareham. He instigated the idea of a new institution for the study of art, and convinced his friend the industrialist and collector Samuel Courtauld to found the Courtauld Gallery, to which Lord Lee bequeathed his own collection.

The *Madonna of the Veil* was widely acclaimed as a Botticelli masterpiece when it first appeared in the 1930s. However, soon after it entered the Courtauld Gallery the former director of the National Gallery, Sir Kenneth Clark, noticed that the Madonna's rosebud lips and pencilled eyebrows were reminiscent of the silent movie star Jean Harlow, the original 'Blonde Bombshell'. Close examination indicated that damage to the surface could have been mechanically induced and recent scientific investigation shows that some of the pigments were only available since the eighteenth century, and that their finely ground consistency is indicative of commercial manufacture. The presence of areas purposefully coloured to suggest the ageing of pigments confirmed that the work was made with the intention to mislead.

The picture is now believed to be by Umberto Giunti, a teacher at the Institute of Fine Arts in Siena with a reputation for producing convincing forgeries. MM

PROVENANCE

Lord Lee of Fareham, Arthur Hamilton (1st Viscount), bought 1930; bequeathed to The Courtauld Gallery, 1947

LITERATURE

London 1990, pp. 34–5, no. 7; King 1994, pp. 8–13; Villiers 2004

44

THE SPANISH FORGER

Susannah and the Elders, c.1900

Body colour with gilt enrichments, 20.5 × 14.5 cm
Accepted by HM Government in lieu of Inheritance Tax and allocated to the Victoria and Albert Museum, 2008
Victoria and Albert Museum, London
(V&A: E.529–2008)

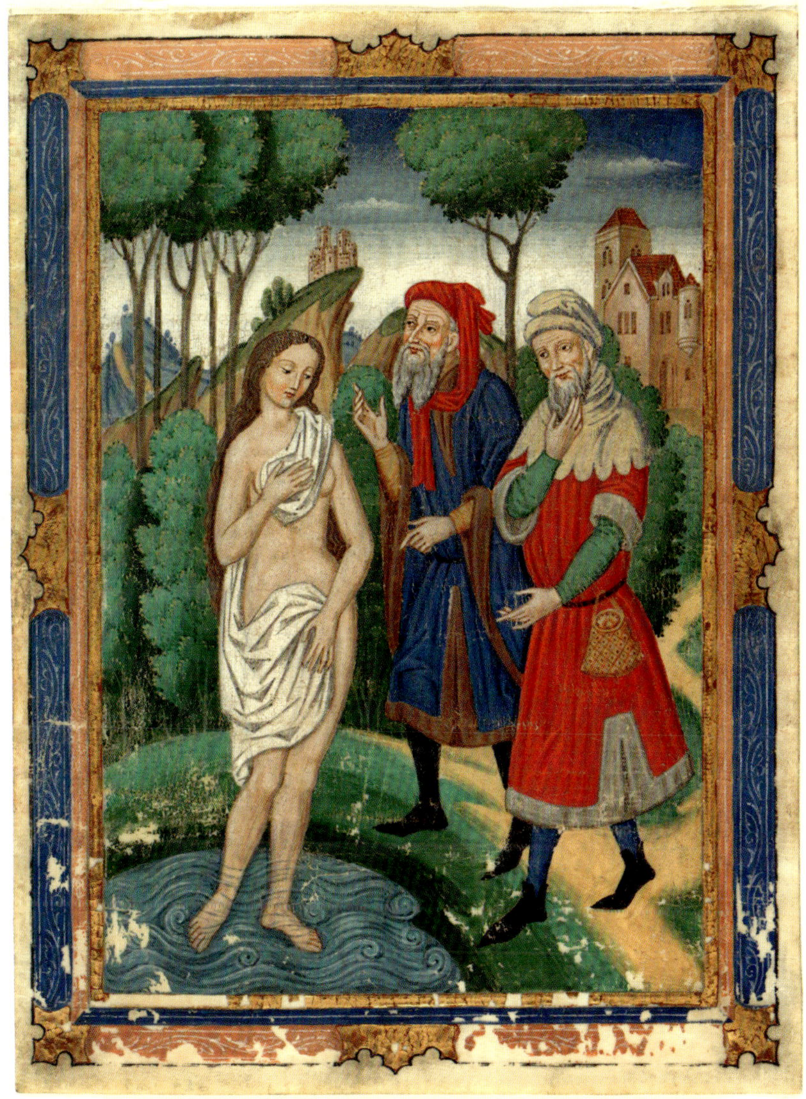

The Spanish Forger capitalized on the taste for medieval paintings and illuminations, widespread between the later nineteenth and early twentieth centuries. His dainty figures, typically set before steep hills and castles, derive from illustrated books on the Middle Ages. He takes his name from a painting attributed to a Spanish master, but was probably active in Paris.

This is one of five miniatures added to the backs of cuttings from text pages of an old Italian choir book. Its subject is taken from the biblical Apocrypha (Susannah 15–24). The costume of the elders and the castellated landscape recall Franco-Flemish manuscripts of around 1400 but the figure of Susannah resembles Venus in Botticelli's *Birth of Venus*, of which a colour reproduction was published by the Arundel Society in 1870 (cat. 81). Such anachronisms as this exposed the works of the Spanish Forger as fakes. ME

PROVENANCE

Mr Brown (d. c.1925), Switzerland; his wife, bequeathed to Maria Teweles, California; Kerrison Preston, Surrey; Jean F. Preston; accepted by HM Government in lieu of Inheritance Tax and allocated to the Victoria and Albert Museum, 2008

LITERATURE

New York 1978, p. 56, no. L.65, fig. 184; Burgio, Clark and Hark 2009

45

‘Mrs. John Lavery as “Primavera”, from Botticelli’s Famous Picture’, *The Sphere*, 20 December 1913

Illustrated newspaper, 30 × 41.5 cm (page)
National Art Library, Victoria and Albert Museum, London (38041800848343)

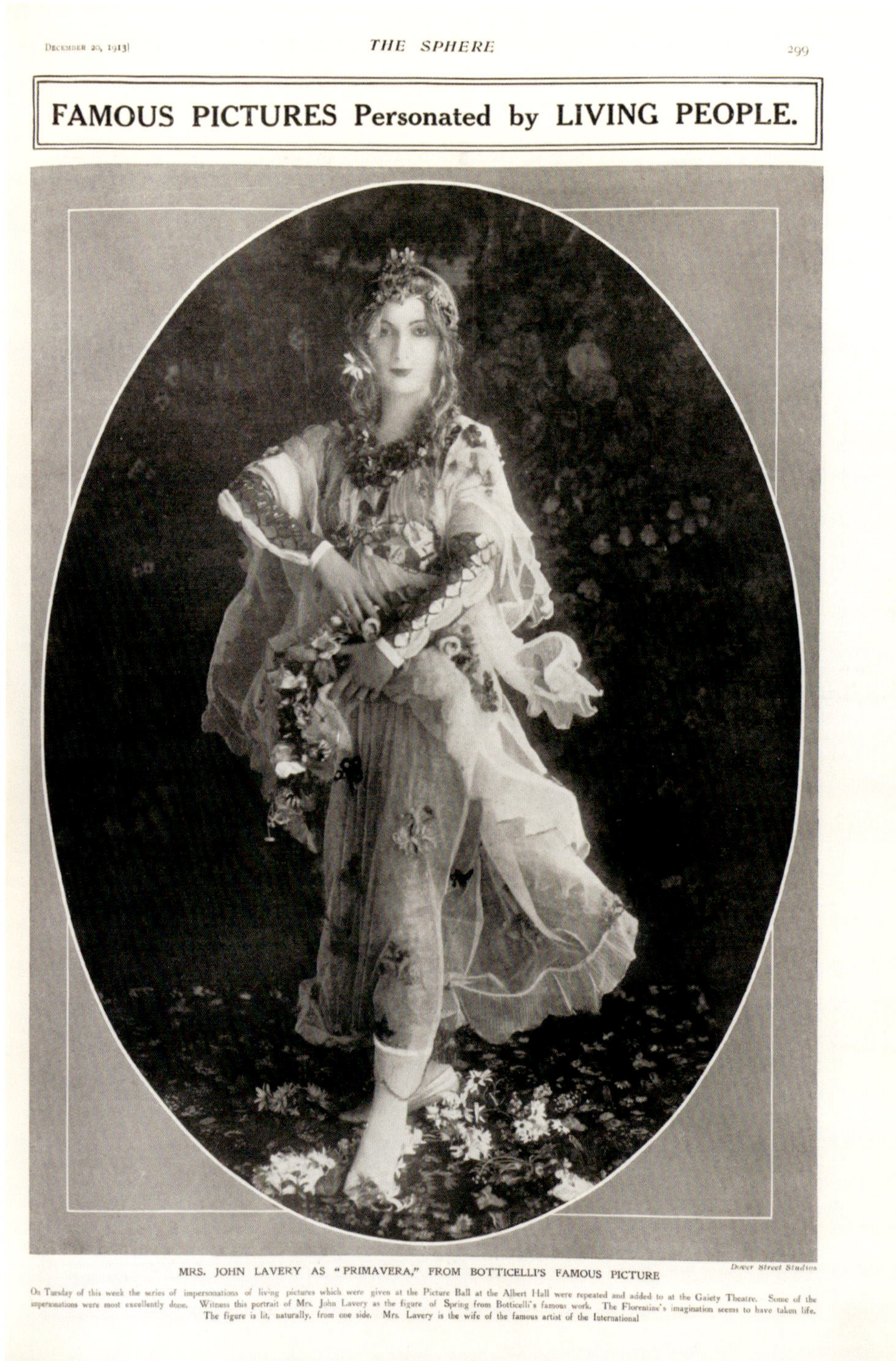

December 20, 1913] THE SPHERE 299

FAMOUS PICTURES Personated by LIVING PEOPLE.

Dover Street Studios

MRS. JOHN LAVERY AS "PRIMAVERA," FROM BOTTICELLI'S FAMOUS PICTURE

On Tuesday of this week the series of impersonations of living pictures which were given at the Picture Ball at the Albert Hall were repeated and added to at the Gaiety Theatre. Some of the impersonations were most excellently done. Witness this portrait of Mrs. John Lavery as the figure of Spring from Botticelli's famous work. The Florentine's imagination seems to have taken life. The figure is lit, naturally, from one side. Mrs. Lavery is the wife of the famous artist of the International

This illustration depicts Hazel, Lady Lavery, the American wife of the Irish portrait painter Sir John Lavery. A society beauty, she regularly appeared in the pages of illustrated magazines such as *The Sphere* and *Tatler*. Lady Lavery first dressed as Flora from Botticelli’s *Primavera* for a ‘Picture Ball’ at the Royal Albert Hall on 4 December 1913, in which several well-known ladies, inspired by celebrated paintings, dressed as ‘moving art’ to raise money for the ‘invalid kitchens’ of London’s East End. A reviewer described her as ‘transfigured ... in her white flowered costume’. When the event was repeated on 20 December at the Gaiety Theatre it was reported in this full-page feature. The caption describes how ‘the Florentine’s imagination seems to have taken life’.

The original photograph was made by Dover Street Studios Ltd, which specialized in theatrical portraiture. The atmospheric use of light, falling dramatically from one side, emphasizes the sheer material of Lady Lavery’s dress. MM

PROVENANCE
National Art Library

LITERATURE
‘Albert Hall spectacle explores history through moving art’, *Guardian*, 4 December 1913; *The Sphere*, 20 December 1913, p. 299; McConkey 1993, pp. 134–5

46

ANONYMOUS

Isadora Duncan Dancing, early twentieth century

Video footage, four seconds
The Isadora Duncan Dance Foundation

In her autobiography, the dancer and choreographer Isadora Duncan described her first visit to Florence around 1902, during which she sat for days before Botticelli's *Primavera*, seeking to understand the movement depicted in the picture: 'the soft undulation of the flower covered earth, the circle of nymphs and the flight of the zephyrs, all assembling around the central figure, half Aphrodite, half Madonna, who indicates the procreation of spring in one significant gesture.'

Duncan later declared that her meditation on how the Three Graces in the painting seem to move with their draperies gently floating in the wind provided inspiration for her radically new 'Dance of the Future'. Her aim was to 'dance this picture and give to others this message of love'. The short film sequence shown in the exhibition is the only surviving footage of Isadora Duncan dancing. The relationship to Botticelli's work is intensified by the outdoor setting and the loose, expressive drapery. MM

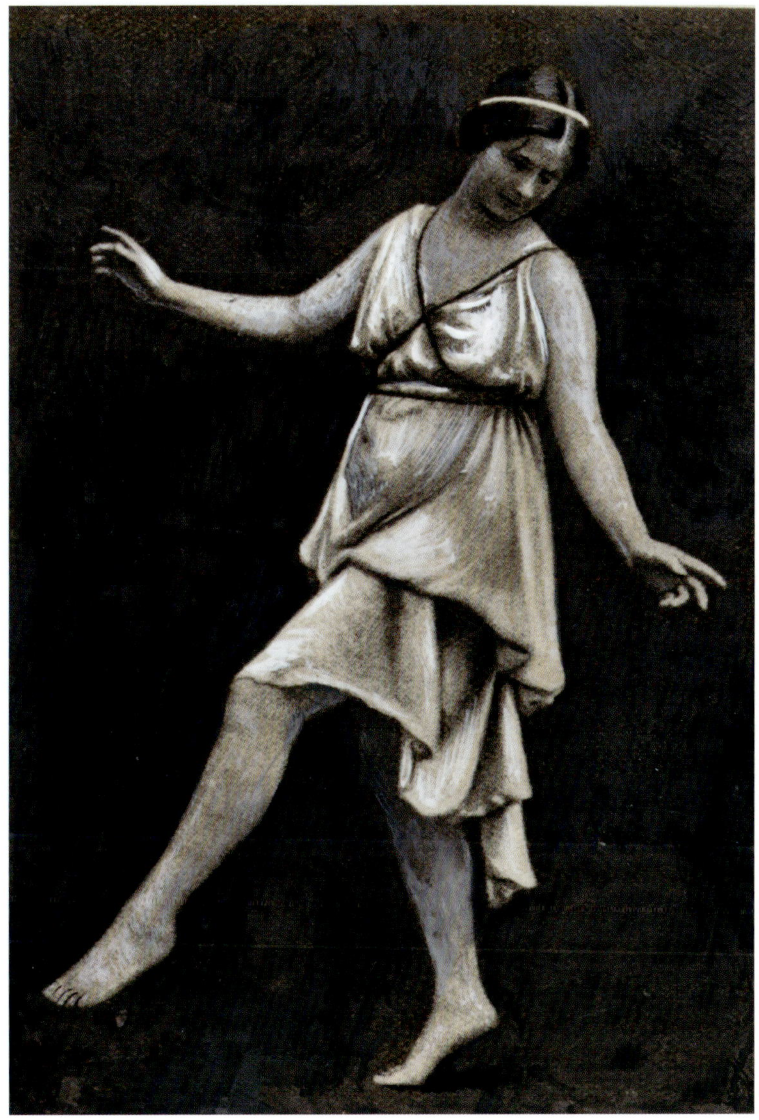

FIG. 70
ANONYMOUS
Photograph of Isadora Duncan dancing, 1904

PROVENANCE
The Isadora Duncan Dance Foundation

LITERATURE
Duncan 1928, pp. 123–4; Ghilardotti and Carizzoni 2006, p. 33

47

LEONARDO BISTOLFI (1859–1933)

First International Exhibition of Modern Decorative Art (*Prima Esposizione Internazionale d'Arte Decorativa Moderna*), 1902

Poster, lithograph in eight colours, 110 × 144.5 cm
Staatsbibliothek, Berlin

BERLIN ONLY

The poster for the *International Exhibition of Modern Decorative Art* (Turin, 1902) depicts four young women dancing a delicate roundelay in a spring meadow, the letters 'ARS', formed momentarily by a length of ribbon fluttering in the breeze, playing around them. In terms of form, it relates both to Japanese prints (the blossoming branches) and to the rhythmically expressive linearity typical of Botticelli, whose dancing Graces from *Primavera* are reinterpreted here in the context of art nouveau (in Italian, the *stile floreale*). Its designer Leonardo Bistolfi was one of the most sought-after sculptors of his day, an admirer of fifteenth-century art and vice-president of the organizing committee of the 1901 *esposizione*, which garnered a great deal of attention across Europe, representing a high point of art nouveau. SH

PROVENANCE

Emporium 1901; Turin 1994–5, p. 446, no. 356

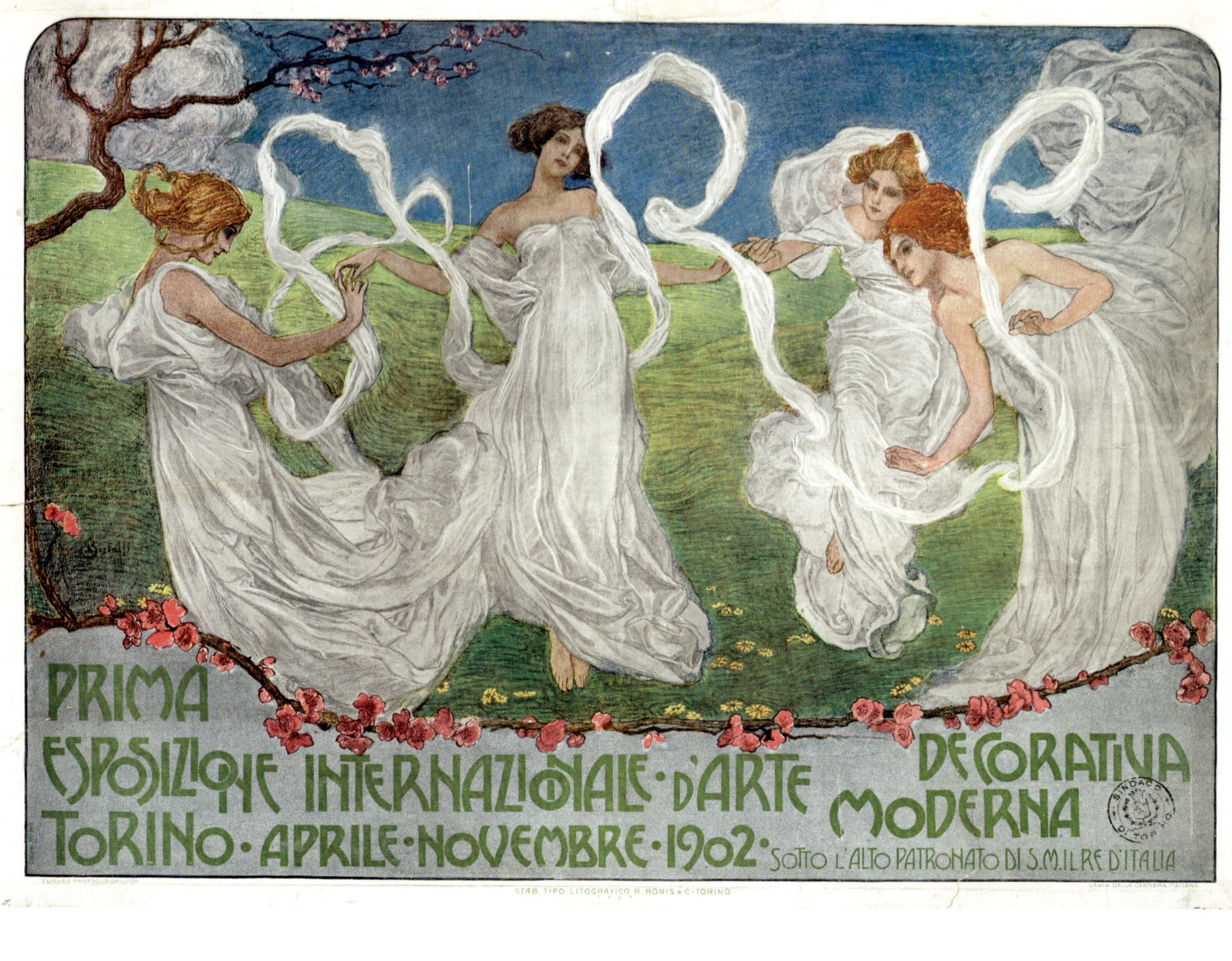

48

ATTILIO FORMILLI (1866–1933)

Festival of Art and Flowers, Florence 1896–97, 1896

Poster, 149 × 70 cm
Kunstbibliothek, Staatliche Museen zu Berlin
(O.S.1976, 10/MID.-NR. 14064196)
BERLIN ONLY

Victoria and Albert Museum, London
(V&A: E.2433-1938)
LONDON ONLY

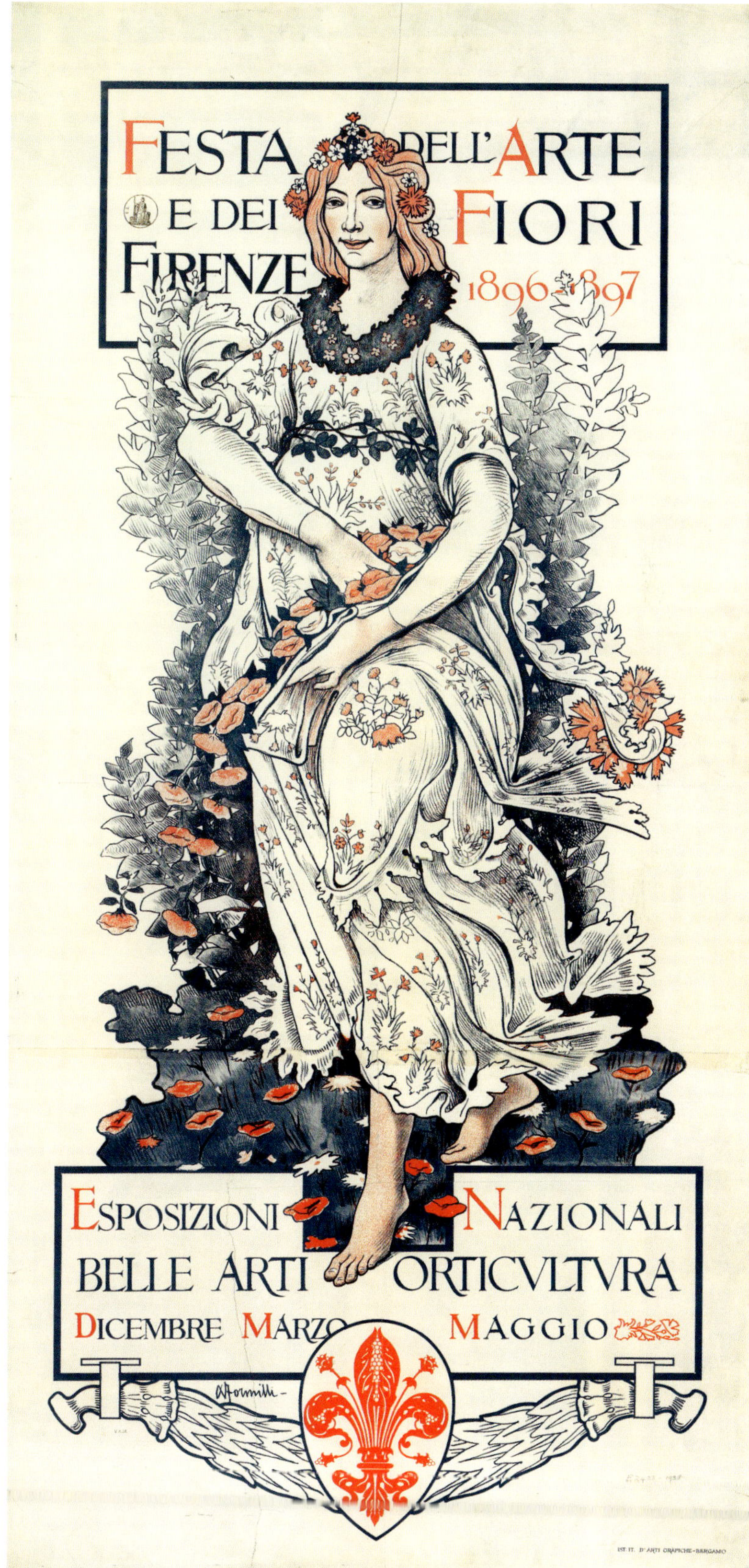

On the occasion of its 50th anniversary in 1896–7, the Florentine Società delle Belle Arti organized an extremely successful art exhibition, supported by the Società Toscana di Orticultura, in an area of the centre of Florence that had recently undergone a radical process of urban transformation. This presented the major international art movements of the past five decades, including many very prominent artists (Giovanni Segantini, Puvis de Chavannes, Claude Monet, Edward Burne-Jones, Arnold Böcklin and Fernand Khnopff, among others), as well as a diverse supporting programme of cultural events and a horticultural exhibition. The blossom-strewing Flora from Botticelli's *Primavera* functioned as an ambassador for this cultural event, which had more than 100,000 visitors: 'of all the Old Masters, [Botticelli was] the one who was most *en vogue*' at that time. It is the earliest example of a company using a Botticelli 'character' for promotion. SH

LITERATURE
Pratesi 1990; Pratesi and Uzzani 1991, pp. 5–36

49

ETTORE XIMENES
(1855–1926)
La Rinascita, 1895
(cast in bronze 1897)

Bronze, wooden base, 214 × 120 × 95 cm
Galleria Nazionale d'arte moderna, Rome (1362)

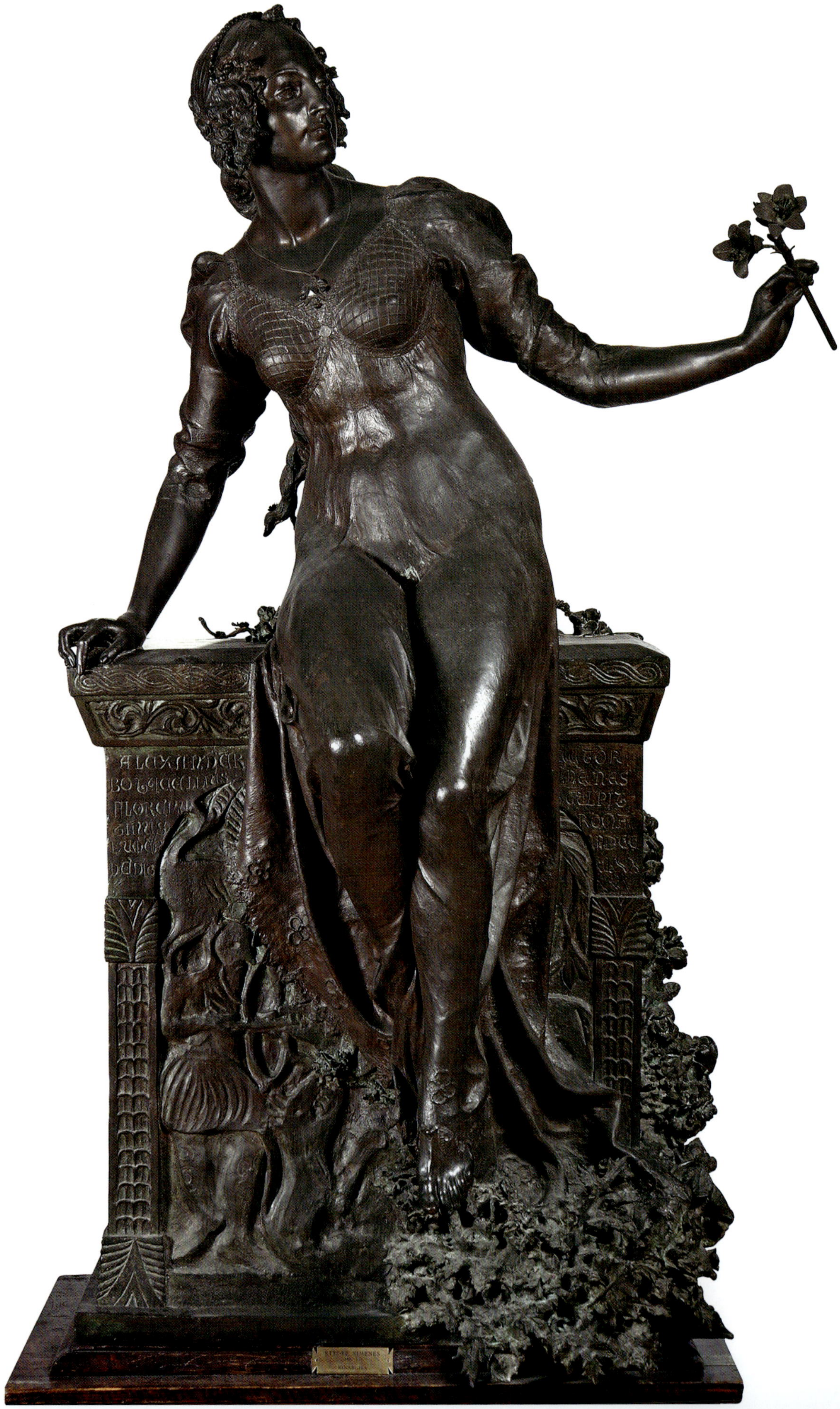

Ximenes was involved in several official monumental projects celebrating the achievements of the Italian nation, which had been unified in 1871. These include statues of Garibaldi in Palermo (1887) and of Dante in New York and Washington (1921).

La Rinascita represents an allegory of the Renaissance ('Rinascimento'). The figure's sheer drapery and hairstyle were inspired by Botticelli's female figures, in particular the Three Graces in *Primavera* (see fig. 8): a source acknowledged by the inscription on the edge of the base: 'Alexander Botticellius Florentinus lumen dedit' ('The Florentine Alessandro Botticelli gave light'). The original plaster was exhibited at the first Venice Biennale in 1895, where it was seen by the Minister of Public Instruction who commissioned a cast for the recently founded national collection of modern art in Rome. A cast was also exhibited at the 1900 Paris Exposition Universelle.

This exercise in the Italian so-called 'Liberty' style combines Pre-Raphaelite, symbolist and neo-Renaissance elements. It marks a significant juncture in the official reception of Botticelli's aesthetic in Italy at the end of the nineteenth century. AD

PROVENANCE
Bought by the Galleria Nazionale d'arte moderna in 1897

LITERATURE
Willard 1902, pp. 192–3, 799, 812; Benzi 2001, pp. 84–5

50

GIULIO ARISTIDE SARTORIO (1860–1932)

Madonna of the Angels (Magnificat), 1895

Oil on canvas, diameter 123 cm
Private collection

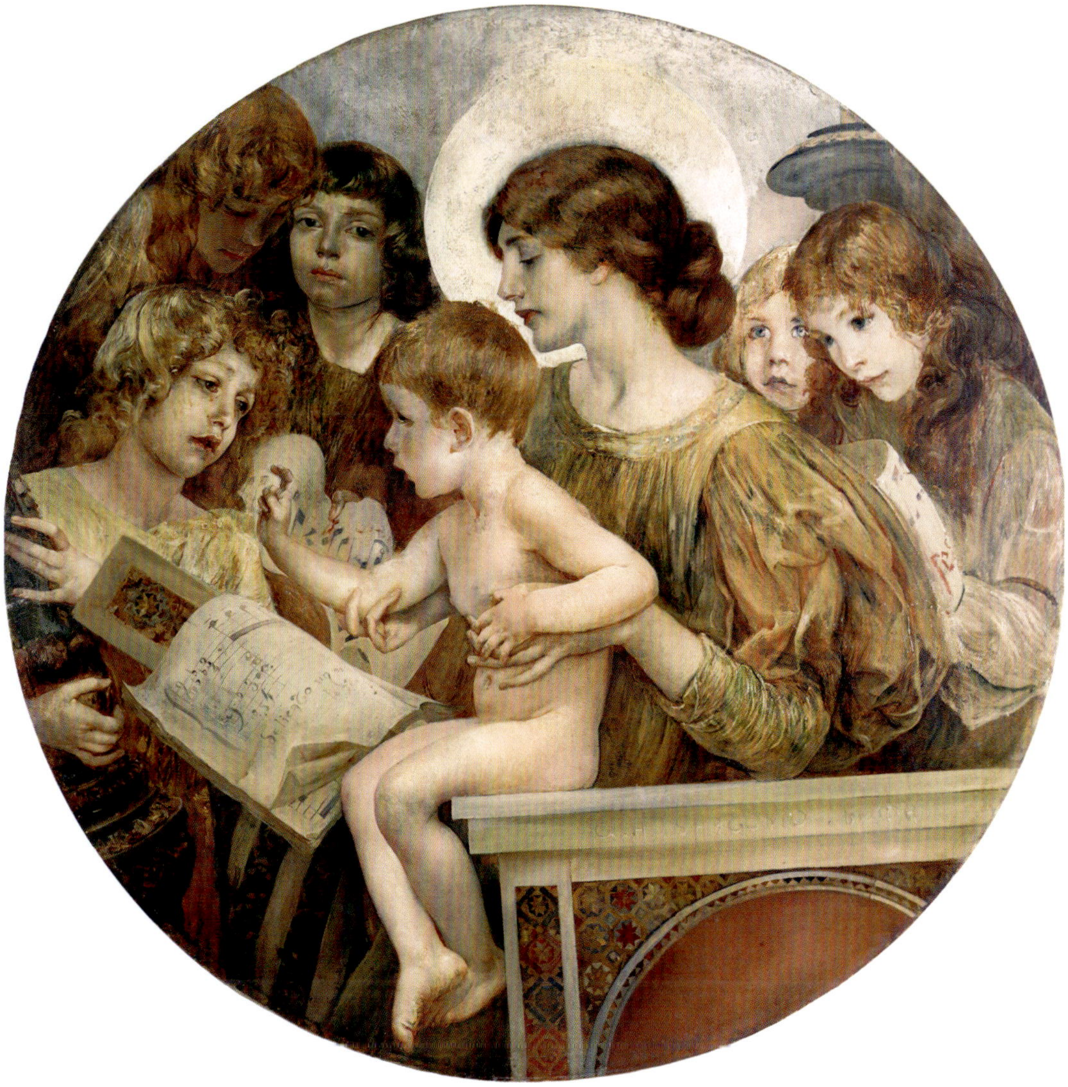

This tondo represents Marie Hardouin, the wife of the poet Gabriele D'Annunzio, as the Virgin, and Gabriellino, one of their sons, as the Christ Child. The subtitle and curvilinear aesthetic pay tribute to its source of inspiration: Botticelli's *Madonna del Magnificat* in the Uffizi (see under cat. 117). The artist had visited Britain in 1894 and shared the Pre-Raphaelites' interest in Renaissance art. The red hair of the female figures suggests a debt to Dante Gabriel Rossetti, about whom Sartorio wrote for *Il Convito*, a periodical founded by D'Annunzio, a leader of the Italian Aesthetic movement 'Liberty'.

Sartorio had previously provided the illustrations for D'Annunzio's *Isaotta Guttadàuro* (1886), a lavish volume which paid homage to the Quattrocento poetry of Angelo Poliziano and Lorenzo de' Medici, as well as the pictorial imagery of the Pre-Raphaelites. AD

PROVENANCE

Angela Sartorio; Augusto Jandolo; sold 1937; by descent to present owner

LITERATURE

Esposizione 1895, p. 128, no. 300; Panzacchi 1895, p. 649; Angeletti and Natali 1904, pp. 52–3; Sartorio 1907, p. 622; Rome 1933, p. 46, no. 34, fig. XVII; Mimita Lamberti 1982; Fugazza 1988, p. 105; Benzi 2001, pp. 83–4; Miracco 2006, p. 174

51

ETIENNE AZAMBRE (1859–1935)

At the Louvre, 1894

Oil on canvas, 62 × 42 cm
Musée du Louvre, Paris (RF 1978-30)

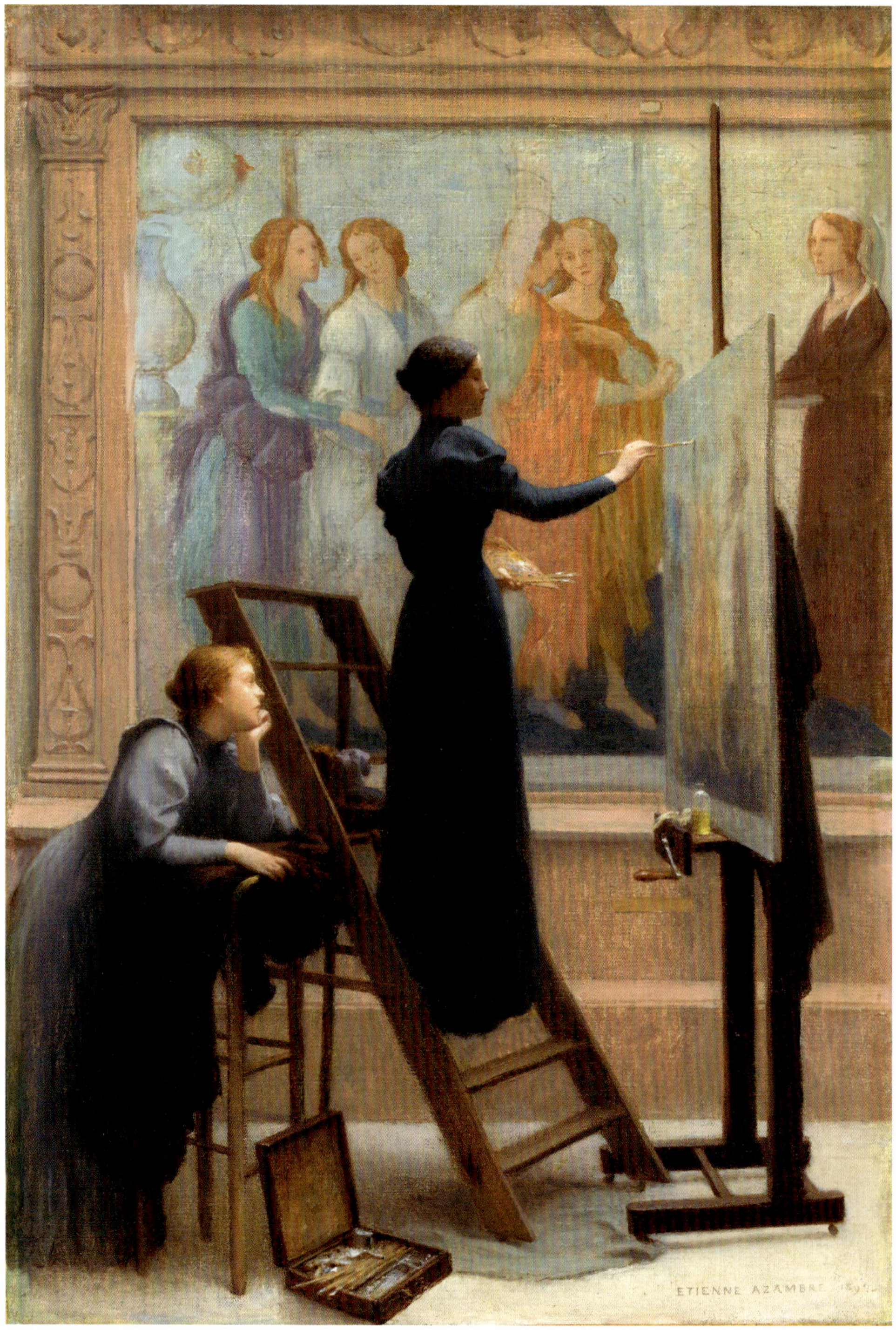

This painting testifies to the extraordinary popularity in the late nineteenth century of the two Botticelli frescoes from the Villa Lemmi, which were put on display at the Louvre in 1882 (depicted here is the fresco of *Giovanna degli Albizzi Receiving a Gift of Flowers from Venus*, see under cat. 62 and fig. 45). The register, which copyists of pictures in the Louvre had to sign, shows that many copyists of the frescoes were women or had English names.

Etienne Azambre creates a harmonic continuity between the gentle female figures in the fresco and those in front of it, all of whom seem to be enveloped in the same air and light. This painting also documents the sight that greeted visitors to the Louvre as they climbed the steps of the Daru staircase – after dutifully viewing the *Nike of Samothrace* – until the extensive renovation in 1934. Presented in pseudo-Renaissance frames, the frescoes were displayed either side of the entrance to the gallery dedicated to French painting, though the view would frequently have been blocked by the ladders and easels of the copyists. Today the frescoes are set into a wall in the passageway to the right of the *Nike*. GM

PROVENANCE
Gift from the Société des amis du Louvre, 1978

LITERATURE
Paris 1993, p. 66, no. 16

52

EVELYN DE MORGAN
(1855–1919)

Flora, 1894

Oil on canvas, 198.1 × 86.3 cm
De Morgan Collection
(P_EDM_0017)

Evelyn De Morgan was a regular visitor to Florence from a young age. Following a decline in the health of her husband in 1893 the couple spent six months there every winter until 1914. *Flora*, painted 17 years after De Morgan's *Cadmus and Harmonia* (cat. 67), is related to the subject of that name in Botticelli's *Primavera*, then on display at the Accademia di Belle Arti.

The contrapposto stance, clothing and flowing hair not only recall the figure of Flora but also that of Venus in the *Birth of Venus*. The extensive use of spring flowers in the drapery and the background are similarly reminiscent of *Primavera* and the roses in Flora's hand have traditional associations with love. De Morgan employed a gold background, such as those in early Florentine paintings, but painted over it in a way that is occasionally found as late as the seventeenth century, for example in the works of Carlo Dolci. This innovative use of a traditional material imbues the image with a glowing effect, which emerges as highlights in the hair and costume.

The Italian inscription alludes to its Florentine origins:

> I came down from Florence and am Flora
> This city takes its name from flower
> Among the flowers I was born and now by a change of home
> I have my dwelling among the mountains of Scotia
> Welcome, and let me treasure amid northern mists be dear to you.

Flora was purchased by De Morgan's patron, the Liverpool shipowner William Imrie. MM

PROVENANCE
William Imrie 1894; Miss Imrie; his sale, Christie's, London, 28 June 1907 (lot 123), bt. Gooden and Fox; Countess Bathurst; Mrs Stirling; De Morgan Foundation

LITERATURE
Gordon 1996, pp. 9, 20, no. 42; Smith 2002, pp. 89–92

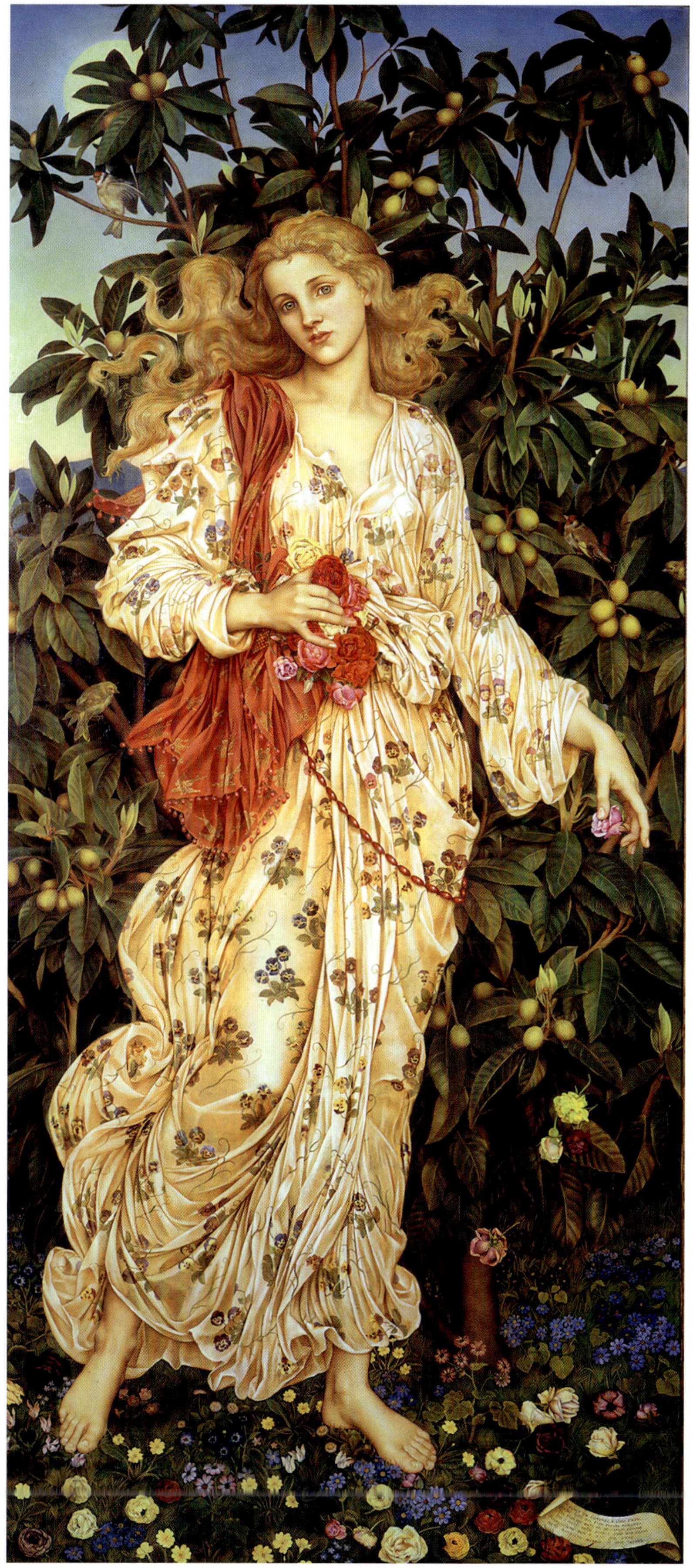

53

ANONYMOUS

Botticelli's 'Primavera', before 1871

Albumen print, 23.9 × 37.2 cm
Ashmolean Museum, Oxford (WA.RS.REF.110)

PROVENANCE
Presented by John Ruskin to the Ruskin School of Drawing (University of Oxford), 1875; transferred to the Ashmolean Musuem, c.1949

LITERATURE
Murray's Handbook 1891, p. 28; Ledger 1978, pp. 189–92; Lightbown 1978, vol. 2, pp. 51–3; Samuels 1979, pp. 298, 378–9; Westgarth 2009, p. 82; Acton 2010, n.p. (photograph of 'Professor Costantini')

During the early years of photography permission to reproduce works from the Royal Galleries of Florence (the Uffizi and Palazzo Pitti) was highly restricted. In December 1857 the director Luca Bourbon Del Monte explained that 'up to the present day … no matter how many experiments have been made … oil paintings do not come out well, [and] no permission has been given to copy the pictures in the Royal Galleries'. This policy changed in 1860 when the Alinari brothers demonstrated they could photograph paintings to a 'fairly satisfying' standard. This set a precedent for others, such as the anonymous photographer of this albumen print.

In 1871 Ruskin became the first Slade Professor of Fine Art at the University of Oxford, where he founded the Ruskin School of Drawing. As teaching aids he assembled a diverse collection of 1,470 objects including photographs, prints and drawings by himself and other artists. These were divided into four categories: standard, reference, educational and rudimentary. This photograph of Botticelli's *Primavera* was in the educational series together with depictions of foliage. Ruskin catalogued it as '5 Aphrodite and the Spring (Sandro Botticelli). P'. The P identified it as a photograph. MM

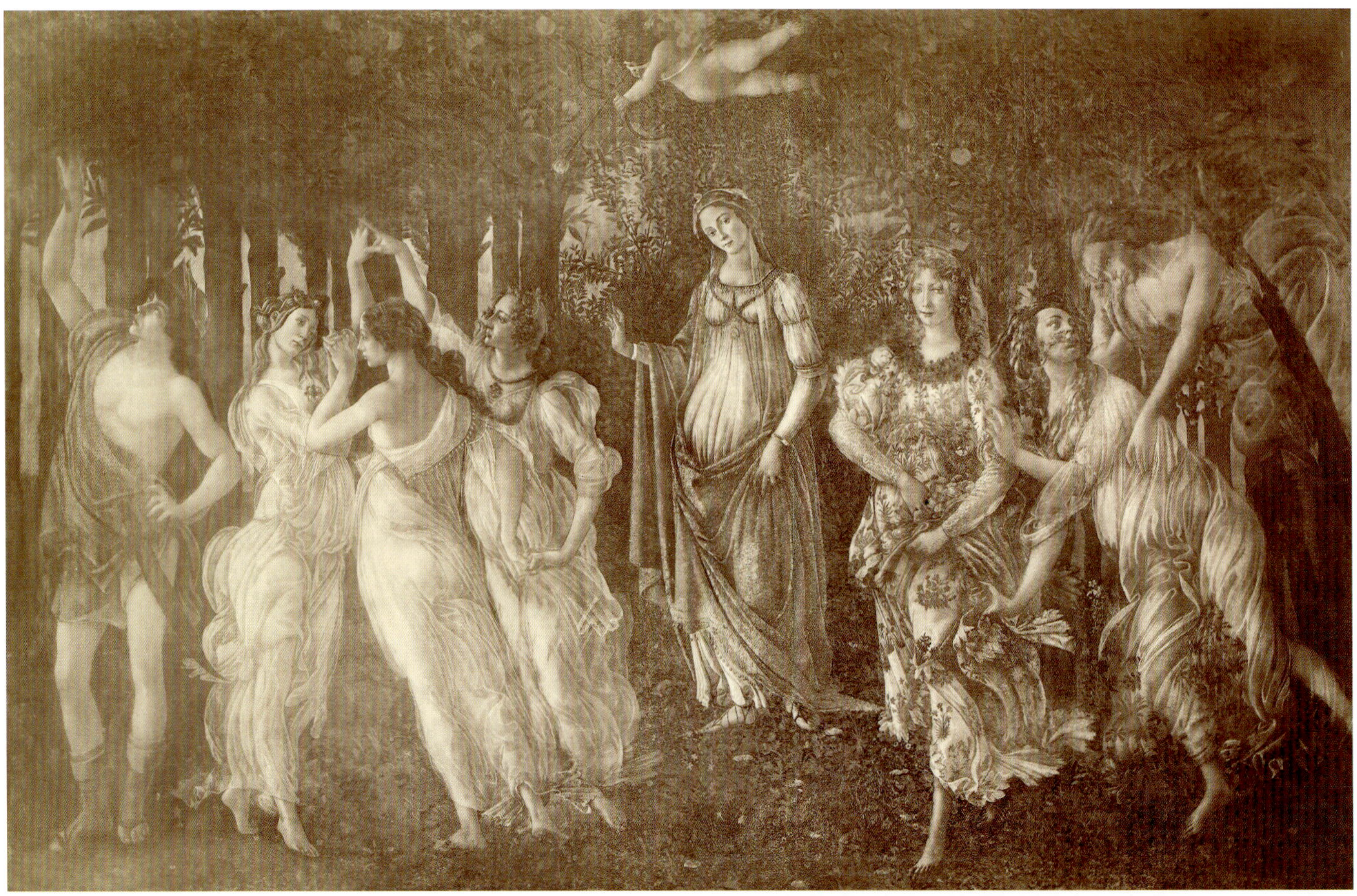

54

EMILIO COSTANTINI
(active c.1888–1902)
after BOTTICELLI

Primavera, before 1888

Watercolour on paper, 53.2 × 82.6 cm
Victoria and Albert Museum, London
(V&A: E.34-1995)

PROVENANCE
The Arundel Society; given in 1897 to the National Gallery; transferred to the Victoria and Albert Museum, 1995

LITERATURE
Murray's Handbook 1891, p. 28; Ledger 1978, pp. 189–92; Lightbown 1978, vol. 2, pp. 51–3; Samuels 1979, pp. 298, 378–9; Westgarth 2009, p. 82; Acton 2010, n.p. (photograph of 'Professor Costantini')

Botticelli's *Primavera* was first recorded in 1550 with the *Birth of Venus* (fig. 10) at the Medici Villa Castello. By 1638 they had been joined there by the artist's *Pallas and the Centaur* (cat. 164). From 1815 *Primavera* was displayed at the Uffizi, but in 1853 it was transferred to the Accademia, before returning to the Uffizi in 1919.

Emilio Costantini was a Florentine art dealer and restorer, whose 'speciality water-colour copies of the old masters' were advertised in 1891 as 'facsimiles guaranteed' with 'highest recommendations from English and foreign gentlemen'. He collaborated with Bernard Berenson, notably over the sale of Raphael's *Portrait of Tommasso Inghirami* to Isabella Stewart Gardner in 1898, but Berenson later denounced him as a notorious forger.

This is one of six copies of Florentine fifteenth-century paintings commissioned from Costantini around 1888–91 by the Arundel Society (see cat. 81). One of the Society's co-founders was John Ruskin, whose interest in Botticelli is apparent from his photographic collection and his own copies after flowers and foliage in *Primavera* (see cats 53, 72).

Despite winning a medal at the 1862 International Exhibition in South Kensington, the Society's reproductions were unable to compete with photographs, and it was wound up in 1897. When its chromolithograph of this watercolour by the German lithographer Wilhelm Greve was published in 1888, the figure of Flora was criticized by the *Athenaeum* reviewer as a 'haggard, hard-featured, and big-nosed wench – a passion-worn actress or less respectable person'. Nevertheless, at the turn of the century *Primavera* was one of Botticelli's most admired works. AD

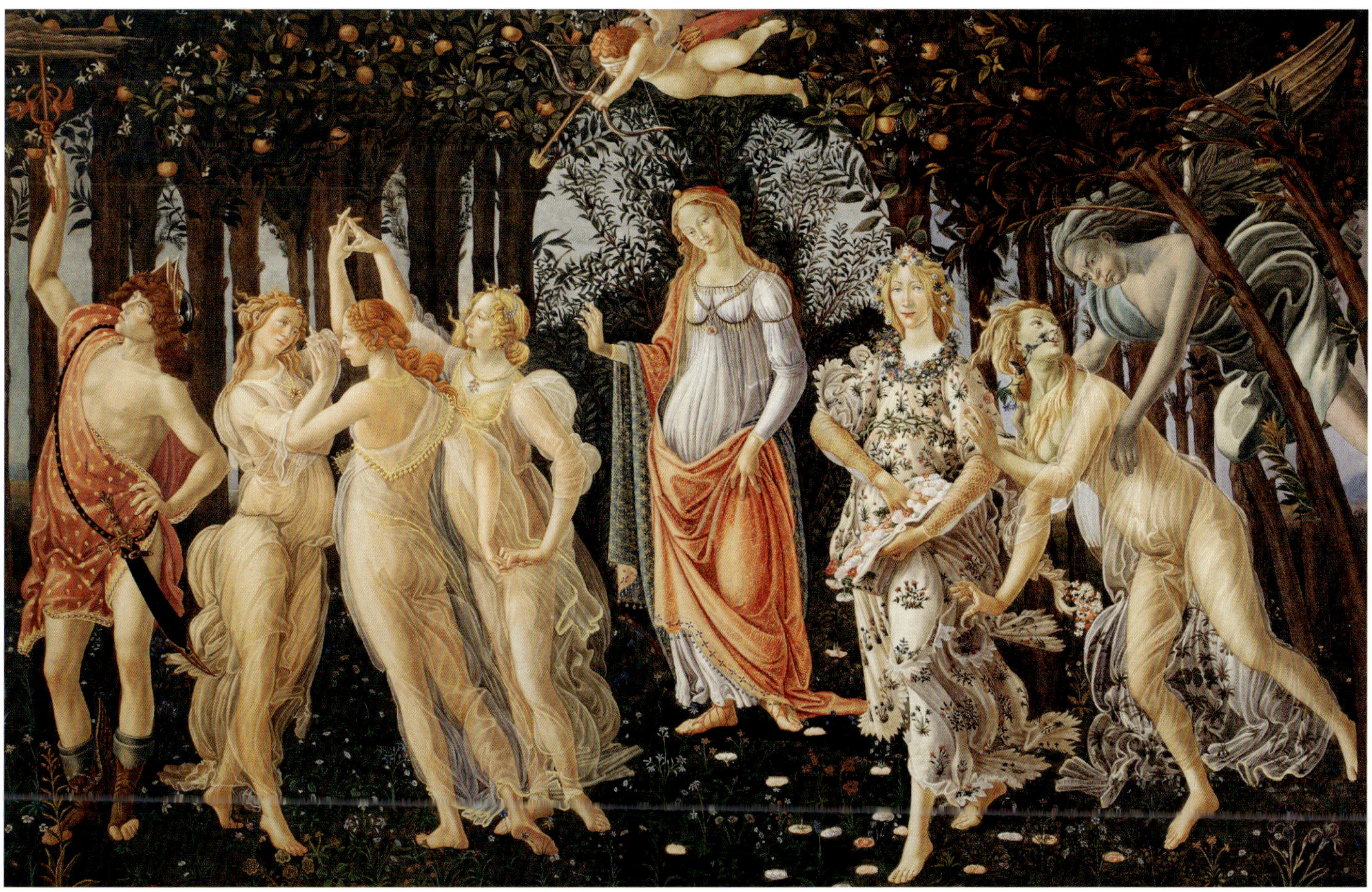

55

AUBREY BEARDSLEY
(1872–1898)
Portrait of Sandro Botticelli, 1893

Graphite on tan wove paper, laid down, 35.5 × 20 cm
The Richard Norton Fund and the Kate, Maurice R. and Melvin R. Seiden Special Purchase Fund in memory of Frederick Deknatel and in honour of Virginia Deknatel
Harvard Art Museums / Fogg Museum, Cambridge MA (2004.91)

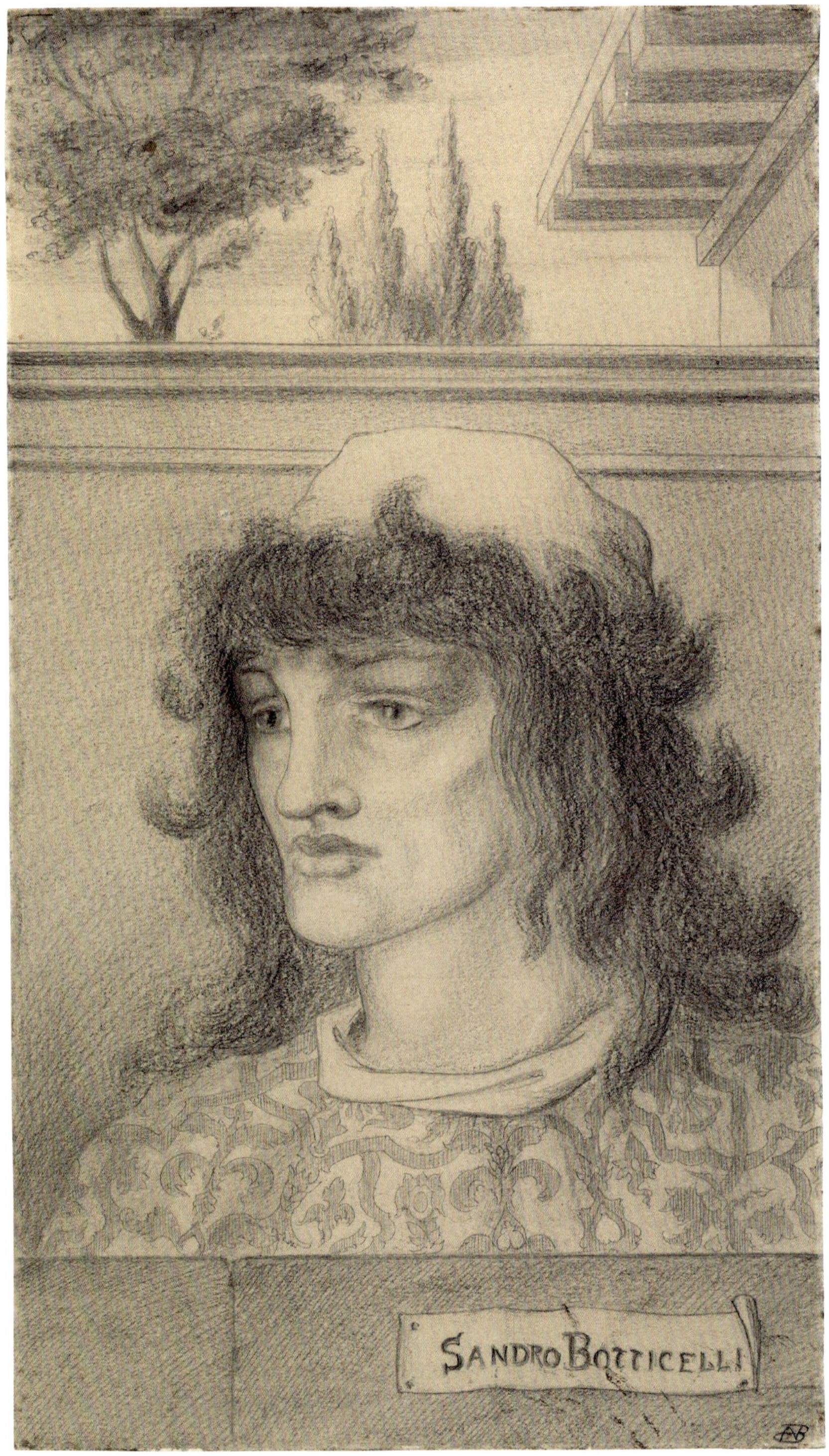

Despite his lack of formal training, Beardsley had a genius for black and white illustration. His mentor, the Pre-Raphaelite painter Edward Burne-Jones, transmitted to him a taste for the early Italian masters Andrea Mantegna and Botticelli, whose works were often confused until their oeuvres were defined. Two Botticelli bust-length portraits of young men in caps (fig. 33 and cat. 163), were once believed to be self-portraits of Masaccio, but the foreground motif of the parapet with a label is often found in paintings by the Venetian master Giovanni Bellini while the soft handling of this drawing is more suggestive of the *sfumato* of Giorgione or Leonardo da Vinci.

Beardsley gave this drawing to his friend Aymer Vallance, who noted that it was 'a reconstruction of the Florentine painter's physiognomy from his extant works, to illustrate Aubrey Beardsley's theory that every artist tends to reproduce his own physical type' – an idea which may be traced back to Leonardo's *Treatise on Painting*. Following his reinterpretation by Walter Pater in 1870, Botticelli became an attractive role model for *fin-de-siècle* artists and writers, including the decadent Frederick William Rolfe, styled Baron Corvo, as well as Beardsley. ME

PROVENANCE

Given by Aubrey Beardsley to Aymer Vallance; James Tregaskis, London; Desmond Coke, London, by 1919; Sotheby's, New York, 11–12 January 1999 (lot 578); purchased by Harvard University Art Museums, 2004

LITERATURE

Vallance 1898, pp. 365, 367; Ross 1909, pp. 72–3, no. 47; Gallatin 1945, p. 30, no. 242; Marillier 1967, p. 83, pl. 38; Weinberg 1995, pp. 220, 222; Arcade Auction 1999 (lot 578)

56

JOSEPH PENNELL
(1857–1926)
Primitives: Copying Botticelli, the National Gallery, 1891

Etching, 17.4 × 12.5 cm
Inscribed and signed by the artist: To the Mr + Mrs Blums / "The day before Xmas" / in the National Gallery / London / drawn, etched and printed by / Joseph Pennell
Allinson Gallery, Storrs CT

The Philadelphia illustrator and writer Joseph Pennell moved to England in 1884. He produced numerous etchings and lithographs, and wrote extensively, often with his wife, Elizabeth Robins, most notably their *Life of James McNeill Whistler*, published in 1908.

This print depicts a female artist copying *The Virgin and Child with St John and an Angel*, now attributed to Botticelli's workshop (cat. 118). It is one of three etchings Pennell made in 1891 of copying in the National Gallery; the others are *A Manufactory of Constable's Paintings* (12.3 × 19.8 cm) and *Copying Turner's Paintings, National Gallery* (12.5 × 20.2 cm). The inclusion of Botticelli together with the two best-known painters of the English school is indicative of the canonical status his work had attained by 1891. This print was probably published in an edition of 35, and this proof impression was dedicated to E.C Blum, President of the Brooklyn Museum. ME

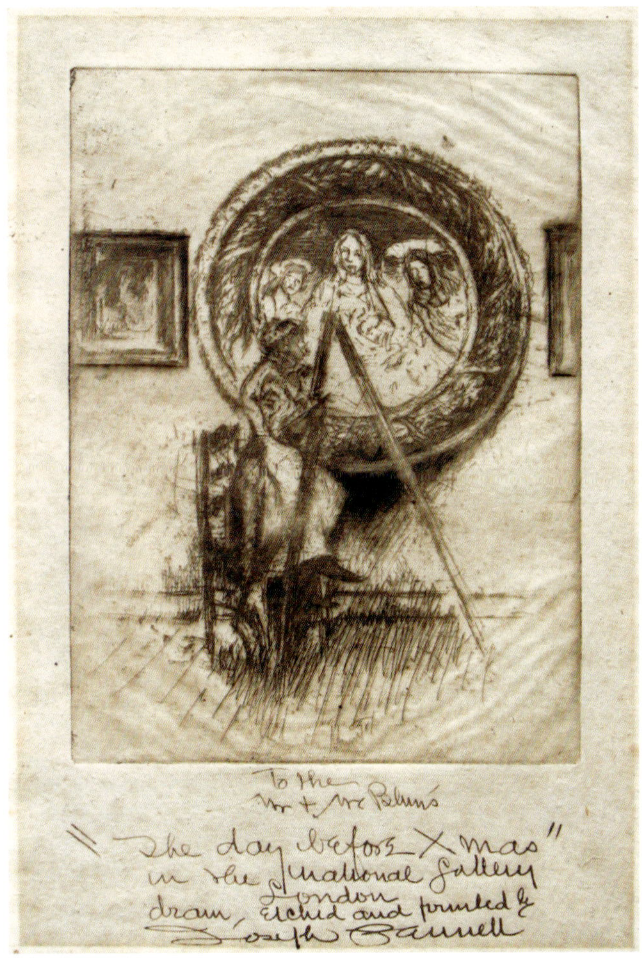

PROVENANCE
The artist's unique presentation proof for Edward Charles Blum (1863–1946) and his wife

LITERATURE
Wuerth 1928, p. 53, no. 155

57

MORRIS & CO., after WILLIAM MORRIS (1834–1896)

Design for 'The Orchard, or 'The Seasons' tapestry, c.1890

Pencil, pen and ink, watercolour heightened with Chinese white, bodycolour, 49.4 × 66.7 cm
Inscribed: 'Greenery' and 'The Seasons', with measurements '16'0" × 7'0"
Victoria and Albert Museum, London
(V&A: E.544–1939)

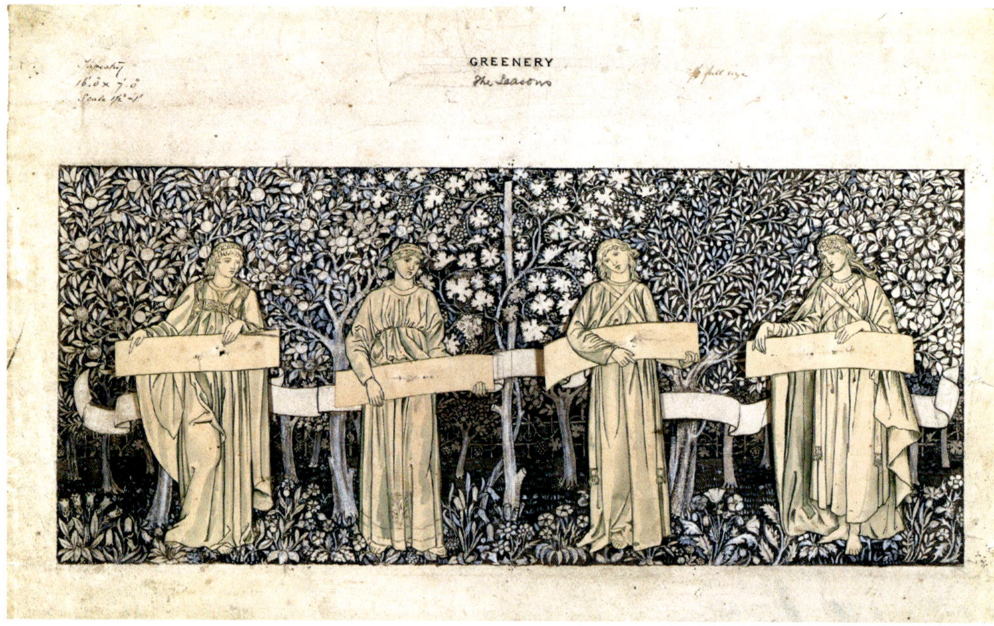

58

WILLIAM MORRIS (1834–1896) and JOHN HENRY DEARLE (1860–1932), woven at Merton Abbey by Morris & Co.

The Orchard, 1890

Tapestry woven in wool, silk and mohair on a cotton warp, 221 × 472 cm
Inscribed with verse: 'Midst bitten mead....'
Victoria and Albert Museum, London
(V&A: 154–1898)

In 1869 William Morris wrote a poem on the theme of the four seasons titled 'The Lapse of the Year', and his friend Edward Burne-Jones painted the seasons as four standing female allegorical figures in 1869–70. Burne-Jones later became Morris's principal designer of tapestries. This design is one-eighth the size of the completed tapestry. Its figures derive, with modifications, from those used as angels in Morris's ceiling decorations for Jesus College, Cambridge, of 1866. Drawn on re-used paper cut-outs, they were stuck onto a background of fruit trees and a trellis fence by Morris's assistant John Henry Dearle.

These bold figures bearing white banners with contrasting black borders recall the fifteenth-century sibyls in marble intarsia on a black ground from the pavement of Siena Cathedral, which Morris would have seen when he and Burne-Jones visited Tuscany in 1873. The tall, slender figures in high-waisted dresses are of the Botticellian type which Burne-Jones made very much his own.

Following the design, the tapestry was woven by William Knight, William Sleath and John Martin supervised by John Henry Dearle, who reported that: 'The colouring as well as the general design are by Mr Morris and parts of the figures have been woven by his own hand'. Perhaps motivated by the desire of clients for an original work, this was William Morris's first attempt to design a figurative tapestry and was

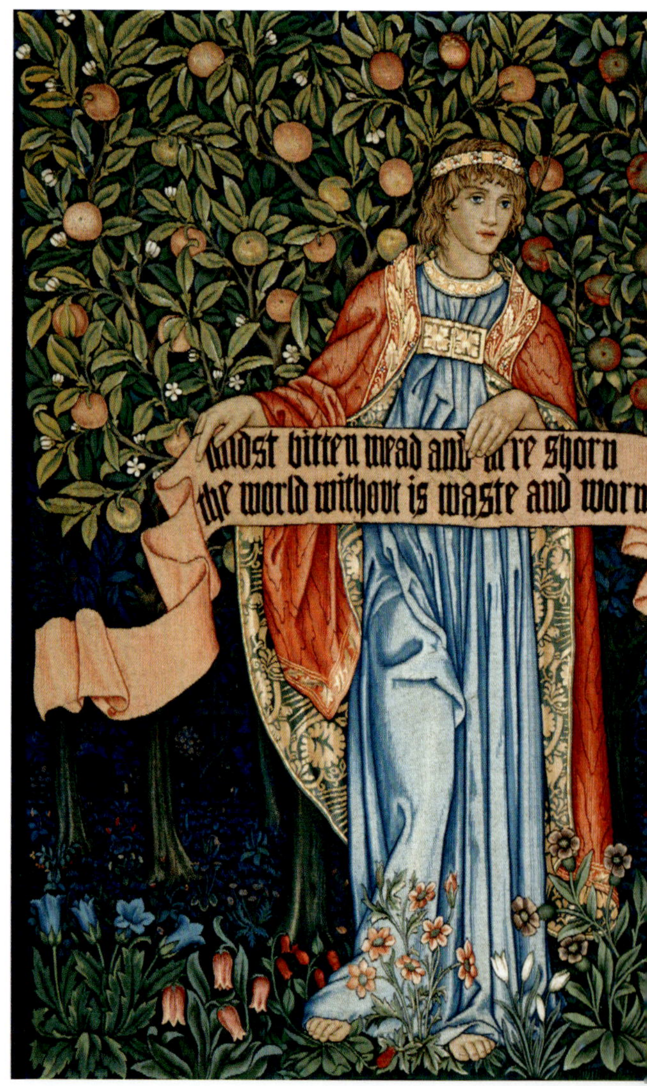

PROVENANCE
Purchased from Morris & Co. for £405, 1898

LITERATURE
London 1893, p. 132, no. 170

exhibited as an 'Arras Tapestry Designed by William Morris' at the New Gallery in 1893. Failing to find a buyer, it was later purchased by the South Kensington Museum.

The tapestry depicts a row of allegorical women representing the four seasons, from winter on the left to spring on the right, among bluebells, tulips, daisies, pansies, daffodils, primroses, carnations and other flowers before an orange and an apple tree, a grape vine, and myrtle and pear trees. Their scrolling banner bears the text of Morris's poem 'The Orchard', which he composed for the tapestry. The verse celebrates the return of spring, and ends: 'And hangs aloft from tree to tree / The banners of the Spring to be'. This subject and the tall elegant figures in an orchard setting are reminiscent of Botticelli's *Primavera*, which was itself copied shortly after as a tapestry by Morris & Co. ME

PROVENANCE

Purchased from Morris & Co. for £7 4s, 13 April 1939

LITERATURE

London 1996, p. 288, no. M.122

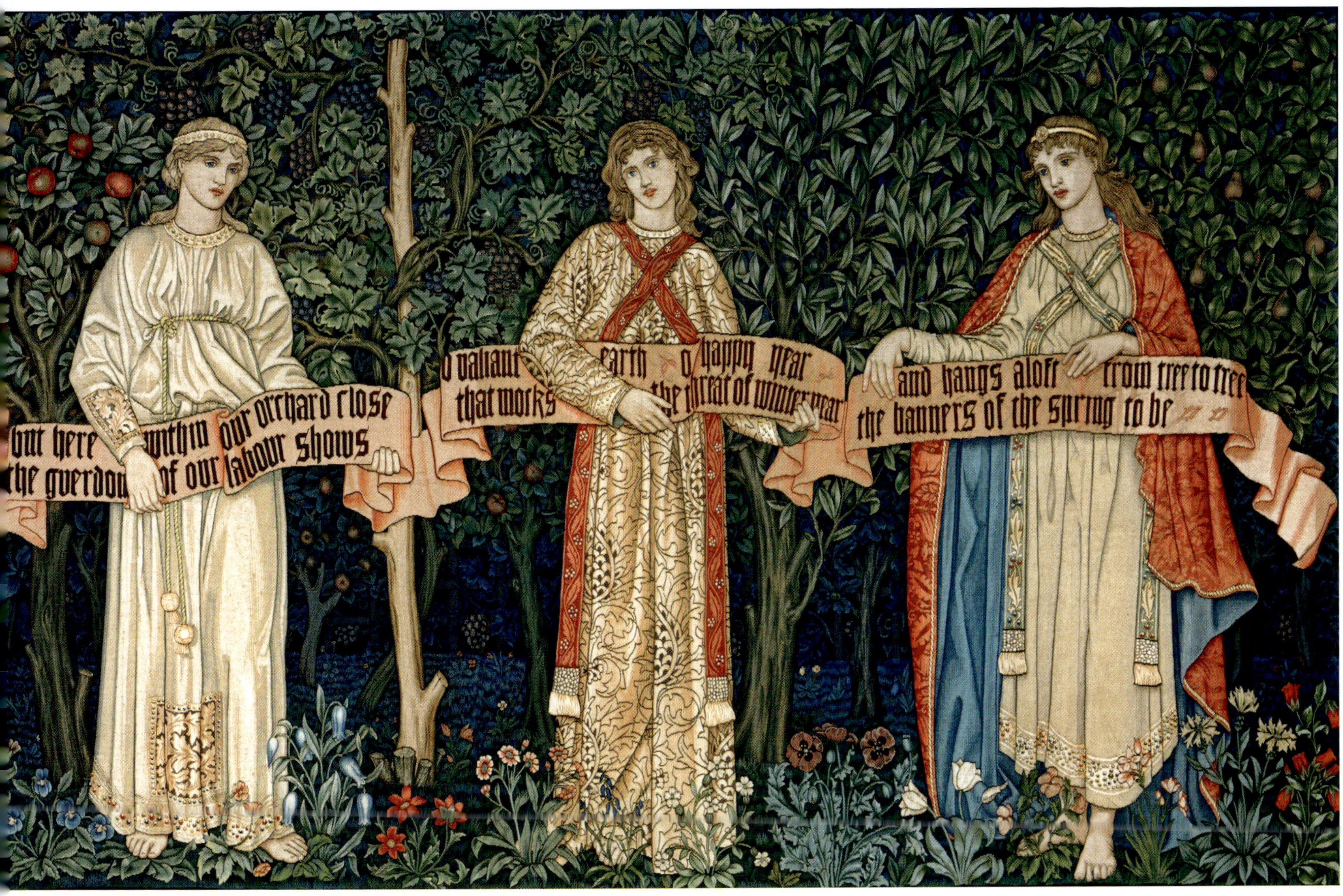

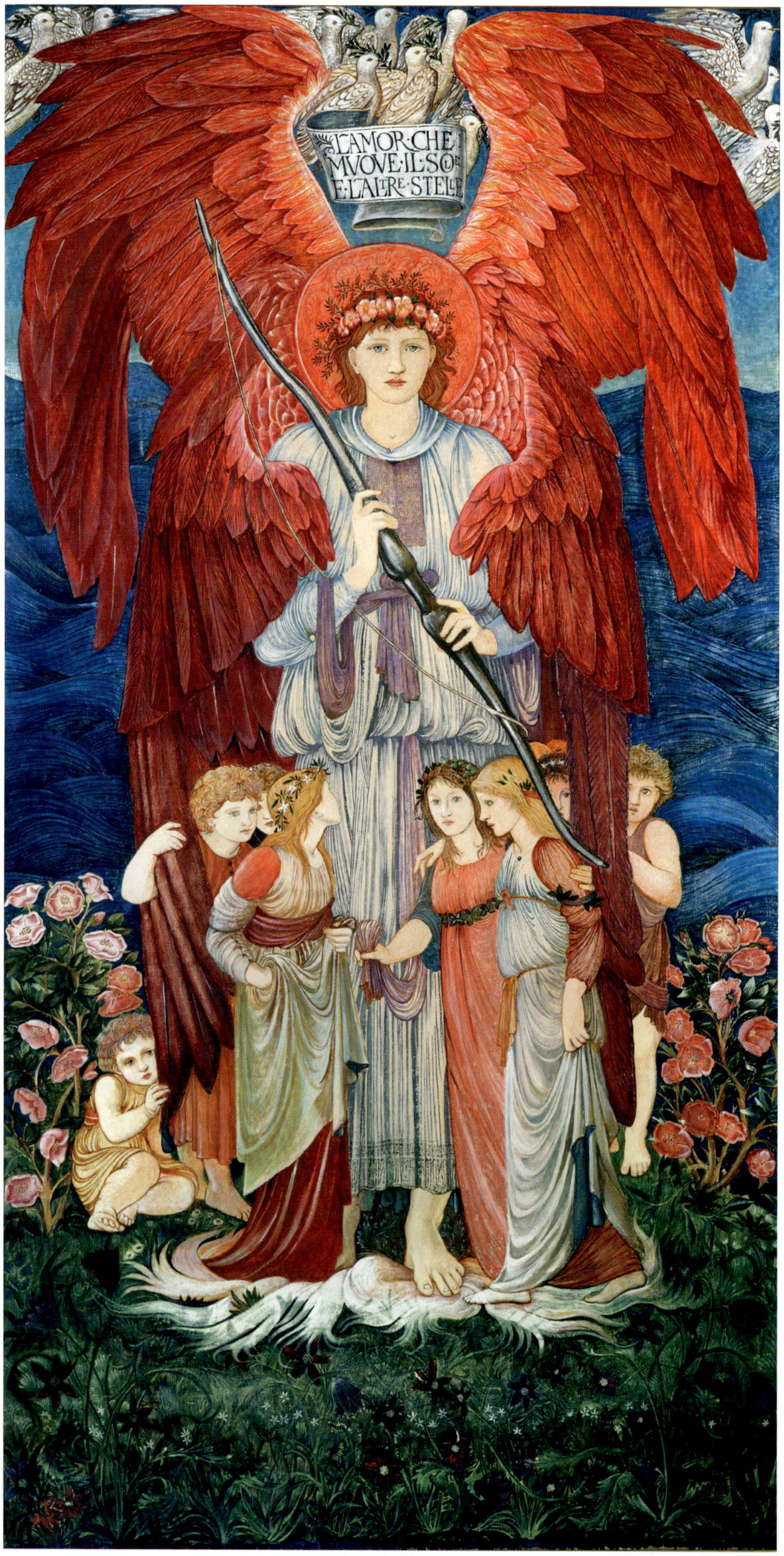

59

EDWARD BURNE-JONES (1833–1898)

Love, 1880s

Watercolour on paper, 211 × 107 cm
Given by the Hon. Mrs Margaret Post
Victoria and Albert Museum, London (V&A: E.838–1937)
LONDON ONLY

This cartoon depicts a winged figure of Love carrying a bow and towering over children in a garden of flowers, with doves bearing olive branches above. The hieratic frontal pose of the monumental allegorical figure and the way its wings protectively encircle the children are reminiscent of Piero della Francesca's *Madonna della Misericordia* in Sansepolcro, which had been reproduced in the *Legends of the Madonna* (1852) by the popular art historian Anna Jameson. Burne-Jones was an early admirer of Piero, whom he listed with Botticelli among his nine favourite artists following his visit to Italy in 1871. The drapery of the figures is Botticellian.

The Italian text in the scroll at the top – 'L'amor che move il sole e l'altre stelle' (the love that moves the sun and the other stars) – is the last line of Dante's *Divine Comedy*. This acknowledges that the poet's love is also the mechanism of the world, and specifically relates this work to Dante's vision of Love, a subject which also fascinated Botticelli, Dante Gabriel Rossetti and Simeon Solomon (cats 60, 85).

Burne-Jones made several such designs for needlework. The present example was embroidered as a panel by Frances Graham, later Lady Homer, and exhibited at the fifth Arts and Crafts Exhibition in 1896. Graham also modelled for the artist, and after her marriage in 1883, Burne-Jones added anemones, symbolic of rejected love and death, to his painting of her. Their scarlet and purple colours on a cobalt and turquoise background are repeated here. MM

PROVENANCE
Made by the artist for Lady Homer; by descent to the Hon. Mrs Margaret Post who gave it to the Victoria and Albert Museum in 1937

LITERATURE
Cheles 1998; New York 1998–9, p. 280, no. 130

60

DANTE GABRIEL ROSSETTI (1828–1882)

The Day Dream, 1880

Oil on canvas, 158.7 × 92.7 cm
Victoria and Albert Museum, London (V&A: CAI.3)

This painting is based on a sketch of Jane Morris made by Rossetti at Kelmscott Manor in 1872, which hung in the artist's Chelsea studio. It was seen there by the art collector Constantine Ionides, who commissioned this full-scale painting of the subject for 700 guineas in 1879.

Rossetti worked on the picture throughout 1880, originally under the title 'Vanna Primavera'. This referred to a passage in Dante's *Vita Nuova* in which a woman named Giovanna but called 'Primavera' walks before the poet's love Beatrice, just as spring precedes summer. Rossetti's working title suggests that he originally envisaged this figure as personifying spring, as does Flora in Botticelli's *Primavera*. Rossetti originally intended the figure to hold spring flowers: snowdrops, suggestive of 'chaste yearning', and a primrose. However, as the former were not in flower when the sycamore was in leaf and the latter seemed too delicate in the model's hands, he replaced them with a sprig of honeysuckle, which has more sensual connotations. The vibrant green dress causes the woman to appear enveloped by the rich surrounding foliage.

Rossetti repeatedly reworked the position of the head and hands. Abandoning the subject of spring, he renamed the work *The Day Dream*, perhaps alluding to Dante's *Vita Nuova*, which uses the literary device of a dream. The artist was inspired by the medieval poet's themes of courtly love to develop his own poems and paintings in celebration of beautiful women. Distracted from the book in her lap, the figure gazes pensively out but does not engage directly with the viewer, creating a 'mood of dreamlike contemplation'. In his accompanying sonnet Rossetti wrote:

> Within the branching shade of Reverie
> Dreams even may spring till autumn; yet none be
> Like woman's budding day-dream spirit-fann'd.

MM

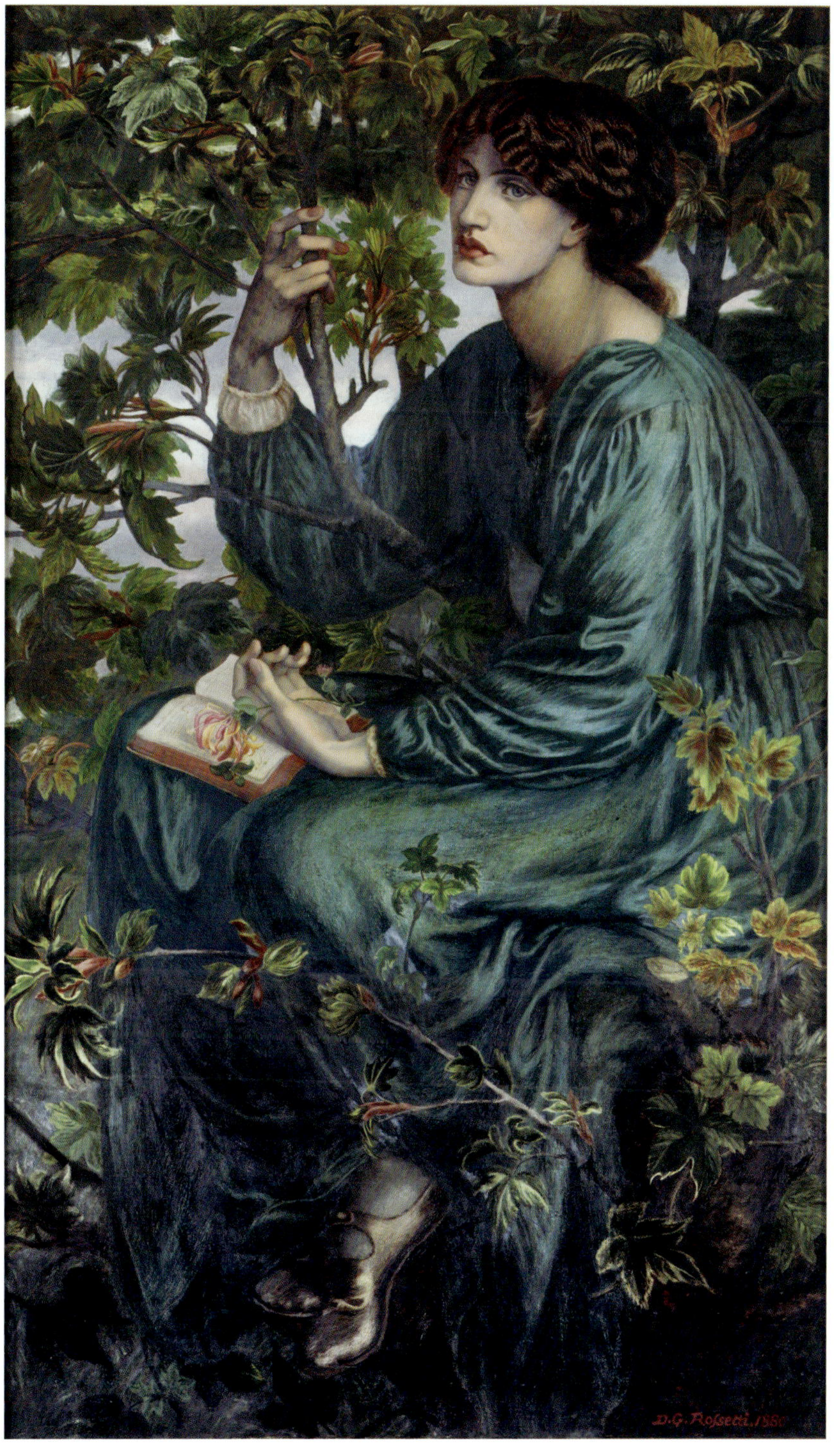

PROVENANCE
Commissioned by Constantine Alexander Ionides by 31 October 1879, finished by December 1880; bequeathed to the Victoria and Albert Museum in 1901

LITERATURE
Long 1925, pp. 53–4; Surtees 1971, pp. 153–4, no. 259; Liverpool and Amsterdam 2003–4, p. 216, no. 274

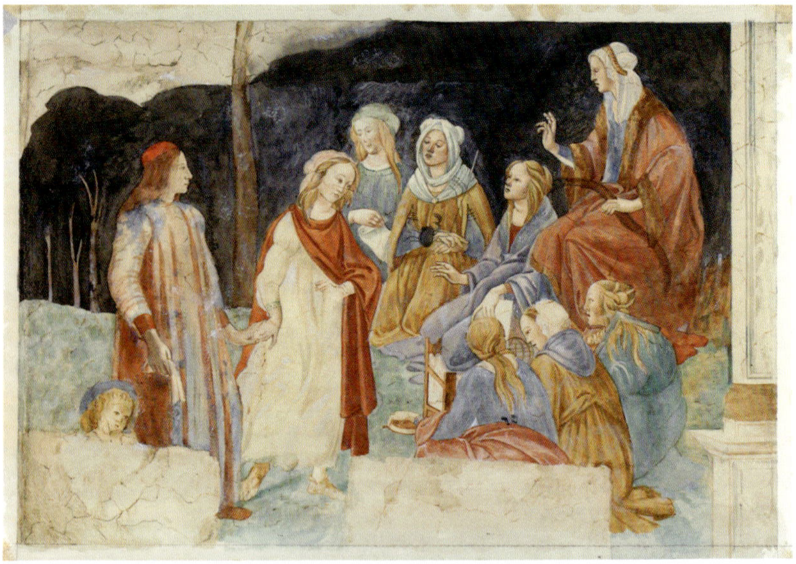

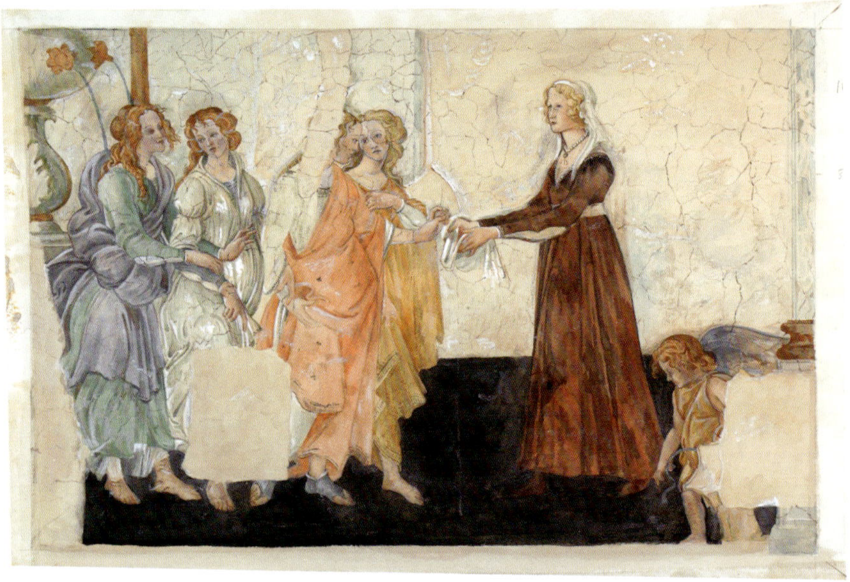

61, 62

WILLIAM GEORGE PAULSON TOWNSEND (1868–1941)
after BOTTICELLI

Lorenzo Tornabuoni Presented by Grammar to Prudentia and the Liberal Arts, 1882–94

Watercolour with white highlights, 29.7 × 42.1 cm
Victoria and Albert Museum, London (V&A: 386–1894)

Giovanna degli Albizzi Receiving a Gift of Flowers from Venus, 1882–94

Watercolour with white highlights, 31 × 45.1cm
Victoria and Albert Museum, London (V&A: 385–1894)

The discovery of the frescoes in the Villa Lemmi in Florence, long hidden under whitewash, was a landmark in Botticelli studies, but the damage sustained by their removal was still regretted by Herbert Horne in 1908. With the aid of the wealthy art historian Charles Ephrussi, the frescoes were purchased in 1882 by the Louvre for 46,517 francs, the equivalent of £923 each. This was, for example, comparable with the £905 Constantine Ionides paid the same year for Edward Burne-Jones's *The Mill* (cat. 73), and proportionate to the £315 he had spent three years earlier on Botticelli's *Portrait of a Lady known as Smeralda Bandinelli* (cat. 162). The celebrity of the Lemmi frescoes is apparent from their display at the top of the main staircase of the Louvre, facing the *Nike of Samothrace*, the ancient Greek marble whose discovery in 1863 was a source of great national pride in France (see also essay the by Gabriel Montua).

The South Kensington Museum (now the V&A) acquired numerous plaster casts, electrotypes, photographs, drawings and watercolours of works of art for study purposes. W.G. Paulson Townsend was an architect, designer and tutor at the Royal College of Needlework. In 1897 and 1898 the museum paid him £20 and £12 for measured drawings of ornamental metalwork.
ME

PROVENANCE
Copied by W.G.P. Townsend; from whom purchased for £10 each by the South Kensington Museum in 1894

LITERATURE
List of Works 1896, p. 57; Lightbown 1978, vol. 2, pp. 60–2, nos B44 and B45

63

CHARLES FAIRFAX MURRAY (1849–1919) after BOTTICELLI

Lorenzo Tornabuoni Presented by Grammar to Prudentia and the Liberal Arts, 1881

Watercolour and bodycolour over graphite on paper, 56 × 81.5 cm
Ashmolean Museum, Oxford (WA.RS.WAL.02)

In 1873 three frescoes by Botticelli were discovered under coats of whitewash in the Villa Lemmi, Florence. Despite their poor preservation two of the fragments were transferred to canvas and purchased by the Louvre in 1882, while the third was too badly damaged and remained *in situ*. The frescoes are believed to celebrate the marriage of Lorenzo Tornabuoni and Giovanna degli Albizzi. Here, the young Lorenzo is introduced to the seven Liberal Arts: Rhetoric, Dialectics, Arithmetic, Grammar, Geometry, Astronomy and Music.

Ruskin commissioned copies of both the transferred works from Murray in 1879 and these were completed prior to the Louvre's purchase of the originals. They show the damage the frescoes had sustained during their lost years and as a result of their removal. This copy was one of several displayed by Ruskin for teaching 'on the Walls of the School, or standing on cabinets' at his School of Drawing in Oxford. Murray had completed the first of the two by June 1880. Ruskin proclaimed it 'the first finished drawing of yours with which I have been entirely satisfied' and 'just and true to its utterly divine original'. He thought Murray 'a heaven-born copyist' and a letter of October 1881 records that Ruskin paid the considerable sum of £100 for the pair. MM

PROVENANCE

Commissioned by John Ruskin in 1879 and presumably later presented to the Ruskin School of Drawing (University of Oxford)

LITERATURE

Lightbown 1978, vol. 2, pp. 61–3, no. B45; Elliott 2000, pp. 84–5

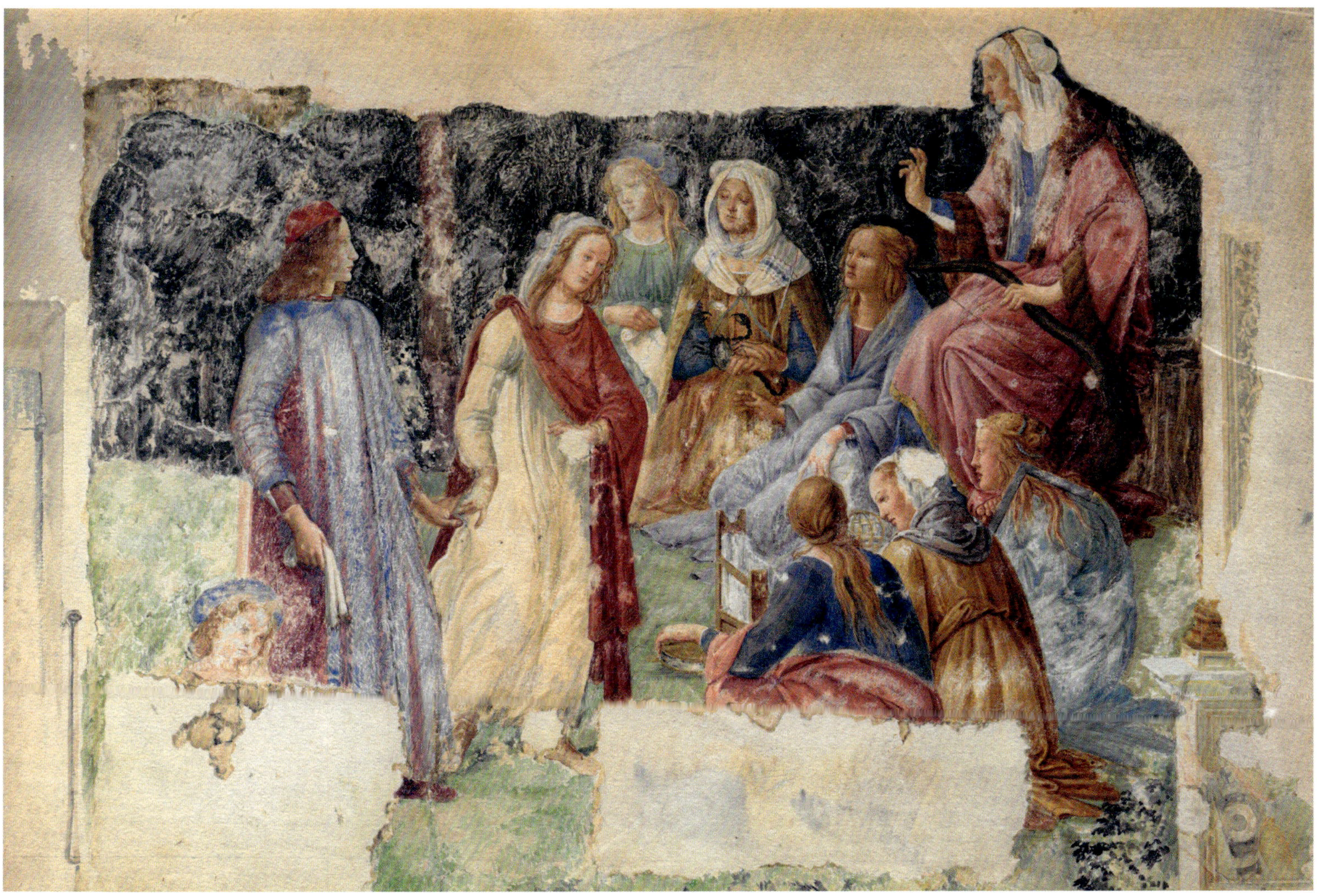

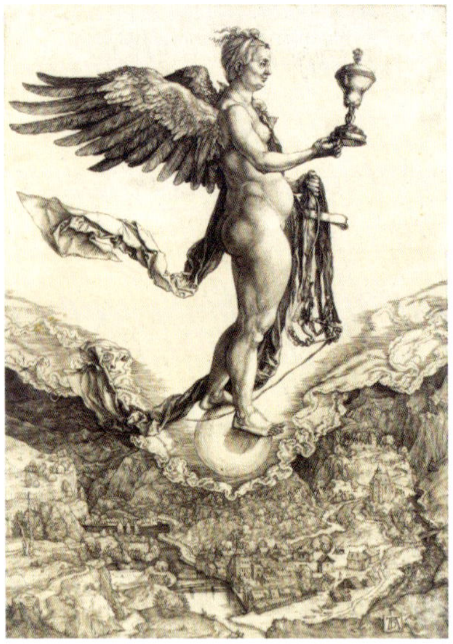

FIG. 71
ALBRECHT DÜRER (1471–1528)
Nemesis, 1502
Engraving, 33.2 × 23.1 cm
V&A: E.587–1940

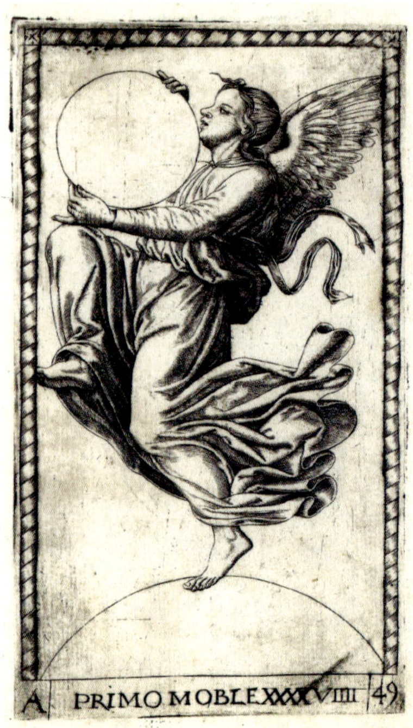

FIG. 72
Prime Mover, from series of fifteenth-century Italian engravings known as 'The Tarrocchi Cards of Mantegna'
Engraving, 18 × 10.1 cm
The British Museum, London (1895,0617.149)

64

EDWARD BURNE-JONES (1833–1898)

Evening, 1870

Watercolour, body colour and gum arabic on paper, 79.3 × 56.5 cm
Private collection
LONDON ONLY

The first of a series of allegorical figures floating in the night sky, this watercolour was exhibited by Burne-Jones at the Old Water-Colour Society in 1870 with four others, including the controversial *Phyllis and Demophoön* (fig. 39). The composition is indebted to two of his favourite artists; the subject of a female allegorical figure hovering above a landscape derives from Albrecht Dürer's famous engraving *Nemesis* (fig. 71), but its figure type and fluttering drapery are inspired by Botticelli, most probably the airborne angels in the *Mystic Nativity* (1500), then in the Fuller Maitland collection, which had been exhibited at Manchester in 1857 and Leeds in 1868 (cat. 101).

In 1870 a reviewer in the *Art Journal* criticized this 'non-descript being, neither fowl nor fish, and yet scarcely human. The colour, too, is like nothing in heaven above or on the earth beneath', while F.G. Stephens in the *Athenaeum* admired its 'grace and sentiment', but considered it 'grand poetry expressed in bad grammar'. The work was bought by the artist's friend, the aristocrat and painter George Howard. The next watercolour of the series, *Night*, was painted in 1870 for the businessman Frederick Craven, and Burne-Jones supplemented it in 1872 with a version of the present work, titled *The Evening Star*. MM

PROVENANCE
Purchased from the artist by George Howard, later 9th Earl of Carlisle, and thence by descent; Christie's, London, 12 December 2013 (lot 53); private collection

LITERATURE
The Times, 27 April 1870, p. 4; *Athenaeum*, no. 2218, 30 April 1870, p. 586; *Spectator*, 7 May 1870, p. 585; Society of Painters 1870; London 1997, p. 130, no. 26

65

EDWARD BURNE-JONES (1833–1898)

Luna, 1872–5

Oil on canvas, 101 × 71 cm
Private collection
LONDON ONLY

The last of Burne-Jones's series of allegorical female figures in the night sky, and the only one painted in oils, this work was described by the artist in 1872 as 'an oil picture of Luna – in tones of blue', but was not completed until 1875. Like the earlier watercolour of *Evening*, its starting point was provided by a Renaissance print; in this case the angelic figure standing on a globe titled the *Prime Mover*, from a series of fifteenth-century Italian engravings known as 'The Tarrocchi Cards of Mantegna', of which impressions had been purchased in 1845 by the British Museum (fig. 72). The elongated figure type with clinging and fluttering drapery is distinctly Botticellian.

Burne-Jones exhibited eleven paintings at the Grosvenor Gallery in 1878 including *Luna*, which was praised by William Michael Rossetti in *The Academy* as 'a lovely colour-invention of veiled though brilliant blue tints'. It was brought by Alexander (Aleco) Ionides, the youngest brother of Constantine Ionides. Considered lost for many years, *Luna* reappeared in 2009 at the posthumous sale of Yves Saint Laurent in Paris. MM

PROVENANCE
Purchased from the artist by Alexander Ionides, his widow; sold Christie's, London, 15 May 1902 (lot 21); purchased by Agnew R.H. Benson; Yves Saint Laurent; his sale, Christie's, Paris, 23–5 February 2009 (lot 91)

LITERATURE
The Times, 2 May 1878, p. 7; *The Illustrated London News*, 4 May 1878, p. 411; *The Academy*, 18 May 1878, p. 466; Hind 1910, pp. 217–33, 255, no. 49; Zucker 2000, pp. 1–8, 60, no. 049a; Saint Laurent 2009 (lot 91)

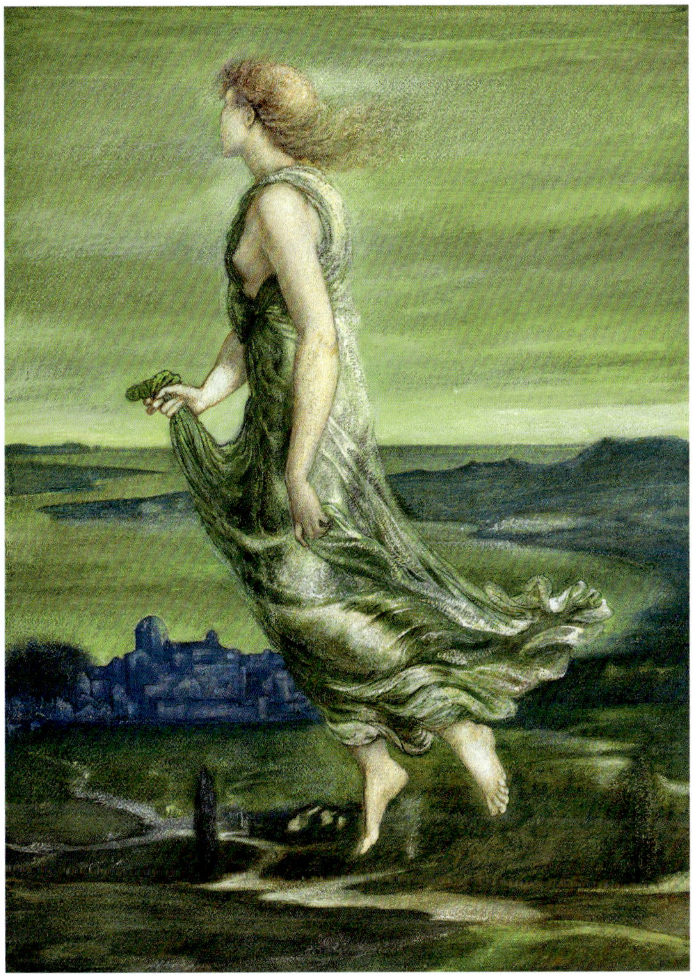

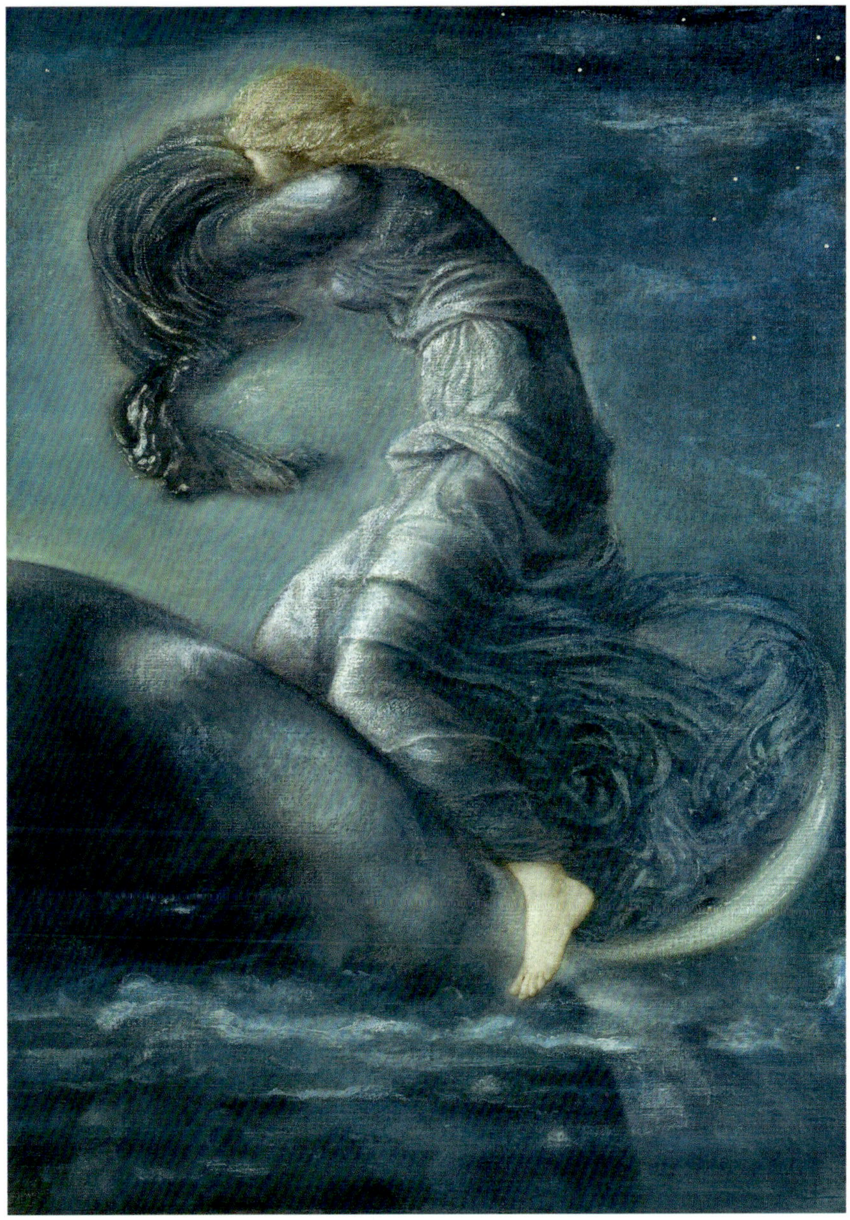

66

WILLIAM BOUGUEREAU (1825–1905)

Birth of Venus, 1879

Oil on canvas, 300 × 215 cm
Musée d'Orsay, Paris (RF 253)
BERLIN ONLY

For his depiction of the *Birth of Venus*, William Bouguereau drew on iconography developed by Botticelli: the already adult goddess stands in a contrapposto pose on a shell. As with Botticelli, who included the Cypriot shore, the surrounding figures suggest shallow waters near land. Unlike the Florentine goddess, however, who fits the archetype of the *Venus pudica*, the nineteenth-century Venus bares all the charms of her S-shaped body as she rises from the foam, lifting her arms to her hair. The central figure had previously appeared at the left-hand margin of the group painting *Nymphaeum* (The Haggin Museum, Stockton, California), completed the year before, and is reminiscent of Jean-Auguste-Dominique Ingres's *Venus Anadyomene* (1848; Musée Condé, Chantilly). However, it was Raphael and his fresco *Triumph of Galatea* (1514; Villa Farnesina, Rome) that inspired the creatures surrounding Bouguereau's Venus: nymphs and centaurs, putti and dolphins. Like Venus herself, however, these bodies – closely entwined and wetly shimmering – exhibit a greater degree of sensuality than their Renaissance counterparts. In 1902, in his *Oreads* (Musée d'Orsay, Paris), Bouguereau would further develop the motif of the putti spiralling up into the sky and seeming to disappear into the ether behind Venus, turning them into a veritable wave of female flesh. GM

PROVENANCE
Acquired from the artist by the French state in 1879 for the Musée du Luxembourg, Paris; on loan to the Musée des Beaux-Arts, Nantes, 1920–79; transferred to the Musée d'Orsay, Paris, 1979

LITERATURE
Lobstein 2006, pp. 210–14; Bartoli and Ross 2010, p. 188; Jung 2014, p. 184–5

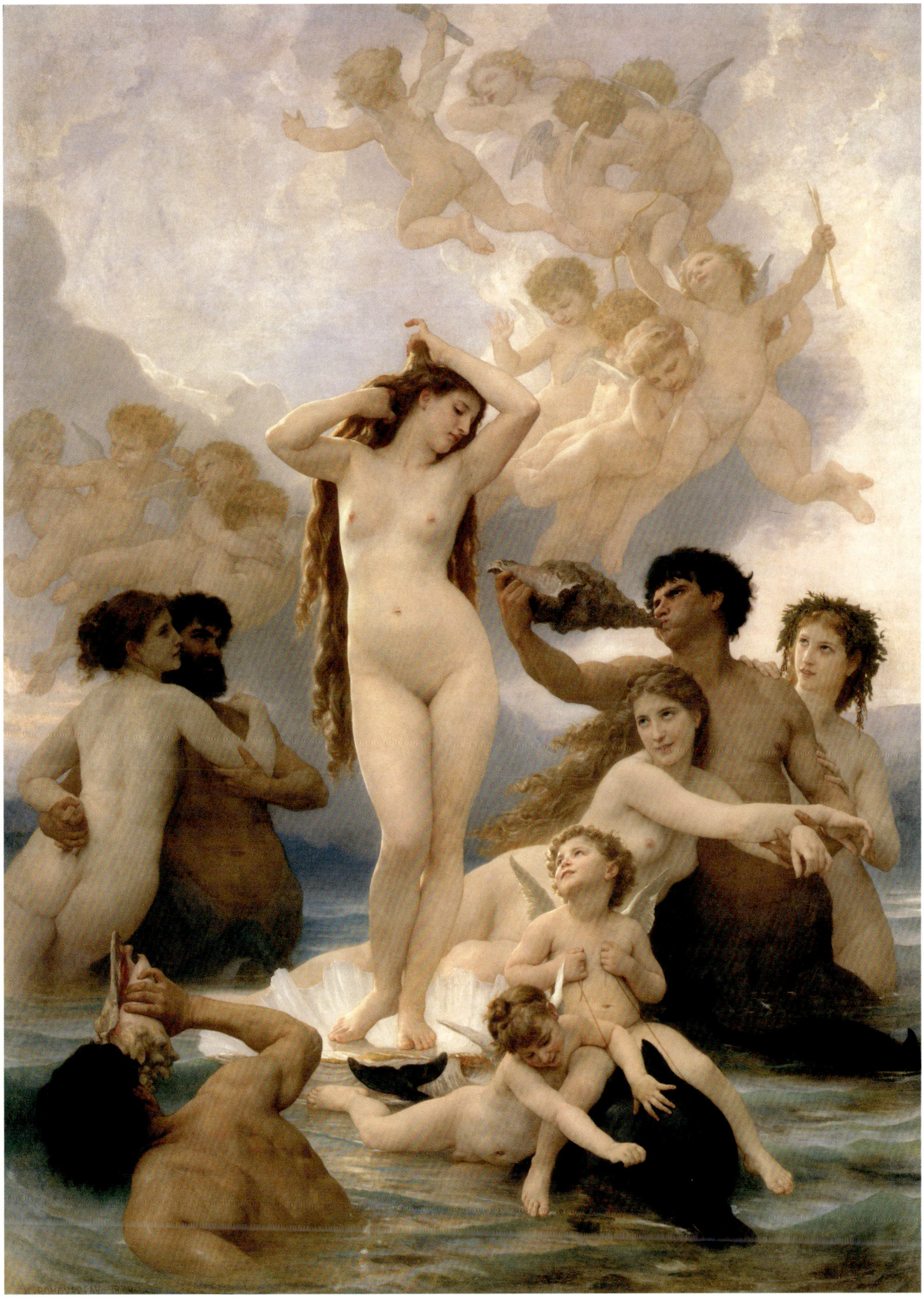

67

EVELYN DE MORGAN
(1855–1919)
Cadmus and Harmonia, 1877

Oil on canvas, 102 × 45 cm
De Morgan Collection
(P_EDM_0041)

Evelyn De Morgan (née Pickering), who was probably introduced to art of the Italian Renaissance by her uncle John Roddam Spencer-Stanhope, a minor Pre-Raphaelite, studied at the National Art Training School and the Slade School of Art in London. She painted *Cadmus and Harmonia* after a visit to Florence in 1876–7.

The subject is from Ovid's *Metamorphoses* (Book IV, 563–603). After Cadmus is changed by Mars into a serpent his wife Harmonia begs for a similar fate, which is duly granted. Here, De Morgan shows her in the embrace of her transfigured husband, in the form of a beautiful maiden rather than the elderly woman of the original tale.

The figure of Harmonia, protectively encircled by the serpentine form of Cadmus reminiscent of the Caduceus of Mercury, echoes the central figure in Botticelli's *Birth of Venus*, which De Morgan had copied as a student, with a snake in place of the luscious hair of Venus. This idealized nude, elongated like Botticelli's figure, suggests a revised aesthetic for feminine beauty, more lithe and lean than the buxom type usual earlier in the nineteenth century. De Morgan uses spring flowers to represent spiritual awakening, a trope repeated in later works such as *Flora* (cat. 52).

An excerpt of Ovid's text was displayed alongside the painting when it was first exhibited in 1877 at the Dudley Gallery (no. 22), where it sold for £60. MM

PROVENANCE
Sir Charles Dilke; Mrs Stirling as bt. 1926; De Morgan Foundation

LITERATURE
Gordon 1996, p. 15, no. 5; Smith 2002, pp. 65–6

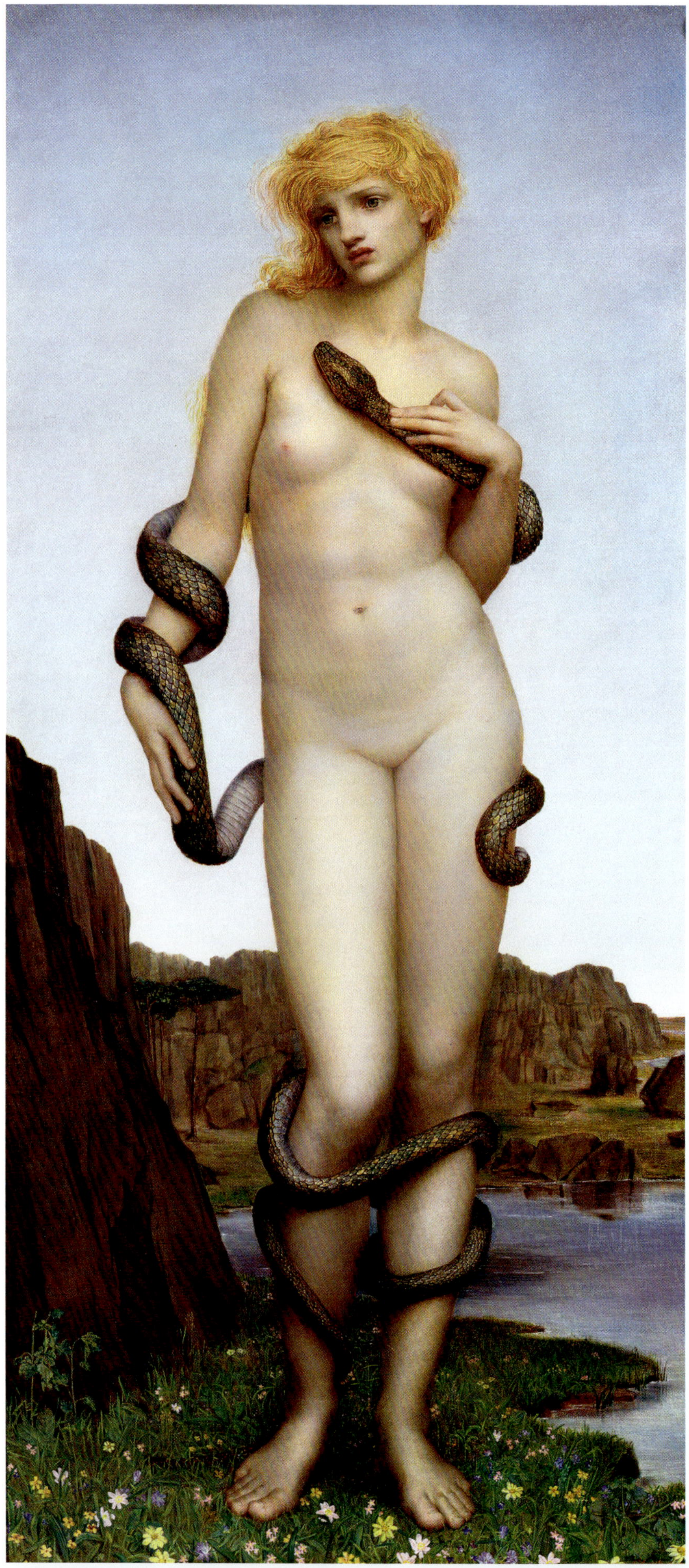

68

WALTER CRANE
(1845–1915)
The Renaissance of Venus, 1877

Oil and tempera on canvas, 138.4 × 184.1 cm
Tate, London (N02920)

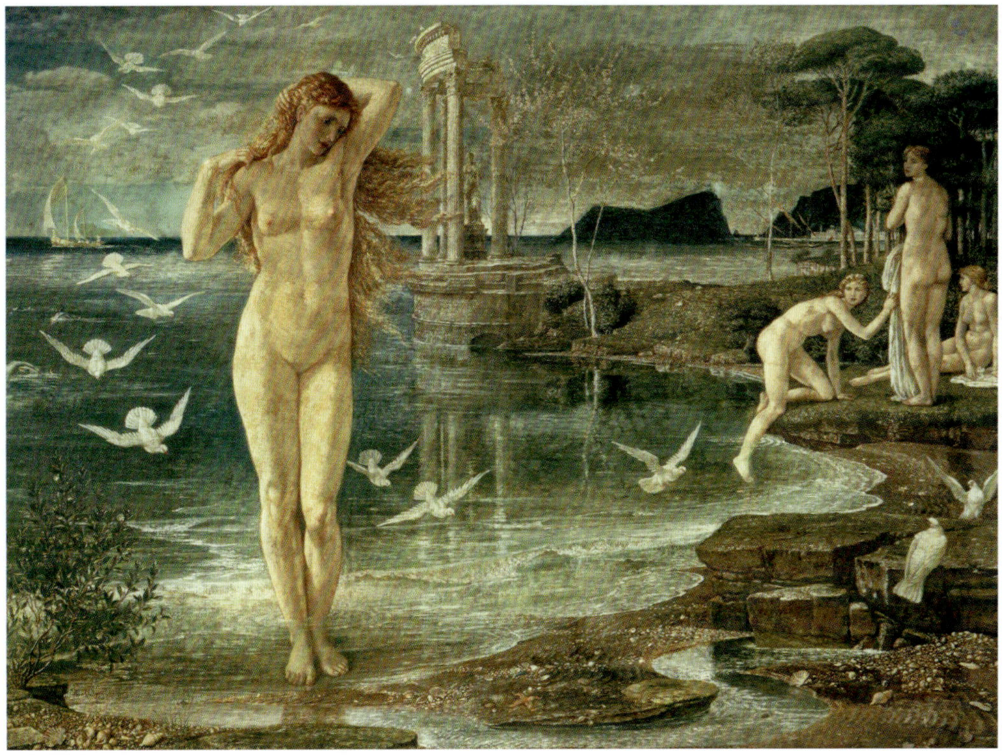

Recalling his eighteen-month Italian honeymoon in 1871–2, Crane remarked that 'Botticelli was not at that time … rediscovered by the critics … but I shall never forget the charm of his beautiful "Spring" and the "Venus"'. This composition paraphrases that of Botticelli's *Birth of Venus*, and its title may refer to Walter Pater's *Studies in the History of the Renaissance* (1873). The attitude of Venus dressing her hair and the alarmed nymph scrambling from the water probably derive from William Mulready's *Bathers Surprised*, a painting inspired by Titian and shown at the South Kensington Museum in 1864. Crane recalled that 'Mulready … was particularly interesting to my father, who frequently took us to the gallery'. In the background a ruined circular colonnade like the temple of Vesta at Tivoli houses a statue resembling the Venus de Milo in the Louvre, which Crane had admired in 1866. The marine theme is continued with the shell decorations on the frame.

This painting was admired at the Grosvenor Gallery in 1877 by the wealthy collector Frederick Richards Leyland, but remained unsold until 1882 when it was purchased in £50 instalments by the painter George Frederic Watts. A friend of his told Crane 'Mr. Watts … says in all pictures old and new he never saw such an exquisite silvery tone … We speculate how far it is tempera and how far oil, will you give us a little light?' The mixed medium Crane used to achieve a fresco-like effect has darkened with age. While in Rome in 1883 the artist painted a picture titled *La Primavera* of a woman in wind-blown drapery picking daffodils, which he sold to Alexander Ionides. ME

PROVENANCE
Exhibited at the Grosvenor Gallery, London, in 1877; purchased in 1882 for £300 by George Frederic Watts, by whose wish presented by Mrs Watts to the Tate Gallery, 1913

LITERATURE
Crane 1907, pp. 44, 91, 125, 231–4; Heleniak 1980, pp. 153–60, 220–1; London 1989, pp. 88–9; O'Neill 2010, pp. 19–20, 23–7, 32–5, 37

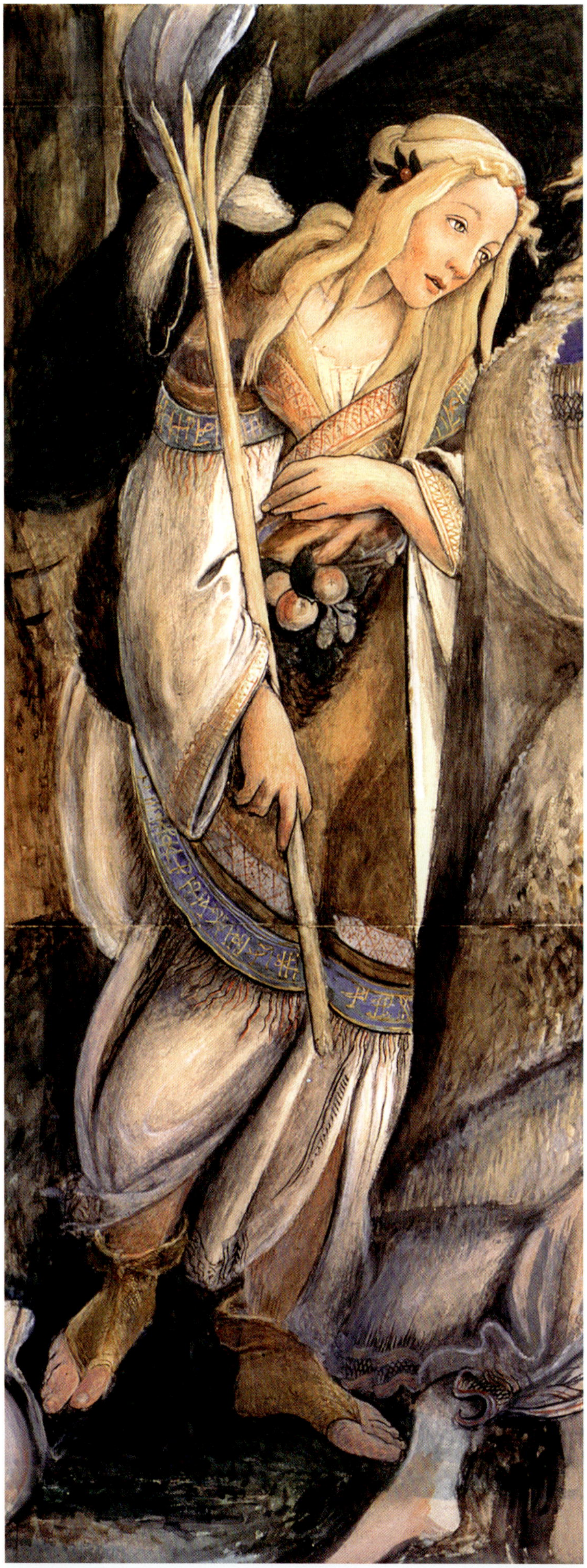

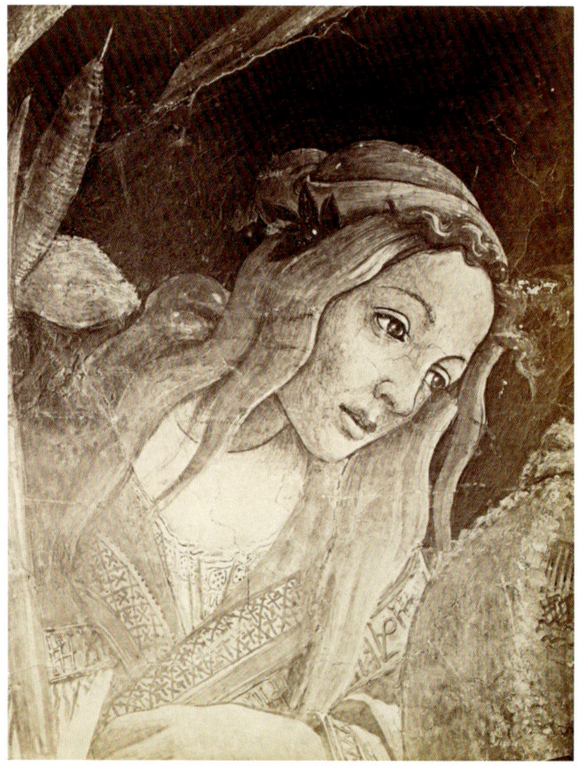

69

JOHN RUSKIN (1819–1900) after BOTTICELLI

Zipporah, 1874

Pencil, watercolour and bodycolour, 143 × 54 cm
Ruskin Library, Lancaster University (1996P0880)

This is a copy of part of Botticelli's fresco of *The Temptation of Moses* in the Sistine Chapel, and represents the daughter of Jethro who became the wife of Moses. Ruskin described his large watercolour 'as nearly a facsimile as I can make it'. After studying Botticelli's frescoes in 1872 he pronounced his preference for these works over Michelangelo's far more celebrated Sistine frescoes.

Ruskin began *Zipporah* in May 1874, and took fifteen days to complete it. Notes in his diary reflect Ruskin's keen interest in the costume of the figure and the 'ill done' lettering around its border, as well as ruminations on the significance of the characters. He discussed these at length with Charles Fairfax Murray who was also at work on copies for Ruskin at the time of his visit. Ruskin wrote to his acquaintance Charles Eliot Norton on 19 June 1874 that he had 'done Botticelli's Zipporah successfully'.

Ruskin used this work as a teaching aid for a lecture on Botticelli of 4 December 1874, in which he characterized Zipporah as 'the Etruscan Athena'. He later lent it to an exhibition at Brighton in 1876 with a woodcut of Athena, examining the association between the two figures further in his accompanying catalogue entry. In this text he also sought to understand the role of Botticelli's Sistine Chapel frescoes within his wider oeuvre. MM

PROVENANCE
Sotheby's, London, 20 May 1931 (lot 45); purchased by John Howard Whitehouse; entered the Ruskin Library in the John Howard Whitehouse collection

LITERATURE
Gamble 1999; Lancaster 2009, p. 2

70

FRATELLI ALINARI

Photograph of Zipporah, from Botticelli's fresco of 'The Temptation of Moses' in the Sistine Chapel, c.1872

Albumen print, 43.3 × 32.7 cm
Presented by John Ruskin
Ashmolean Museum, Oxford (WA.RS.REF.108.a)

The photographic company of Fratelli Alinari was founded in Florence in 1852 by Leopoldo Alinari with his brothers Giuseppe and Romualdo. Known as 'The Firm', important early commissions included supplying Prince Albert with photographs of Raphael drawings in 1858. Alinari's truthful and scientific approach to recording art and architecture was in direct accord with the ideals of John Ruskin, who praised the precision and beauty of its work, and commissioned the company to photograph Botticelli's frescoes in the Sistine Chapel at the Vatican, the results of which were published in 1876.

Ruskin used such photographs extensively in his lectures and recommended students to copy them. He gave four prints from *The Temptation of Moses*, including 'Zipporah' and 'Moses', to the teaching collection of the Ruskin School of Drawing in Oxford. MM

PROVENANCE
Presumably given by John Ruskin to the Ruskin School of Drawing (University of Oxford); first recorded in the Ruskin School of Drawing in 1906; transferred to the Ashmolean Museum, c.1949

LITERATURE
Maffioli 2003, pp. 10, 15–16

71

CHARLES HERBERT MOORE
(1840–1930)

Girdle of Roses from the Figure of 'Spring' by Botticelli, in the Academy of Florence, c.1877–8

Watercolour and white gouache over graphite on off-white card, 28.1 × 39.6 cm
Transfer from the Fine Arts Department, Harvard University
Harvard Art Museums/ Fogg Museum, Cambridge MA
(1926.33.71)

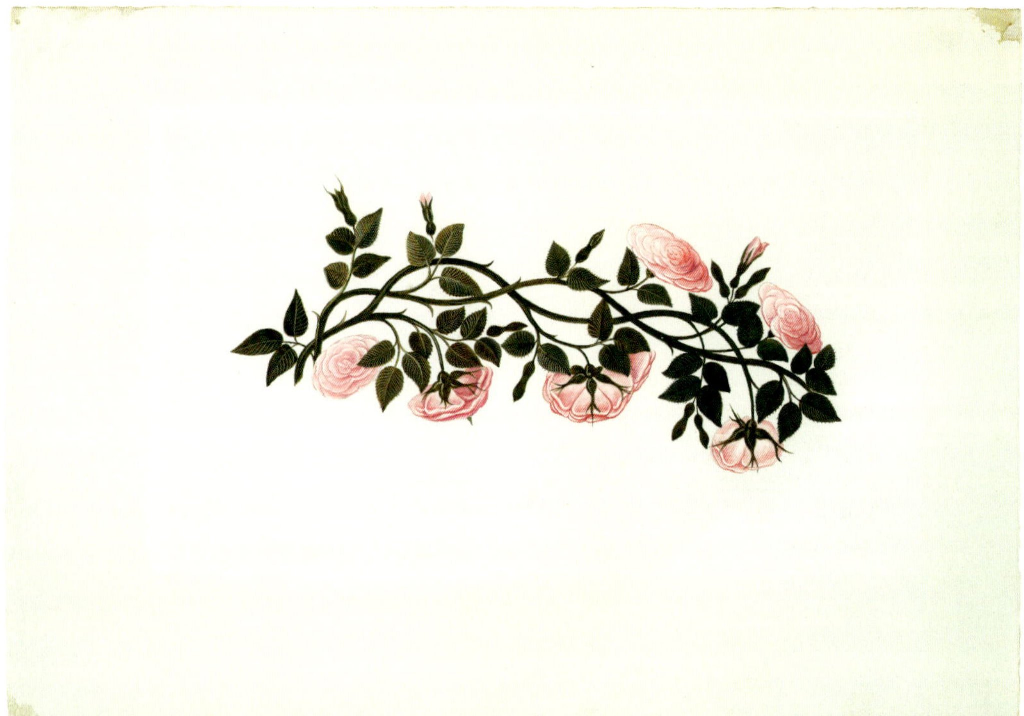

This study after *Primavera* demonstrates the impact of Botticelli's remarkable sense of ornament on art and design. Moore was co-founder in 1863 of the American Society for the Advancement of Truth in Art, which subscribed to Pre-Raphaelite ideals. His acquaintance Charles Eliot Norton, Harvard's first Professor of Fine Arts, facilitated his appointment at Harvard, first to the scientific school in 1871 and from 1874 to teach fine arts at the main college. Moore and Norton were influential promoters of Ruskinian ideas in America, and shared Ruskin's moral concern for truth and his preference for medieval and early Renaissance paintings.

In 1876 Moore visited Europe to collect teaching material for his lectures and to meet Ruskin. For almost two years, often in Ruskin's company, he made copies or 'fac-similes' of works of art such as this *Girdle of Roses* from *Primavera*. On his return to Harvard, Moore followed Ruskin's example and assembled drawings, paintings, photographs and copies as a teaching collection. That year an illustration of the *Girdle of Roses* was published in his *Catalogue, with Notes, of Studies and Fac-similes from Examples of the Works of Florence and Venice*, intended for the instruction of his students. In 1896–1909 Moore served as the first director of the Fogg Museum at Harvard. MM

PROVENANCE
Fine Arts Department, Harvard University, Cambridge MA; transferred to Fogg Museum, 1926

LITERATURE
Moore 1878, p. 28, no. 50; Cambridge 2007, pp. 37–9, 47–9; Stebbins et al. 2008, p. 250, no. 240

72

JOHN RUSKIN
(1819–1900)
Sketch of a Few Leaves in the Background of Botticelli's 'Primavera', before 1871

Watercolour and bodycolour over graphite on wove paper, 45.7 × 32 cm
Ashmolean Museum, Oxford (WA.RS.ED.252)

Ruskin intended this sketch of myrtle leaves to serve as a practical teaching aid. Like other pictures and photographs of foliage in his possession, in his catalogue of these it immediately follows a photograph of Botticelli's *Primavera* (cat. 53) and is described as 'A sketch of a few leaves in the background'.

Writing of fourteenth-century painters in his *Mornings in Florence* (1860) Ruskin remarked that 'No Florentine painter … painted leaves as well as that, till you get down to Sandro Botticelli, who did them much better'. In the same publication he coined the telling axiom 'If you can paint one leaf you can paint the world'. Nevertheless, Ruskin made few studies directly from flowers or leaves, more often copying such details from works by other artists for use as teaching aids. Roses from *Primavera* provided the source for the vignette on the title page of his periodical *Fors Clavigera*. MM

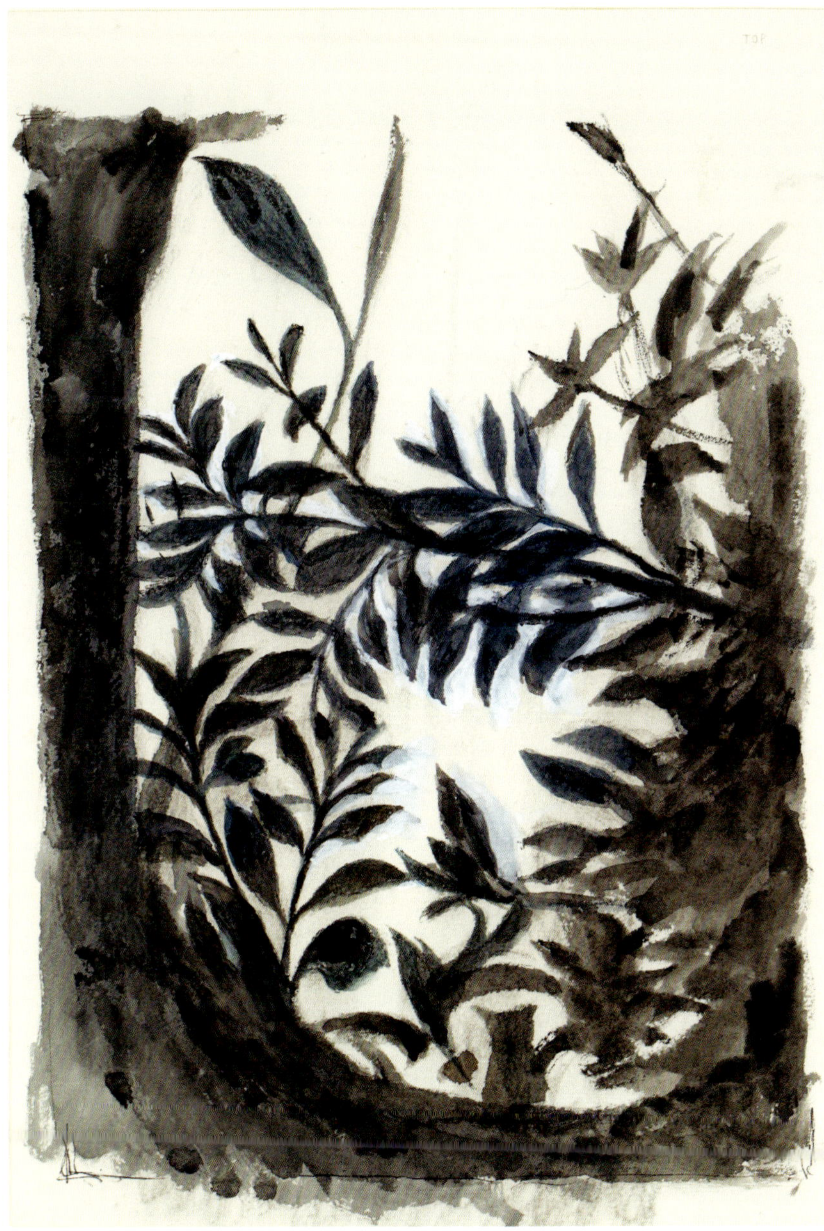

PROVENANCE
Given by John Ruskin to the Ruskin School of Drawing (University of Oxford), 1875; transferred to the Ashmolean Museum, c.1949

LITERATURE
Ruskin 1875–7; Lancaster 2009, pp. 15–16

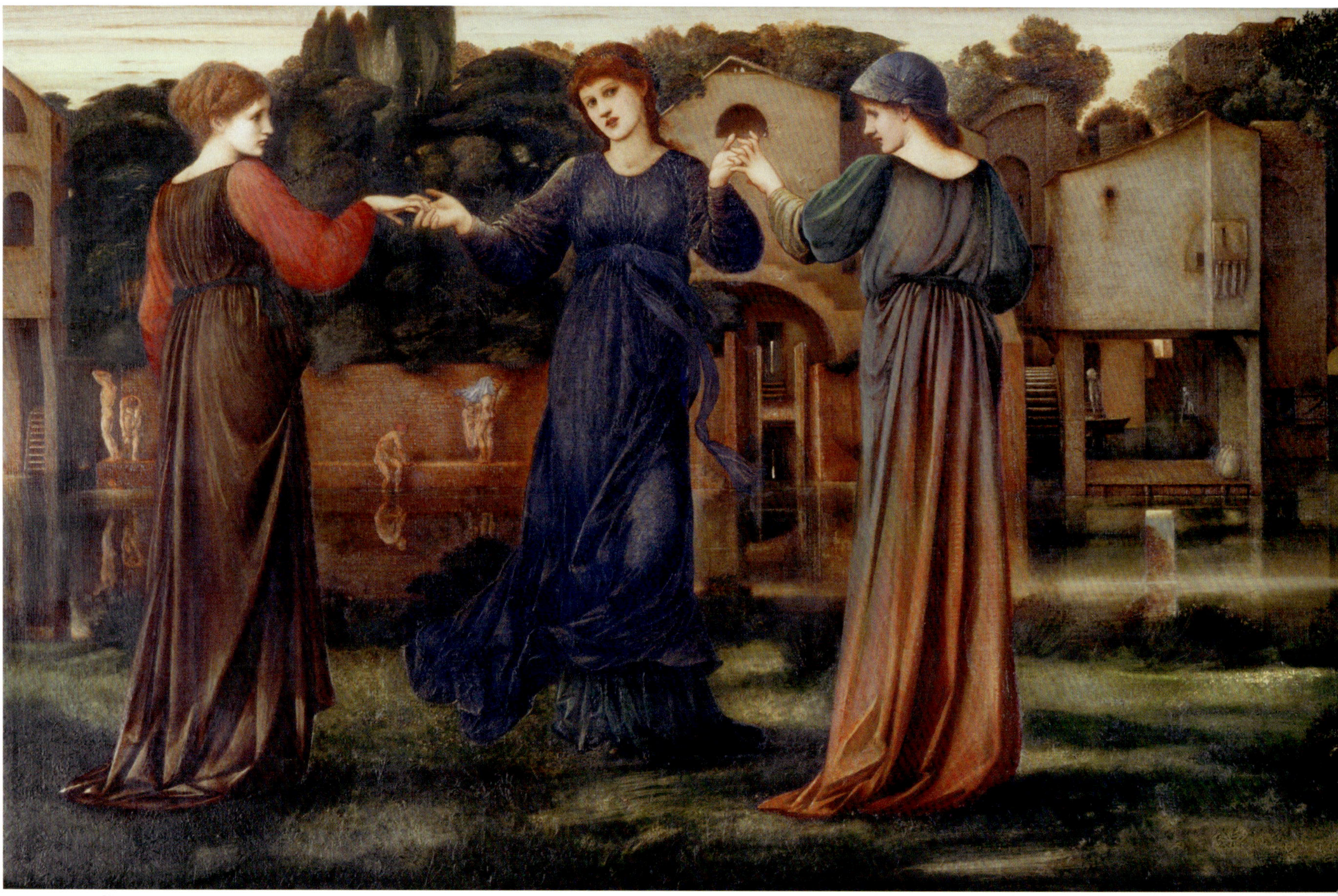

73

EDWARD BURNE-JONES
(1833–1898)

The Mill: Girls Dancing to Music by a River, 1870–82

Oil on canvas, 90.8 × 197.5 cm
Victoria and Albert Museum, London (V&A: CAI.8)

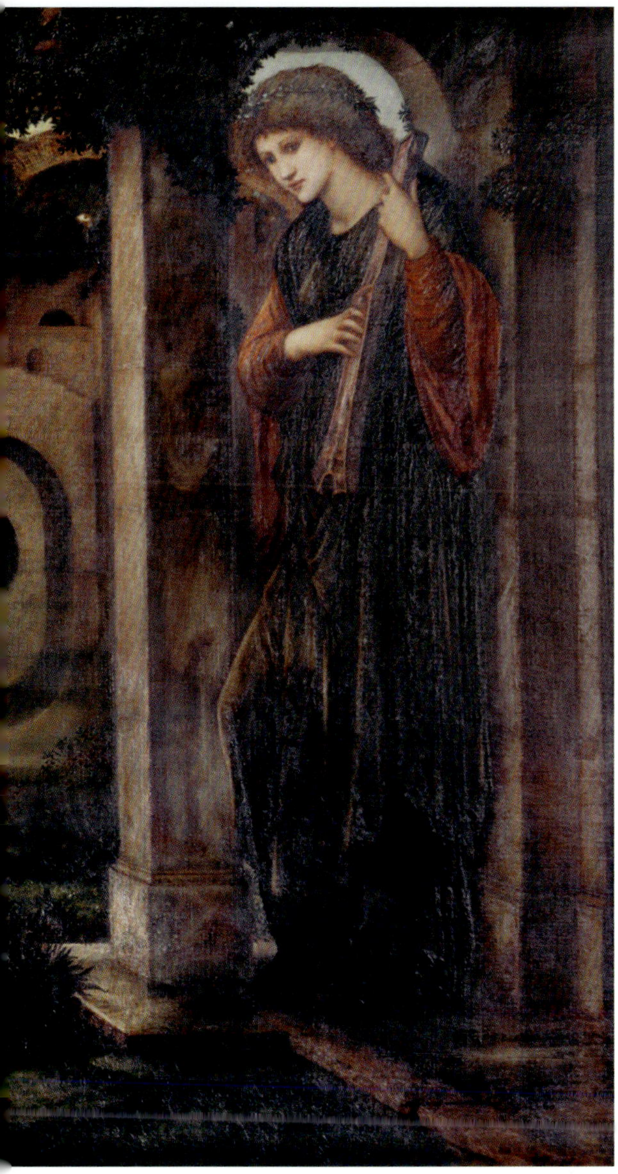

The style of *The Mill* and its apparent subject of the Three Graces dancing to the music of Apollo, derive from Italian Renaissance art. Ionides family papers identify the women as three Anglo-Greek cousins related to the patron and collectively known as 'the Three Graces': Marie Spartali, Aglaia Coronio and Maria Zambaco. Burne-Jones began the painting in 1870 and received £905 for the finished work on 21 April 1882.

The Mill was one of nine paintings exhibited by Burne-Jones in 1882 at the Grosvenor Gallery in London, a principal venue for artists of the Aesthetic movement. Reviewers noted its lack of specific subject matter. The novelist Henry James wrote that while its historic period, setting and the role of the dancers remained indeterminate, the picture was 'an echo of early Italianism' and 'impregnated with the love of Italy'.

The elegant configuration of the three young women may generally be likened to that of the Graces in Botticelli's *Primavera* (fig. 8) which the artist knew well from his visits to Florence. They wear traditional Italian dresses with high waists and fluttering ribbons, like those in Botticelli's paintings. The monumental architecture is evocative of Roman ruins. The mellow tonalities and self-absorbed figures create a dreamlike quality and the painting has been described as representing a state of mind rather than a scene.

Burne-Jones acknowledged that his composition was inspired by *Primavera* and that the bathing figures in the background were borrowed from Piero della Francesca's *Baptism of Christ* (National Gallery, London), but remarked that its true meaning was only understood by 'the few people I care for.' MM

PROVENANCE
Commissioned from the artist by Constantine Alexander Ionides; bequeathed to the Victoria and Albert Museum in 1901

LITERATURE
Long 1925, pp. 8–9; Childs 1990; New York 1998–9, pp. 250–2, no. 111

74

DANTE GABRIEL ROSSETTI (1828–1882)

La Ghirlandata, 1873

Oil on canvas, 124 × 85 cm
Guildhall Art Gallery, London (1059)
LONDON ONLY

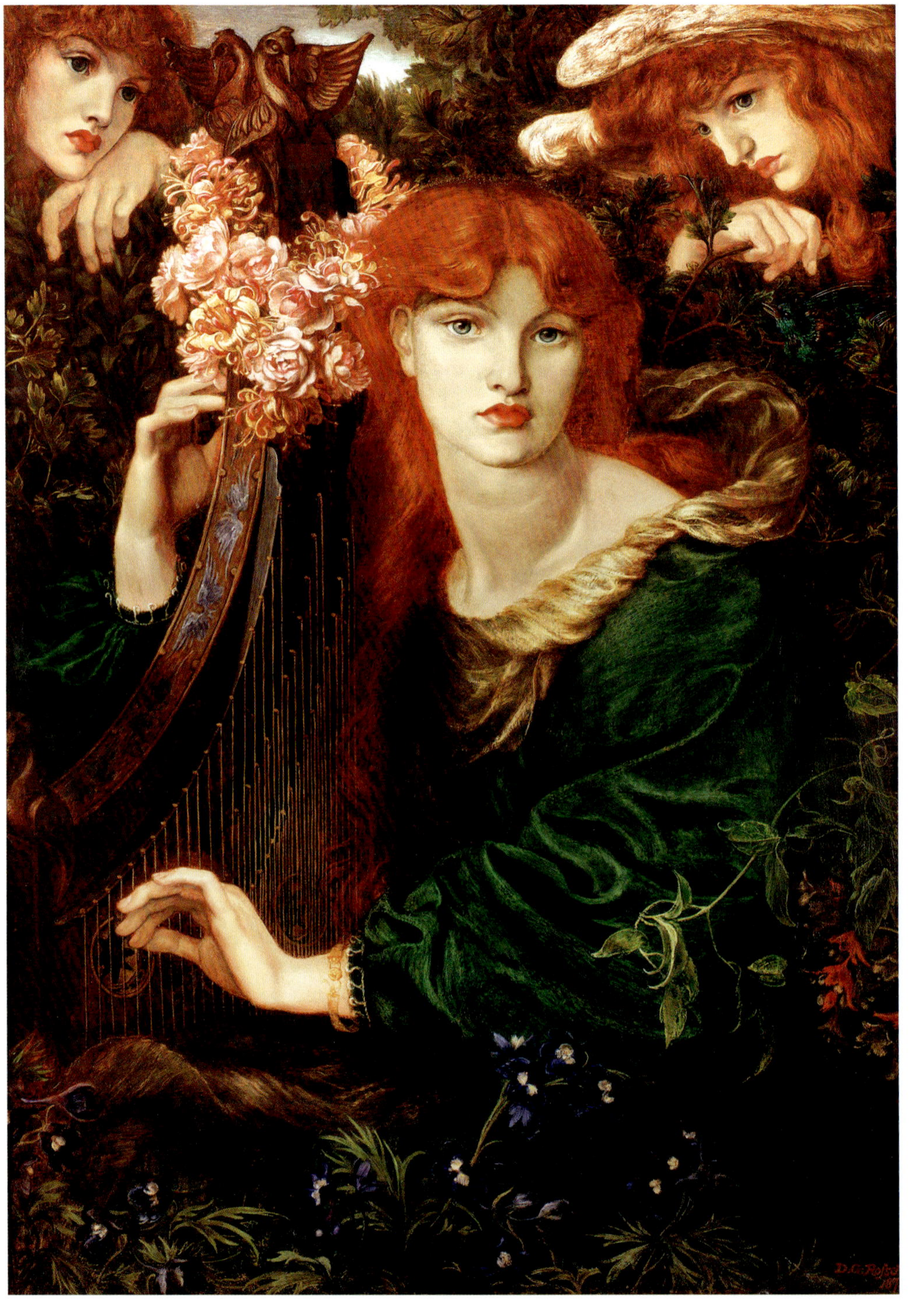

Described by Rossetti as 'The greenest picture in the world', this is one of several three-quarter-length paintings of beautiful women making music he produced between 1865 and 1877. *La Ghirlandata* was painted at Kelmscott Manor, the country house of William Morris, whose eleven-year-old daughter May posed for the angel heads at top right and left. The way these closely flank the central figure recalls the paired angels and saints in two Botticelli workshop tondi of the *The Virgin and Child with St John and an Angel* acquired by the National Gallery in 1855 (cat. 118).

This similarity doubtless accounts for the reaction to *La Ghirlandata* of the Glasgow Liberal MP William Graham. He bought it for 800 guineas from Rossetti, who thought him 'the only buyer I have who is worth a damn'. Graham exhorted the artist to paint a companion for it, saying: 'let it be a fair beautiful woman as like Botticelli as possible, for this one is exactly like Botticelli, and if R[ossetti] will only paint me pictures of this class I will buy nothing else but his, and any old master you can get me.' The collector had declined to purchase Botticelli's *Portrait of a Lady known as Smeralda Bandinelli* (cat. 162) in 1870, when Rossetti offered it to him for £200, but he acquired a Botticelli workshop tondo of the *Virgin and Child*, now in Cambridge (cat. 122). MM

PROVENANCE
Purchased in 1873 for £840 by William Graham; his sale, Christie's, London, 3 April 1886 (lot 117), £1,050; Joseph Ruston; his sale, Christie's, London, 21 May 1898 (lot 50), £3,150; Sir James Ross; his sale, Christie's, London, 8 July 1927 (lot 21), £840; David Croal Thomson, from whom bought the same year for £1,200 by the Guildhall Art Gallery

LITERATURE

Surtees 1971, vol. 1, p. 130, vol. 2, no. 232

75

DANTE GABRIEL ROSSETTI (1828–1882)

La Donna della Finestra, 1870

Pastel on green paper, 84.8 × 72 cm
Whitworth Art Gallery, Manchester (D.1921.35)

Rossetti produced six studies relating to the subject of *La Donna della Finestra* in the 1870s, and a final oil painting in 1879 (fig. 37). These vary in their state of completion and the pose of the model Jane Morris. In this drawing the figure seems more introspective, and the location of the sill to one side, accentuated by the positioning of the hands, suggests that she is turning from the window towards a viewer who has entered the room. Rossetti described the search for beauty as 'the only absolute aim' of art. Other works such as his *Bocca Baciata* (1859) present a striking woman with abundant red hair, a nod to sixteenth-century Venetian portraiture. Conversely this highly finished but incomplete study in pastel focuses on the sitter, whose animated hands suggest feelings of pity and compassion. The work remained unsold in Rossetti's lifetime. MM

PROVENANCE
The artist; his sale (lot 35), £53 11s; S.M. Milne, Milne sale, Sotheby's, London, 21 April 1921 (lot 202); David Croal Thomson; Whitworth Art Gallery 1921, £165

LITERATURE
Surtees 1971, pp. 151–2, no. 255D

76

DANTE GABRIEL ROSSETTI (1828–1882)

La Donna della Finestra, 1870

Coloured chalks on paper, 84.8 × 72.1 cm
Bradford Art Gallery (104.26)

Rossetti's first studies for *La Donna della Finestra* ('the woman at the window') utilize coloured chalks like those used for portrait drawings, and in 1879 he completed an oil version of this composition. Its subject was suggested by a passage in Dante's *Vita Nova* (1295): the poet, distraught at the death of his love Beatrice, notices a beautiful young lady at a window looking on him with compassion. This picture of Jane Morris has no overt narrative, but its attitude is consistent with the inscription from the *Vita Nova* on the scroll in the foreground 'Color d'amore e di pietà sembiante' (the colour of love and appearance of pity).

The influence of Botticelli's early *Portrait of a Lady known as Smeralda Bandinelli* (cat. 162), which Rossetti had purchased in 1867, is apparent in the woman's pose of this figure as if leaning over a window ledge, and her even gaze which meets that of the viewer. The ivy leaves on the ledge, symbols of attachment and fidelity, may relate to the consolation Jane Morris offered him following the death of his wife Elizabeth Siddal. The artist's brother William Michael Rossetti wrote of this work: 'Humanly she is the Lady at the Window; mentally she is the Lady of Pity. This interpretation of soul and body – this sense of an equal and indefeasible reality of the thing symbolized and the form which conveys the symbol – this externalism – are constantly to be understood as the key-note of Rossetti's aim and performance in art.' MM

PROVENANCE
H. Virtue Tebbs, Tebbs sale, Christie's, London, 10 March 1900 (lot 30), £507 3s; presented in 1928 by Asa Lingard to Bradford Art Gallery and Museums

LITERATURE
Rossetti 1889, pp. 107–9; Surtees 1971, pp. 151–2, no. 255A

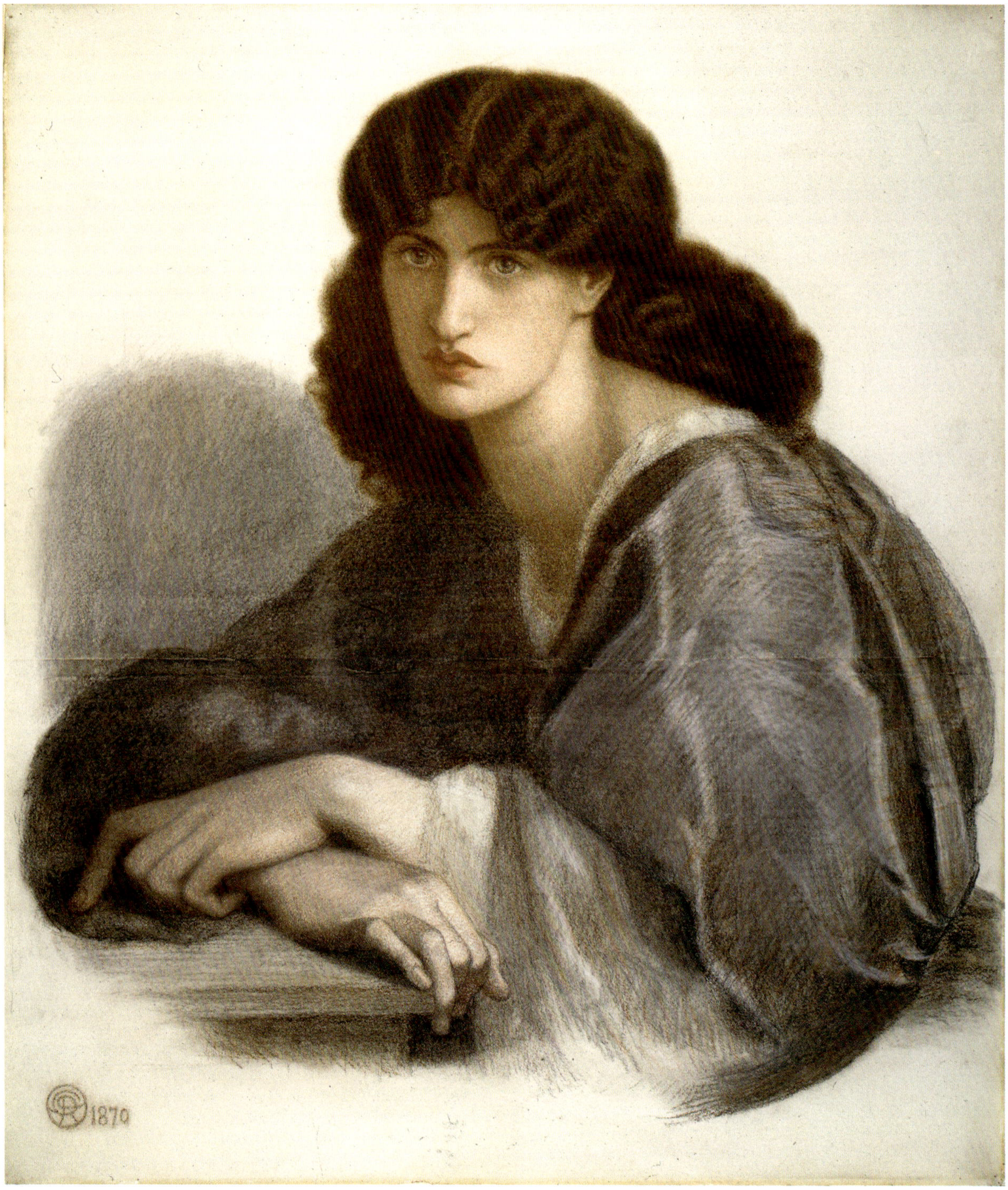

75

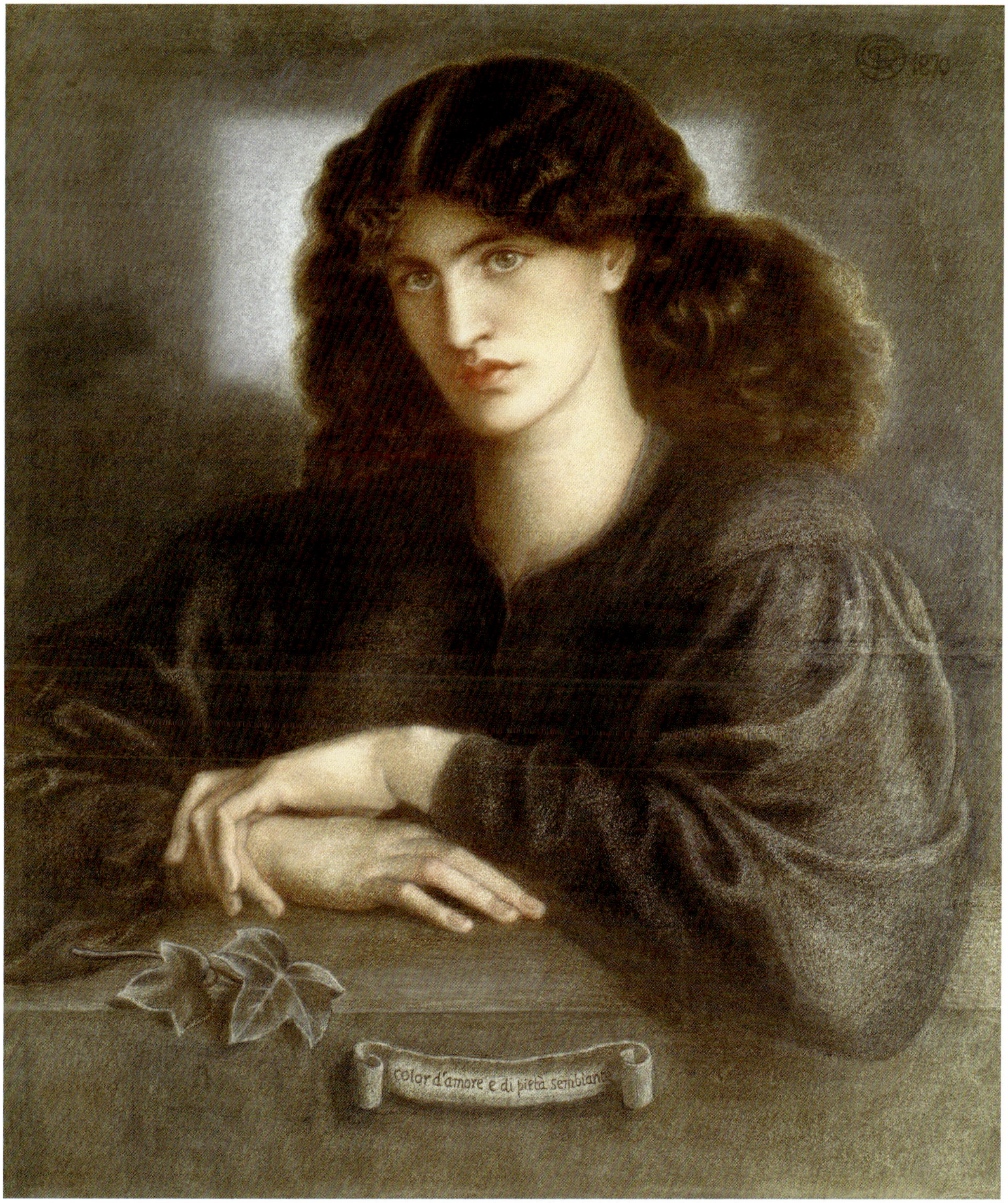

76

77

CHARLES FAIRFAX MURRAY (1849–1919) after BOTTICELLI

Mystic Nativity, 1870s–80s

Watercolour on cream wove paper, 35.6 × 25.5 cm
Harvard Art Museums / Fogg Museum, Cambridge MA
(1970.159)

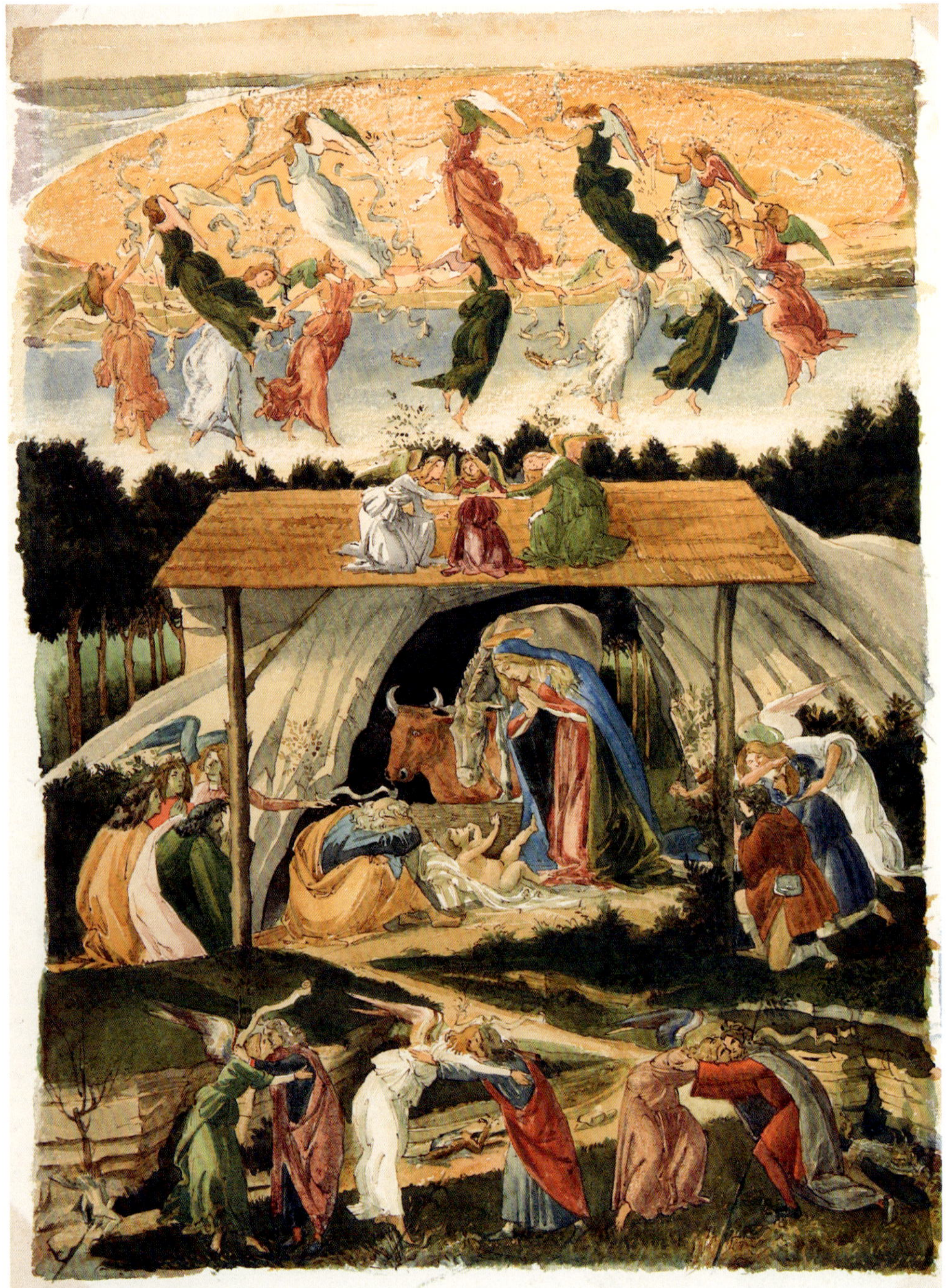

As the *Mystic Nativity* (cat. 101) is Botticelli's only signed painting, it is of fundamental importance to the reconstruction of his oeuvre. This is one of several copies by Murray after works by the Florentine master. It may have been made as early as 1871 when the *Mystic Nativity* was exhibited at the Royal Academy, or after it became more accessible following its purchase by the National Gallery in 1878. Murray lived in Florence between 1878 and 1885 and became an active collector and dealer, influential on the art market in Europe and the United States.

This copy belonged to Charles Eliot Norton, from 1874 the first Professor of Fine Arts at Harvard and a friend and follower of John Ruskin. He knew Murray by 1869, and subscribed to Ruskin's belief in the important role of such copies for artistic instruction and to disseminate knowledge. This copy does not include the long inscription in Greek at the top of the original. MM

PROVENANCE
Charles Eliot Norton, by descent to his daughter Elizabeth Gaskell Norton (by 1908); gift to Edward W. Forbes; bequest to the Fogg Museum, 1970

LITERATURE
Elliott 2000, p. 22

78

CHARLES FAIRFAX MURRAY (1849–1919) after BOTTICELLI
Adoration of the Magi, 1875

Watercolour on paper, 20.8 × 25.7 cm
Collection of the Guild of St George, Museums Sheffield (CGSG00097)

PROVENANCE
Commissioned by John Ruskin in 1875 for the Guild of St George

LITERATURE
Ruskin 1875–7, 30, p. 192; Elliott 2000, p. 66

In 1866 John Ruskin arranged for the young Charles Fairfax Murray to assist Edward Burne-Jones, and he later worked for William Morris, Dante Gabriel Rossetti and George Frederic Watts. In 1873 Ruskin commissioned Murray to copy the Botticelli frescoes in the Sistine Chapel, a project on which they collaborated until their relations soured in 1883. From the early 1870s Ruskin's interests included social projects and in 1875 he opened the museum of the Guild of St George in Sheffield with books, casts, prints, paintings and drawings to serve as a creative and educational resource for local metalworkers. Ruskin considered the 40 or so copies Murray made for the Guild to be 'among the principal treasures we can boast'.

This is one of two copies after Botticelli, which Murray made for Ruskin in 1875. It depicts the so-called *Del Lama Adoration* in the Uffizi, an early work of the 1470s, which includes portraits of the Medici as well as a self-portrait of Botticelli himself, dressed in yellow at the right. Ruskin (*Works*, 30, p. 192) found this copy 'entirely admirable as a picture – and as a copy', and used it in his 'Ariadne Florentina' series of lectures on Florentine art and design. In February 1877 he told Fairfax Murray 'I have presented [your drawing of the King] to the Sheffield museum and want more such, probably as many as you care to do', adding later that year that it was 'producing great and good effect at Sheffield'. MM

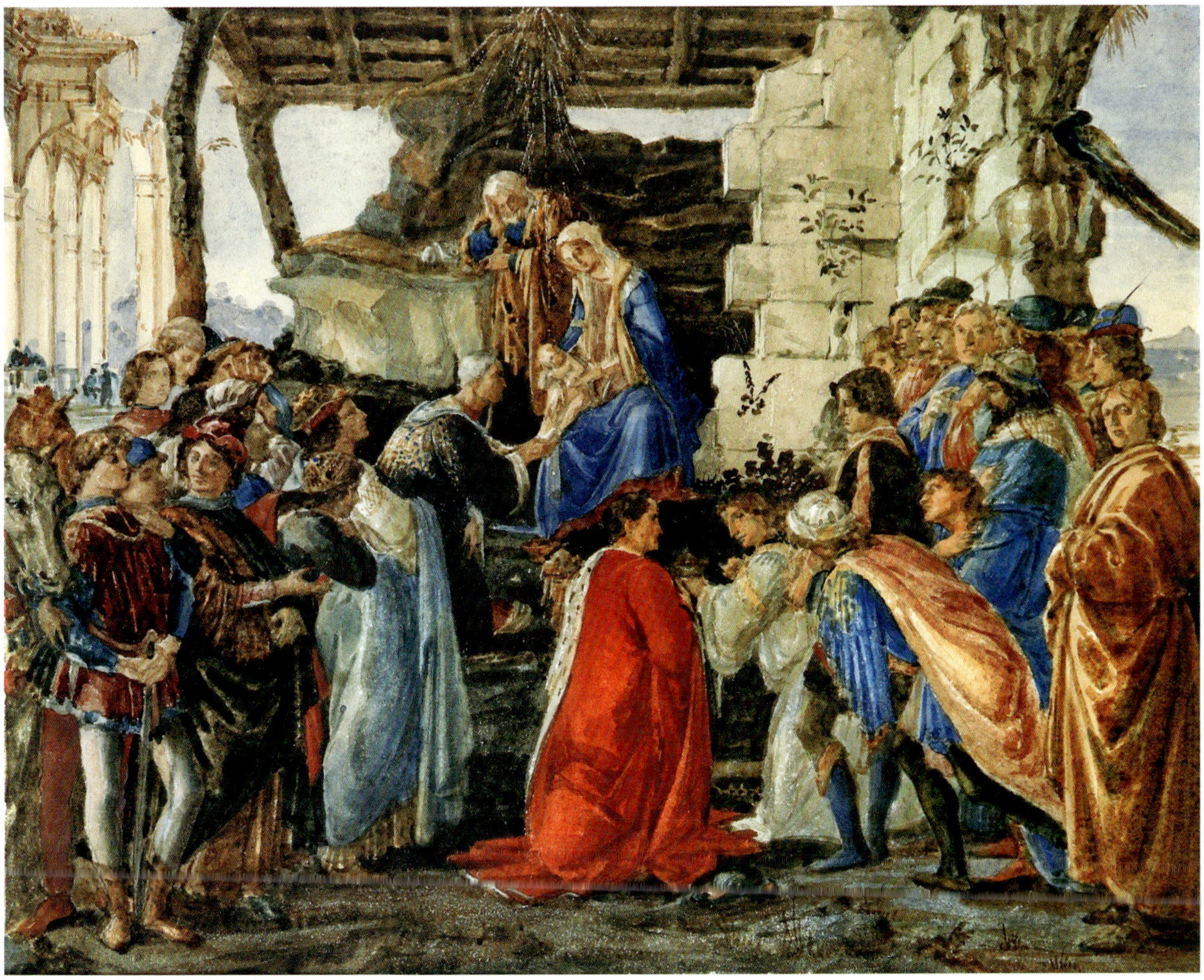

79, 80

EVELYN DE MORGAN (1855–1919) after BOTTICELLI

Detail of The Madonna of the Magnificat, 1870s

Watercolour on paper, 27 × 31.3 cm
De Morgan Collection
(D_EDM_0342)

Detail of the Birth of Venus, 1870s

Watercolour on paper, 36 × 42.6 cm
De Morgan Collection
(D_EDM_0214)

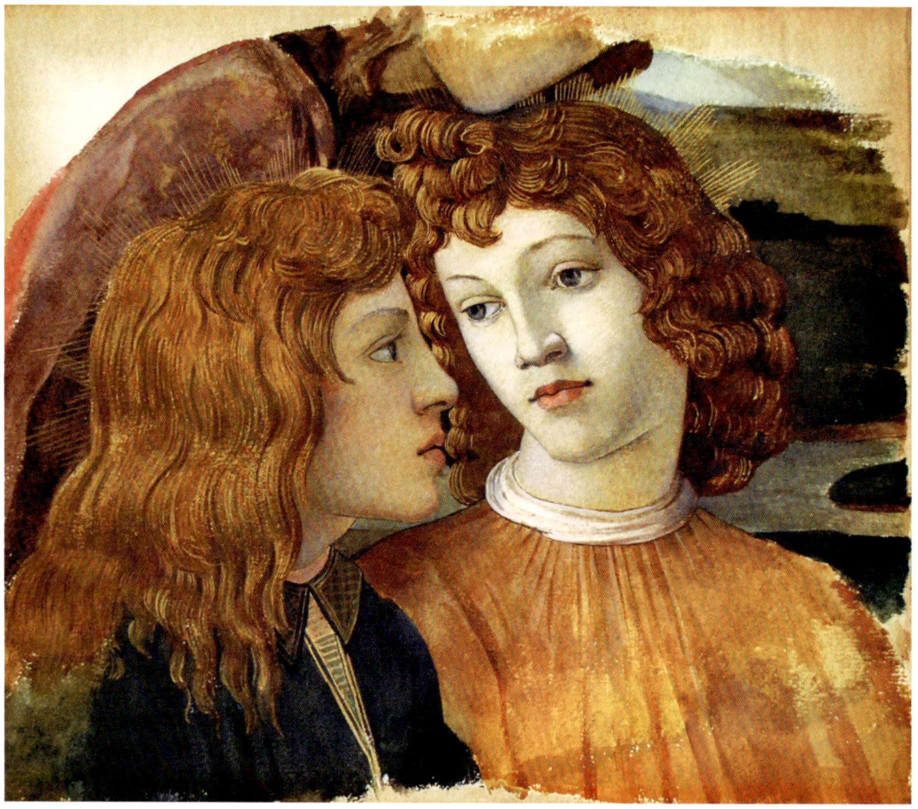

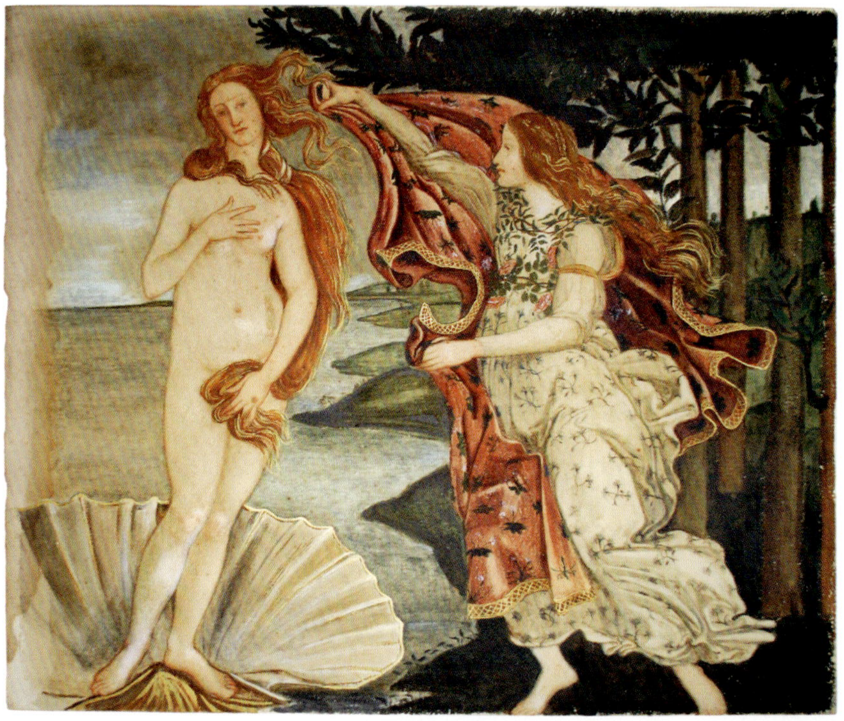

A colour lithograph of Cesare Mariannecci's watercolour after the *Birth of Venus* (cat. 81) was published in 1870 by the Arundel Society, and the heads of the angels in the *Madonna del Magnificat* – then Botticelli's most celebrated painting – were frequently reproduced as photographs. Evelyn De Morgan probably encountered reproductions of both works while still a student at the South Kensington National Art Training School and the Slade School of Art in London. During 1875–7 she made several visits to Florence, where she stayed with her uncle, the painter John Roddam Spencer-Stanhope, of whom his mentor Edward Burne-Jones ruefully remarked that it was 'a great pity he ever saw my work or that he ever saw Botticelli's'. He encouraged his niece to make copies of the Florentine master's work, such as this incomplete study of the right half of the *Birth of Venus* and a more finished watercolour of the angels to the left of the Virgin in the *Madonna del Magnificat*, both in the Uffizi. MM

PROVENANCE
The artist; by descent to her sister Anna Marie Wilhelmina Pickering, by whom they were bequeathed to the De Morgan Foundation who acquired them in 1967

LITERATURE
Gordon 1996, p. 68

81

CESARE MARIANNECCI
(active c.1853–1889)
after BOTTICELLI
Birth of Venus, 1868

Watercolour on paper, 40.3 × 64.2 cm
Victoria and Albert Museum, London
(V&A: E.35–1995)

PROVENANCE
The Arundel Society; given in 1897 to the National Gallery; transferred to the Victoria and Albert Museum, 1995

LITERATURE
Artistical Directory 1856, p. 24; Bonfigli 1860, p. 24; Ledger 1978, pp. 98–107

Botticelli's *Birth of Venus* was first recorded in 1550 with *Primavera* (fig. 8) at the Medici Villa Castello. Several full-scale versions of the figure of Venus against a dark background were painted by the artist's workshop (cats 169, 170). Since 1815 the *Birth of Venus* has been on display at the Uffizi.

Trained in Rome, Mariannecci was a lifelong correspondent of Enrico Ridolfi, who became director of the Uffizi. In 1856–9 he was offering visitors to his Roman studio 'a copious supply' of copies 'in watercolours from the Old Masters, especially of the early Tuscan school', and made photographs of figures in local costume. He moved to Florence in 1859.

This copy was commissioned by the Arundel Society, an association founded in 1848 and named after the seventeenth-century collector Thomas Howard, Earl of Arundel, 'to preserve the record and diffuse a knowledge of the most important remains of painting … [and] to elevate the standard of taste in England' by publishing high quality reproductions (see cat. 54). Mariannecci painted over 85 watercolour copies for the Society, which sold 26 of them to the South Kensington Museum in 1859–68 for prices from £10 to £35. A chromolithograph of this watercolour made by the Berlin lithography firm Storch and Kramer was published in 1870.

One of the first British pictures inspired by the *Birth of Venus* was Walter Crane's *The Renaissance of Venus*, made in 1877 (cat. 68). In the twentieth century Botticelli's composition became one of the most celebrated and frequently copied, reproduced and reinterpreted paintings in the world. AD

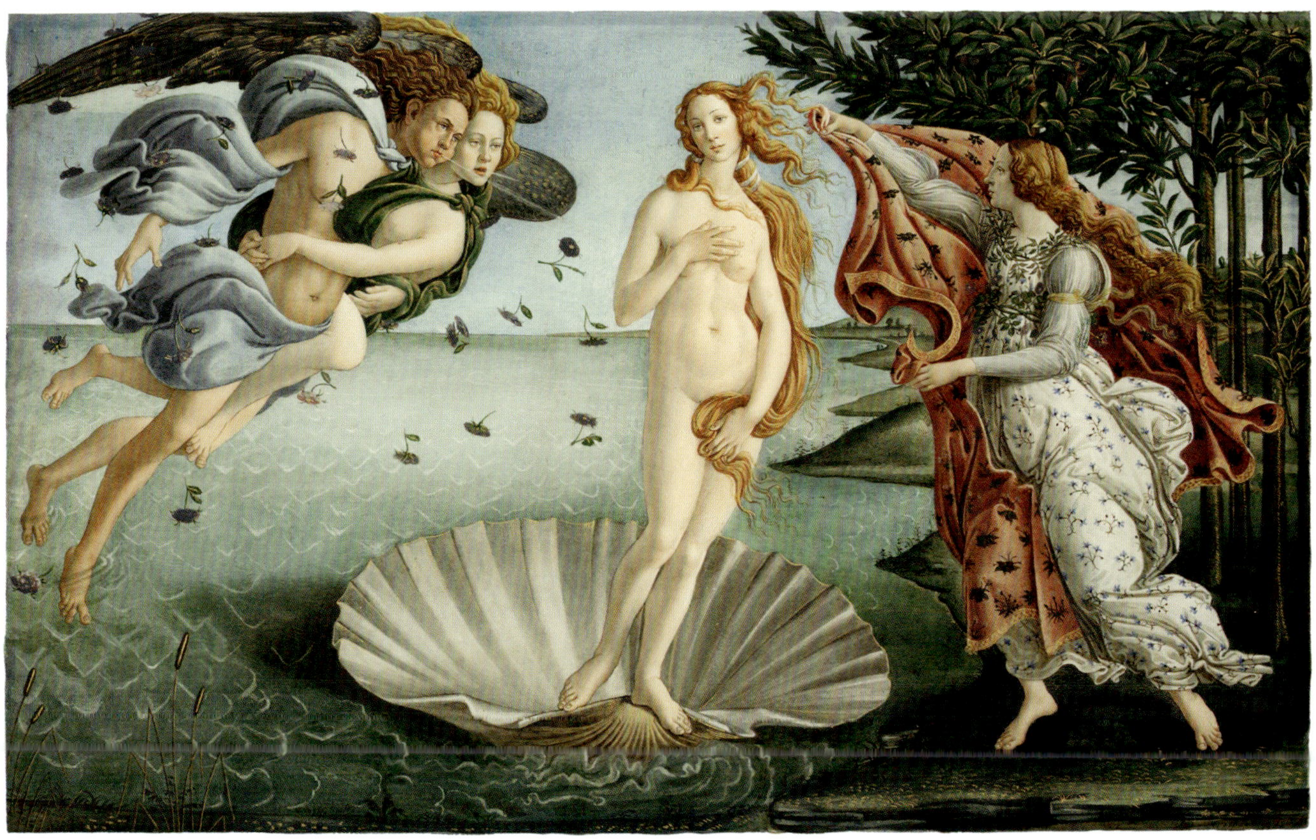

82

GUSTAVE MOREAU (1826–1898) after BOTTICELLI

Birth of Venus, c.1858–9

Oil on canvas, 31 × 46.5 cm
Musée Gustave Moreau, Paris (13622)

PROVENANCE
The artist's estate

LITERATURE
Rome 1996–7, p. 194

Gustave Moreau probably painted this small copy from the original in Florence, towards the end of December 1858 or early 1859. He must have studied this copy closely before painting his own depiction of the subject (cat. 83), but he also showed it to others. Charles Ephrussi, editor of the *Gazette des Beaux-Arts* and intermediary in the Louvre's purchase of the Botticelli frescoes from the Villa Lemmi, wrote to Moreau in 1886, 'Didn't I see a copy of Botticelli's *Birth of Venus* from the Accademia in Florence at your house? We're having an engraving done by Gaujean of that painting for the *Gazette* … He needs some kind of copy to use during his work as a point of reference for the colours, something that will indicate the tonal values. Your copy is better than any other; I believe I saw a most exquisite thing after the aforementioned painting at your studio. If you could let me have this painting for a few hours or days you'd really be doing me a favour.' There is no record of whether Moreau granted this request, but Ephrussi's judgement regarding the copy's fidelity of colour is impressive. GM

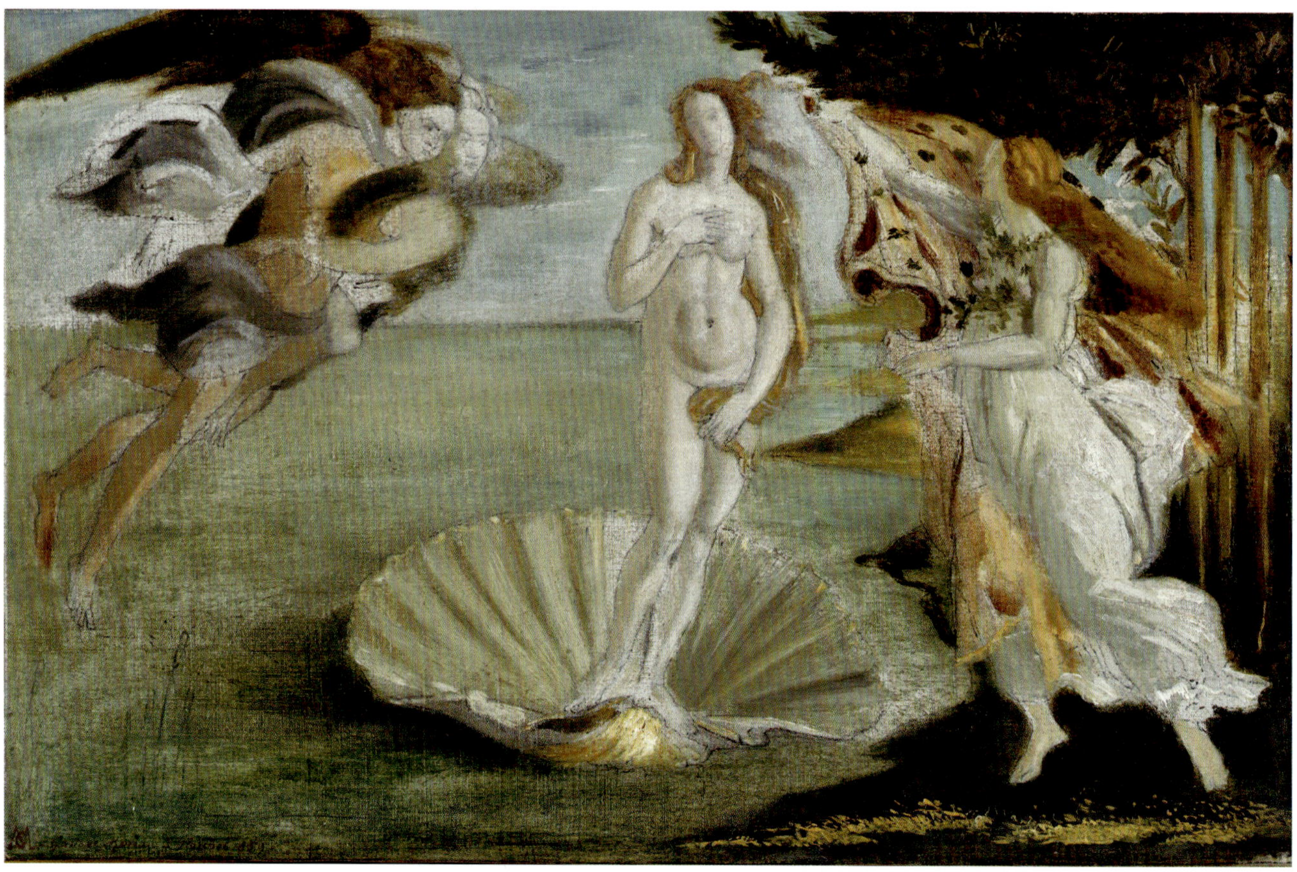

83

GUSTAVE MOREAU
(1826–1898)
Birth of Venus, c.1870

Oil on canvas, 40 × 62 cm
Musée Gustave Moreau, Paris (41)

PROVENANCE
The artist's estate

LITERATURE
Moreau 1974, p. 43

Before turning to his own depiction of the birth of Venus around 1870, Gustave Moreau had already engaged closely with Botticelli's treatment of the subject. In Florence in 1858–9 he produced both a drawing and a colour copy in oil (cat. 82), the fidelity of which in terms of colour was praised by Charles Ephrussi. For his own version of the subject Moreau relegated the additional figures to the background (except for a single putto), concentrating exclusively on Venus in her shell, who has moved from her customary position in the centre of the image to the left-hand side, her right arm cast behind her. While in Botticelli's painting the goddess is depicted in bright daylight among gentle waves, Moreau sets the scene in more puzzling surroundings. Although Venus herself is brightly lit from the left, large parts of the background look like a night scene. It is also unclear whether Venus is in some sort of hollow or cave. This strange atmosphere, as well as the bright, seemingly unfinished section to the right, lend Moreau's painting an unmistakeably symbolic character, with which he also stamped many other mythological or biblical scenes. GM

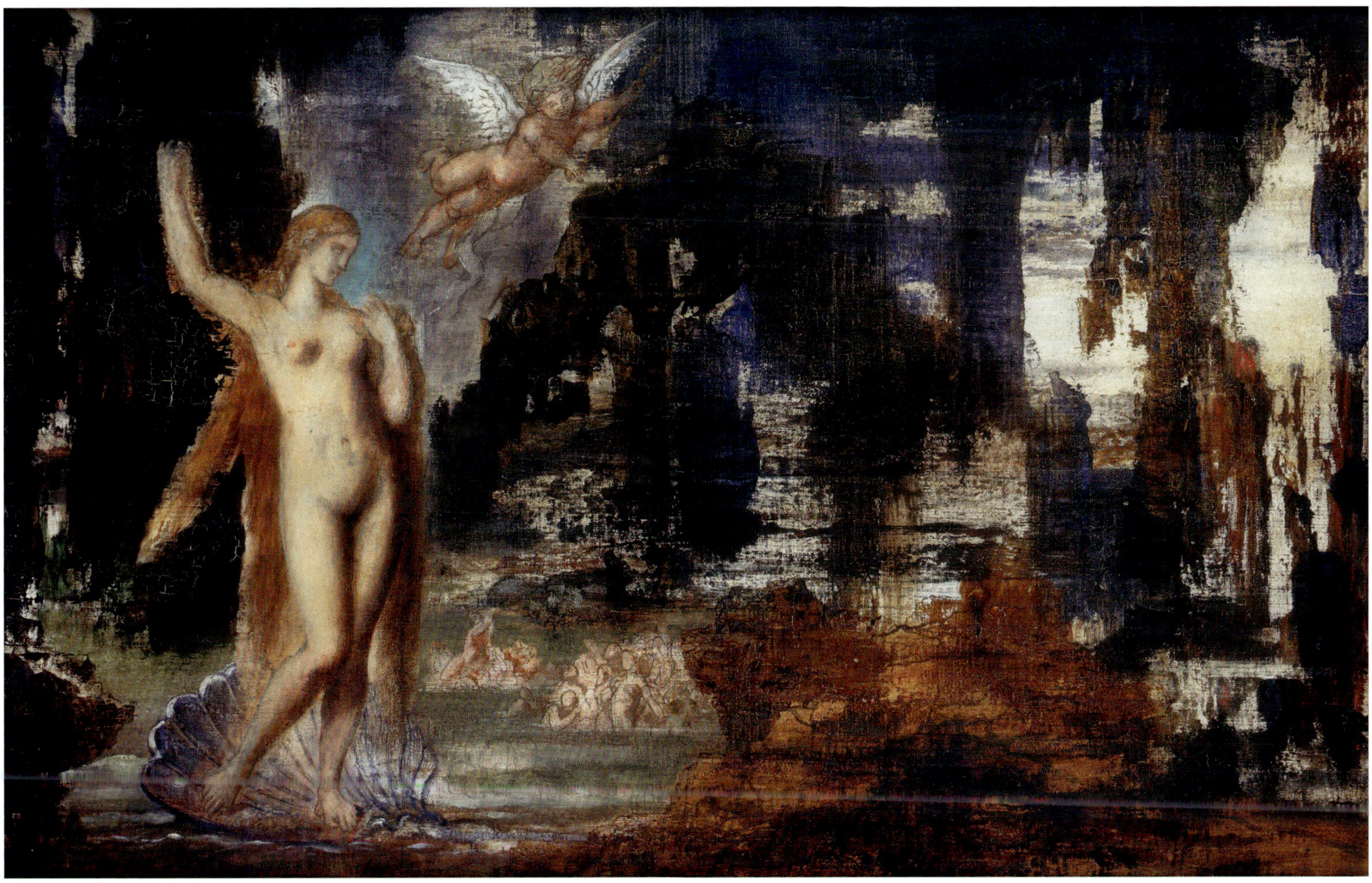

84

ARNOLD BÖCKLIN
(1827–1901)

Birth of Venus, 1868–9

Oil on canvas, 135.5 × 79 cm
Hessisches Landesmuseum, Darmstadt (8767)

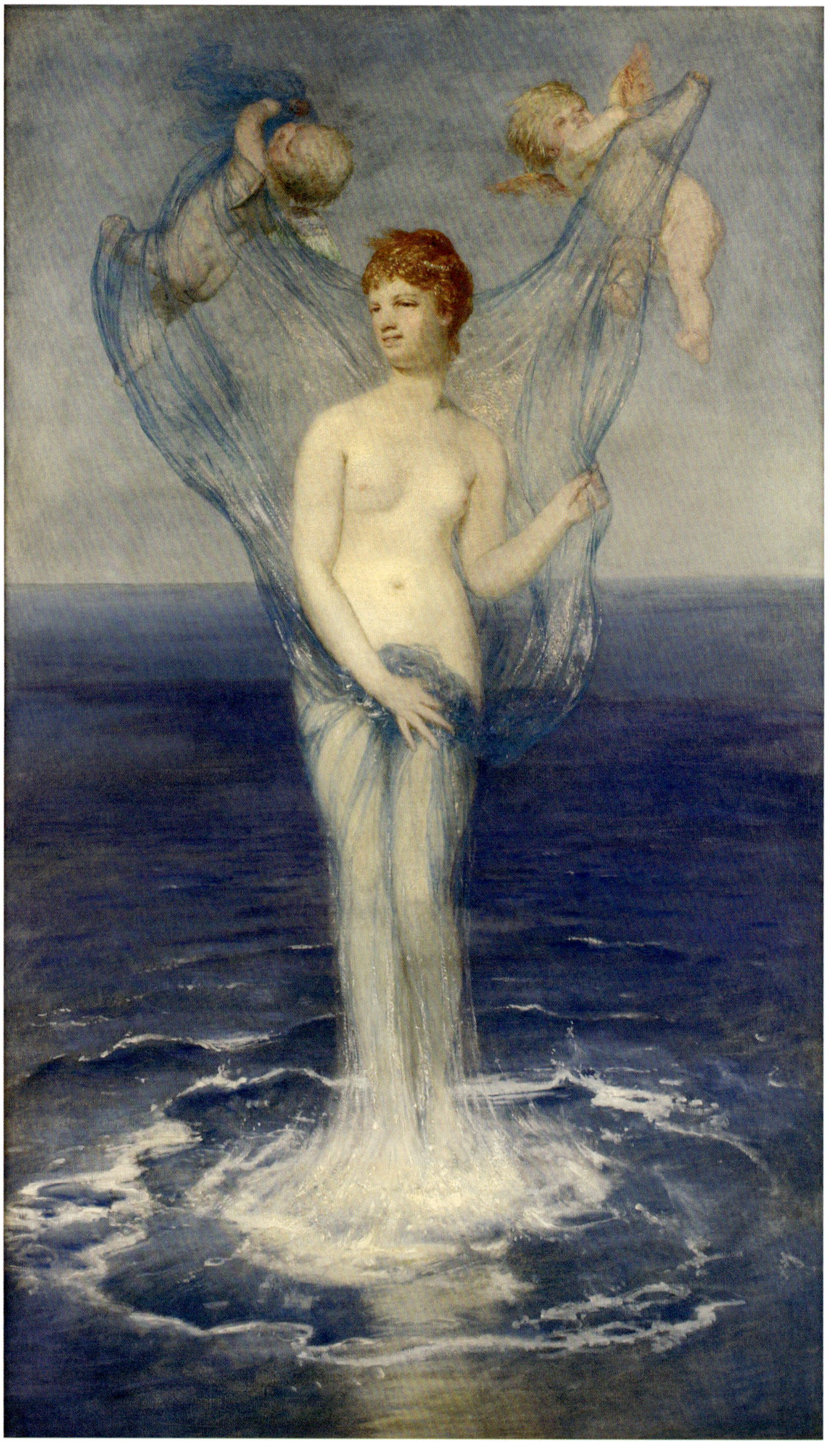

In formal terms, Böcklin's depiction of Venus is remarkable: it is systematically executed in a wide range of shades of blue, interrupted only by flesh tones and a few flecks of white froth in the sea spray. Böcklin skilfully portrayed the foaming water in the shape of a shell, from which emerges Venus – born from the waves. This subtle reference establishes a direct connection to Botticelli. Böcklin observed that this shell-like wave provided a compositional counterweight to the veil held by two putti in the upper half of the painting. The rest was to remain empty, 'imbuing Venus alone with interest and significance' (as noted by his friend Rudolf Schick in a diary entry of 30 January 1869). The Swiss art historian Jacob Burckhardt nonetheless repeatedly requested Böcklin to add to this painting. Perhaps wearied by this persistent lobbying, the artist left the *Birth of Venus* unfinished, and instead incorporated the sea monster and additional putti suggested by Burckhardt at the top and bottom of a smaller painting of *Venus Anadyomene*, dated 1872 and now in Saint Louis Art Museum. GM

PROVENANCE
1898 Maximilian Freiherr von Heyl, Darmstadt; various owners; Sigmund Buchenau, Niendorf/Lübeck; 1938 Karl Haberstock, Berlin; 'Führermuseum', Linz; acquired by The Federal Republic of Germany; since 1968 on permanent loan in Darmstadt

LITERATURE
Andree 1998, pp. 326–7, no. 227

85

SIMEON SOLOMON
(1840–1905)
Love in Autumn, 1866

Oil on canvas, 84 × 66 cm
Private collection

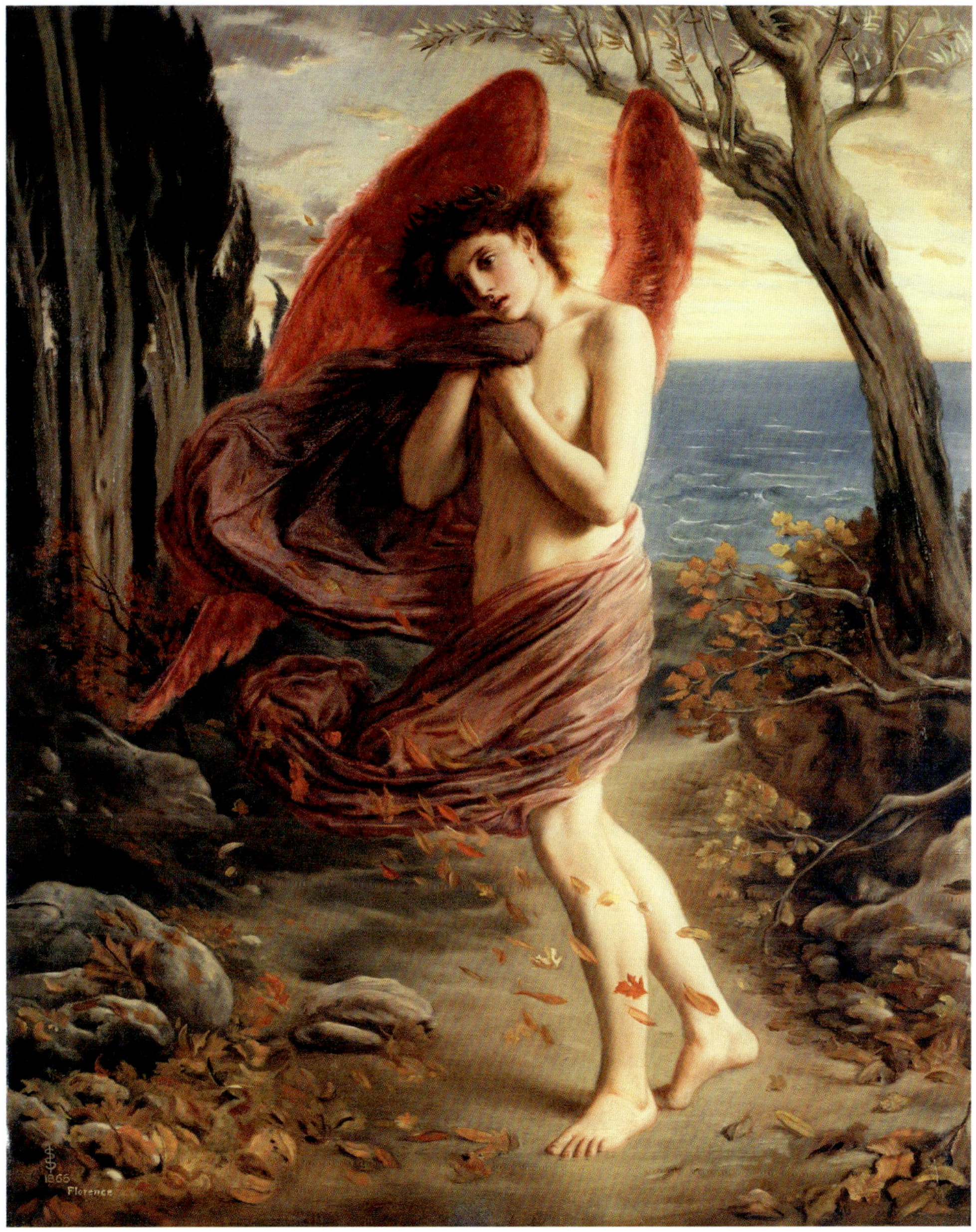

By the mid-1860s Solomon was friendly with Dante Gabriel Rossetti and Edward Burne-Jones, and was working in a Pre-Raphaelite style. This work was painted during his first visit to Florence. When it was displayed in 1872 at the Dudley Gallery as 'Eros being blown by autumn winds...' the artist was chided for depicting Cupid as 'a well-grown youth'. Interpreted as an allegory of love growing cold in the autumn of life, it was given the title *Love in Winter* when exhibited posthumously at the Royal Academy in 1906.

The figure and its drapery are modelled on those of Zephyr blowing the goddess of love to shore in Botticelli's *Birth of Venus*, which Solomon would have recently seen. Also derived from the airborne wind god are the 'badly drawn legs' criticized in 1872 by the reviewer for the *Athenaeum* as seemingly inadequate to support this standing figure. The present work is one of the first British paintings derived from Botticelli's mythologies. MM

PROVENANCE
Mrs William Coltart, 1906; private collection

LITERATURE
Athenaeum, 2 November 1872, p. 569; *The Art-Journal*, 1 December 1872, p. 309; London 1906, p. 28; Birmingham 2005–6, pp. 144–6

86

GUSTAVE MOREAU (1826–1898) after BOTTICELLI

Page of Studies with St Onuphrius, 1862

Pencil on paper, 10 × 6.1 cm
Musée Gustave Moreau, Paris (4556)
BERLIN ONLY

Gustave Moreau copied Botticelli's work not only during his travels in Italy in 1858–9, but also later in Paris. When the Campana collection purchased by Napoleon III was exhibited there in 1862, Moreau made copies of numerous works, including a panel from Botticelli's workshop, the *Noli me tangere*, now in Avignon (cat. 139). He copied the figure on the far right, the Egyptian hermit St Onuphrius: like St Sebastian, a rare male nude. GM

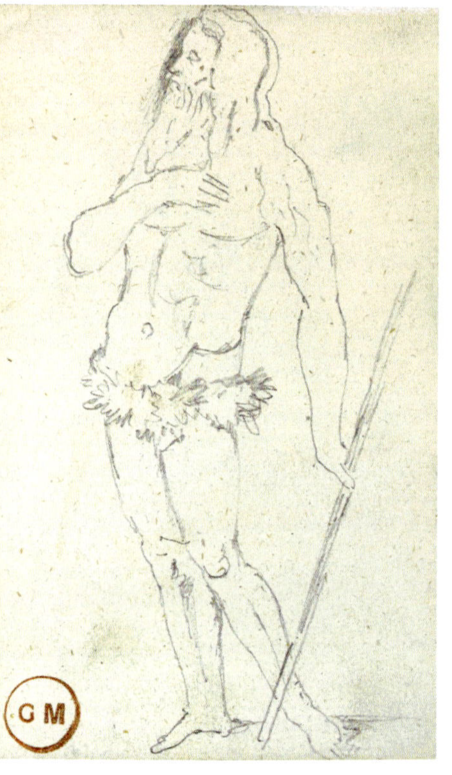

PROVENANCE
The artist's estate

LITERATURE
Bittler and Mathieu 1983, p. 205; Forest 2009, p. 862

87

ATTRIBUTED TO
IGNAZIO ZOTTI
(1806–c.1865) after BOTTICELLI
Portrait of a Lady, before 1837

Graphite and watercolour on paper, 19.4 × 12.9 cm
Tate, London (T 09476)

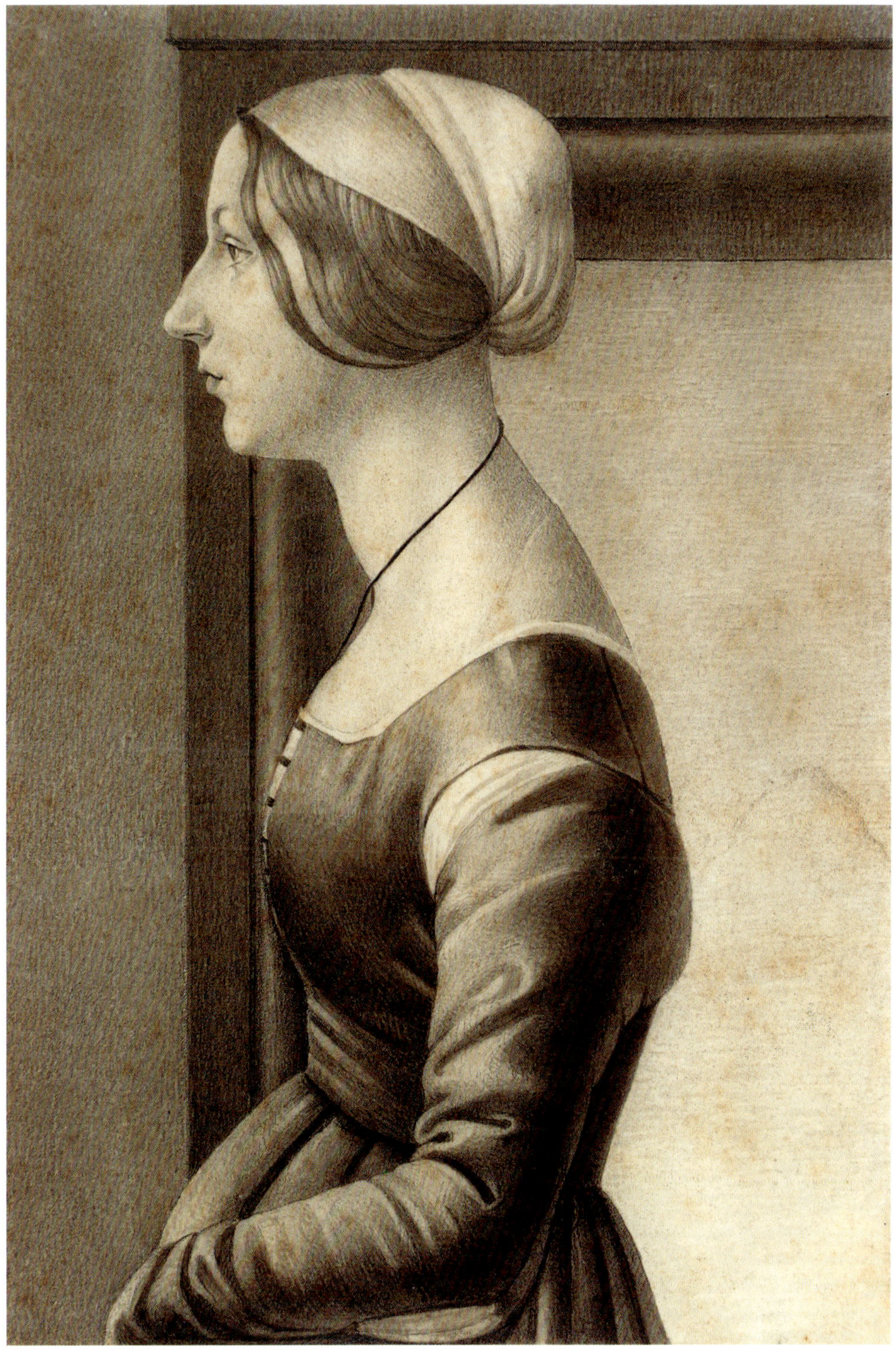

This drawing is a copy of a portrait of an unidentified woman first listed in the inventory of the Galleria Palatina at the Palazzo Pitti in 1829 (cat. 160), and published with an attribution to Botticelli by Giovanni Masselli in Luigi Bardi's *L'Imperiale e Reale Galleria Pitti* (1837), illustrated with an engraving by Luigi Calamatta after a drawing by Ignazio Zotti. In his commentary, Masselli called the lady 'the lover of Giuliano de' Medici', and speculated as to whether she should be identified as Simonetta Vespucci or Fioretta Gorini, the mother of Pope Clement VII. Other identifications of the sitter have been suggested, and later authors, with the exception of Berenson and Lightbown, have accepted the attribution to Botticelli, or his workshop.

This drawing entered the Tate Gallery with over 3,000 watercolours and drawings assembled by the distinguished connoisseur Paul Oppé, who attributed it to George Price Boyce. However, as this fine drawing eschews colour for tones of grey and exactly matches the size of the engraving published by Luigi Bardi in 1837, it is probably its preparatory study by the Florentine portrait painter Ignazio Zotti. His knowledge of early paintings was acknowledged in 1844 by his neighbour, the sculptor Giovanni Duprè and in 1856–8 by the dealer Otto Mündler. ME

PROVENANCE
Paul Oppé; purchased by the Tate Gallery with assistance from the National Lottery through the Heritage Lottery Fund, 1996

LITERATURE
Bardi 1837, pp. 29–31, pl. 11; Duprè 1886, p. 133; Lightbown 1978, vol. 2, pp. 210–11, no. F7 (with previous bibliography); Anderson 1985, pp. 132, 166, 190, 220; Frankfurt 2009–10, pp. 184–7, no. 14; Milan 2010–11, pp. 30, 32, fig. 30

88, 89

EDGAR DEGAS
(1834–1917) after BOTTICELLI
Venus, 1858–9

Graphite on paper, 30 × 22.5 cm
Private collection

GUSTAVE MOREAU
(1826–1898)
Portrait of Edgar Degas in the Uffizi, 1859

Graphite on paper, 15.3 × 9.4 cm
Musée Gustave Moreau, Paris (des. 12703)
BERLIN ONLY

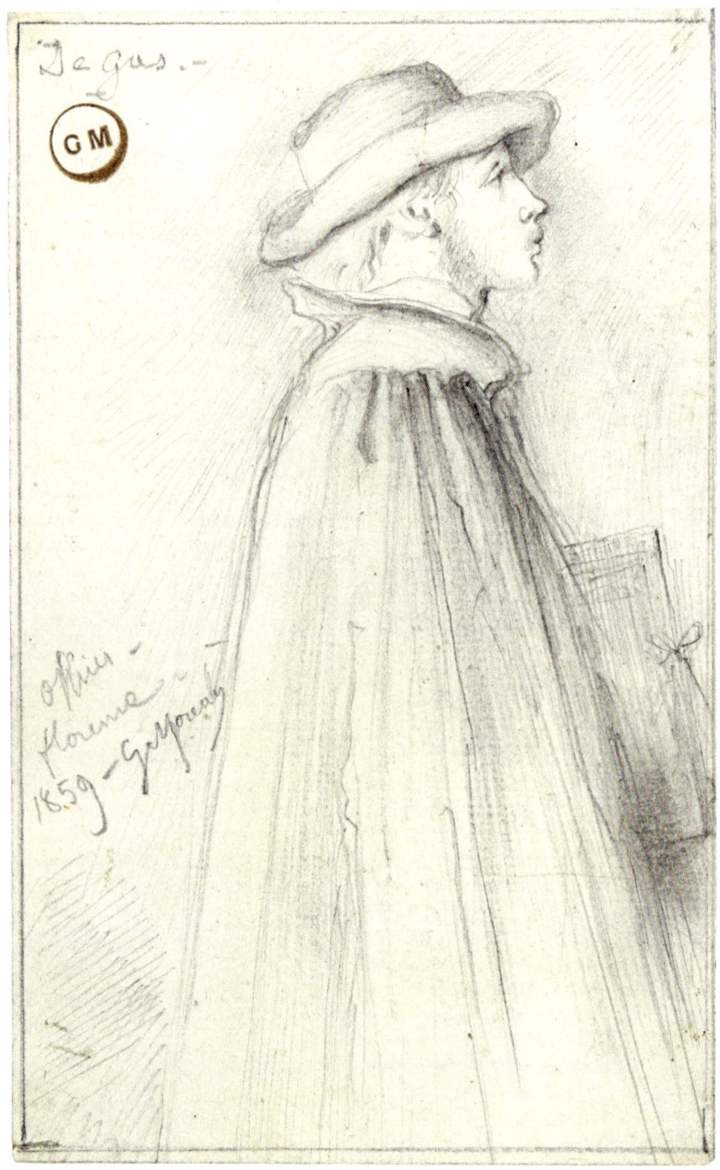

The display of Botticelli's *Birth of Venus* in the Uffizi, first confirmed in a gallery guide of 1844, as well as the publication of reproductions of this composition (cats 97, 98), set the stage for the popularization of this image, which is today firmly anchored in our global visual memory. Initially, French authors and artists were most enthusiastic about the painting. It was not the debt of Botticelli's Venus to the antique sculptural form of the Medici Venus, but rather her aloof grace, interpreted as unclassical, that spoke to visitors such as the Goncourt Brothers in 1855.

During his stay in Florence in 1858–9, Degas made drawings after the painting, extracting the figure of Venus from the composition as a whole. The combination of strong contours and the soft modelling of her nude body, achieved through extremely delicate hatching, is striking. Drawing after the Old Masters was a fundamental part of academic training, although this model was not representative of the traditional academic canon. Nonetheless, Degas's enthusiasm for the nudes of Jean-Auguste-Dominique Ingres (see cat. 92) made him receptive to Botticelli's *Venus*. Walter Pater similarly remarked in 1870 that the Renaissance painter's *Venus* reminded him of 'the faultless nude studies of Ingres'. RR

PROVENANCE
CAT. 88 Sold from the artist's estate in 1919
CAT. 89 The artist's estate

LITERATURE
CAT. 88 Boston and Paris 2011–12, p. 24, no. 25; Karlsruhe 2014–15, p. 247, no. 114
CAT. 89 Boston and Paris 2011–12, p. 24

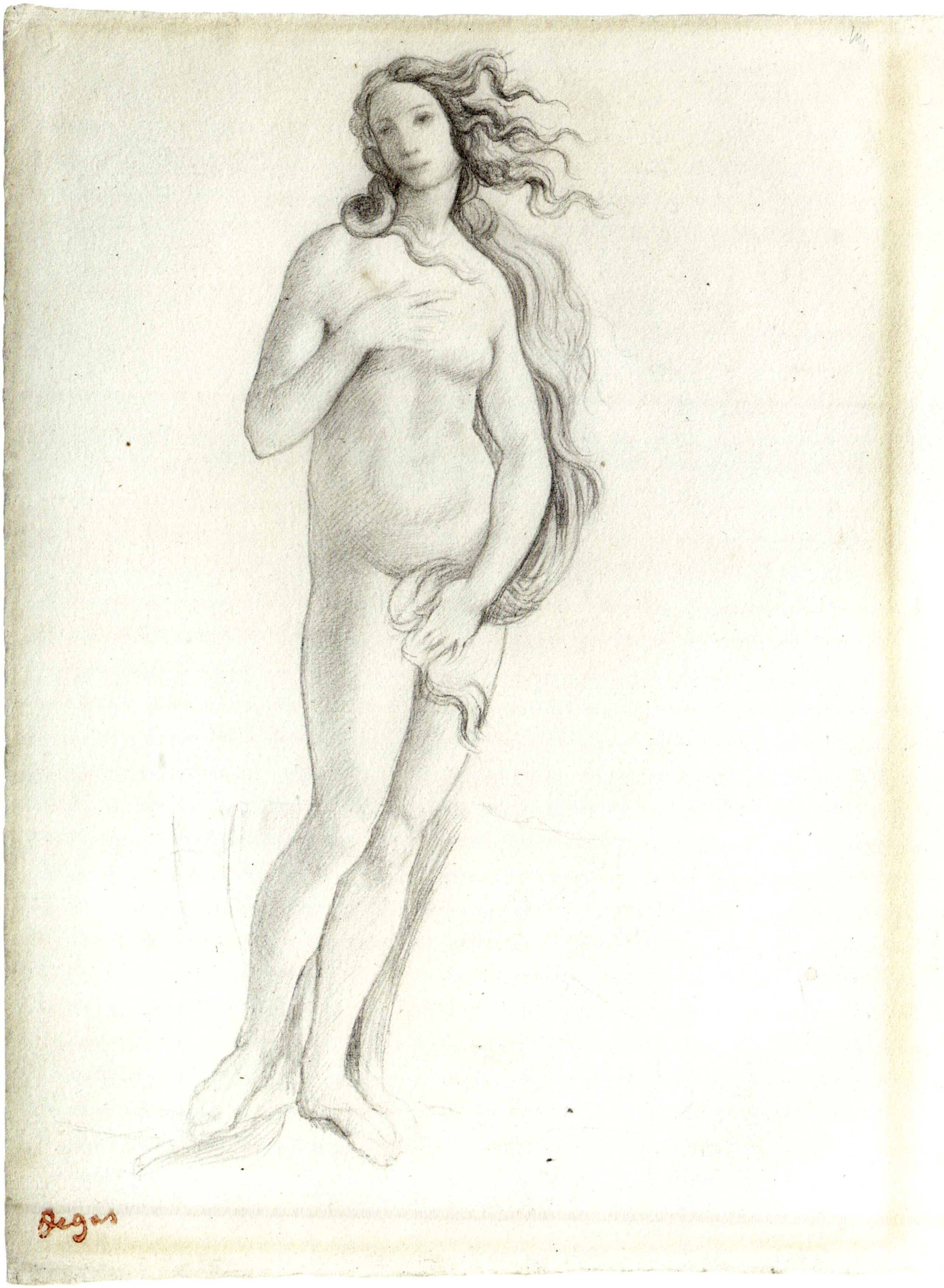

90, 91

JEAN-AUGUSTE-DOMINIQUE INGRES (1780–1867)

Venus, 1815–20

Lead point on glued paper, 26.7 × 15.2 cm
Musée Ingres, Montauban (867.2301)
LONDON ONLY

Venus, 1815–20

Pen and ink and lead point on paper, 18.8 × 9.9 cm
Musée Ingres, Montauban (867.2302)
BERLIN ONLY

Ingres was extremely methodical in his working practice, producing numerous preparatory drawings for his compositions, and often reworking them over an extended period. These two examples are physically and conceptually related to the paintings *Venus Anadyomene* (Musée Condé, Chantilly) and *The Source* (cat. 92). The earlier, damaged sheet was probably made in Florence between 1815 and 1820 and bears quotations from the second Homeric *Hymn to Aphrodite* as well as additional notes including the comment 'she is ashamed of her nudity'. This statement epitomizes the puritanical anxiety over depictions of the female body that had become widespread in France following the Jacobin Revolution. In his attempt to represent ideal beauty Ingres expresses Venus's modesty through a *pudica* gesture inspired by Botticelli's *Birth of Venus*. AD

PROVENANCE
Bequeathed by the artist to the city of Montauban, 1867

LITERATURE
Alazard 1950, p. 40; Rome 1968, no. 11 (col. 1); Vigne 1995, p. 157, nos 849 and 850 (with previous bibliography)

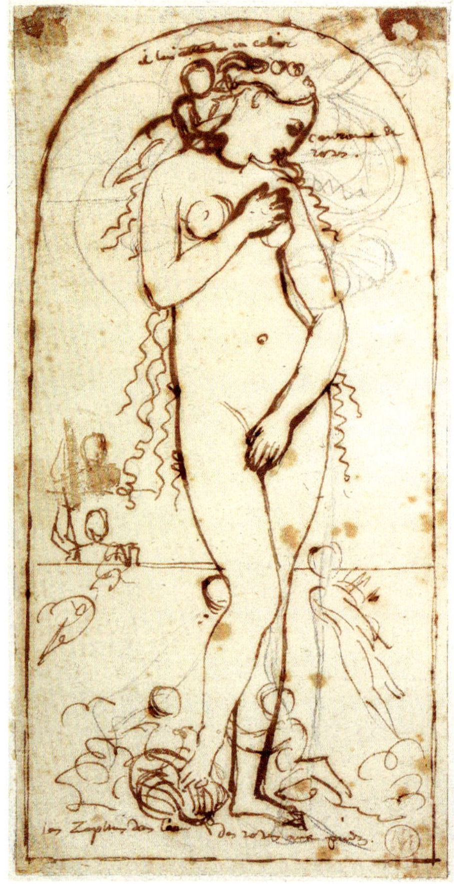

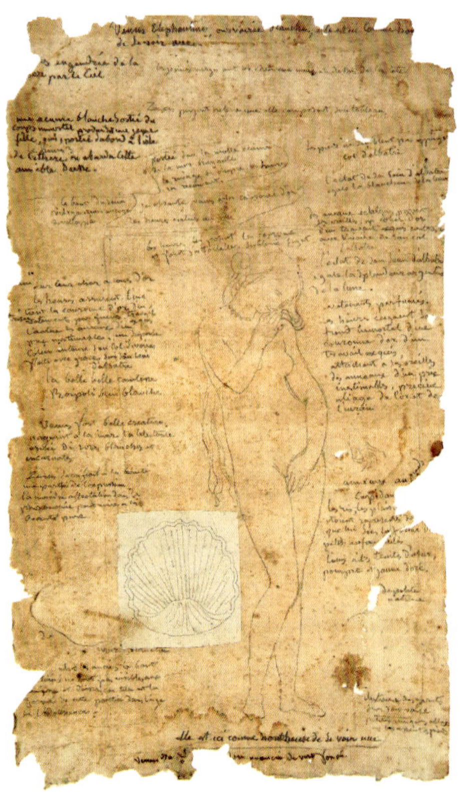

92

JEAN-AUGUSTE-DOMINIQUE INGRES (1780–1867), PAUL BALZE (1815–1884) and ALEXANDRE DESGOFFE (1805–1882)

The Source, 1820–56

Oil on canvas, 163 × 80 cm
Musée du Louvre, Paris, on long-term loan to Musée d'Orsay, Paris (RF 219)

In August 1820 Ingres returned to Florence, and began work on *The Source*, a subject he had previously explored during an earlier stay there with *Venus Anadyomene* (Musée Condé, Chantilly), begun in 1806. The two paintings draw on Botticelli's *Birth of Venus*, which had been on public display at the Uffizi since 1815, and probably on Botticelli workshop versions of Venus set against a plain dark background (cats 169, 170). Both of Ingres's paintings took decades to complete: the *Venus* in 1848 and *The Source* in 1856 with the help of his assistants Paul Balze and Alexandre Desgoffe.

These long periods of gestation are typical of Ingres's slow working practice and obsessive perfectionism in pursuit of an ideal of female beauty. This required multiple versions and revisions of his subject. Surviving drawings (cats 90, 91) show the protracted evolution of the figure of Venus. While devoted principally to Raphael, Ingres also shared Botticelli's simple curvilinear style and bright, albeit subdued, palette. A contemporary critic, Léon Lagrange, likened Ingres's technical achievement and pure rendering of lines to Botticelli's art, while lamenting that the latter remained little known in France.

The Source became one of Ingres's most popular works and was often engraved. In 1862 it was exhibited at the International Exhibition in London (no. 79). Théodore de Banville dedicated a poem to the nymph, while Théophile Gautier admired its combination of ideal and realistic. Count Duchâtel, a minister of Napoleon III, outbid his competitors and paid the considerable sum of 25,000 francs for *The Source*, which he displayed surrounded with aquatic flowers and large plants to increase the *trompe-l'oeil* effect of this Botticellian nymph. AD

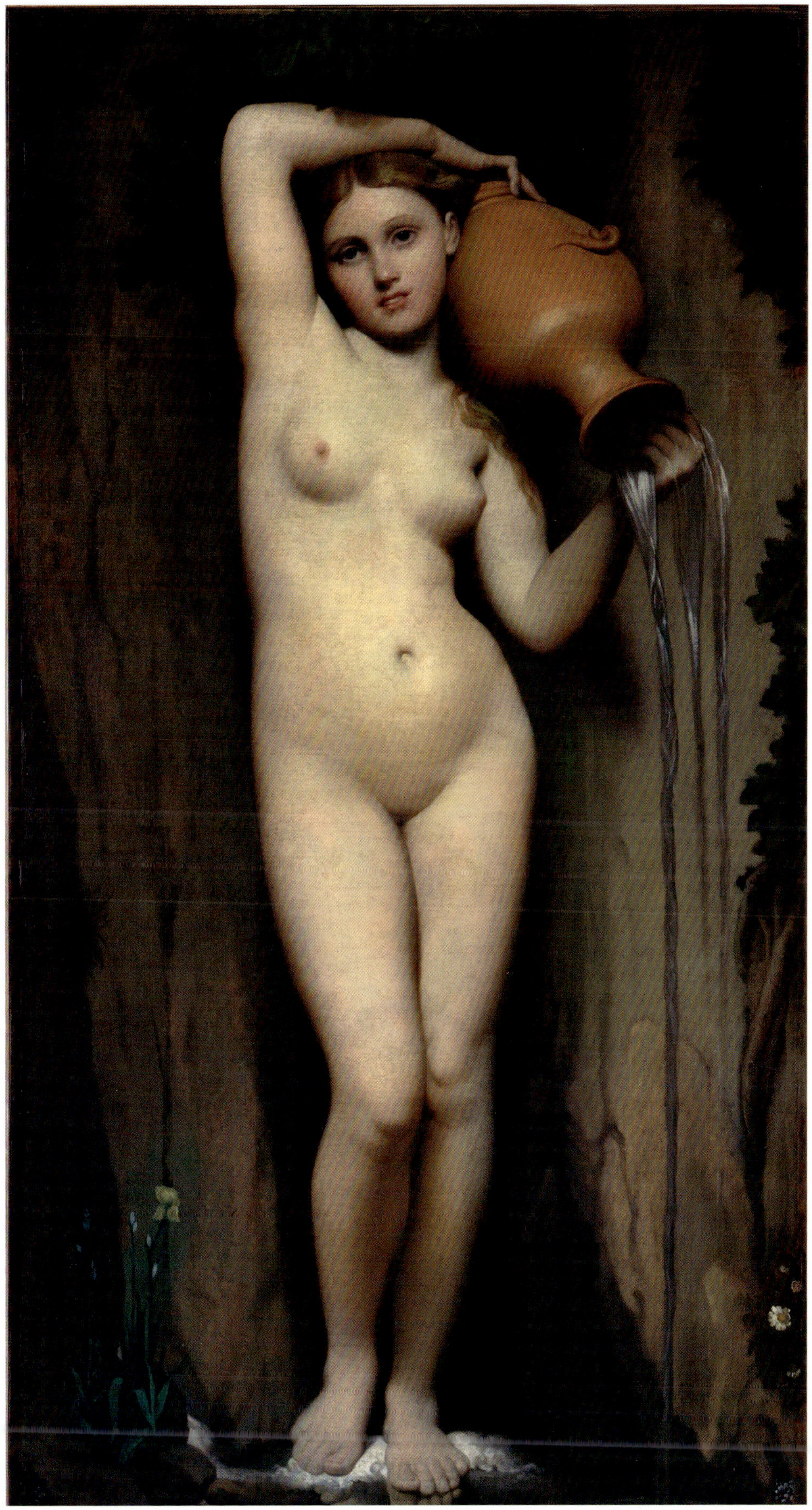

PROVENANCE

1857, bought by Count Charles-Marie Tanneguy Duchâtel for 25,000 francs, bequeathed in 1878 by his widow to the Louvre; on long-term loan at the Musée d'Orsay, Paris, since 1986

LITERATURE

Gautier 1857; Delaborde 1954, no. 279; Camesasca 1968, no. 154; Ternois 1980, pp. 114–15, 171

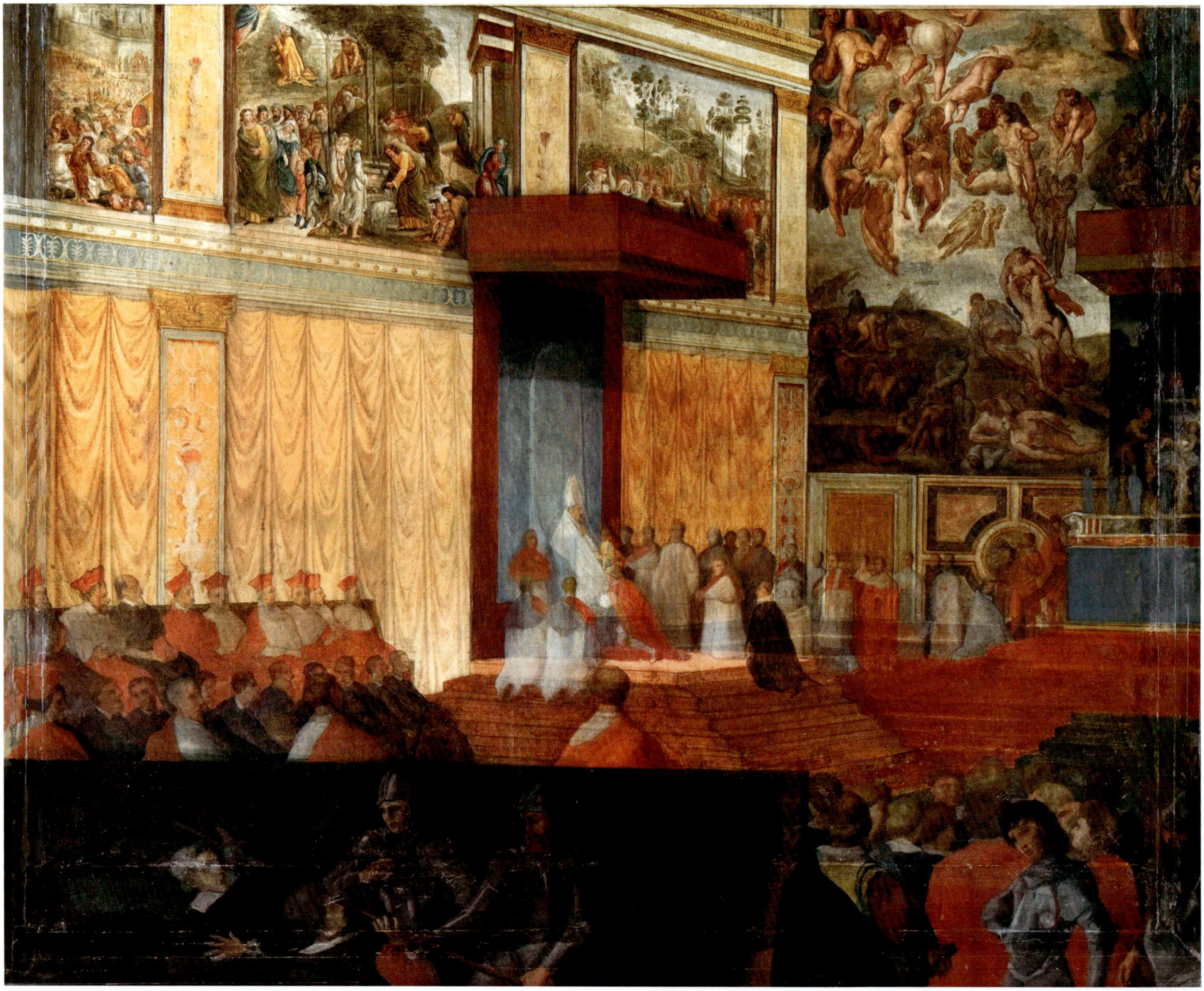

93

JEAN-AUGUSTE-DOMINIQUE INGRES (1780–1867)

Investiture of a Roman Prefect in the Sistine Chapel, 1848

Oil on canvas on wood, 81 × 98 cm
Musée Ingres, Montauban (MI 867.101)

When Ingres arrived in Rome in 1806, he was impressed by the grandeur and ceremony of the Vatican. He recalled this atmosphere in his work even decades later, and in 1836, as director of the Académie Française in Rome, he invited the architect Eugène Viollet-le-Duc to a Christmas Eve mass in the Sistine Chapel. In 1814 he produced the first of three oil paintings featuring a near-identical interior view of the chapel as a backdrop to a pontifical ceremony (National Gallery of Art, Washington), with a smaller version following in 1820 (Louvre, Paris). The Pope and other dignitaries are treated in much the same manner as the imposing décor. Michelangelo's monumental wall fresco *The Last Judgement* can be clearly made out, as can the older frescoes from the 1480s on the south wall, in particular Botticelli's *Scenes from the Life of Moses* (cat. 94) to the left of the baldachin-crowned papal throne. There are no more detailed studies of this fresco among Ingres's sketches, but the final work suggests close observation of the original, and represents one of the first encounters of a nineteenth-century artist with Botticelli. Ingres imbued the architectural background with the greatest significance in the version produced in 1848, where he painted the surroundings himself *d'après nature* while a pupil copied the central figures from Agostino Tassi's *Investiture of Taddeo Barberini by Urban VIII* (1631–33, Museo di Roma). GM

PROVENANCE
1851, gift of the artist

LITERATURE
Ternois 1965, no. 181; Paris 2014–15b, p. 189

94

J.B.L.G SÉROUX D'AGINCOURT (1730–1814) after BOTTICELLI

The Rebellion against Moses, 1823

Etching, 32.2 × 50.3 cm
National Art Library, Victoria and Albert Museum, London (38041800898215)

This engraving (at bottom left) after frescoes by Botticelli and others in the Sistine Chapel is from the final volume of Jean-Baptiste-Louis-Georges Séroux d'Agincourt's six-part treatise *Histoire de l'art par les monumens*. The author settled in Rome in 1779 where he befriended the leading neo-classical sculptor Antonio Canova, Johann Wolfgang von Goethe, François-René Chateaubriand and Stefano Borgia, an important collector of Italian 'Primitives'. Séroux d'Agincourt was a follower of the influential art historian Johann Joachim Winckelmann, and his treatise was the result of 35 years of dedicated research. It was one of the earliest surveys of the history of architecture, sculpture and painting, and used engravings to illustrate the continuity of art from Antiquity to the Renaissance. A number of skilled draughtsmen, engravers and architects were employed to reproduce the chosen works, and some of the illustrations were based on drawings by the author. MM

PROVENANCE
Purchased

LITERATURE
Séroux d'Agincourt 1811–23, vol. 2, pp. 162–3; vol. 3, p. 168; vol. 6, pl. clxxiii ('Moses Punishing Corah and his Company, after Botticelli's Fresco in Rome')

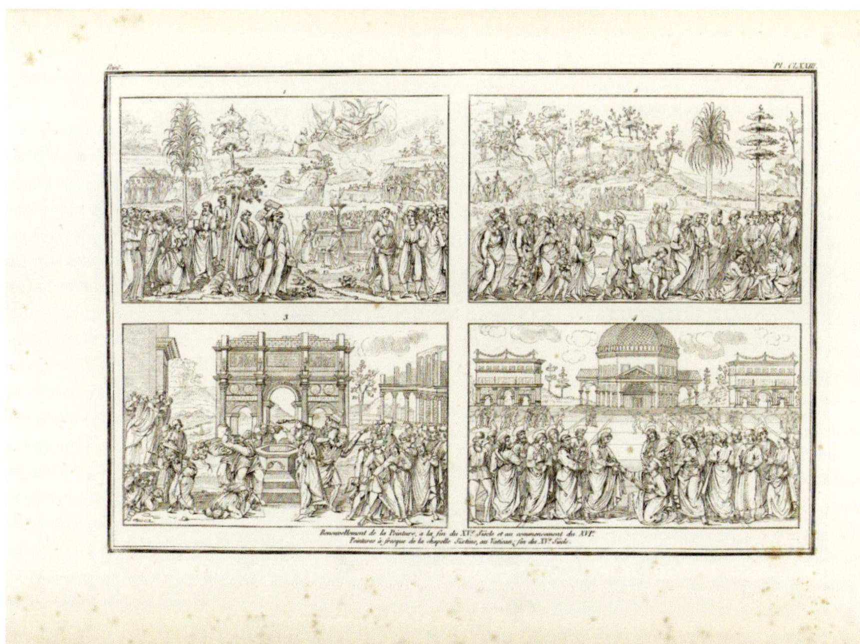

95

FRANZ (1786–1831) and JOHANNES (1788–1860) RIEPENHAUSEN after BOTTICELLI

The Calumny of Apelles, 1808

Pen and ink over black chalk on paper, 37.2 × 54 cm
Inscribed at bottom left: 'Sandro Botticelli pinx Riepenhausen del. Firenze 1808'
Collection Booth-Clibborn, London

The Riepenhausen brothers trained at Göttingen and were introduced to 'Primitive' art by the writer and collector Carl Friedrich von Rumohr, whom they accompanied to Italy in 1805. This line drawing is a copy of Botticelli's *Calumny of Apelles*, a painting mentioned by Vasari and on display at the Uffizi since 1778. It is one of a group of drawings after early paintings made by the brothers during a four-month stay in Florence in 1808 for a series of four illustrated volumes they were planning with the title *Geschichte der Malerei in Italien*. In the event, only the first volume, dealing with the fourteenth century, was published, at Tübingen in 1810. The brothers sent their publisher in 1816 a further 17 drawings mainly after fifteenth-century pictures 'from the most beautiful epoch of painting in Italy', whcih are now in the Schiller Nationalmuseum in Marbach. This and another drawing by the Riepenhausen brothers of 'a mystic subject' after Botticelli were acquired by Dominique-Vivant, Baron Denon, the first director of the Louvre, probably for his own illustrated history of art, which remained unfinished at his death. ME

PROVENANCE
Baron Dominique-Vivant Denon, his sale 1826 (part of lot 881); acquired in 2006

LITERATURE
Pérignon 1826 (Lugt 11164), p. 202, lot 881; Levey 1960, p. 296; Schröter 1997, pp. 213–91; Stendal 2001, pp. 122–8, 131–6; London 2011–12, pp. 72–3, no. 15

96

JULIUS SCHNORR VON CAROLSFELD (1794–1872) after BOTTICELLI

Scene from the Life of St Zenobius, 1819

Pen and brown ink and grey-brown wash over graphite on paper, 21 × 24.6 cm
Inscribed at bottom left: 'Florenz, d. 13 Juny 1819', with the artist's monogram; and at bottom right: 'nach Alless. Botticelli'
Collection Booth-Clibborn, London

Following studies in Vienna, Schnorr moved in 1817 to Rome, where he remained for ten years. There he became a leading member of the Nazarene brotherhood of expatriate German artists, who greatly admired the Italian masters of the fifteenth century. In 1819 Schnorr fell ill with malaria and visited Florence to recuperate. During his stay, he made this copy of a predella panel from Botticelli's altarpiece of *St Zenobius*, then probably still owned by his friend, the art dealer Johann Metzger. Schnorr's drawing utilizes an outline style derived ultimately from the English artist John Flaxman, who had earlier been impressed by the Italian 'Primitives'. In 1823 Botticelli's panel was purchased by Carl Friedrich von Rumohr, who sold it to Schnorr's friend and patron, the artist and collector Johann Gottlob von Quandt. ME

PROVENANCE
Purchased from Karl & Faber, Munich, 29 November 2005 (lot 429)

LITERATURE
London 2011–12, pp. 294–5, no. 86

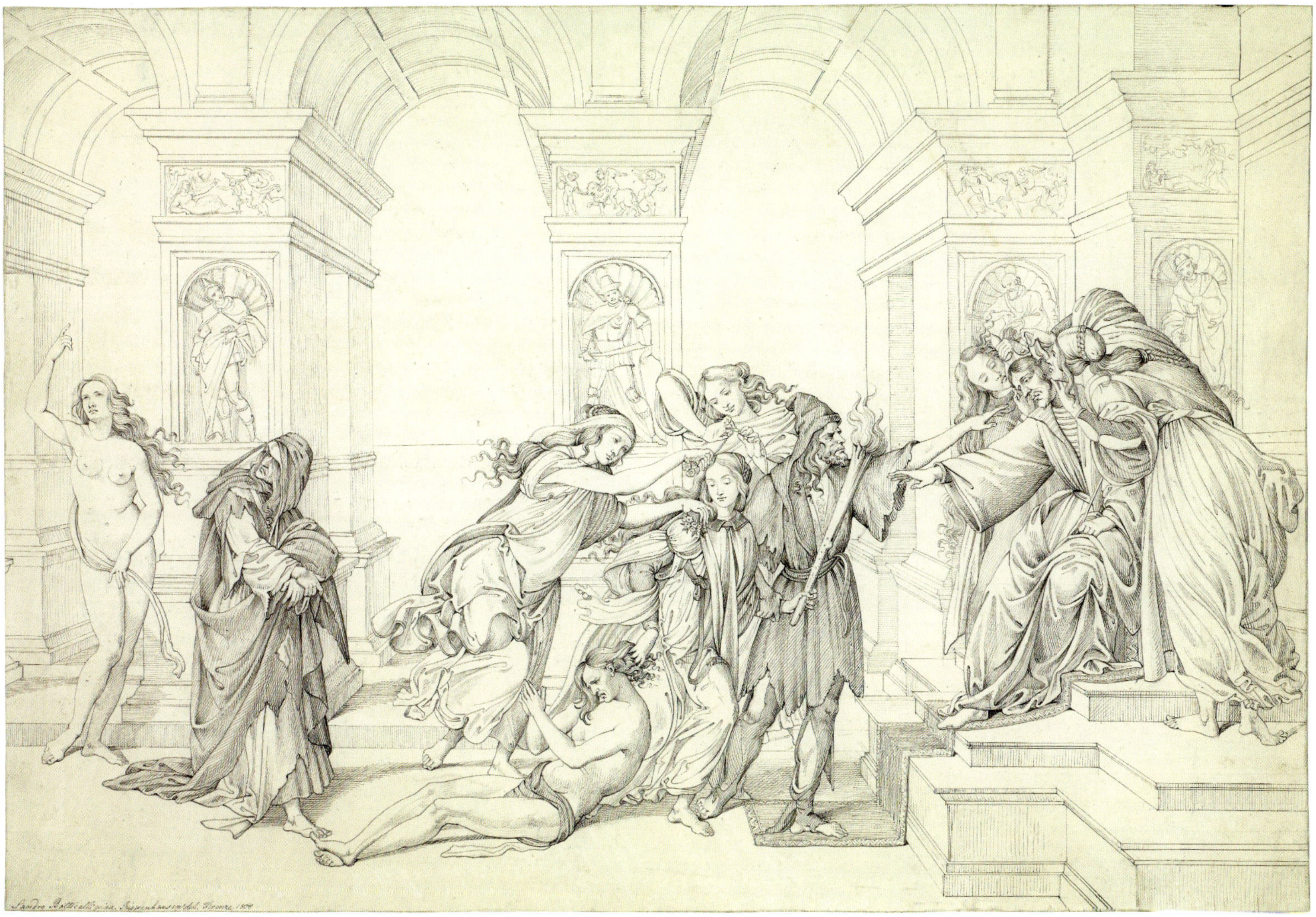

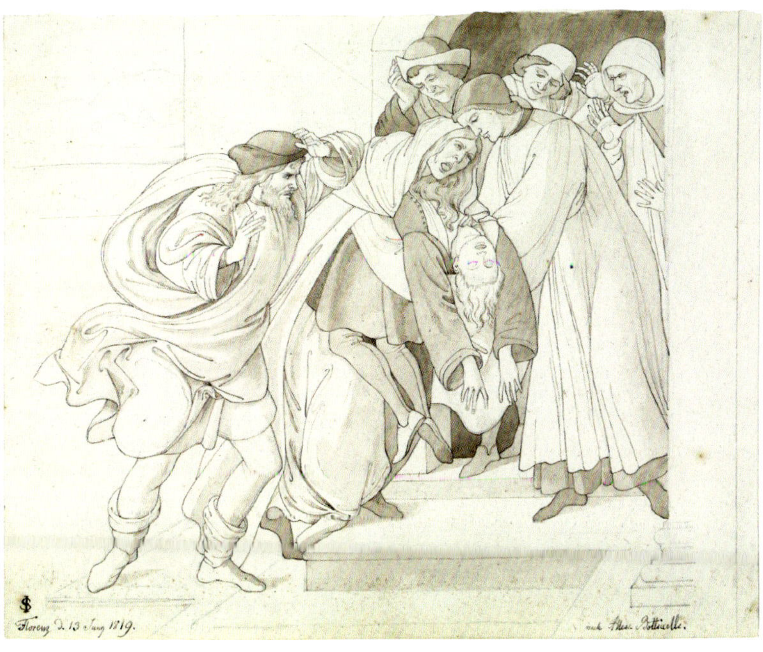

97

FRANCESCO CLERICI AND G. LANGUINETTI (dates unknown) after BOTTICELLI

Birth of Venus, 1841–6

Etching, 25.5 × 34.4 cm (sheet)
The British Museum, London (1857,0411.29)

98

GIUSEPPE ROSSI AND ANGELO TRICCA (dates unknown) after BOTTICELLI

Birth of Venus, 1840

Etching, 45.5 × 29.3 cm (plate)
Staatsbibliothek, Berlin

BERLIN ONLY

PROVENANCE
CAT. 97 Imperiale e Reale Galleria 1841–7
CAT. 98 Rosini 1839–47, vol. 2, fig. 55

Following the display of the *Birth of Venus* in the east corridor of the Uffizi sometime between 1840 and 1844, a large-format reproduction of the painting was published in a volume titled *Imperiale e reale Galleria di Firenze*. Very much in the tradition of royal gallery publications, this reproduced lavish prints of major works in the collection. Around the same time, a reproduction of the *Birth of Venus* appeared in Giovanni Rosini's *Storia della pittura italiana esposta coi monumenti*, an illustrated history of Italian painting. Clerici's and Rossi's etchings initiated the reproduction history of Botticelli's *Birth of Venus*, which still flourishes today. RR

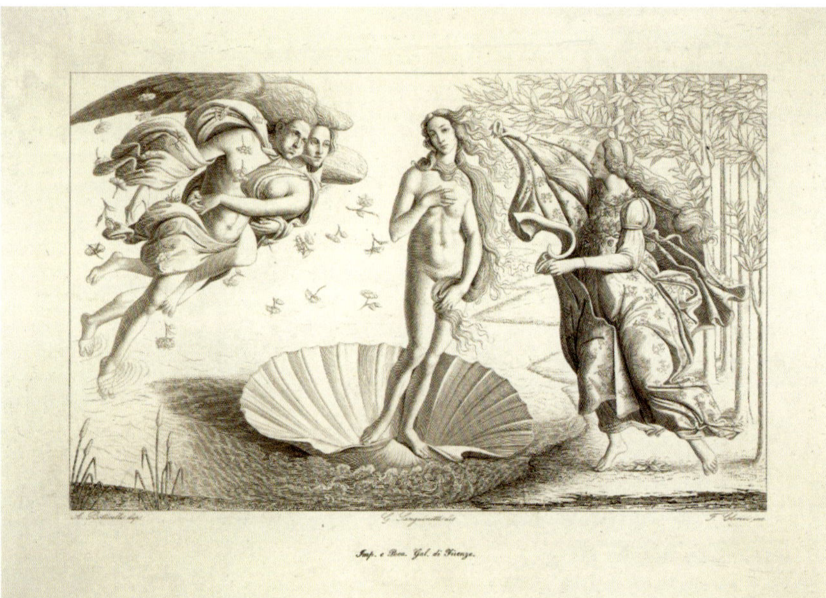

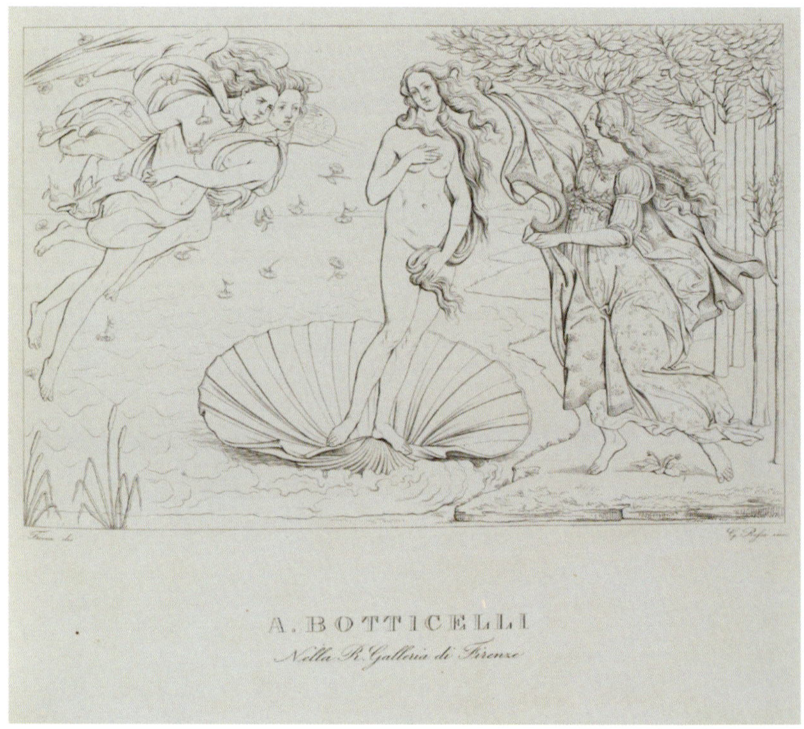

99

MATTEO CARBONI (1768–1805) after BOTTICELLI

The Virgin and Child with Four Angels and Six Saints. Plate from Lastri's 'L'Etruria pittrice', 1791

Etching, 29 × 41.5 cm (plate)
Private collection
BERLIN ONLY

National Art Library, Victoria and Albert Museum, London (38041800870040)
LONDON ONLY

Marco Lastri's book *L'Etruria Pittrice*, published in two volumes in 1791 and 1795, is a milestone of art-historical writing. Not only does it use artists' biographies to tell the story of Tuscan painting from the tenth century to the present, but it also features 120 reproductions as prints. To illustrate Botticelli's oeuvre, Lastri had an engraving made of an altar painting in the Florentine church of San Barnaba, noting that it was especially representative of his style. The altarpiece, which was moved to the Accademia in 1808 and the Uffizi in 1919, today attracts less attention from contemporary visitors than the other Botticelli paintings on display. At the end of the eighteenth century, however, this work was seen as particularly expressive, and was captured in what was probably the earliest accurate reproduction of a painting by the artist. RR

LITERATURE
Lastri 1791–5, vol. 1, no. 18

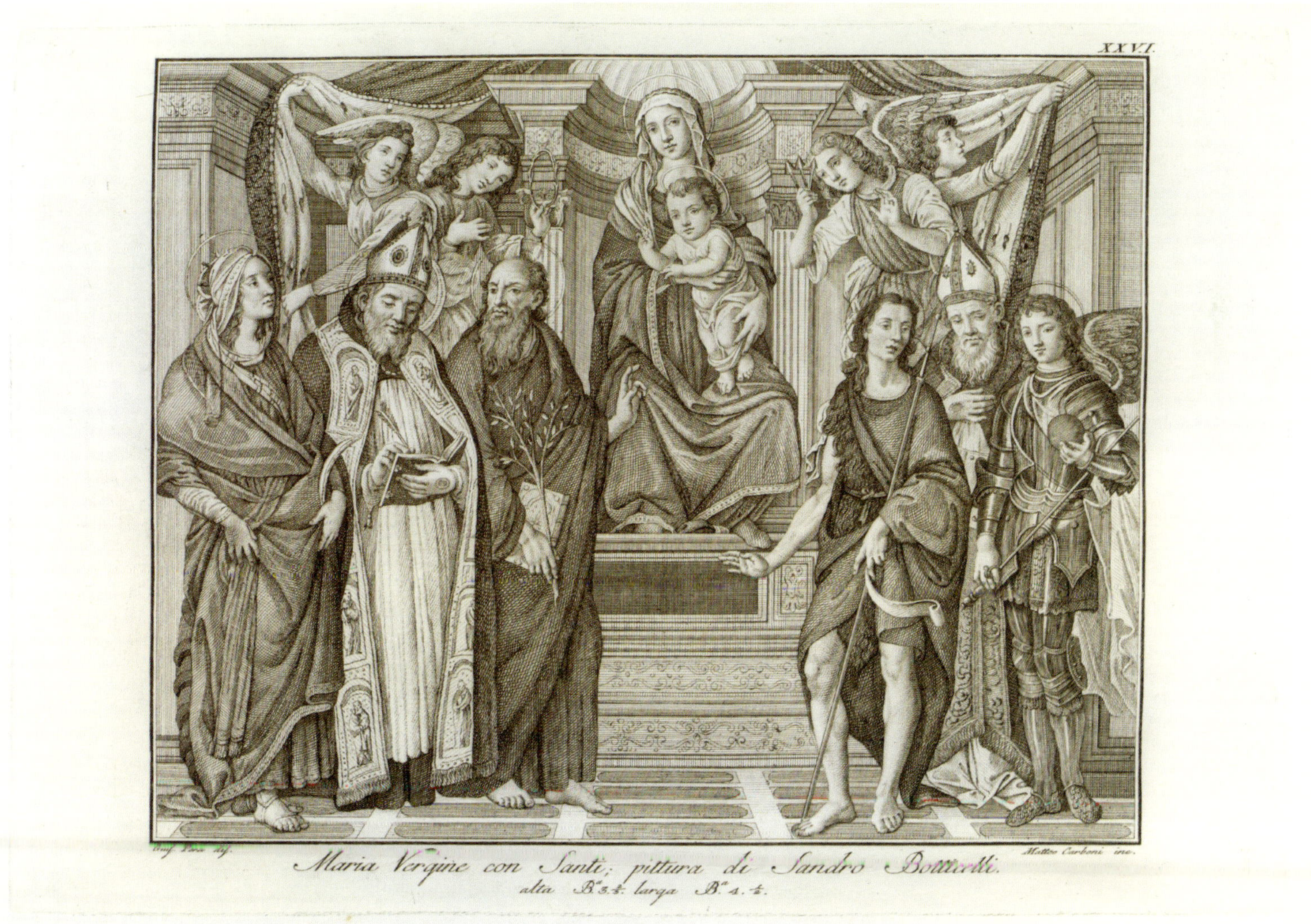

100

JOHN FLAXMAN
(1755–1826)

Dante's Inferno, canto XVI, l. 25–6, 1792–3

Graphite, pen and grey ink on laid paper;
from an album of drawings for *The Divine Comedy*,
58 sheets plus 2, 13.1 × 19.2 cm
Fitzwilliam Museum, Cambridge (Ms. No. 736, fol. 50r)

PROVENANCE
Charles Bale; his sale Christie's, London, 13 May 1881 (lot 382);
Charles Fairfax Murray, by whom given in 1912

LITERATURE
Berlin, Rome and London 2000–1, pp. 19, 78–81; Salvadori 2005, pp. 84–5, 273–5

This sheet is in an album of preparatory sketches by the English sculptor John Flaxman for 111 illustrations to Dante's *Divine Comedy*, commissioned in Rome by Thomas Hope in 1792. The finished drawings are in the Houghton Library at Harvard University (PF MS TYP 26.4). Several of Flaxman's designs are related to Botticelli's ink drawings of *The Divine Comedy* (cats 147–53; see the essay by Mark Evans in this volume). In this sheet the balletic poses of the damned souls of the Florentine noblemen resemble by the corresponding figures, tortured by a rain of fire, at the top right of Botticelli's illustration of the same passage of the *Inferno*, in the Biblioteca Apostolica Vaticana (cat. 149).

Seven of Botticelli's Dante drawings had entered the Vatican Library by the 1690s, and the remainder were acquired by the Duke of Hamilton between 1803 and 1819. This volume of Flaxman's drawings belonged to the artist and art dealer Charles Fairfax Murray, who copied works by Botticelli in Florence for John Ruskin (cat. 63), and procured for him a painting of the *Virgin and Child* (cat. 127) from Botticelli's workshop. ME

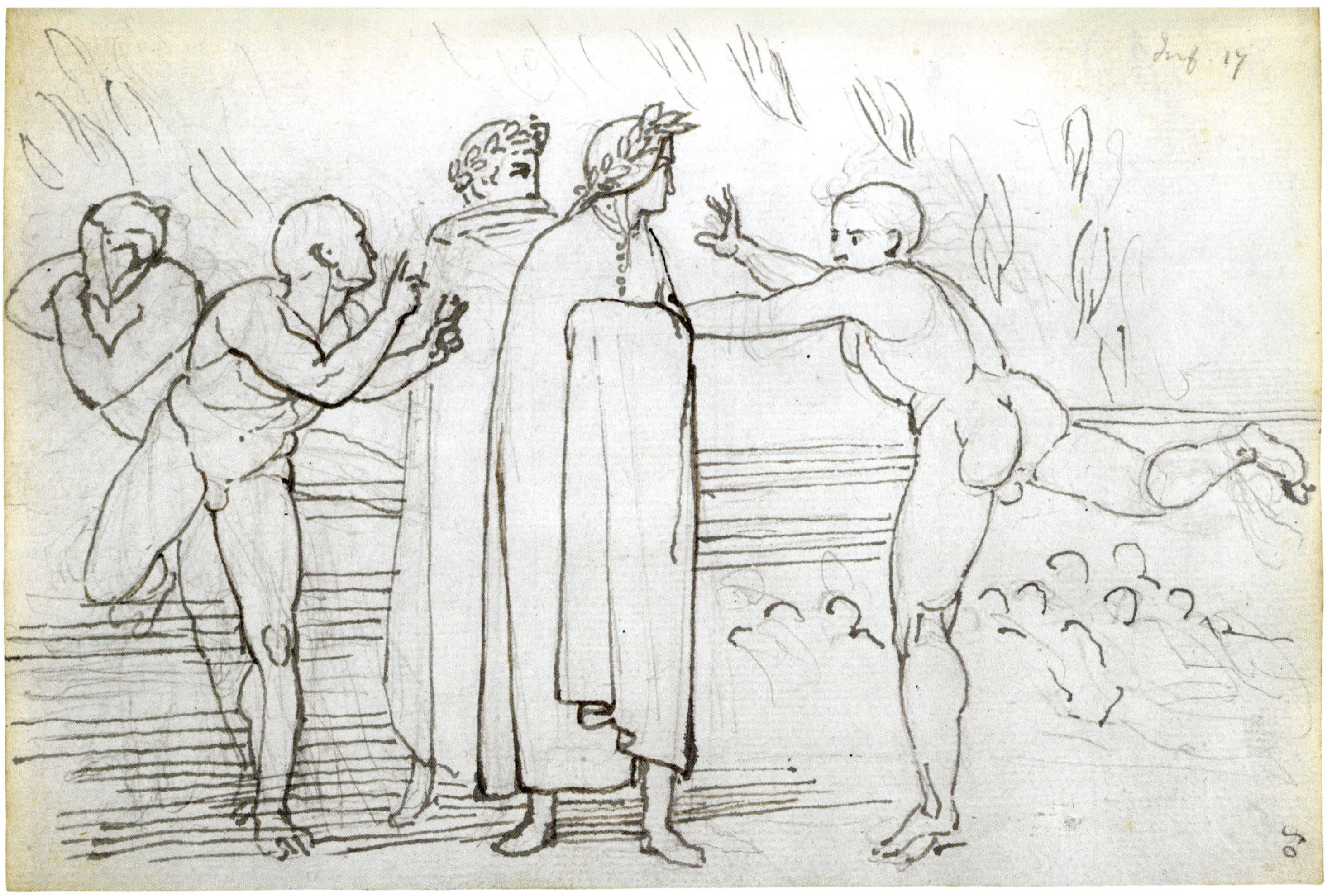

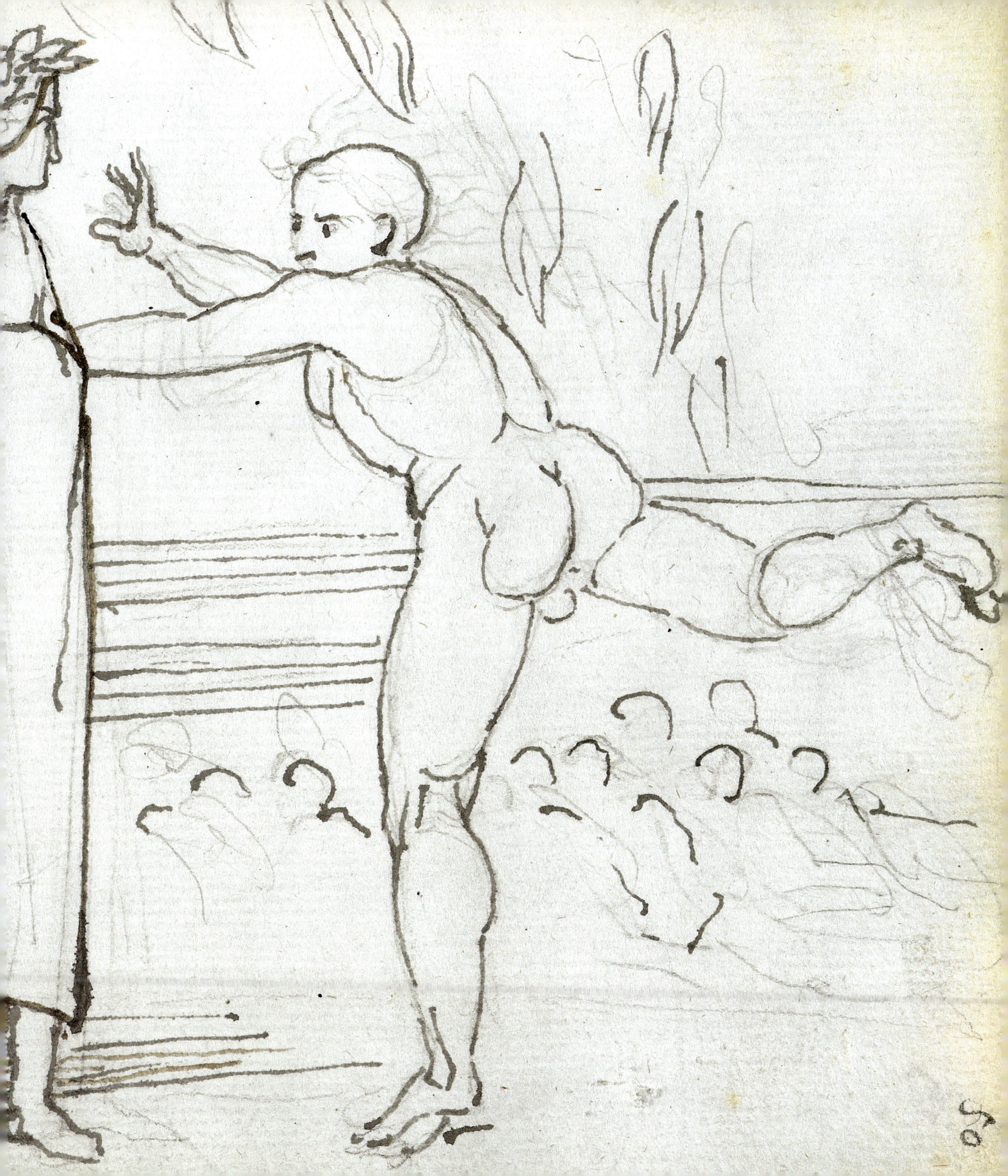

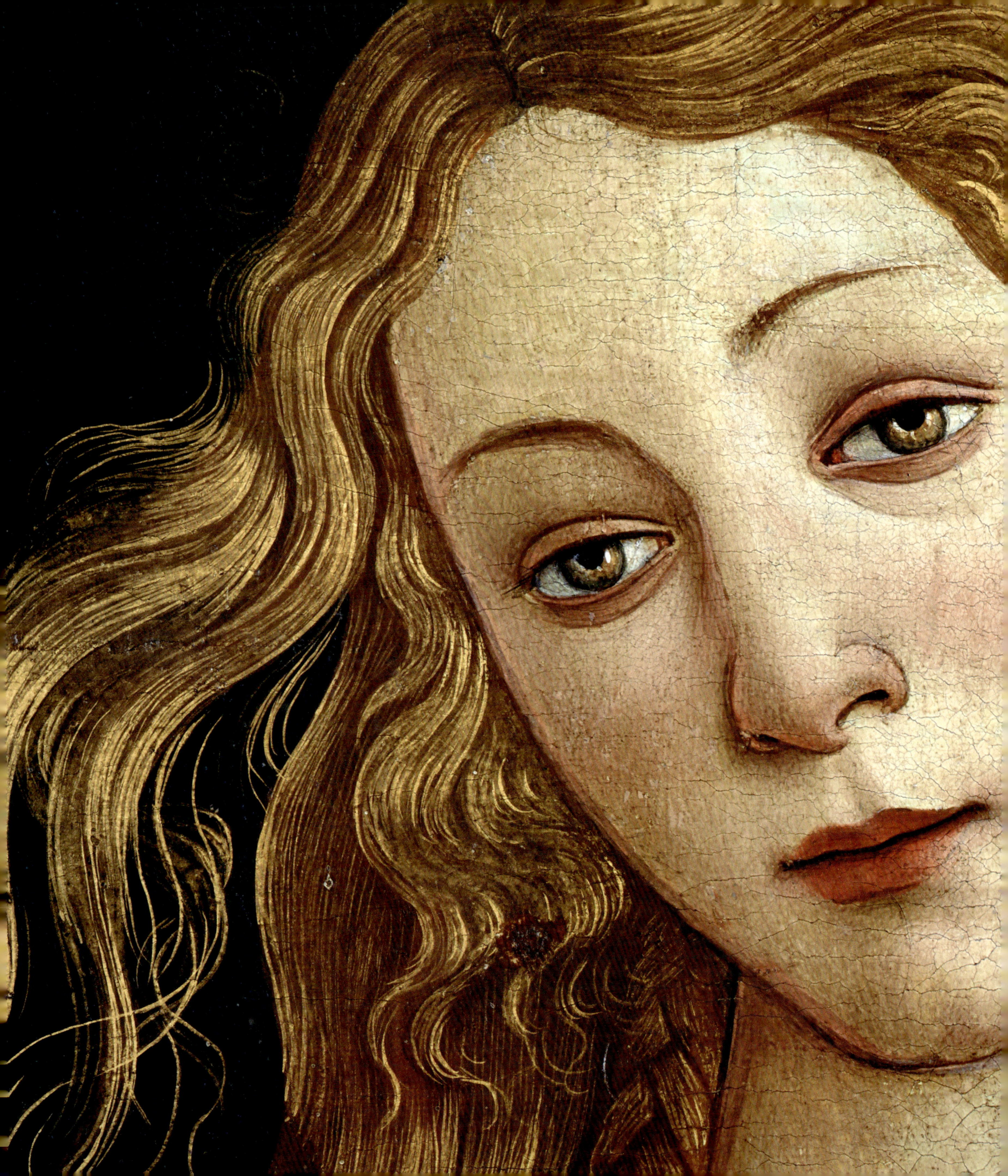

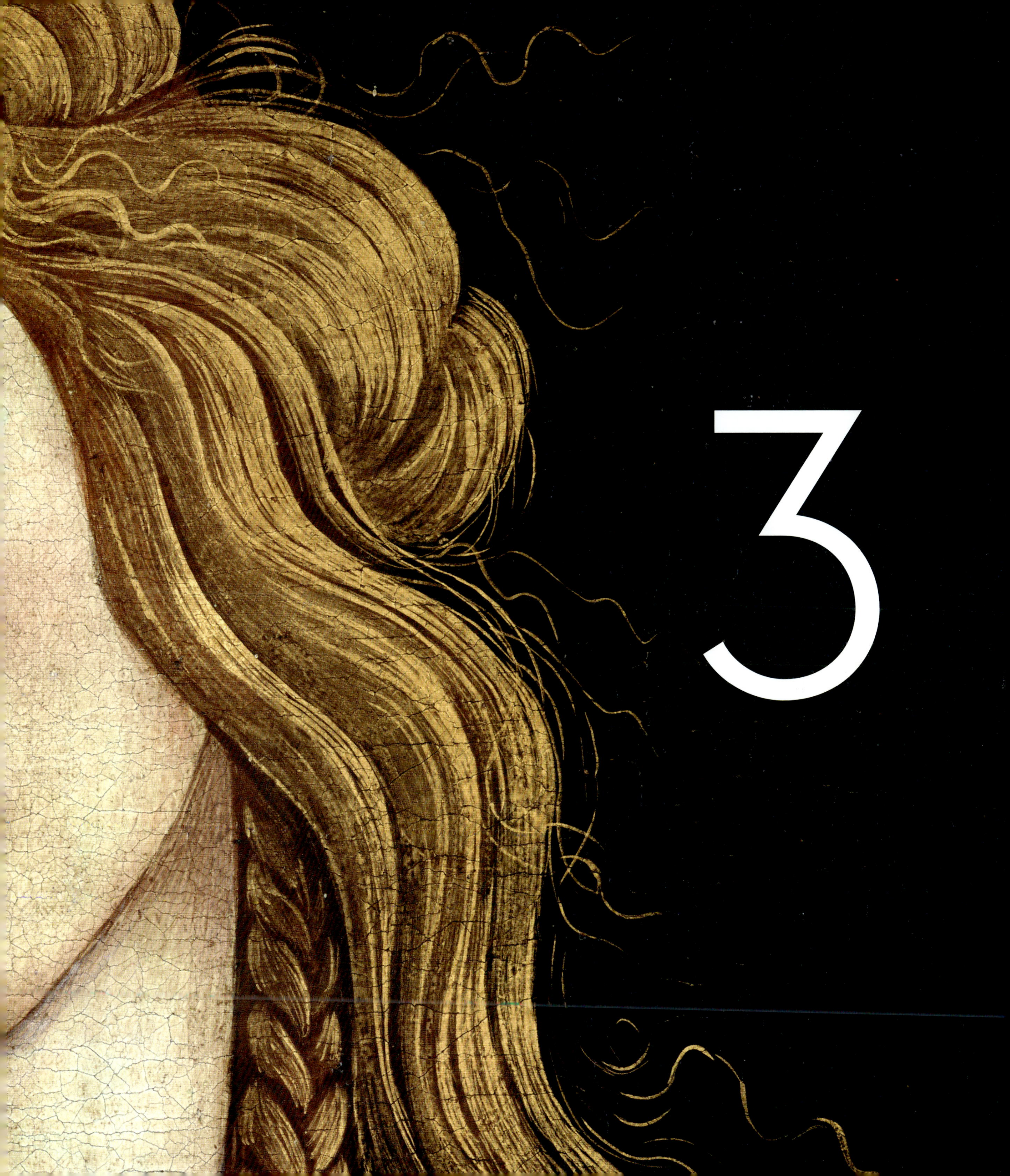

3

101

SANDRO BOTTICELLI
(c.1445–1510)
Mystic Nativity, 1501
(Florentine year 1500)

Tempera on canvas, 108.6 × 74.9 cm
The National Gallery, London (NG 1034)

Botticelli's only signed and dated painting, this work bears a cryptic inscription in Greek: 'This picture, at the end of the year 1500, in the troubles of Italy, I, Alessandro, painted in the half time after the time, at the time of the fulfilment of the eleventh of Saint John, in the Second Woe of the Apocalypse; in the loosing of the devil for three and a half years; then he shall be chained according to the twelfth, and we shall see him ... as in this picture.'

The pioneering collector William Young Ottley, who brought this work to England around 1800, remarked that it was 'a very interesting specimen of the fancy of its author'. It is assumed the inscription alludes to the political upheavals caused by the invasion of Italy by the French king Charles VIII in 1494 and the exile of the Medici, and foresees the eventual triumph of Florence, as prophesized by the Dominican preacher Savonarola. It may have been painted as a devotional work for a follower of the friar (possibly a member of the Aldobrandini family).

The disproportionate scale of the figure of the Virgin and lack of conventional perspective are characteristic of Botticelli's 'archaic' late style. This work was widely exhibited in Manchester and Leeds, the Royal Academy, Burlington Fine Arts Club and the South Kensington Museum between 1857 and the 1870s. The Pre-Raphaelite painter and critic William Bell Scott thought this 'most delightful and valuable' picture 'a superb poetic creation' in 1871. Later commentators surmised that Botticelli himself composed the inscription and interpreted the painting as 'one of the greatest documents of Joachimistic thought'. It has been associated with Botticelli's *Mystic Crucifixion* (cat. 132), also apparently of Savonarolian inspiration, although it is unclear whether Botticelli was himself a follower of the Dominican friar. AD

PROVENANCE
Possibly Villa Aldobrandini, Rome; first recorded in the sale of William Young Ottley, Christie's, London, 25 May 1811 (lot 32), £42; Fuller Maitland collection, 1847; The National Gallery, London, 1878, purchased for £1,500

LITERATURE
Scott 1871, p. 90; Weinstein 1970, p. 335; Lightbown 1978, vol. 2, pp. 99–101, no. B90 (with previous bibliography); Pons 1989; Caneva 1990, pp. 132–3, no. 72; Hatfield 1995; Plazzotta 1999; Paris and Florence 2003–4, p. 15, fig. 2; Cecchi 2005, pp. 348–50; Zöllner 2005, no. 85

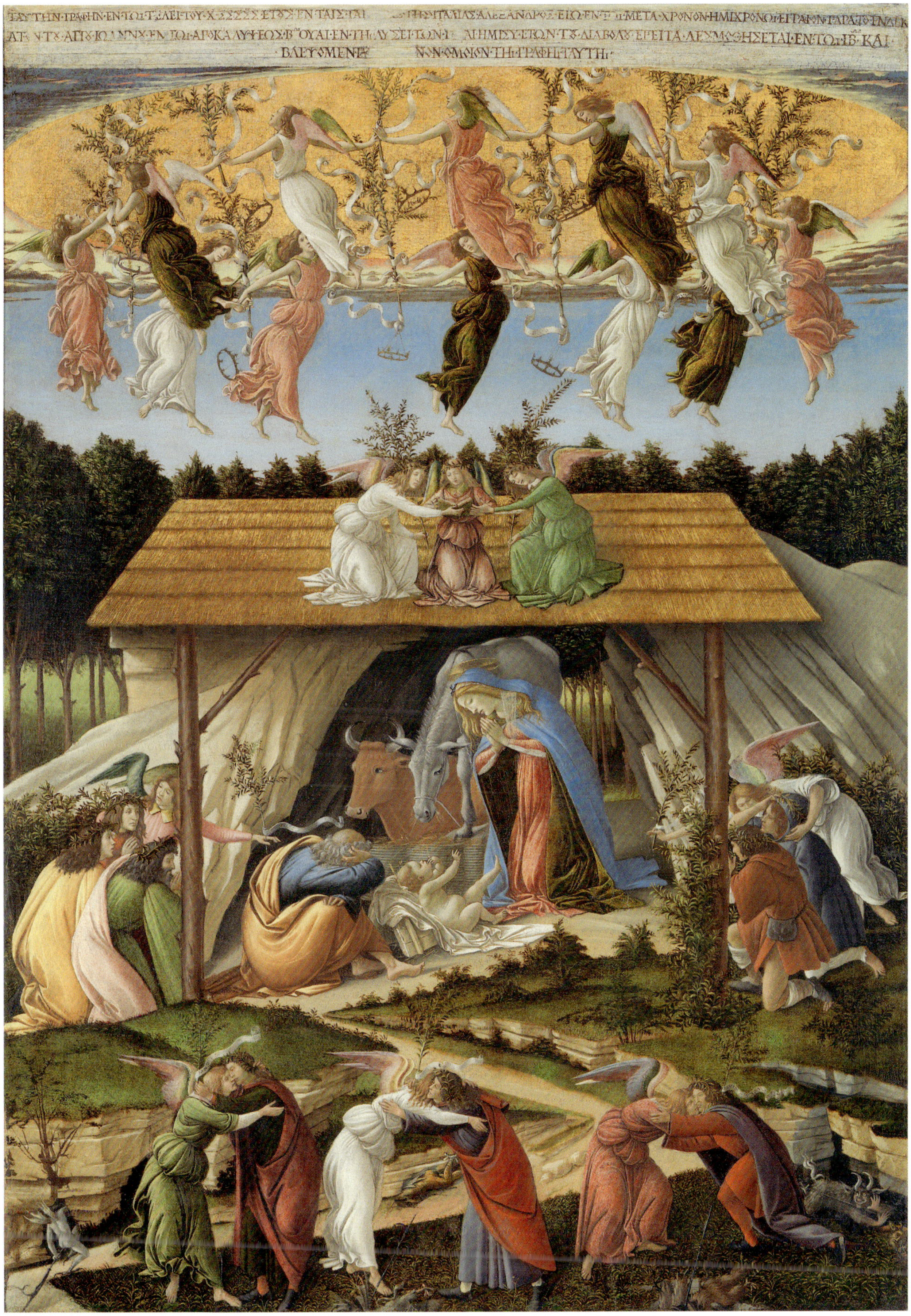

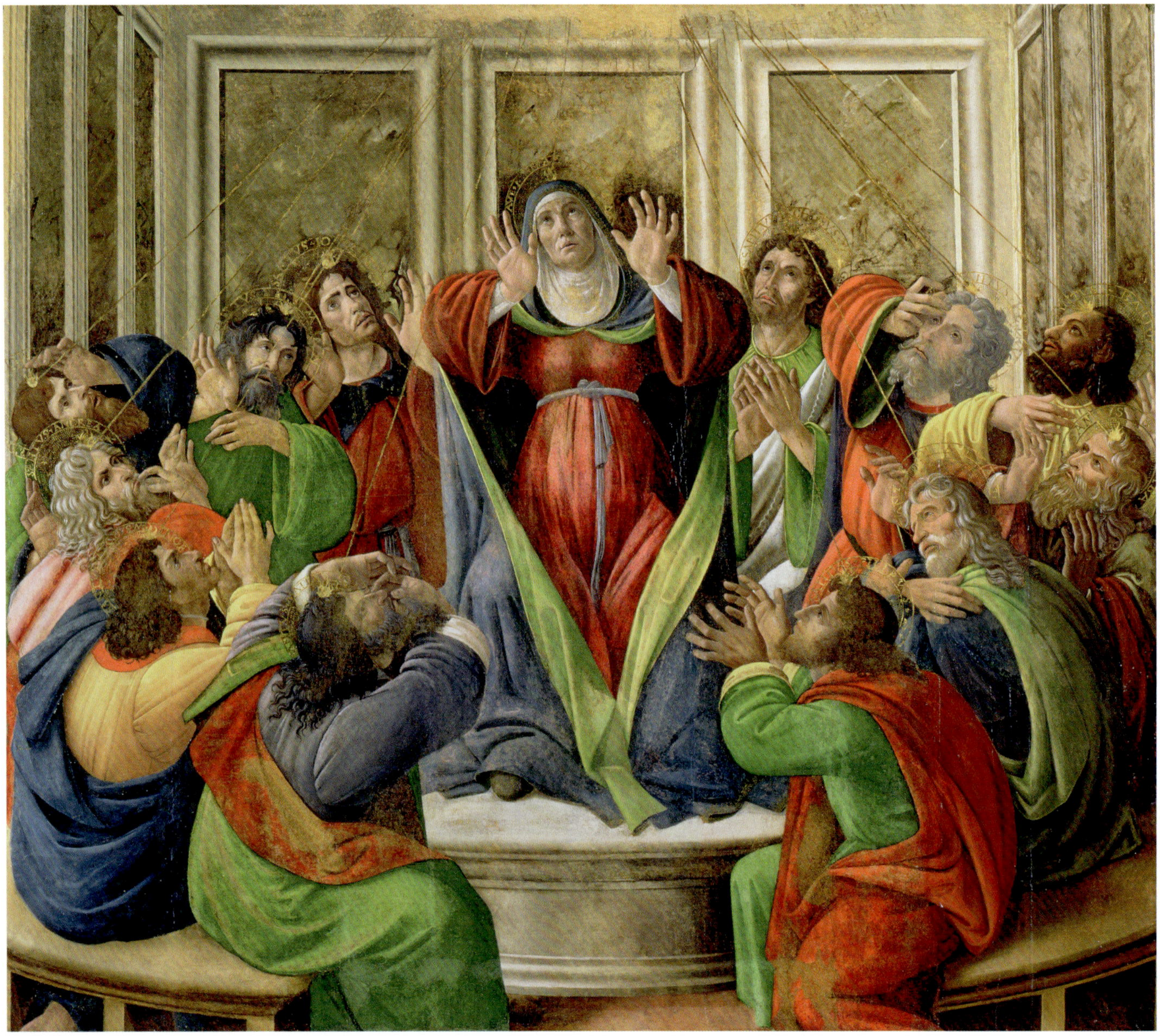

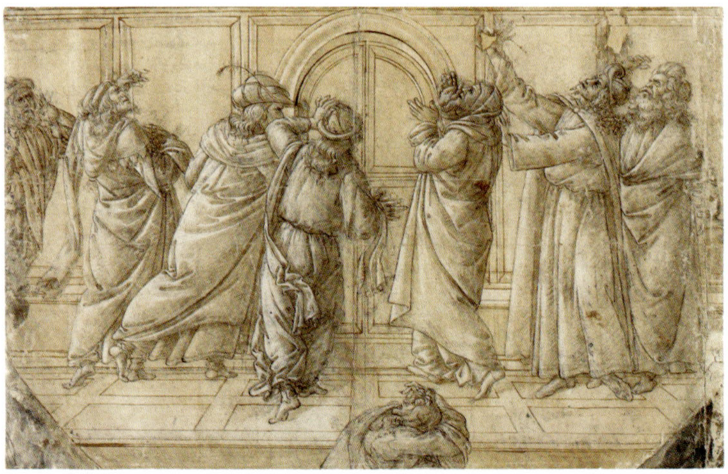

102

SANDRO BOTTICELLI (c.1445–1510) and workshop

Pentecost, 1505

Tempera on wood, 207 × 229.8 cm
Birmingham Museums Trust (1959P31)
Purchased with the assistance of the National Art Collections Fund, 1959

LONDON ONLY

PROVENANCE
Commissioned from the artist by the Compagnia dello Santo Spirito in Montelupo, 1505; Michele and Luigi Gamberini, Bologna, 1872; the Abbé Hyères, Lyons, by 1874, when purchased by Sir Francis Cook, Richmond; by descent; The Trustees of the Cook Collection; sold Sotheby's, London, 25 June 1958; Julius F. Weitzner, from whom purchased with the assistance of the National Art Collections Fund, 1959

LITERATURE
Cannon-Brookes 1968; Lightbown 1978, vol. 2, pp. 150–1, no. C64; Waldman 2009

The scene depicts Pentecost; after Christ's Ascension, the descent of the Holy Spirit on the Apostles and the Virgin Mary granted the ability to speak in foreign languages to spread the word of Christ: 'Suddenly there came a sound from heaven as of a rushing mighty wind, and it filled all the house where they were sitting. And ... cloven tongues like as of fire ... sat upon each of them. And they were all filled with the Holy Ghost, and began to speak with other tongues...' (Acts 2: 2–4).

This heavily damaged panel has been cut at the edges and much overpainted. An apparently autograph Botticelli drawing in Darmstadt of gesticulating male figures grouped around a closed door and looking up (cat. 103) has been plausibly identified as a study for the lower part of this composition. As in a fourteenth-century depiction, the Pentecost could have appeared as though at an open loggia on an upper storey. Most commentators have attributed this design to Botticelli, and its execution to his assistants.

Louis Waldman recently discovered what is evidently the contract for this work, dated 14 May 1505, between Botticelli and the Compagnia dello Santo Spirito in Montelupo, a small town 20 kilometres southwest of Florence. This specifies payment of 70 florins for an altarpiece of the Pentecost, with thirteen large figures, measuring overall about 4.67 × 2.92 cm. One of Botticelli's few surviving contracts, and for his largest known panel painting, it shows he was receiving major commissions near the end of his life, albeit from provincial patrons at a modest fee for such a large undertaking. His highly expressive design was rather crudely interpreted. ME

103

SANDRO BOTTICELLI (c.1445–1510)

The Devout Jews at Pentecost, 1500s

Black chalk, pen and brown ink, brown wash with white gouache, on paper, 23.1 × 36.5 cm
Hessisches Landesmuseum, Darmstadt (AE.1285)

LONDON ONLY

PROVENANCE
In the Darmstadt collection by 1896

LITERATURE
Schönbrunner and Meder 1896–1908, vol. 5, pp. 1900–1, fig. 578; Berenson 1903b, no. 572; Horne 1908, p. 322; Venturi 1925, p. 108; Yashiro 1929, p. 245; Gamba 1936, p. 213, no. 1; Mesnil 1938, pp. 173–4, pl. CI; Paris 1971–2, pp. 15–16, no. 2; Lightbown 1978, vol. 2, pp. 167–8, no. D16; Bergsträsser and Marker 1998, pp. 118–11, no. 45; Berlin, Rome and London 2000–1, p. 371, Appendix no. 22; Cecchi 2005, pp. 365–7; Zöllner 2005, p. 292, no. D16; Frankfurt 2009–10, pp. 340–1, no. 73; Waldman 2009, p. 111ff., fig. 3.12

Jacques Mesnil, in his monograph on Botticelli published in 1938, was the first to relate this remarkable drawing, whose subject remained unidentified for a long time, with the painting of the *Pentecost* now in Birmingham (cat. 102). This depicts the 'Jews, devout men, out of every nation under heaven' who have gathered in Jerusalem and 'were confounded, because every man heard [the Apostles] speak in his own language' (Acts 2: 5–6). The present drawing almost certainly records the missing lower half of the painting as the juxtaposition of the two reveals a two-tier composition evidently based on Trecento Florentine examples, which is a characteristic trait of Botticelli's late style. Both works were typically regarded as studio productions of marginal significance until 2009 when Louis Waldman published the contract for the painting, dated 14 May 1505.

This exciting new discovery challenges Vasari's account of Botticelli's final decade. It proves that *Pentecost*, probably Botticelli's largest painting and one of his most ambitious compositions, was commissioned directly from the artist shortly before his death, prompting a reappraisal of the powerful expressionistic style of his late period. AD

104, 105

SANDRO BOTTICELLI
(c.1445–1510)
Two Fragments of an Adoration of the Magi, 1480s–90s

Umber tempera on prepared linen,
30.9 × 23.4 cm and 44.2 × 37.1 cm
Fitzwilliam Museum, Cambridge (910 and 2888)

William Young Ottley brought these fragments back from Italy, engraved them in 1809 with an attribution to Fra Filippo Lippi, Botticelli's master, and published them in the first volume of *The Italian School of Design* in 1823. They originally formed part of the same composition. The fragments were subsequently acquired by the celebrated English painter Sir Thomas Lawrence, who owned one of the greatest collections of Old Master drawings. Two fragments entered the collection of the Fitzwilliam Museum in 1918. A third fragment was purchased by the collector George Salting and passed by exchange to the artist, dealer and collector Charles Fairfax Murray, who admired Botticelli and copied several of his compositions (cat. 63). It is now in the Pierpont Morgan Library in New York.

Hermann Ulmann, in his 1893 monograph on Botticelli, was the first to suggest an attribution to the artist, and Herbert Horne regarded the fragments as pieces from a copy after a lost original, perhaps the destroyed *Adoration* formerly in the Palazzo Vecchio, which survives in an early copy in the Uffizi. Although considered as a preparatory study by most authors, the technique (umber tempera), support and scale suggest that these fragments are the remains of an underdrawing rather than a grisaille (monochrome picture). Botticelli painted numerous versions of this subject and another *Adoration* by the master, now in the Uffizi, was left unfinished and coloured by a later hand. A relationship with Leonardo da Vinci's famous unfinished composition of the same subject has been already noted. The present composition is evidently one of Botticelli's many versions and replicas of a successful design, which was perhaps retained unfinished for reference in his workshop. AD

PROVENANCE
William Young Ottley; his sale, T. Philipe, London, 13 June 1814 (lots 733 and 734); Sir Thomas Lawrence (Lugt 2445); William Russell (Lugt 2648); his sale, Christie's, London, 11 December 1884 (lots 393 and 394): the *Holy Family* (lot 393) was bought by W.S. Brough of Leek for £1 10s (Lugt 2652); by descent to H.H. Brindley (Brough's nephew), who gave it to the museum in 1918 – the *Adoration* was bought by Mr James Knowles for £3 (lot 394); then by G.T. Clough at Sotheby's, London, in 1896, who gave it to the museum in 1913

LITERATURE
Lightbown 1978, vol. 2, pp. 111–13, nos B98 and B99 (with previous bibliography); Florence 1992, nos 14.11 and 12

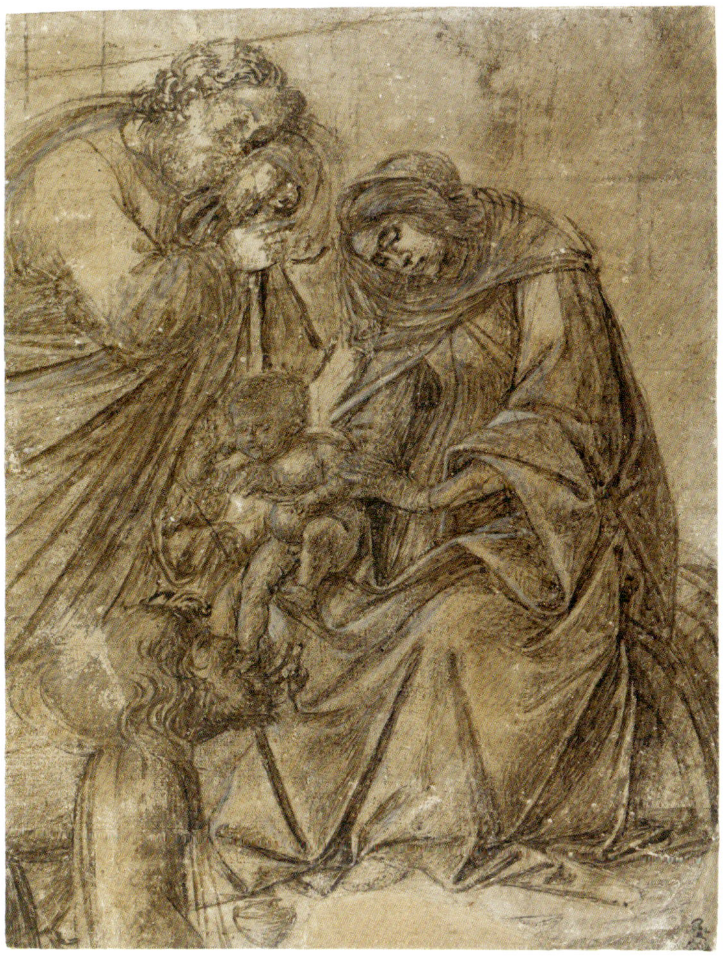

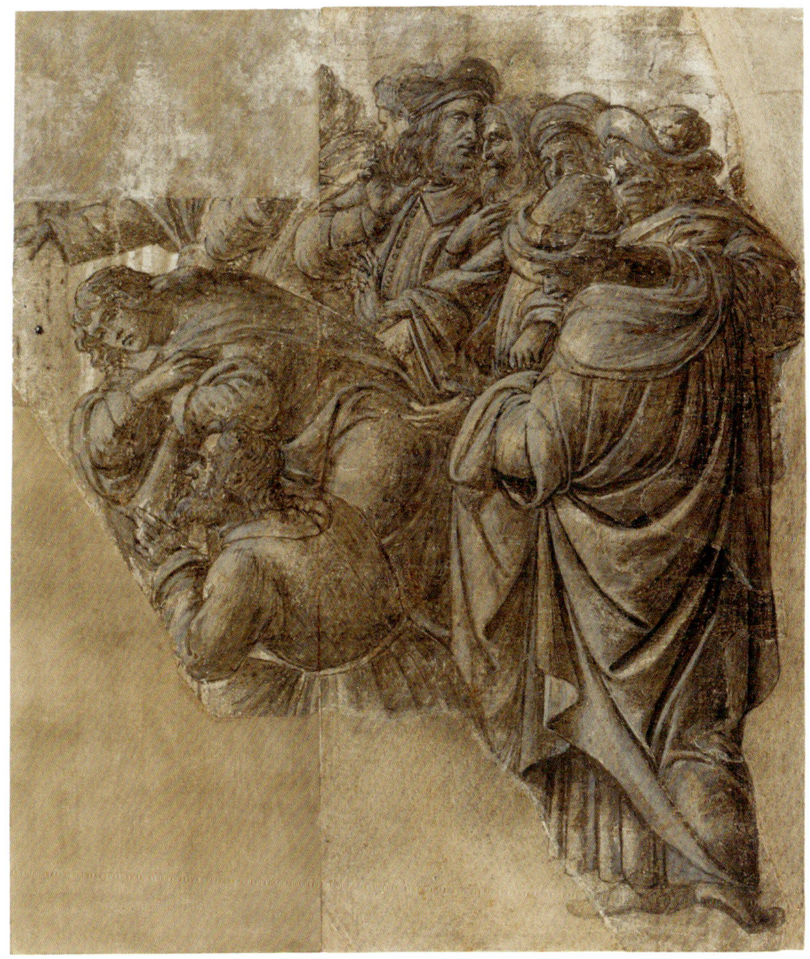

106

SANDRO BOTTICELLI
(c.1445–1510)

The Virgin and Child Enthroned with St John the Baptist and St John the Evangelist
(Bardi Altarpiece), 1485

Tempera on poplar, 185 × 180 cm
Gemäldegalerie, Staatliche Museen zu Berlin (106)
BERLIN ONLY

On 3 August 1485, the merchant Giovanni d'Agnolo de' Bardi paid 75 florins to 'Sandro del Botticiello' to create an altarpiece for his chapel in the Florentine church of Santo Spirito. Two florins were intended for the expensive blue pigment, 38 for the gold he used and for the preparation of the panel, and 25 'for his brush', meaning that he himself would produce the work. In 1550 Vasari described the careful execution of the piece, writing that 'some olive trees and palms' were to be seen in it. As early as 1629, the altarpiece was replaced with a Baroque painting.

Two hundred years later, the Berlin Museum acquired a panel from the Florentine art dealer Fedele Acciai (he had apparently bought it from the Bardi family), which has been unanimously identified ever since as the Botticelli altarpiece from Santo Spirito described in sources. Not only is it excellently preserved, but the quality of the painting and the complex subject, focused around the glorification of the Virgin, as well as the seemingly so well-documented circumstances of its creation, have since led the painting to be considered Botticelli's religious masterpiece, and his authorship has seldom been called into question. RR

PROVENANCE
Acquired via Carl Friedrich von Rumohr from the art dealer Fedele Acciai in 1829

LITERATURE
Waagen 1830, p. 54, no. I.169; Lightbown 1978, vol. 2, pp. 56–7, no. B42; Blume 1995; Zöllner 2005, pp. 227–8, no. 51

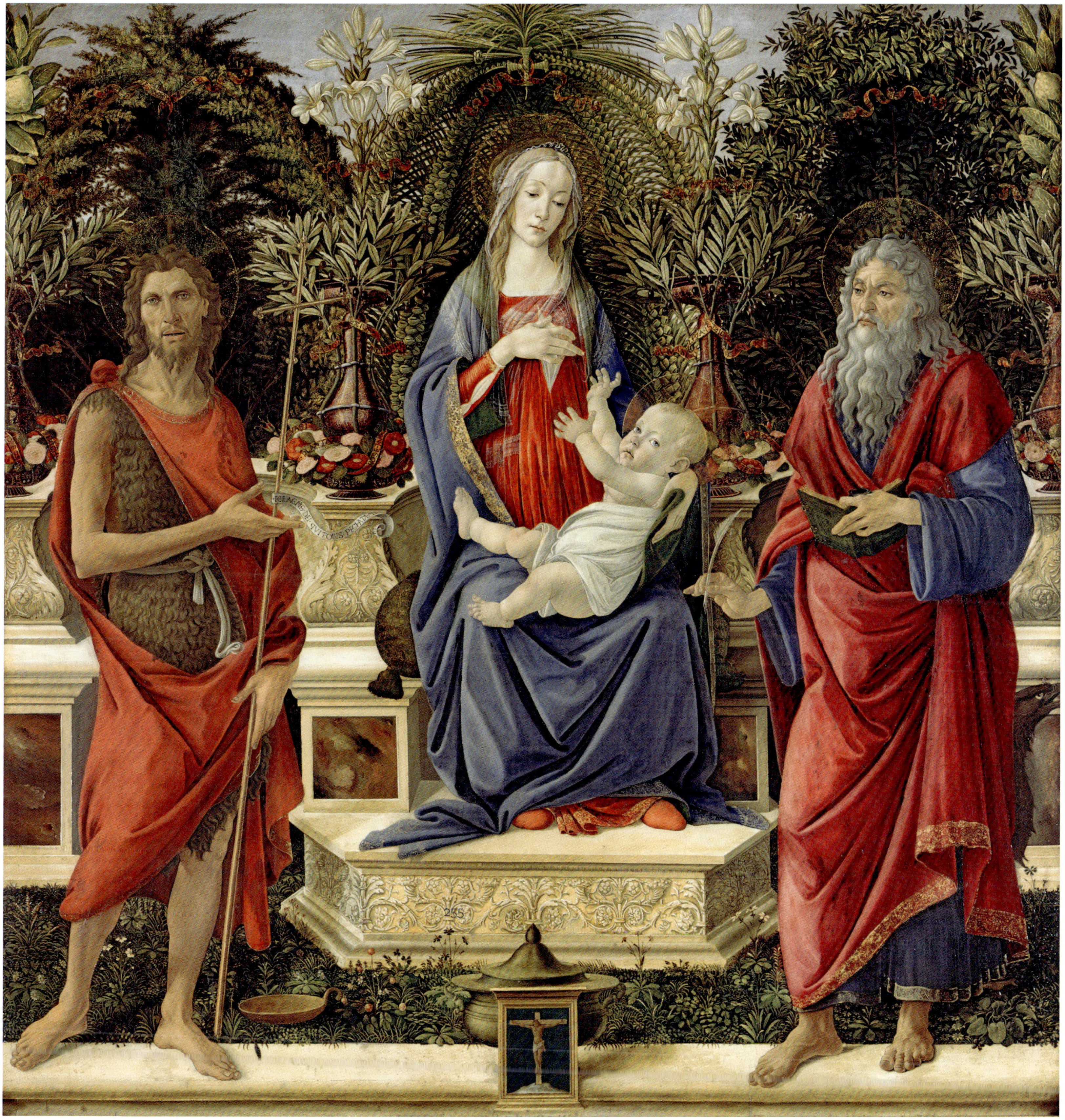

107

SANDRO BOTTICELLI
(c.1445–1510)
The Virgin and Child with an Angel, c.1465

Tempera on poplar, 115 × 77 cm
Palais Fesch, Musée des Beaux-Arts, Ajaccio
(852-1-59)
BERLIN ONLY

This unusual depiction of a standing, full-length Virgin and Child with an attending angel once formed part of the immense art collection of Cardinal Joseph Fesch, half-uncle to Napoleon Bonaparte, who participated in his Italian campaign, and was later Archbishop of Lyons and Ambassador to the Holy See. Prior to 1815 it was probably in his Paris residence, and later accompanied him into exile at the Palazzo Falconieri in Rome. After his death, in 1843 the painting was part of his bequest of numerous early Italian works to his home town of Ajaccio in Corsica. The Roman inventory of Fesch's estate (1839) and the catalogue of his collection (1841) list a total of four paintings by Botticelli (or in his style). However, this panel is described in the inventory as a damaged work 'in the manner of Fra Filippino [*sic*] Lippi', by which is presumably meant Botticelli's teacher, the Carmelite monk Fra Filippo Lippi (and not his son), to whose style this type of Madonna is clearly indebted (see also cat. 111). Appearing as a Botticelli in the museum's catalogues (1880; 1892), the panel was published as by Botticelli in Luisa Vertova's monograph, and since then has been unanimously accepted as one of his earliest works. SH

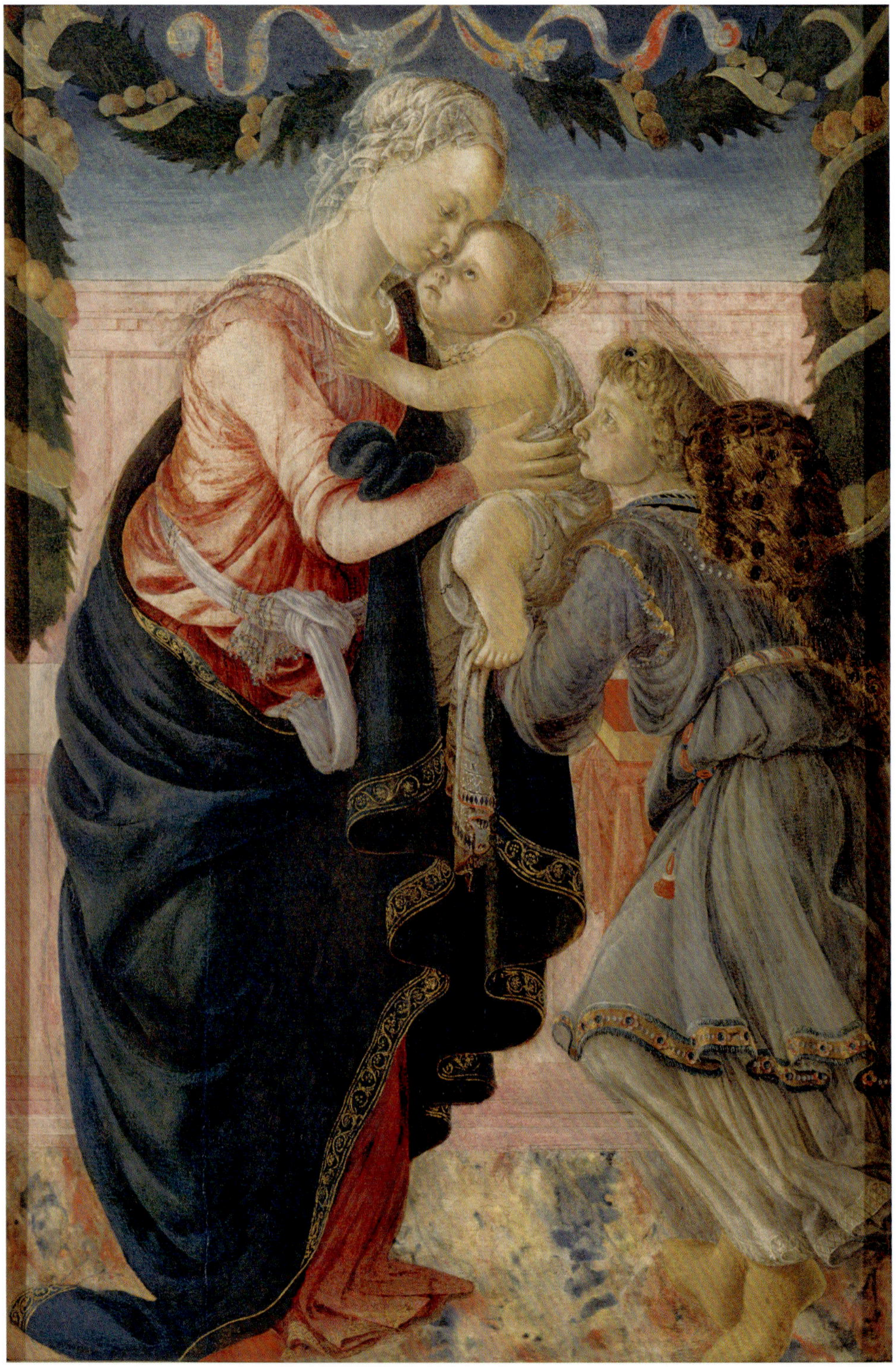

PROVENANCE

Joseph Fesch collection, Paris and Rome; 1852, Musée Fesch, Ajaccio (1843 bequest)

LITERATURE

Peraldi and Novellini 1880; Peraldi and Novellini 1892; Vertova 1948; Paris 1956, p. 40, no. 57; Lightbown 1978, vol. 2, p. 12, no. B3; Thiébaut 1987, pp. 72–3, no. 6; Florence 2004, pp. 198–200, no. 28

108

SANDRO BOTTICELLI
(c.1445–1510)

The Virgin and Child
(Campana Madonna), c.1467–70

Tempera on poplar, 72 × 51 cm
Musée du Petit Palais, Avignon (M.I. 480)
BERLIN ONLY

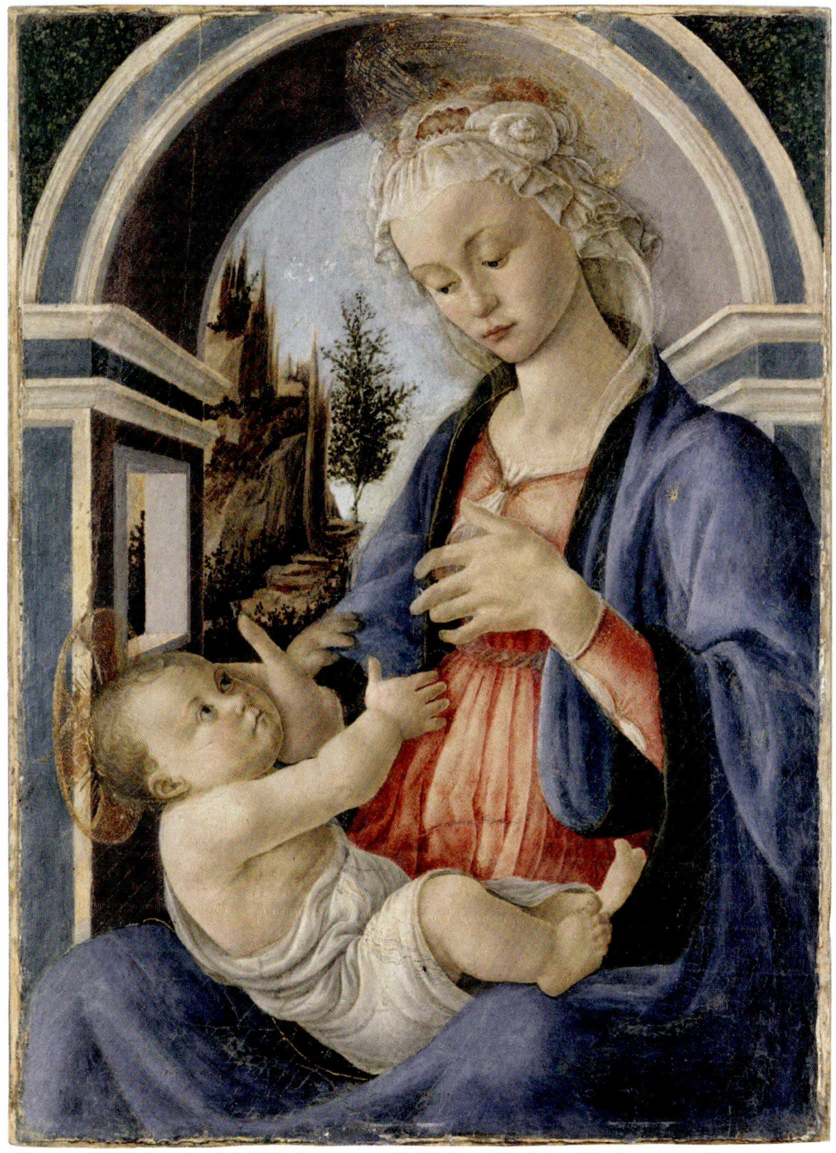

This *Madonna lactans* (nursing Madonna) was part of the encyclopaedic art collection assembled around the mid-nineteenth century in Rome by Giampietro Campana. Director of the Monte di Pietà, the pawnbroker to the Papal States, and an occasional dabbler in archaeology, Campana was convicted of embezzlement in 1858, whereupon the French state acquired his confiscated paintings *en bloc* (see cats 123, 125, 139). In 1862 these were exhibited in Paris under the name of the 'Musée Napoléon III', initially planned as a museum for art and design in the manner of London's South Kensington Museum, now the Victoria and Albert Museum (founded in 1852). After this project came to nothing, despite vehement protests, the collection was distributed among a number of museums in the French provinces, and was not reunited until 1977, at Avignon. Thanks not least to being stored in a peripheral location, this painting was long ignored by researchers and its old attribution to Fra Filippo Lippi (Museo Campana, 1858) remained uncontested until well into the twentieth century. Berenson identified it as from Botticelli's workshop, and the painting is now generally considered one of the master's earliest independent visual creations, an assessment based on the extreme delicacy of its execution. SH

PROVENANCE
Until 1858 in the Campana collection, Rome; 1862, Musée Napoléon III, Paris; 1863, Musée du Louvre (salles de la colonnade), Paris; 1872–1956, transferred to the Musée de Périgueux; 1956–76, Musée du Louvre, Paris; 1976, transferred to Avignon

LITERATURE
Museo Campana 1858, p. 24, no. 201; Paris 1956, pp. 40–1, no. 58; Lightbown 1978, vol. 2, p. 17, no. A14; Laclotte and Moench 2005, p. 81, no. 50

109

SANDRO BOTTICELLI (c.1445–1510) *The Virgin and Child with an Angel* (Chigi Madonna), 1470s

Tempera and oil on wood, 85.2 × 65 cm
Isabella Stewart Gardner Museum, Boston
(P27W73)
LONDON ONLY

Giovanni Morelli attributed this important early work to Botticelli about 1890 when it was in the Chigi collection. On the advice of Bernard Berenson it was purchased by the energetic Boston collector Isabella Stewart Gardner for the huge price of £13,000. For infringing export regulations Prince Chigi was fined a colossal sum, which was reduced on appeal to under 10/-. After two years of concealment, the painting caused a sensation when shown at Colnaghi's in 1901. It was one of the first works by Botticelli to enter an American collection.

In this composition the corn and grapes symbolize bread and wine and prefigure Christ's Passion. At least four further versions exist. One from the Palazzo Panciatichi in Florence passed through several collections, including that of the Philadelphia millionaire Joseph Widener, a founding benefactor of the National Gallery of Art, Washington, and was acquired by the dealer Joseph Duveen. This was sold at Christie's, New York, on 28 January 2015. AD

PROVENANCE
Duke of Ariccia, Palazzo Chigi, Rome; sold by Prince Mario Chigi to Edmond Despretz for Colnaghi's; July 1899, Colnaghi's, London, bought Isabella Stewart Gardner

LITERATURE
Horne 1908, p. 35; Lightbown 1978, vol. 2, pp. 23–4, no. B9; Boston 1997, pp. 30–1; Paris 2003–4, p. 59, fig. 2; Zöllner 2005, p. 192, no. 16; Cecchi 2005, pp. 102–5; Körner 2006, pp. 30–1; Frankfurt 2009–10, pp. 42–3, fig. 27

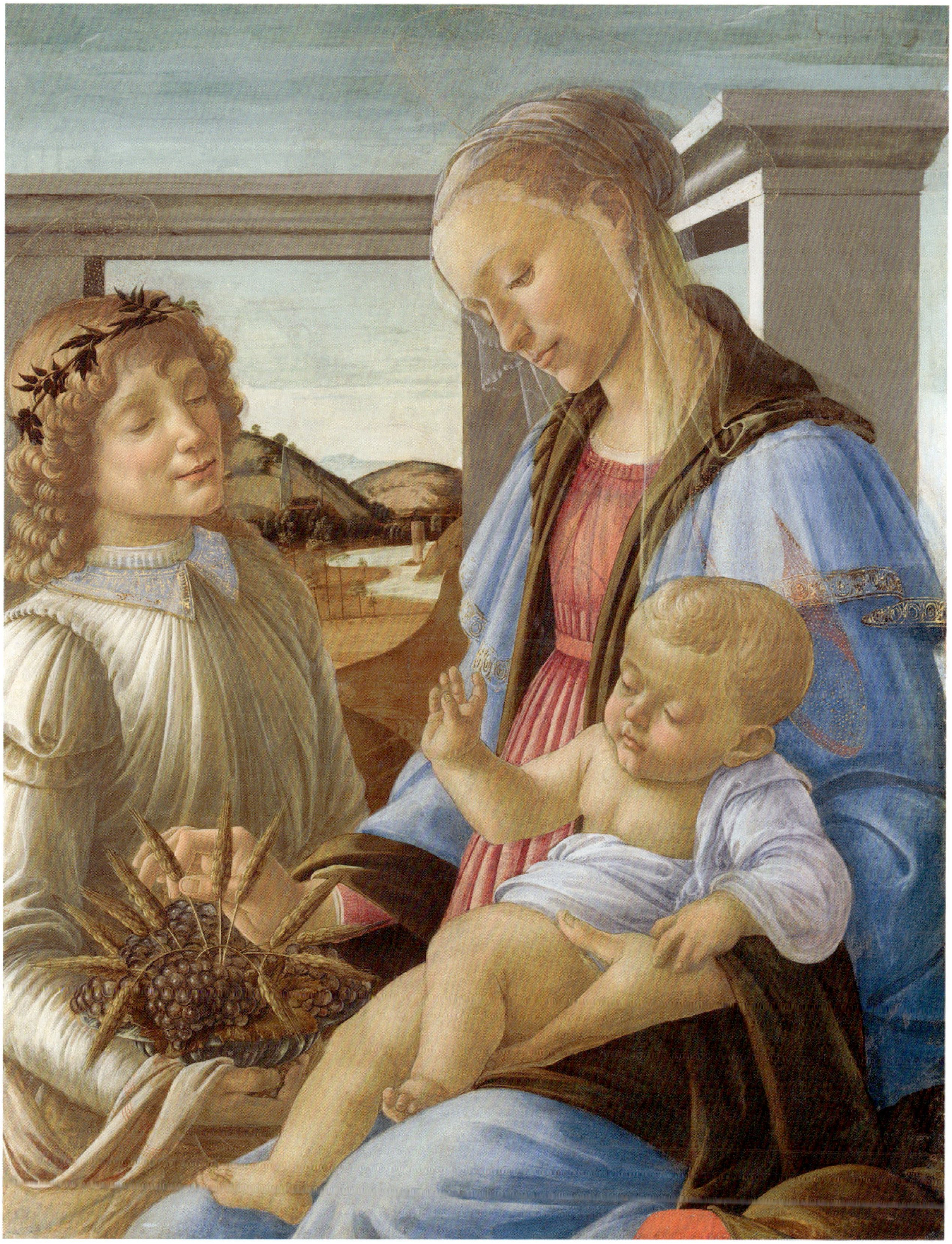

110

SANDRO BOTTICELLI (c.1445–1510)

The Virgin and Child with the Young St John the Baptist, c.1468

Tempera on poplar, 90 × 67 cm
Musée du Louvre, Paris (286)
BERLIN ONLY

This unusually well preserved panel, commonly called the Madonna of the Roses, was among the first works by Botticelli publicly exhibited outside Italy. In 1824 it was purchased for Louis XVIII at the 'Musée Européen' of the Parisian dealer Mauco in the rue du Temple. Attributed to Botticelli, it was shown in the Grande Galerie at the Louvre, and from 1841 in the Salle des Sept Maîtres. Reproduced as an engraving in 1872 by Claude-Ferdinand Gaillard, it inspired a number of artists (see cat. 40). According to G.F. Waagen (1839) 'everything, especially the noble profile of Mary, exudes the finer feelings of Filippino' (meaning Botticelli's pupil Filippino Lippi, the son of his teacher Fra Filippo Lippi). Since Ulmann (1893) it has been generally considered one of the earliest depictions of the Virgin from the master's own hand. Various later workshop productions were based on this composition (see cats 126, 127). It has been suggested that the young St John the Baptist was contributed by an assistant. SH

PROVENANCE
Edme Antoine Durand collection; the dealer Mauco, from whom acquired for Louis XVIII in 1824

LITERATURE
Waagen 1839, p. 408, no. 894; Villot 1849, p. 30, no. 81; Mündler 1850, p. 49, no. 81; Both de Tauzia 1878, p. 118, no. 184; Plan-catalogue 1882, p. 81, no. 184; Ulmann 1893, p. 34; Lightbown 1978, vol. 2, p. 18, no. B1; Sécherre 2005, pp. 168–9

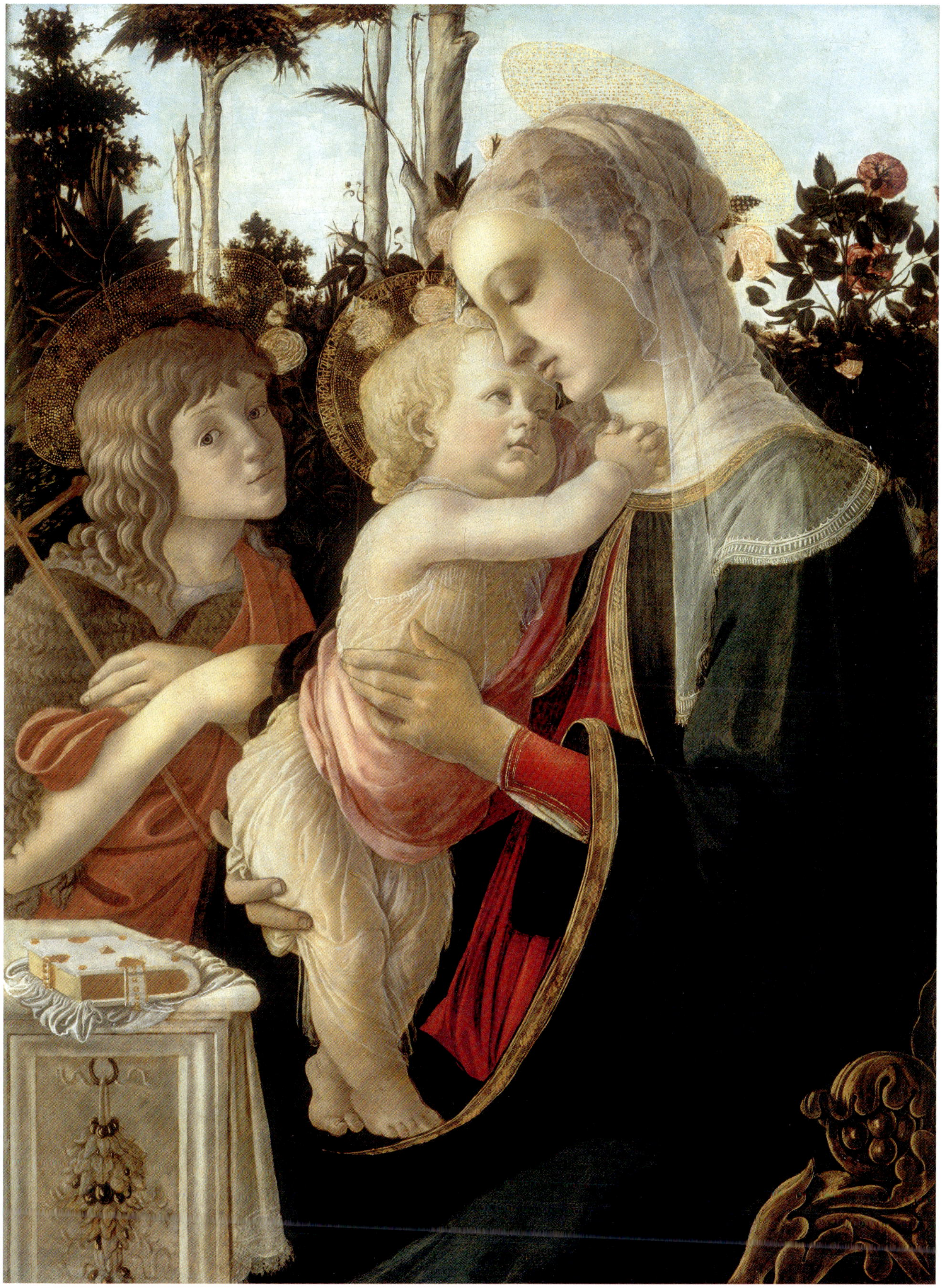

111

SANDRO BOTTICELLI (c.1445–1510)

The Virgin and Child (Madonna del Mare), 1475–80

Tempera on wood, 40.3 × 28.4 cm
Galleria dell' Accademia, Florence (8456)

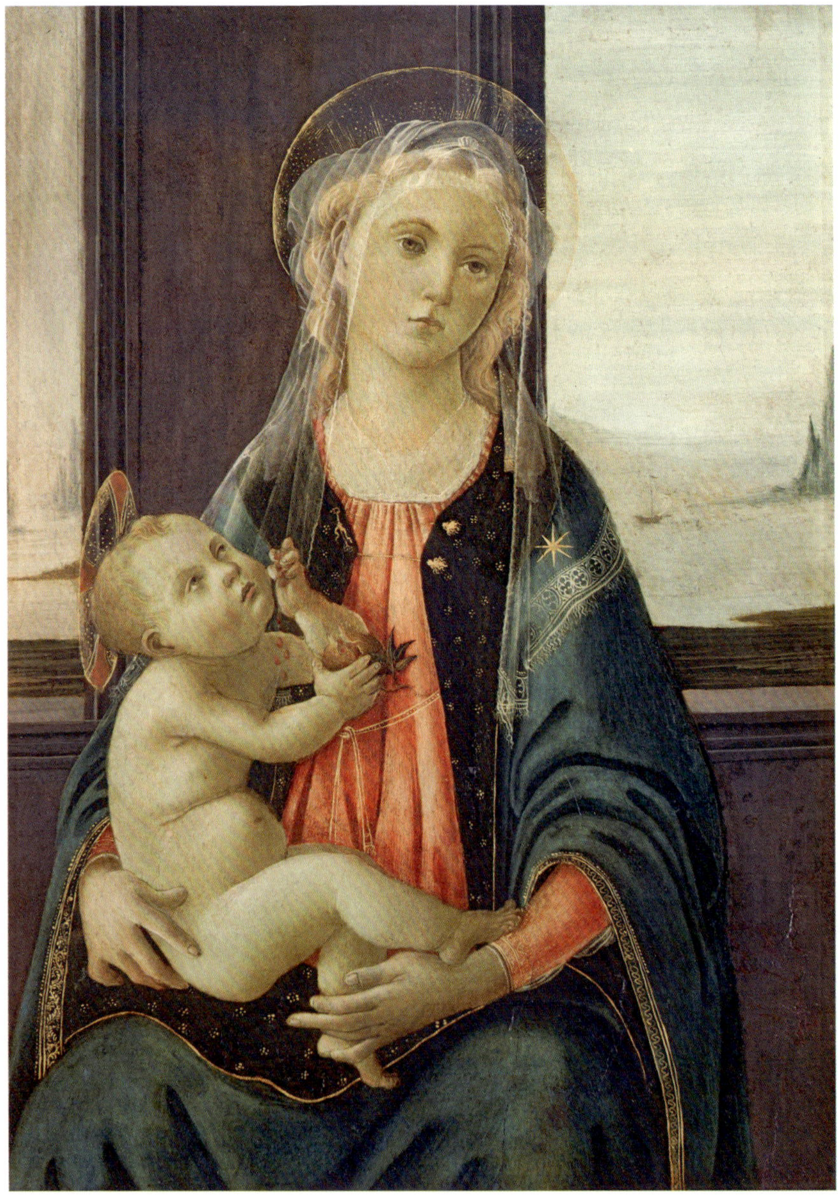

The painting takes its name from the seascape in the background and the golden star of the Virgin's mantle alludes to her Latin denomination as *Stella maris* (Star of the Sea). The pomegranate held by the Christ Child symbolizes the Church and its seeds allude to the blood of Christ. From the female Benedictine convent of Santa Felicità, secularized during the Napoleonic occupation of Florence, the work was transferred to the Accademia around 1809.

First attributed to Botticelli in 1893, this painting has been associated with the Raczyński Tondo (cat. 113). Other scholars have attributed it to Filippino Lippi, who was Botticelli's disciple in 1472–3, and to the workshop of Andrea del Verrocchio, who may also have studied with Botticelli's master Fra Filippo Lippi. Formerly heavily overpainted, this panel was restored in 1956. It has marked stylistic affinities with Filippino Lippi and Botticelli, but the nature of this relationship is elusive. AD

PROVENANCE

Convent of Santa Felicità, Florence; 1809 Accademia, Florence; 1934 Uffizi; 1936 Accademia

LITERATURE

Lightbown 1978, vol. 2, p. 207, no. F3; Bonsanti 1987, p. 39; Zambrano and Nelson 2004, p. 359, no. R6; Frankfurt 2009–10, pp. 276–7, no. 47

112

WORKSHOP OF
SANDRO BOTTICELLI (c.1445–1510)
The Virgin and Child with a Goldfinch, c.1500–10

Oil, tempera and gold on wood, 74.3 × 40.6 cm
Private collection, London, courtesy of Moretti Fine Art

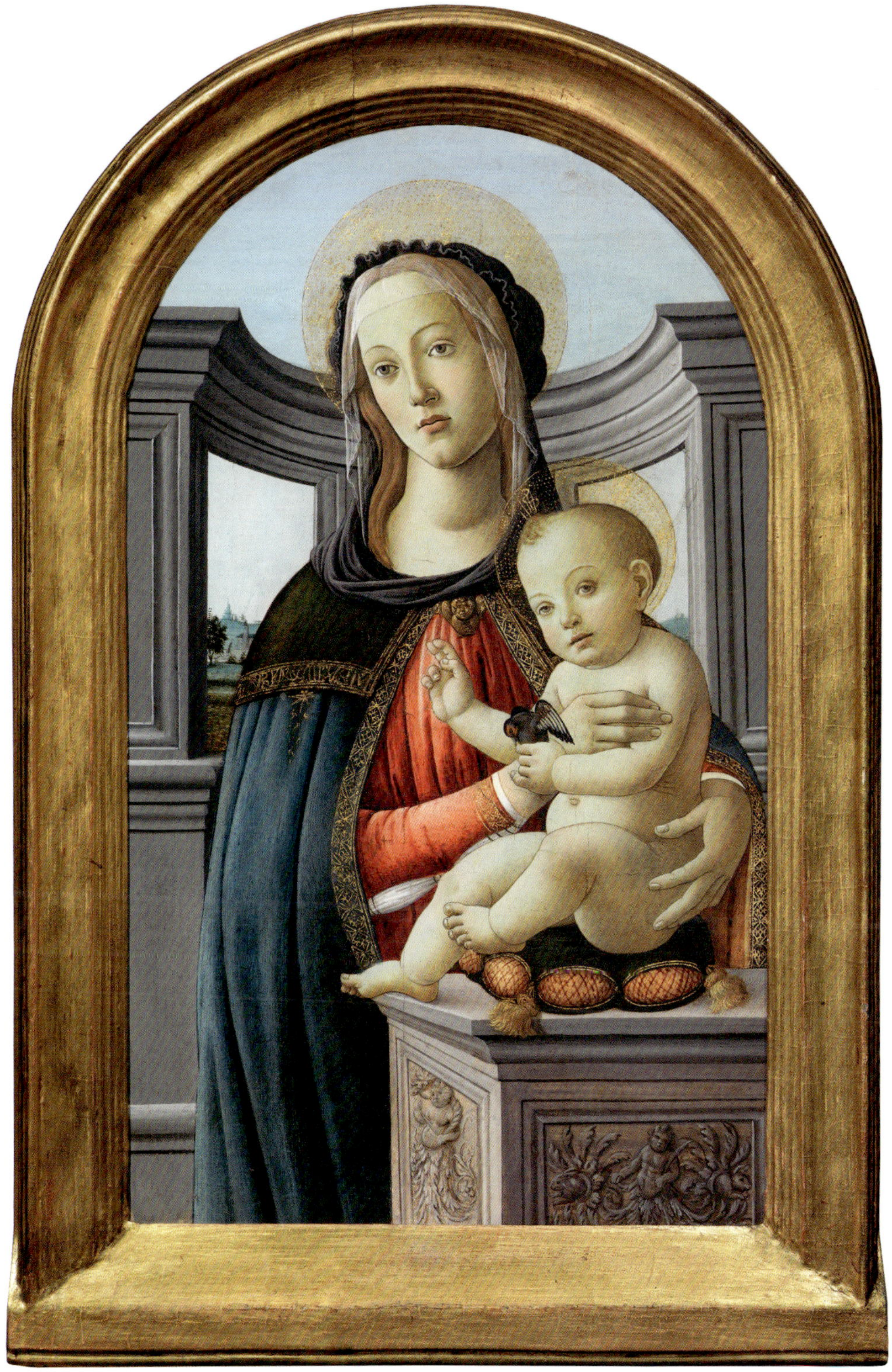

This painting is one of a series of half-length compositions in which the figure of the Virgin is taken from that in Botticelli's San Barnaba altarpiece, a work generally dated to the 1480s and now in the Uffizi. The semi-circular architectural motif in the background retains the shape of the niche-shaped throne in the San Barnaba altarpiece, but opened up to reveal a distant landscape. The blessing Christ Child is derived from the corresponding but now much over-painted figure in the Sant' Ambrogio altarpiece, usually dated to the 1470s and also in the Uffizi. The grotesques on the foreground altar suggest a date around 1500–10.

Alessandro Contini-Bonacossi, whose spectacular collection is now in the Uffizi, rivalled Joseph Duveen as a dealer and became one of Mussolini's chief financial advisers. Contini-Bonacossi sold this painting to the banker and Jewish philanthropist Felix Warburg, who doubtless consulted his elder brother Aby Warburg, an authority on Botticelli. It was displayed in the stained glass conservatory of Warburg's mansion on 1109 Fifth Avenue, a French Gothic palace commissioned by C.P.H Gilbert in 1906–8 and now part of the Jewish Museum in New York. Warburg's collection included tapestries, sixteenth- and seventeenth-century prints, illuminated manuscripts and sculptures and other early Italian paintings. AD

PROVENANCE

Count Alessandro Contini-Bonacossi, Rome and New York; sold in 1927 to Felix M. Warburg, New York; given in his memory in 1941 by his wife and children to the Metropolitan Museum of Art, New York (41.116.1); sold Christie's, New York, 29 January 2014 (lot 102); private collection, London, courtesy of Moretti Fine Art

LITERATURE

Marle 1931, p. 241, fig. 148; Birmingham 1967, pp. 286–8; Zeri and Gardner 1971, p. 166; Fredericksen and Zeri 1972, pp. 34, 319, 608; Lightbown 1978, vol. 2, p. 122, no. C13; Pons 1989, no. 77

113

SANDRO BOTTICELLI (c.1445–1510)

The Virgin and Child with Eight Angels (Raczyński Tondo), c.1477

Tempera on poplar, diameter 136.5 cm
Gemäldegalerie, Staatliche Museen zu Berlin (102 A)
BERLIN ONLY

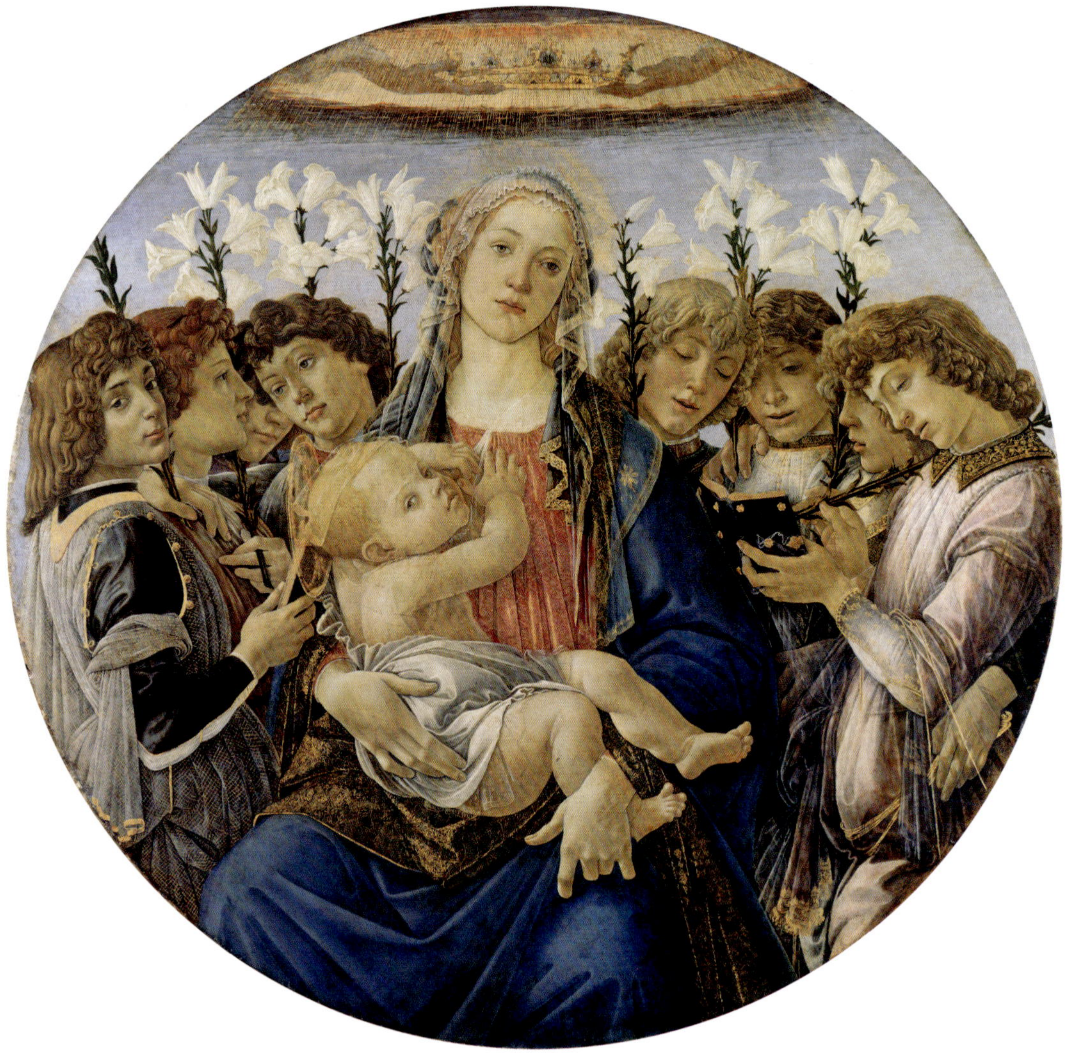

This tondo was brought to Paris from Italy by one of Napoleon's officials, and in 1824 it was purchased by Count Atanazy Raczyński for 2,500 francs. By 1827 at the latest the count was living in Berlin, serving as a chamberlain and diplomat for the King of Prussia. He became more famous, however, as a collector and writer on art. His collection of paintings, which mostly consisted of works by contemporary German artists, was initially exhibited, from 1834, at his house on Unter den Linden and later, from 1847, in a newly constructed palace that was torn down in 1883 to make space for the Reichstag building. The collection was subsequently loaned to the Royal Museums, at first in the Nationalgalerie. It was only in 1904 that the tondo was grouped together with other Botticelli paintings in the recently opened Kaiser Friedrich Museum.

In the catalogue of his collection, Raczyński drew a connection between his painting and one mentioned by Giorgio Vasari as being in San Francesco (today San Salvatore) al Monte in Florence, where evidence of it could be found as late as 1677. Of all the surviving tondi, the Berlin painting, with its eight singing angels wearing white lilies as a symbol of the Virgin's purity, does indeed correspond most closely to the description of the painting in San Francesco. RR

PROVENANCE

Acquired by the French War Commissioner Revil in Italy; in 1824 purchased from him by Count Raczyński in Paris; on permanent loan to the Royal (later State) Museums from 1884; in 1954 acquired by the Federal Republic of Germany and the German states from the Raczyński family

LITERATURE

Raczyński 1847, pp. 3–4, no. 2; Raczyński 1853, pp. 19–29, no. 45; Schasler 1855–6, vol. 2, p. 288; Rave 1956; Lightbown 1978, vol. 2, pp. 53–4, no. B40; Zöllner 2005, p. 225, no. 48

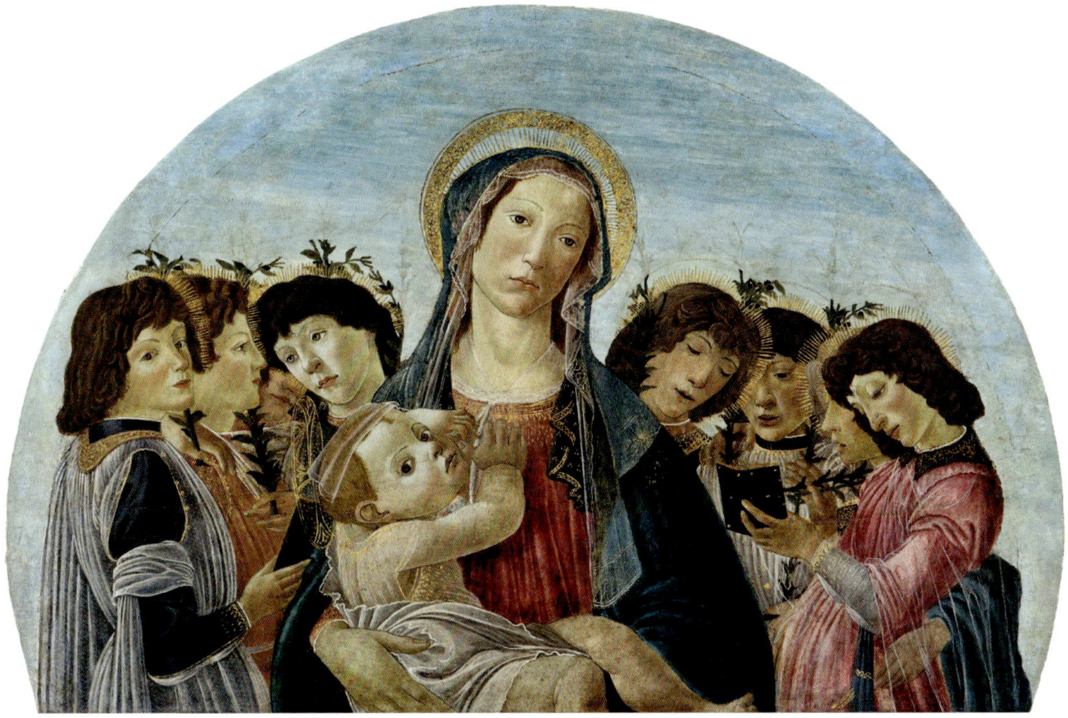

114

WORKSHOP OF
SANDRO BOTTICELLI
(c.1445–1510)
The Virgin and Child with Angels,
c.1480–90

Tempera on wood, 43.5 × 64 cm
Lindenau-Museum, Altenburg (101)

This panel is first documented, attributed to Botticelli, in the 1848 catalogue of the Lindenau collection by the artist and art historian Johann Gottlob von Quandt and Heinrich Wilhelm Schulz, director of the antiquities collection in Dresden. It may have been procured by Dr Emil Braun, secretary to the German Archaeological Institute in Rome, a friend who supplied many of Lindenau's pictures. This is a half-size replica, lacking its bottom third, of the large Botticelli tondo formerly owned by Count Atanazy Raczyński, which has been in Berlin since 1834 (cat. 113). The present work was recognized by Crowe and Cavalcaselle in 1870 as a workshop production.

Vasari mentions 'a Madonna in a round picture by the hand of Sandro' with eight angels 'the size of life' – probably the Raczyński Tondo – of which 'a pupil of his called Biagio … made a round picture exactly like', which 'Sandro sold … for six florins of gold to a citizen'. The biographer further states as an example of Botticelli's 'very pleasant humour' that he played a trick on Biagio by sticking on the angels red paper hats, which he later removed. The fragmentary Lindenau Tondo may be the copy mentioned by Vasari, who relates how Botticelli's students painted replicas of his compositions, which he sold on their behalf. ME

PROVENANCE

By 1848 in the collection of Bernhard August von Lindenau, by whom bequeathed to the Lindenau-Museum in Altenburg

LITERATURE

Oertel 1961, p. 155, no. 101; Lightbown 1978, vol. 2, pp. 53–5, under no. B40; Florence 2005, pp. 66–7, no. 7; O'Malley 2013b, pp. 9–10, 16, 19, 21–3, 26–8

115, 116

WORKSHOP OF
SANDRO BOTTICELLI
(c.1445–1510)

The Virgin and Child with Five Angels (two fragments), c.1485

Tempera on poplar, 36 × 27.3 and 36.5 × 28 cm
Kunstmuseum, Bern (74)

These oval paintings are both fragments of a reduced-scale workshop replica of Botticelli's famous tondo in the Uffizi. Whether the tondo was cut into oval pendants following damage or to serve some decorative purpose is unknown. The two fragments were probably acquired in Florence around the mid-nineteenth century by the history painter Franz Adolf von Stürler. From a patrician family in Bern, he was a pupil and friend of Ingres, and from 1829–53 lived in Italy, mainly in Florence, where he became fascinated by and formed a collection of early Italian paintings. Between 1844 and 1848 he and Luigi Mussini, a member of the Italian 'Purismo' movement, ran a drawing school, which sought to revive the traditions of Florentine artists' workshops of the 1300s and 1400s. Botticelli's example encouraged Von Stürler's interest in Dante's *Divine Comedy*, for which he produced numerous illustrations from 1840 onwards. SH

PROVENANCE
Bequest of Adolf von Stürler in 1881, received 1902

LITERATURE
Wagner 1974, pp. 105–8; Lightbown 1978, vol. 2, pp. 42–4, no. B29; Bätschmann and Fehlmann 2002; Fehlmann 2002; Bern 2002–3, pp. 136–7, no. 17

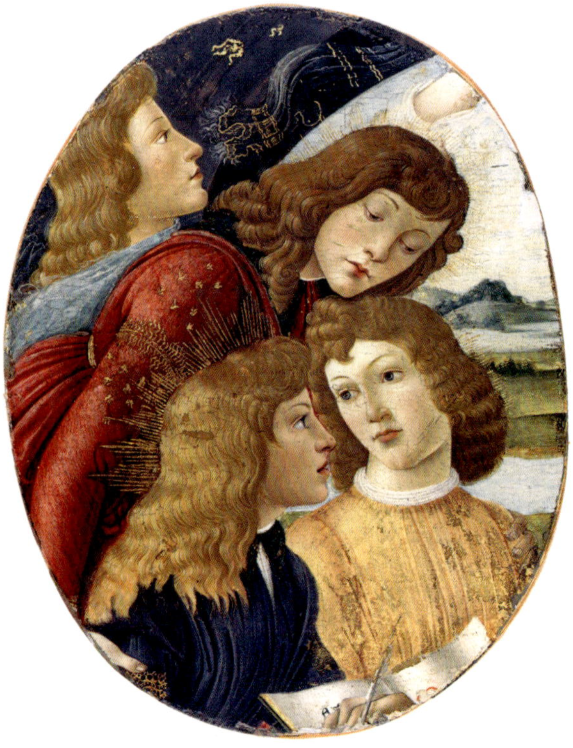

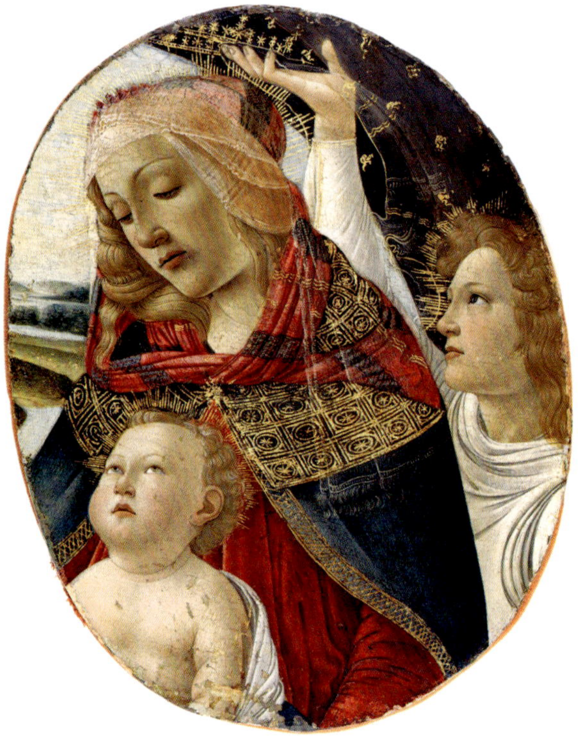

117

WORKSHOP OF
SANDRO BOTTICELLI
(c.1445–1510)

Virgin and Child with Four Angels (Madonna del Magnificat), 1485

Tempera on wood, diameter 114 cm
Musée Fabre, Montpellier (D79.1.2)

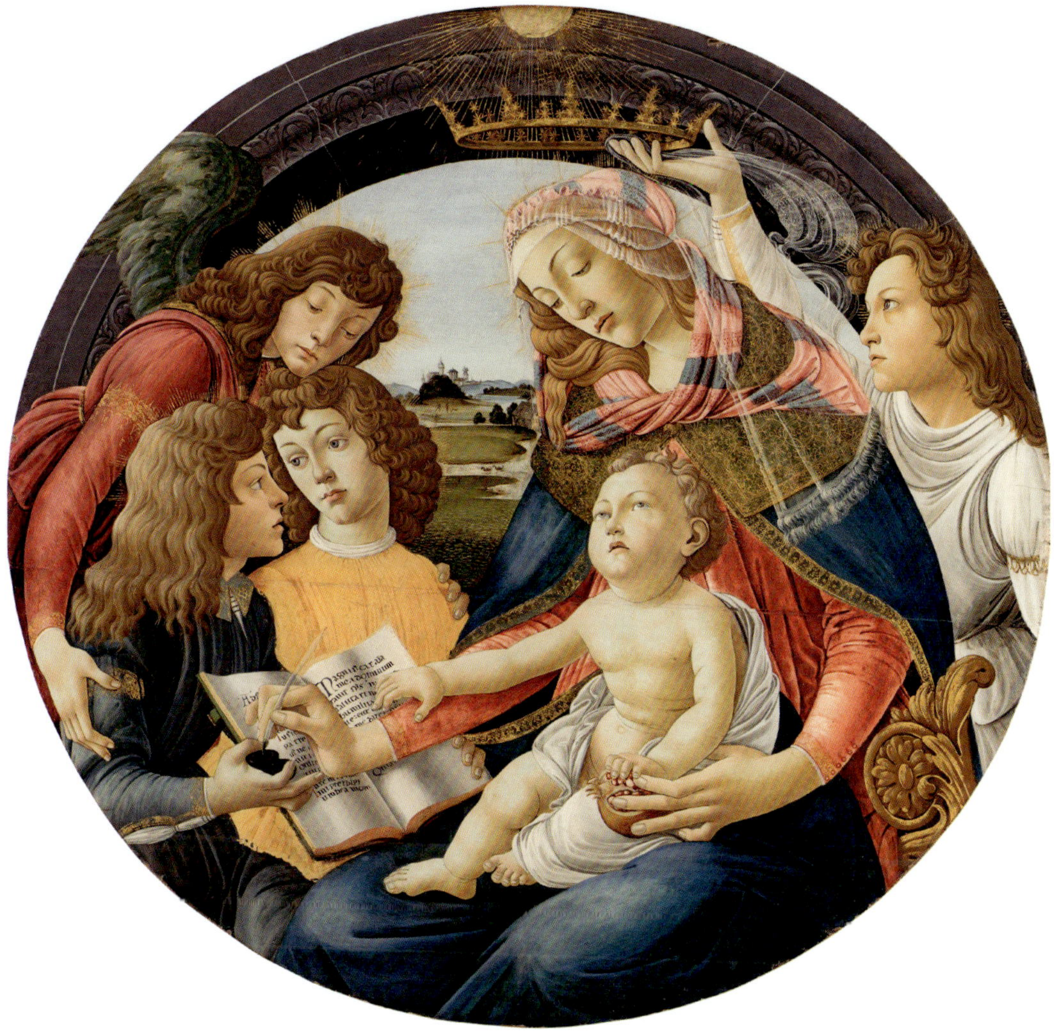

This tondo is now recognized as a version of the *Madonna del Magnificat* in the Uffizi. In 1812 it entered the Musée Napoléon in Paris, and was thought at the time to be the only work by Botticelli in that collection (another was then wrongly attributed to Cimabue, cat. 128), although Vivant Denon had actually selected a quite different painting for the museum while in Florence (see the author's essay in this volume, pp. 52–3). Today it is difficult to imagine the celebrity acquired by the tondo in consequence of its presence in Paris. In 1814 it represented Botticelli at the vast exhibition of the 'Écoles Primitives' in Paris. In 1821 the painting was published by Charles Paul Landon as a line engraving. G.F. Waagen referred to it in 1839 as 'an exquisite work from the middle and best period of the Master'. It was on account of the publicity surrounding this painting that the primary version in the Uffizi – until then ascribed to 'the German School' – was recognized for the first time as by Botticelli. Their fortunes are now reversed, and today it is the Uffizi version that is by far the more famous of the two. The Paris tondo, now regarded merely as a workshop replica, was transferred to Montpellier in 1979. RR

PROVENANCE
1811, Galleria dell'Accademia, Florence; 1812, Musée Napoléon (later Musée du Louvre), Paris; since 1979 Musée Fabre, Montpellier

LITERATURE
Landon 1810–21, vol. 4, 1821, pp. 31–2, pl. 13; Waagen 1839, p. 408; Blumer 1936, p. 280, no. 184; Lightbown 1978, vol. 2, p. 43, no. B29a; Preti Hamard 1999, p. 508

118

WORKSHOP OF
SANDRO BOTTICELLI
(c.1445–1510)
The Virgin and Child with St John and an Angel, c.1490

Tempera on wood, diameter 84.5 cm
The National Gallery, London (NG 275)

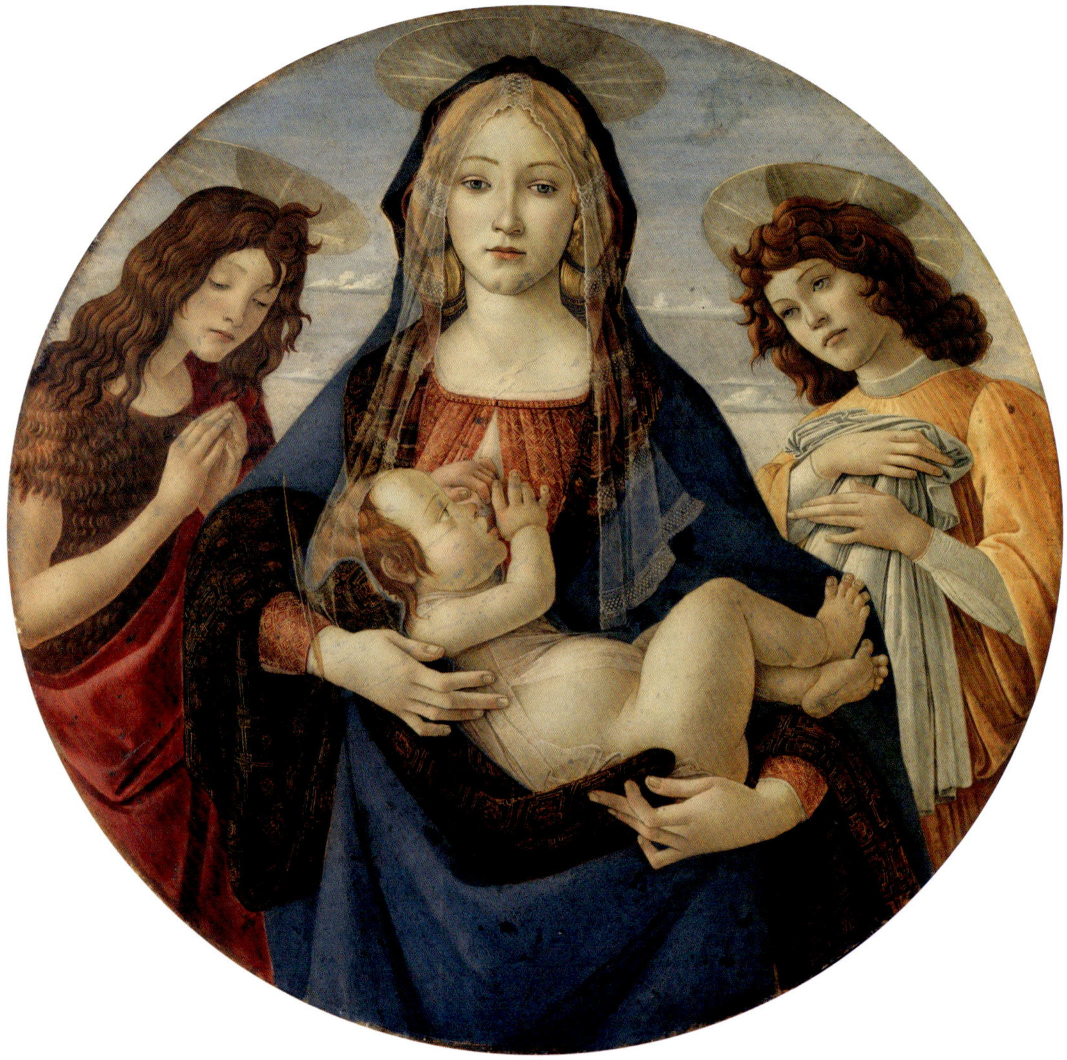

In 1855 this tondo was one of the first works attributed to Botticelli to enter the National Gallery. Shortly after its acquisition G.F. Waagen considered it a fine autograph work and stressed the 'expression of purity' of the Virgin and the 'humble adoration' of St John the Baptist and the angel; an outlook which tallies with the mid-nineteenth-century conception of Botticelli as a 'pious artist'. He assumed it belonged to the architect Giuliano da Sangallo, whose name is written on the reverse, but who may instead have designed its frame. A number of surviving versions attest to the popularity of the composition. A copy by the wealthy artist and suffragette Christiana, Lady Herringham, who founded the Society of Painters in Tempera in 1901 and played a major role in establishing the National Art Collections Fund in 1903, was given in 1918 to Bedford College London (now University of London, Royal Holloway; P1104).

In 1864 Crowe and Cavalcaselle considered it 'not a fine example', and since 1893 most commentators have assigned it to the artist's workshop. In 1930, Fiocco published the painting as 'A newly discovered tondo by Botticelli', but it was ignored by Berenson and Mesnil. Now generally regarded as the work of a skilled assistant, the picture remains popular with the public to judge from its frequent reproduction on consumer products such as mobile phone covers. AD

PROVENANCE
Owned by the Abbate Carlo Bianconi of Bologna and Milan; Giovanni Giuseppe Bianconi, from whom purchased in 1855

LITERATURE
Waagen 1857, p. 54; Lightbown 1978, vol. 2, p. 132, no. C30 (with previous bibliography); Pons 1989, p. 80, no. 94; Caneva 1990, p. 141, no. 7A

119

WORKSHOP OF
SANDRO BOTTICELLI
(c.1445–1510)

Virgin and Child with the Young St John the Baptist, 1480s

Tempera on wood, diameter 78 cm
Private collection

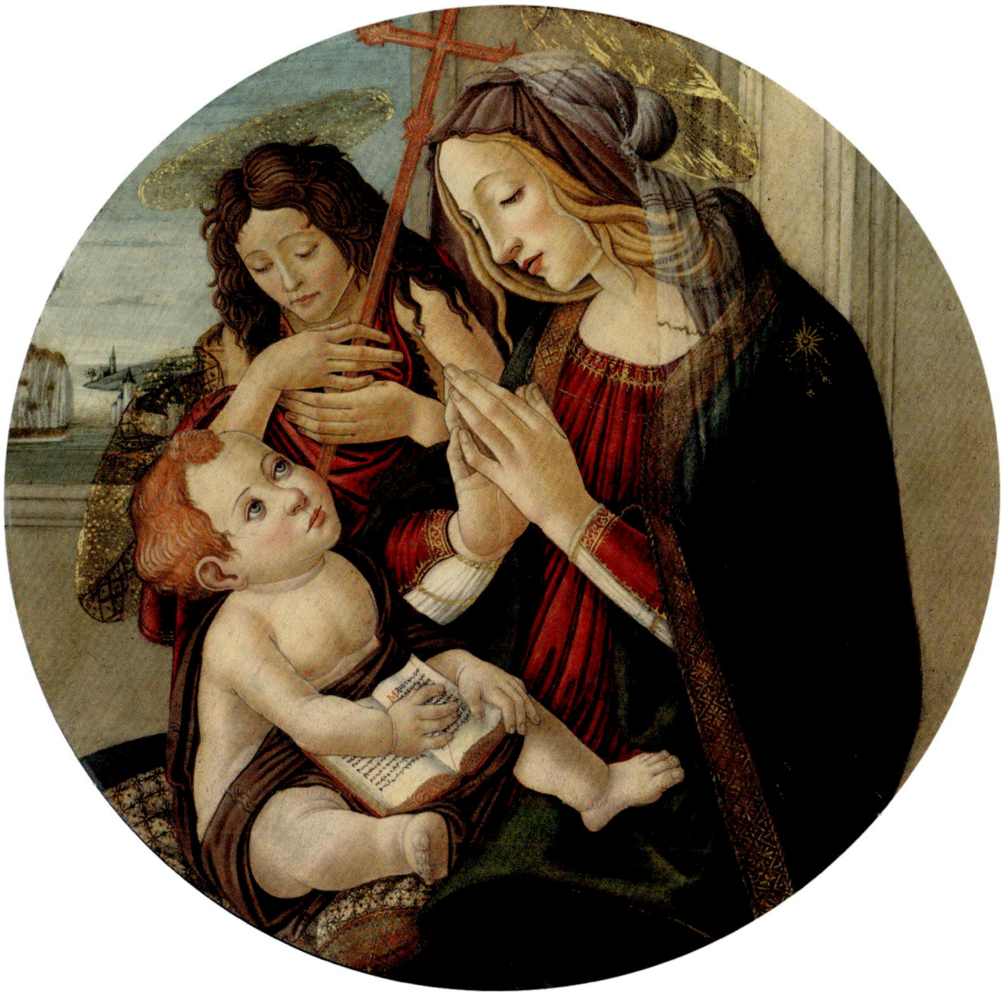

Formerly in the collection of Léopold Leclanché, who translated Vasari's *Lives* into French (1841), this tondo was purchased in Paris in 1892 by the Polish count Karol Lanckoroński. Perhaps advised by Bernard Berenson, he assembled a major collection, strong in early Italian panels, and himself wrote a book on painted cassone. His father-in-law Prince Karl Max von Lichnowsky also owned a work attributed to Botticelli (cat. 137) and his daughter Karolina Lanckorońska became an art historian. A photograph shows the tondo in 1903 in a prominent location above a cassone panel in the Italian room of the Lanckoroński Palace in Vienna. After the Nazi seizure of the collection, this work was acquired in 1942 by the unscrupulous *Reichsmarschall* Hermann Göring, to the annoyance of Adolf Hitler, who believed that works of art confiscated in Austria should remain there. It was restituted after the Second World War.

Considered by Ulmann in 1893 to be a late autograph work, later scholars have attributed this painting to Botticelli's workshop. The composition appears with minor variations in at least two further versions: an upright format in the Museum of Fine Arts, Boston, and another tondo formerly in the Hay collection, Washington. All three may derive from a common prototype. AD

PROVENANCE

Paris, Leclanché collection; sold Galerie Georges Petit, Paris, 25 May 1892 (lot 3); Vienna, Lanckoroński collection; confiscated and acquired by Hermann Göring; Munich, Central Collecting Point, receipt of 5 August 1945; restituted to the Lanckoroński family; Florence, Salocchi collection; sold Sotheby's, New York, 29 January 2015 (lot 125)

LITERATURE

Lightbown 1978, vol. 2, p. 139, no. C44(b); Miziolek 1995, p. 30, no. 3; Boston 1997, pp. 54–5; Kanter 1997, p. 176; Yeide 2009, p. 399, no. A1337, repr. p. 187 (as School of Botticelli by Andrea Vecchietti); Isell 2010, pp. 243–0; Winiowicz-Wolska 2010, vol. 1, pp. 473, 509, no. 65; vol. 2, p. 27; Skubiszewska and Kuczman 2010, pp. 20, 21, 23–4

120

WORKSHOP OF
SANDRO BOTTICELLI
(C.1445–1510)
The Virgin Adoring the Child with the Young St John the Baptist, 1480s–90s

Tempera on wood, diameter 86.4 cm
Amgueddfa Cymru – National Museum Wales, Cardiff
(NMW A 241)

This painting was bought in Rome in 1842 by William Fuller Maitland, an enthusiastic collector of early Italian and northern paintings. G.F. Waagen visited his collection in 1851 and considered it autograph; praising the 'earnest and noble sentiment' of the heads and finding the infant Christ 'lightly and transparently coloured … truer to nature in the forms than is usual for him'. It was lent to the Royal Academy in 1873.

The painting's attribution was later complicated by the discovery of several related versions and Berenson ascribed it to the artist's workshop. It is now generally considered a replica of a larger tondo formerly owned by the Marchese Patrizi in Rome, which by 1889 had passed to George Salting, who bequeathed it to the National Gallery in 1910. The picture also resembles a rectangular version of the subject now in the Landesmuseum, Hanover, which was already in Berlin by the 1820s. It was purchased in 1922 by the pioneering British collector of French Impressionism, Gwendoline Davies, who also owned another Botticelli workshop picture, *Virgin and Child with a Pomegranate*.

Paintings of the Virgin and Child were widely used in the fifteenth century for private devotion and Botticelli's master, Fra Filippo Lippi, specialized in this type of image. The versions of this composition show how successful designs were replicated as a commercial strategy. AD

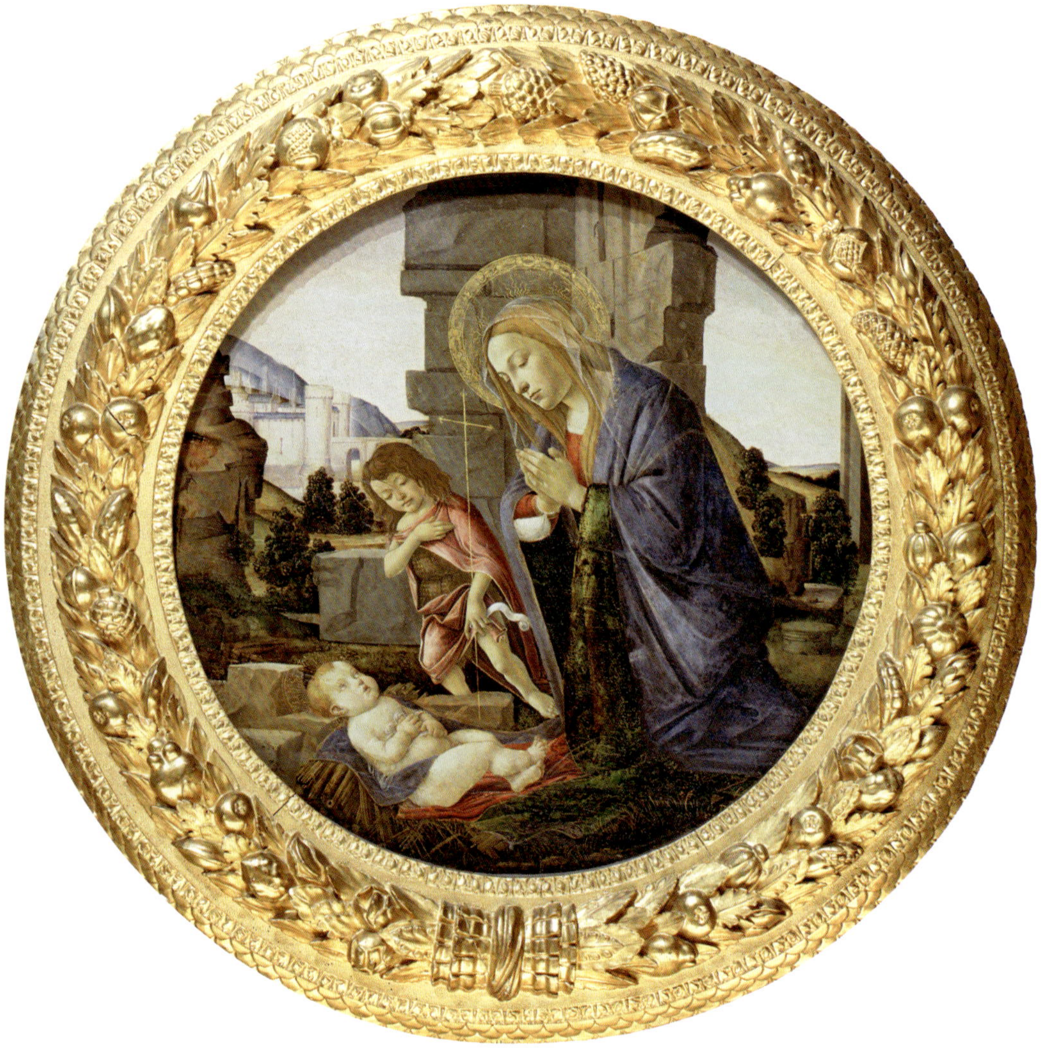

PROVENANCE
Purchased in Rome in 1842 by William Fuller Maitland; sold Christies, London, 14 July 1922 (lot 53); bought by Hugh Blaker for Gwendoline Davies; bequeathed to the National Museum of Wales, 1952

LITERATURE
Waagen 1854, vol. 3, p. 3; Catalogue 1955, p. 135, no. 747; Lightbown 1978, vol. 2, pp. 153–4, no. C68b (with previous bibliography)

121

SANDRO BOTTICELLI
(c.1445–1510) and workshop

The Holy Family with the Young St John the Baptist, 1480s/90s

Tempera on wood, diameter 90.2 cm
Faringdon collection, Buscot Park (47)

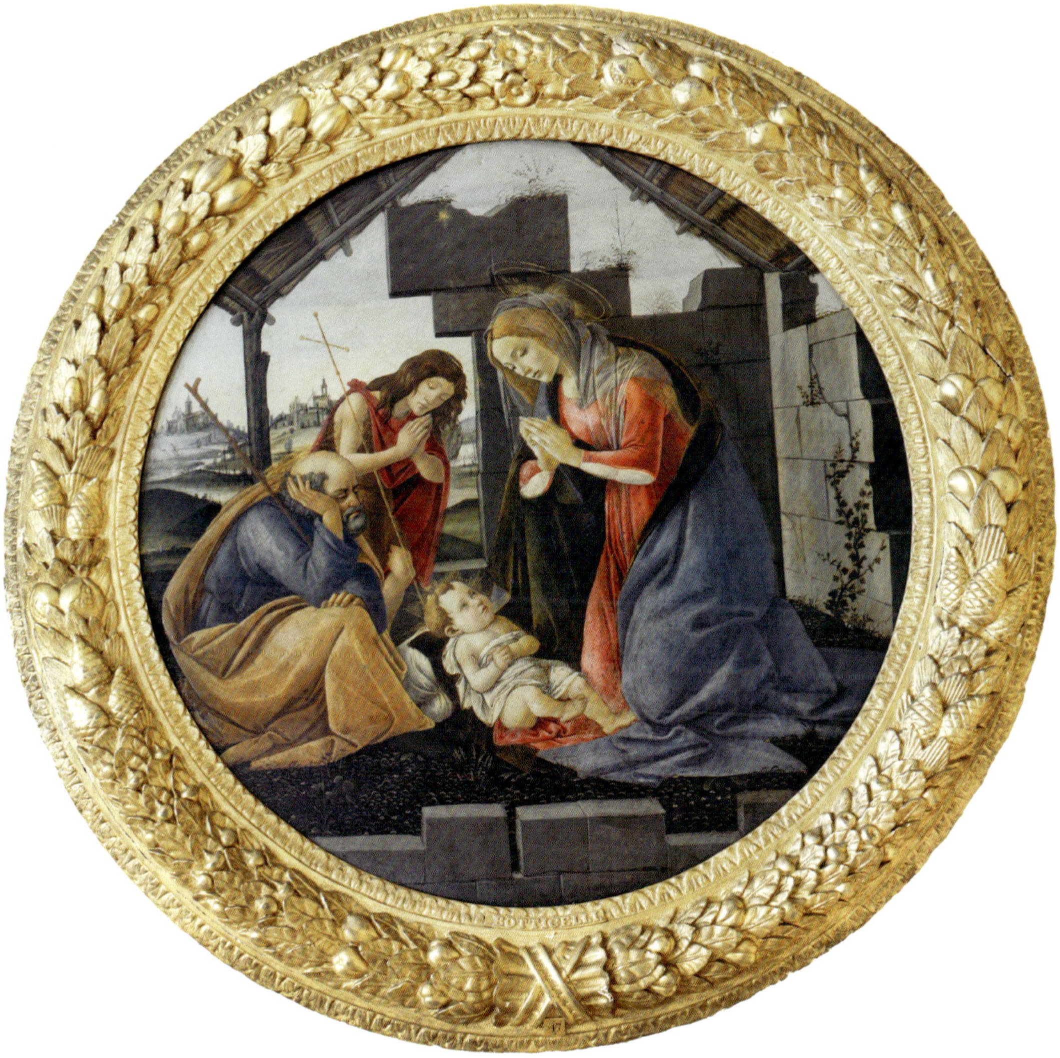

This is an elaboration of a composition which exists in several Botticelli workshop variants (cat. 120), with the addition of more elaborate architecture, the infant St John replaced with an adolescent figure similar to that in a half-length tondo (cat. 119), and an added crouching St Joseph resembling that in the *Mystic Nativity* of 1500 (cat. 101). St Joseph is taken from a surviving squared-off preparatory study and a related drawing of *The Adoration of the Child* is in the Uffizi.

G.F. Waagen considered this 'an inferior work of the master's late time' following his visit in 1851 to the collection of Lord Ward, whose most important pictures had previously belonged to Cardinal Fesch and Count Bisenzio in Rome. When it was exhibited at the Royal Academy in 1871 (no. 299), the painter William Bell Scott doubted 'whether or not it is really from the hand of the master'. The tondo was also shown at the New Galleries in 1893 (no. 108) and has generally been regarded as a workshop product. Recently, Francis Russell proposed that it is substantially autograph, a view supported by Everett Fahy and Laurence Kanter. AD

PROVENANCE
William Ward, 1st Earl of Dudley, by 1851; 2nd Earl of Dudley, sold Christie's, London, 25 June 1892 (lot 50); Wickham Flower by 1893; his sale Christie's, London, 17 December 1904 (lot 43); bought by Agnew, from whom acquired by Alexander Henderson, later 1st Lord Faringdon; by descent

LITERATURE
Waagen 1854, vol. 2, p. 231; Lightbown 1978, vol. 2, p. 138, no. C42

122

WORKSHOP OF
SANDRO BOTTICELLI
(c.1445–1510)
The Virgin and Child, 1490s

Oil on wood, diameter 80.7 cm
Fitzwilliam Museum, Cambridge (M.9)

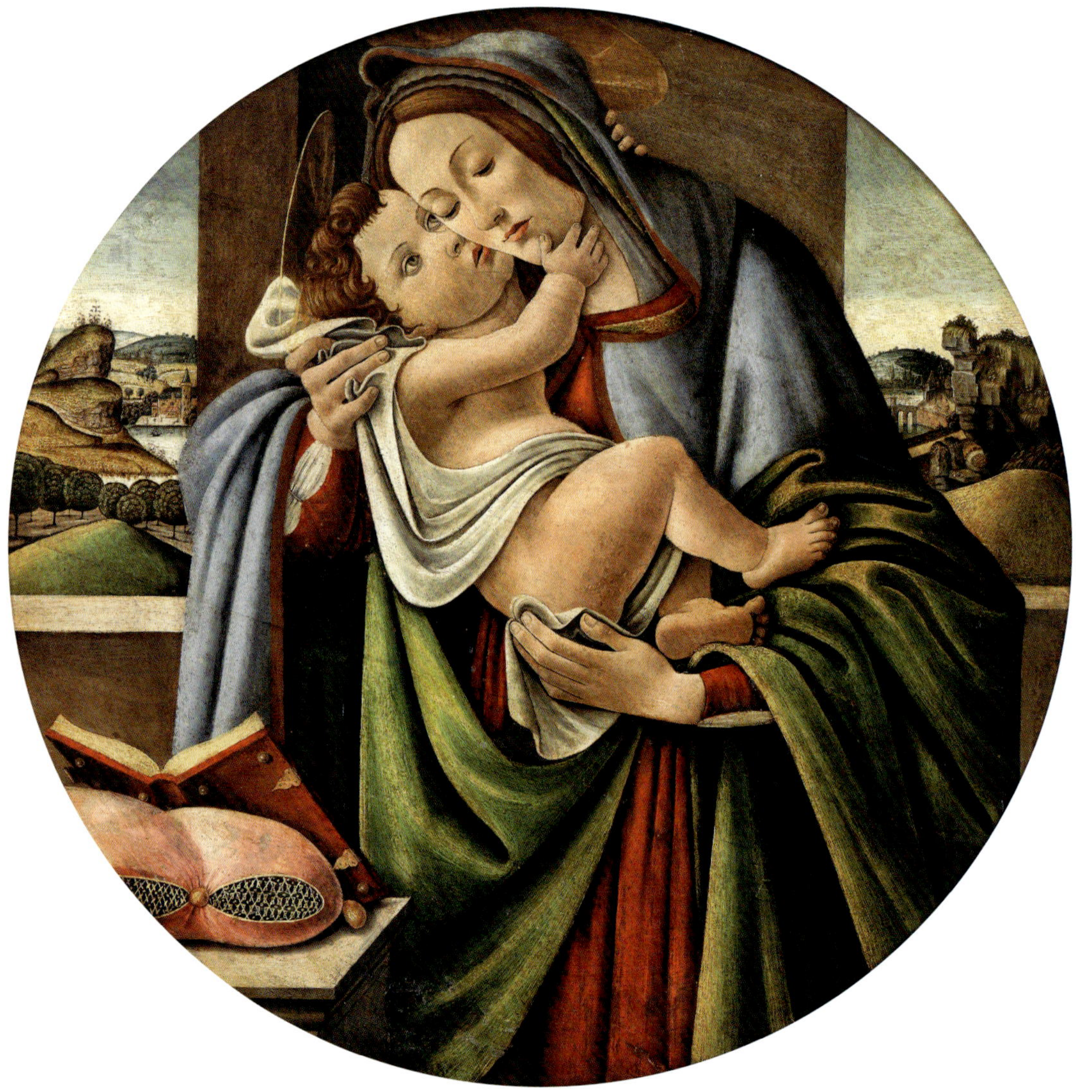

This painting was part of the fine collection, strong in early Italian pictures, owned by the Glasgow merchant and Liberal MP William Graham. He began to collect in the 1860s and became an important patron of the Pre-Raphaelite Brotherhood. In 1874 he wrote to Dante Gabriel Rossetti 'I do think of all the old [masters] Boticelli [*sic*] and Mantegna give me most pleasure', but could only afford studio works by them. In 1870 Rossetti offered Graham Botticelli's *Portrait of a Lady known as Smeralda Bandinelli*, now in the Victoria and Albert Museum (cat. 162). He declined it, but later purchased a chalk version of the composition it inspired, Rossetti's *La Donna della Finestra*. Graham spent freely on the pictures of his friends Rossetti and Edward Burne-Jones, assembling major groups of pictures by both artists. When in 1873 he bought Rossetti's *La Ghirlandata* (cat. 74), he remarked: 'this one is exactly like Botticelli.'

Graham recognized that the present work was a studio production, and it made £40 in his sale. Such circular tondi were a speciality of Botticelli's workshop and the present work is now thought to derive from a largely autograph example in the Cleveland Museum of Art, from the Lazzaroni collection in Rome, which exists in several versions, one in the Musée Fabre, Montpellier and another in the Musée du Petit-Palais, Avignon (cat. 123). AD

PROVENANCE
William Graham, sold Christie's, London, 8 April 1886 (lot 239) as 'School of Botticelli', brought Colnaghi; bequeathed by Charles Brinsley Marlay to the Fitzwilliam Museum, 1912

LITERATURE
Lightbown 1978, vol. 2, pp. 124–5, no. C19(3); Garnett 2000

123

WORKSHOP OF
SANDRO BOTTICELLI
(c.1445–1510)

The Virgin and Child with the Young St John the Baptist, after 1485–90

Tempera on wood, diameter 75 cm
Musée du Petit Palais, Avignon (20720)

The provenance of this tondo can be traced back to the enormous Roman collection of art and antiquities belonging to Giampietro Campana. Assembled in the mid-nineteenth century to form a kind of universal museum with encyclopaedic aspirations, the collection featured an unusually high number of works from the 'resurgence of painting in Italy from the era of the Byzantine School to Raphael' (see cats 108, 125). In the catalogue of the 'Museo Campana', whose paintings were purchased by the French state, there are no fewer than eleven items ascribed to Botticelli or his circle. This tondo was then considered to be 'in the manner of Botticelli', a judgement that has largely endured to this day. The high quality of the painting's execution suggests that it was produced at his workshop, after his cartoon and in close consultation with the master. There are at least six other, slightly different versions of this composition in existence (including those at the Museum of Art, Cleveland and the Galleria Estense, Modena). SH

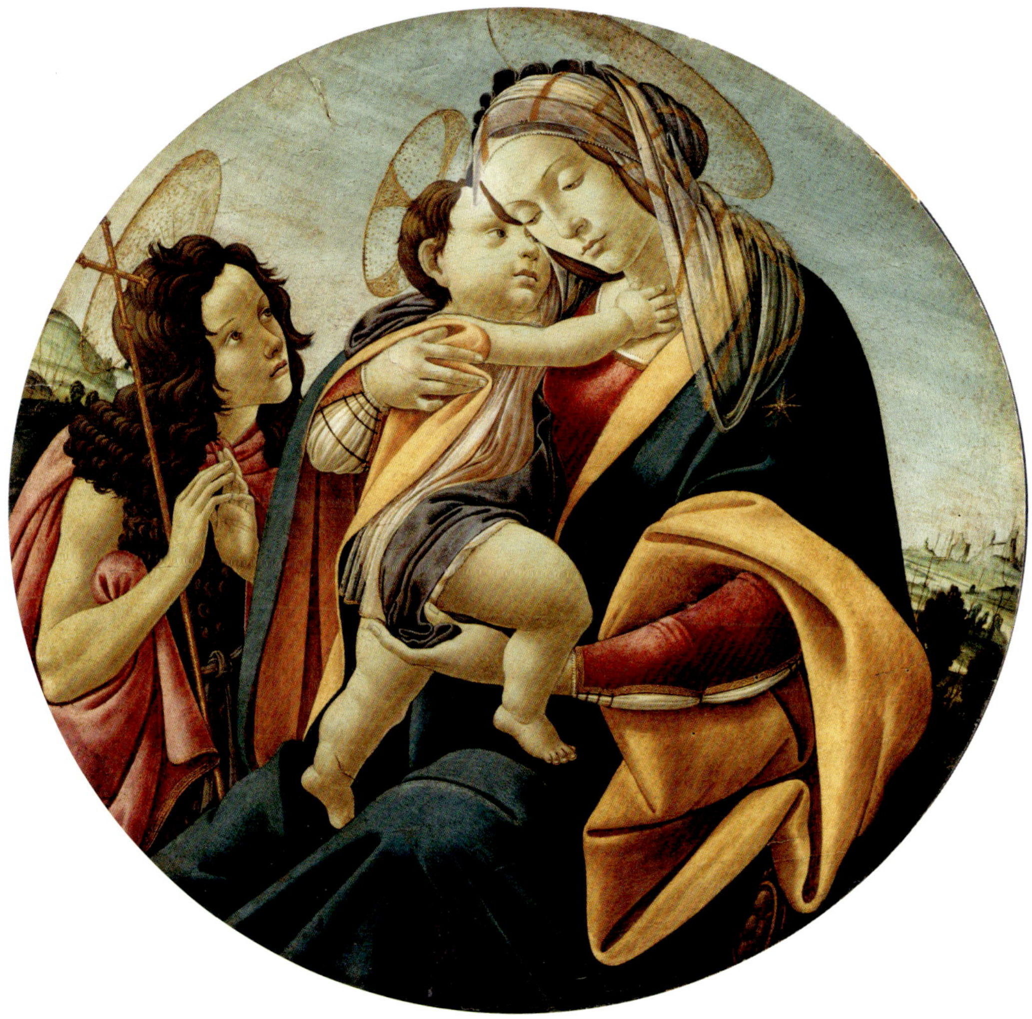

PROVENANCE

Until 1858 in the Campana collection, Rome; 1862, Musée Napoléon III, Paris; 1863, Musée du Louvre, Paris; 1863–1977, transferred to Montpellier; 1977, transferred to Avignon

LITERATURE

Museo Campana 1858, p. 28, no. 231; Lightbown 1978, vol. 2, pp. 124–5, no. C19; Laclotte and Moench 2005, p. 82, no. 52

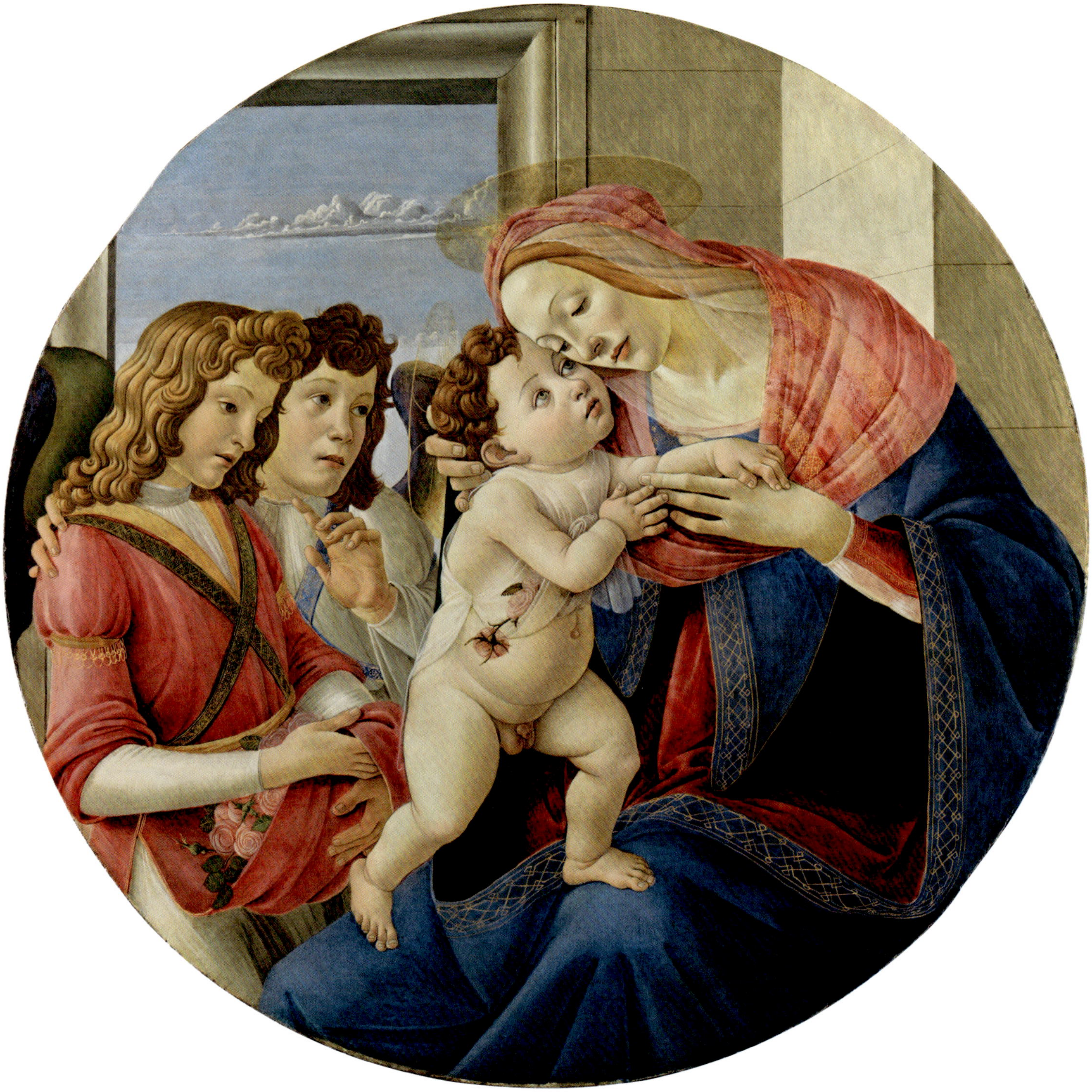

124, 125

SANDRO BOTTICELLI (c.1445–1510)

The Virgin and Child with Two Angels, c.1490

Tempera on poplar, diameter 115 cm
Gemäldegalerie, Akademie der bildenden Künste, Vienna (GG-1133)

WORKSHOP OF SANDRO BOTTICELLI (c.1445–1510)

The Virgin and Child with an Angel, c.1500

Tempera on poplar, diameter 93 cm
Musée du Petit-Palais, Avignon (20254)

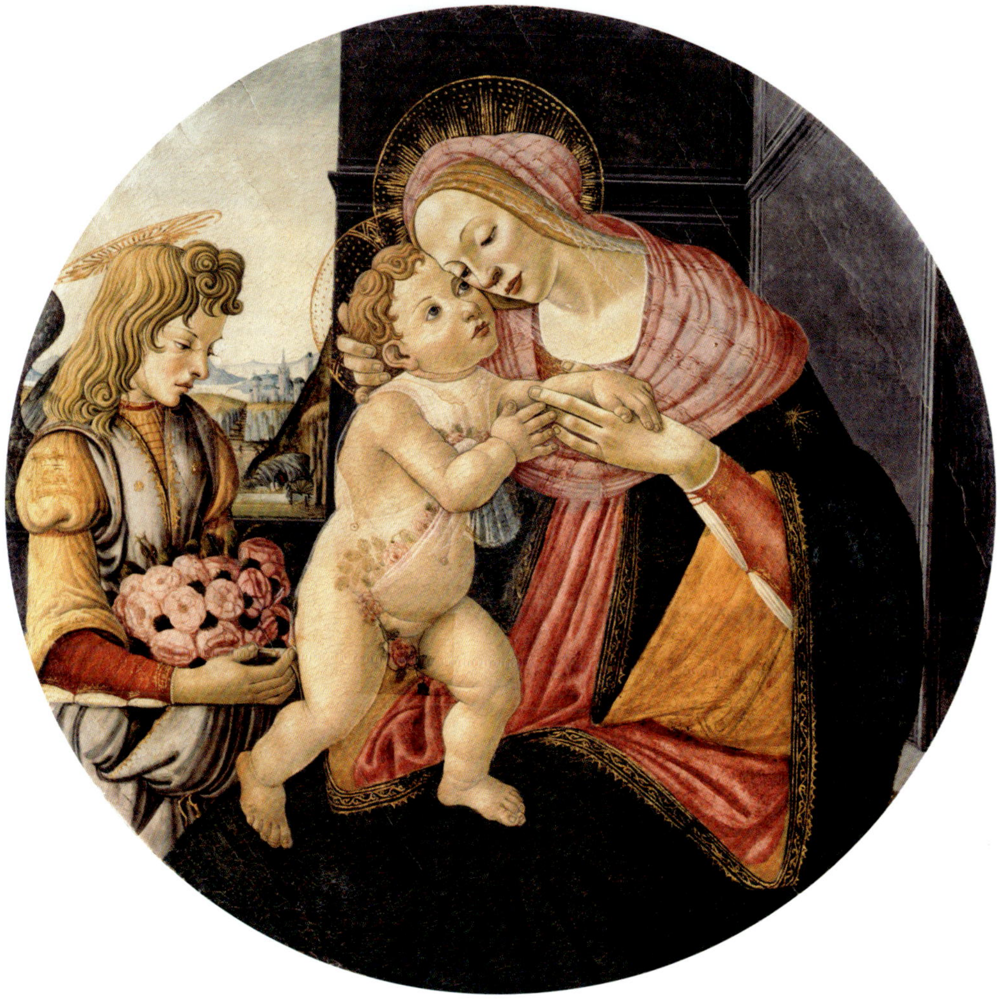

As early as 1879 Wilhelm von Bode described the painting now in Vienna, which he had seen in Florence. Its elaborate composition demonstrates Botticelli's intensive and continually renewed engagement with the tondo format. Because of the somewhat harsh execution of the details, it was frequently attributed to the artist's workshop, but the high quality of its composition suggests that it is a faithful autograph copy of a lost original. The superior quality of the Vienna tondo is evident from comparison with a surviving workshop copy, formerly in the Campana collection, and now in Avignon (cat. 125). This shows how Botticelli's linear style lends itself to schematic simplification when repeated by less practised colleagues.

The painting in Vienna is one of more than 58 works that Prince Johann II of Liechtenstein gave to the Academy in that city between 1879 and 1925. These included important early Italian pictures, traditionally under-represented in the imperial collections, which made the gallery of the Academy the foremost centre for the study of early Renaissance painting in Vienna. This is all the more remarkable since the gallery was originally conceived as a collection of examples for training art students. RR

PROVENANCE

CAT. 124 1879 in the Palazzo Canigiani, Florence; Prince Johann II of Liechtenstein, by whom given in 1881 to the Academy of Fine Arts, Vienna

CAT. 125 Campana collection, Rome; 1862, Musée Napoleon III, Paris; 1863–1962, Musée de Rouen; since 1976 Musée du Petit-Palais, Avignon

LITERATURE

CAT. 124 Burckhardt and Bode 1879, vol. 2, p. 544; Ulmann 1893, pp. 122–3; Lightbown 1978, vol. 2, pp. 128–9, no. C25; Trnek 1997, pp. 82–4; Fleischer 2005, p. 42

CAT. 125 Museo Campana 1858, p. 20, no. 233; Catalogue Musée Napoléon III 1862, p. 58, no. 233; Lightbown 1978, vol. 2, p. 129, no. C25d; Laclotte and Moench 2005, p. 82, no. 54

126

WORKSHOP OF
SANDRO BOTTICELLI
(c.1445–1510)
The Virgin and Child with the Young St John the Baptist,
1480s

Tempera on canvas, transferred from wood, 93.6 × 76.2 cm
Städel Museum, Frankfurt am Main (1064)

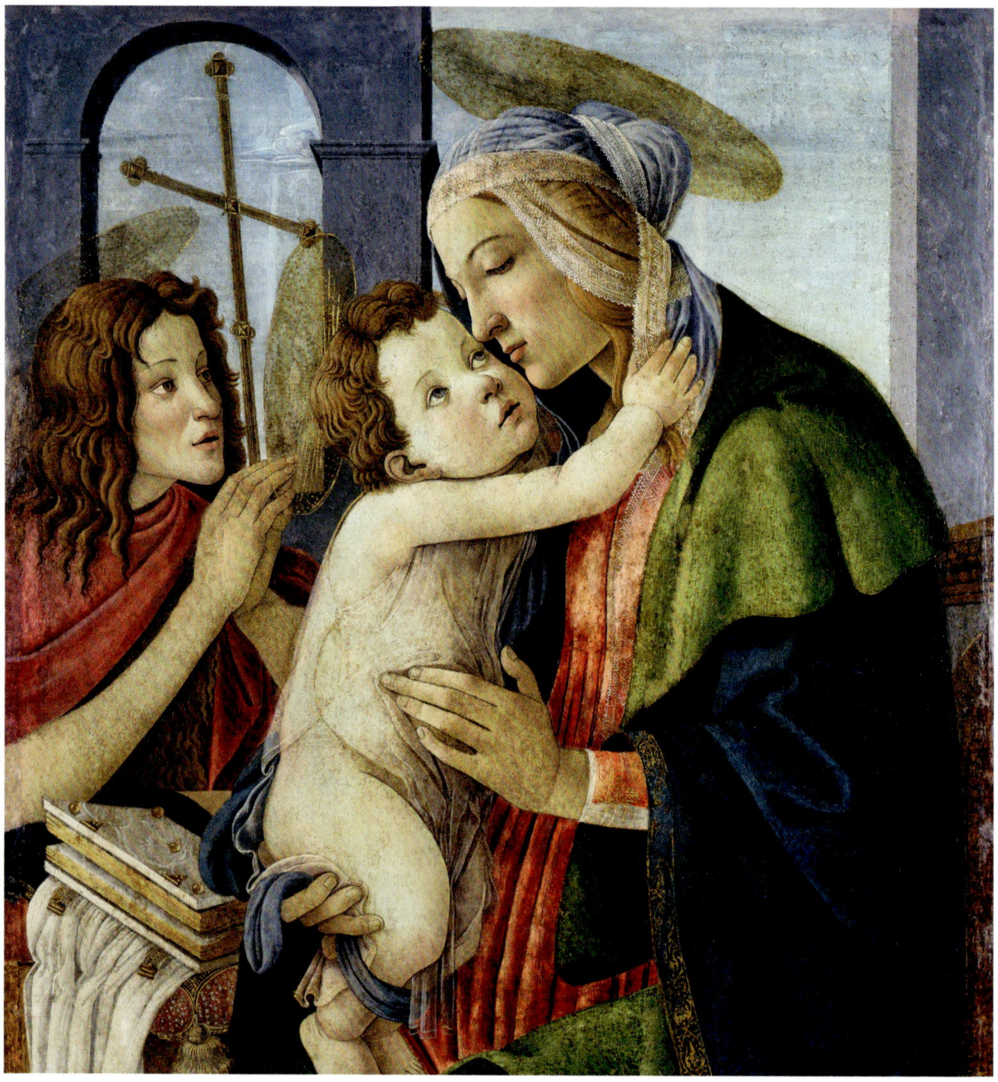

This popular variant on a much earlier Botticelli outdoor composition exists in four versions. One reputedly owned by William Beckford was praised in 1854 by G.F. Waagen as 'Very nobly conceived, and admirably executed' and later acquired by the Liverpool shipowner Frederick Richards Leyland, who was also a patron of Dante Gabriel Rossetti and Edward Burne-Jones. Another was purchased from an English collection by the Dresden Gemäldegalerie in 1874, while a third remains in Florence, at the Palazzo Vecchio. The present work was the first of these to enter a public collection. Their close correspondence suggests all four were made from the same cartoon. A simplified version of this composition, lacking the figure of St John but with a landscape background, was purchased by John Ruskin in 1877 (cat. 127). ME

PROVENANCE
By 1869 owned by the Munich librarian Widmann, by whom lent that year to an exhibition of Old Master paintings at the Königlichen Kunstausstellungsgebäude, Munich; purchased for 2,000 Guilders by the Frankfurter Kunstverein for the Städelsche Kunstinstitut

LITERATURE
Waagen 1854, vol. 2, p. 127; Lightbown 1978, vol. 2, pp. 126–7, no. C22(1), Gaertringen 2004, pp. xvii, 345–54; O'Malley 2013b, pp. 24–30

127

WORKSHOP OF
SANDRO BOTTICELLI
(c.1445–1510)
The Virgin and Child,
probably 1480s

Tempera on wood, 88 × 57.9 cm
Ashmolean Museum, Oxford (WA1932.1)

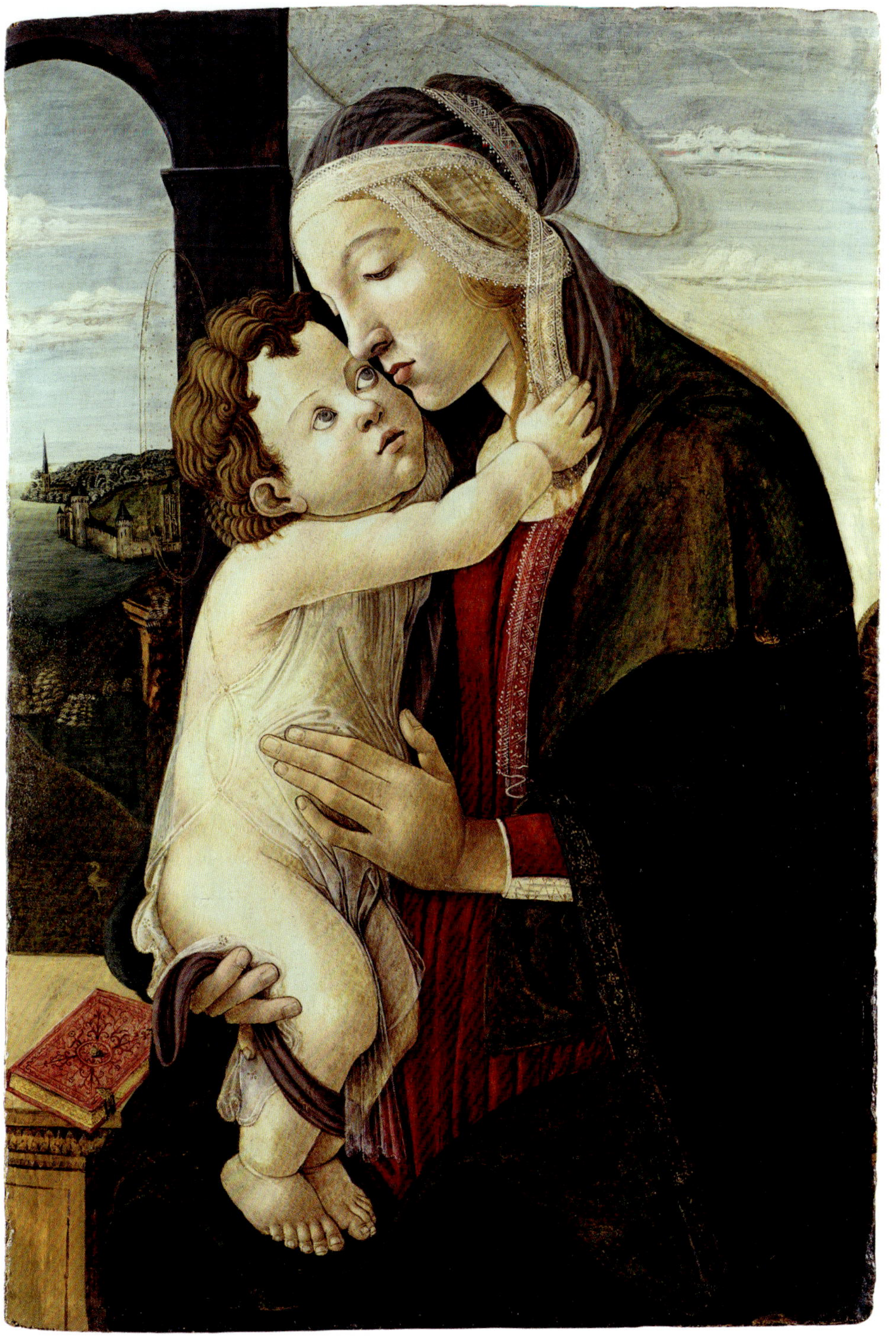

Charles Fairfax Murray was in Italy in the mid-1870s, copying works by early Italian masters for John Ruskin and occasionally acquiring works of art for him. Murray brought this painting to the critic's attention in November 1877, and sent him photographs of it. Ruskin purchased the *Virgin and Child* for £300, but when it arrived in Oxford he was appalled and complained: 'the Botticelli … is so ugly that I've not dared show it to a human soul. Your buying such an ugly thing has shaken my very trust in you.'

Noting that he believed the painting 'to be a work of [Botticelli's] old age', Murray sent a photograph of it to Frederic Burton, Director of the National Gallery, who observed that it is one of several versions of the same composition. The earliest, a work of about 1468 still under the influence of Fra Filippo Lippi, entered the Louvre in 1824, and variants in Frankfurt (cat. 126) and elsewhere attest to the continued use of the composition in Botticelli's workshop for many years, plausibly into the 1480s. In the present version an additional figure of the young St John has been removed and the background altered. MM

PROVENANCE
Purchased by John Ruskin in 1877; Sotheby's, London, 20 May 1931 (lot 122); presented by the Art Fund to the Ashmolean Museum, 1932

LITERATURE
Letter of 22 December 1877 to Charles Fairfax Murray (Pierpont Morgan Library); Lloyd 1977, pp. 36–7; Lightbown 1978, vol. 2, pp. 127–8, no. C23(4); Elliot 2000, pp. 81–2 (purchase price incorrectly given as £5,000); London 2000, p. 145; O'Malley 2013b

128

WORKSHOP OF
SANDRO BOTTICELLI
(C.1445–1510)
The Virgin and Child, 1480s

Tempera on wood, 63 × 47 cm
Palais des Beaux-Arts, Lille (P 789)

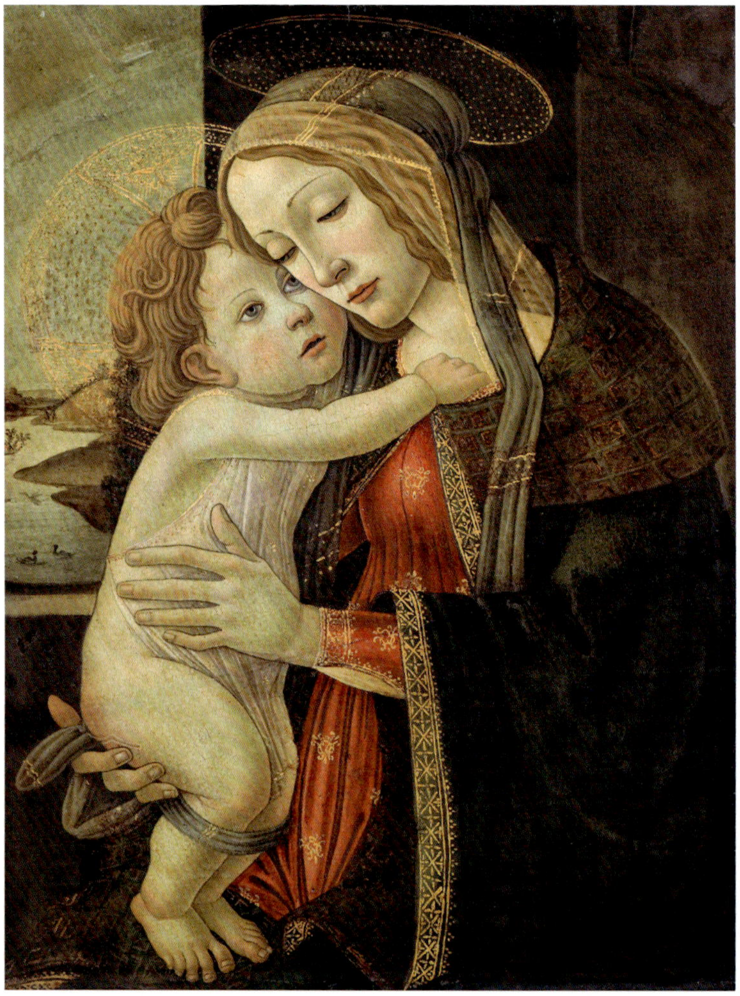

This painting can be traced back to early exhibitions of Botticelli's work in the Louvre (see cat. 117). It is one of many versions of the Virgin Mary cheek to cheek with the Christ Child (other examples are in the National Gallery, London, and in Oxford, cat. 127) that echo the Byzantine archetype of the 'Eleusa', or the Virgin of Tenderness. This painting was probably in the famous Farnese collection, which was moved to Naples around 1735. From there it was transferred to Paris in 1803, where it was ascribed to Cimabue. In 1839 the director of the Berlin Museum, G.F. Waagen, attributed it for the first time to the school of Botticelli.
RR

PROVENANCE
In the Royal Palace of Capodimonte, Naples, until 1802; from 1803–4 in the Musée Napoléon (later the Louvre), Paris; in 1872 transferred to Lille

LITERATURE
Waagen 1839, p. 402; Blumer 1936, p. 277, no. 167; Lightbown 1978, vol. 2, p. 128, no. C23(3); Brejon de Lavergnée 1999, p. 152

129

WORKSHOP OF
SANDRO BOTTICELLI
(c.1445–1510)

The Virgin and Child with the Young St John the Baptist, c.1500

Tempera on poplar, diameter 86 cm
Gemäldegalerie, Staatliche Museen zu Berlin (1582)

BERLIN ONLY

This painting is closely related to a tondo in the Galleria Borghese, Rome, appropriating its composition at a proportionally smaller scale. In both works, the figures are depicted in an interior space with a clearly defined sense of perspective. In Berlin, however, these are reduced to the Virgin and Child and a young St John the Baptist, while the painting in Rome also features six singing angels. This is an interesting example of the way in which Botticelli's workshop reproduced successful works not only as exact copies, but also – with an eye to a wider circle of customers – through smaller reductions with simplified details. Except for a loan to the Angermuseum, Erfurt, between 1884 and 1920, this tondo has remained largely in store at the Gemäldegalerie.
RR

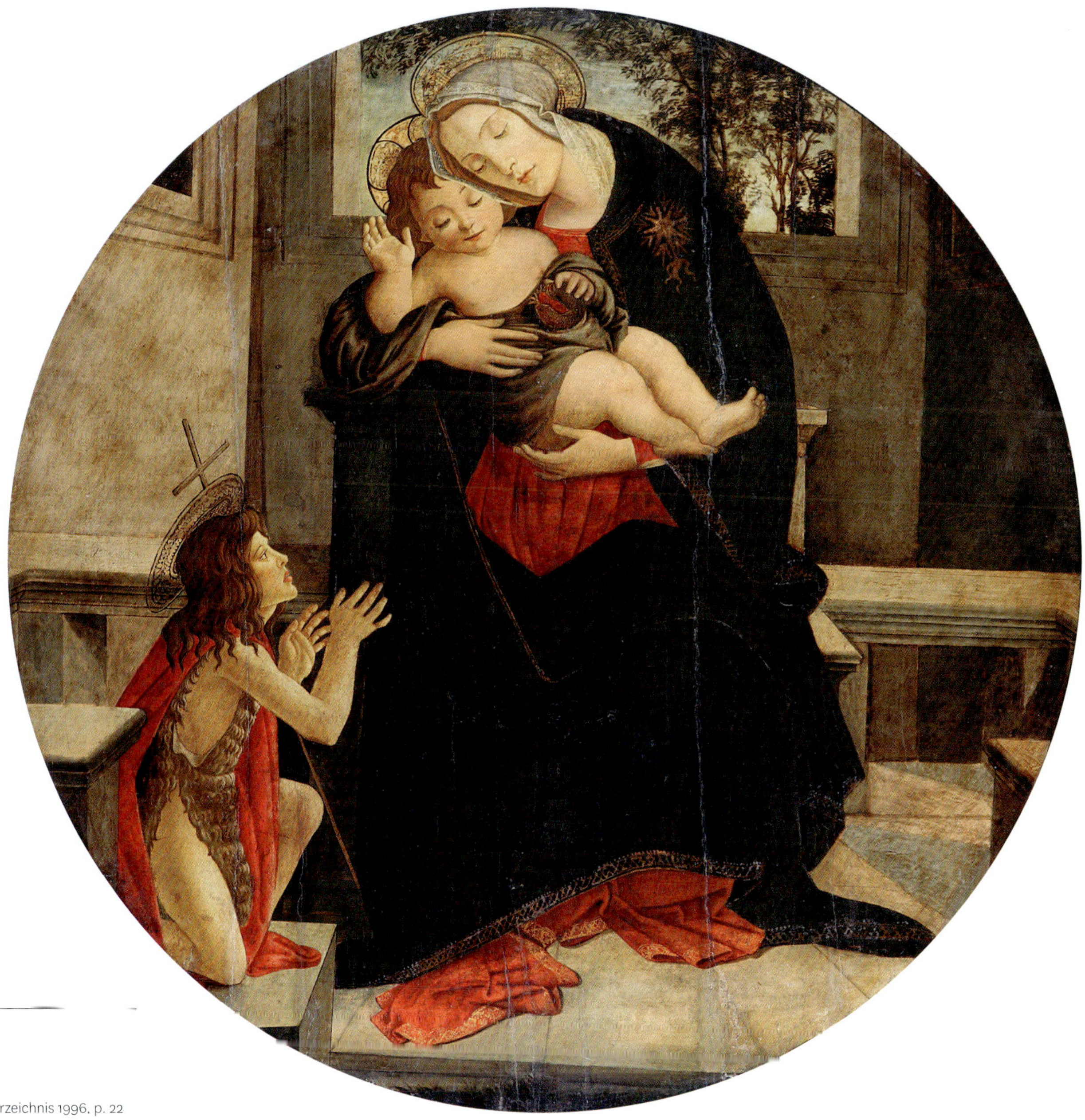

PROVENANCE
Acquired before 1884

LITERATURE
Vorratsverzeichnis 1886, p. 212; Gesamtverzeichnis 1996, p. 22

130

SANDRO BOTTICELLI
(c.1445–1510) and workshop
The Virgin and Child with the Young St John the Baptist, 1480s

Tempera on canvas, 130.7 × 91.4 cm
The Barber Institute of Fine Arts, Birmingham (43.10)
LONDON ONLY

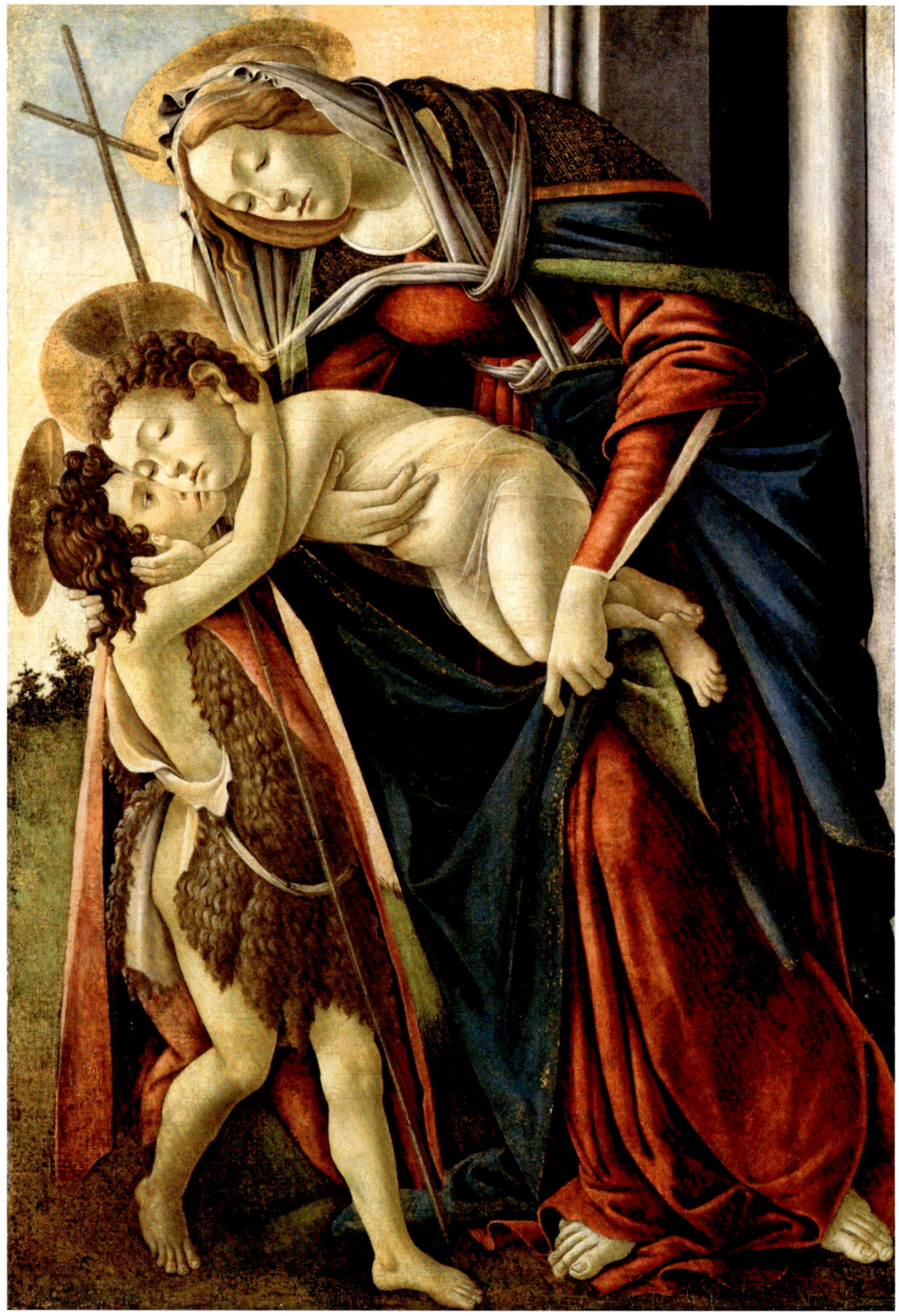

This painting is probably based on the same cartoon as an identical composition of the same dimensions, but in reverse, in the Palazzo Pitti. The latter was published with an attribution to Botticelli by Luigi Bardi in 1842 but both pictures may repeat a lost original. The 'celebrated Mrs. Jamieson', as Thomas Carlyle calls her, described it as 'a quaint picture by Botticelli … very dry in colour, and faulty in drawing, but beautiful for the sentiment'. The present work is first documented in the collection of the scholarly dealer Henry Farrer, who reputedly knew 'so much about old masters that his opinion is constantly asked for, paid for, and considered conclusive'. It was attributed to Botticelli in Farrer's sale, and made the respectable sum of 56 guineas.

Botticelli's highly efficient workshop produced numerous replicas of such images to meet the high demand for devotional paintings. The dramatic arrangement of the figures, almost covering the entire surface of the canvas, is typical of the artist's expressive late style and can be found in works of similar date such as *The Flight into Egypt* (cat. 131). AD

PROVENANCE
Henry Farrer FSA; his sale Christie's, London, 15 June 1866 (lot 157); Captain the Hon. J. Carnegie; Col. Scrymscoure-Steuart-Fothringham; bought by the museum from Colnaghi's, 1943

LITERATURE
Bardi 1842, pl. 23; Jameson 1852, pp. 274–5; Lightbown 1978, vol. 2, pp. 139–40, no. C45b; Pons 1989, p. 83, no. 107a

131

SANDRO BOTTICELLI
(c.1445–1510) and workshop
The Flight into Egypt, 1490s–1510

Tempera on canvas, 151 × 89 cm
Institut de France
Musée Jacquemart-André, Paris (739)

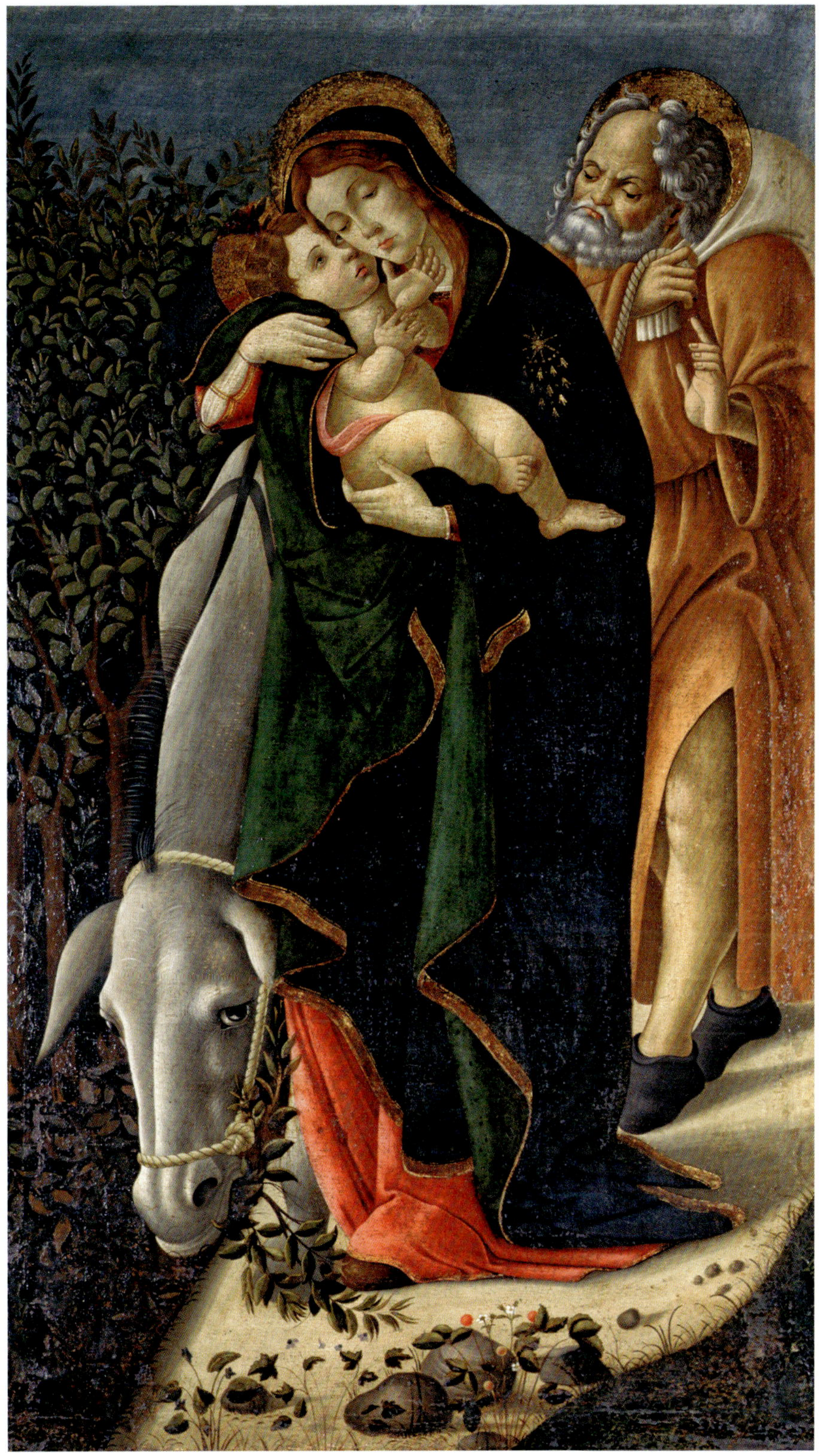

Advised by Wilhelm von Bode, director of the Kaiser Friedrich Museum, Edouard André and his wife the painter Nélie Jacquemart assembled a remarkable collection of early Italian pictures and works of art in the 'musée italien' on the first floor of their Parisian palace. Earlier French collectors such as Comte James-Alexandre de Pourtalès-Gorgier (see cats 162, 163) had acquired works by Botticelli, but Eugène Delacroix criticized the 'superficial judgement' of dispersing the early Italian paintings acquired with the Campana collection in 1862 to regional museums. The Louvre finally acquired two major works by Botticelli in 1882: the Lemmi frescoes (see under cats 61, 62).

This painting was acquired five years later from the Florentine dealer and connoisseur, Stefano Bardini, whose clients included J. Pierpont Morgan and the South Kensington Museum. Bernard Berenson later recommended the Jacquemart-André collection as a model to Isabella Stewart Gardner when she established her own museum in Boston.

Attributed to Botticelli by Bode and Ulmann (1893), this painting was subsequently recognized as a workshop production. Zeri likened it to another 'archaic' late work, the *Madonna and Child with the Young St John* in the Palazzo Pitti, and its replica in the Barber Institute, Birmingham (cat. 130), which he interpreted as evidence of the continued activity of Botticelli's assistants, even after their master's death. These monumental figures occupying the entire surface of the canvas are remarkably expressive creations by a highly distinctive and idiosyncratic master. AD

PROVENANCE
Purchased in 1887 from Stefano Bardini, Florence

LITERATURE
Lightbown 1978, vol. 2, pp. 139–40, no. C46 (with previous bibliography); Zeri 1985; Pons 1989, pp. 98–9, no. 149; Paris 2003–4, pp. 146–9, no. 17

132

SANDRO BOTTICELLI (c.1445–1510)

Mystic Crucifixion, c. 1500

Oil and tempera on linen, transferred from wood, 72.4 × 51.4 cm
Harvard Art Museums/Fogg Museum, Cambridge MA (1924.27)
Friends of the Fogg Art Museum Fund

Clinging to the base of Christ's cross is a kneeling woman, probably Mary Magdalene. The small creature slipping from her clothing evidently represents evil, and alludes to the delivery of the faithful from sin through Christ's sacrifice. On the other side of the cross is an angel, brandishing his executioner's sword in a threatening gesture and holding up an animal – probably a lion (the heraldic emblem of Florence known as the 'Marzocco'). In the background is visible the Florentine skyline (fig. 73) with its cathedral dome, campanile, baptistry and fortified Bargello, and above hover two shields with a red cross on a white field: the coat of arms of the Florentine people. The dark clouds retreat, yielding to the splendour of God the Father, represented at top left. The theme of this mystical scene appears to be the reformation of Florence.

In 1908 Herbert Horne attributed this painting to Botticelli, and associated it with the influence of the Dominican Girolamo Savonarola, who in 1490–8 preached against the immoral conduct of the prosperous citizens and clergy of Florence. This specific connection is not entirely convincing, as the need for moral purification had been a common theme of Florentine religious movements and imagery since the time of Dante. In 1920, the still disputed attribution to Botticelli was emphatically confirmed by Wilhelm von Bode. Remarkably, this view has since remained unanimous, despite the painting's rather poor condition and atypical iconography. It was perhaps because of the lack of a firm basis for this attribution that Bode made no effort to acquire the painting for Berlin when it was on the market between 1922 and 1924. SW

PROVENANCE
Probably from the Palazzo Medici-Riccardi, Florence; the Emil Peyre collection, Paris; until 1913 the Edouard Aynard collection, Lyon; the Marczell von Nemes collection, Munich and F. Kleinberger; acquired by the Fogg Art Museum, Cambridge MA in 1924

LITERATURE
Horne 1908, pp. 301–2; Lightbown 1978, vol. 2, p. 94, no. B81; Lesnick 1990; Hankins 1997; Savonarola 2002, pp. 75, 153–7, 191, 509; Zöllner 2005, pp. 175–8, 264; Körner 2006, pp. 376–7, no. IV

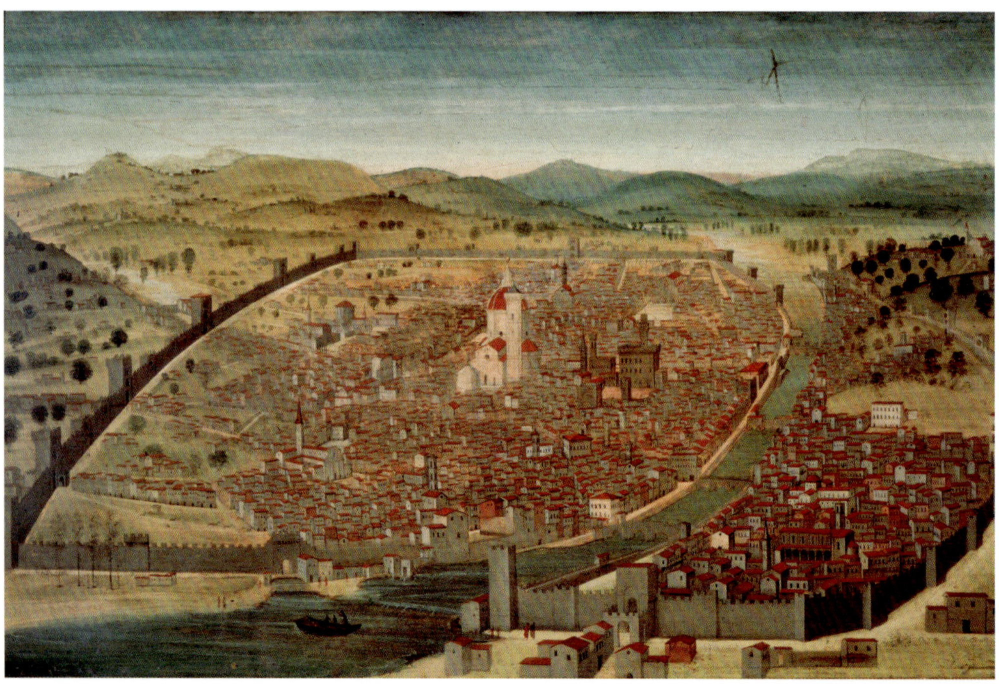

FIG. 73
Attributed to FRANCESCO ROSSELLI (1445–1513) and workshop
View of Florence from the South-West, c.1495
Tempera on wood, 146 × 96 cm
Private collection

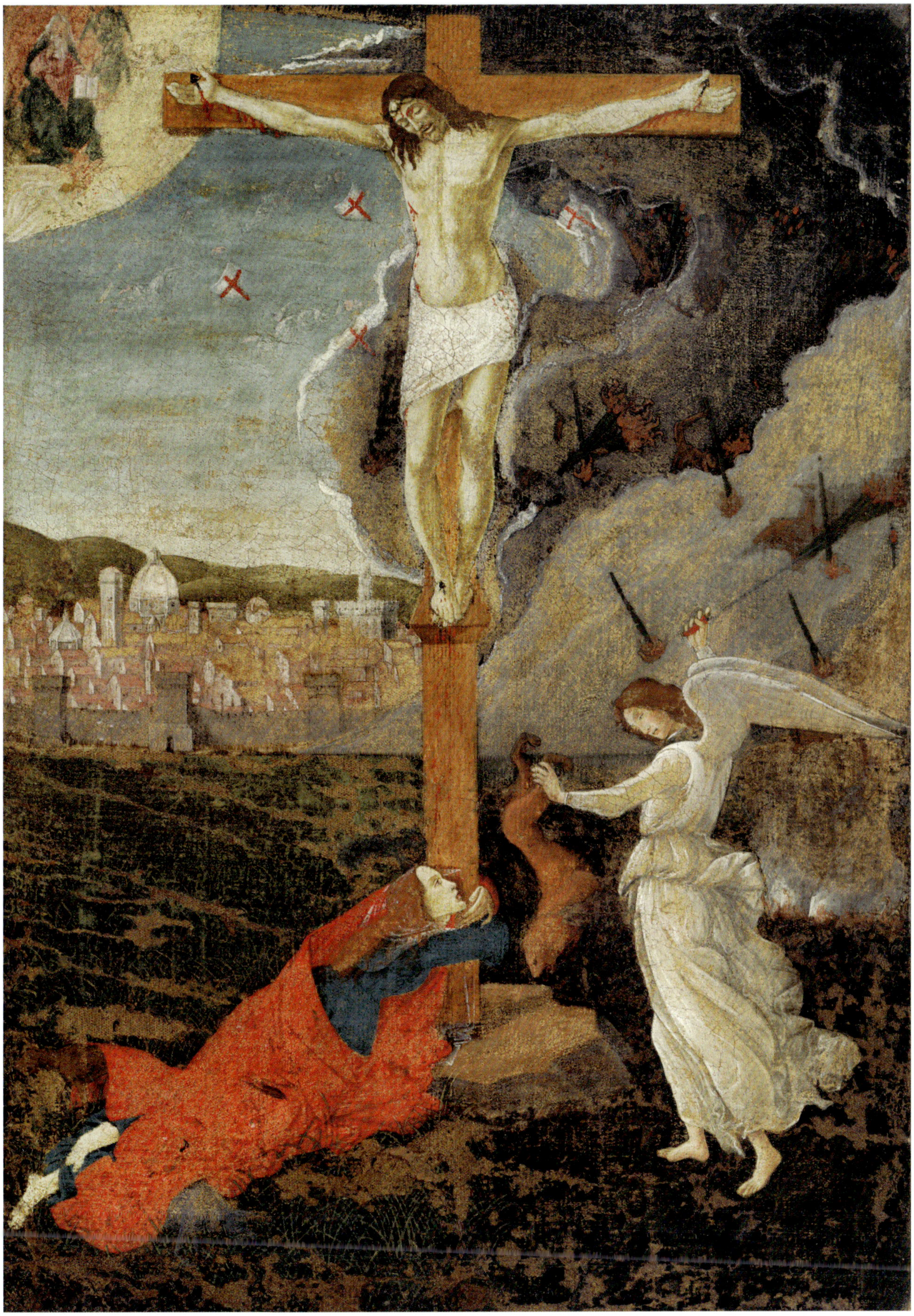

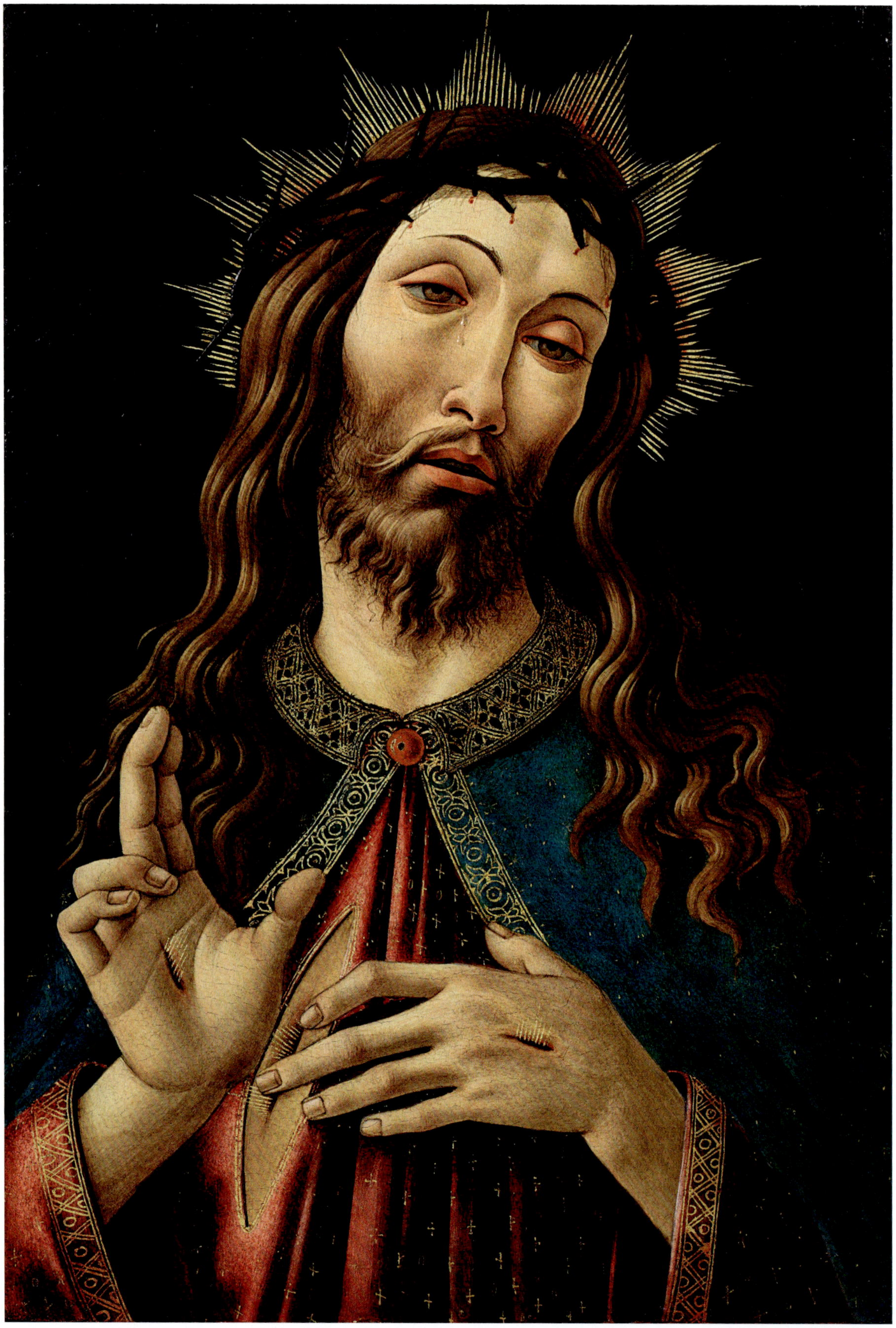

133

SANDRO BOTTICELLI
(c.1445–1510)

Christ the Redeemer (Man of Sorrows), c.1495–1505

Tempera and gold on wood, 47.6 × 32.3 cm
Accademia Carrara, Pinacoteca di Arte Antica, Bergamo (928-1891)

LONDON ONLY

This painting was acquired in Florence before 1865 by the art collector and connoisseur Giovanni Morelli. Its lost pendant, a *Mother of Sorrows*, was formerly owned by a daughter of Tsar Nicholas I, the Grand Duchess Maria Nikolaevna, who lived in Florence from 1862. The subject matter of such devotional diptychs was inspired by imported Netherlandish paintings, which in the time of Savonarola were widely considered especially devout. Several related compositions survive, in Detroit, Berlin (cat. 134) and Oxford (cat. 135). Scholars have been divided in opinion as to whether this example was painted by Botticelli or a painter of his school.

Morelli sought to devise a 'scientific method' of attribution, based on the representation of idiosyncratic elements such as ears and hands, and wrote to a friend in 1860 that he should buy early pictures 'to better study the technical specificities of these masters'. He remarked: 'Among Sandro Botticelli's characteristic forms I will mention the hand, with bony fingers – not beautiful, but always full of life; the nails … are square with black outlines…' AD

PROVENANCE
Acquired in Florence by Giovanni Morelli and bequeathed to the Accademia Carrara, 1891

LITERATURE
Morelli 1892, p. 35; Lightbown 1978, vol. 2, pp. 140–1, no. C48 (with previous bibliography); Zeri and Rossi 1986, pp. 95–6, no. 20; Pons 1989, p. 99, no. 151; Cecchi 2005, pp. 332, 364 n. 103; Milan 2010–11, pp. 80–3, no. 7

134

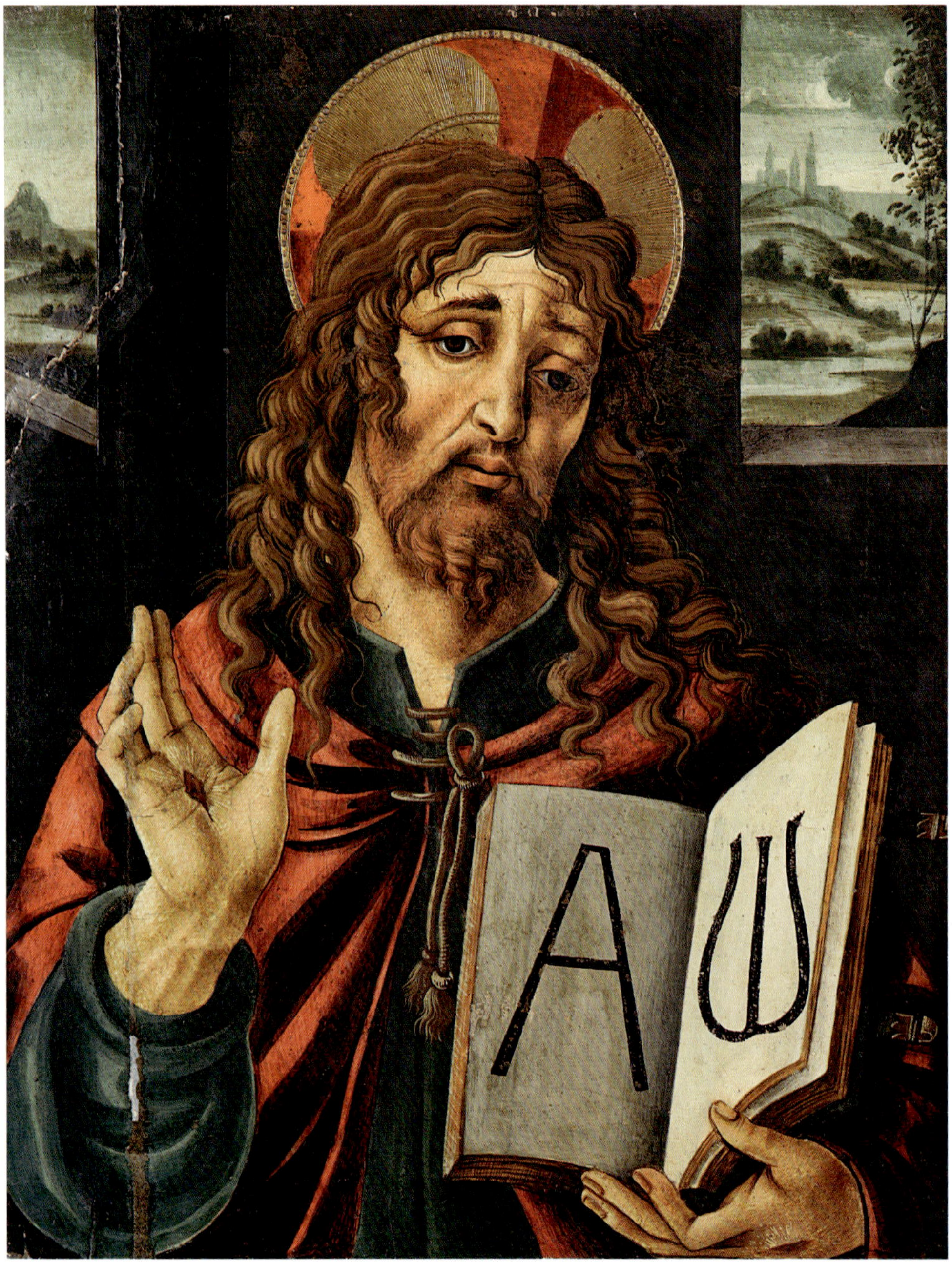

WORKSHOP OF
SANDRO BOTTICELLI (c.1445–1510)
Christ the Redeemer, c.1500

Tempera on poplar, 57 × 43 cm
Gemäldegalerie, Staatliche Museen zu Berlin (1286)

This panel represents a particular iconographic type, showing Christ crowned with thorns, his hand raised in benediction. The version in Bergamo, from the collection of Giovanni Morelli (cat. 133), may be the closest to Botticelli's original conception, but there are numerous variants in existence. The Berlin version omits the crown of thorns, while Christ's left hand holds the Book inscribed with the Greek letters 'Alpha' and 'Omega' (Revelation 22: 13). Like another example in Oxford, which is stylistically very different in terms of the execution of the face and hair (cat. 135), the background shows an interior room with two views over the country-side. The painting was acquired as part of the Solly collection but was apparently never exhibited in the Gemäldegalerie, or given to one of the royal palaces, as were other works not required by the museum. It was lent to the art collection of the University of Bonn between 1884 and 1936. RR

PROVENANCE
Edward Solly; acquired as part of his collection in 1821

LITERATURE
Vorratsverzeichnis 1886, p. 19; Gesamtverzeichnis 1996, p. 22

135

FOLLOWER OF
BOTTICELLI (c.1445–1510)
Christ the Redeemer, c.1490–1500

Tempera on wood, 39.8 × 20 cm
Christ Church Oxford, Fox-Strangways Gift, 1828 (JBS 38)

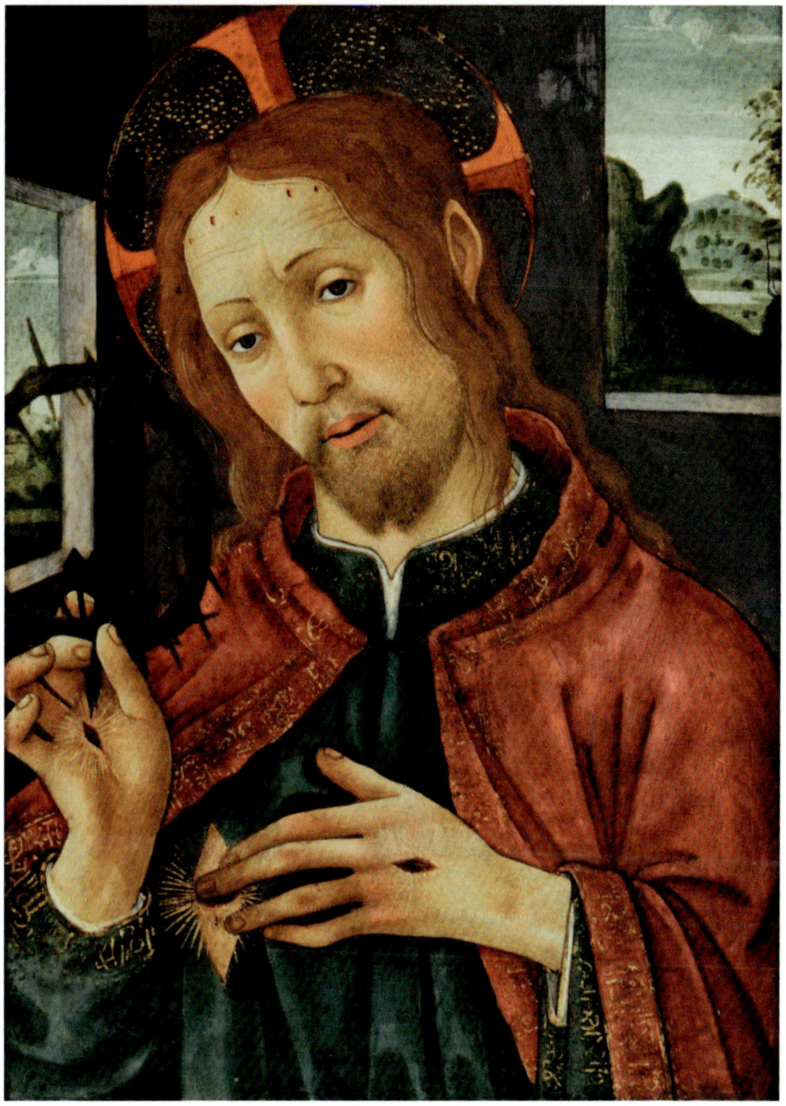

The diplomat W.T.H. Fox-Strangways was a pioneering collector of early Italian art, whose major gift of paintings to Christ Church Oxford in 1828 included the present panel. Although attributed in 1833 to Andrea del Castagno, its presence by this date in a British collection represents a milestone in the reconstruction of Botticelli's oeuvre.

This hieratic image of Christ displaying his wounds derives from imported Netherlandish paintings such as those of Hans Memling. Savonarola's preaching intensified the demand for such devotional works in Florence (see cats 133, 134). Horne noted in 1908 that 'so little individual character have these various copies and imitations, that it seems impossible for the student to do more than trace their design to its origins, ... such a panel as that at Christ Church, Oxford, is to be connected with his school only by the analogy of its subject.' He and Yashiro suggested it is a copy of a work now in the Kress collection, with an attribution to Jacopo del Sellaio. AD

PROVENANCE
Florence, Cinelli collection; Fox-Strangways Gift, 1828

LITERATURE
Catalogue 1833, no. 123 (as Castagno); Horne 1908, p. 119; Borenius 1916, no. 35; Marle 1931, p. 271; Byam Shaw 1967, p. 51, no. 38, pl. 52; Lightbown 1978, vol. 2, pp. 141–2, under no. C49

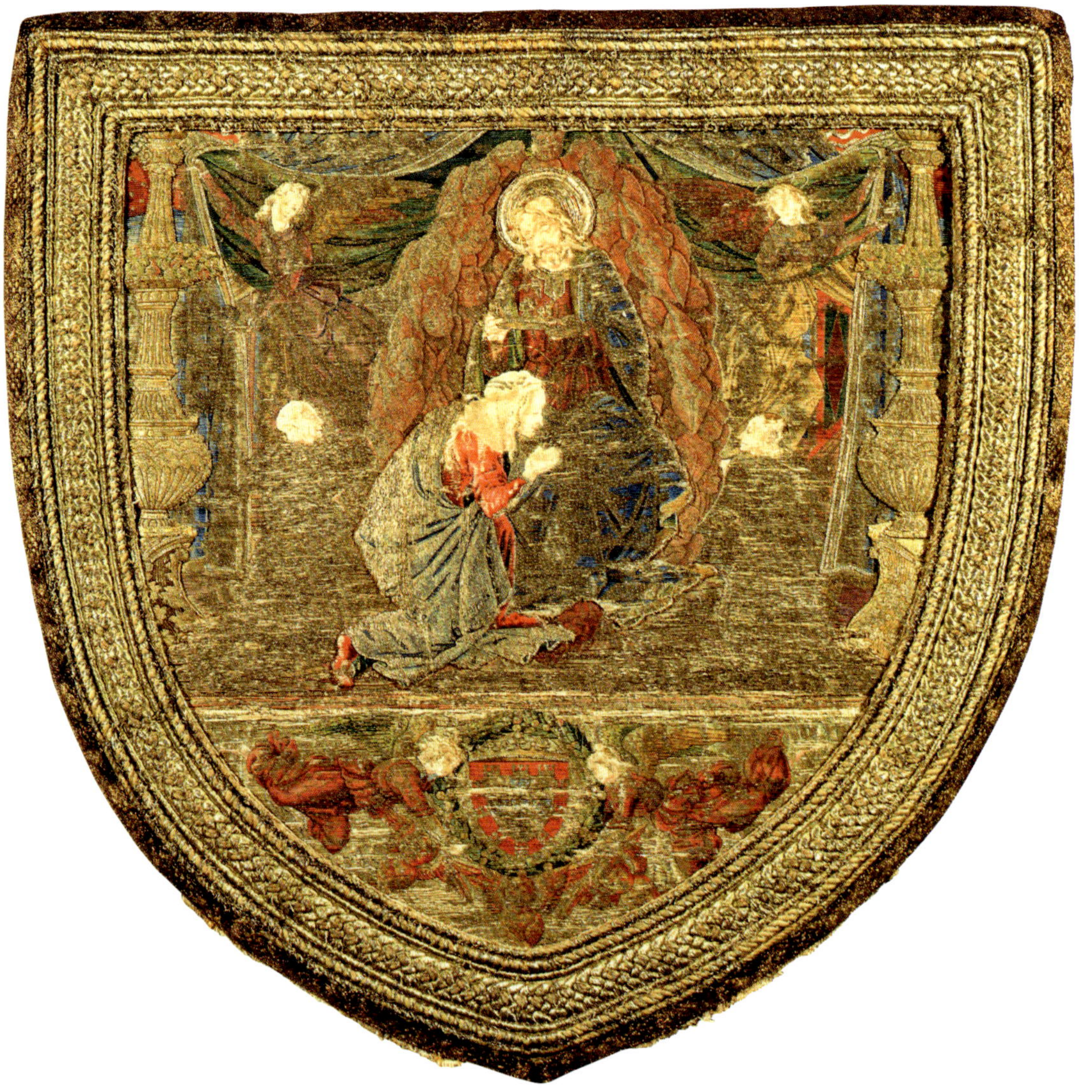

136

DESIGNED BY
SANDRO BOTTICELLI
(c.1445–1510)

The Coronation of the Virgin
(hood of a cope), c.1485–90

Coloured silk embroidery with gold thread in appliqué technique on silk taffeta and linen,
46.5 × 46.2 cm
Museo Poldi Pezzoli, Milan (444)

BERLIN ONLY

This elaborately worked embroidery originally decorated the back of a cope. It bears the arms of Portugal, probably those of King John II (r.1477/81–95), who may have commissioned the vestment for the church of San Miniato al Monte in Florence, where his uncle was buried. It is one of the few surviving textiles after a cartoon by Botticelli, whose prominent role as an innovative designer of liturgical cloths was acknowledged by Giorgio Vasari.

The hood consists of two separately worked parts, the lower of which includes its patron's coat of arms. The upper part, depicting the Coronation of the Virgin with two saints, probably originally belonged to a different item of liturgical clothing and stylistically seems rather later; only subsequently was it carefully joined to the other part.

Another embroidery with a similar design, but without the coat of arms or saints, was formerly in the private collection of Giuseppe Bertini, and is now in the collection of the Castello Sforzesco in Milan. SH

PROVENANCE

The Milanese art dealer Giuseppe Goldberg, from whom acquired as a 'cappuccio antico del '400' by the museum's director Giuseppe Bertini in 1889 for 200 lire, and attributed to Botticelli soon thereafter

LITERATURE

Garzelli 1973; Poldi Pezzoli [1989]; Milan 2010–11, pp. 70–3, no. 5; Florence 2011–12, pp. 222–3, no. 7.15

137

WORKSHOP OF
SANDRO BOTTICELLI
(c.1445–1510)

The Coronation of the Virgin, with St Anthony Abbot, St John the Baptist, St Julian and St Francis, c.1475–1500

Tempera on canvas, transferred from wood,
100.3 × 153 cm
The Jules Bache Collection, 1949
The Metropolitan Museum of Art, New York (49.7.4)

According to Duveen Bros., who sold this painting for $287,500 to their regular client Jules Bache in 1928, it had formerly belonged to the Pre-Raphaelite painter Edward Burne-Jones. In the interim it was owned by Prince Karl Max von Lichnowsky, German ambassador to the Court of St James's at the outbreak of the First World War, whose son-in-law Count Karol Lanckoroński also owned a work attributed to Botticelli (cat. 119).

Burne-Jones also owned a Botticelli workshop tondo of the *Annunciation, with Raphael and Tobias*, which had formerly been in the collection of his friend and patron William Graham (see also under cat. 122). A regular visitor to Italy, Burne-Jones affirmed in 1871 that Botticelli was one of his favourite artists. This subject may have appealed to him because of his fondness for two further Botticelli pictures of the 'coronation of the Virgin' with 'heaven beginning about 6 inches over the tops of our heads', which he mentioned in letters to Agnes Graham in Florence in 1876, requesting her to examine one with a spy glass on his behalf.

This work was attributed to Botticelli by Berenson in 1927, who dated it not after 1486, while Zeri dated it around 1500 and ascribed it to a follower, perhaps influenced by Raffaellino del Garbo. ME

PROVENANCE

Sir Edward Coley Burne-Jones, London; Prince Karl Max von Lichnowsky, Chuchelná, Czechoslovakia; Jules S. Bache, New York; bequeathed to the Metropolitan Museum of Art, 1949

LITERATURE

Burne-Jones 1904, vol. 2, pp. 64–5; Duveen 1941, n.p., no. 103; Zeri and Gardner 1971, pp. 164–6; Lightbown 1978, vol. 2, pp. 146–7, no. C55; Russell 1978; Simpson 1986, pp. 214, 293; Pons 1989, p. 132, no. 152

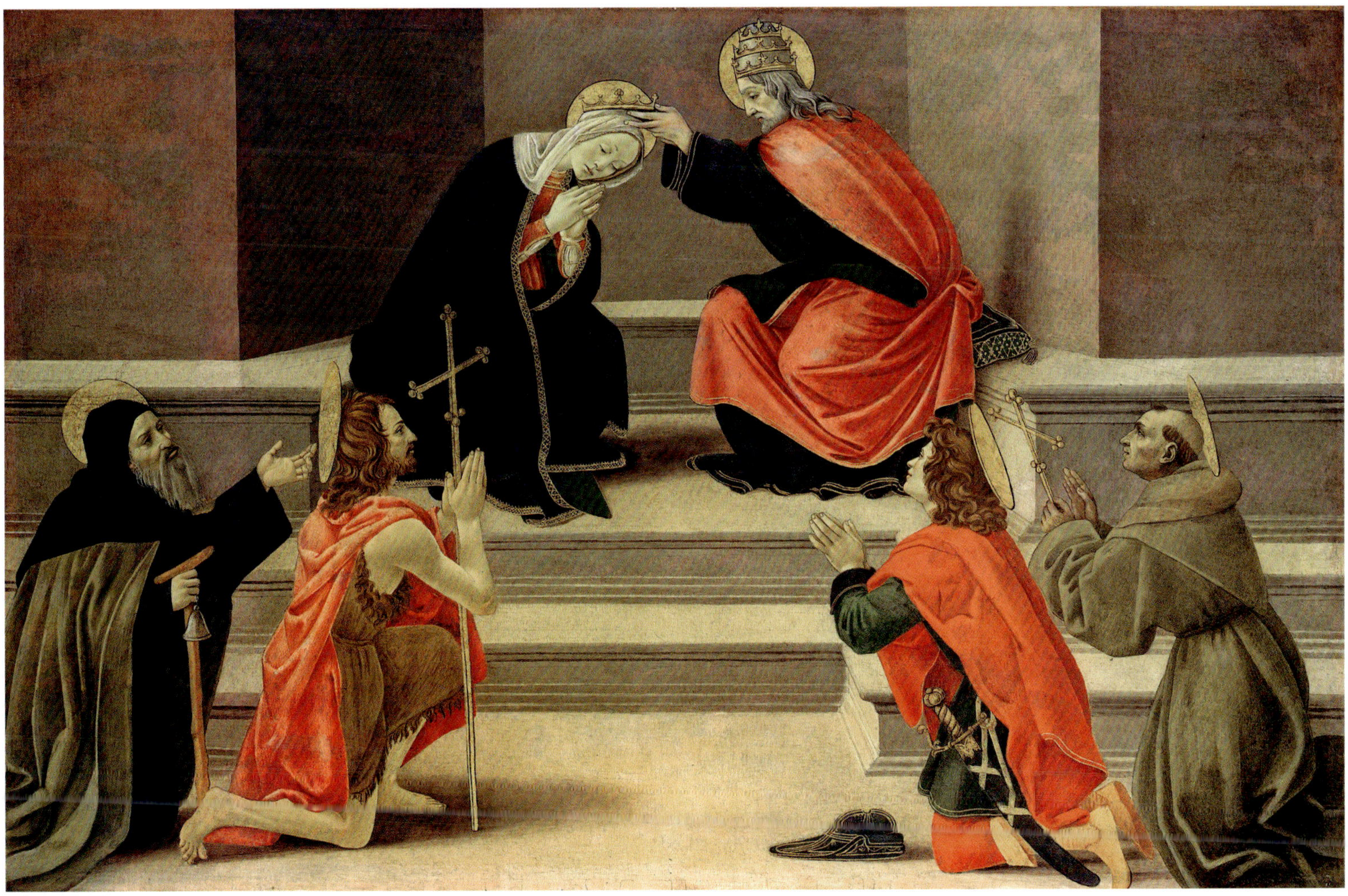

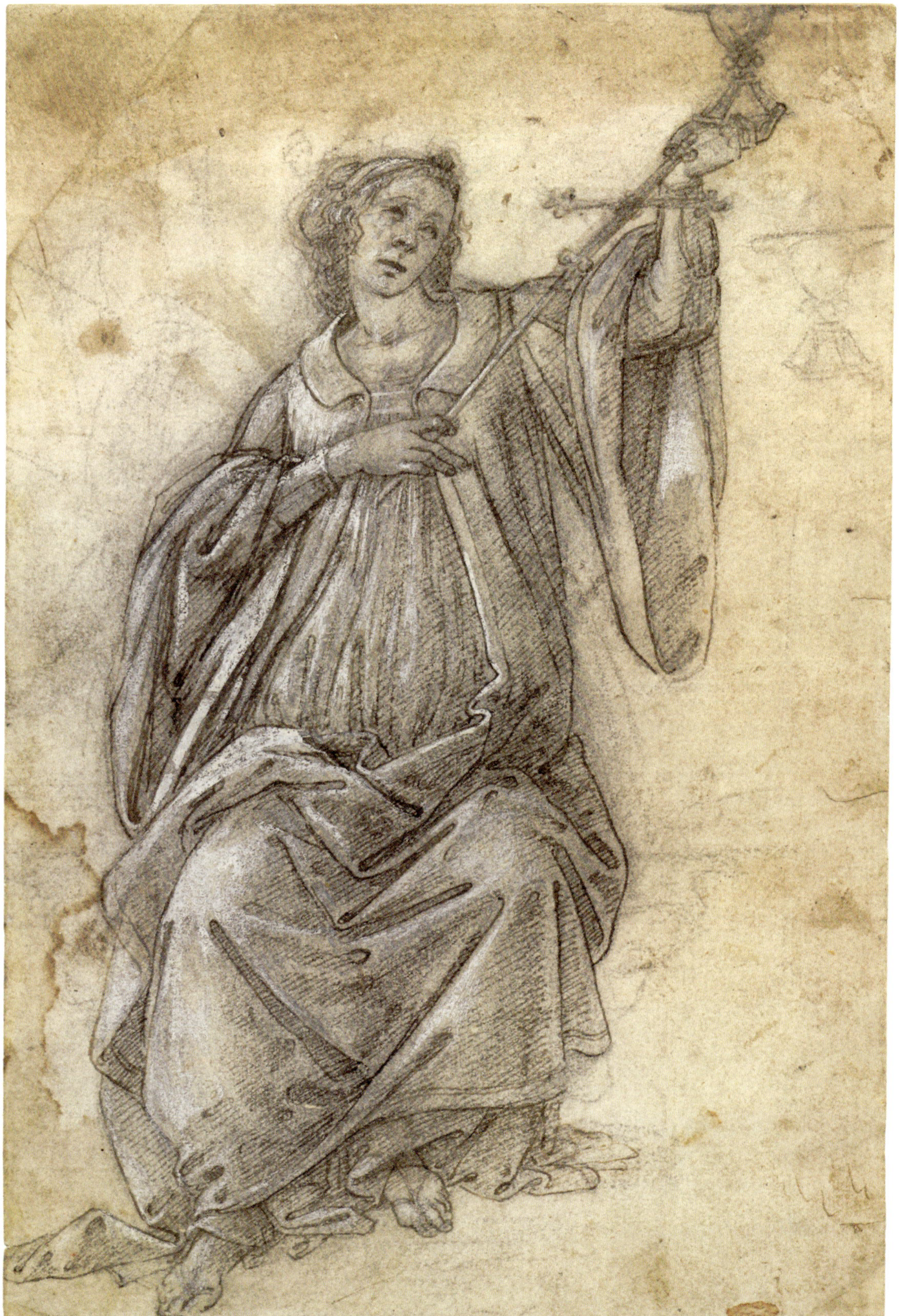

138

SANDRO BOTTICELLI
(c.1445–1510)
Allegorical Figure of Faith with a Cross and a Chalice, Paten and Host, c.1490–1500

Black chalk, pen and brown ink, wash,
heightened with lead white on paper, 25 × 16.5 cm
The British Museum, London (1895,0915.448)

This drawing shows an allegorical representation of Faith holding a cross and a chalice, paten and host, all consecrated for the celebration of the Eucharist, the sacrifice of Christ for humankind. It was acquired by John Charles Robinson who identified it as an autograph work by Botticelli, a view supported by most subsequent authors.

In comparison with the ethereal *Allegory of Abundance or Autumn* (cat. 165), the present drawing appears angular and heavily shaded. However the reworking and many pentimenti show it is an original idea based on Botticelli's early allegory of Fortitude of around 1470 in the Uffizi. The apocalyptic preaching of Savonarola was allegedly an influence on Botticelli's late style (see also cat. 132).

The purpose of this drawing is unclear, but it may have belonged to a series of the three theological virtues (with Hope and Charity) often associated with the four secular cardinal virtues (Temperance, Justice, Prudence and Courage). AD

PROVENANCE

Sir John Charles Robinson; sold to John Malcolm of Poltalloch in 1860; acquired from Col. John Wingfield Malcolm, 1895

LITERATURE

Robinson 1876, p. 9, no. 15; Berenson 1938, vol. 3, p. 192, no. 578; Popham and Pouncey 1950, vol. 1, pp. 16–17, no. 25, vol. 2, pl. XXII (with previous literature); Grassi 1956, p. 63, Grassi [1961], no. 59; Lightbown 1978, vol. 2, p. 164, no. D8; Chapman in Berlin, London and Rome 2000–1, p. 370, no. 21; Faietti in London and Florence 2010–11, pp. 178–9, no. 38

139

WORKSHOP OF
SANDRO BOTTICELLI,
(C.1445–1510)

Noli me tangere, after 1490

Tempera on poplar, 24 × 92 cm
Musée du Petit Palais, Avignon (M. I. 544)

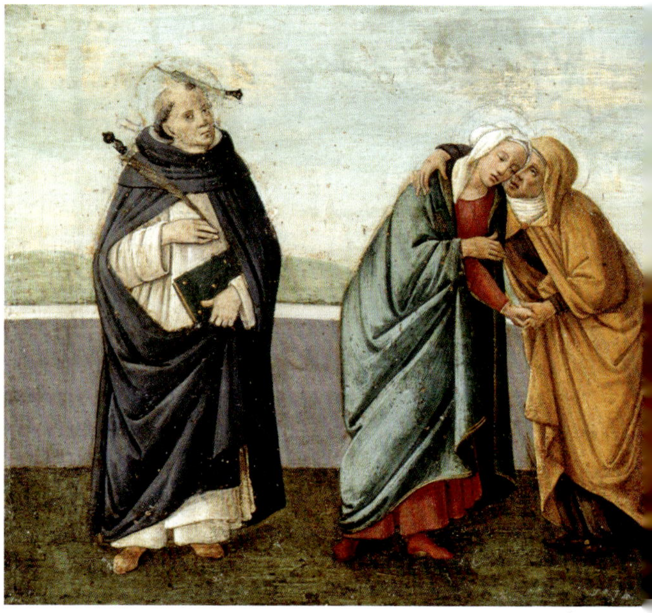

Between two saints – Peter Martyr to the left and Onuphrius to the right – this composition depicts three scenes from the New Testament and the lives of the saints: the Visitation; Jesus appearing to Mary Magdalene (with the words 'noli me tangere'), accompanied by a praying figure (often identified as King David); and the meeting between Saints Francis and Dominic, founders of the principal mendicant orders. Despite their narrative autonomy, the five constituent parts are all situated in the same continuous broad landscape. This unusual panel, probably intended as a predella – the lower element of a larger altarpiece – is today generally considered a late Botticelli, either a workshop piece or autograph (the latter suggested orally by E. Fahy). At the time of its first documented mention it was still attributed to Ghirlandaio: François-Louis-Esprit Dubois, commissioner-general of the police in French-occupied Tuscany from 1809 to 1811, acquired it during his tenure there, and in 1813 sold it on the Parisian market. It was probably first identified as a Botticelli while in the Campana collection (see cat. 108), whose acquisition proved so significant for France. This was where Gustave Moreau saw the painting, and drew the figures of Saints Onuphrius and Peter Martyr, as well as a snippet of the background landscape (see cat. 86). RR

PROVENANCE

By 1813, François-Louis-Esprit Dubois in Florence and Paris; his sale 17–18 March 1813 (lot 17), as by Ghirlandaio; 1841–5, Fesch Collection, Paris and Rome; 1858, Campana collection, Rome; 1862, Musée Napoléon III, Paris; 1863, Musée du Louvre, Paris; 1976, transferred to Avignon

LITERATURE

Garzell Delaroche 1813, p. 10, no. 17; Museo Campana 1858, p. 28, no. 229; Sécherre 2003, pp. 22, 26; Laclotte and Moench 2005, p. 82, no. 53

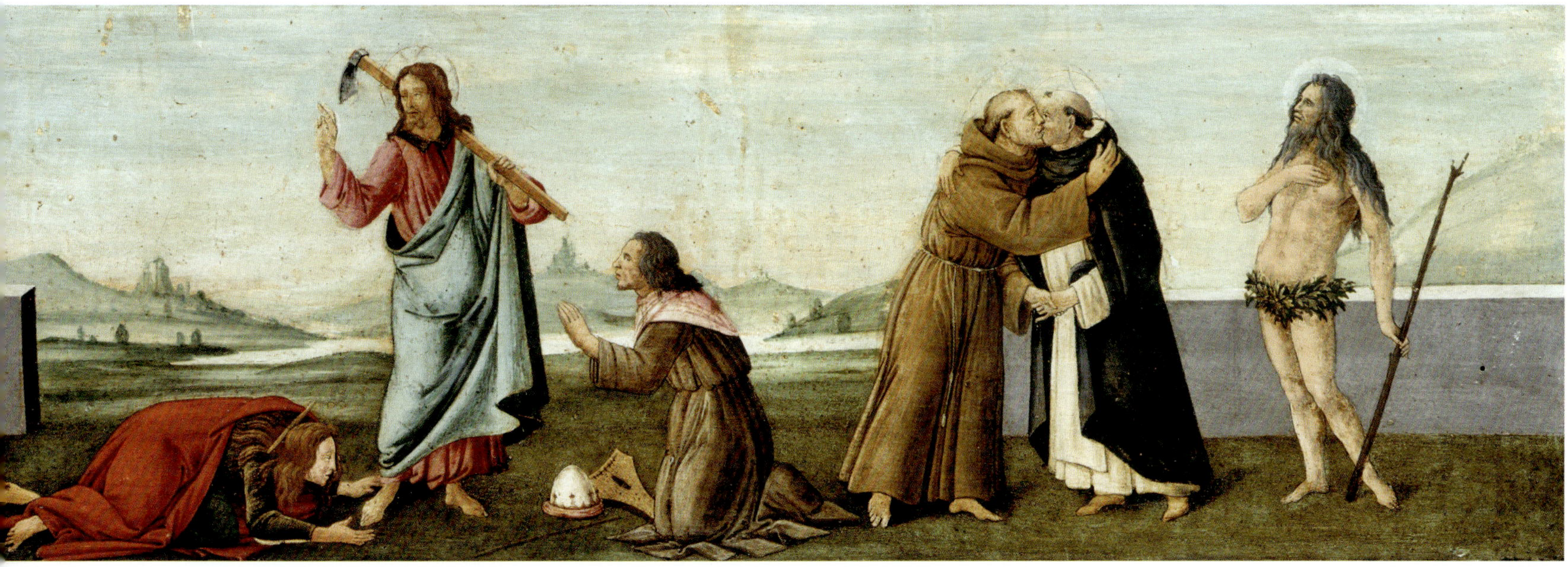

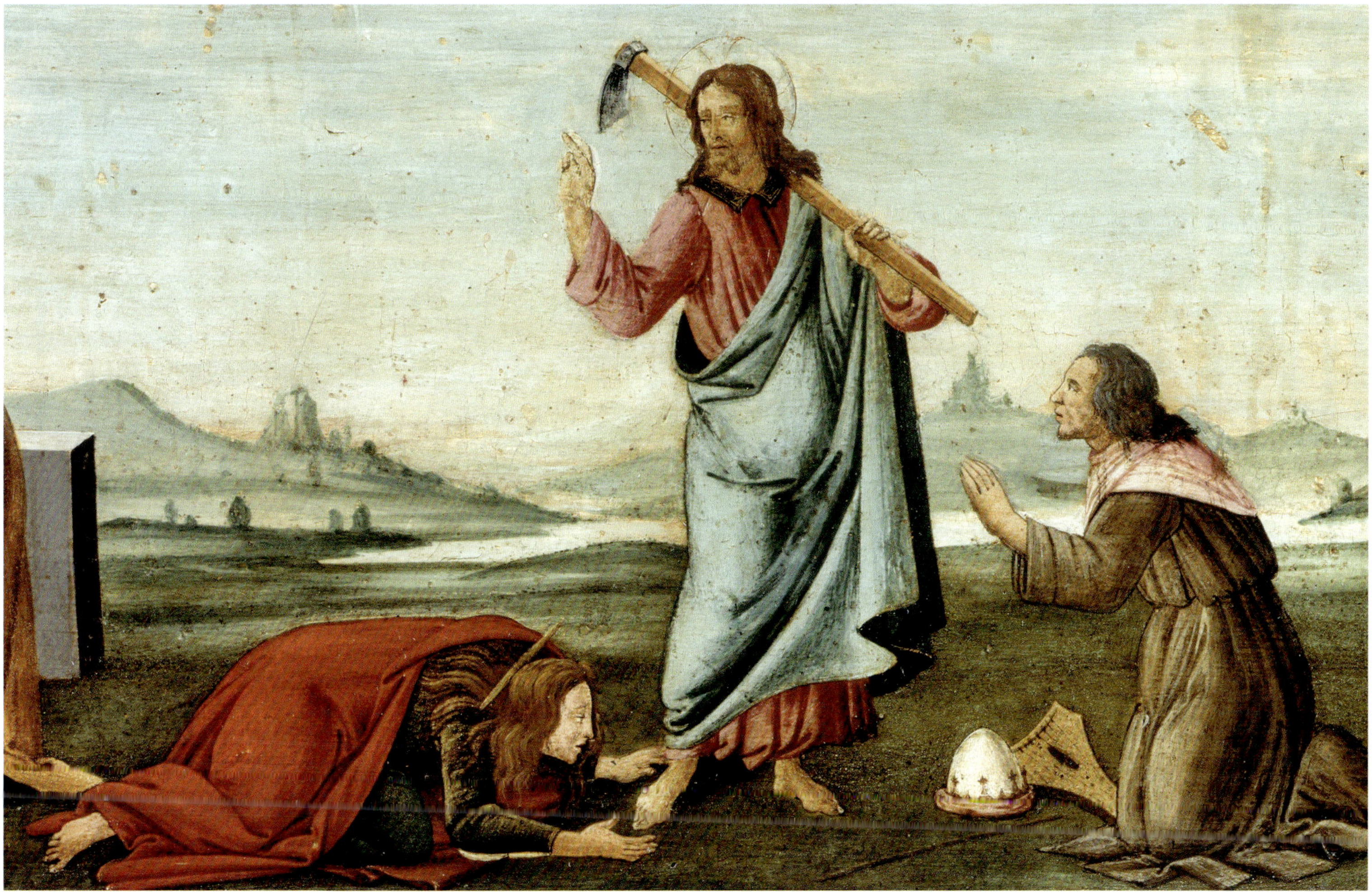

140, 141, 142

SANDRO BOTTICELLI
(c.1445–1510)

The Angel of the Annunciation, and the Virgin Annunciate, c.1490–5

Tempera on canvas, transferred from wood, 45 × 13 cm
Pushkin Museum, Moscow (Ж-1612)

St Jerome in Penitence, c.1490–5

Tempera on canvas, transferred from wood, 44.5 × 26 cm
Hermitage, St Petersburg (ГЭ 4076)

St Dominic Preaching, c.1490–5

Tempera on canvas, transferred from wood, 44.5 × 26 cm
Hermitage, St Petersburg (ГЭ 4077)

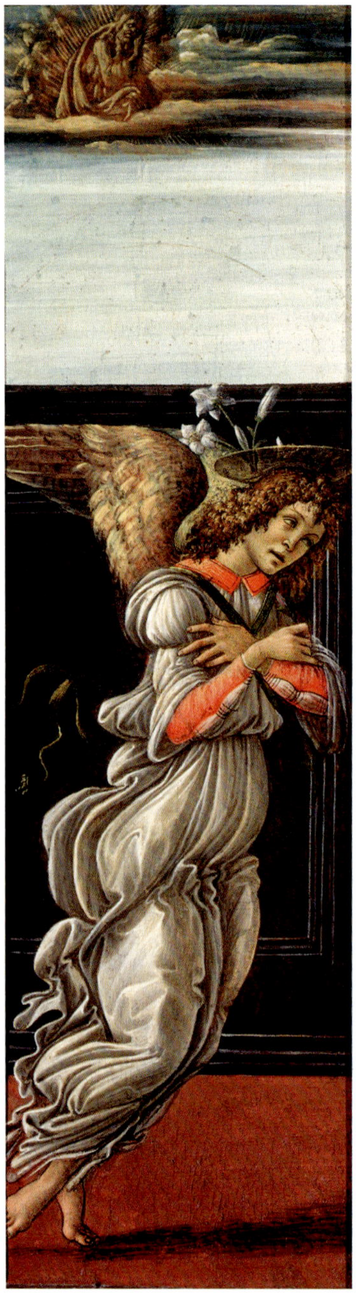

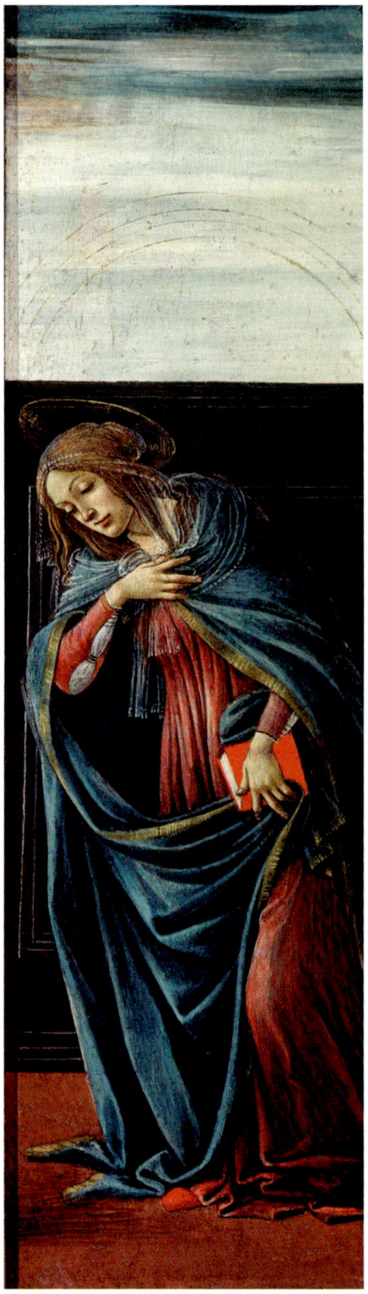

These four images are from the same group. The combined size of the two Annuncation figures is equivalent to one of the two saints, and the grisaille figure of God the Father above the Angel Gabriel closely resembles that of the Judging Christ at the top left of *St Dominic Preaching*. The transfer from panel to canvas has further obscured the original relationship between the works. Their first function – whether as part of a single ensemble or possibly as wings to a *Last Judgement* by Fra Angelico – has been hotly debated, and they have been variously attributed to Botticelli and/or his workshop. The attitude of the Dominican saint, who is gesturing towards an apparition of the Judging Christ, is unusual, and Lazareff interpreted it as a disguised portrait of Savonarola.

All four pictures were first published as late works by Botticelli by Harck in 1896, while in the collection of Count Stroganov. They had probably been acquired by his ancestor Sergei Grigorievitch Stroganov in 1842, the date of a letter by a painter in his service reporting that the count had 'acquired an Annunciation for a lot of money. The praying St Jerome has a very lovely face, but I don't like it as much.' A soldier, the count was an educational reformer and a passionate collector of icons who promoted research into Scythian antiquities and in 1825 founded the first academy of art in Moscow. SH

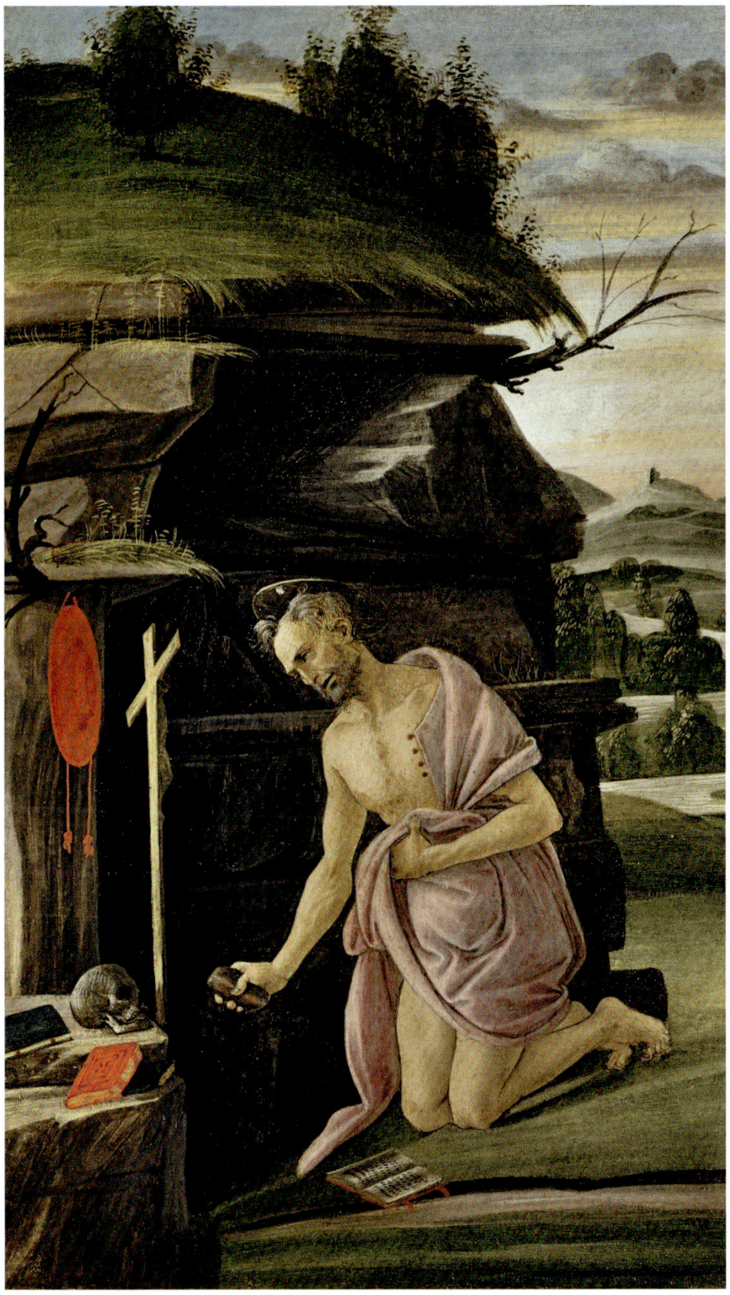

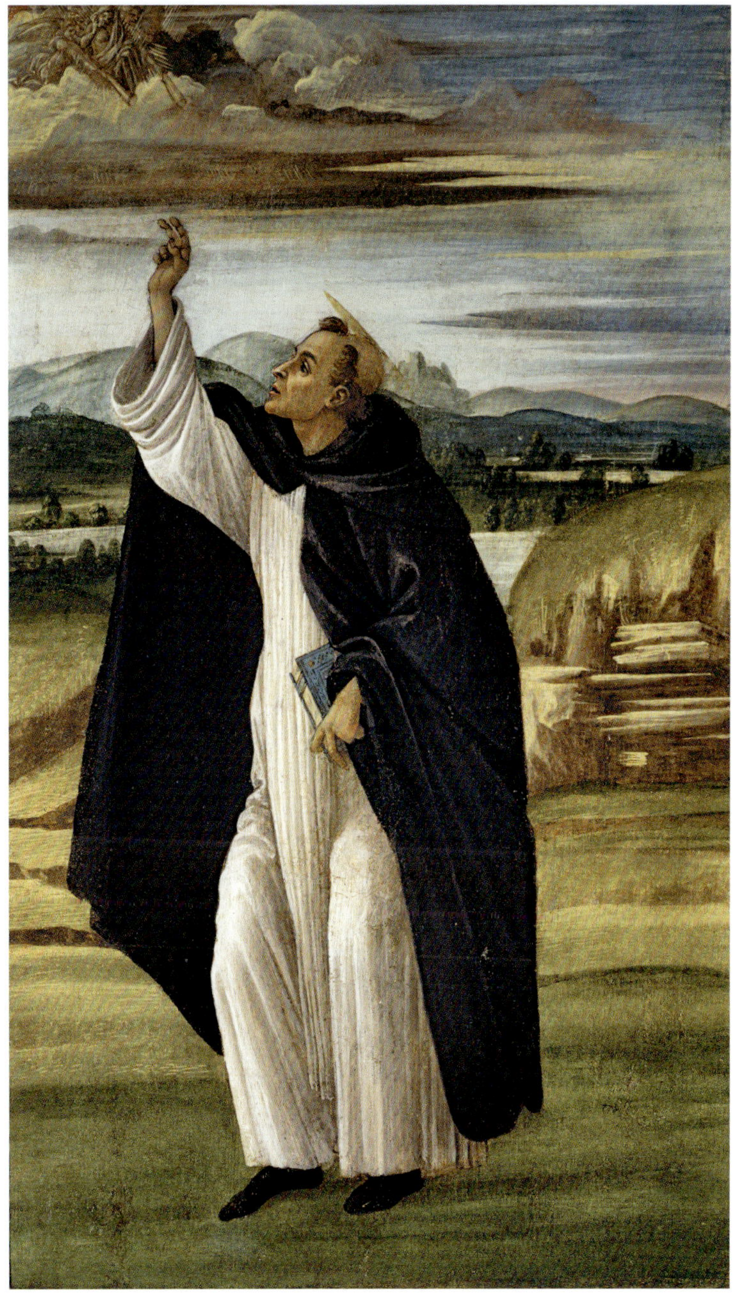

PROVENANCE

CAT. 140 1928, transferred to the Pushkin Museum, Moscow

CATS 141, 142 1842, collection of Sergei Grigorievitch Stroganov; 1896, Palais Stroganov, St Petersburg; 1922, Hermitage, St Petersburg

LITERATURE

Harck 1896, p. 431; Lazareff 1924; Lightbown 1978, vol. 2, pp. 95–6, nos B84 and B85; Marková 2002, pp. 99–102, nos 46 and 47; Florence 2004, p. 276; Zöllner 2005, p. 244–5, no. 64; Kustodieva 2011, p. 187, nos 52 and 53

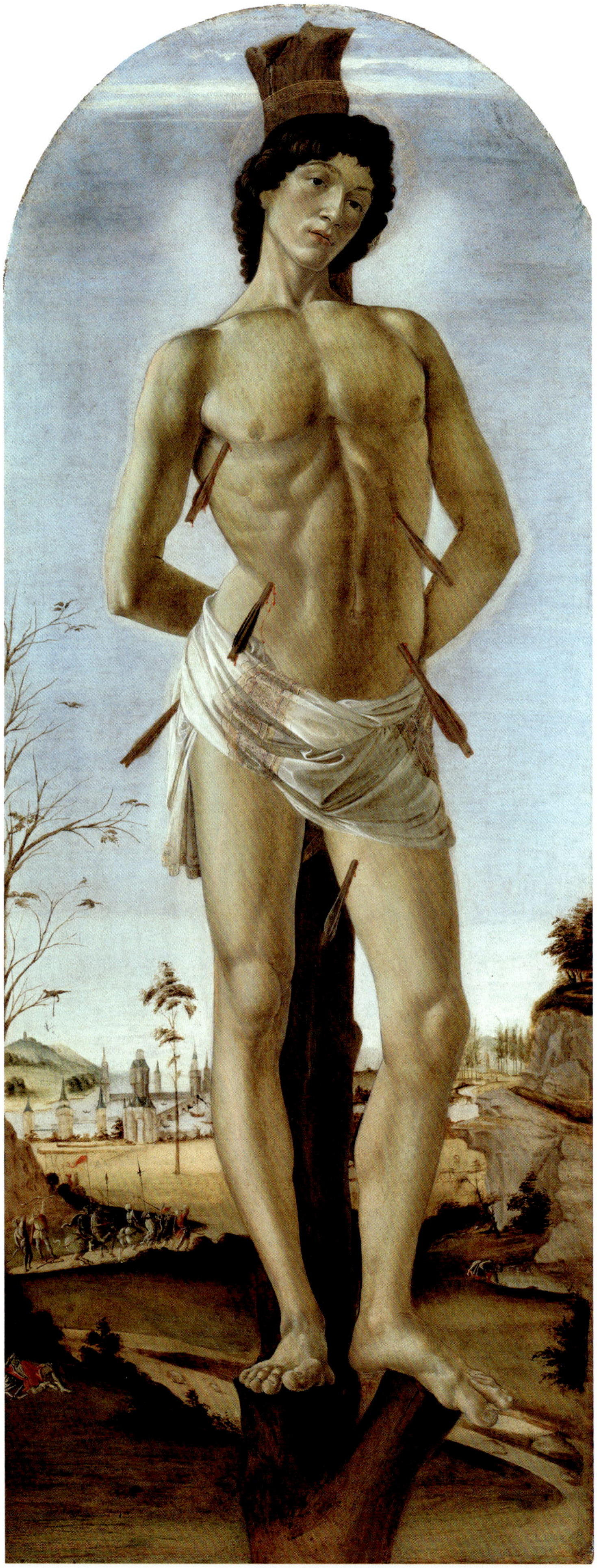

143

SANDRO BOTTICELLI (c.1445–1510)

St Sebastian, 1474

Tempera on wood, 195 × 75 cm
Gemäldegalerie, Staatliche Museen zu Berlin (1128)

BERLIN ONLY

The Roman captain Sebastian underwent a double martyrdom. After having been condemned to death and shot with arrows he was nursed back to health, before being clubbed to death. This strange fate creates a theological parallel with the resurrection of Christ. Botticelli has suggested the saint's survival of his execution by depicting him in perfect physical condition, gazing directly at the viewer. This combination of Christian history with a figure considered typical of antiquity fascinated not only fifteenth-century viewers, but also artists and authors of the *fin de siècle* and the twentieth century (Gabriele D'Annunzio and Rainer Maria Rilke, for instance), and eventually the saint even became stylized as an icon of gay art. The painting was attributed to Antonio del Pollaiuolo when it was acquired for Berlin, remaining so until 1860. After its identification as a Botticelli, Hermann Ulmann proposed that it was the altarpiece that had been in Santa Maria Maggiore in Florence in the sixteenth century.

RR

PROVENANCE

Edward Solly; acquired as part of his collection in 1821

LITERATURE

Waagen 1830, p. 54, no. I.171; Ulmann 1893, pp. 46–8; Lightbown 1978, vol. 2, pp. 27–8, no. B14; Zöllner 2005, p. 195, no. 19

144, 145, 146

BACCIO BALDINI (?1436–1487)
perhaps after Botticelli

Page from the Canto Primo of Dante's 'Divine Comedy', c.1481

Letterpress and engraving, 38 × 22.8 cm
The British Museum, London (1845,0825.440)

The City of Dis and the Punishments of Heresy, c.1481

Engraving, 9.9 × 17.4 cm
The British Museum, London (1845,0825.453)

The Banks of Phlegethon and the Punishments of Sodomy, c.1481

Engraving, 9.6 × 17.2 cm
The British Museum, London (1845,0825.459)

From Giorgio Vasari until William Roscoe at the start of the nineteenth century, Botticelli was primarily remembered as an illustrator of Dante's *Divine Comedy*. According to Vasari this enterprise brought 'infinite disorder to his life' and made him 'neglect his work'. Vasari probably knew the engravings of the printed edition of the *Divine Comedy* published in Florence in 1481 by Niccolò di Lorenzo della Magna with a commentary by Cristoforo Landino, a professor at the Studio (Florence University), and an important member of the Medici circle, but did not connect them directly with Botticelli.

The genesis of these illustrations is unclear: they bear some resemblance to the drawings of the same subject now in the Vatican and Berlin (see cats 147–53), but often reverse those compositions and focus on particular details. The engravings had already been linked with Botticelli before the related drawings reappeared, but their relationship remains unclear and it is not certain that Botticelli designed the engravings.

This was the first edition of Dante's poem to be illustrated with engravings. As the text was printed in raised type and the illustrations from incised metal plates (intaglio), each had to be printed separately, either by running the sheet through two presses or by printing the engravings on separate sheets and pasting them in later. This complicated procedure doubtless accounts for the variable and incomplete number of illustrations in the surviving copies of the 1481 edition. The printer left space for 96 illustrations but only 19 were made and most copies of the book do not include all of them.

The attribution of the engravings to Baccio Baldini occurred in the late eighteenth century when he was rediscovered by critics who noticed that the early accounts of Vasari and the art historian and biographer Filippo Baldinucci stated that Baldini had little skill in drawing and therefore often used to turn to Botticelli for assistance with his engravings. Although neither of these early authorities specifically mentions the Dante engravings, it was inferred that Baldini had executed them. In the late nineteenth century a number of scholars questioned the attribution to Baldini of a large proportion of surviving early Florentine engravings – Aby Warburg referred to him as the 'mythical Baldini' – and it is still subject to debate. AD

PROVENANCE

Heineken 1768, vol. 1, p. 28; Bartsch 1803, XIII.175.37; Hind 1938–48, vol. 1, p. 100; Clark 1976, p. 9; Keller 2000–1, p. 326, fig. 66

CANTO PRIMO DELLA PRIMA CANTICA O VERO COMEDIA DEL DIVINO POETA FIORENTINO DANTHE ALEGHIERI : CAPITOLO PRIMO :

N
EL
ME
ZO
DEL
CA
MI
NO
DI
NO
S T
RA
VI
TA

Mi ritrouai peruna ſelua obſcura
che la diricta uia era ſmarrita
Et quanto adire quale era e/ coſa dura
eſta ſelua ſeluaggia et aſpra et forte
che nel penſier rinuoua lapaura
Tanto era amara che pocho e piu morte
ma per tractar del ben chio ui trouai
diro dellaltre coſe chio uho ſcorte
I non ſo ben ridire chomio uentrai
tantera pien diſonno inſu quel puncto
che lauerace uia abbandonai
Ma poi chio fui appie dun colle giunto
la oue terminaua quella ualle
che mhauea dipaur elcor compuncto
Guardai inalto et uidi leſue ſpalle
coperte gia deraggi delpianeta
che mena dricto altrui per ogni calle
Allhor fu lapaura un pocho queta
che nellago del chuor mera durata
lanocte chio paſſai con tanta pieta

h abbiamo narrato non ſolamente lauita del poeta et eltitolo dellibro et che coſa ſia po eta Ma etiam quãto ſia uetuſta et anticha quãto nobile et uaria quanto utile et ioconda tal doc trina. Quanto ſia efficace a muouere lhumane mẽti; et quãto dilecti ogni liberale ĩgegno. Ne giudicammo da tacere quanto in ſi diuina diſci plina ſia ſtata la excellentia dello ingegno del noſtro poeta. Inche ſiſono ſtato piu brieue che forſe non ſi conuerebbe; conſideri chi legge che lanumeroſa et quaſi infinita copia dellecoſe del le quali e neceſſario tractare miſſorza non uolẽ do chel uolume creſca ſopra modo; a inculcare et inuiluppare piutoſto che explicare: et diſtẽ dere moltecoſe et maxime quelle lequali quãdo ben taceſſi non pero ne reſtera obſcura la expo ſitione del teſto. Verremo adunque aquella. Ma perche ſtimo non eſſer lectore alcuno ne di ſi baſſo ingegno; ne di ſi pocho giudicio: che ha uendo inteſo; quanto ſia et laprofondita et ua rieta della doctrina; et la excellentia et diuinita dello ingegno delnoſtro toſcano; et fiorentino poeta; non ſi perſuada che queſto principio delprimo canto debba per ſublimita et grande za eſſer pari alla ſtupenda doctrina dellechoſe che ſeguitano: pero con ogni induſtria in ueſti gheremo che allegoricho ſenſo arechi ſeco que ſto mezo delcamino: et che coſa ſia ſelua Diche ueggio non piccola differentia eſſere ſtata tra glinterpreti et expoſitori diqueſta cantica. Im pero che alchuni dicono: che il mezo della uita humana e el ſonno moſſi; credo dalla ſententia dariſtotele dicendo lui nellethica neſſuna diffe rentia eſſere tra felici; et miſeri nella meta della uita per che lenocti che ſono lameta del tempo cinducono ſonno: et daquello naſce che ne bene nemale ſentir poſſiamo. Ilperche uogliono que ſti: che el poeta pongha el mezo della uita per la nocte; et lanocte pelſonno; ad notare che queſto poema non ſia altro che una uiſione che gliap parue dormẽdo per laquale hebbe cognitõe del le coſe dallui deſcripte ĩ queſte tre comedie. Di cono adũque che lui imita Ioanni euangeliſta el quale dormẽdo ſopra elpecto di chriſto redemptore hebbe uiſione delle choſe celeſte; ouueramẽte ponghi lanocte dimoſtrando lui hauere cominciato elſuo poema dinocte nella quale raccoglẽdoſi lanimo inſemedeſimo et abſoluendoſi et liberandoſi da ogni cura meglo intenda. Ma benche tale ſententia quadri al poeta: nientedimeno leparole non la dimoſtrono ſenon cõ tanto obſcura ambi guita: che non pare degna della elegantia ditanto poeta. Prima perche nonſeguita che benche nelle reuolutioni deltempo tanto ſpatio occupin lenocti quanto e di; perqueſto dicendo io ſcripſi dinoc te ſintenda io ſcripſi nel mezo della mia eta; perche et nel principio et nelfine della eta humana ſo no lenocti chome nel mezo et ſimilmente e di. Il perche per lamedeſima ragione ſi potrebbe fare tale interpretatione pel di chome per lanocte. Altridicono che uolle pelmezo del camino intende re che nelmezo delleta dette principio alſuo poema. Ma non e unamedſima opinione deltermine della noſtra eta; per che diuerſi ſcriptori diuerſamente ſentono. Ariſtotile nel ſuo de republica

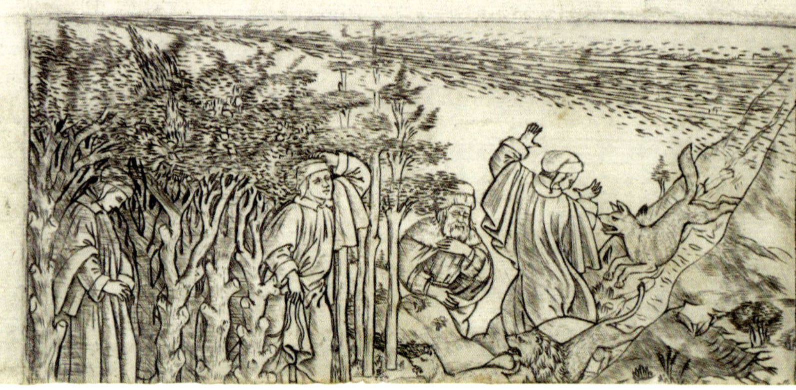

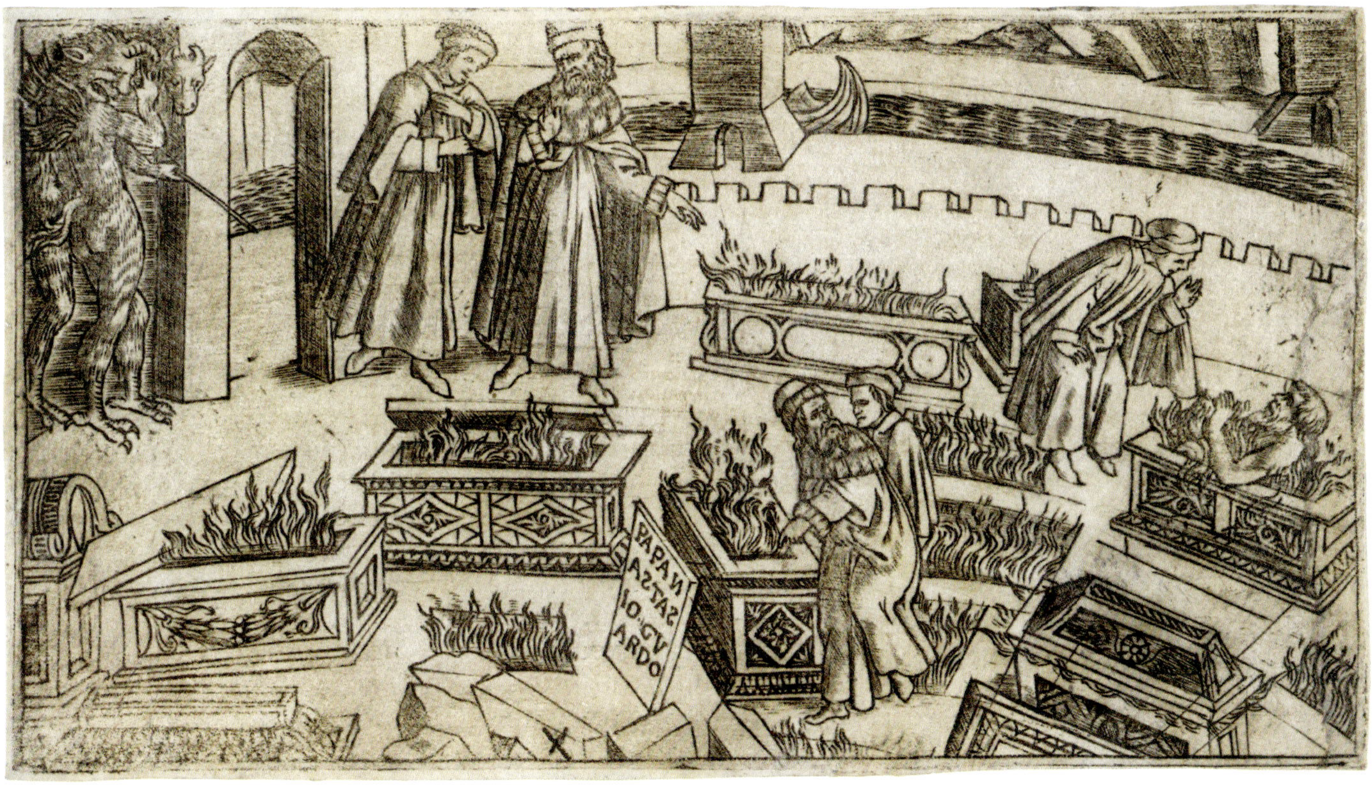
PAPA N
ASTAS
IO.GV
ARDO

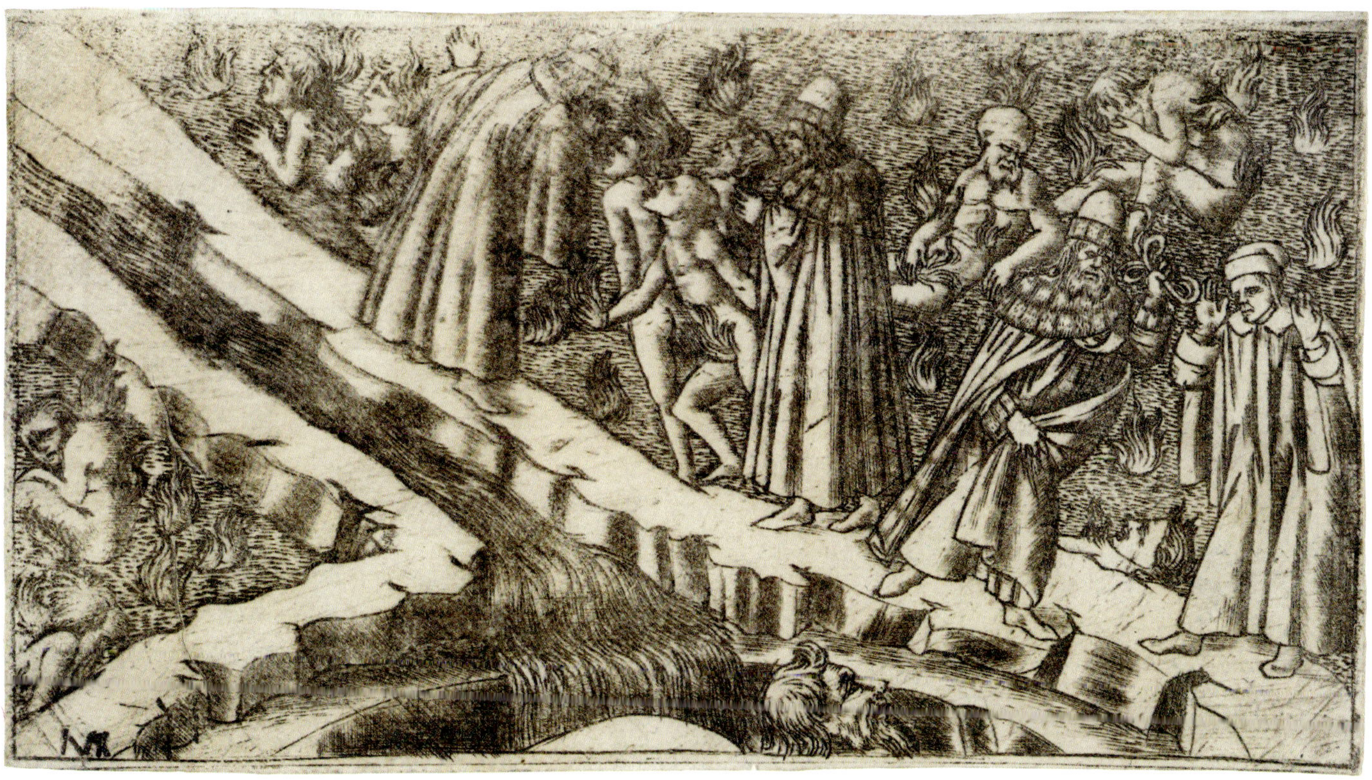

147

SANDRO BOTTICELLI (c.1445–1510)

Fifth Circle, The Furies on the Tower – Help from a Divine Messenger – Entry into the city of Dis (The Divine Comedy, Inferno, canto IX), c.1481–8

Pen and brown ink over metalpoint on vellum, 32.5 × 47.5 cm
Biblioteca Apostolica Vaticana, Vatican City (COD. REG. LAT. 1896, fol. 97v)
LONDON ONLY

This drawing is one of 92 surviving illustrations to Dante's *Divine Comedy*, now divided between the Kupferstichkabinett, Staatliche Museen zu Berlin and the Vatican Library. The text is a long poem relating the journey of its author through the three realms of the afterlife: Hell, Purgatory and Paradise. Hell is imagined as nine descending circles where the souls are punished in ways that either contrast with or resemble the sin of which they are guilty.

The present sheet depicts Dante, accompanied by his guide, the Latin poet Virgil, arriving at and entering the gates of the city of Dis in the fifth circle of Hell. Dante's attention is drawn to the threatening three furies (Alecto, Tisiphone and Megaera) with the head of Medusa on the battlements. An angelic messenger appears and lets them into the city unharmed where they encounter a cemetery full of burning graves containing the souls of heretics.

The earliest mention of these illustrations occurs in a compilation of artists' lives of around 1540 by the so-called Anonimo Magliabechiano, which states that the drawings were made for Lorenzo di Pierfrancesco de' Medici, a younger cousin of Lorenzo the Magnificent and one of Botticelli's most important patrons, who also commissioned *Primavera*, *Birth of Venus* and *Pallas and the Centaur* (see cat. 164). AD

PROVENANCE
Lorenzo di Pierfrancesco de' Medici; Paris, Alexandre Pétau, by 1632; Rome, Queen Christina of Sweden by 1658; Cardinal Ottoboni, future Pope Alexander VIII, in 1689, by whom given to the Biblioteca Apostolica

LITERATURE
Lightbown 1978, vol. 2, p. 174, no. E10 (with previous bibliography); Parronchi 1985, pp. 6–52; Dreyer 1986, vol. 2, pp. 72–3; Berlin, Rome and London 2000–1, pp. 56–7

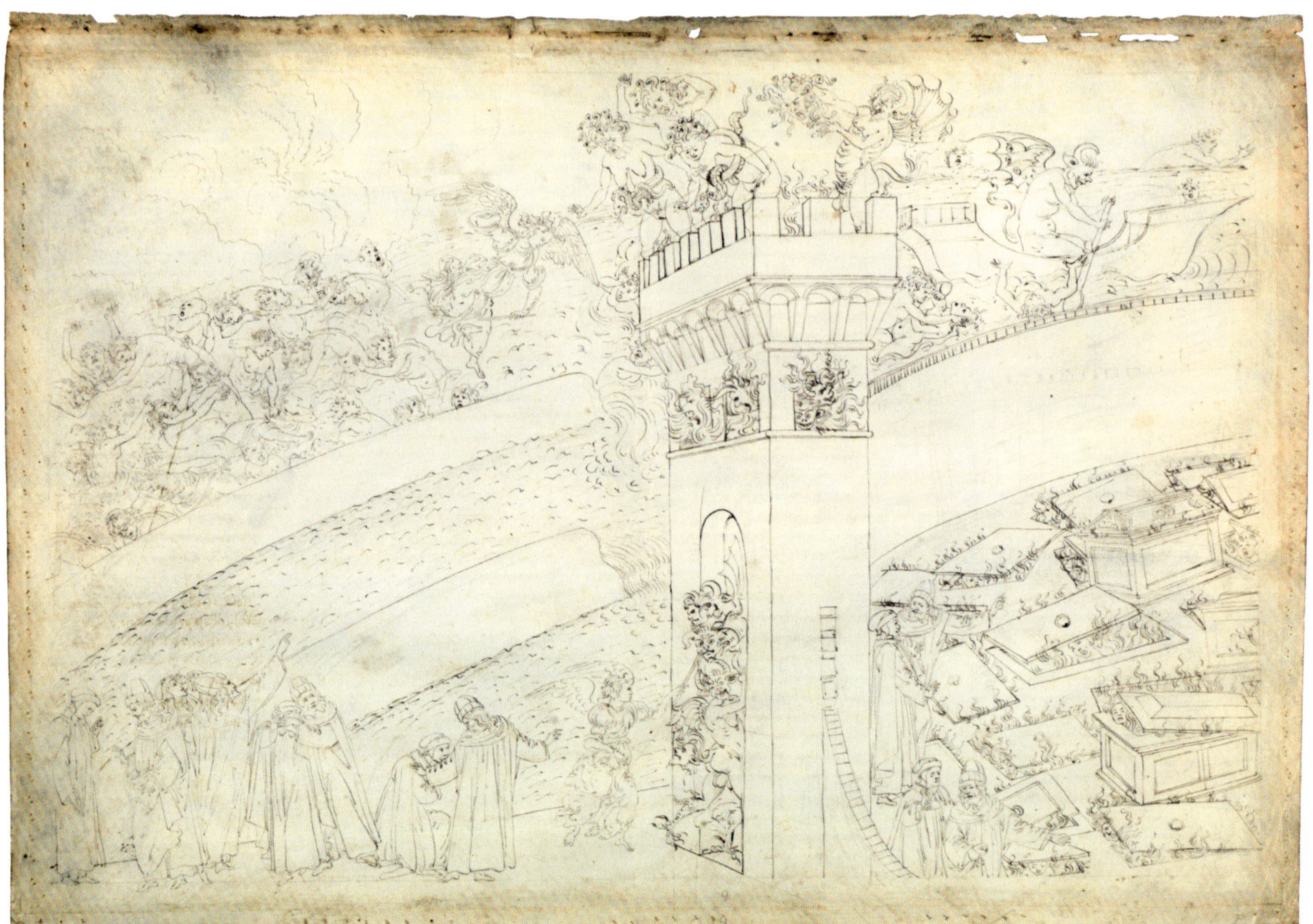

148

SANDRO BOTTICELLI (c.1445–1510)

Seventh Circle, Second Round. The Wood of Thorns: Punishment of Suicides and Profligates – Encounter with Pier della Vigne (The Divine Comedy, Inferno, canto XIII), c.1481–8

Pen and brown ink over metalpoint on vellum, 32.5 × 47.5 cm
Biblioteca Apostolica Vaticana, Vatican City (COD. REG. LAT. 1896, fol. 102r)
LONDON ONLY

In a dense mass of thorny branches, Dante and Virgil are depicted penetrating deep into the seventh circle of Hell. Along the banks of the river of blood moan the souls of suicides, who have been turned into bushes. The harpies, female monsters in the form of a bird with a human head, inhabit the wood and feed on them while other naked souls are chased by hounds and torn into pieces.

Botticelli's cycle was probably executed as an autonomous pictorial narrative, but its precise purpose has caused debate ever since its rediscovery in the late seventeenth century. Most sheets are pen and ink drawings at various stages of completion while only a few were coloured, perhaps by a later hand as happened with Botticelli's designs on another occasion (see under cats 104, 105).

Lines were incised to guide the scribe, Niccolò Mangona, whose text of Dante's verses shows through the verso of the sheet. The text of illuminated manuscripts was usually written prior to the addition of illustration, but in this case it is uncertain whether that procedure was followed. AD

PROVENANCE
Lorenzo di Pierfrancesco de' Medici; Paris, Alexandre Pétau, by 1632; Rome, Queen Christina of Sweden by 1658; Cardinal Ottoboni, future Pope Alexander VIII, in 1689, by whom given to the Biblioteca Apostolica

LITERATURE
Lightbown 1978, vol. 2, p. 174, no. E14 (with previous bibliography); Parronchi 1985, pp. 6–52; Dreyer 1986, vol. 2, pp. 75–6; Berlin, Rome and London 2000–1, pp. 68–9

149

SANDRO BOTTICELLI
(c.1445–1510)

Seventh Circle, Third Round. The Desert of the Burning Sands: the Souls of those who Committed Violence against the Divine Order, Punishment of Sodomites – Encounter with Three Florentine Noblemen and with Geryon (The Divine Comedy, Inferno, canto XVI), c.1481–8

Pen and brown ink over metalpoint on vellum, 32.5 × 47.5 cm
Biblioteca Apostolica Vaticana, Vatican City (COD. REG. LAT. 1896, fol. 98v)
LONDON ONLY

This sheet illustrates the well-known episode of the burning sands where the souls of sodomites are punished for their violence against the divine order. Dante included in his text a number of famous Florentines in order to denounce the corruption and political machinations that afflicted his native city.

The wide horizontal format of these sheets allowed Botticelli to depict a sequence of consecutive events within a single unified composition. Such continuous narrative had been typical of earlier paintings but Botticelli used it to create a pictorial language and narrative style which have puzzled many scholars. The function of these drawings remains unclear; theories range from Lightbown's view that they were created for the artist's own use, to Alessandro Parronchi's hypothesis that they were studies for an unexecuted cycle of frescoes intended for the crossing of Florence Cathedral. Indeed, the viewpoint of the drawings may indicate that these compositions were designed to be seen from below. AD

PROVENANCE
Lorenzo di Pierfrancesco de' Medici; Paris, Alexandre Pétau, by 1632; Rome, Queen Christina of Sweden by 1658; Cardinal Ottoboni, future Pope Alexander VIII, in 1689, by whom given to the Biblioteca Apostolica

LITERATURE
Lightbown 1978, vol. 2, p. 175, no. E17 (with previous bibliography); Parronchi 1985, pp. 6–52; Dreyer 1986, vol. 2, pp. 77–8; Berlin, Rome and London 2000–1, pp. 78–9

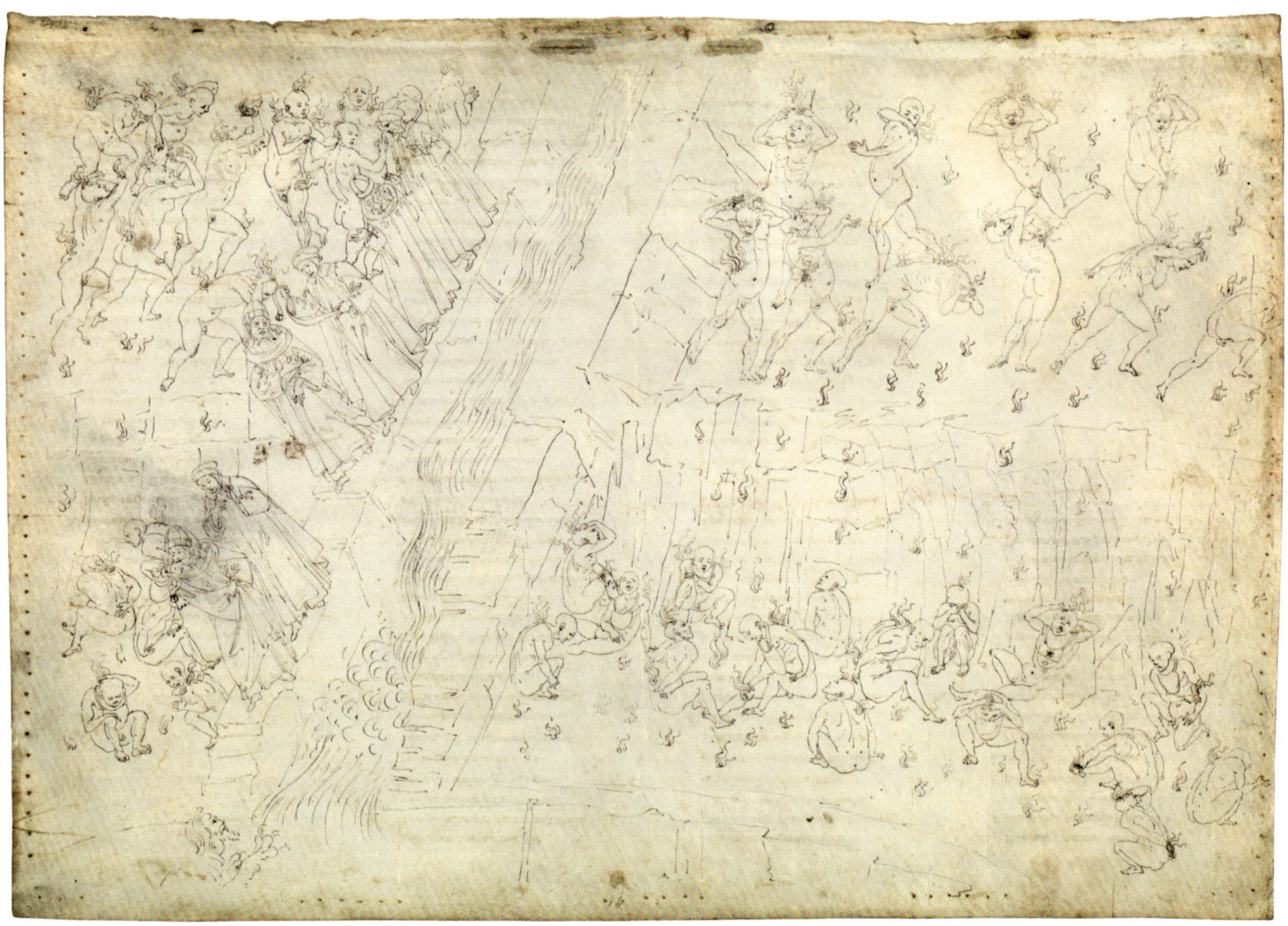

150

SANDRO BOTTICELLI
(c.1445–1510)

The Well of Giants in the Eighth Circle of Hell (The Divine Comedy, Inferno, canto XXXI), c.1481–88

Pen and brown ink over metalpoint on vellum, 32.5 × 47.5 cm
On the verso four columns of text from *Inferno*, canto XXX (pen and brown ink)
Kupferstichkabinett, Staatliche Museen zu Berlin

BERLIN ONLY

From a slightly elevated position, we gaze into the mouth of Hell, which – funnel-like – becomes increasingly narrow as it tapers downwards, ending in a closed circle. Dante and Virgil, wandering through the afterlife, encounter mythical giants standing up to their bellies in a deep well, yet still towering above the two poets. We recognize Nimrod, the horn-blower, who triggered the confusion of tongues, Ephialtes, his chains wound around him five times, as well as Briareus, Tityus, Typhoeus and Antaeus, who bends down to put Dante and Virgil on the icy ground of hell. The giants look like classical statues, betraying nothing of their raw natural power. Their faces, too, are characterized less by blind rage than by intense contemplation. Stylistically, they display distinctly Pollaiuolo-esque features, and are very similar to Botticelli's faces in the Bardi altarpiece (cat. 106) and the centaur in the painting of *Pallas and the Centaur* (cat. 164). DK

PROVENANCE
Giovanni Claudio Molino, Paris by 1803; Duke of Hamilton's collection (COD. HAM. 201) by 1819; acquired 1882

LITERATURE
Berlin, Rome and London 2000–1, p. 120

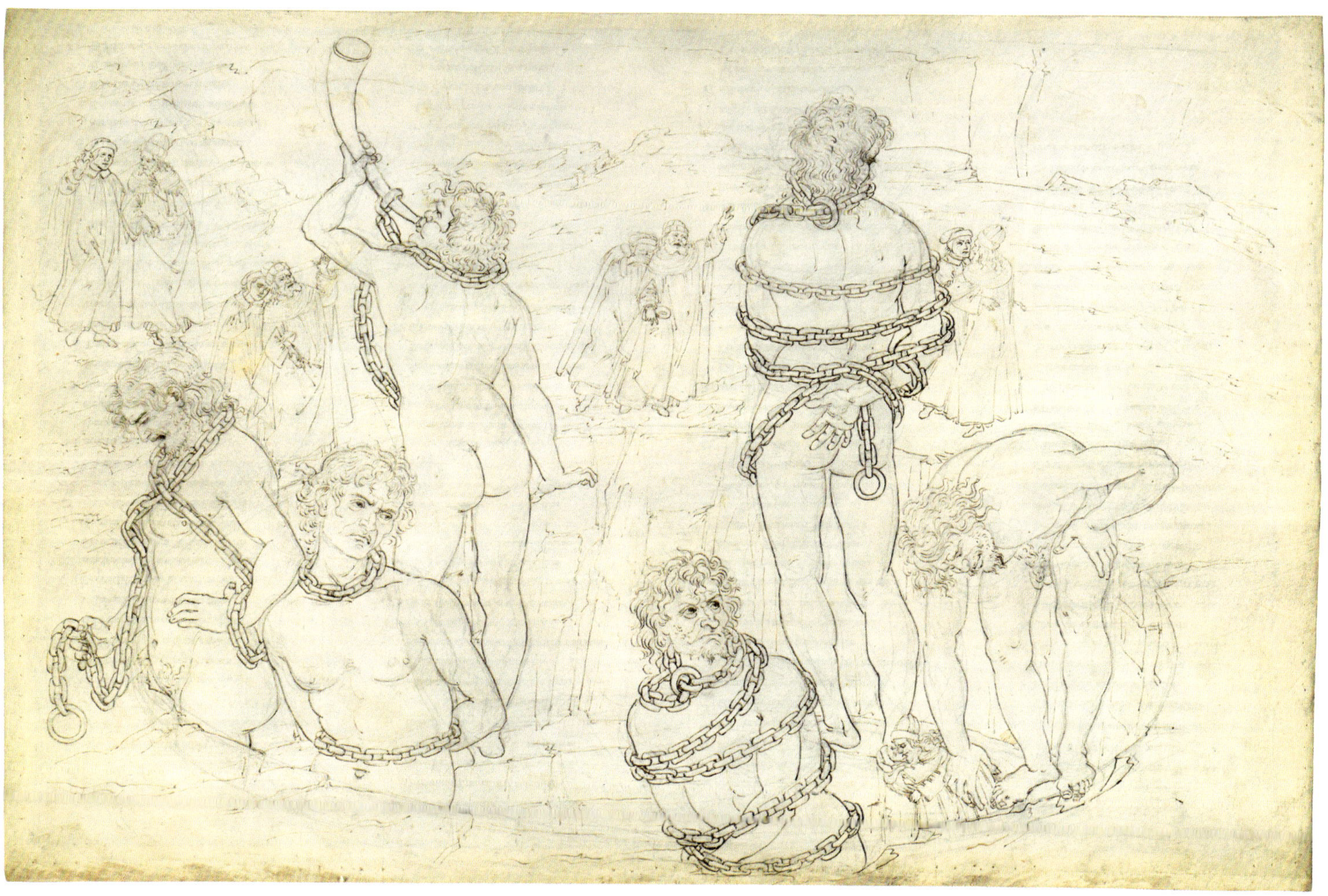

151

SANDRO BOTTICELLI
(c.1445–1510)

Arrival of Souls on the Island of the Mount of Purgatory, Dante Meets Casella (The Divine Comedy, Purgatory, canto II), c.1488–92

Pen and brown ink over metalpoint on vellum, 32.5 × 47.5 cm
On the verso four columns of text from *Purgatorio*, canto I (pen and brown ink)
Kupferstichkabinett, Staatliche Museen zu Berlin

BERLIN ONLY

After striding through hell, Dante and Virgil have arrived on the island of the Mount of Purgatory. We recognize them first, standing at the lower edge of the page and observing a radiant angel on the left guiding a ship without rudder or sail towards the shore, bringing happily chanting souls to the island. Among them is the composer Casella, who embraces his old friend Dante and starts to sing. The angel's boat on the left, his departure and the crowd of penitents surging to the right remain in a delicate metalpoint underdrawing, and have not been reworked with pen and ink. The extreme animation of this scene and the group depiction of the souls are in total contrast to the isolation and stasis of the eternal torments of hell. They augur the perfection of the souls' humanity, which will be brought about through their sufferings in Purgatory. DK

PROVENANCE

Giovanni Claudio Molino, Paris by 1803; Duke of Hamilton collection (COD. HAM. 201) by 1819; acquired 1882

LITERATURE

Berlin, Rome and London 2000–1, p. 138

152, 153

SANDRO BOTTICELLI (c.1445–1510)

Beatrice and the Virtues in the Earthly Paradise, Dante Bathes in the River Eunoe (The Divine Comedy, Purgatory, canto XXXIII), c.1488–92

Pen and brown ink over metalpoint on vellum, 32.5 × 47.5 cm
On the verso four columns of text from *Purgatorio*, canto XXXII (pen and brown ink)
Kupferstichkabinett, Staatliche Museen zu Berlin
LONDON ONLY

At the top of the Mount of Purgatory sit the Seven Virtues in the guise of women, lamenting the fate of the Church as Beatrice, like the Virgin Mary at the foot of the Cross, listens to them and sighs. At her behest the women move towards the right, with Dante, Statius and Matilda following them. Bare trees grow green and begin to bloom as they pass by. Their towering trunks and spreading branches are reminiscent of the setting of Botticelli's *Nastagio* paintings, and of the burgeoning, diverse vegetation in the Bardi altarpiece (cat. 106) and *Primavera*. The delicate yet firm lines are not used here to establish a sense of three-dimensionality, in keeping with the mystical visions of this place. The wanderers eventually reach a spring in the upper right-hand corner, and Matilda immerses Dante in the waters of the River Eunoe. He is renewed by this baptism, rejuvenated like a young plant with fresh leaves – 'pure and ready to ascend to the stars'. DK

PROVENANCE
Giovanni Claudio Molino, Paris by 1803; Duke of Hamilton collection (COD. HAM. 201) by 1819; acquired 1882

LITERATURE
Berlin, Rome and London 2000–1, p. 214

Dante Sees God as a Brightly Shining Point of Light Surrounded by Choirs of Angels in the Ninth Sphere of Paradise (Crystal Heaven or Primum Mobile) (The Divine Comedy, Paradise, canto XXVIII), c.1492–5

Pen and brown ink over metalpoint on vellum, 32.5 × 47.5 cm
On the verso four columns of text from *Paradiso*, canto XXVII (pen and brown ink)
Kupferstichkabinett, Staatliche Museen zu Berlin

In the ninth sphere of Paradise Dante sees a light reflected in Beatrice's eyes. He turns around to find the source and is blinded by a tiny yet radiantly bright point of light resting in the very centre of the heavens. It is surrounded by circling choirs of angels. The hierarchy of this celestial host, descending from Seraphim, Cherubim and Thrones through Dominions, Strongholds and Powers to Principalities, is indicated by various attributes, but also written on the right-hand side of the drawing. Botticelli has signed this page – not as a proud artist, but as a plea for intercession for himself and his work, humbly submitted to an angel in the lower left-hand corner, who holds a tablet bearing his name: Sandro / di ma / riano. DK

PROVENANCE
Giovanni Claudio Molino, Paris by 1803; Duke of Hamilton collection (COD. HAM. 201) by 1819; acquired 1882

LITERATURE
Berlin, Rome and London 2000–1, p. 276

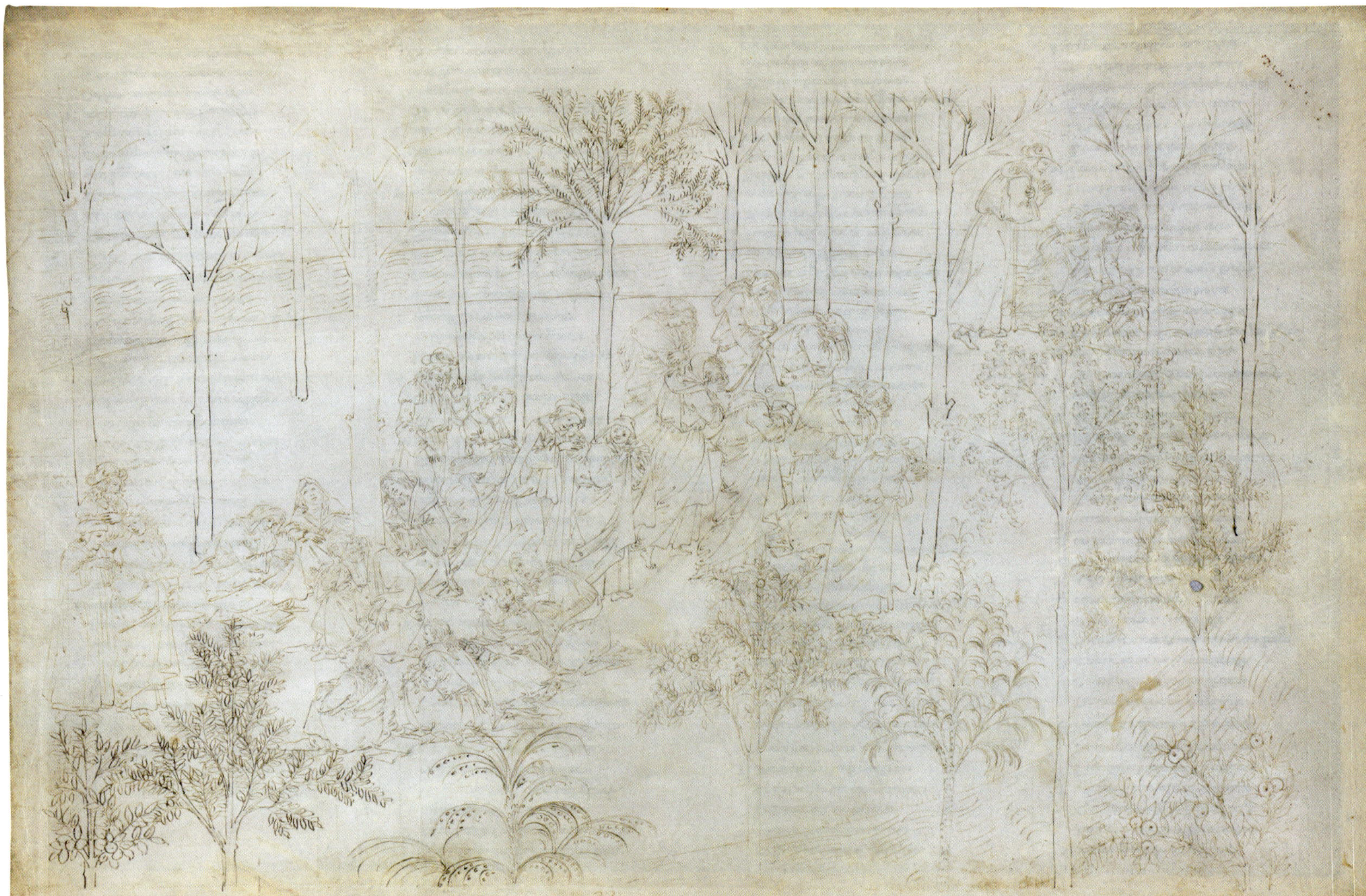

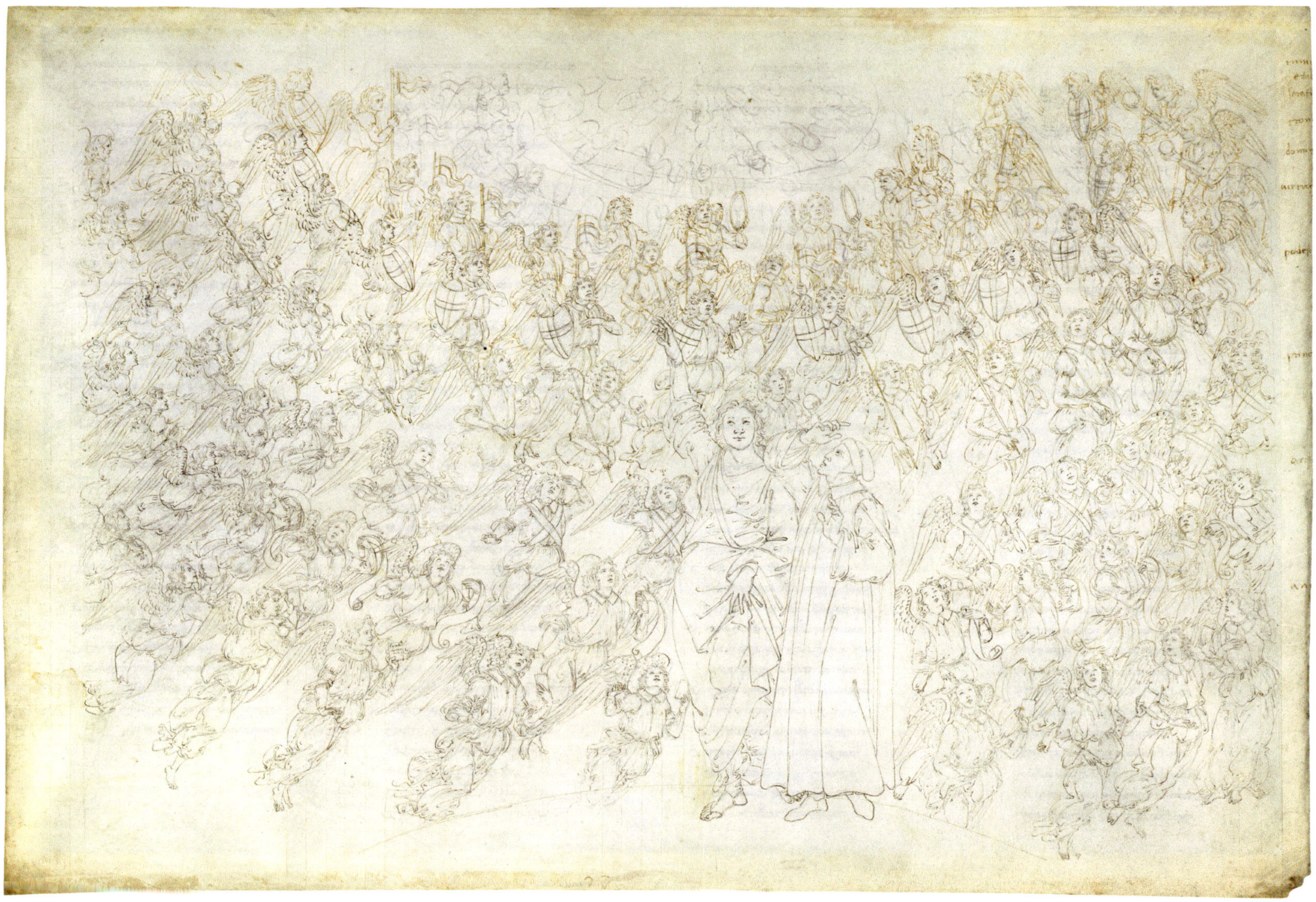

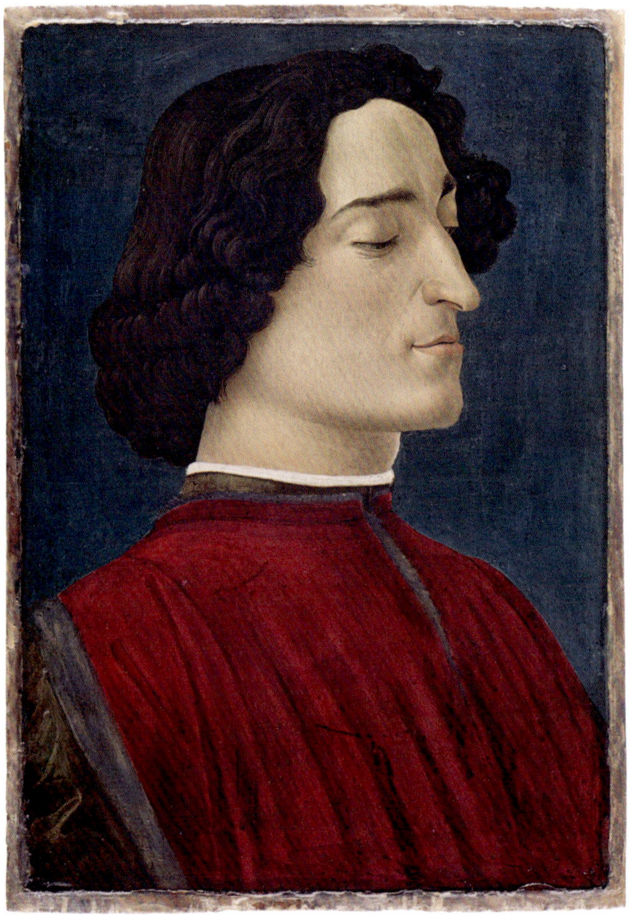

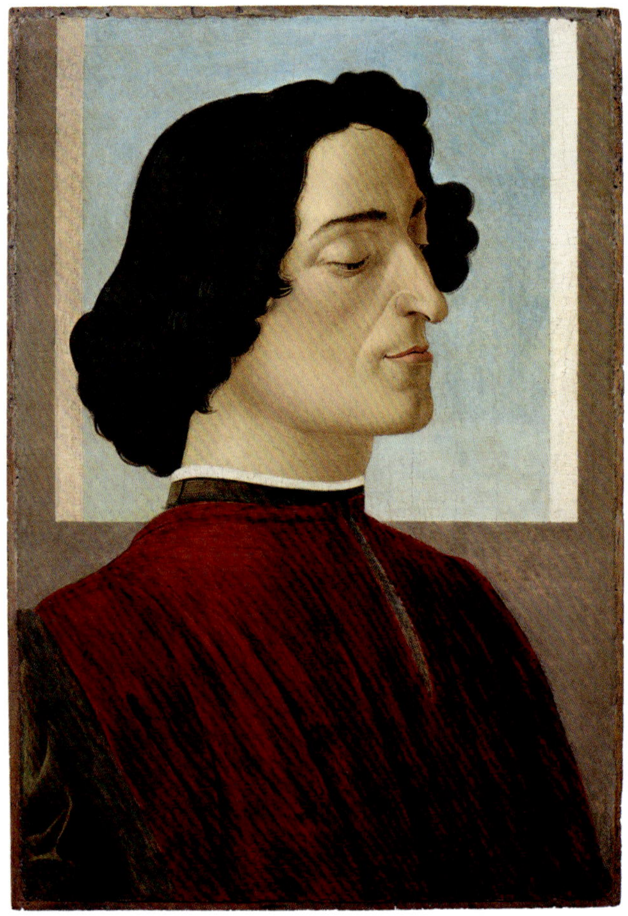

154, 155

SANDRO BOTTICELLI
(c.1445–1510)

Portrait of Giuliano de' Medici, 1478

Tempera on poplar, 56.8 × 38.5 cm
Gemäldegalerie, Staatliche Museen zu Berlin (106B)

Portrait of Giuliano de' Medici, 1478

Tempera on poplar, 56.8 × 38.5 cm
Accademia Carrara, Pinacoteca di Arte Antica, Bergamo (58MR00006)

LONDON ONLY

PROVENANCE

CAT. 154 Acquired in 1878 from the Palazzo Strozzi, Florence, for the Gemäldegalerie

CAT. 155 Acquired in 1883 in Florence by Giovanni Morelli; 1891 bequeathed by him to the Accademia Carrara

LITERATURE

Meyer and Bode 1878, p. 44; Morelli 1893, vol. 3, p. 11–13; Lightbown 1978, vol. 2, p. 30, nos B18, B19; Zöllner 2005, p. 201, nos 27, 28; Zambrano in Milan 2010–11, pp. 54–7, no. 1; Weppelmann in Berlin and New York 2011–12, pp. 174–6, nos 50, 51

This likeness of Giuliano de' Medici, brother of Lorenzo the Magnificent, is often associated with its sitter's murder during the 'Pazzi Conspiracy'. The assassins, who struck on 26 April 1478, also targeted Giuliano's more famous brother, attempting to destabilize the political dominance of the Medici family in Florence. According to some interpretations, this portrait, which has survived in several versions, was intended to show its owners' steadfast loyalty to the Medici. More recent readings, however, see not a reference to death in Giuliano's lowered (but not closed) eyes, but rather a politically motivated presentation of him as a contemplative and humble citizen.

The version from the Palazzo Strozzi, which is now in Berlin, was formerly ascribed to Pollaiuolo until Wilhelm von Bode reattributed it to Botticelli. This was disputed by Giovanni Morelli who considered it a workshop copy of another version of the portrait, in his possession since 1883, and which he bequeathed to the Accademia Carrara. In contrast to the flat blue background of the Berlin picture, in the latter an open window appears behind the sitter. Another version of this portrait surfaced in 1942 (now in the National Gallery of Art, Washington). The superior quality of the Berlin version and the more complex composition of the Washington version have variously been cited as evidence for attributing them to Botticelli himself. RR

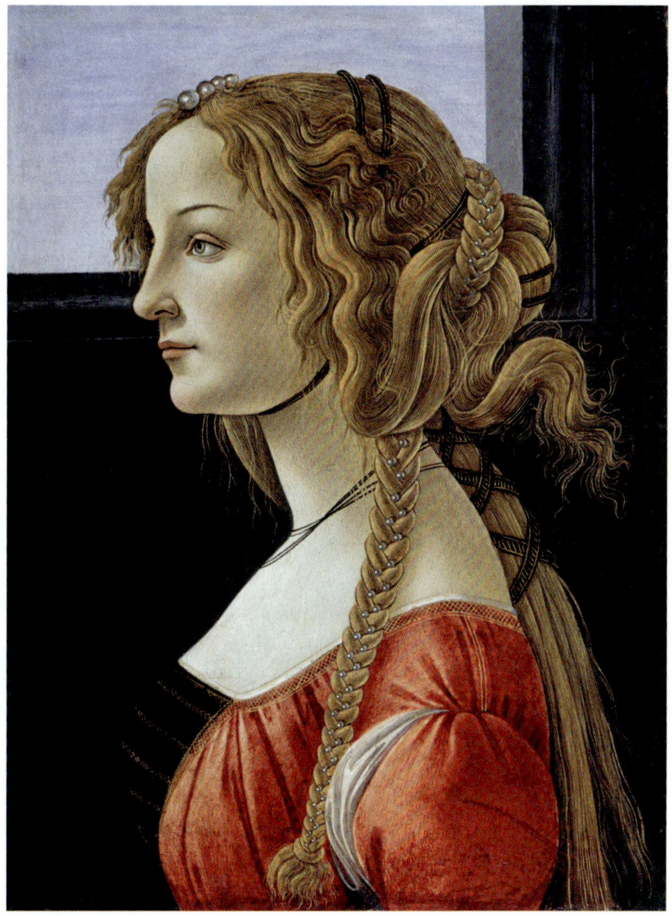

156

SANDRO BOTTICELLI
(c.1445–1510)

Ideal Portrait of a Lady ('Simonetta Vespucci'), c.1475–80

Tempera on poplar, 47.5 × 35 cm
Gemäldegalerie, Staatliche Museen zu Berlin (106 A)

When this painting was purchased, it was identified with the portrait of Simonetta Vespucci mentioned by Giorgio Vasari in his life of Botticelli. As early as 1829, Carl Friedrich von Rumohr had acquired for Berlin a portrait of a woman that he believed was this same image, known only through Vasari's *Lives* (cat. 159). In 1888, however, Wilhelm von Bode argued that the more recently acquired painting was more probably a 'work of the imagination, completely invented by Sandro'. Comparison with Botticelli's depictions of the Virgin and Venus in the Berlin museum shows how the artist repeated a similar idealized female archetype. Subsequent research supports the notion that the painting is an idealized image rather than an accurate likeness of Simonetta. To what extent this is an autograph work by Botticelli is still debated. Giovanni Morelli declared it a delightful piece from the master's own hand, to which his adversary Bode acidly retorted that of all the Berlin Botticellis, Morelli had issued only this comparatively insignificant work his 'lasciapassare' (entry permit). RR

PROVENANCE

Acquired in 1875 from the Palazzo Medici-Riccardi, Florence

LITERATURE

Meyer and Bode 1878, p. 44; Bode 1888, pp. 484–6; Morelli 1893, vol. 3, p. 11; Bode 1906, p. 245; Lightbown 1978, vol. 2, p. 117, no. C4; Zöllner 2005, pp. 57–8, 201, no. 40; Weppelmann in Berlin and New York 2011–12, pp. 121–3, no. 19

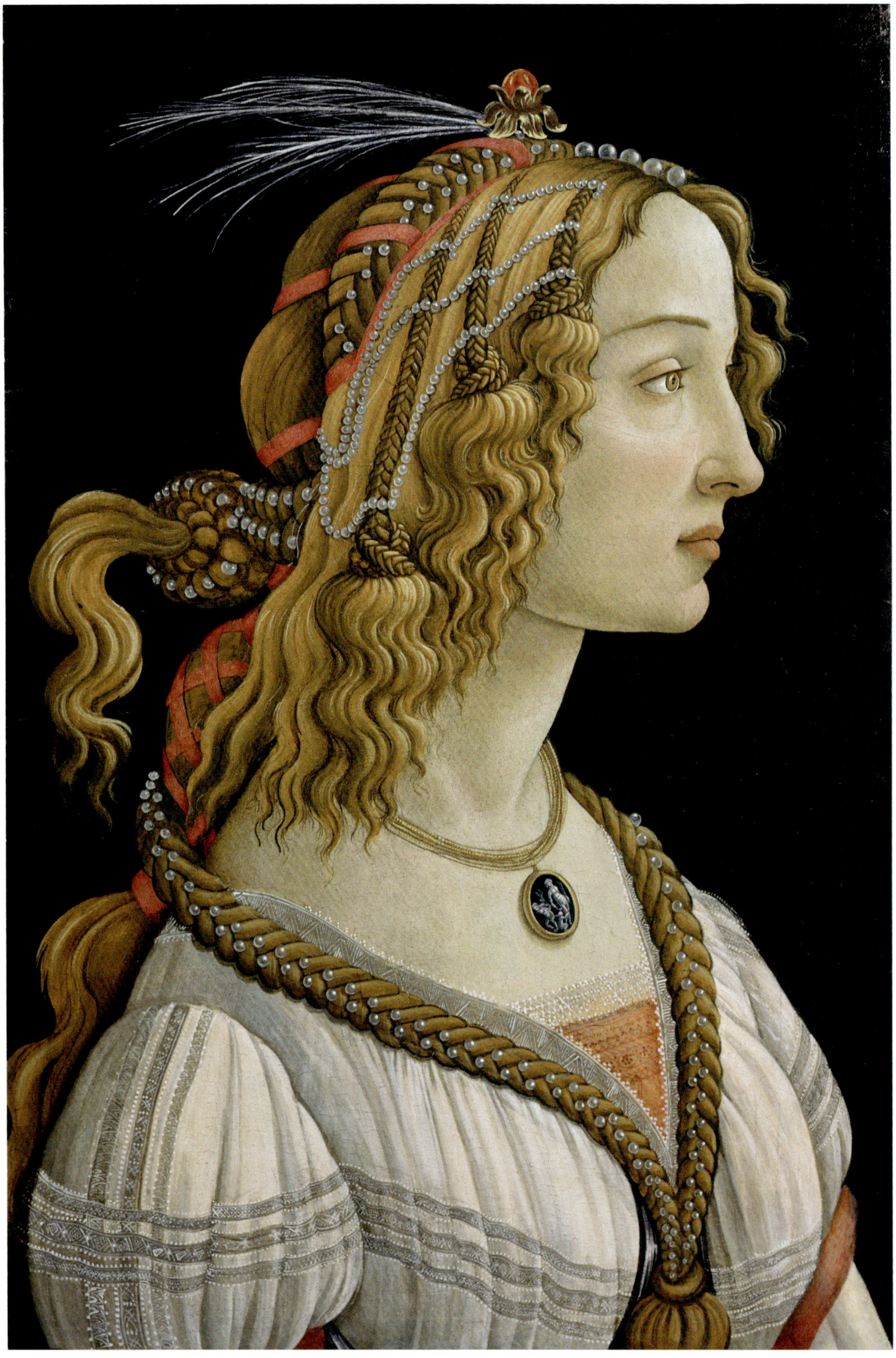

157

SANDRO BOTTICELLI (c.1445–1510)

Ideal Portrait of a Lady ('Simonetta Vespucci'), 1475/85

Tempera on poplar, 82 × 54 cm
Städel Museum, Frankfurt am Main (936)

This 'colossal bust portrait' was attributed in 1849 to Botticelli, and then identified as Lucrezia Tornabuoni, the wife of Piero di Cosimo de' Medici. The picture was likened to 'a study of the antique' in 1864 by Crowe and Cavalcaselle, who considered it autograph, as have most later writers. A silverpoint study of the head from Botticelli's workshop (now in the Ashmolean Museum, Oxford) lacks the pendant cameo, which Warburg recognized as a reversed copy of a famous antique carnelian of *Apollo and Marsyas* owned by Lorenzo de' Medici. The portrait has itself been likened to a cameo, and similar ideal female profiles appear, at a smaller scale, in earlier Florentine marble reliefs of Roman empresses by Mino da Fiesole and Desiderio da Settignano.

A smaller portrait, also by Botticelli and reputedly from the Palazzo Medici-Riccardi (cat. 156), depicts the same sitter facing in the opposite direction, with a similarly elaborate coiffure but in contemporary dress, before a window. Three further versions survive, with variations in the hairstyle and costume (cat. 158). Following Warburg (1893), these portraits have been associated with a beloved of Lorenzo's brother Giuliano (see under cats 154, 155), mentioned by Vasari as in the Medici collection. This probably represented Simonetta Vespucci, who was praised by the poet Angelo Poliziano: 'She is fair-skinned, unblemished white, and white is her garment … the ringlets of her golden hair descend on a forehead humbly proud.'

Following her tragic early death, Simonetta was likened to Dante's Beatrice and Petrarch's Laura as an ideal of virtuous beauty. The large size of this portrait suggests that it was displayed at a high level. Humbler likenesses of celebrated *belle donne* later decorated maiolica plates. ME

PROVENANCE

By 1830 in the possession of the Frankfurt art dealer Christian Franz Eberhard-Winter, from whom purchased for 1,400 guilders in 1849 by the Städelsche Kunstinstitut, Frankfurt

LITERATURE

Lightbown 1978, vol. 2, pp. 116–17, no. C3; Washington 2001–2, pp. 182–5, no. 28; Gaertringen 2004, pp. 325–44; Körner 2006, pp. 266–71; Caglioti 2008; Frankfurt 2009–10, pp. 152–5, no. 1; Berlin and New York 2011–12, pp. 120–3, no. 20

158

SANDRO BOTTICELLI
(c.1445–1510)
Allegorical Portrait of a Lady,
1475–85

Tempera on canvas, 57.6 × 40 cm
Private collection

When first exhibited in 1885–6 at the Royal Academy (no. 196), this painting was attributed to Botticelli and titled 'La Bella Simonetta'. Its facial mask closely resembles that of the Botticelli portrait also often identified as Simonetta Vespucci, since 1875 in Berlin (cat. 156). However, the sitter in the present work is posed before a coastal landscape, her coiffure and dress are more ornate, and she expresses milk from a bare breast. This unusual gesture also appears in a lost antique cameo of a bacchante formerly owned by Lorenzo de' Medici, and in the late fifteenth-century Martelli Mirror at the Victoria and Albert Museum. That celebrated North Italian bronze has a Latin inscription translatable as 'Nature encourages what necessity demands', and is probably an allegory of procreation.

Botticelli's female portrait in Frankfurt (cat. 157) includes a depiction of another antique cameo owned by Lorenzo de' Medici, and the coiled snake device of his cousin Lorenzo di Pierfrancesco appears in Piero di Cosimo's portrait at Chantilly, which was previously also ascribed to Botticelli. This bare-breasted beauty with elaborately plaited blonde hair is depicted in front of a coastal landscape and identified by an inscription as Simonetta Vespucci. The recurrence of Medicean devices supports the identification of these related portraits by or associated with Botticelli as ideal representations of this reputed lover of Giuliano de' Medici (cats 154, 155). ME

PROVENANCE
Probably Sir John Salusbury Trelawny and by descent to his son-in-law John Barton Sterling; purchased around 1890 by Sir Frederick Cook; by descent; sold at an unknown date

LITERATURE
Pope-Hennessy 1964, vol. 1, pp. 325–9, no. 359; Lightbown 1978, vol. 2, pp. 154–5, no. C70; Geronimus 2006, pp. 48–75; Frankfurt 2009–10, pp. 160–3, no. 4

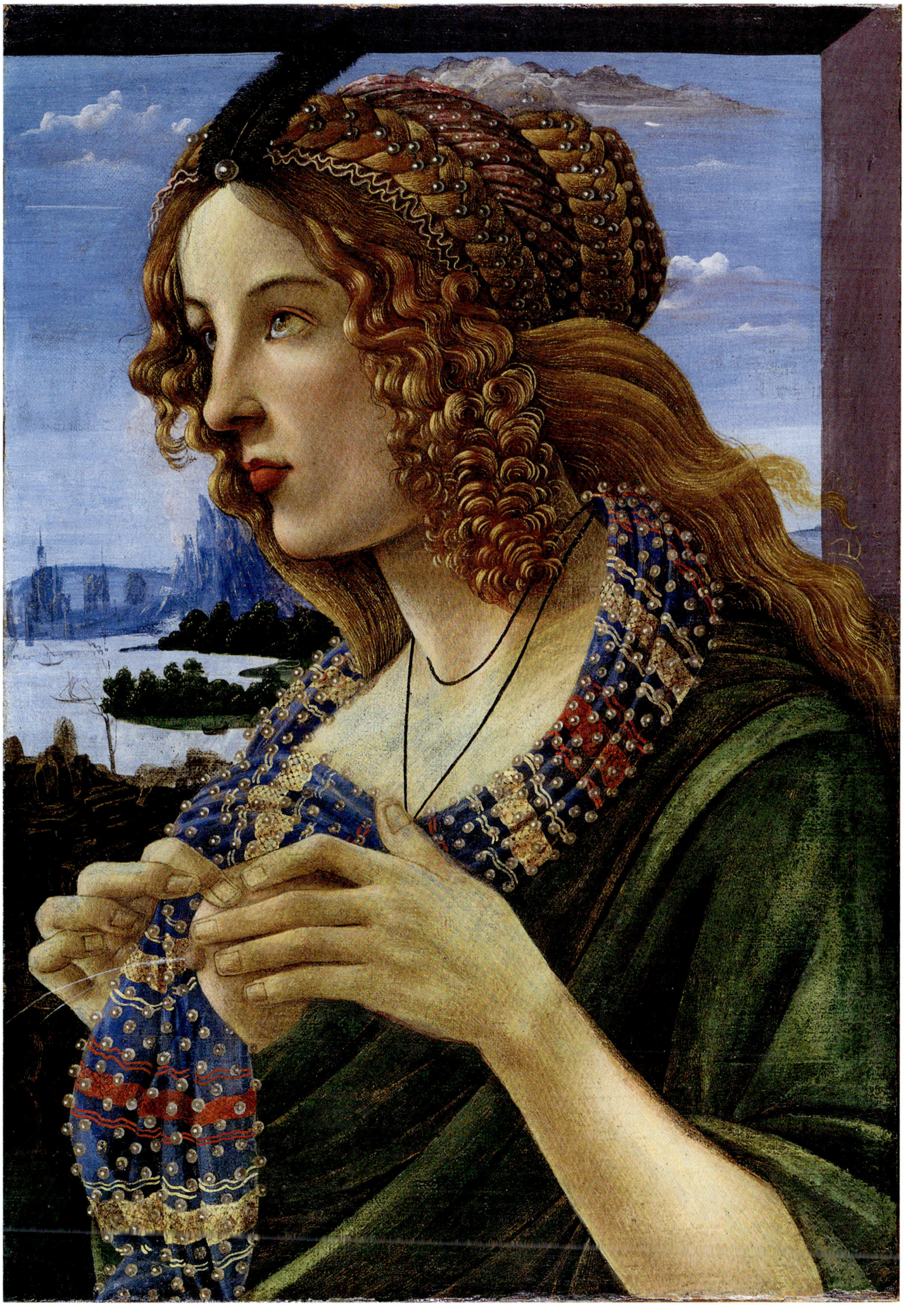

159

RAFFAELLINO DEL GARBO (?)
(?1466–1524)

Portrait of a Lady, 1485–90

Tempera on wood, 38.7 × 24.8 cm
The Museum of Fine Arts, Houston (44.554)

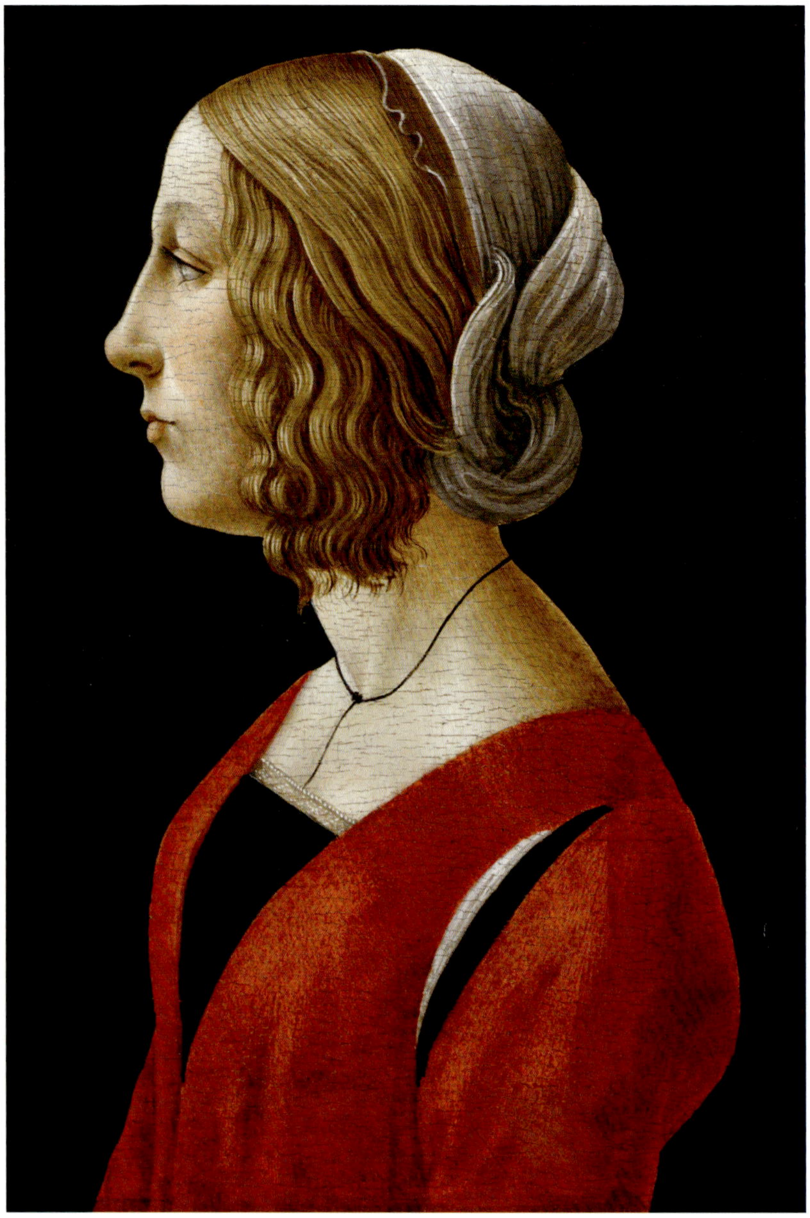

This portrait of a lady in strict profile was attributed to Botticelli – or rather, to his workshop – until the 1970s. When Carl Friedrich von Rumohr acquired it for the newly founded Berlin Museum in 1829, he believed it to be the portrait of Simonetta Vespucci, the celebrated beloved of Giuliano de' Medici, described by the biographer Giorgio Vasari. This was the first painting to be identified as the Vespucci portrait, which is known only from Vasari's text. Several others would follow. In 1875, when Wilhelm von Bode purchased another portrait of Simonetta ascribed to Botticelli (cat. 156), he lost interest in the first one, now considered simply in the 'style of Botticelli'. In 1924, it was exchanged with the art dealer Paul Cassirer for a Dutch landscape. RR

PROVENANCE
Acquired in 1829 for the Royal Museum, Berlin; traded with Paul Cassirer, Berlin in 1924; 1932, Kurt Glogowski, Berlin; 1933, Percy S. Straus, New York; 1944, acquired by the Museum of Fine Arts, Houston, as part of the Straus collection

LITERATURE
Waagen 1830, p. 59, no. I.159; Lightbown 1978, vol. 2, p. 156, no. C75; Wilson 1996, pp. 150–3, no. 12; Frankfurt 2009–10, p. 194, no. 17

160

SANDRO BOTTICELLI
(c.1445–1510)

Portrait of a Lady
(La bella Simonetta), 1485–90

Tempera on wood, 61.3 × 40.5 cm
Galleria Palatina, Florence (pal. n. 353)

BERLIN ONLY

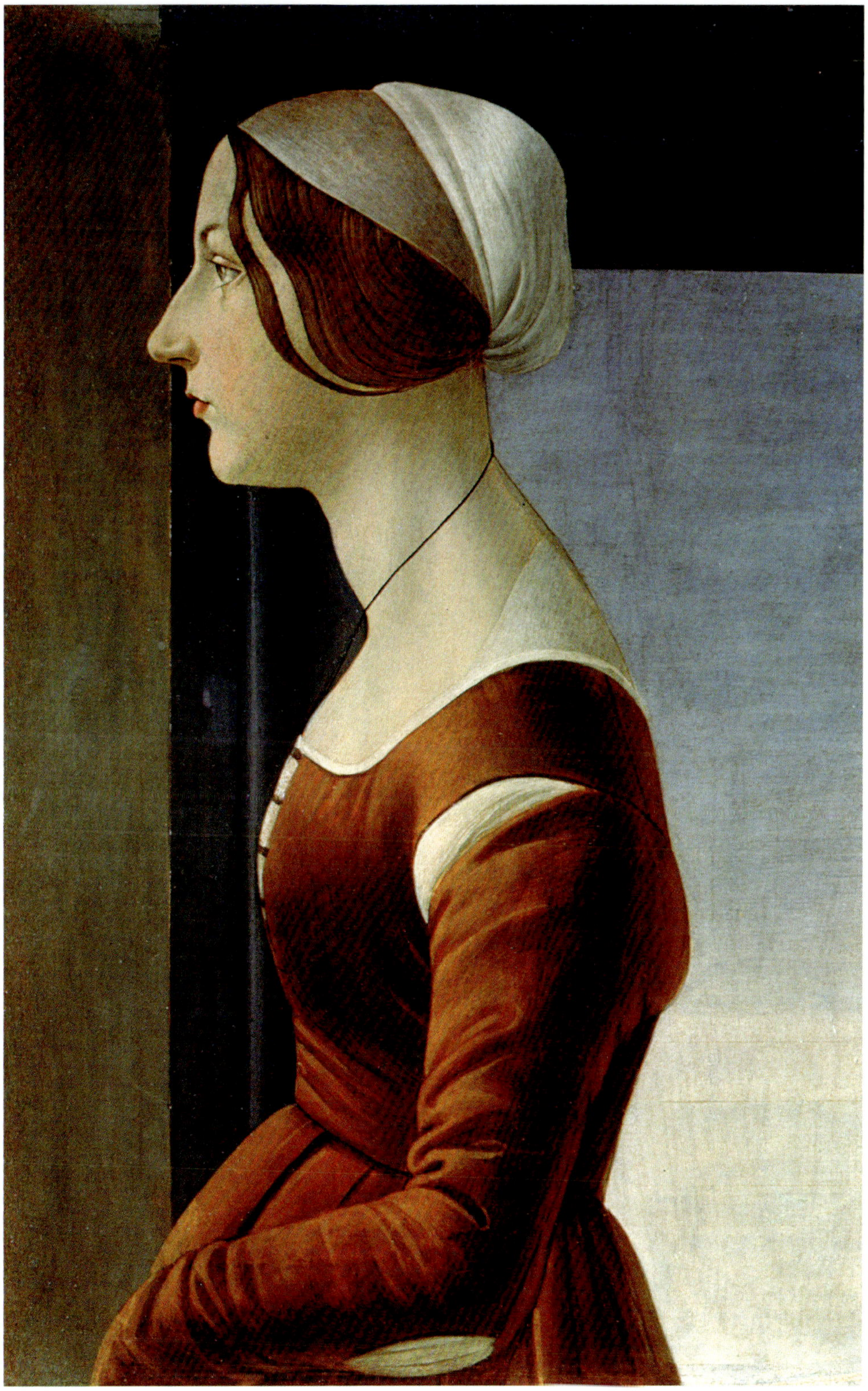

This painting was first attributed to Botticelli in 1834, and the sitter identified as Simonetta Vespucci. Like many of his depictions of women (see cat. 157), it was associated with a painting of Simonetta, said to be Giuliano de' Medici's lover, which is known solely because it was mentioned by Vasari. It is striking how vastly *La bella Simonetta*'s features differ in many of these apparent portraits. Botticelli's authorship having been repeatedly called into question, it has recently been suggested that this painting in the Galleria Palatina is an imitation – or even a forgery – dating from the seventeenth century. Most authors, however, remain convinced of its attribution to Botticelli. An engraving of the painting was published as early as 1837. This was based on a preparatory drawing by Ignazio Zotti (cat. 87). RR

PROVENANCE
Since 1829 in the inventory of the Galleria Palatina

LITERATURE
Lightbown 1978, vol. 2, pp. 210–11, no. F7; Chiarini and Padovani 2003, vol. 2, p. 92, no. 121; Zöllner 2005, p. 278, no. 97; Frankfurt 2009–10, p. 184, no. 14

161

SANDRO BOTTICELLI (c.1445–1510)

Portrait of a Lady with the Attributes of St Catherine, c.1475 (?)

Tempera on poplar, 81.3 × 53.2 cm
Lindenau-Museum, Altenburg (100)

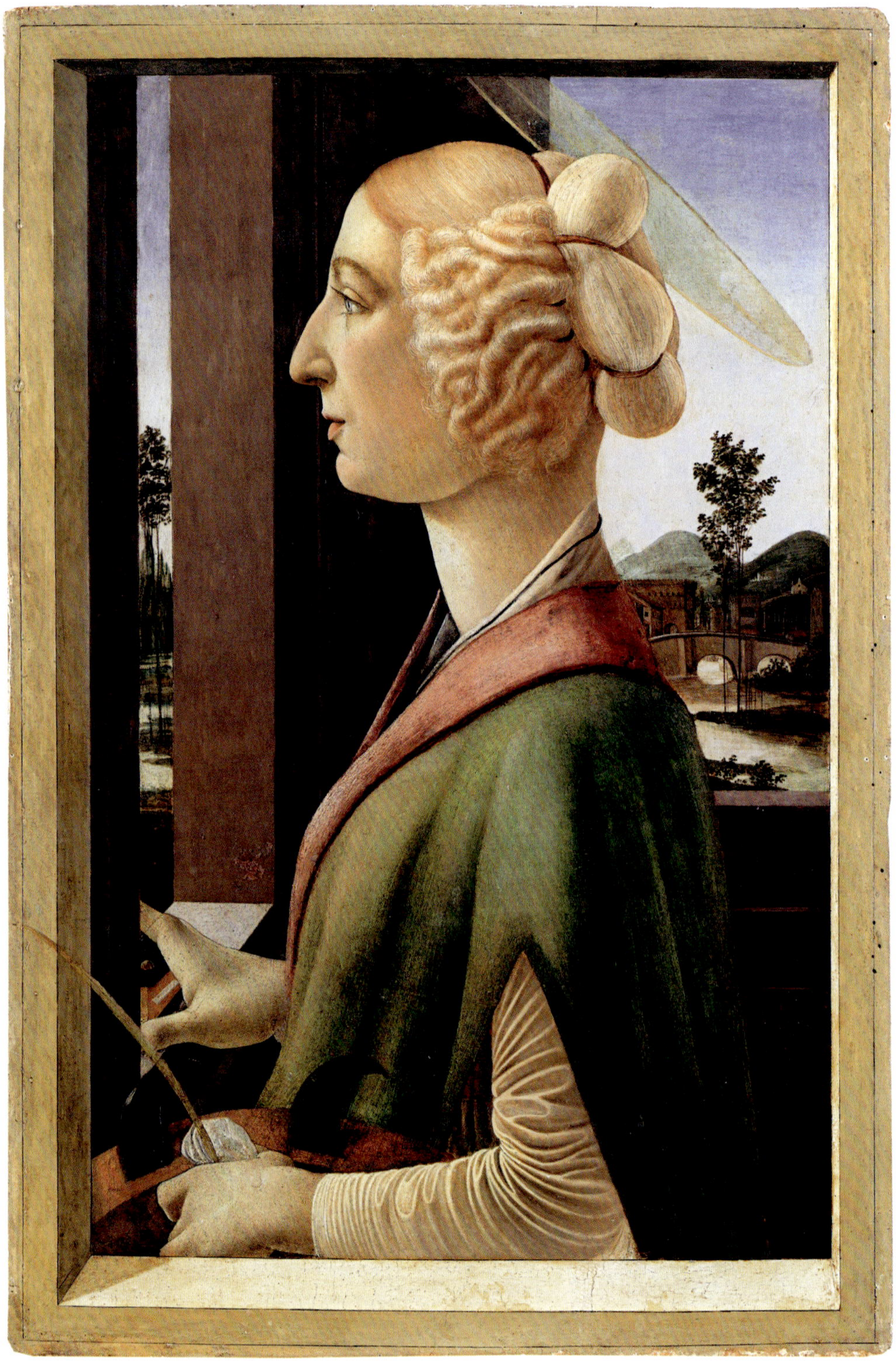

In a setting like that of Botticelli's *Portrait of a Lady known as Smeralda Bandinelli* (cat. 162), with window embrasures on three sides, stands a half-length blonde woman with a striking profile, gazing out through a window to the left. Behind her is a view of a riverside city with landmarks reminiscent of Florence (the Palazzo Spini, Porta San Niccolò and San Miniato al Monte, for instance). The woman's hands are large and prominent, while the attributes of St Catherine – a martyr's palm, wheel and halo – were added later, perhaps by a different artist. The same is true of the green cloak, which hides most of her original clothing – richly decorated and with a high waist – but now visible only under X-radiography. Originally a portrait, the painting was later revised to serve as an image of a popular saint.

In 1847, bearing an attribution to the Milanese school, the panel was purchased by Emil Braun (who thought it to be by Andrea del Verrocchio) for the pioneering collection of early Italian paintings assembled by the Saxon statesman Bernhard August von Lindenau, who founded the public museum which bears his name. In the first Altenburg catalogue (1848), the painting was given to Domenico Ghirlandaio, and August Schmarsow (1897) reattributed it to his rival Botticelli. The identification of the sitter as Caterina Sforza may now be discounted, thanks to the discovery that the attributes of St Catherine were added later. SH

PROVENANCE

Export seal from the Milanese Academy; purchased by Dr Emil Braun in Rome in 1847 for 40 scudi; by 1848 in the collection of Bernhard August von Lindenau, by whom bequeathed to the Lindenau-Museum in Altenburg

LITERATURE

Schmarsow 1897, p. 181; Oertel 1961, pp. 151–4; Lightbown 1978, vol. 2, p. 160, no. 31; Florence 2005, pp. 60–5, no. 6; Frankfurt 2009–10, pp. 188–90, no. 15; Hamburg 2011–12, pp. 182–3, no. 30

162

SANDRO BOTTICELLI (c.1445–1510)

Portrait of a Lady known as Smeralda Bandinelli, c.1470–5

Tempera on poplar, 65.7 × 41 cm
Victoria and Albert Museum, London (V&A: CAI.100)

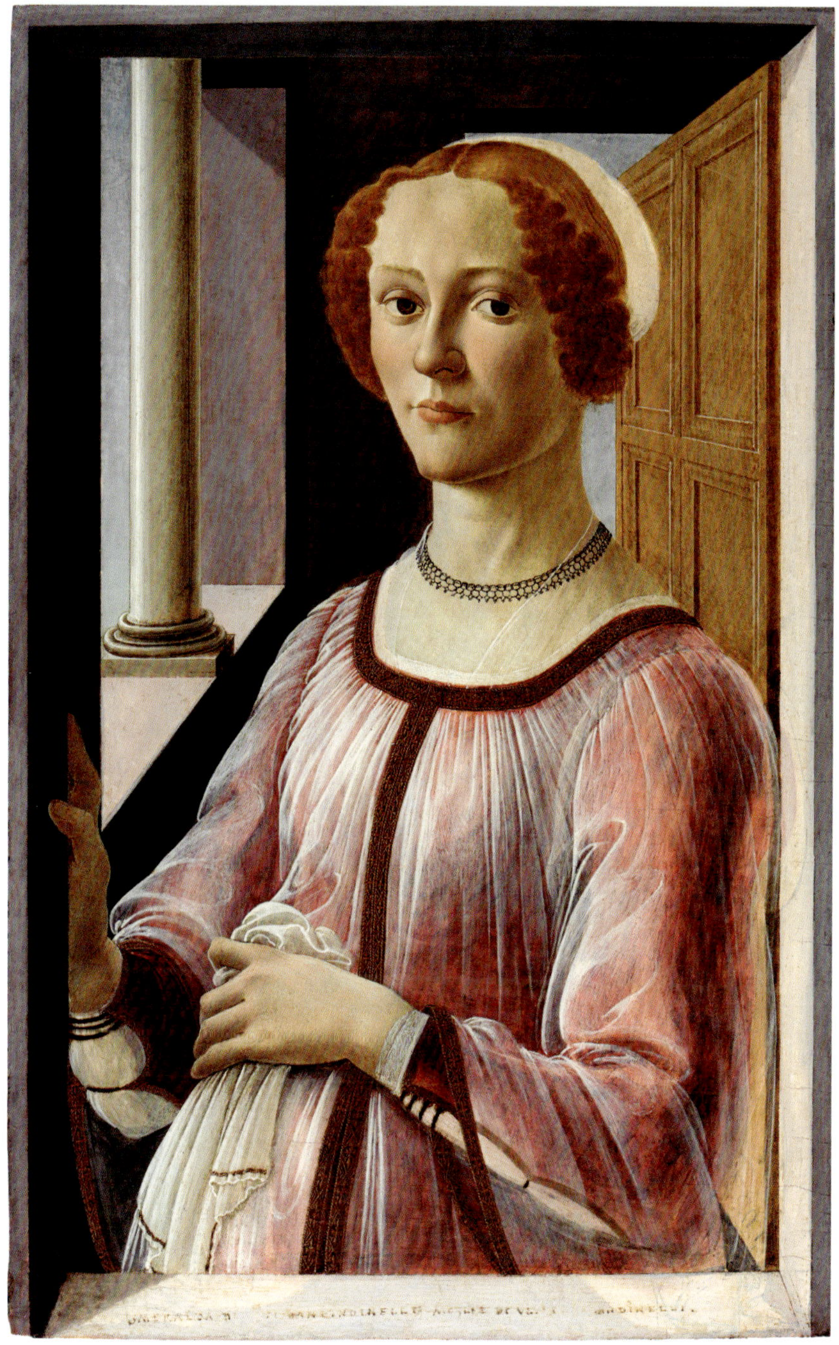

This painting shows signs of being deliberately vandalized, possibly because the sitter's direct glance challenged the expectations of female modesty customary in the Renaissance; a feature recently characterized as 'one of the boldest inventions in Florentine fifteenth-century portraiture'. The Italian inscription on the window sill identifies the subject as Smeralda Bandinelli, wife of Viviano de' Brandini and grandmother of the sixteenth-century sculptor Baccio Bandinelli. She would have been in her early thirties at the time this portrait was painted. The inscription was probably added by her descendant Baccio Bandinelli the younger.

Already attributed to Botticelli by 1841, this work was purchased in 1867 by the Pre-Raphaelite painter and poet Dante Gabriel Rossetti, who fancied that the sitter was also the model for the figure of Venus in Botticelli's *Primavera*. Inspired by this portrait and a poem in Dante's *Vita Nova*, Rossetti portrayed a beautiful young woman at half-length (cats 75, 76) titled 'The woman at the window'. Botticelli was also thoroughly familiar with Dante, and may have intended similar poetic associations in this picture. A key work in the Victorian rediscovery of Botticelli, the painting was exhibited in London in 1872 and again in 1893–4, following its sale to Rossetti's patron Constantine Alexander Ionides.

A full-scale copy in tempera on panel by Christiana, Lady Herringham, was given in 1918 to Bedford College, London (now University of London, Royal Holloway, P0451). ME

PROVENANCE
Perhaps painted for Smeralda Bandinelli, née Donati; by 1636 probably Baccio Bandinelli the younger; by 1841 James-Alexandre de Pourtalès-Gorgier, Paris; by descent; sold March 1865 for 3,400 francs; Colnaghi, sold Christie's, London, 23 March 1867 (lot 1970), bought Howell for £20 for Dante Gabriel Rossetti; by whom sold in 1880 for £315 to Constantine Alexander Ionides; bequeathed to the Victoria and Albert Museum in 1901

LITERATURE
Lightbown 1978, vol. 2, pp. 28–9, no. B15; London 1999–2000, p. 327, no. 83; Washington 2001–2, pp. 172–4, no. 25; Weinberg 2004; Berlin and New York 2011–12, pp. 112–14, no. 14

163

SANDRO BOTTICELLI (c.1445–1510)

Portrait of a Young Man c.1480–5

Tempera on wood, 43.5 × 46.2 cm
Andrew W. Mellon Collection
National Gallery of Art, Washington DC (1937.1.19)

This painting is first documented, misidentified as a self-portrait by Masaccio, in the collection of Baron Jean-Antoine-Joseph Fauchet, resident in Florence as prefect of the Napoleonic Département de l'Arno in 1809–14. He was on good terms with the director of the Uffizi, and acquired many Italian pictures, which were offered for sale in 1816. The *Portrait of a Young Man* then realised only 40 francs (less than £2 sterling), and was apparently bought in. By 1841 it had passed to Comte James Alexandre de Pourtalès-Gorgier, who also owned Botticelli's *Portrait of a Lady known as Smeralda Bandinelli* (cat. 162). Since both pictures show traces of similar vandalism, they may have an earlier shared history.

Generally accepted since the 1890s as an autograph work by Botticelli of the 1480s or early 1490s, this portrait elicited lyrical praise from Bernard Berenson in 1922: 'I held my breath and murmured "Is it YOU? Is it possible" I felt the symptoms described by Sappho as love at first sight ... True, it is more "Botticellian" than any other Botticelli in existence ... this completest note of his own music...'

The sitter's costume of a brown fur-trimmed doublet and a red cap is similar to that depicted in Botticelli's *Portrait of a Young Man*, also formerly misidentified as a Masaccio self-portrait, and bought in 1859 by the National Gallery in London (fig. 33; see essays by Mark Evans and Susanna Avery-Quash in this volume). His tipped head and gesture of one hand to his breast suggest deference, implicitly to the portrait's owner. ME

PROVENANCE

Baron Jean-Antoine-Joseph Fauchet; his sale 2 April 1816 (no. 32), as by Masaccio; by 1841 James-Alexandre de Pourtalès-Gorgier; by descent; sold March 1865 for 2,600 francs; Henri-Joseph-François, baron de Triqueti; by descent; sold Paris, 4 May 1886; Baron Arthur de Schickler; by descent; sold June 1920 to Duveen Brothers, London and New York with Wildenstein, New York and Arnold Seligmann, Paris; by 1924 Clarence H. Mackay, New York; Duveen Brothers; purchased 15 December 1936 by the A.W. Mellon Educational and Charitable Trust, Pittsburgh; by which given to the National Gallery of Art, Washington, in 1937

LITERATURE

Regnault-Delalande 1816, p. 10, no. 32; Lightbown 1978, vol. 2, pp. 78–9, no. B67; Boskovits and Brown 2003, pp. 176–80, no. 1937.1.19; Sécherre 2003

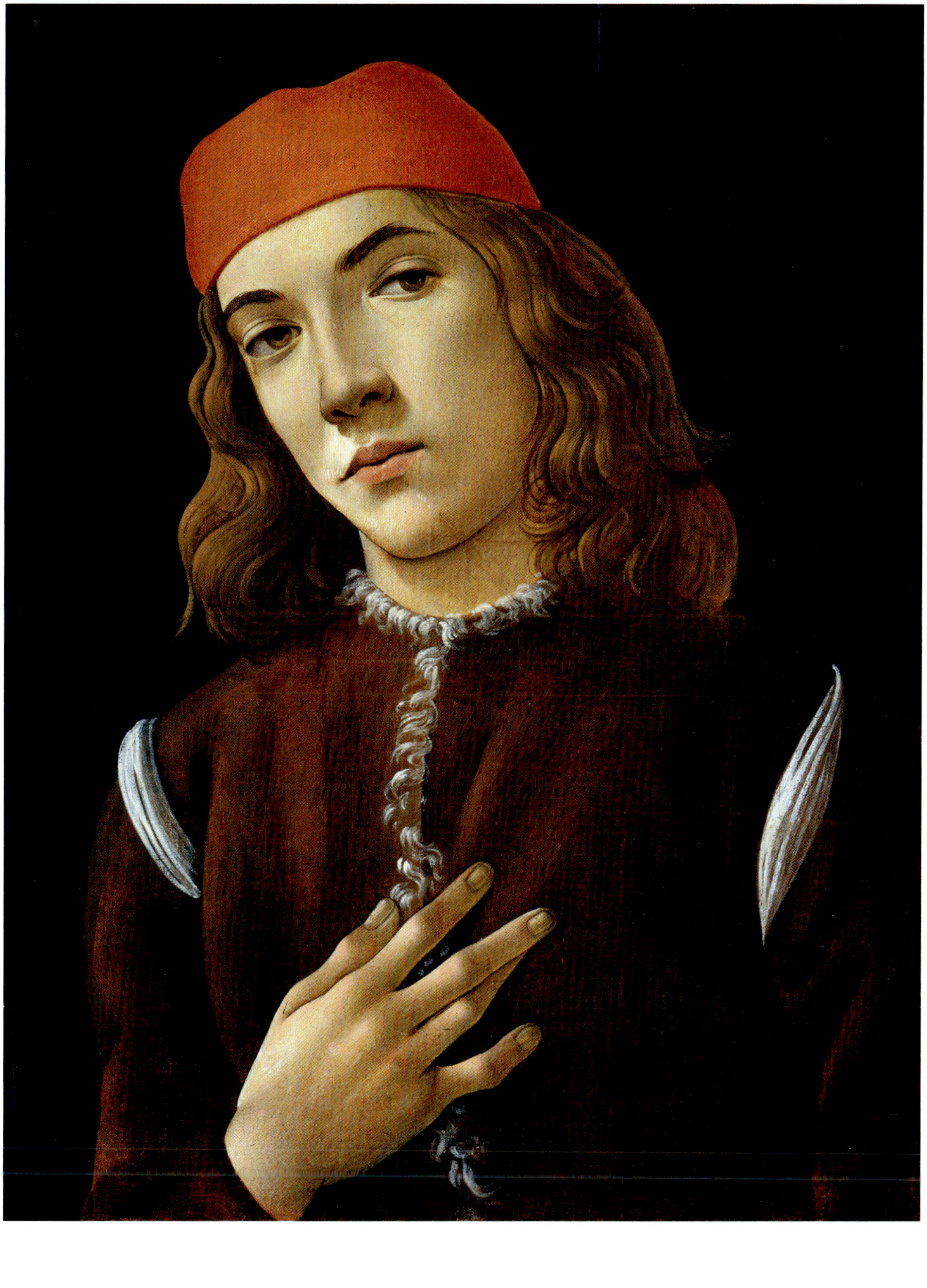

164

SANDRO BOTTICELLI (c.1445–1510)

Pallas and the Centaur, c.1482

Tempera on canvas, 207 × 148 cm
Galeria degli Uffizi, Florence (1890)
LONDON ONLY

This painting, now considered a masterpiece, is mentioned in an inventory of 1498 which describes it as hanging above a door in an antechamber of the palace on via Larga in Florence, owned by Lorenzo and Pierfrancesco de' Medici, cousins of Lorenzo the Magnificent. It was transferred in the 1540s to Villa Castello where it was displayed until at least 1761 beside Botticelli's *Primavera* and *Birth of Venus* (see figs 8, 10). Around 1856 *Pallas and the Centaur* was transferred to private apartments at the Palazzo Pitti where it was rediscovered in 1895 by the English painter and art dealer resident in Florence, William B. Spence. Enrico Ridolfi, then director of the Uffizi, immediately put it on public display.

Its rediscovery, announced in *La Nazione* on 2 March 1895, created a sensation and Bernard Berenson enthused in 1896: 'every line, every indentation ... appeals so vividly to the sense of touch that our fingers feel as if they had everywhere been in contact ... imagine shapes having the supreme life of line you may see in the contours of licking flames, and yet possessed of all the plasticity of something which caresses the hand that models it to its own desire!' Count Plunkett observed in 1900 that its discovery 'has done more to win the public into recognition of [Botticelli's] merits than even the enthusiasm of Mr Ruskin accomplished'.

Intense debates began immediately. In 1895 Ridolfi misidentified it as the lost standard of Giuliano de' Medici described by Vasari as 'Pallas on a device of great branches ... the size of life', sometimes associated with the tapestry *Minerva Pacifica* (cat. 166), woven from a cartoon by Botticelli for Guy de Baudreuil. Lightbown and Cecchi suggest it was a wedding gift from Lorenzo de' Medici to his nephew and godson, Lorenzo di Pierfrancesco, on his marriage in 1482 to Semiramide d'Appiano.

Uncertainty as to the circumstances of the commission and the interpretation of the figures contributed to the concept of Botticelli as a renovator of antique mythology and a Neoplatonist artist. The female figure has been variously identified as Virgil's heroine Camilla (*Aeneid*, 11) or Pallas the goddess of wisdom (Fulgentius, *Images of the Gods*), while Gombrich interpreted the subject as an allegory of Reason subduing Passion, a moral theme derived from Marsilio Ficino. Other interpretations have been proposed since, but it remains unclear whether the allegory was intended to convey a specific poetic, philosophical or political message. AD

PROVENANCE
Medici collection; transferred to Villa Castello; after 1856 transferred to private apartments in Palazzo Pitti; 1895 transferred to the Uffizi

LITERATURE
Lightbown 1978, vol. 2, pp. 57–60, no. B43; Meltzoff 1987, pp. 168–73; Pons 1989, pp. 67–8; Caneva 1990, pp. 76–7; Luchinat 2001, pp. 167–70; Paris 2003–4, pp. 122–7; Cecchi 2005, pp. 202–5; Zöllner 2005, p. 213; Deimling in Hatfield 2009, pp. 63–104; Frankfurt 2009–10, pp. 214–17, no. 26

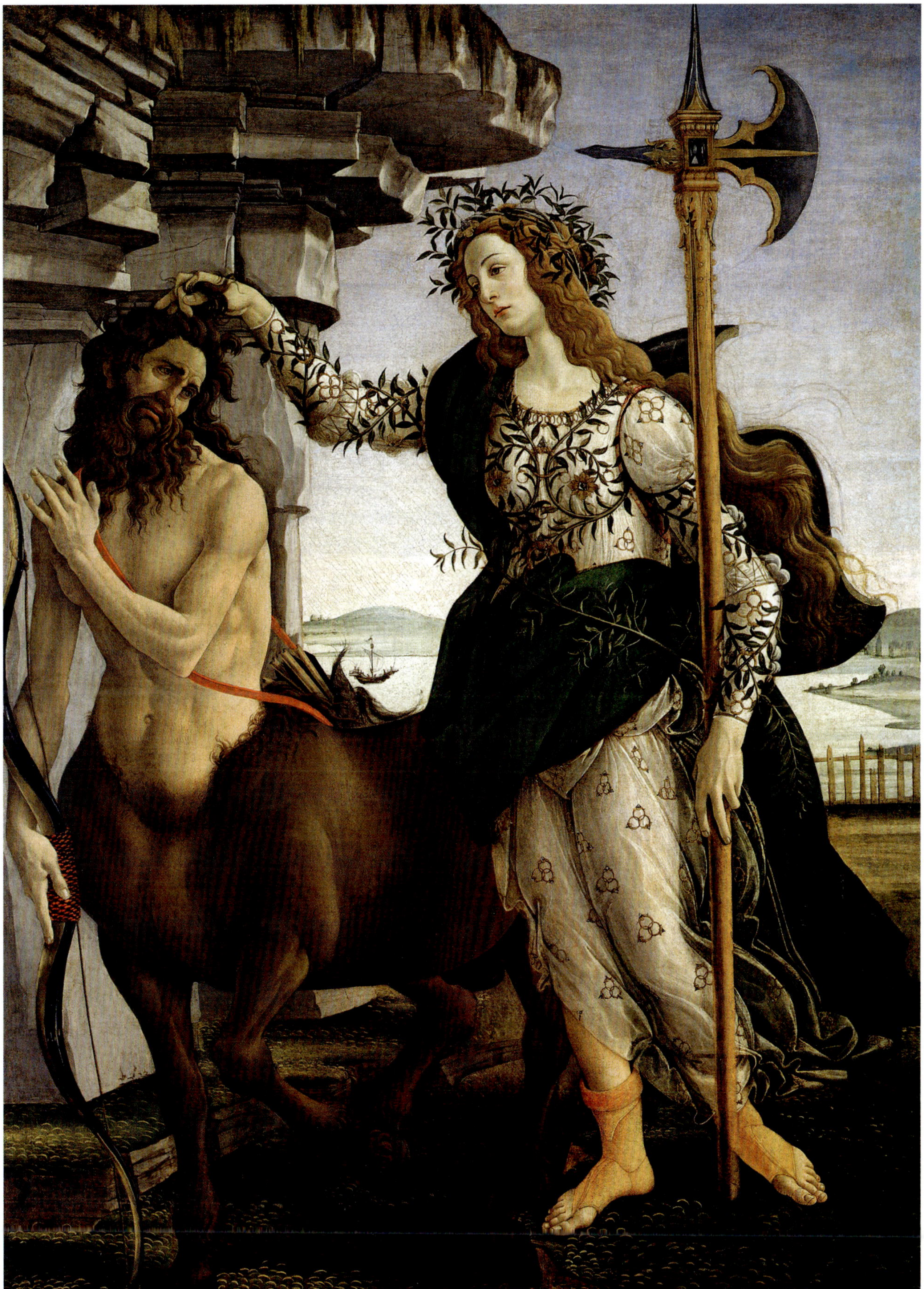

165

SANDRO BOTTICELLI (c.1445–1510)

Allegory of Abundance or Autumn, c.1480–5

Black and red chalk, pen and brown ink, brown wash, heightened with lead white, on paper with an irregular orange-red ground consisting mainly of red lead, 31.7 × 25.2 cm
The British Museum, London (1895,0915.447)
LONDON ONLY

This drawing is unique within Botticelli's graphic corpus and is often counted as one of the most beautiful drawings of the fifteenth century. Its central figure, a delicate image of feminine beauty, recalls at least three graceful nymphs with a dancing gait: Flora and Venus clad in loose floating drapery from *Primavera* and the nude Venus in the *Birth of Venus*, both from the late 1470s. The pose is also reminiscent of the figure of Pallas in *Pallas and the Centaur* (*c.*1482; cat. 164) and the sheet may be intermediate in date between this work and *Primavera*.

Although Warburg suggested a derivation from Ovid's *Metamorphoses* (Book IX, 8), Botticelli's remarkable invention can convey multiple meanings and be adapted to a variety of contexts including an allegory of Abundance or Autumn such as the painting in the Musée Condé, Chantilly, which was perhaps based on the present study. The unfinished section of this drawing shows an autumnal cornucopia – according to legend, Hercules had snapped the horn from the head of the river god Achelous while in the form of a bull – with a retinue of putti carrying bunches of grapes.

This drawing was sold twice at auction in London, with an attribution to Andrea Mantegna in 1801 and to Andrea del Verrocchio in 1856. It was then reputedly in a mount designed by Giorgio Vasari, who owned several drawings by Botticelli. Herbert Horne recorded that a trace of this mount remained in 1908, but it has since disappeared.

John Charles Robinson, then superintendent of the South Kensington Museum (now Victoria and Albert Museum), attributed the work to Botticelli and sold it in 1860 with the rest of his remarkable collection of Old Master drawings to one of the leading collectors of his day, John Malcolm of Poltalloch. The drawing, which had previously belonged to the poet Samuel Rogers, was exhibited at the Grosvenor Gallery in London (no. 846) in 1877–8, and at the Ecole des Beaux-Arts in Paris (no. 21) in 1879. In 1895, it was acquired with the rest of the Malcolm collection by the British Museum. AD

PROVENANCE

Giorgio Vasari?; Greffier F. Fagel, his sale T. Philipe, London, 29 May 1801 (lot 115) as Mantegna; bought by Samuel Rogers; his sale Christie's, London, 6 May 1856 (lot 923); M. Moore; Sir John Charles Robinson; sold to John Malcolm of Poltalloch in 1860; acquired from Col. John Wingfield Malcolm, 1895

LITERATURE

Robinson 1876, p. 9, no. 14; Warburg 1898 (repr. in Warburg 1999, p. 159); Popham and Pouncey 1950, vol. 1, p. 16, no. 24; Lightbown 1978, vol. 2, p. 162, no. D3 and under no. C8; Van Cleave 1994, pp. 238–9; Rubin in London 1999–2000, p. 335, no. 87; Chapman in Berlin, Rome and London 2000–1, p. 367, no. 19; Davies 2001; Cecchi 2005, p. 226; Zöllner 2005, p. 283, no. D4; Körner 2006, p. 262; Van Cleave 2007, p. 70; Faietti in London and Florence 2010–11, pp. 174–5, no. 36

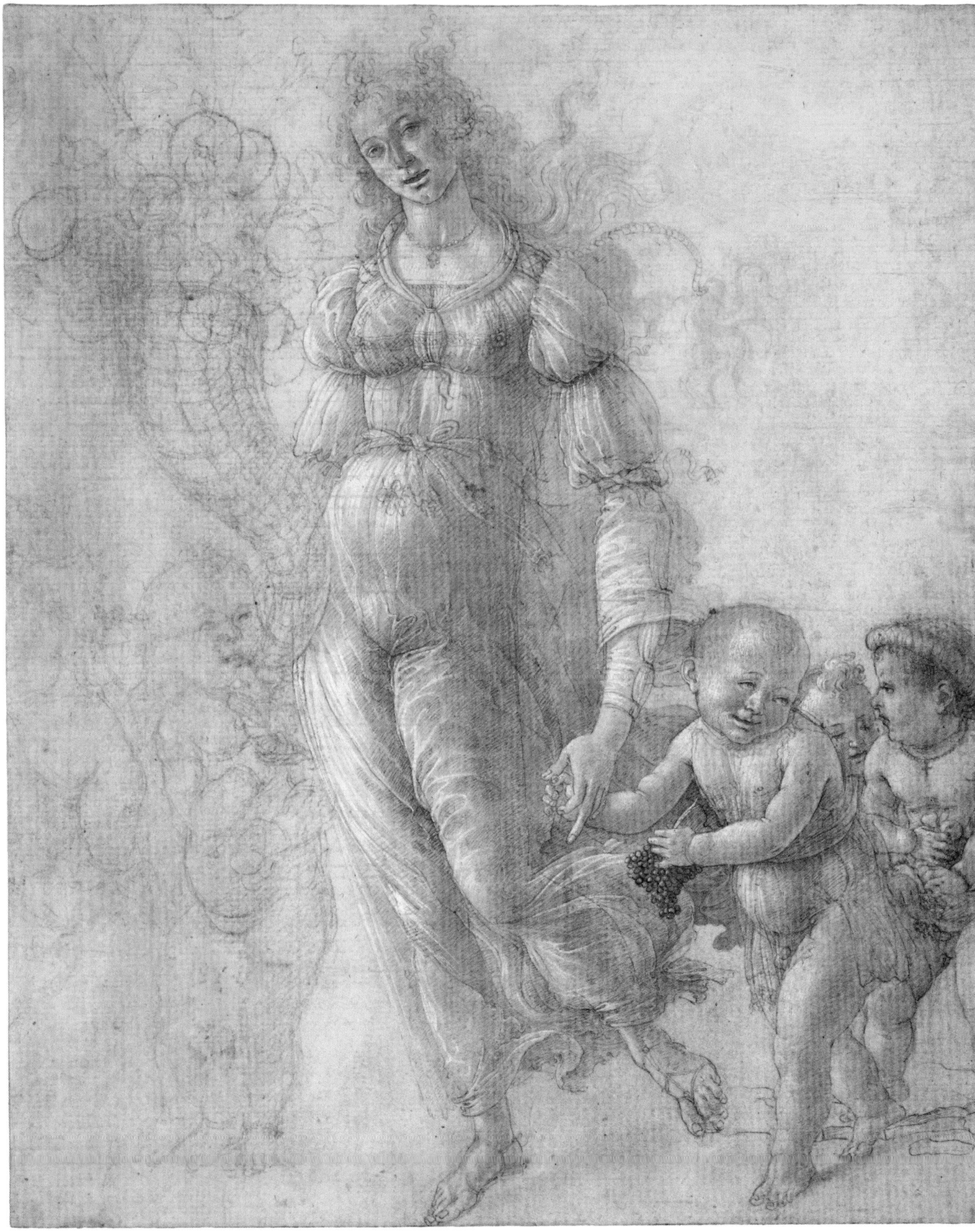

166

DESIGNED BY
SANDRO BOTTICELLI
(c.1445–1510)

Minerva Pacifica, c.1494–1500

Fragment of tapestry, warp in wool and weft in wool and silk, 257 × 156 cm
Private collection

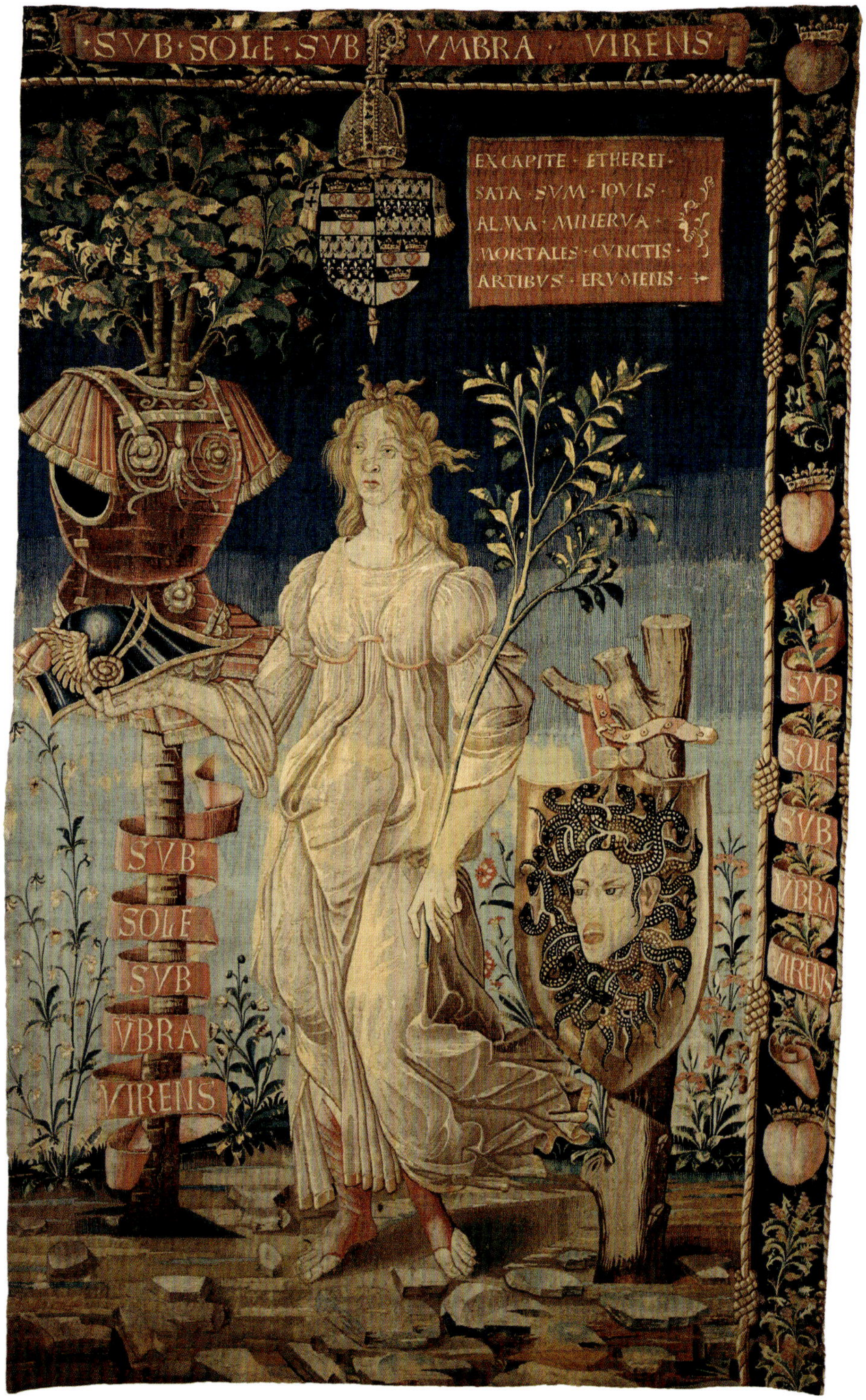

This tapestry was published in 1889 by Eugène Müntz as the frontispiece of the first volume of his monumental *Histoire de l'art pendant la Renaissance* and was discussed by Horne and Warburg in 1903. It was exhibited in *L'Art Italien de Cimabue à Tiepolo* at the Petit Palais in Paris in 1935. The attribution of the design to Botticelli has since been generally accepted and two related drawings in Florence and Oxford may record preparatory studies. The figure closely resembles Flora in Botticelli's *Primavera* and its composition may relate to a lost banner painted by the artist for Giuliano de' Medici (see under cats 154, 155). This work testifies to Botticelli's skill as a tapestry designer.

One of the first Franco-Flemish tapestries designed by an Italian artist, its coat of arms indicates that it was woven for Guy de Baudreuil, secular abbot of Saint-Martin-aux-Bois from 1491 to 1530, who visited Florence on behalf of the French king Charles VIII. At the top appears his motto: 'Sub sole sub umbra virens'. The goddess Minerva is identifiable by her attributes of an olive branch, armour and the shield with the head of Medusa while the inscription suggests that she is depicted here as a Neoplatonist allegory of peace and wisdom: 'Ex capite etherei [n]ata sum Iovis alma Minerva mortales cunctis artibus erudient'. AD

PROVENANCE

Count Guy de Baudreuil, Abbot of Saint-Martin-des-Bois; private collection

LITERATURE

Chastel 1958, pp. 262–3; Lightbown 1978, vol. 2, pp. 166–7, no. D15 (with previous bibliography); Horne 1986, p. 529; Dempsey 1992, p. 136, fig. 26; Meoni 1998–2007, vol. 1, pp. 26–7 nn. 90–1; Paris 2003–4, pp. 176–7, no. 26; Cecchi 2005, pp. 299–300; Zöllner 2005, pp. 286–7; Körner 2006, p. 286ff.; Roeck 2009, p. 120; Frankfurt 2009–10, p. 27, no. 27

167

SANDRO BOTTICELLI
(c.1445–1510)

Head of a Youth, 1470s

Pen and brown ink, heightened with white, on pink prepared paper, diameter 7.3 cm
The British Museum, London (1895,0915.450)

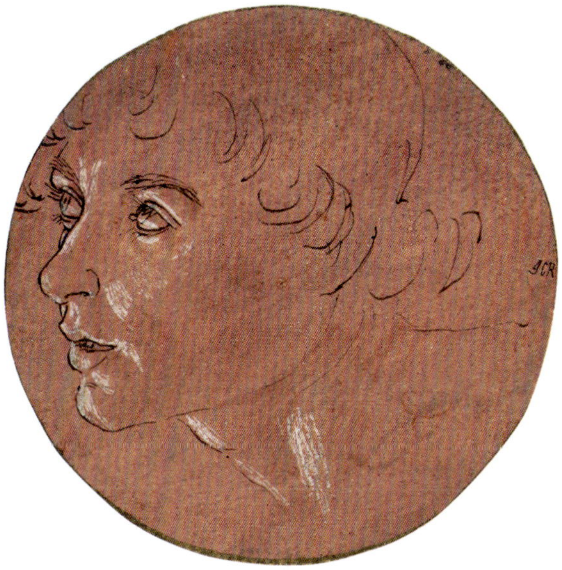

According to John Charles Robinson, this drawing belonged to the art-loving diarist John Perceval, 1st Earl of Egmont. Robinson considered it 'intrinsically excellent' and ascribed it to Botticelli with the proviso that this required 'further consideration and comparison'. Berenson initially attributed this fragment to an artistic personality of his own creation, 'Amico di Sandro', whom he later disavowed, and subsequently listed it as autograph.

The technique employed here is typically Florentine and can be related to Botticelli's formative years as a goldsmith and a niello engraver. The facial type is reminiscent of Fra Filippo Lippi, and Lorenza Melli has recently pointed out that it may be a study for the head of Mercury in *Primavera*. If so, it would be one of the very few preparatory drawings for a finished painting by Botticelli. It most likely dates from the 1470s, soon after Botticelli became an independent master. With cats 138 and 165, this drawing entered the remarkable collection of John Malcolm of Poltalloch, which was acquired by the British Museum in 1895. AD

PROVENANCE

Reputedly John Perceval, 1st Earl of Egmont; John Charles Robinson; sold to John Malcolm of Poltalloch in 1860; acquired from Col. John Wingfield Malcolm, 1895

LITERATURE

Robinson 1876, p. 9, no. 17; Berenson 1903b, vol. 2, p. 3, no. 50; Berenson 1938, vol. 2, p. 58, no. 567A, fig. 197; Popham and Pouncey 1950, vol. 1, p. 17, no. 26 (with further literature); Lightbown 1978, vol. 2, p. 161, no. D1; Chapman in Berlin, London and Rome 2000–1, no. 14; Melli in Frankfurt 2009–10, pp. 101–2, fig. 63

168

WORKSHOP OF
SANDRO BOTTICELLI
(c.1445–1510)

The Judgement of Paris, c.1485–88

Tempera on wood, 81 × 197 cm
Fondazione Giorgio Cini, Galleria di Palazzo Cini, Venice (40015)

BERLIN ONLY

This large-scale panel, which remained little known for many years, was originally a *spalliera* used to decorate a domestic interior. The panel depicts Paris judging who is the most beautiful of the three rival goddesses Juno, Minerva and Venus, and deciding in favour of the goddess of love. Utilizing a common repertoire of preparatory drawings and copies was customary workshop practice. For instance, the depiction of a shipyard in the left background of this composition repeats a motif from Botticelli's fresco of *The Punishment of Korah* (1482) in the Sistine Chapel. Several hands could work on a painting, while the master himself took responsibility for its stylistic consistency and ultimate quality control.

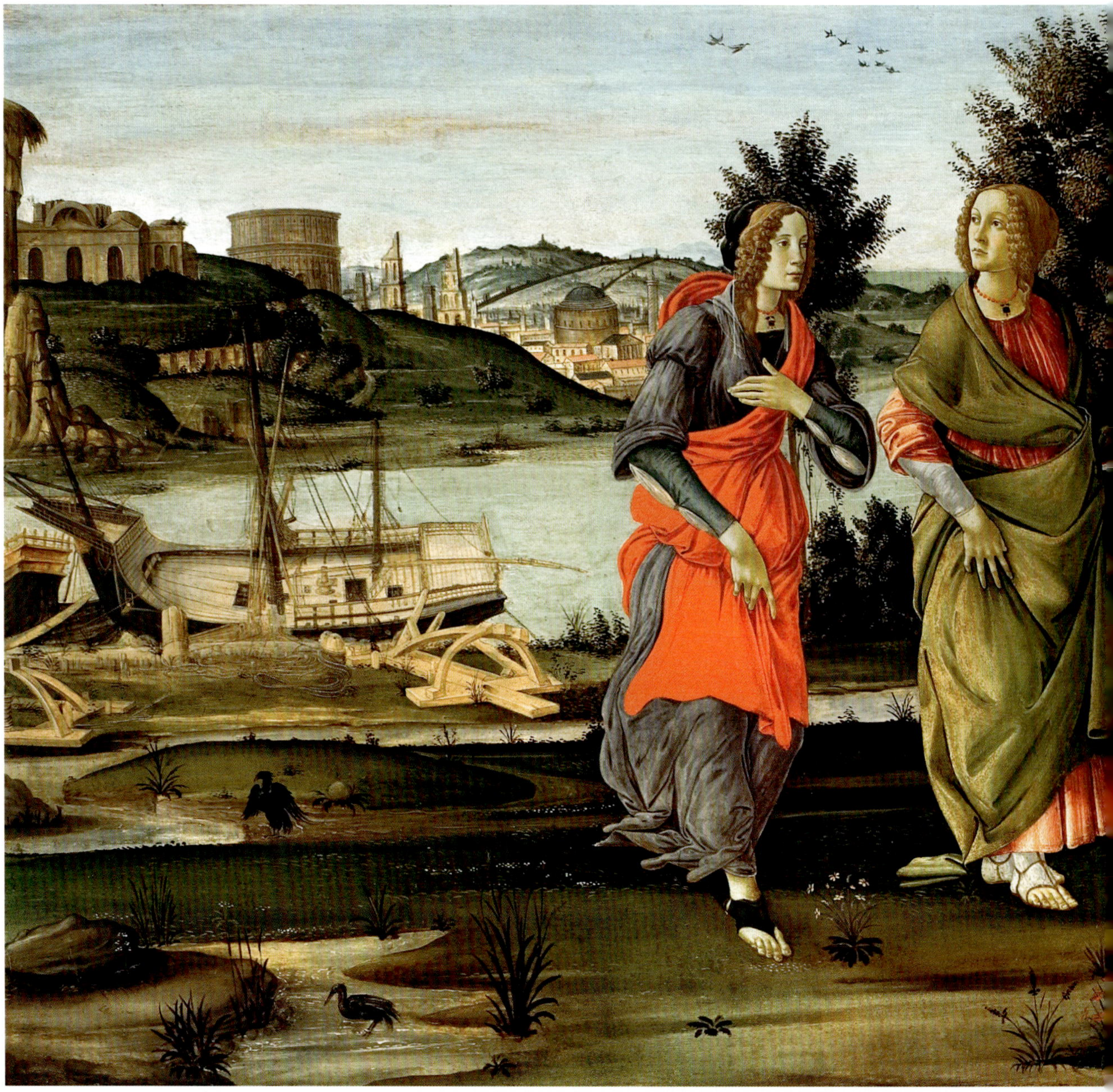

A label on the reverse of the panel shows that it was formerly part of 'Etruria pittrice', a large collection of early Tuscan paintings owned by the noble connoisseur and dealer Alfonso Tacoli-Canacci, resident in Florence. In 1789 he unsuccessfully offered his collection to Charles IV of Spain and Duke Ferdinand I of Parma. The label on the reverse and Tacoli-Canacci's manuscript catalogue both ascribe this work to Botticelli. It is therefore surprising that an alternative attribution to Mantegna appears in the catalogue raisonné of his collection, published in 1796. SH

PROVENANCE

By 1789, collection of Alfonso Tacoli-Canacci, Florence; 1801 inherited by his nephew Pietro and by descent in the Bagnesi-Bellincini family, Modena; 1942 purchased by Vittorio Cini

LITERATURE

Florence 1949, p. 64; Zeri et al. 1984, pp. 27–9; Florence 1992–3, pp. 137–8, no. 4.2; Florence 2004, pp. 250–3, no. 41; Buonacore 2005, pp. 103, 233, no. 491; Frankfurt 2009–10, pp. 232–5, no. 33; Florence 2014, pp. 211–15

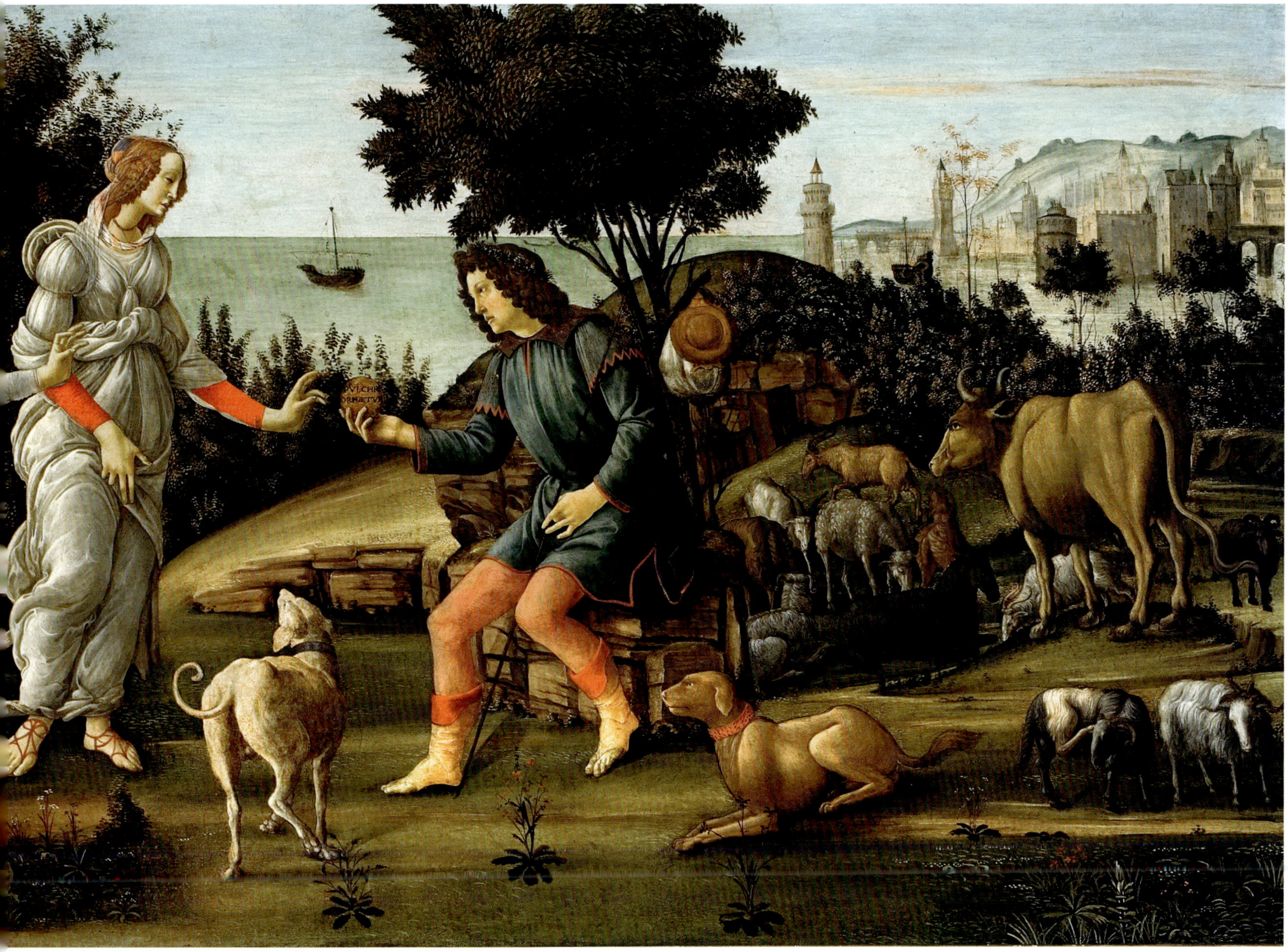

169, 170

SANDRO BOTTICELLI,
(c.1445–1510) and workshop (?)
Venus, 1490s

Oil on canvas, transferred from wood, 147 × 77 cm
Galleria Sabauda, Turin (172)

SANDRO BOTTICELLI,
(c.1445–1510) and workshop (?)
Venus, 1490s

Canvas, 158.1 × 68.5 cm
Gemäldegalerie, Staatliche Museen zu Berlin (1124)

Even during Botticelli's lifetime, one of his contemporaries, Antonio Billi, acknowledged that the artist painted 'the most beautiful naked women'. Three surviving examples are attributed to Botticelli and his workshop: in Berlin, in Turin and formerly in a private collection in Geneva. These monumental nudes, among the earliest secular instances in post-classical European painting, were inspired by the antique figure of the *Venus pudica*: Venus covering her nakedness. Though the most famous classical example, known as the *Venus de' Medici*, only arrived in Florence in the seventeenth century, there is evidence that other versions could be seen there as early as the fourteenth century. The relationship between this antique sculpture and Botticelli's *Venus* in Berlin was noted in the Berlin gallery's first catalogue in 1830. However, neither G.F. Waagen nor Carl Friedrich von Rumohr, who had just purchased the Bardi altarpiece (cat. 106) and what may well be the first *Simonetta* (cat. 159) in Florence, saw its connection with Botticelli's *Birth of Venus*. A revised edition of the Berlin catalogue in 1878 pointed out the connection, now referring to the present work as a 'study' executed for the Florentine 'Birth', a designation that Wilhelm von Bode confirmed in 1888, while in 1890 his colleague Julius Meyer thought it to be from Botticelli's own hand. In 1893, in explicit opposition to Bode, Giovanni Morelli claimed the Berlin painting was most likely a workshop copy after the Florentine original. Venturi and Yashiro thought the Turin Venus autograph, while Lightbown considered it to be a workshop production. Botticelli's incorporation of this classical type into a multi-figure composition in the Florentine painting, as well as her return to isolation in the Berlin and Turin pictures, helps us to understand the universal popularity today of his *Venus*: its enduring adaptability into other visual contexts is in part due to its statuesque character. RR

PROVENANCE

CAT. 169 Purchased in Florence in 1844 by the Revd Walter Davenport Bromley; sold Christie's, London, 12–13 June 1863 (lot 170); Ashburton collection, Bath House; Baron Marochetti; Riccardo Gualino, Turin; given to the Galleria Sabauda in 1928

CAT. 170 Edward Solly; acquired as part of his collection in 1821

LITERATURE

CAT. 169 Waagen 1857b, pp. 166–7; Venturi 1925, pp. 55–7; Yashiro 1929, p. XXI, 243; Lightbown 1978, vol. 2, pp. 121–2, no. C12; Frankfurt 2009–10, no. 35, pp. 236–9

CAT. 170 Waagen 1830, p. 53, no. 167; Meyer and Bode 1878, p. 45; Bode 1888, p. 486; Meyer 1890, pp. 5, 8–9; Morelli 1890–3, vol. 3, p. 13; Lightbown 1978, vol. 2, pp. 120–2, no. C10; Frankfurt 2009–10, no. 34, pp. 236–9

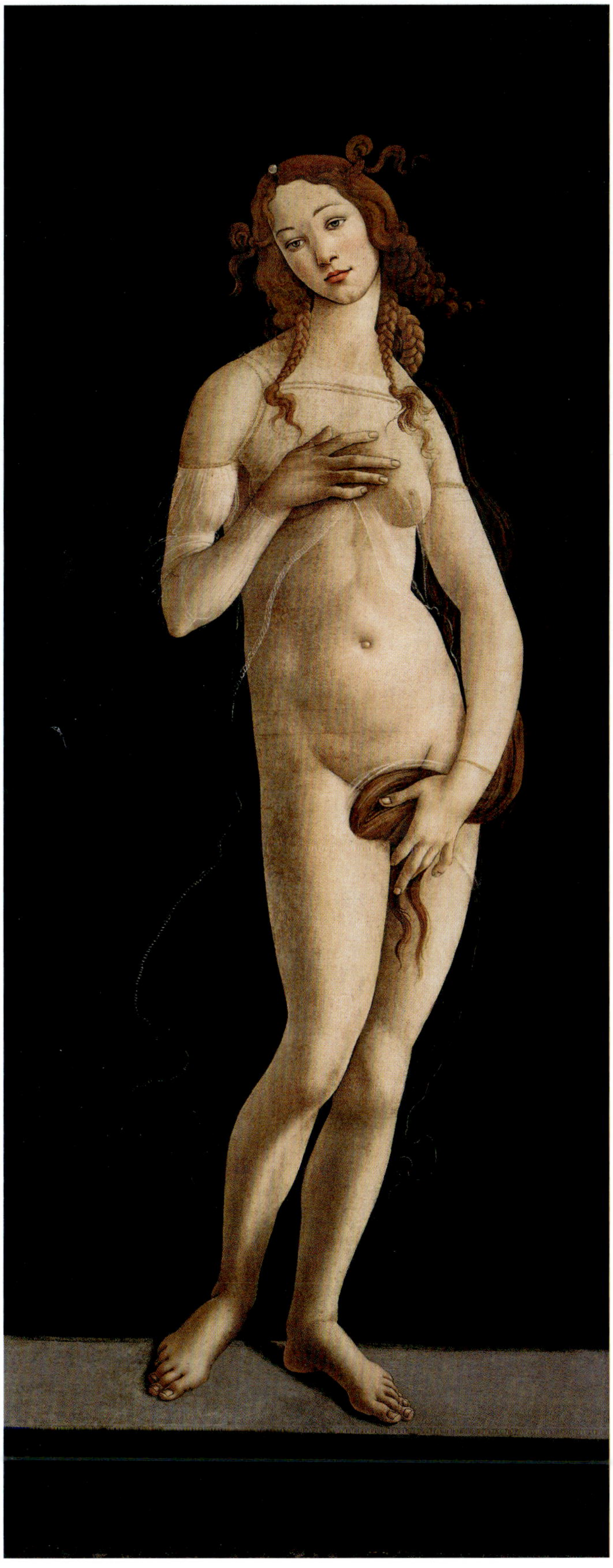

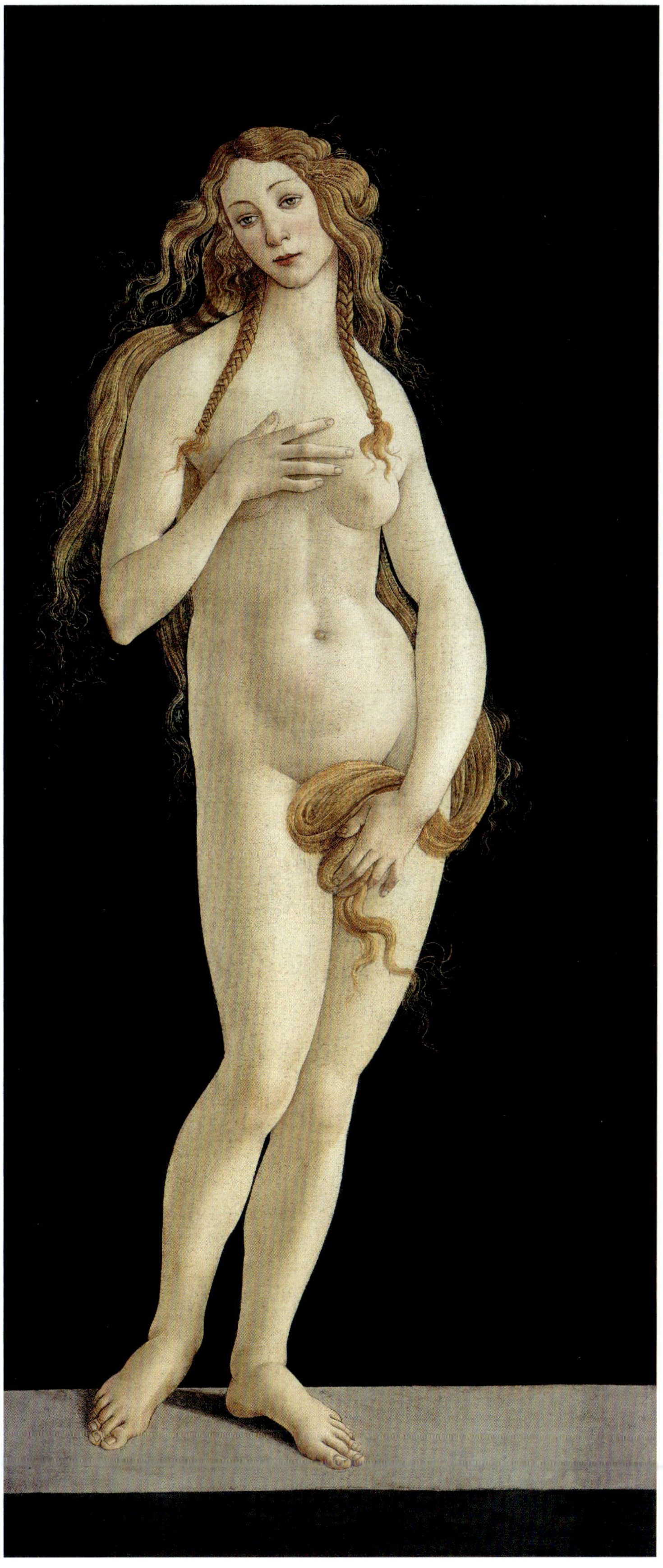

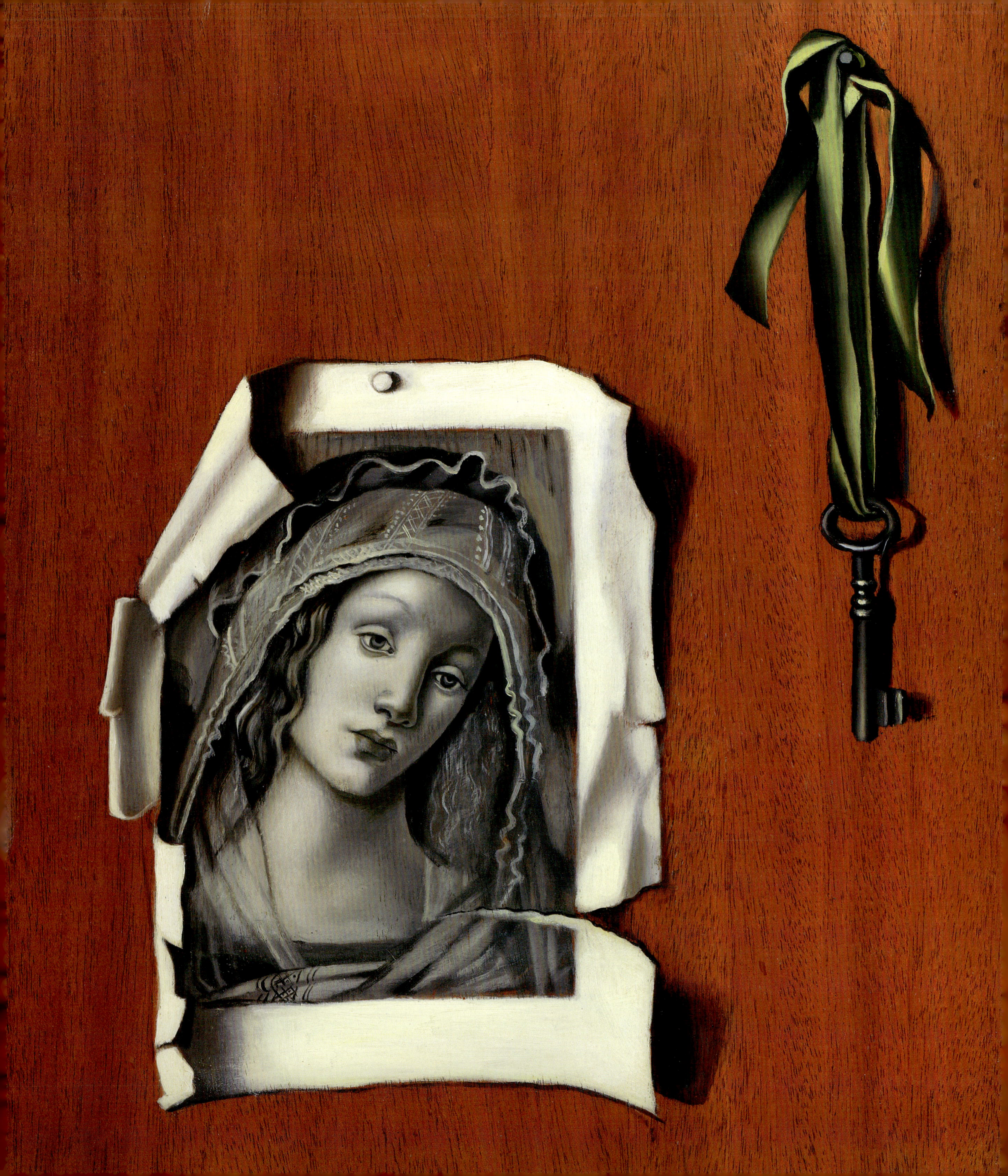

Notes

INTRODUCTION, pp. 10–15

Ana Debenedetti, Mark Evans, Ruben Rebmann and Stefan Weppelmann

1 Gombrich 1945, p. 7; Levey 1960; Weinberg 2004; Melius 2010.
2 Eliot 1951, p. 15.
3 Alberti 2004, p. 88. See the essay by Ana Debenedetti in this volume.
4 Aby Warburg, 'Sandro Botticelli's *Birth of Venus* and *Spring*: An Examination of Concepts of Antiquity in the Italian Early Renaissance' (1893), in Warburg 1999, pp. 92–3, 125.
5 Filippo Baldinucci (1681), cited in Fermor 1998, p. 126ff.
6 Baxandall 1972, pp. 26–7, 77–81, 152.
7 Alberti 1988, p. 156; Alberti 2004, p. 71.
8 Ibid., p. 75.
9 Richter 1949, p. 65, cited in Freedberg 1989, p. 361.
10 Vasari 1912–14, vol. 3, p. 250.
11 See the essays by Dagmar Korbacher, Mark Evans and Ruben Rebmann in this volume.
12 Podro 1982, pp. 1–3.
13 Evans 2011.
14 *Report from the Select Committee on Arts and their Connection with Manufactures*, House of Commons, London 1836, Part 1, p. 11, no. 8, cited in Evans 2011, p. 66. See the essays by Ruben Rebmann and Susanna Avery-Quash in this volume.
15 London 2007, p. 34; Warner 1992, pp. 3–4.
16 *The Literary Gazette*, 9 June 1849, p. 433, cited in London 1984, p. 69.
17 Brigstocke, Marchand and Wright 2010, pp. 3, 89; Kugler 1855, p. 200 and facing ill.; Burckhardt 1879, p. 63. Kugler's *Handbuch* first appeared in 1837, and his student Burckhardt's *Cicerone* in 1855. For Pater and Ruskin see the essays by Ulrich Rehm and Stephen Calloway in this volume.
18 John Ruskin, *Fors Clavigera*, Letter 22, 19 September 1872, cited in London 2000, p. 145; Ruskin 1903–12, vol. 27, pp. 371–2.
19 Letter of 22 December 1877 to Charles Fairfax Murray (Pierpont Morgan Library); cited in London 2000, p. 145.
20 See the essays by Mark Evans and Elizabeth Prettejohn in this volume.
21 Rossetti 1911, p. 232.
22 See the essays by Elizabeth Prettejohn and Susan Owens in this volume. Haweis 1879, pp. 97–9; Stern 2004, pp. 5–10.
23 London 1980, pp. 18–19; Liverpool 1900, p. 104, no. 1447. The 'Angel Panel' was priced in 1900 at £35 and survives in the drawing room of a house designed by Rathbone in Wilmslow, Cheshire. We are grateful to Joseph Sharples for this information.
24 Nichols 1998, pp. 42–3. Debussy remarked in 1889 that his favourite painters were then Botticelli and Gustave Moreau; Lockspeiser 1979, p. 119 n. 1.
25 Royal Collection Trust, RCIN 19551; http://www.royalcollection.org.uk/collection/19551/spring (accessed 22 February 2015). Copying famous paintings for the Gobelins manufactory had by the later nineteenth century ceased to be a principal task of the pensioners at the French Academy, but the copy remained an essential part of their curriculum and Degas advised his own students to be 'thoroughly imbued' with Florentine painters of the fifteenth century; Boime 1971, pp. 3, 122–7.
26 Körner 2006, p. 383; Gamble 1999; Smith 2005; Karpeles 2008, pp. 12–13, 16–18, 22–3, 50–3, 62–3, 102–3. See also the essay by Gabriel Montua in this volume.
27 Aby Warburg, 'Sandro Botticelli's *Birth of Venus* and *Spring*. An Examination of Concepts of Antiquity in the Italian Early Renaissance' (1893) and 'Botticelli' (1898), both in Warburg 1999, pp. 112, 158; Horne 1908, p. xviii. See also the essays by Caroline Elam and Gerhard Wolf in this volume.
28 Kurt W. Forster, 'Introduction', and Warburg (1893) in Warburg 1999, pp. 10–13, 89; see also Rampley 1997, pp. 41–55.
29 Lee and Anstruther-Thomson 1912; Burdett 2011.
30 Berenson 1896, p. 71. See also Lee and Anstruther-Thomson 1912, p. 112; Gagel 2010; Alison Brown, 'Bernard Berenson and "Tactile Values" in Florence', pp. 1–22; http://berenson.itatti.harvard.edu/berenson/items/show/3021 (accessed 22 February 2015). See also the essay by Oliver Tostmann in this volume.
31 Wölfflin 1952, pp. xi, 13.
32 Cited in Simonson 2013, p. 116.
33 Ibid., pp. 114–16.
34 Ibid., p. 116.
35 For these tableaux, see McConkey 1993, pp. 134–5.
36 Haskell 2000.
37 Ibid.; Braun 2005. Braun's essay states incorrectly that *Primavera* was included in these exhibitions.
38 Haskell 2000, pl. 31; Braun 2005, fig. 77.
39 The *Birth of Venus* was illustrated in colour facing the frontispiece of the exhibition catalogue, and received four pages of text, twice as much as any other work. See also the essay by Stefan Weppelmann in this volume.
40 See also the essays by Sonnet Stanfill and Riccardo Venturi in this volume.
41 See Rip Cronk, 'Art on the Rebound'; http://www.rcronk.com/venicereconstituted.html (accessed 22 February 2015).
42 Wells 2004, pp. 129, 133.
43 Munchausen's encounter with Venus occurs in chapter 20 of Rudolph Erich Raspe's *The Surprising Adventures of Baron Munchausen*, first published in 1785.
44 For appropriation or quotational art, see Belting 2001, pp. 405–26; Nelson and Shiff 2003, pp. 116–28; Evans 2009.
45 See the essay by Stefan Weppelmann in this volume.
46 See also the essay by Toshio Watanabe in this volume.
47 See for example Hatfield 2009; O'Malley 2013b.
48 See the essay by Caroline Campbell in this volume.
49 Ishizu and Zeki 2011; reported in *Art News Headlines*, 16 May 2011 http://www.escapeintolife.com/art-news/art-news-headlines-may-16-2011 (accessed 22 February 2015).

BOTTICELLI AND THE BOTTEGA, pp. 24–9

Caroline Campbell

This essay draws on the unpublished research of Sally Korman on the Botticelli workshop, undertaken with Marika Spring and Martin Wyld in 2001–2. I am indebted to Sally for her generosity in letting me make use of her work.

1 Lightbown 1978, vol. 1, pp. 155–6; Cecchi 2005, pp. 75–90; Körner 2006, pp. 290–310; O'Malley 2013a, pp. 197–204; O'Malley 2013b. The only other Renaissance painter whose work bears comparison with Botticelli, for his similar reliance on outlined forms and

dependence on an efficient workshop, is the Wittenberg painter Lucas Cranach the elder.

2 Baxandall 1972, p. 26. 'Sandro de Botticello pictore Excellen[mo] in tavola et in muro: le cose sue hano aria virile et sono cum optima ragione et integra proportione.'
3 For a summary of fifteenth-century Florentine workshop structure and practice, see Rubin 2007, pp. 62–9, 325–7.
4 See Cecchi 2005, pp. 30–57, 60–93.
5 Cennini 1960, p. 2; Santi 1976; Rubin 2007, p. 73.
6 Vasari 1981, vol. 3, p. 310.
7 Discussed in relation to Botticelli by Cecchi 2005, p. 41.
8 Holmes 1999, p. 15; Holmes 2004, p. 39; O'Malley 2013b, p. 11.
9 It should be noted that Fra Filippo Lippi, as a friar, was not obliged to keep to the guild system (or accept its jurisdiction): see Rubin 2007, pp. 66–9; for Jacopo di Domenico di Papi da San Giorgio, see Lightbown 1978, vol. 1, p. 154; Cecchi 2005, pp. 75–80; O'Malley 2013a, pp. 163–6.
10 Lightbown 1978, vol. 1, p. 154; Cecchi 2005, pp. 75–90; O'Malley 2013a, pp. 163–6.
11 Zambrano and Nelson 2004, pp. 103–16.
12 The summary given by Lightbown 1978, vol. 1, pp. 69–99, remains useful; see also Dempsey 1992; Zöllner 2005, pp. 64–84, 120–41.
13 Cecchi 2005, pp. 184–200; Zöllner 2005, pp. 86–99.
14 Lightbown 1978, vol. 1, pp. 100–14; Körner 2006, pp. 310–29.
15 Lightbown 1978, vol. 2, pp. 115–60; Körner 2006, esp. pp. 290–310; O'Malley 2013b, pp. 24–32.
16 Davies 1961, pp. 110–18.
17 Cecchi 2005, p. 226; Körner 2006, pp. 269–70.
18 Körner 2006, pp. 270–2.
19 Davies 1961, p. 111; Körner 2006, p. 301, ill. 201.
20 Davies 1961, p. 111 nn. 5–8.
21 Richter 1898, pp. 63–4; Davies 1961, p. 111.
22 Unpublished notes by Sally Korman, 2001–2.
23 Körner 2006, pp. 291–6; O'Malley 2013b, pp. 25–6.
24 Körner 2006, pp. 290–4.
25 O'Malley 2013a, pp. 200–5.
26 Davies 1961, pp. 99–101, 116–17; Letter from Lady Elizabeth Eastlake to William Boxall, 9 June 1874 (NGA 1/1/77/8).
27 Nethersole 2010.
28 Musée du Louvre, Paris, RF 1299.
29 Vasari 1981, p. 311.
30 Yashiro 1925, p. 157.
31 Philadelphia Museum of Art, John G. Johnson Collection, cats 44–7. We await eagerly the publication of Carl Brandon Strehlke and Mark Tucker's further research into the four surviving parts of this predella.
32 Körner 2006, p. 290.
33 For the fullest published study to date, see North 1997. Graeme Barraclough, Aviva Burnstock, Scott Nethersole and Karen Serres at the Courtauld Institute and Gallery, London, are pursuing further research into and technical study of the Convertite altarpiece.
34 North 1997.
35 Baxandall 1972, p. 26.

BOTTICELLI: BETWEEN NEOPLATONISM AND SAVONAROLA, pp. 30–5
Ana Debenedetti

1 *The Enneads* I, 6, 4; Plotinus 1991.
2 Whether this new Platonic Academy was a formal school or an institution with regular meetings is still a controversial subject among scholars. See for instance Hankins 1990; Field 1988.
3 The Renaissance reception of the mythological gods comes at the end of a long process rooted in the past centuries. See for instance Seznec 1953.
4 The most important of these was that of the Roman architect Vitruvius, which laid down precise rules governing the mathematical proportions used in the construction of buildings. Vitruvius drew parallels between these proportions and those of the ideal human figure, a concept famously illustrated by Leonardo da Vinci in his drawing of 'Vitruvian Man'.
5 Leon Battista Alberti is considered the father of modern art with the publication of his treatise *On Painting* first in Latin in 1435 [*De pictura*] followed by a vernacular version the following year [*Della pittura*]. His treatise on architecture written in Latin was published after in death in 1485 with a dedication to Lorenzo the Magnificent by Angelo Poliziano. Until then, the artistic practice was considered a mechanical activity. During the fifteenth century, a new category of learned artists fought to elevate the artistic activity to the dignity of the Liberal Arts. See Kristeller 1990.
6 See the letter titled *Prospera in fato fortuna, vera in virtute felicitas* in Ficino 1576, vol. 2, pp. 805–6.
7 Post 1914, pp. 257–63.
8 See Warburg 1999, pp. 86–156; Gombrich 1972, pp. 31–81; Wind 1958; Panofsky 1960. See also Ferruolo 1955.
9 Cecchi 2005, p. 178 n. 99; see Poliziano, *Stanze per la giostra*.
10 Savonarola was made a prior of the convent of San Marco in 1491, he consolidated further his power by taking over the convents of Fiesole, Prato and Pisa.
11 Vasari 1912–14, vol. 3, p. 251.
12 Pater 1893; Horne 1980, p. 189; Müntz 1891, pp. 26ff. For a discussion against Botticelli's involvement in Savonarola's sect, see Davies 1961, p. 105; Cecchi 2005, p. 296.
13 The inscription reads, as quoted in Davies 1961, p. 103: 'I Sandro painted this picture, at the end of the year 1500 (?), in the troubles of Italy in the half time after the time according to the 11th chapter of St John in the second woe of the Apocalypse in the loosing of the devil for three and a half years then he will be chained according to the 12th chapter and we shall see clearly ... as in this picture.'
14 See for instance Villari 1859–61; Ridolfi 1952. See Weinstein 1970, pp. 3–14.
15 Garin 1952, pp. 37–9.
16 See for instance, Filippino Lippi, *Crucifixion with the Virgin and St Francis*, formerly in the Kaiser Friedrich Museum, Berlin; and Domenico Ghirlandaio and workshop, *Resurrection*, Statens Museum for Kunst, Copenhagen.
17 Ficino, *De amore*, IV, 3: 'Nunc autem puros colores, lumina, vocem unam, fulgorem auri et argenti candorem, scientiam, anima, que omnia simplicia sunt, pulchra delectant' (author's translation).

THE PORTRAIT OF A LADY KNOWN AS *SMERALDA BANDINELLI*, pp. 36–41
Mark Evans

1 Kauffmann 1973, pp. 37–9; Lightbown 1978, vol. 2, pp. 28–9, no. B15; London 1999–2000, p. 327; Washington 2001–2, pp. 172–3; Berlin and New York 2011–12, pp. 112–14.
2 Dubois 1841, p. 10, no. 21.
3 Kauffmann 1973, pp. 37–9.
4 Patricia Lee Rubin, in London 1999–2000, p. 327.
5 Costaras and Richardson 2012–14.
6 Dante 2001, section XXXV.
7 Illustrated in Randolph 2002, pp. 102–3.
8 Cited by Dale Kent in Washington 2001–2, p. 26.
9 The Metropolitan Museum of Art, New York, gift of Henry G. Marquand, 1889; in Washington 2001–2, pp. 106–7.
10 Lindenau-Museum, Altenburg, variously dated to the 1470s or 1480s; Oertel 1961, pp. 15, 151–4; Lightbown 1978, p. 160.
11 Lightbown 1978, vol. 2, p. 37, no. B24.
12 Noted by Louis Waldman and reported by Patricia Lee Rubin and Alison Wright in London 1999–2000, p. 327. See also Waldman 2004, pp. x–xii.
13 Cramer 2000, pp. 192, 212–16; Boisset 2005, pp. 187–206.
14 Pourtalès's fortune was estimated in 1817 at 2 million francs; Langer 2006, p. 262. This was the equivalent in 1817 of £82,000, according to Denzel 2010, p. 286.
15 *Catalogue of the distinguished Collection of Select and Beautiful Paintings by the most Eminent Masters of the Dutch and Flemish Schools; formed during the last thirty years by the Count Pourtales*, Mr. Phillips, 73, New Bond Street, London, 19 and 20 May 1826 (Lugt 11181; copy annotated with prices in the library of the National Gallery).
16 Dubois 1841; Dawson and Uphill 1972, p. 91.
17 Middleton 1996.
18 That it could be visited every Wednesday from January to May was noted by Charles Eastlake in 1860; Avery-Quash 2011, p. 552; Foucart-Walter 2000.
19 Weinberg 2004, pp. 21–2. The total for the sale was 2,804,897 francs; Boisset 2005, p. 198; for the 1865 exchange rate of 25.193 francs : £1 see Denzel 2010, p. 288.
20 The Hals was bought for 700 guilders and sold for 51,000 francs; Ingamells 1992, pp. 135–8. The Antonello was reputedly bought for 750 francs and sold for 113,500 francs; Rome 2006, p. 242. For the 1822 exchange rate of 100 guilders : £8.195 see Denzel 2010, p. 20 and for the 1835 rate of 25.491 francs : £1 and the 1865 exchange rate of 25.193 francs : £1 see Denzel 2010, pp. 287, 288.
21 The former, now in Washington, sold for 2,600 francs and the latter for 3,400 francs; Lightbown 1978, vol. 2, pp. 78–9, no. B67; Kauffmann 1973, p. 39; Denzel 2010, p. 288.
22 Weinberg 2004, pp. 20, 23.
23 Rossetti fixed a label stating this on the reverse of the picture; ibid., p. 24.
24 Surtees 1971, pp. 151–2; Weinberg 2004, p. 26.
25 London 1872, no. 270, 'A Portrait – Sandro Botticelli, Panel 25½ × 15½ in. Lent by D.G. Rosetti [*sic*] Esq.'; Weinberg 2004, pp. 24–5.
26 Evans and Vandenbrouck 2012, pp. 28–9, 35; Surtees 1971, pp. 153–4.
27 Letter of 16 May 1880, in Bryson and Troxell 1976, p. 152.
28 Evans and Vandenbrouck 2012, pp. 22–45.

THE STORY OF BOTTICELLI'S DRAWINGS FOR DANTE'S *DIVINE COMEDY*, pp. 42–4

Dagmar Korbacher

1 Vasari 1987, p. 520.
2 The British Museum, London, Department of Prints and Drawings (inv. no. 1895,0915.447); see London and Florence 2010–11, p. 174, no. 36 (Marzia Faietti); Levey 1960, p. 292; Popham and Pouncey 1950, p. 16.
3 See Levey 1960, p. 293.
4 The British Museum, London, Department of Prints and Drawings (inv. no. 1855,0811.1/98), and Musée du Louvre, Paris, Département des Arts Graphiques (inv. nos RF 1475-1556, RF 425, 427, 428); see Elen 1995, pp. 213–22; nos 21, 22; pp. 425–63.
5 See Schulze Altcappenberg 2000, pp. 28–31.
6 See Stapleford 1995, p. 397.
7 Biblioteca Nazionale di Firenze, Florence, Cod. Magliabechiano, XVII, 17, fol. 84; quoted in Stapleford 1995, p. 408.
8 See Dombrowski 1992, p. 24 n. 1.
9 Gabinetto Disegni e Stampe degli Uffizi, Florence, inv. no. 3474F; see Stoltz 2011, esp. pp. 65–8 (on older literature); Brunner 1999, p. 52.
10 Bonhams, London (Knightsbridge), Old Master Drawings (Auction 10511), 9 July 2003, lot 21 (pen and brown ink over red chalk on vellum, 311 × 469 mm); Musei Civici, Reggio Emilia (Collezione Villani; pen and brown ink on vellum, 265 × 487 mm); see Reggio Emilia 2000–1, p. 133, no. IDV 68 (kindly brought to my attention by Maria Ludovica Piazzi).
11 See Schulze Altcappenberg 2000, p. 22.
12 Strzygowski 1885–6; Strzygowski 1887.
13 See Clarke 1819, p. 260.
14 See Waagen 1854, vol. 3, p. 307.
15 Pater 1986, p. 40.
16 *The Times*, 4 November 1882, p. 5, quoted in Watts 1993, p. 59.
17 Swinburne 1901, p. 326; see Levey 1960, p. 302.
18 Ruskin 1903–12, vol. 22, *Ariadne Florentina*, Lecture 1: 'Definition of the Art of Engraving', p. 305; vol. 23, Lecture 8: 'Botticelli', p. 265.
19 Pater 1986.
20 Ruskin 1903–12, vol. 22, *Ariadne Florentina*, Lecture 6: 'Design in the Florentine Schools of Engraving (Sandro Botticelli)', pp. 422–62; see also Weinberg 1987.
21 See Watts 1995, p. 81.
22 See Watts 1993, p. 61; Watts 1995, p. 87.
23 Ruskin 1903–12, vol. 27, letter 22, 19 September 1872, pp. 371–2.
24 See Vasari 1987, pp. 516–17; Pater 1986, p. 34.
25 See Keller 2000; Bellini 1990, esp. pp. 47–8.
26 Watts 1995, p. 91.
27 See Bertram 1950, p. 483; see also Havely 2014, pp. 244–59 *passim*.
28 See Watts 1995, pp. 93–7; Fulford 1981, pp. 122–8; Bode 1930, vol. 1, p. 198.
29 See Lippmann 1887.
30 See Berlin, Rome and London 2000–1.
31 See Cologne 2011–12, pp. 112–21.
32 See Voigt 2014.

THE CRITICAL FORTUNES OF VASARI'S BOTTICELLI IN THE NINETEENTH CENTURY, pp. 48–9

Ulrich Rehm

1 Vasari 1971, vol. 3, pp. 511–21, here p. 517.
2 See Rehm 2009; Waldman 2009.
3 Rio 1836, p. 343.
4 Pater 1912, pp. 50–62, p. xiv.
5 Ibid., p. 54.
6 Ibid., p. xiii.
7 Ibid., p. 64.
8 Ibid., pp. 55–7.
9 Ibid., pp. 53–4.
10 Ruskin 1903–12, vol. 22, 1906, p. 424; see also vol. 23, 1906, pp. 266, 277; Lottes 1996, p. 248.
11 Bullen 1994, pp. 223–7; Cherry 1998, pp. 205–6.
12 Ruskin 1903–12, vol. 23, 1906, p. 266.
13 Ibid., vol. 27, 1907, pp. 371–2.
14 Ibid., p. 375.
15 Rehm 2009, pp. 215–23.
16 Bode 1921, p. 174.

BOTTICELLI ENTERS THE MUSEUM: THE REDISCOVERY OF A PAINTER AND THE INVENTION OF THE PUBLIC ART MUSEUM, pp. 50–5

Ruben Rebmann

1 This includes several misattributions, for example Botticini's altarpiece of the three archangels, today in the Uffizi (inv. 1890 no. 8359), Bocchi-Cinelli 1677, p. 147.
2 Ibid., p. 16.
3 Ibid., p. 559, probably in the choir, where it was to be found in the eighteenth century.
4 Ibid., p. 144.
5 Archivio di Stato di Firenze, Guardaroba Medicea 826, fol. 77v, no. 379M. Leopoldo had also acquired another tondo, then thought to be by Botticelli, that today is attributed to Botticini. Mosco 1982, p. 41. The picture has been at the Galleria Palatina since 1828 (Pal. 347).
6 Archivio Storico delle Gallerie Fiorentine, Filza XIII, 1780, no. 141; Spalletti 2010, p. 50.
7 Zacchiroli 1783, vol. 3, p. 106.
8 Wolf 2013, p. 320.
9 Zacchiroli 1783, vol. 3, p. 101.
10 Spalletti 2008, p. 109. The sequence began with Andrea Rico, dated to the eleventh century, and ended with Cigoli in the seventeenth century.
11 La Galerie de Florence 1800, pages unnumbered [p. 36].
12 Denon 1999, vol. 2, p. 880.
13 Blumer 1936, p. 280; Musée Fabre, Montpellier, D79.1.2.
14 Preti Hamard 1999, p. 235.
15 Blumer 1936, p. 280; Palais des Beaux-Arts, Lille, p. 789.
16 As the 'École Allemande' in gallery guidebooks from 1807 and 1813. It was purchased in 1784 from Ottavio Magherini, who was also unable to identify it: 'Pare opera del fine de XV. secolo, e sarebbe desiderabile il sapere, o il potere indovinare l'autore, ma ne il Magherini hà potuto indicarlo, ne io fin qui ho saputo scoprirlo.' Archivio Storico delle Gallerie Fiorentine, Filza XVIII, 1785, no. 2.
17 Galerie Impériale et Royale de Florence 1816, p. 64, listed as a Botticelli.
18 On the history of the establishment of the Berlin museum, see Vogtherr 1997; Gaehtgens 2012.
19 Dietl 1993.
20 By way of comparison, Schinkel valued an early painting by Raphael, later referred to as the Solly Madonna, at only 5,000 thalers, Skwirbles 2009, p. 89.
21 Palica 2009, p. 77.
22 Wesenberg 1992, pp. 73–7.
23 Galerie Impériale et Royale de Florence 1816, p. 186. No longer listed: Galerie Impériale et Royale de Florence 1822, p. 171.
24 Description 1854, p. 62, and also, without further evidence, Lightbown 1978, vol. 2, p. 52.
25 Galerie Impériale et Royale de Florence 1844, p. 71. In the previous, fifteenth edition of the guide from 1840 (as well as earlier ones), it does not appear.
26 Archivio Storico delle Gallerie Fiorentine, Filza XXXIX, 1815, no. 13, letter from 8.5.1815: 'Tra i quadri che S.A.R. ha ordinato trasportarsi dal Palazzo Pitti ai magazzini della R. Guardaroba in Palazzo Vecchio, tre ne esistono che io crederei opportuni per guarnire i corridori di questa I. e R. Galleria. Il primo è una gran tela antica di Sandro Botticelli, esprimente la Nascita di Venere, che fa accompagnatura con altra dello stesso autore, già qui esistente tra i quadri della Scuola Toscana, ambedue fatte per la Casa Medici e a ragione commendate dal Vasari.'
27 Goncourt 1991, p. 91: 'Ce tableau c'est une *Naissance de Vénus* où c'est ne plus la Vénus brune de l'antiquité, mais une Vénus qui parait avoir pris naissance sur le Valpurgis [*sic*]: le type de la femme blonde du Nord… .'
28 Letter from Degas to Moreau from 21 September 1858: 'Je vous condurai devant un Botticelli à l'Académie des beaux-arts, que je suis sur que vous ne connaissez pas. C'est une allégorie. J'aime mieux ne vous en rien dire et vous mettre l'eau à la bouche.' Quoted in Moreau 2002, p. 451.
29 Lagrange 1862, p. 544.
30 Guida Accademia 1883, pp. 30–43.
31 Catalogo 1881, p. 121.
32 Catalogue 1905, pp. 219–20.
33 Waagen 1830, pp. 53–61.
34 Kaiser Friedrich Museum 1904, pp. 123–4.

BOTTICELLI AND THE GEORGIANS, pp. 56–61

Mark Evans

1 Symonds 1899, p. 181 n. 1, cited by Hoch 2005, p. 75.
2 Gent 1981, p. 72.
3 Peacham 1906, p. 154. Mountford entered Trinity College, Cambridge in 1594, was awarded the degree of doctor of divinity in 1620 and instituted Rector of Thorley in 1619. He held various clerical benefices until 1643 when he was ejected from his livings by Parliament, but became a Prebendary of Ely in 1644; http://friends-stjames.org/John_Mountford.htm (accessed 9 October 2014).
4 Peacham 1906, pp. 137–54; Hale 1996, pp. 58–9.
5 Aglionby 1685; Hale 1996, pp. 58–9.
6 Aglionby 1685, pp. 70–1. Levey 1960, pp. 292–3.
7 Richardson 1754, p. 49. The painting was in the 'Closet of Madama', perhaps that of Anna Maria Luisa de' Medici, who later bequeathed her family's art collection to the Tuscan state.
8 I am obliged to Ruben Rebmann for the former information (personal communication of 24 October 2014); Levey 1960, p. 293; Lightbown 1986, pp. 412–13; Lightbown 1978, vol. 2, pp. 35–7.
9 Gibson-Wood 2003, pp. 160–1; Levey 1960, p. 293. Four drawings from Richardson's collection, formerly attributed to Botticelli but now ascribed to Lorenzo di Credi or Filippino Lippi, are in the British Museum; Popham and Pouncey 1950, vol. 1, pp. 29–30, 86.

10 Ingamells 1997, pp. 532–3; Belsey 2014a.
11 Fleming 1955.
12 Ibid., p. 206; Cole and Middeldorf 1971; Smith 1972; Lightbown 1978, vol. 1, pp. 119–20 and vol. 2, pp. 85–6. According to an exchange rate of £20.72 : 100 ducati di banco and 126.92 ducati di banco : 100 scudi d'oro; Denzel 2010, pp. 40, 150. The problematic Lippi was purchased in 1771 for 30 sequins.
13 Ingamells 1997, pp. 635–7, 745–6; Belsey 2014b.
14 Watson 1940. Patch acquired detached fragments of frescoes ascribed by Vasari to Giotto but now attributed to Spinello Aretino, which he engraved and sold on to English collectors; Davies 1961, pp. 498–500; Morris and Hopkinson 1977, pp. 205–6.
15 Cited in Maser 1973, p. 193; Patch 1770; Compton 1960–1, pp. 35, 38.
16 Patch 1770, no. I, 'The Portrait of Masaccio / il ritratto di Masaccio'. The latter are now in the National Gallery, London (NG 626) and the National Gallery of Art, Washington (inv. 19); Lightbown 1978, vol. 1, p. 114 and vol. 2, pp. 65, 78–9.
17 *Catalogue of a select and valuable collection of Italian, French and Flemish Pictures*, Christie's, London, 12 May 1804, lot 82 (annotated copy in the Rijksbureau voor Kunsthistorische Documentaties, The Hague; http://lugt.idcpublishers.info, accessed 13 October 2014). Smith was elected an FSA in 1794 and attended meetings regularly in the earlier years of his fellowship, exhibiting various antiquities there in 1800–1 (personal communication from Adrian James, 15 October 2014). See also Compton 1960–1, pp. 32, 38; Ros 1866, p. 281, and Morris and Hopkinson 1977, pp. 20, 114, 152, 157, 171, 172, 173.
18 Dubois 1841, p. 4, no. 4; reprinted in *Catalogue des tableaux Anciens & Modernes Qui composent les Collections de Feu M. Le Comte de Pourtalès-Gorgier*, rue Tronchet 7, Paris 1865, p. 32, no. 87.
19 Findlen 2012, pp. 100–5; Findlen 2013.
20 Mazza and Tomasello 2004, pp. 52, 169, 207, 211, 302, 303.
21 Lanzi 1822, pp. 61–2.
22 Knowles 1831, p. 183.
23 Ibid., p. 184. For Fuseli's borrowings from Botticelli see Schiff 1973, pp. 99, 102, 447, 493–5.
24 Berlin, Rome and London 2000–1, pp. 20–2; Greco 1990a, pp. 261–80.
25 MacNaughton 2014.
26 Morris and Hopkinson 1977, pp. 1–4, 100, 125, 206, 212, 275–6.
27 *Catalogue of the very select and valuable library of William Roscoe Esq*, Mr. Winstanley, Marble Street, Liverpool, 19 August–3 September 1816, lot 999 (copy with prices in the Walker Art Gallery, Liverpool); *Catalogue of the genuine and entire collection of drawings and pictures, the property of William Roscoe Esq*, Mr. Winstanley, Marble Street, Liverpool, 23–8 September 1816, lots 39 and 40 (Lugt 8970; copy with prices in the Rijksbureau voor Kunsthistorische Documentaties, The Hague). I am grateful to Martin Hopkinson, Timothy Stevens and Xanthe Brooke for this information (personal communications of 9, 18 and 28 November 2014). See also Roscoe 1846a, p. 284; Roscoe 1846b, vol. 2, p. 350; Mazza and Tomasello 2004, p. 169; Keller 2000, pp. 332–3.
28 The grangerized six-volume set of Thomas Roscoe's translation of Lanzi was bequeathed in 1950 by the widow of Roscoe's grandson to Liverpool Central Library (pressmark 86–A4).
29 Lugt 1921, pp. 391, 406, nos 2183 and 2112 respectively; Berenson 1961, vol. 2, p. 155, no. 842 A-2**.
30 Turner 2014; Brigstocke, Marchand and Wright 2010; Marchi 2013, pp. 66–117.
31 *Catalogue of the rich and extensive collection of original drawings by the great masters formed by William Young Ottley*, T. Philipe, London, 6 June 1814, lots 205–7, 733–5; Lightbown 1978, vol. 1, pp. 134–8 and vol. 2, pp. 99–101, 112–13.
32 Lightbown 1978, vol. 1, pp. 134–8 and vol. 2, pp. 99–101.
33 Ingamells 1997, pp. 361–4, 521–2; Salvadori 2005.
34 Brigstocke, Marchand and Wright 2010, pp. 3, 89; Irwin 1979, pp. 34–43.
35 Cited in Irwin 1979, pp. 95–104.
36 Compare, for example, the illustrations to *Inferno*, canto VIII (machicolations on towers), XVI (running figures), XVII (figure of Geryon with crescent-shaped barb on tail), XXII (screaming mask), XXIII (cowled hypocrites and crucified sinner with inverted face), XXIX (massive arched stone bridge), XXXI (bearded giant), XXXIV (figure of Lucifer) and *Purgatory*, canto XI (souls bent double under boulders), XVIII (running souls), XIX (prone soul with face in crook of arm), XX (soul glancing up), XXI (folds of Dante's cloak), XXI (inverted tree) XXIII (running souls in attitude of prayer), XXVI (souls in flames), XXIX (candlesticks with drip pans and trailing striations); Salvadori 2005, pp. 68–9, 84–7, 98–101, 112–13, 116–17, 126–7, 162–3, 176–87, 192–3, 198–9; Berlin, Rome and London 2000–1, pp. 54–5, 78–83, 96–101, 116–17, 120–1, 128–9, 160–1, 176–87, 192–3, 200–1.
37 Clarke 1819, p. 260; '*Dante Alighieri, La Commedia, MS. on vellum, oblong folio.* Saec. XV. This fine MS ... is ornamented with eighty-eight original designs supposed to be executed by the hand *of Sandro Botticelli*, or some other eminent Florentine artist'; Munby 1972, pp. 10, 75, 113–14, 146–7, 155–6; Watts 1995, pp. 91–2.
38 Munby 1972, pp. 77–8; Eschapasse 2001, pp. 99–115. Gemmett 2000, pp. 92–3, 140, 142, 151, 191, 214, 241.
39 Letters of 10 January 1831 and 3 April 1833, in Gemmett 2000, pp. 53, 196.
40 Brigstocke, Marchand and Wright 2010, pp. 356, 520, 571. An engraving after a Botticelli portrait of a lady was published in 1807 with an attribution to Cimabue and another of the Sistine fresco of *Moses Punishing Korah* appeared in 1823 in Séroux d'Agincourt's delayed *L'Histoire de l'Art par les monuments*; Levey 1960, pp. 294, 296.
41 For the Renaissance painters most admired in the early nineteenth century see Haskell 1987, pp. 90–115.
42 Bindman 2005; Vaughan 1979, pp. 2, 30, 41, 74, 123–8, 130, 140, 145, 183, 192.
43 London 2011–12, pp. 72–3, 294–5. The Riepenhausen drawing was one of two intended for a volume of the *Geschichte der Malerei in Italien* which remained unpublished, and was later acquired by Dominique-Vivant, Baron Denon, the first director of the Louvre; Levey 1960, p. 296. Schnorr's drawing perhaps brought Botticelli's panel to the attention of his friend, Johann Gottlob von Quandt, who later acquired the painting.

THE LOVE AFFAIR WITH FLORENCE, pp. 62–7
Stephen Calloway

1 From a conversation between Burne-Jones and Freda Stanhope (niece of his old friend Spencer Stanhope) on the last afternoon of his life. Quoted (unsourced) in Dentler 1964, p. 36; the painter's widow gives a more prosaic version of the sentiment in Burne-Jones 1904, vol. 2, p. 347: '[Time spent in] Florence is your most delightful time of year, and the rest is nothing.'
2 Lee 1880, p. 33.
3 Oliphant 1876, p. xv.
4 *Memoriale di molto statue et picture sono nella inclyta cipta di Florentia per mano di sculptori & pictori excellenti moderni & antiqui, tracto dalla propria copia di Messer Francesco Albertini prete Fiorentino. Anno domini 1510.* Horne 1908, p. ix, cites a 'unique copy' in the Biblioteca Riccardiana.
5 On the Arundel Society, see Ledger 1978. The famous Arundel large colour lithographs after Botticelli were published fairly late in the society's history: the *Birth of Venus* in 1870 and *Primavera* not until 1888.
6 Steegman 1947, p. 123.
7 On Lindsay and the wider reception of his book, see Steegman 1947 and Edinburgh 2000.
8 *Praeterita*, in Ruskin 1903–12, vol. 30, p. 359.
9 Ibid.
10 'The Autumn in Florence' (1873), reprinted in James 1909, p. 376.
11 Ibid.
12 See Horne 1908, p. xi.
13 Swinburne 1868; Pater 1870, reprinted in Pater 1873, pp. 39–51.
14 Pater 1873, p. 51.
15 Ibid., p. 45.
16 Horne 1908, p. xiii.
17 It was generally held that income went three times further in Italy when compared with living expenses in England.
18 *Ariadne Florentina*, in Ruskin 1903–12, vol. 22, p. 395.
19 'Italy Revisited' (1877), reprinted in James 1909, p. 175.
20 Forster 1908, ch. 5.
21 James 1909, pp. 176–7.
22 Ibid.

BOTTICELLI AND VICTORIAN ART COLLECTING, pp. 68–75
Susanna Avery-Quash

1 See Lightbown 1978, vol. 2, p. 23. Mrs Gardner's first major acquisition was Botticelli's *The Tragedy of Lucrezia*, which she bought in 1894 through Colnaghi's and Berenson.
2 A fact noted by Howard 1999, p. 75.
3 Turner 1996, vol. 4, p. 503.
4 See Passavant 1836; Waagen 1854; Waagen 1857.
5 Reproduced in Caldesi and Montecchi 1858. Although misattributed, this is likely to be one of the first photographic illustrations of a Botticelli painting.
6 Layard 1903, vol. 2, p. 231 (letter from Layard to Lady Eastlake, from Florence, 13 November 1865).
7 Horne 1908, p. xii.
8 Rossetti 1895, vol. 1, p. 264.
9 Report 1836, response by Gustav Waagen, p. 5.
10 Smith 1895, vol. 2, p. 76.
11 Layard 1903, vol. 2, p. 231.
12 Letter from Eastlake to R.N. Wornum, 14 September 1863 (NGA 5/152/7).
13 Quoted in Levey 1960, p. 300.
14 See 'Notes on paintings' (NGA 1/1/20/11). In September 1867 Waagen noted in a letter to von Quandt (NGA 1/1/18/11) that

although Botticelli was by now 'a name', the Quandt Botticelli would be interesting in Britain 'only to a very small public and consequently would be difficult to sell'.

15 Eastlake had been 'at one time in treaty' for some of the Barker Botticellis ('two of the long Botticellis', including the *Venus and Mars*); see letter from Layard to Boxall, 28 December 1873 (NGA 1/1/74/12).

16 The Farinola Botticelli (*The Last Communion of St Jerome*) was offered to the nation more than once. For instance, in 1898 Herbert Horne offered it for 30,000 lire. Although Burne-Jones expressed the greatest admiration for it, and Lord Carlisle was interested, the negotiation came to nothing as the then director, Sir Edward Poynter, said it was too expensive, ill drawn and the head of St Jerome was too small. See Horne 1986, pp. xi, 402–4. I am grateful to Caroline Elam for drawing this episode to my attention.

17 See a paragraph describing the Botticellis lent by Barker in the *Athenauem*, no. 2192 (30 October 1869), p. 568.

18 For the painting's chequered attribution history, see http://collections.vam.ac.uk/item/O17317/portrait-of-a-lady-known-painting-botticelli-sandro/ (accessed 5 December 2014).

19 Popham and Pouncey 1950, vol. 1, pp. 15–17.

BOTTICELLI AND THE PRE-RAPHAELITES, pp. 76–81

Elizabeth Prettejohn

1 The price may have been 20 guineas (rather than pounds); see Weinberg 2004, p. 24.

2 Surtees 1971, nos 207, 255, 233.

3 Pater 1870.

4 Jerome McGann, 'The Poetry of Dante Gabriel Rossetti (1828–1882)', and Elizabeth Prettejohn, 'The Painting of Dante Gabriel Rossetti', in Prettejohn 2012, pp. 89–102, 103–15.

5 For a fuller account see Prettejohn 2007, pp. 228–31.

6 See Rossetti's note to his sonnet 'For Spring, by Sandro Botticelli', in Rossetti 1911, p. 232.

7 Dante Gabriel Rossetti to Jane Morris, 16 May 1880, in Fredeman 2002–10, vol. IX, p. 180 (letter 80.175).

8 See the relevant chapter by Mark Evans in this volume; Weinberg 2004, p. 23.

9 See for example Haskell 1976, pp. 174–8 and *passim*; Kermode 1985.

10 Rossetti 1895, vol. 1, p. 264.

11 Melius 2010, p. 129 and ch. 4, 'Against Aestheticism'.

12 It is unclear whether the Rossetti family or the Pre-Raphaelite circle knew of the volume of Botticelli's drawings for Dante's *Divine Comedy* in the Hamilton collection before its sale in 1882; see Watts 1995. Burne-Jones acquired reproductions of the drawings in 1885; see Burne-Jones 1904, vol. 2, p. 147.

13 Horne 1980, p. xvii.

14 New York 1998–9, pp. 85, 141–2; Horne 1980, p. xviii (William Michael Rossetti); Swinburne 1868, pp. 22–6; Ward 2011–12, pp. 62–4 (Solomon); Crane 1907, p. 125. For Millais see Susanna Avery-Quash's essay in this volume.

15 Swinburne 1868, p. 23. The tapestries of the Morris firm seem imbued with reminiscences of *Primavera* (a reproduction of which is clearly visible hanging on the wall in photographs of Morris's workroom at Kelmscott House).

16 Dante Gabriel Rossetti to Jane Morris, 1 August 1879, in Fredeman 2002–10, vol. VIII, pp. 323–4 (letter 79.122).

17 See Birmingham 2005–6, p. 147; Melius 2010, pp. 14–18, 22–4.

18 Rossetti was also fascinated by the *Mystic Nativity* (NG 1034), then in the Fuller Maitland collection but repeatedly exhibited in the years before its acquisition by the National Gallery in 1878.

19 See Burne-Jones 1904, vol. 2, pp. 64–5.

20 La Sizeranne 1898, p. 222.

21 Horne 1980, p. xix.

22 Ibid., p. xviii; Warburg 1999, p. 112.

BEARDSLEY AND BOTTICELLI, pp. 82–5

Susan Owens

1 Hind 1925, p. vii.

2 Ross 1909, pp. 40, 42.

3 Ibid., p. 14.

4 From a letter to G.F. Scotson-Clark of July 1891; Maas, Duncan and Good 1970, p. 19. The Rossetti drawings in Gurney's collection were a pen and wash version of *The Death of Lady Macbeth* and a preparatory graphite study for *A Vision of Fiametta* (Surtees 1971, nos 242B and 252A respectively), both of which Gurney had purchased from the posthumous sale of Rossetti's work held at Christie's, London, in May 1883.

5 Surtees 1971, nos 170 and 195 respectively. Although no illustrated book about Rossetti was published until 1894 (Esther Wood's *Dante Rossetti and the Pre-Raphaelite Movement*), Beardsley would have seen photographic reproductions of his paintings of the kind produced by Frederick Hollyer.

6 Ross 1909, pp. 16–17. Matthew Sturgis suggests that his source was an article by Helen Zimmern entitled 'Angels in Art', in the journal *Atalanta*, vol. 5, no. 51 (December 1891), which illustrates two Botticelli tondi: Sturgis 1998, p. 87.

7 Pater 1873, pp. 48–9.

8 See Wakeman 1973, pp. 126–40.

9 See Calloway 1998, pp. 31–3; Sturgis 1998, pp. 71–5.

10 From a letter to G.F. Scotson-Clark of around September 1891; Maas, Duncan and Good 1970, p. 28.

11 Vallance, whom Beardsley met early in 1892, was to become William Morris's biographer. It was through Vallance that Beardsley met Robert Ross.

12 Aymer Vallance, 'List of Drawings by Aubrey Beardsley', in Ross 1909, pp. 72–3, no. 47.

13 Beardsley's portrait distinctly resembles Botticelli's *Portrait of a Man Holding a Medallion of Cosimo de' Medici* in the Uffizi, attributed to Botticelli since 1883.

14 From the letter to G.F. Scotson-Clark of July 1891; Maas, Duncan and Good 1970, p. 19.

15 The Madonna Beardsley saw in Leyland's collection is the *Virgin and Child with the Young St John*, Lightbown no. C38; the '4 pictures for Nastagio' are Lightbown nos B35, 36, 37 and 38. The editors of the *Letters of Aubrey Beardsley* misinterpret Beardsley's handwriting here and give 'Mastagio [?]' for Nastagio (Maas, Duncan and Good 1970, p. 19).

16 This drawing was published in volume IV of the *Yellow Book* in January 1895.

17 Ross 1909, p. 41.

18 See Calloway 1998, p. 201.

BOTTICELLI'S PATH TO MODERNITY: CONTINENTAL RECEPTION 1850–1930, pp. 86–91

Gabriel Montua

1 See the essay by Ulrich Rehm in this volume.

2 Bann 2004, p. 25; Haskell 1976, pp. 9–10.

3 Letter from Edgar Degas to Gustave Moreau, 27 September 1858, in Moreau 2002, pp. 450–2.

4 Lacambre 1992, pp. 79–80.

5 Paris 2014–15a, p. 23.

6 Bode 1997, p. 118.

7 Letters from Henri Evenepoel to his father, 4 and 8 April 1893, in Evenepoel 1923, pp. 10–11.

8 On the reception of the Pre-Raphaelites in France and Burne-Jones's influence on Parisian theatres and set design, see Lethève 1959, pp. 322–3.

9 Mirbeau 1993a, p. 88.

10 Huysmans 1955, p. 170; for a comparison between the pictures Huysmans mentions and the Paris exhibition see Lethève 1959, p. 321.

11 Lorrain 2007, pp. 266–70, here p. 267; on the reception of the Pre-Raphaelites in France, see Lethève 1959.

12 Mirbeau 1993b, pp. 156, 162. I wish to thank J.-C. Lebensztejn for drawing my attention to this article.

13 Ibid., p. 159. Maurice Denis, diary entry from 18 December 1887, in Denis 1957, p. 67.

14 Huysmans 2006, p. 474.

15 Bredekamp 2000, pp. 71–82; Paris 1999–2000, pp. 231–2; sources regarding Charles Ephrussi's role in the purchase can be found in the documentation of the frescoes in the Louvre (RF 321 and 322).

16 On the reception of the Pre-Raphaelites in Italy and the development of the *Stile Liberty*, see Pieri 2007; Oxford and Ravenna 2010.

17 Dresden 2000, pp. 23–6, no. 19.

18 Picabia 1978, p. 186.

19 Pierre 2002, pp. 215–33, 231.

20 See the essay by Stefan Weppelmann in this volume.

HERBERT HORNE'S BOTTICELLI, pp. 94–101

Caroline Elam

1 Elam 2009, n. 1, citing letter from Horne to Roger Fry, 1913: '... I belong to the good old days of Queen Victoria'; see also, more precisely, in Horne's *Memorie autobiografiche* (AH, H.VI.4): 'I do not belong to the already remote and classic epoch of "1880". My period, alas, was a whole decade later. My contemporaries ... flourished in the last years of the Victorian era.' For Horne's biography, see especially Saxl 1957; Fletcher 1970 and 1980; Crawford 2014.

2 Elam 2009.

3 Fletcher 1980. See also Horne's letters from Florence to Edgar Jepson in London (SU, HPHL). Among these, particularly interesting was Muriel Broadbent, later Mrs Edith Catherine 'Amaryllis' Hacon, sitter to Charles Haselwood Shannon, William Rothenstein and Charles Conder.

4 Horne 1908, pp. 326, 344.

5 For his collection, see a whole series of catalogues, including Collobi Ragghianti 1966; Garofalo 2000; Paolini 2002.

6 Saxl 1957, on the 'torrid and the frigid intertwined', but see also Elam 2009, for continuity.

7 Letter to Randall Davies, 1912, cited in Davies 1916, 'Introduction', and in Elam

2009, p. 188. For the palace and its restoration, see Preyer 1993 and 2000.

8 Horne 1908; Horne 1980.

9 Fry 1908. For further tributes by Fry to Horne, see Fry 1916 and 1926. Horne had designed the *Burlington Magazine*'s front cover, bound volumes cover and initial letters, as well as contributing an article to the first issue; see Elam 2009.

10 Such as Francesco Albertini's 1510 guidebook to Florence or Condivi's *Life of Michelangelo*. See illustrations in Elam 2009.

11 The only painting he had not seen among those he classified as autograph was the *Adoration of the Magi* now in the National Gallery of Art, Washington, then in St Petersburg (Horne 1908, pp. 103–4). Mary Berenson supplied him with notes: see letter from Horne to Berenson, 27 May 1902 (AB).

12 Horne 1987.

13 Horne 1908, pp. ix–xv (xv–xxi in the 1980 reprint). Levey 1960 remains essential reading.

14 Pater 1870; reprinted in Pater 1873.

15 Morelli's attributions to Botticelli are to be found in Morelli 1890–3, vol. 1, pp. 43, 98–9, 105–11; vol. 2, pp. 135, 336; vol. 3, pp. 10–15.

16 Crowe and Cavalcaselle 1864–6, vol. 2, pp. 414–30; Crowe and Cavalcaselle 1911, pp. 249–73.

17 Berenson described Horne as the 'great man of the next generation' (Samuels 1979, p. 62). In fact Berenson, Fry, Horne and Warburg were all of the same generation.

18 This rather unsuccessful episode, involving the Carfax Gallery and Robert Ross, is discussed in Elam 2009, pp. 177–8. Mary Berenson's diaries of 1896–8 (AB) are packed with references to Horne.

19 Horne 1903, reviewed by Fry 1903; see Elam 2009, pp. 178–9.

20 Berenson 1965, pp. 79–80. For the deathbed visit, see Strachey and Samuels 1983, pp. 207–9; Samuels 1987, pp. 203–4.

21 'Ihr ist eigentlich der einzige richtig cultiverte Zeitgenosse', letter from Aby Warburg to Mary Warburg, 16 October 1902 (WIA, GC), cited in Roeck 2009, p. 128.

22 On Horne: 'long English cranium, pallid, thin moustache turned up at the ends, struggles with a stammer' ('Englischer Langschädel, bleich, dürftiger augestellter Schnurrbart, kämpft gegen Stottern'); on Berenson: 'cold blue eyes, pushy and snobbish, an affected sharpness ([I am] to publish documents for him), no enthusiasm' ('Berenson kalte blaue Augen, Streber und Snob, eine affectirte Schärfe (Dokumente für ihn publizieren), kein Enthusiasmus' (WIA, III.10.2, 101r-v), cited, with slightly different translation, in Roeck 2009, pp. 128, 160.

23 'Der liebe Gott steckt im detail'; see Gombrich 1986, p. 13 n. 1.

24 Reprinted in Berenson 1901, pp. 46–69. For a thorough account, see Zambrano's discussion in Berenson 2005, and a crucial recent contribution by Nelson 2009.

25 For the Smeralda, see in this volume, pp. 36–41; for the Pitti portrait (once called *La bella Simonetta*), which I believe to be a superb autograph piece, but is often doubted and even called a fake, see cat. 160, and see the excellent entry by Nicoletta Pons in Paris and Florence 2003–4, p. 226, no. 36; for the Giuliano, see in this volume, cat. 154, 155.

26 Berenson 1901, pp. 67–9.

27 This is extremely well disentangled by Nelson 2009, analysing Horne's letters to Fry in Sutton 1985.

28 Berenson 1932.

29 Sutton 1985, pp. 146–53, for this and many other letters on the Philadelphia panels. See also the rich account in Strehlke 1989. They were bought by J.G. Johnson of Philadelphia, and we can agree with Horne that they 'are surely the most important of all his Italians'. Sutton 1985, p. 153.

30 Berenson 1913, pp. 27–9; Horne 1913.

31 Yashiro 1925. The issue is too complex to be gone into here, but essentially critics fall into three camps: those who date both Courtauld *Trinity* and the predella early as from the Convertite (Yashiro 1925 etc.); those who accept the Convertite origin for both but date them late (e.g. Bode 1925, pp. 84–5, 141; Lightbown 1978, vol. 1, pp. 75–8; Cecchi 2005, pp. 290–1; Körner 2006, pp. 361–3); and those who prefer to date the predella early and associate it with another candidate for the Convertite altarpiece the *Virgin and Child with Saints* in the Uffizi (Gamba 1931, pp. 595–8, 1936, pp. 103–5; Mesnil 1938, pp. 31–3; Preyer 1999, pp. 285–6). Padoa Rizzo 2001 has argued that both altarpieces came from the Convertite, but still associates the Philadelphia predella with the *Trinity*. Whatever the status of the Courtauld panel, in my view the predella must be early, as Berenson and Horne concluded.

32 WIA, letter cited at note 29 above: 'Der Frühling sei für den anderen Lorenzo/ di Piero Francesco [*inserted above line*]/ gemalt in dessen Besitz Castello war er 1478.'

33 It still remains a problem, as Bode pointed out (Bode 1925, ch. 4) that Lorenzo di Pierfrancesco, born in 1463, was very young to have commissioned *Primavera* around 1478, which seems to be its likely date on stylistic grounds. His father had died in 1476. Shearman 1975 published an inventory of 1498 listing *Primavera* hung in Lorenzo di Pierfrancesco's town palace in Via Larga, the earliest mention of the painting.

34 Letter from Warburg to Horne, 15 November 1902 (WIA, GC). Warburg's letter is cited in Roeck 2009, p. 129, but translated back from the German translation in the original edition of his book.

35 Warburg 1898. I do not know if Horne ever read this article, which was so in tune with his own views.

36 Warburg 1999, p. 157.

37 Ibid., citing Müller-Walde 1897, p. 165. Warburg translates the Milanese agent's comments as: 'seine Werke haben männlichen Ausdruck und sind mit Überlegung und Proportion gemacht.'

38 Horne 1908, for example, pp. III, 353.

39 Ibid., pp. 52–4, 101. Out of tact, Horne does not explicitly attribute the idea to Warburg.

40 WIA, GC, letter from Warburg to Bode, 7 May 1920: 'er war Architekt von Haus aus, und es fehlte ihm doch wohl neben seinem unglaublich ausdauernden Sinn für das Urkundliche ein Stück wissenschaftliche Phantasie, um die für sich noch heute zweifellose Beziehung zwischen dem Simonetta-Kult und dem Reich der Venus und der Geburt nachzufühlen, einzusehen.'

41 Fry 1908, p. 84.

42 Kermode 1985.

43 *Memorie autobiografiche* (AH, H.VI.4).

44 Bode 1921; Bode 1925, p. 3. Bode also published the Botticelli volume in the 'Klassiker der Kunst' series, Bode 1926.

45 Mesnil 1930. Mesnil's own monograph (Mesnil 1938) stressed Botticelli's role as an excellent artisan, appreciated by the populace as well as the elite.

WARBURG'S BOTTICELLI AND BOTTICELLI'S NYMPH, pp. 102–5

Gerhard Wolf

1 Warburg (1898) 1998, pp. 61–8, here p. 63; trans. in Warburg (1898) 1999, pp. 157–64, here p. 157. See also Melius 2010, on Warburg, esp. p. 129ff.

2 Warburg (1893) 1998, pp. 1–57; Warburg (1893) 2010, pp. 39–123; trans. in Warburg (1893) 1999, pp. 89–156.

3 Warburg (1893) 1998, 'Preface', p. 5.

4 From the extensive bibliography I mention only: Gombrich 1945; Wind 1958; Levi D'Ancona 1983 with an exploration of the botanical world of *Primavera*; Dempsey 1968, Dempsey 1992. While Warburg believed the *Birth of Venus* and *Primavera* were a pair taken from the Medici villas of Castello or Careggi, by now it has been shown that *Primavera* (probably created in 1485) was initially placed in Lorenzo di Pierfrancesco de' Medici's city palace with its counterpart, Botticelli's *Minerva and the Centaur*, while the *Birth of Venus* was made for an unknown location, before Botticelli's work in the Sistine Chapel. On the reconstruction of *Primavera*'s position in the city palace belonging to a branch of the Medici family, see Rohlmann 1996. For a critique of the Neoplatonic reading of the image with regard to its research history and interpretation in terms of a Lucretian understanding of nature, see Bredekamp 2009.

5 Warburg (1893) 1998, p. 37.

6 Papapetros 2014.

7 Warburg (1893) 1998, p. 54.

8 On the relationship between Chloris and Flora in this context see Wind 1958, p. 116ff. For the relevant passage in Ovid, see *Fasti* V, 195: 'Chloris eram quae Flora vocor.'

9 Warburg (1893) 1998, p. 45ff.

10 Ibid., p. 55.

11 Ibid., p. 54.

12 Ibid., p. 61–8, here p. 68.

13 Ibid.

14 Warburg (1912) 1998, pp. 459–81, here p. 477.

15 Ibid., p. 478.

16 Warburg (1898) 1998, p. 66; on the *ninfa* see the fragment of correspondence with Jolles in Warburg (1900) 2010, pp. 198–210, as well as – from the rich literature – esp. Huber 1993, pp. 443–60; Dempsey 2004; Didi-Huberman 2005, pp. 331–60.

17 Warburg (1898) 1998, p. 63.

18 See London 1993, p. 111ff.; Gamble 1999, pp. 381–94. On Ruskin's erotic desires regarding Botticelli's Graces, see his correspondence in London 1993, p. 113.

BERNARD BERENSON AND AMERICA'S DISCOVERY OF SANDRO BOTTICELLI, pp. 106–9

Oliver Tostmann

1 Gennari Santori 2004; Rubin 2000; Miller 1992. I am grateful to Christopher T. Richards and Vanessa Sigalas for their many suggestions and words of advice.

2 Bo 1967 offers an overview.

3 Boskovits and Brown 2003, pp. 145–80.

4 See most recently, Connors and Waldman 2014; Cohen 2013; Samuels 1987; Samuels 1979; Washington 1979.

5 Berenson 1896; Berenson 1903b.
6 Berenson 1900, pp. 69–70.
7 Berenson 1913; Berenson and Roberts 1916.
8 Hadley 1987, pp. 17–26.
9 Prior to 1894 there were some paintings in American collections that were erroneously ascribed to Botticelli. See, for instance, White 1853, p. 14; Sirén 1916, p. 135.
10 Sandro Botticelli, *Virgin and Child*, tempera on wood, 84 × 63 cm, Isabella Stewart Gardner Museum, Boston.
11 Sandro Botticelli and workshop, *The Nativity*, tempera on wood, tondo, diameter: 30 cm, Isabella Stewart Gardner Museum, Boston.
12 Miller even speaks of a 'Botticelli madness' in Boston during this period; Miller 1992, p. 11.
13 Melius 2010, pp. 46–103; see also the excellent online exhibition on Berenson as a student at Harvard: http://berenson.itatti.harvard.edu/berenson/ (accessed 10 March 2015). Many books by Ruskin as well as Pater's *Marius the Epicurean* (1885) are held in Gardner's library.
14 Sandro Botticelli, *Virgin and Child with St John the Baptist*, tempera on wood, 123.8 × 84.4 cm, Museum of Fine Arts, Boston.
15 Letters from W.S. Bigelow to Isabella Stewart Gardner dated 12 March 1895 and 31 March 1895. See also a letter from Richard Norton to Isabella Stewart Gardner dated 14 September 1898. The three letters are in the archives of the Isabella Stewart Gardner Museum in Boston.
16 See a letter from Berenson to Isabella Stewart Gardner dated 1 August 1894, in Hadley 1987, p. 39.
17 Howard 2014.
18 Secrest 2004.
19 Duveen 1941, nos 100–6.
20 Brown 2014, esp. p. 278ff. See also Clark 1960.

BOTTICELLI, YUKIO YASHIRO AND THE SCHOLARSHIP ON WESTERN ART IN JAPAN, pp. 110–13
Toshio Watanabe

1 Isozaki and Yoshida 1977, p. 67.
2 Tokyo 1986, pp. 269–77.
3 Yashiro 1972, pp. 86–9.
4 Ibid., p. 83.
5 See the essay by Caroline Elam in this volume.
6 See the essays by Caroline Elam and Gerhard Wolf in this volume.
7 Yashiro 1972, pp. 83–6.
8 Yashiro 1929, p. xiv.
9 Ibid., pp. xviii–xix.
10 Yashiro 1972, pp. 101–2.

BOTTICELLI AND FASHION, pp. 114–19
Sonnet Stanfill

1 British *Vogue*, 6 July 1938, p. 50.
2 Blum 2007, p. 180.
3 Suzy Menkes, 'Poppy Seeds', *Vogue.com*, 9 June 2014, http://www.vogue.co.uk/news/2014/06/10/suzy-menkes-vogue-column-poppy-delevingne- wedding-dress-pucci-dundas (accessed 2 December 2014).
4 Sarah Mower, 'Alexander the Great', American *Vogue*, 19 April 2011, http://www.vogue.com/865444/alexander-the-great/ (accessed 2 December 2014).
5 Suzy Menkes, 'A Giant Step Forward for Womankind', 8 October 2006, *International Herald Tribune*.
6 *Harpers Bazaar*, April 2007, quoted on the website of the Metropolitan Museum of Art, http://blog.metmuseum.org/alexandermcqueen/dress-sarabande (accessed 2 December 2014).
7 Evans 2003, p. 187.

FILMING BOTTICELLI IN POST-WAR ITALY, pp. 120–123
Riccardo Venturi

1 'On pourrait considérer notre rapport à la peinture sous cet aspect: ce ne sont pas des images immobiles, mais plutôt des photogrammes chargés de mouvement qui proviennent d'un film qui nous manque. Il faudrait les rendre à ce film (vous aurez reconnu le projet d'Aby Warburg)': Agamben 1998, p. 66.
2 V., 'Cinema. I film sulla danza', *Il Progresso d'Italia* (Bologna), 7 July 1949.
3 'l'interpretazione cinematografica di un quadro o di un gruppo di quadri, a scopi narrativi', 'l'unico genere che abbia qualcosa da vedere con il cinema', '*L'allegoria della primavera* fonde le visioni del Botticelli in un solo mondo ideale e trascendente di forme armoniose', Vito Pandolfi, '"Documentari" di Emmer', *Mondo Operaio*, 26 November 1949.
4 'Si Emmer, par une destruction créatrice, mais destruction quand même, impose une nouvelle façon d'être, une nouvelle existence aux tableaux, n'y a-t-il pas là une erreur? Il ne le semble pas.' Claude Cariguel and Luciano Emmer, *Ecran français*, 26 December 1949.
5 Kracauer 1960, pp. 195–6.
6 Gasparini 1995, p. 65.
7 Luciano Emmer, cited in Bo 1988, p. 46.
8 Di Genova 2009, cited in Scremin 2010, p. 11.
9 Ragghianti 1952, p. 264. Strangely, in the otherwise well-researched study by Steven Jacobs, the name of Ragghianti does not appear (Jacobs 2011).
10 Gasparini 1995, p. 61.
11 See Michaud 2000.
12 Of *Fantasia* Ragghianti noted: 'In this film there was no respect for the the point of view of the artist: the point of view is part of the work, it is not external or extraneous, the work is born from the painter, with the point of view that he establishes', Gasparini 1995, p. 65.
13 See on this Venturi 2010.

BRANDING VENUS: BOTTICELLI AS MIRRORED IN AMERICAN ART SINCE 1940, pp. 124–31
Stefan Weppelmann

1 Miller 1992 considered the reception of the Italian Renaissance in the United States, and the fate of Botticelli in particular, during the period between 1860 and 1920.
2 For filmed documentation of the mermaids, see Home Movies, Medicus collection, New York World's Fair, 1939–40, reel 6, 1939; https://archive.org/details/0639_HM_Medicus_collection_New_York_Worlds_Fair_1939–40_Reel_6_15_01_00_00 (accessed 19 January 2015).
3 See Bedarida 2012, p. 151.
4 For a description of the room, see *New York Herald Tribune*, 26 January 1940, and the article in *Corriere d'America*, 26 January 1940.
5 *Christian Science Monitor* (Boston), 11 January 1940.
6 MoMA Archive, press release dated 8 April 1940.
7 Bedarida 2012, p. 151 and n. 12.
8 MoMA Archive, memo from Jack Graham Jr to Miss Hall, 28 February 1940.
9 For Offner 1927, p. 6, Botticelli's achievement was 'the marriage of the feminine principle of singing line to bodily structure…'.
10 Berenson 1952, p. 85.
11 See Barolsky 1982, p. 472 and Barolsky 2010, p. 43.
12 Breslin 1993, pp. 212–16.
13 Phillips Collection, Washington DC.
14 Phillips 1926, p. 9: 'We need such Italians of the Quattrocento as Piero di Cosimo, Piero della Francesca, Botticelli and Signorelli.'
15 Greenberg 1940, 'Towards a Newer Laocoon' (quoted in Lüdeking 1997, p. 75): 'The history of avant-garde painting is that of a progressive surrender to the resistance of its medium; which resistance consists chiefly in the flat picture plane's denial of efforts to "hole through" it for realistic perspectival space.… Painting abandons chiaroscuro and shaded modelling. Brush strokes are often defined for their own sake. Primary colors, the "instinctive," easy colors, replace tones and tonality.'
16 Auther 2004, p. 341: 'Greenberg used the decorative as a critical device to distinguish "high" abstract painting from "decoration" defined as a form of surface attractiveness masquerading as art.' On Greenberg's distinction between abstraction and decoration see ibid., pp. 342–55.
17 Letter from a certain Giorgiana Allen, Briarcliff, dated 10 January 1940, in the *New York Sun*, 12 January 1940.
18 See the essay by Sonnet Stanfill in this volume.
19 For example, the thoroughbred stallion Botticelli, born in England, which won numerous international competitions and gave the name Botticelli a certain buzz in the media, associating it with concepts such as sportsmanship, elegance and speed.
20 On the reasons for the reorganization see Berti 1978, p. 77. The reopening took place on 28 January 1978.
21 See Berlin 2002.
22 7 December 2006, Christie's, London, *Virgin and Child*.
23 Christie's, New York. According to an article in the *Daily Telegraph*, 16 October 1999, p. 3, the Kimbell Museum of Art, Fort Worth, offered 25 million US dollars for the *Virgin Adoring the Sleeping Christ* (Wemyss collection) when it was up for sale (Scottish National Gallery, Edinburgh).
24 See the essay by Toshio Watanabe in this volume.
25 *The Birth of Venus* (after Botticelli), 2009, oil on canvas, 177 × 269 cm, private collection (formerly Galerie Rothamel).

Bibliography

Archival sources; abbreviations

AB	Archivio Berenson, Villa I Tatti, Settignano, Florence
AH	Archivio Horne, Fondazione Horne, Florence
NGA	National Gallery Archive, London
SU, HPHL	Herbert Percy Horne Letters, 1891–1912, Stanford University Library, Special Collections
WIA	Warburg Institute Archive
GC	General Correspondence

Selected books from the Warburg Institute Library relevant to Botticelli are available at the following address: warburg.sas.ac.uk/library/digital-collections/botticelli

ACTON 2010
Acton Photograph Archive, 3, *Research and Conservation at Villa La Pietra*, New York 2010

AGAMBEN 1998
Giorgio Agamben, *Image et mémoire* (Arts et Esthétique, 14), Paris 1998

AGLIONBY 1685
William Aglionby, *Painting Illustrated in Three Dialogues ... with the Lives of the Most Eminent Painters, from Cimabue to the time of Raphael and Michaelangelo*, London 1685; reprinted in *The Printed Sources of Western Art*, ed. Theodore Besterman, vol. 2, Portland, Oregon 1972

ALAZARD 1950
Jean Alazard, *Ingres et l'Ingrisme*, Paris 1950

ALBERTI 1988
Leon Battista Alberti, *On the Art of Building in Ten Books*, trans. Joseph Rykwert, Neil Leach and Robert Tavernor, Cambridge MA 1988

ALBERTI 2004
Leon Battista Alberti, *On Painting*, trans. Cecil Grayson, London 2004

AMSTERDAM AND LOS ANGELES 2009
David LaChapelle, *The Rape of Africa*, with texts by Wim Pijbes and Colin Wiggins, exh. cat., Galerie Alex Daniels, Amsterdam; David DeSanctis Gallery, Los Angeles 2009

ANDERSON 1985
Jaynie Anderson, 'The Travel Diaries of Otto Mündler, 1855–1858', *The Walpole Society*, vol. 51 (1985)

ANDERSON 1996
Jaynie Anderson, 'The Political Power of Connoisseurship in Nineteenth-Century Europe: Wilhelm von Bode versus Giovanni Morelli', in *Jahrbuch der Berliner Museen 38. Beiheft. Kennerschaft. Kolloquium zum 150sten Geburtstag von Wilhelm von Bode*, ed. Thomas W. Gaehtgens and Peter-Klaus Schuster, 1996, pp. 107–19

ANDREE 1998
Rolf Andree, *Arnold Böcklin. Die Gemälde*, Basel and Munich 1998

ANGELETTI AND NATALI 1904
Roberto Angeletti and Ermanno Natali, *Gli artisti a Roma. Medaglioni. IX. Aristide Sartorio,* Sulmona 1904

ARCADE AUCTION 1999
Arcade Auction: Old Master and 19th Century European Art, Sotheby's, New York, 11–12 January 1999

ARGAN 1957
Carlo Giulio Argan, *Botticelli* (Der Geschmack unserer Zeit, 19), Geneva 1957

ARTISTICAL DIRECTORY 1856
The Artistical Directory, Rome 1856

AUTHER 2004
Elissa Auther, 'The Decorative, Abstraction, and the Hierarchy of Art and Craft in the Art Criticism of Clement Greenberg', *Oxford Art Journal*, vol. 27, no. 3 (2004), pp. 341–64

AVERY-QUASH 2011
Susanna Avery-Quash, 'The Travel Notebooks of Sir Charles Eastlake', *The Walpole Society*, vol. 73 (2011)

BANN 2004
Stephen Bann, 'Paul Delaroche à l'hémicycle des Beaux-Arts. L'histoire de l'art et l'autorité de la peinture', *Revue de l'art*, no. 146 (April 2004), pp. 21–34

BARCELONA ET AL. 2004–5
Fèlix Fanés (ed.), *Dalí: Cultura de masses*, exh. cat., CaixaForum, Barcelona et al. 2004–5

BARDI 1837
Luigi Bardi, *L'Imperiale e Reale Galleria Pitti*, vol. 1, Florence 1837

BARDI 1842
Luigi Bardi, *Galerie du Palais Pitti*, vol. 3, Florence 1842

BAROLSKY 1982
Paul Barolsky, 'Walter Pater and the Poetry of Nothingness', *The Antioch Review*, vol. 40, no. 4 (Autumn 1982), pp. 469–78

BAROLSKY 2010
Paul Barolsky, 'Walter Pater and the Aesthetics of Abstraction', *Source: Notes in the History of Art*, vol. 29, no. 4 (2010), pp. 43–5

BARTOLI AND ROSS 2010
Damien Bartoli and Frederick C. Ross, *William Bouguereau: Catalogue Raisonné of his Painted Work*, New York 2010

BARTSCH 1803
Adam von Bartsch, *Le Peintre graveur*, vol. 2, Vienna 1803

BÄTSCHMANN AND FEHLMANN 2002
Marie Therese Bätschmann and Marc Fehlmann, *Adolf von Stürler (1802–1881). Zwischen Duccio und Ingres*, Bern 2002

BAXANDALL 1972
Michael Baxandall, *Painting and Experience in Fifteenth-Century Italy: A Primer in the Social History of Pictorial Style*, Oxford 1972

BAXANDALL 1985
Michael Baxandall, *Patterns of Intention: On the Historical Explanation of Pictures*, New Haven and London 1985

BEDARIDA 2012
Raffaele Bedarida, 'Operation Renaissance: Italian Art at MoMA, 1940–1949', *Oxford Art Journal*, vol. 35, no. 2 (2012), pp. 147–69

BELL 1892
Malcolm Bell, *Edward Burne-Jones: A Record and Review*, London 1892

BELLINI 1990
Paolo Bellini, 'Le due serie di disegni del Botticelli per la Commedia', in Torre de' Passeri 1990, pp. 41–50

BELSEY 2014a
Hugh Belsey, 'Hugford, Ignazio Enrico', *Oxford Dictionary of National Biography*; http://www.oxforddnb.com/view/article/14048 (accessed 10 October 2014)

BELSEY 2014b
Hugh Belsey, 'Mann, Sir Horatio', *Oxford Dictionary of National Biography*; http://www.oxforddnb.com/view/article/17945 (accessed 13 October 2014)

BELSEY 2014c
Hugh Belsey, 'Patch, Thomas', *Oxford Dictionary of National Biography*; http://www.oxforddnb.com/view/article/21521 (accessed 13 October 2014)

BELTING 2001
Hans Belting, *The Invisible Masterpiece*, London 2001

BENZI 2001
Fabio Benzi, *Il liberty in Italia*, Milan 2001

BERENSON 1895
Bernard Berenson, 'Ulmann's Botticelli', *Revue Critique d'Histoire et de Littérature*, vol. 29, no. 5 (1895), pp. 88–95

BERENSON 1896
Bernard Berenson, *The Florentine Painters of the Renaissance with an Index to their Works*, New York and London 1896

BERENSON 1900
Bernard Berenson, *The Florentine Painters of the Renaissance with an Index to their Works*, 2nd rev. ed., New York and London 1900

BERENSON 1901
Bernard Berenson, *The Study and Criticism of Italian Art: I*, London 1901

BERENSON 1903a
Bernard Berenson, 'Alunno di Domenico', *The Burlington Magazine*, vol. I, no. 1 (April 1903), pp. 2, 6–7, 10–13, 16–21

BERENSON 1903b
Bernard Berenson, *The Drawings of the Florentine Painters: Classified, Criticized and Studied as Documents in the History and Appreciation of Tuscan Art*, 2 vols, London and New York 1903

BERENSON 1913
Bernard Berenson, *Catalogue of a Collection of Paintings and Some Art Objects. Volume I: Italian Paintings*, Philadelphia 1913

BERENSON 1932
Bernard Berenson, *Italian Pictures of the Renaissance: A List of the Principal Artists and Their Works with an Index of Places*, Oxford 1932

BERENSON 1938
Bernard Berenson, *The Drawings of the Florentine Painters*, 3 vols, Chicago 1938

BERENSON 1952
Bernard Berenson, *The Italian Painters of the Renaissance*, London 1952

BERENSON 1961
Bernard Berenson, *I disegni dei pittori fiorentini*, 3 vols, Milan 1961

BERENSON 1963
Bernard Berenson, *Sunset and Twilight: From the Diaries of 1947–1958*, ed. Nicky Mariano, New York 1963

BERENSON 1965
Bernard Berenson, *The Selected Letters of Bernard Berenson*, London 1965

BERENSON 2005
Bernard Berenson, *Amico di Sandro, con un saggio di Patrizia Zambrano*, Milan 2005

BERENSON AND ROBERTS 1916
Bernard Berenson and William Roberts, *Pictures in the Collection of P.A.B. Widener at Lynnewood Hall, Elkins Park, Pennsylvania: Early Italian and Spanish Schools*, Philadelphia 1916

BERGSTRÄSSER AND MÄRKER 1998
Gisela Bergsträsser and Peter Märker, *Hundert Zeichnungen alter Meister aus dem Hessischen Landesmuseum Darmstadt*, Leipzig 1998

BERLIN 2002
Kira Perov (ed.), *Bill Viola: Going Forth By Day*, exh. cat., Deutsche Guggenheim, Berlin 2002

BERLIN 2011–12
Sherin Najjar and Stefan Weppelmann (eds), *Botticelli–Grey*, exh. cat., Gemaldegalerie, Staatliche Museen zu Berlin 2011–12

BERLIN AND NEW YORK 2011–12
Keith Christiansen and Stefan Weppelmann (eds), *Gesichter der Renaissance. Meisterwerke italienischer Portrait-Kunst / The Renaissance Portrait: From Donatello to Bellini*, exh. cat., Bode Museum, Berlin; Metropolitan Museum of Art, New York 2011–12

BERLIN, ROME AND LONDON 2000–1
Hein-Th. Schulze Altcappenberg (ed.), *Sandro Botticelli. Der Bilderzyklus zu Dantes Göttlicher Komödie / Sandro Botticelli: The Drawings for Dante's Divine Comedy*, exh. cat., Kupferstichkabinett Berlin; Scuderie Papali al Quirinale, Rome; Royal Academy of Arts, London 2000–1

BERN 2002–3
Marc Fehlmann and Gaudenz Freuler (eds), *Die Sammlung Adolf von Stürler. In Memoriam Eduard Hüttinger (1926–1998)*, exh. cat., Kunstmuseum Bern 2002

BERTI 1978
Luciano Berti, 'La Sala del Botticelli agli Uffizi', *Prospettiva*, vol. 13 (1978), pp. 76–7

BERTRAM 1950
Anthony Bertram, 'The English Discovery of Botticelli', *Journal of the Society of Arts*, vol. 98, no. 4819 (1950), pp. 468–84

BINDMAN 2005
David Bindman, 'John Flaxman: Sculptor and Illustrator', in Salvadori 2005, pp. 12–15

BIRMINGHAM 1967
Stephen Birmingham, *'Our Crowd': The Great Jewish Families of New York*, New York 1967

BIRMINGHAM 2005–6
Colin Cruise, *Love Revealed: Simeon Solomon and the Pre-Raphaelites*, exh. cat., Birmingham Museums and Art Gallery, Birmingham 2005–6

BITTLER AND MATHIEU 1983
Paul Bittler and Pierre-Louis Mathieu, *Catalogue des dessins de Gustave Moreau*, Paris 1983

BLACKWOOD 2004
Jonathan Blackwood, *Portrait of a Young Scotsman: A Life of Edward Baird, 1904–1949*, London 2004

BLONDEL 1999
Alain Blondel, *Tamara de Lempicka: Catalogue Raisonné, 1921–1979*, Lausanne 1999

BLUM 2007
Dilys Blum, *Shocking! The Art and Fashion of Elsa Schiaparelli*, Philadelphia 2007

BLUME 1995
Andrew C. Blume, 'Giovanni de' Bardi and Sandro Botticelli in Santo Spirito', *Jahrbuch der Berliner Museen*, vol. 37 (1995), pp. 169–83

BLUMER 1936
Marie-Louise Blumer, 'Catalogue des peintures transportées d'Italie en France de 1796 à 1814', *Bulletin de la Société d'histoire de l'art français*, vol. 2 (1936), pp. 244–348

BO 1967
Carlo Bo, *L'opera completa del Botticelli*, Milan 1967

BO 1988
Fabio Bo, 'Luciano Emmer. Memorie di un neorealista "rosa"', in *I Festival del cinema italiano*, Rome 1988

BOCCHI-CINELLI 1677
Le Bellezze della Città di Firenze. Di Sacri Templi, di Palazzi i più notabili artifizi e più preziosi si contengono. Scritte già da M. Francesco Bocchi ed ora da M. Giovanni Cinelli ampliate ed accresciute, Florence 1677

BOCK 2014
Julia Bock, *Die stille Macht vertrauter Motive. Bewusste und unbewusste Adaption, Zitation und Wahrnehmung von Kunst in der Populärkultur und ihr möglicher Nutzen für die Museumspädagogik*, Göttingen 2014

BODE 1888
Wilhelm von Bode, 'La Renaissance au musée de Berlin. Les peintres florentines du XVème siècle', *Gazette des Beaux-Arts*, vol. 37 (1888), pp. 472–89

BODE 1906
Wilhelm von Bode, 'Eine Verkündigung Botticellis in der Sammlung Huldschinsky zu Berlin', *Jahrbuch der Königlich Preußischen Kunstsammlungen*, vol. 27 (1906), pp. 245–8

BODE 1921
Wilhelm von Bode, *Sandro Botticelli*, Berlin 1921

BODE 1925
Wilhelm von Bode, *Sandro Botticelli*, trans. F. Renfield and F.L. Rudston Brown, London 1925

BODE 1926
Wilhelm von Bode, *Botticelli. Des Meisters Werke in 155 Abbildungen* (Klassiker der Kunst, 30), Stuttgart 1926

BODE 1997
Wilhelm von Bode, *Mein Leben* (1930), ed. Thomas W. Gaehtgens and Barbara Paul, 2 vols, Berlin 1997

BOIME 1971
Albert Boime, *The Academy and French Painting in the Nineteenth Century*, London and New York 1971

BOISSET 2005
Olivier Boisset, 'Les antiques du comte James-Alexandre de Pourtalès-Gorgier (1776–1855): une introduction', in *Collections et Marché de l'Art en France 1789–1848*, ed. Monica Preti Hamard and Philippe Sénéchal, Rennes 2005, pp. 187–206

BOLOGNA 2007
Germano Celant and Gianfranco Maraniello (eds), *Vertigo: A Century of Multimedia Art from Futurism to the Web*, exh. cat., Museo d'Arte Moderna di Bologna 2007

BONFIGLI 1860
F. Salverio Bonfigli, *Guide to the Studios in Rome with Much Supplementary Information*, Rome 1860

BONN 2014
Klaus Honnef (ed.), *Ulrike Rosenbach. Weiblicher Energie Austausch, 1972–2013. Werkblock Frauenbilder*, exh. cat., LVR-LandesMuseum Bonn 2014

BONSANTI 1987
Giorgio Bonsanti, *La Galleria dell'Accademia, Firenze: Guida e catalogo completo*, Florence 1987

BORENIUS 1916
Tancred Borenius, *Pictures by the Old Masters in the Library of Christ Church, Oxford*, Oxford, 1916

BOSKOVITS AND BROWN 2003
Miklós Boskovits and David Alan Brown (eds), *Italian Paintings of the Fifteenth Century (The Collections of the National Gallery of Art)*, Oxford 2003

BOSSAGLIA-MACLEAN 1987
Rossana Bossaglia, 'The Iconography of the Italian Novecento in the European Context', trans. Howard Rodger MacLean, *The Journal of Decorative and Propaganda Arts*, vol. 3 (Winter 1987), pp. 52–65

BOSTON 1997
Laurence B. Kanter, *Botticelli's Witness: Changing Style in a Changing Florence*, exh. cat., Isabella Stewart Gardner Museum, Boston 1997

BOSTON AND PARIS 2011–12
George T.M. Shackelford and Xavier Rey (eds), *Degas and the Nude*, exh. cat., Museum of Fine Arts, Boston; Musée d'Orsay, Paris 2011–12

BOTH DE TAUZIA 1878
L[éonce] Both de Tauzia, *Notice des tableaux exposés dans les galleries du Musée National du Louvre, 1re partie: Ecoles d'Italie et d'Espagne*, Paris 1878

BRAUN 2005
Emily Braun, 'Leonardo's Smile', in *Donatello among the Blackshirts: History and Modernity in the Visual Culture of Fascist Italy*, ed. Claudia Lazzaro and Roger J. Crum, Ithaca and London 2005, pp. 173–86

BREDEKAMP 2000
Horst Bredekamp, 'Berenson, Horne, Warburg & Co. Die Geschichte der Kunstgeschichte in Marcel Prousts "Auf der Suche nach der verlorenen Zeit"', in *Jenseits der Grenzen. Festschrift für Thomas Gaehtgens*, ed. U. Fleckner, M. Schieder and M. Zimmermann, Cologne 2000, pp. 71–82

BREDEKAMP 2009
Horst Bredekamp, *Sandro Botticelli – Primavera: Florenz als Garten der Venus*, 2nd rev. ed., Berlin 2009

BREJON DE LAVERGNÉE 1999
Arnauld Brejon de Lavergnée, *Musée des Beaux-Arts de Lille. Catalogue sommaire illustré des peintures. Écoles étrangères*, Paris 1999

BRESLIN 1993
James E.B. Breslin, *Mark Rothko: A Biography*, Chicago 1993

BRIGSTOCKE, MARCHAND AND WRIGHT 2010
Hugh Brigstocke, Eckart Marchand and Alison Wright, 'John Flaxman and William Young Ottley in Italy', *The Walpole Society*, vol. 72 (2010), pp. 341–70

BROWN 2014
David Alan Brown, 'Bernard Berenson and Paul Sachs: Teaching Connoisseurship', in Connors and Waldman 2014, pp. 269–82

BRUNNER 1999
Michael Brunner, *Die Illustrierung von Dantes Divina Commedia in der Zeit der Dante-Debatte (1570–1600)*, Munich 1999

BRYSON AND TROXELL 1976
John Bryson and Janet Camp Troxell (eds), *Dante Gabriel Rossetti and Jane Morris: Their Correspondence*, Oxford 1976

BULLEN 1994
J.B. Bullen, *The Myth of the Renaissance in Nineteenth-Century Writing*, Oxford 1994

BUONACORE 2005
Vincenzo Buonacore, *Il marchese Alfonso Tacoli-Canacci: 'Onesto gentiluomo smaniante per la Pittura'*, Reggio Emilia 2005

BURCKHARDT 1879
Jacob Burckhardt, *The Cicerone: An Art Guide to Painting in Italy*, trans. Mrs A.H. Clough, ed. J.A. Crowe, London 1879

BURCKHARDT AND BODE 1879
Jacob Burckhardt, *Der Cicerone. Eine Anleitung zum Genuss der Kunstwerke Italiens*, 4th ed., 2 vols, Leipzig 1879

BURDETT 2011
Carolyn Burdett, '"The subjective inside us can turn into the objective outside": Vernon Lee's Psychological Aesthetics', *Interdisciplinary Studies in the Long Nineteenth Century*, no. 12 (2011), pp. 1–31; www.19.bbk.ac.uk

BURGIO, CLARK AND HARK 2009
Lucia Burgio, Robin J.H. Clark and Richard R. Hark, 'Spectroscopic investigation of modern pigments on purportedly medieval miniatures by the "Spanish Forger"', *Journal of Raman Spectroscopy*, vol. 40, no. 12 (December 2009), pp. 2031–6

BURNE-JONES 1904
Georgiana Burne-Jones, *Memorials of Edward Burne-Jones*, 2 vols, London 1904 (reprint London 1993)

BUSCOT PARK 2004
Buscot Park and The Faringdon Collection, London 2004

BYAM SHAW 1967
James Byam Shaw, *Paintings by Old Masters at Christ Church Oxford*, London 1967

CAGLIOTI 2008
Francesco Caglioti, 'Fifteenth-century Reliefs of Ancient Emperors and Empresses in Florence: Production and Collecting', in *Collecting Sculpture in Early Modern Europe*, ed. Nicholas Penny and Eike D. Schmidt, New Haven and London 2008, pp. 67–109

CALDESI AND MONTECCHI 1858
Leonida Caldesi and Eugenio Montecchi, *Gems of the Art Treasures Exhibition, Manchester 1857*, London and Manchester 1858

CALLOWAY 1998
Stephen Calloway, *Aubrey Beardsley*, London 1998

CAMBRIDGE 2007
Theodore E. Stebbins Jr and Virginia Anderson, *The Last Ruskinians: Charles Eliot Norton, Charles Herbert Moore, and Their Circle*, exh. cat., Fogg Art Museum / Harvard University Art Museums, Cambridge MA 2007

CAMESASCA 1968
Ettore Camesasca, *L'opera completa di Ingres*, Milan 1968

CAMFIELD 1979
William Camfield, *Francis Picabia: His Art, Life and Times*, Princeton 1979

CAMPBELL 1975
Margaret Campbell, *Dolmetsch: The Man and His Work*, London 1975

CANEVA 1990
Caterina Caneva, *Botticelli: catalogo completo dei dipinti*, Florence 1990

CANNON-BROOKES 1968
Peter Cannon-Brookes, 'Botticelli's Pentecost: An Interpretation', *Apollo*, vol. LXXXVI, no. 74 (April 1968), pp. 274–8

CATALOGO 1881
Catalogo della R. Galleria degli Uffizi di Firenze, Florence 1881

CATALOGUE 1833
A Catalogue of the Collection of Pictures in the Library at Christ Church, Oxford 1833

CATALOGUE 1905
Catalogue de la Galerie Royale des Uffizi à Florence, Florence 1905

CATALOGUE 1955
Catalogue of Oil-Paintings (National Museum of Wales), Cardiff 1955

CATALOGUE 1984
Paintings, drawings and watercolours from the Studios of the Late Harry Bush, R.O.I. 1883–1957 and Noel Laura Nisbet, R.I. (Mrs Harry Bush), 1887–1956, London 1984

CATALOGUE MUSÉE NAPOLÉON III 1862
Catalogue des tableaux, des sculptures de la Renaissance et des majoliques du musée Napoléon III, Paris 1862

CECCHI 2005
Alessandro Cecchi, *Sandro Botticelli*, Milan 2005

CENNINI 1960
Cennino Cennini, *The Craftsman's Handbook, 'Il libro dell'Arte. Cennino d'Andrea Cennini*, trans. Daniel J. Thompson Jr, New York 1960

CHASTEL 1958
André Chastel, *Botticelli*, Milan 1959

CHELES 1998
Luciano Cheles, 'Copie ed echi di Piero in Inghilterra', in *Piero Interpretato. Copie, giudizi e musealizzazione di Piero della Francesca*, ed. Cecilia Prete and Ranieri Varese, Ancona 1998, pp. 13–38

CHERRY 1998
Bridget Cherry, *The Buildings of England. London 4 North*, London 1998

CHIARINI AND PADOVANI 2003
Marco Chiarini and Serena Padovani, *La Galleria Palatina e gli Appartamenti Reali di Palazzo Pitti. Catalogo dei dipinti*, 2 vols, Florence 2003

CHURCHMAN 1993
Michael Churchman, 'The Founders', in *High Ideals and Aspirations: The Nelson Atkins Museum of Art, 1933–1993*, Kansas City 1993, pp. 7–15

CLARK 1960
Kenneth Clark, 'Bernard Berenson', *The Burlington Magazine*, vol. CII, no. 690 (September 1960), pp. 381–6

CLARK 1976
Kenneth Clark, *The Drawings by Sandro Botticelli for Dante's Divine Comedy, After the Originals in the Berlin Museums and the Vatican*, London 1976

CLARKE 1819
William Clarke, *Repertorium Bibliographicum; or, Some Account of the Most Celebrated British Libraries*, London 1819

COGEVAL 2013
Guy Cogeval, *Le Musée d'Orsay à 360 degrés*, Paris 2013

COHEN 2013
Rachel Cohen, *Bernard Berenson: A Life in the Picture Trade*, New Haven and London 2013

COLE AND MIDDELDORF 1971
Bruce Cole and Ulrich Middeldorf, 'Masaccio, Lippi, or Hugford?', *The Burlington Magazine*, vol. CXIII, no. 822 (September 1971), pp. 500–7

COLLOBI RAGGHIANTI 1966
Licia Collobi Ragghianti, *Disegni inglesi della Fondazione Horne in Firenze*, Cremona 1966

COLOGNE 2011–12
Kasper König and Thomas Trummer (eds), *Vor dem Gesetz. Skulpturen der Nachkriegszeit und Räume der Gegenwartskunst*, exh. cat., Museum Ludwig, Cologne 2011–12

COMPTON 1960–1
Michael Compton, 'William Roscoe and Early Collectors of Italian Primitives', *The Liverpool Libraries, Museums & Art Committee Bulletin*, vol. 9 (1960–1), pp. 26–51

CONNORS AND WALDMAN 2014
Joseph Connors and Louis A. Waldman (eds), *Bernard Berenson: Formation and Heritage* (Villa I Tatti Series, 31), Cambridge MA 2014

COSTARAS AND RICHARDSON 2012–14
Nicola Costaras and Clare Richardson, 'Condition Report: "Smeralda Bandinelli"', V&A Conservation Department, London 2012–14

COX AND FORD 2003
Julian Cox and Colin Ford, *Julia Margaret Cameron: The Complete Photographs*, Los Angeles and London 2003

CRAMER 2000
Robert Cramer, *Les Pourtalès: 1300–2000*, Saint Pierre de Vassols 2000

CRANE 1907
Walter Crane, *An Artist's Reminiscences*, London 1907

CRAWFORD 2014
Alan Crawford, 'Horne, Herbert Percy', *Oxford Dictionary of National Biography*; http://www.oxforddnb.com/view/article/37570 (accessed 13 October 2014)

CROW 2005
Thomas Crow, 'Cosmic Exile: Prophetic Turns in the Life and Exile of Robert Smithson', in *Robert Smithson*, ed. Eugenie Tsai and Cornelia Butler, exh. cat., Museum of Contemporary Art, Los Angeles; Dallas Museum of Art, Dallas; The Whitney Museum of American Art, New York 2005, pp. 32–89

CROWE AND CAVALCASELLE 1864–6
Joseph Archer Crowe and Giovanni Battista Cavalcaselle, *A New History of Painting from the II to the XVI Century*, 3 vols, London 1864–6

CROWE AND CAVALCASELLE 1911
Joseph Archer Crowe and Giovanni Battista Cavalcaselle, *A History of Painting in Italy. Umbria, Florence and Siena from the Second to the Sixteenth Century. Vol. IV, Florentine Masters of the Fifteenth Century*, ed. R. Langton Douglas and G. De Nicola, London 1911

DALÍ 1998
Salvador Dalí, *The Collected Writings of Salvador Dalí*, ed and trans. Haim Finkelstein, Cambridge 1998

DANTE 2001
Dante Alighieri, *La Vita Nuova: 'The New Life' of Dante Alighieri*, trans. A.S. Kline, 2001, http://www.poetryintranslation.com/PITBR/Italian/TheNewLifeIV.htm (accessed 23 September 2014)

DAVIES 2001
Helen Davies, 'Sir John Charles Robinson and John Malcolm of Poltalloch: Collecting Italian Old Master Drawings in Nineteenth-Century England', *Apollo*, vol. CLIII, no. 469 (March 2001), pp. 35–42

DAVIES 1961
Martin Davies, *National Gallery Catalogues: The Earlier Italian Schools*, London 1961

DAVIES 1916
Randall Davies (ed.), *Exhibition of the Herbert Horne Collection of Drawings with Special Reference to the Works of Alexander Cozens, with Some Decorative Furniture and Other Objects of Art*, London 1916

DAWSON AND UPHILL 1972
Warren R. Dawson and Eric P. Uphill, *Who was Who in Egyptology*, London 1972

DELABORDE 1870
Henri Delaborde, *Ingres: sa vie, ses travaux, sa doctrine, d'après les notes manuscrites et les lettres du maître*, Paris 1870

DELAROCHE 1813
H. Delaroche, *Catalogue d'une collection de tableaux des Écoles D'Italie*, H. Delaroche and M. Balbastre, Hôtel Bullion, rue J.J. Rousseau, Paris 1813

DEMPSEY 1968
Charles Dempsey, 'Mercurius Ver: The Sources of Botticelli's Primavera', *Journal of the Warburg and Courtauld Institutes*, vol. 31 (1968), pp. 251–73

DEMPSEY 1992
Charles Dempsey, *The Portrayal of Love: Botticelli's Primavera and Humanist Culture at the Time of Lorenzo the Magnificent*, Princeton 1992

DEMPSEY 2004
Charles Dempsey, 'L'amore e la figura della ninfa nell'arte di Botticelli', in Florence 2004, pp. 25–37

DENIS 1957
Maurice Denis, *Journal, vol. 1 (1884–1904)*, Paris 1957

DENON 1999
Vivant Denon, directeur des musées sous le Consulat et l'Empire. Correspondance (1802–1815), ed. Marie-Anne Dupuy, 2 vols, Paris 1999

DENTLER 1964
Clara Louise Dentler, *Famous Foreigners in Florence, 1400–1900*, Florence 1964

DENZEL 2010
Markus A. Denzel, *Handbook of World Exchange Rates, 1590–1914*, Farnham 2010

DESCRIPTION 1854
Description de l'I. et R. Académie des Beaux Arts de Florence, 2nd ed., Florence 1854

DIDI-HUBERMAN 2005
Georges Didi-Huberman, 'Bewegende Bewegungen: die Schleier der Ninfa nach Aby Warburg', in *Ikonologie des Zwischenraums. Der Schleier als Medium und Metapher*, ed. Johannes Endres, Barbara Wittmann and Gerhard Wolf, Munich 2005, pp. 331–60

DIETL 1993
Maria Dietl, 'The Picture Gallery of Berlin: The Formation of the Solly Collection', in *Giovanni Morelli e la cultura dei conoscitori*, ed. Giacomo Agosti, 3 vols, Bergamo 1993, vol. 1, pp. 49–59

DILLENBERGER 1998
Jane Daggett Dillenberger, *The Religious Art of Andy Warhol*, New York and London 1998

DOMBROWSKI 1992
Damian Dombrowski, *Die Divina Commedia als Stätte der Ganzheit. Sandro Botticellis Dante-Visionen*, unpublished MA thesis, Westfälische Wilhelms-Universität, Münster 1992

DOMBROWSKI 1996
Damian Dombrowski, 'Beobachtungen zu Botticellis Dante-Illustrationen', *Deutsches Dante-Jahrbuch*, vol. 71 (1996), pp. 45–75

DRESDEN 2000
Gabriele Werner (ed.), *Wilhelm Lachnit. Gemälde 1899–1962*, exh. cat., Staatliche Kunstsammlungen Dresden; Gemäldegalerie Neue Meister, Dresden 2000

DREYER 1984
Peter Dreyer, 'Botticelli´ s Series of Engravings of 1481', *Print Quarterly*, vol. 1, no. 2 (1984), pp. 111–15

DREYER 1986
Peter Dreyer, *Dantes Divina commedia mit den Illustrationen von Sandro Botticelli*, facsimile edition, 2 vols, Zurich 1986

DUBOIS 1841
Léon-Jean-Joseph Dubois, *Description des tableaux faisant partie des collections de M. Pourtalès-Gorgier*, Paris 1841

DUNCAN 1928
Isadora Duncan, *My Life*, London 1928

DUPRÈ 1886
Giovanni Duprè, *Thoughts on Art and Autobiographical Memoirs*, trans. E.M. Peruzzi, Boston 1886

DUVEEN 1941
Duveen Pictures in Public Collections of America: A Catalogue Raisonné with Three Hundred Illustrations of Paintings by the Great Masters, which have passed through the House of Duveen, New York 1941

EASTON AND HOLROYD 1974
Malcolm Easton and Michael Holroyd, *The Art of Augustus John*, London 1974

EDINBURGH 2000
Nicolas Barker et al., *A Poet in Paradise: Lord Lindsay and Christian Art*, exh. cat., National Gallery of Scotland, Edinburgh 2000

ELAM 2009
Caroline Elam, 'Herbert Horne: "A Kind of Posteritorious Distinction"', in Hatfield 2009, pp. 169–226

ELEN 1995
Albert Jan Elen, *Italian Late Medieval and Renaissance Drawing-Books from Giovannino de'Grassi to Palma Giovane: A Codicological Approach*, Leiden 1995

ELIOT 1951
T.S. Eliot, 'Tradition and the Individual Talent' (1921), in *Selected Essays*, London 1951

ELLIOT 1992
Patrick Elliot, *Edward Baird, 1904–1949*, Edinburgh 1992

ELLIOTT 2000
David B. Elliott, *Charles Fairfax Murray: The Unknown Pre-Raphaelite*, Lewes 2000

EMPORIUM 1901
E.T., 'Il cartellone della La Esposizione Internazionale d'Arte Decorativa Moderna (Cronachetta artistica)', *Emporium*, vol. 13 (1901), pp. 477–9

ESCHAPASSE 2001
Anne Eschapasse, 'William Beckford in Paris, 1788–1844: "Le Faste Solitaire"', in *William Beckford, 1760–1844: An Eye for the Magnificent*, ed. Derek E. Ostergard, New Haven and London 2001, pp. 99–115

ESPOSIZIONE 1895
I Esposizione Internazionale d'Arte della Città di Venezia, Venice 1895

EVANS 2003
Caroline Evans, *Fashion at the Edge: Spectacle, Modernity and Deathliness*, New Haven and London 2003

EVANS 2009
David Evans, *Appropriation*, London and Cambridge MA 2009

EVANS 1996
Mark Evans, 'Augustus John and Art History', in *Themes and Variations: The Drawings of Augustus John, 1901–1931*, London 1996, pp. 13–16

EVANS 2011
Mark Evans, 'Raphael and Pre-Raphael in England and Germany, 1815–71', in *Art and Design for All: The Victoria and Albert Museum*, ed. Julius Bryant, exh. cat., Victoria and Albert Museum, London 2011, pp. 63–73

EVANS AND VANDENBROUCK 2012
Mark Evans and Melanie Vandenbrouck, '"A Collection as a Man of Taste Would Wish to Live With": Constantine Ionides at Home', *The Decorative Arts Society Journal*, vol. 36 (2012), pp. 22–45

EVENEPOEL 1923
Henri Evenepoel, *Gustave Moreau et ses élèves. Lettres d'Henri Evenepoel à son père*, ed. Edouard Michel, Paris 1923

FEHLMANN 2002
Marc Fehlmann, '"Vingt petites peintures très anciennes sur fond d'or". Die Sammlung Adolf von Stürler', in Bern 2002–3, pp. 8–21

FERMOR 1995
Sharon Fermor, 'Botticelli and the Medici', in *The Early Medici and their Artists*, ed. Francis Ames-Lewis, London 1995, pp. 169–85

FERMOR 1998
Sharon Fermor, 'Poetry in Motion: Beauty in Movement and the Renaissance Concept of *leggiadria*', in Frances Ames-Lewis and Mary Rogers (eds), *Concepts of Beauty in Renaissance Art*, Aldershot 1998, pp. 124–33

FERRUOLO 1955
Arnolfo B. Ferruolo, 'Botticelli's Mythologies, Ficino's "De Amore", Poliziano's "Stanze Per La Giostra": Their Circle of Love', *The Art Bulletin*, vol. 37, no. 1 (March 1955), pp. 17–25

FICINO 1576
Marsilio Ficino, *Opera omnia*, Basel 1576

FIELD 1988
Arthur Field, *The Origins of the Platonic Academy of Florence*, Princeton 1988

FINDLEN 2012
Paula Findlen, 'Uffizi Gallery, Florence: The Rebirth of a Museum in the Eighteenth Century', in *The First Modern Museums of Art: The Birth of an Institution in 18th- and early 19th-century Europe*, ed. Carole Paul, Los Angeles 2012, pp. 73–111

FINDLEN 2013
Paula Findlen, 'The 2012 Josephine Walters Bennett Lecture: The Eighteenth-Century Invention of the Renaissance: Lessons from the Uffizi', *Renaissance Quarterly*, vol. 66, no. 1 (Spring 2013), pp. 1–34

FLEISCHER 2005
Martina Fleischer, *Gemäldegalerie der Akademie der bildenden Künste Wien*, London 2005

FLEMING 1955
John Fleming, 'The Hugfords of Florence' (part II), *The Connoisseur*, vol. CXXXVI, no. 549 (November 1955), pp. 197–206

FLETCHER 1970
Ian Fletcher, 'Herbert Horne: The Earlier Phase', *English Miscellany*, vol. 21 (1970), pp. 117–57

FLETCHER 1980
Ian Fletcher, *Rediscovering Herbert Horne: Poet, Architect, Typographer, Art Historian*, Greensboro 1980

FLORENCE 1949
Licia Ragghianti Collobi (ed.), *Lorenzo il Magnifico e le arti*, exh. cat., Palazzo Strozzi, Florence 1949

FLORENCE 1992
Annamaria Petrioli Tofani (ed.), *Il disegno Fiorentino del Tempo di Lorenzo il Magnifico*, exh. cat., Gabinetto disegni e stampe, Uffizi, Florence 1992

FLORENCE 1992–3
Mina Gregori et al., *Maestri e botteghe. Pittura a Firenze alla fine del Quattrocento*, exh. cat., Palazzo Strozzi, Florence 1992–3

FLORENCE 2004
Daniel Arasse et al., *Botticelli e Filippino: L'inquietudine e la grazia nella pittura fiorentina del Quattrocento*, exh. cat., Palazzo Strozzi, Florence 2004

FLORENCE 2005
Miklós Boskovits (ed.), *Da Bernardo Daddi al Beato Angelico a Botticelli: Dipinti fiorentini del Lindenau-Museum di Altenburg*, exh. cat., Museo di San Marco, Florence 2005

FLORENCE 2011–12
Ludovica Sebregondi et al., *Denaro e bellezza. I banchieri, Botticelli e il rogo delle vanità*, exh. cat., Palazzo Strozzi, Florence 2011–12

FLORENCE 2012–13
Antonello Negri (ed.), *Anni '30. Arti in Italia oltre il fascismo*, exh. cat., Palazzo Strozzi, Florence 2012–13

FLORENCE 2014
Angelo Tartuferi (ed.), *La Fortuna dei primitivi. Tesori d'arte dalle collezioni italiane fra sette e Ottocento*, exh. cat., Galleria dell'Accademia, Florence 2014

FORD 2003
Colin Ford, *Julia Margaret Cameron: A Critical Biography*, Los Angeles 2003

FOREST 2009
Marie-Cécile Forest (ed.), *Gustave Moreau: Catalogue sommaire des dessins, Musée Gustave Moreau*, Paris 2009

FORSTER 1908
E.M. Forster, *A Room with a View*, London 1908

FOUCART-WALTER 2000
Elisabeth Foucart-Walter, 'Le Portrait du Comte de Pourtalès-Gorgier', *Revue du Louvre*, vol. 1 (February 2000), pp. 39–54

FRANCINI 2009
Antonella Francini, 'Herbert Horne and an English "Fable" for Botticelli', in Hatfield 2009, pp. 227–50

FRANKFURT 2009–10
Andreas Schumacher (ed.), *Botticelli, Likeness, Myth, Devotion*, exh. cat., Städel Museum, Frankfurt am Main 2009–10

FRANKFURT AND LONDON 2007–8
Bodo Brinkmann (ed.), *Cranach*, exh. cat., Städel Museum, Frankfurt am Main; Royal Academy of Arts, London 2007–8

FREDEMAN 2002–10
William E. Fredeman et al. (eds), *The Correspondence of Dante Gabriel Rossetti*, 9 vols, Cambridge 2002–10

FREDERICKSEN AND ZERI 1972
Burton B. Fredericksen and Federico Zeri, *Census of Pre-nineteenth-century Italian Paintings in North American Public Collections*, Cambridge MA 1972

FREEDBERG 1989
David Freedberg, *The Power of Images: Studies in the History and Theory of Response*, Chicago and London 1989

FRIEDEWALD 2014
Boris Friedewald, *Meisterinnen des Lichts – Große Fotografinnen aus zwei Jahrhunderten*, Munich 2014

FRY 1901
Roger Fry, 'The Symbolism of Signorelli's "School of Pan"', *Monthly Review*, vol. 5 (1901), pp. 110–14

FRY 1903
Roger Fry, 'Review of the Life of Leonardo da Vinci by Giorgio Vasari, translated with a commentary by H.P. Horne', *Athenaeum* (1903), pp. 323–4

FRY 1908
Roger Fry, 'Mr Horne's Book on Botticelli', *The Burlington Magazine*, vol. XIII (April–September 1908), pp. 83–7

FRY 1916
Roger Fry, 'Mr. Herbert P. Horne and Mr. William Cleverly Alexander', *The Burlington Magazine*, vol. XXIX, no. 158 (May 1916), pp. 81–2

FRY 1926
Roger Fry, 'Sandro Botticelli', *The Burlington Magazine*, vol. XLVIII, no. 277 (April 1926), pp. 196–200

FUGAZZA 1988
Stefano Fugazza, 'D'Annunzio e la fotografia', in *Gabriele D'Annunzio e la promozione delle arti*, ed. R. Bossaglia and M. Quesada, Milan and Rome 1988, pp. 51–4

FULFORD 1981
Roger Fulford (ed.), *Beloved Mama: Private Correspondence of Queen Victoria and the German Crown Princess, 1878–1885*, London 1981

GAEHTGENS 2012
Thomas W. Gaehtgens, 'Altes Museum, Berlin: Building Prussia's First Modern Museum', in Paul 2012, pp. 285–303

GAERTRINGEN 2004
Rudolf Hiller von Gaertringen, *Italienische Gemälde im Städel 1300–1550: Toskana und Umbrien*, Mainz 2004

GAGEL 2010
Mandy Gagel, '1897, A Discussion of Plagiarism: Letters Between Vernon Lee, Bernard Berenson, and Mary Costelloe', *Literary Imagination*, vol. 12, no. 2 (2010), pp. 154–79

LA GALERIE DE FLORENCE 1800
La Galerie de Florence, Basel 1800

GALERIE IMPÉRIALE ET ROYALE DE FLORENCE 1816
Galerie Impériale et Royale de Florence. Nouvelle Édition ornée des Planches de la Vénus de Médicis de celle de Canova et de l'Apollon, Florence 1816

GALERIE IMPÉRIALE ET ROYALE DE FLORENCE 1822
Galerie Impériale et Royale de Florence, Florence 1822

GALERIE IMPÉRIALE ET ROYALE DE FLORENCE 1844
Galerie Impériale et Royale de Florence. Seizième Édition ornée de planches, Florence 1844

GALLATIN 1945
Albert Eugene Gallatin, *Aubrey Beardsley: Catalogue of Drawings and Bibliography*, New York 1945

GAMBA 1931
Carlo Gamba, 'Dipinti fiorentini di raccolte americane all'Esposizione di Londra', *Dedalo*, vol. 11 (1931), pp. 3–5

GAMBA 1936
Carlo Gamba, *Botticelli*, Milan 1936

GAMBLE 1999
Cynthia J. Gamble, 'Zipporah: a Ruskinian enigma appropriated by Marcel Proust', *Word & Image*, vol. 15, no. 4 (October–December 1999), pp. 381–94

GANCITANO 2012
Christian Gancitano, *'Kawaiizzazioni' di Tomoko Nagao*, Olgiate Olona 2012

GARIN 1952
Eugenio Garin, *L'umanesimo italiano*, Bari 1952

GARNETT 2000
Oliver Garnett, 'The Letters and Collection of William Graham – Pre-Raphaelite Patron and Pre-Raphaelite Collector', *The Walpole Society*, vol. 62 (2000), pp. 145–343

GAROFALO 2000
Cristiana Garofalo, *Da Raffaello a Rubens. Disegni della Fondazione Horne*, Florence 2000

GARZELLI 1973
Annarosa Garzelli, *Il ricamo nella attività artistica di Pollaiolo, Botticelli, Bartolomeo di Giovanni*, Florence 1973

GASPARINI 1995
Massimo Gasparini, 'Conversazione con C.L. Ragghianti', in *Carlo L. Ragghianti. I critofilm d'arte*, ed. Antonio Costa, Udine 1995

GAUTIER 1857
Théophile Gautier, 'La Source: Nouveau tableau de M. Ingres', *L'Artiste* (1 February 1857), pp. 113–14

GEMMETT 2000
Roger J. Gemmett (ed.), *The Consummate Collector: William Beckford's Letters to His Bookseller*, Norwich 2000

GENNARI SANTORI 2004
Flaminia Gennari Santori, *The Melancholy of Masterpieces: Old Master Paintings in America 1900–1914*, Milan 2004

GENOVA 2009
Arianna di Genova, 'Se Bosch danza su ritmi infernali. Intervista a Roman Vlad', *Alias*, vol. 3 (October 2009)

GENT 1981
Lucy Gent, *Picture and Poetry 1560–1620: Relations between Literature and the Visual Arts in the English Renaissance*, Leamington Spa 1981

GERONIMUS 2006
Dennis Geronimus, *Piero di Cosimo: Visions Beautiful and Strange*, New Haven and London 2006

GESAMTVERZEICHNIS 1996
Gemäldegalerie Berlin. Gesamtverzeichnis, ed. Henning Bock et al., Berlin 1996

GHILARDOTTI AND CARIZZONI 2006
Arianna Ghilardotti and Pier Giorgio Carizzoni, *Isadora Duncan, Pina Bausch: Danza dell'anima, liberazione del corpo*, Milan 2006

GIBSON 1997
Ian Gibson, *The Shameful Life of Salvador Dalí*, London 1997

GIBSON-WOOD 2003
Carol Gibson-Wood, '"A Judiciously Disposed Collection": Jonathan Richardson Senior's Cabinet of Drawings', in *Collecting Prints and Drawings in Europe c.1500–1750*, ed. Christopher Baker, Caroline Elam and Genevieve Warwick, Aldershot and Burlington VT 2003, pp. 155–71

GLÜHER 2005
Gerhard Glüher (ed.), *Ulrike Rosenbach. Wege zur Medienkunst 1969 bis 2004*, Cologne 2005

GOLDTHWAITE 2009
Richard A. Goldthwaite, *The Economy of Renaissance Florence*, Baltimore 2009

GOMBRICH 1945
Ernst H. Gombrich, 'Botticelli's Mythologies: A Study in the Neo-Platonic Symbolism of his Circle', *Journal of the Warburg and Courtauld Institutes*, vol. 8 (1945), pp. 7–60 (reprinted in Gombrich 1972, pp. 31–81)

GOMBRICH 1972
Ernst H. Gombrich, *Symbolic Images: Studies in the Art of the Renaissance*, London 1972

GOMBRICH 1986
Ernst H. Gombrich, *Aby Warburg: An Intellectual Biography*, Oxford 1986

GONCOURT 1991
Edmond and Jules de Goncourt, *L'Italie d'hier. Notes de voyage, 1855–1856*, Paris 1991

GORDON 1996
Catherine Gordon (ed.), *Evelyn De Morgan: Oil Paintings*, London 1996

GRASSI 1956
Luigi Grassi, *Il disegno italiano dal Trecento al Seicento*, Rome 1956

GRASSI [1961?]
Luigi Grassi, *I disegni italiani del Trecento e Quattrocento: scuole fiorentina, senese, marchigiana, umbra*, Venice n.d. [1961?]

GRECO 1990a
Luigi Greco, 'Un libraire italien à Paris à la veille de la Révolution', *Mélanges de l'Ecole française de Rome. Italie et Méditerranée*, vol. 102, no. 2 (1990), pp. 261–80

GRECO 1990b
Luigi Greco, 'Un libraire italien à Paris: Gian Claudio Molini (1724–1812)', *Mélanges de la Bibliothèque de la Sorbonne*, vol. 10 (1990), pp. 103–21

GRENDLER 2006
Paul F. Grendler, *The European Renaissance in American Life*, Westport 2006

GUIDA ACCADEMIA 1883
Guida della R. Galleria Antica e Moderna e Tribuna del David di Eugenio Pieraccini, Sesta Edizione, Prato 1883

HADLEY 1987
Rollin Van N. Hadley (ed.) *The Letters of Bernard Berenson and Isabella Stewart Gardner, 1887–1924*, Boston 1987

HALE 1996
John Hale, *England and the Italian Renaissance: The Growth of Interest in its History and Art*, London 1996

HAMBURG 2009–10
Lillian Bassman & Paul Himmel: Die erste Retrospektive, ed. Ingo Taubhorn and Brigitte Woischnik, exh. cat., Haus der Photographie, Hamburg 2009–10

HAMBURG 2011–12
Ortrud Westheider and Michael Philipp (eds), *Die Erfindung des Bildes. Frühe italienische Meister bis Botticelli*, exh. cat., Staatliches Lindenau-Museum, Altenburg, Hamburg 2011–12

HANKINS 1990
James Hankins, 'Cosimo de' Medici and the "Platonic Academy"', *Journal of the Warburg and Courtauld Institutes*, vol. 53 (1990), pp. 144–62

HANKINS 1997
James Hankins, 'Florence between Lorenzo de' Medici and Savonarola', in *Botticelli's Witness: Changing Style in a changing Florence*, ed. Laurence B. Kanter et al., Boston 1997, pp. 13–20

HARCK 1896
Fritz Harck, 'Notizen über italienische Bilder in Petersburger Sammlungen', *Repertorium für Kunstwissenschaft*, vol. 19 (1896), pp. 413–34

HASKELL 1976
Francis Haskell, *Rediscoveries in Art: Some Aspects of Taste, Fashion and Collecting in England and France*, Oxford 1976

HASKELL 1987
Francis Haskell, 'The Old Masters in Nineteenth-Century French Painting', in *Past and Present in Art and Taste: Selected Essays*, New Haven and London 1987, pp. 90–115

HASKELL 2000
Francis Haskell, 'Botticelli in the Service of Fascism', in *The Ephemeral Museum: Old Master Paintings and the Rise of the Art Exhibition*, New Haven and London 2000, pp. 105–27

HATFIELD 1995
Rab Hatfield, 'Botticelli's Mystic Nativity, Savonarola and the Millennium', *Journal of the Warburg and Courtauld Institutes*, vol. 58 (1995), pp. 88–114

HATFIELD 2009
Rab Hatfield (ed.), *Sandro Botticelli and Herbert Horne: New Research*, Florence 2009

HAVELY 2014
Nicholas Havely, *Dante's British Public: Readers and Texts from the Fourteenth Century to the Present*, Oxford 2014

HAWEIS 1879
Mrs H.R. Haweis, *The Art of Dress*, London 1879

HEINEKEN 1768–9
Karl Heinrich von Heineken, *Nachrichten von Künstlern und Kunst-Sachen*, 2 vols, Leipzig 1768–9

HELENIAK 1980
Kathryn Moore Heleniak, *William Mulready*, New Haven and London 1980

HILLS 2013
Paul Hills, 'Michael Baxandall', in *The Books that Shaped Art History*, ed. Richard Shone and John-Paul Stonard, London 2013, pp. 150–63

HIND 1910
Arthur Mayger Hind, *Catalogue of Early Italian Engravings preserved in the Department of Prints and Drawings in the British Museum*, ed. Sidney Colvin, London 1910

HIND 1938–48
Arthur Mayger Hind, *Early Italian Engraving: A Critical Catalogue with Complete Reproduction of all the Prints Described*, 7 vols, London 1938–48

HIND 1925
Charles Lewis Hind (ed.), *The Uncollected Work of Aubrey Beardsley*, London 1925

HOCH 2005
Adrian S. Hoch, 'The Art of Alessandro Botticelli through the Eyes of Victorian Aesthetes', in John E. Law and Lene Østermark-Johansen (eds), *Victorian and Edwardian Responses to the Italian Renaissance*, Aldershot 2005, pp. 55–85

HOLMES 1999
Megan Holmes, *Fra Filippo Lippi: The Carmelite Painter*, New Haven and London 1999

HOLMES 2004
Megan Holmes, 'Copying Practices and Marketing Strategies in a Late Fifteenth-Century Painter's Workshop', in *Artistic Exchange and Cultural Translation in the Italian Renaissance City*, ed. Stephen J. Campbell and Stephen J. Milner, Cambridge 2004, pp. 38–74

HOLROYD 1974
Michael Holroyd, *Augustus John: A Biography*, vol. 1, London 1974

HORNE 1891
Herbert P. Horne, *Diversi colores*, London 1891

HORNE 1902
Herbert P. Horne, 'Quelques souvenirs de Sandro Botticelli', *Revue Archéologique*, vol. 11 (1902), pp. 3–11

HORNE 1903
Herbert P. Horne, *The Life of Leonardo da Vinci by Giorgio Vasari*, Edinburgh 1903

HORNE 1908
Herbert P. Horne, *Alessandro Filipepi, Commonly Called Sandro Botticelli, Painter of Florence*, London 1908 (reprint Princeton 1980)

HORNE 1913
Herbert P. Horne, 'La tavola d'altare delle Convertite dipinta da Sandro Botticelli', *Rivista d'Arte*, vol. 13 (1913), pp. 147–54

HORNE 1980
Herbert P. Horne, *Botticelli: Painter of Florence*, introduction by John Pope-Hennessy, Princeton, NJ, 1980

HORNE 1986
Herbert P. Horne, *Alessandro Filipepi detto Sandro Botticelli pittore in Firenze*, trans. Caterina Caneva and Serena Gavioli, introduction by Caterina Caneva, with Horne's Addenda A and B, ed. Caterina Caneva and Giovanna Giusti, 2 vols, Florence 1986

HORNE 1987
Herbert P. Horne, *Alessandro Filipepi, Commonly Called Sandro Botticelli, Painter of Florence: Appendix III*, with Horne's addenda A and B, ed. Caterina Caneva and Giovanna Giusti, Florence 1987

HOWARD 1999
Jeremy Howard, 'Renaissance Florence: Inventing the 1470s in the Britain of the 1870s', *British Art Journal*, vol. 1, no. 1 (Autumn 1999), pp. 75–7

HOWARD 2014
Jeremy Howard, 'Art, Commerce, and Scholarship. The Friendship between Otto Gutekunst of Colnaghi and Bernard Berenson', in Connors and Waldman 2014, pp. 33–68

HUBER 1993
Gabriele Huber, 'Warburgs Ninfa, Freuds Gradiva und ihre Metamorphose bei Masson', in *Denkräume zwischen Kunst und Wissenschaft. 5. Kunsthistorikerinnentagung. Hamburg 1991*, ed. Silvia Baumgart and Gotlind Birkle, Berlin 1993, pp. 443–60

HUMFREY 2012
Peter Humfrey, *Glasgow Museums: The Italian Paintings*, London 2012

HUYSMANS 1955
Joris-Karl Huysmans, *À rebours*, Paris 1955

HUYSMANS 2006
Joris-Karl Huysmans, 'Noëls du Louvre', *L'Écho de Paris* (28 December 1898), reprinted in *Joris-Karl Huysmans, Écrits sur l'art 1867–1905*, ed. Patrice Locmant, Paris 2006, pp. 473–8

IMPERIALE E REALE GALLERIA 1841–6
Imperiale e Reale Galleria di Firenze, Societa editrice della Galleria de Firenze, Florence 1841–6

INGAMELLS 1992
John Ingamells (ed.), *The Wallace Collection: Catalogue of Pictures. Vol. 4: Dutch and Flemish*, London 1992

INGAMELLS 1997
John Ingamells, *A Dictionary of British and Irish Travellers in Italy 1701–1800*, New Haven and London 1997

IRWIN 1979
David Irwin, *John Flaxman 1755–1826*, London 1979

ISELT 2010
Kathrin Iselt, *'Sonderbeauftragter des Führers': der Kunsthistoriker und Museumsmann Hermann Voss (1884–1969)*, Weimar 2010

ISHIZU AND ZEKI 2011
Tomohiro Ishizu and Semir Zeki, 'Toward A Brain-Based Theory of Beauty', 6 July 2011; http://www.plosone.org/article/info:-doi%2F10.1371%2Fjournal.pone.0021852 (accessed 4 July 2015)

ISOZAKI AND YOSHIDA 1977
Yasuhiko Isozaki and Chizuko Yoshida (eds), *Tōkyō bijutsu gakkō no rekishi* [History of Tokyo School of Fine Arts], Tokyo 1977

JACHEC 1998
Nancy Jachec, 'Modernism, Enlightenment Values, and Clement Greenberg', *Oxford Art Journal*, vol. 21, no. 2 (1998), pp. 123–32

JACOBS 2011
Steven Jacobs, *Framing Pictures: Film and the Visual Arts*, Edinburgh 2011

JAFFE 1992
Irma B. Jaffe (ed.), *The Italian Presence in American Art 1860–1920*, New York 1992

JAMES 1909
Henry James, *Italian Hours*, London and Boston 1909

JAMESON 1852
Anna Jameson, *Legends of the Madonna*, London 1852

JENA 2002
Erik Stephan (ed.), *Joel-Peter Witkin: Compassionate Beauty*, exh. cat., Städtische Museen Jena, Jena 2002

JOANNIDES 1995
Paul Joannides, 'Late Botticelli: Archaism and Ideology', *Arte Cristiana*, vol. 73, no. 768 (1995), pp. 163–78

JORDANOVA 2012
Ludmilla Jordanova, *The Look of the Past: Visual and Material Evidence in Historical Practice*, Cambridge 2012

JUNG 2014
Didier Jung, *William Bouguereau. Le peintre roi de la Belle Époque*, Paris 2014

KAISER FRIEDRICH MUSEUM 1904
Führer durch das Kaiser Friedrich Museum herausgegeben von der Generalverwaltung, Berlin 1904

KANTER 1997
Laurence B. Kanter, *Italian Paintings in the Museum of Fine Arts, Boston. Volume 1: 13th–15th Century*, Boston 1997

KARLSRUHE 2012
Ariane Mensger (ed.), *Déjà-Vu? Die Kunst der Wiederholung von Dürer bis YouTube*, exh. cat., Staatliche Kunsthalle Karlsruhe 2012

KARLSRUHE 2014–15
Alexander Eiling (ed.), *Degas. Klassik und Experiment*, exh. cat., Staatliche Kunsthalle Karlsruhe 2014–15

KARPELES 2008
Eric Karpeles, *Paintings in Proust: A Visual Companion to 'In Search of Lost Time'*, London 2008

KAUFFMANN 1973
C. M. Kauffmann, *Catalogue of Foreign Paintings. Vol. 1: Before 1800*, London 1973

KELLER 2000–1
Peter Keller, 'The Engravings in the 1481 Edition of the "Divine Comedy"', in Berlin, Rome and London 2000–1, pp. 326–33

KEMP 1977
Martin Kemp, 'Botticelli's Glasgow "Annunciation": Patterns of Instability', *The Burlington Magazine*, vol. CXIX, no. 888 (March 1977), pp. 181–4

KERMODE 1985
Frank Kermode, 'Botticelli Recovered', in *Forms of Attention*, Chicago and London 1985, pp. 1–32

KING 1994
A. King, *An Evaluation of Selected Methods of Technical Examination in the Detection of Forgeries*, Research Project, Department of Conservation and Technology, Courtauld Institute of Art, London 1994

KNOWLES 1831
John Knowles (ed.), *The Life and Writings of Henry Fuseli*, vol. 3, London 1831

KÖRNER 2006
Hans Körner, *Botticelli*, Cologne 2006

KOTZ 1990
Mary Lynn Kotz, *Rauschenberg: Art and Life*, New York 1990

KRACAUER 1960
Siegfried Kracauer, *Theory of Film: The Redemption of Physical Reality*, Oxford and New York 1960

KRISTELLER 1990
Paul Oskar Kristeller, 'The Modern System of Arts: A Study in the History of Aesthetics', *Journal of the History of Ideas*, vol. 12, no. 4 (October 1951), pp. 496–527 (reprinted in *Renaissance Thought and the Arts: Collected Essays*, Princeton 1990, pp. 123–227)

KUGLER 1855
Franz Kugler, *Handbook of Painting: The Italian Schools*, part I, 3rd ed., ed. Charles Eastlake, London 1855

KUSTODIEVA 2011
Tatjana Kustodieva, *Museo Statale Ermitage. La pittura italiana dal XIII al XVI secolo*, Milan 2011

LACAMBRE 1992
Geneviève Lacambre, 'Documentation et création: l'exemple de Gustave Moreau', in *Usages de l'image au XIXe siècle*, ed. Stéphane Michaud, Paris 1992, pp. 79–92

LACLOTTE AND MOENCH 2005
Michel Laclotte and Esther Moench, *Peinture italienne musée du Petit Palais Avignon*, Paris 2005

LAFFAILLE 1977
Maurice Laffaille, *Raoul Dufy. Catalogue raisonné de l'oeuvre peint*, vol. 4, Geneva 1977

LAGRANGE 1862
Léon Lagrange, 'Catalogue des dessins des maîtres exposés dans la Galerie des Uffizi à Florence', *Gazette des Beaux-Arts*, vol. 12 (1862), pp. 535–54

LANCASTER 2009
Stephen Wildman, *Ruskin and the Old Masters*, exh. cat. Ruskin Library and Research Centre, Lancaster 2009

LANDON 1810–21
Charles Paul Landon, *Annales du Musée et de l'École Moderne des Beaux-Arts. Recueil de gravures au trait*, 4 vols, Paris 1810–21

LANGER 2006
Laurent Langer, 'Les Tableaux Italiens de James-Alexandre Comte de Pourtalès-Gorgier', in *Goût pour la peinture italienne autour de 1800, prédécesseurs concurrents du cardinal Fesch: Actes du colloque*, ed. Philippe Costamagna, Olivier Bonfait and Monica Preti Hamard, Le Musée Fesch, Ajaccio 2006, pp. 261–76

LANZI 1822
Luigi Lanzi, *Storia Pittorica della Italia*, 4th ed., Florence 1822

LASTRI 1791–5
Marco Lastri, *L'Etruria Pittrice, ovvero storia della pittura toscana dedotta dai suoi monumenti che si esibiscono in stampa dal secolo X fino al presente*, 2 vols, Florence 1791–5

LAYARD 1903
Austen Henry Layard, *Sir A. Henry Layard, G.C.B, D.C.L: autobiography and letters from his childhood until his appointment as H.M. ambassador at Madrid / edited by the Hon William N. Bruce, with a chapter on his parliamentary career by the Rt Hon Sir Arthur Otway*, 2 vols, London 1903

LAZAREFF 1924
Victor Lazareff, 'An Unnoticed Botticelli in Petersburg', *The Burlington Magazine*, vol. XLIV, no. 252 (March 1924), pp. 118–26

LEDGER 1978
Tanya Ledger, *A Study of the Arundel Society 1848–1897*, unpublished D.Phil. thesis, University of Oxford, 1978

LEE 1880
Vernon Lee, *Studies of the Eighteenth Century in Italy*, London 1880

LEE AND ANSTRUTHER-THOMSON 1912
Vernon Lee and C. Anstruther-Thomson, *Beauty and Ugliness and other Studies in Psychological Aesthetics*, London 1912

LESNICK 1990
Daniel R. Lesnick, 'Civic Preaching in the Early Renaissance: Giovanni Dominicis Florentine Sermons', in *Christianity and the Renaissance: Image and Religious Imagination in the Quattrocento*, ed. Timothy Verdon and John Henderson, Syracuse 1990, pp. 208–5

LETHÈVE 1959
Jacques Lethève, 'La Connaissance des peintres préraphaélites anglais en France (1855–1900)', *Gazette des Beaux-Arts*, no. 53 (1959), pp. 315–28

LEVEY 1960
Michael Levey, 'Botticelli and Nineteenth-Century England', *Journal of the Warburg and Courtauld Institutes*, vol. 23, no. 3/4 (July–December 1960), pp. 291–306

LEVI D'ANCONA 1983
Mirella Levi D'Ancona, *Botticelli's Primavera: A Botanical Interpretation including Astrology, Alchemy and the Medici*, Florence 1983

LIGHTBOWN 1978
Ronald Lightbown, *Sandro Botticelli*, 2 vols, London 1978

LIGHTBOWN 1986
Ronald Lightbown, *Mantegna*, Oxford 1986

LINZ 1992
Valie Export, exh. cat., OÖ Landesmuseum, Linz 1992

LIPPMANN 1883
Friedrich Lippmann, 'Die Zeichnungen des Sandro Botticelli zur Göttlichen Komödie', *Jahrbuch der Preußischen Kunstsammlungen*, vol. 4 (1883), pp. 63–72

LIPPMANN 1887
Friedrich Lippmann, *Zeichnungen von Sandro Botticelli zu Dante's Göttlicher Komödie nach den Originalen im K. Kupferstichkabinett zu Berlin*, 2 vols, Berlin 1887

LIPPMANN 1921
Friedrich Lippmann, *Zeichnungen von Sandro Botticelli zu Dantes Göttlicher Komödie. Verkleinerte Nachbildungen der Originale im Kupferstichkabinett zu Berlin und in der Bibliothek des Vatikans, mit einer Einleitung und der Erklärung der Darstellungen*, 2nd ed., Berlin 1921

LIST 1896
List of Works of Art Acquired by the South Kensington Museum During the Year 1894, Department of Science and Art of the Committee of the Council on Education, London 1896

LIVERPOOL 1900
Autumn Exhibition, exh. cat., Walker Art Gallery, Liverpool 1900

LIVERPOOL AND AMSTERDAM 2003–4
Julian Treuherz, Elisabeth Prettejohn and Edwin Becker *Dante Gabriel Rossetti*, exh. cat., Walker Art Gallery, Liverpool; Van Gogh Museum, Amsterdam 2003–4

LLOYD 1977
Christopher Lloyd, *A Catalogue of the Earlier Italian Paintings in the Ashmolean Museum*, Oxford 1977

LOBSTEIN 2006
Dominique Lobstein, *Les Salons au XIXe siècle. Paris, capitale des arts*, Paris 2006

LOCKSPEISER 1979
Edward Lockspeiser, *Debussy: His Life and Mind*, Cambridge 1979

LONDON 1872
Exhibition of the Works of the Old Masters together with Works of Deceased Masters of the British School, Royal Academy of Arts, London 1872

LONDON 1882
Catalogue of the Magnificent Collection of Manuscripts from Hamilton Palace, Sotheby's, London 1882

LONDON 1893
Arts and Crafts Exhibition Society, fourth exhibition, exh. cat., The New Gallery, London 1893

LONDON 1906
Old Masters, Deceased Masters of the British School and Drawings and Sketches by George Frederick Watts RA, Royal Academy of Arts, London 1906

LONDON 1980
The Birkenhead Della Robbia Pottery 1893–1906, exh. cat., Jeremy Cooper Ltd., London 1980

LONDON 1984
Leslie Parris (ed.), *The Pre-Raphaelites*, exh. cat., Tate Gallery, London 1984

LONDON 1989
John Christian (ed.), *The Last Romantics, The Romantic Tradition in British Art: Burne-Jones to Stanley Spencer*, exh. cat., Barbican Art Gallery, London 1989

LONDON 1990
Mark Jones (ed.), *Fake? The Art of Deception*, exh. cat., British Museum, London 1990

LONDON 1993
Jeanne Clegg and Paul Hayes Tucker (eds), *Ruskin and Tuscany*, exh. cat., Accademia Italiana, London 1993

LONDON 1996
Linda Parry (ed.), *William Morris*, exh. cat., Victoria and Albert Museum, London 1996

LONDON 1997
Andrew Wilson et al., *The Age of Rossetti, Burne-Jones and Watts: Symbolism in Britain 1860–1910*, exh. cat., Tate Gallery, London 1997

LONDON 1999–2000
Patricia Lee Rubin and Alison Wright, *Renaissance Florence: The Art of the 1470s*, exh. cat., National Gallery, London 1999–2000

LONDON 2000
Robert Hewison, Ian Warrell and Stephen Wildman, *Ruskin, Turner and the Pre-Raphaelites*, exh. cat., Tate Britain, London 2000

LONDON 2007
Jason Rosenfeld and Alison Smith, *Millais*, exh. cat., Tate Britain, London 2007

LONDON 2011–12
Giulia Bartrum (ed.), *German Romantic Prints and Drawings from an English Private Collection*, exh. cat., British Museum, London 2011–12

LONDON AND FLORENCE 2010–11
Hugo Chapman and Marzia Faietti (eds), *Fra Angelico to Leonardo: Italian Renaissance Drawings*, exh. cat., British Museum, London; Gabinetto disegni e stampe degli Uffizi, Florence 2010–11

LONG 1925
Basil S. Long, *Catalogue of the Constantine Alexander Ionides Collection*, vol. 1, *Paintings in Oil, Tempera and Water-colour, together with certain of the Drawings*, London 1925

LORRAIN 2007
Jean Lorrain, 'Pall Mall Semaine', *L'Écho de Paris* (11 May 1895), reprinted in *Jean Lorrain, Chroniques d'art 1887–1904*, ed. Thalie Rapetti, Paris 2007, pp. 266–70

LOTTES 1996
Wolfgang Lottes, 'Appropriating Botticelli: English Approaches 1860–1890', in *Icons, Texts, Iconotexts: Essays on Ekphrasis and Intermediality*, ed. Peter Wagner, Berlin and New York 1996, pp. 236–61

LUCHINAT 2001
Cristina Acidini Luchinat, *Botticelli: Allegorie mitologiche*, Milan 2001

LÜDEKING 1997
Karlheinz Lüdeking (ed.), *Clement Greenberg: Die Essenz der Moderne. Ausgewählte Essays und Kritiken*, Amsterdam and Dresden 1997

LUGT 1921
Frits Lugt, *Les Marques de collections de dessins et d'estampes*, Amsterdam and Leipzig 1921

MAAS, DUNCAN AND GOOD 1970
Henry Maas, J.L. Duncan and W.G. Good (eds), *The Letters of Aubrey Beardsley*, London and Rutherford 1970

MacNAUGHTON 2014
Donald A. MacNaughton, 'Roscoe, William', *Oxford Dictionary of National Biography*; http://www.oxforddnb.com/view/article/24084 (accessed 16 October 2014)

MAFFIOLI 2003
Monica Maffioli, *Fratelli Alinari: Photographers in Florence*, Florence 2003

MAHER 2012
Jimmy Maher, *The Future was Here: The Commodore Amiga*, Cambridge MA 2012

MARCHI 2013
Andrea G. De Marchi, *Revelations: Discoveries and Rediscoveries in Italian Primitive Art*, Florence 2013

MARILLIER 1967
Henry Currie Marillier, *The Early Work of Aubrey Beardsley*, New York 1967

MARLE 1931
Raimond van Marle, *The Development of the Italian School of Paintings, XII, The Renaissance Painters of Florence in the 15th century: The Third Generation*, The Hague, 1931

MARRA 1999
Michele Marra (ed.), *Modern Japanese Aesthetics: A Reader*, Honolulu 1999

MARRA 2002
Michael F. Marra (ed.), *Japanese Hermeneutics: Current Debates on Aesthetics and Interpretation*, Honolulu 2002

MASER 1973
Edward A. Maser, 'Giotto, Masaccio, Ghiberti and Thomas Patch', in *Festschrift Klaus Lankheit*, ed. Wolfgang Hartmann, Cologne 1973, pp. 192–9

MATTISON 2003
Robert S. Mattison, *Robert Rauschenberg. Breaking Boundaries*, New Haven and London 2003

MAZZA AND TOMASELLO 2004
Miriam Fileti Mazza and Bruna Tomasello (eds), *Catalogo delle pitture della Regia Galleria compilato da Giuseppe Bencivenni già Pelli. Gli Uffizi alla fine del Settecento*, Florence 2004

McCONKEY 1993
Kenneth McConkey, *Sir John Lavery*, Edinburgh 1993

MELIUS 2010
Jeremy Melius, *Art History and the Invention of Botticelli*, PhD thesis, University of California, Berkeley, 2010, https://escholarship.org/uc/item/98r1q0mq (accessed 25 September 2014)

MELTZOFF 1987
Stanley Meltzoff, *Botticelli, Signorelli and Savonarola: Theologia poetica and Painting from Boccaccio to Poliziano*, Florence 1987

MEONI 1998–2007
Lucia Meoni, *Gli arazzi nei musei fiorentini: la collezione medicea: catalogo completo*, 2 vols, Livorno 1998–2007

MESNIL 1930
Jacques Mesnil, 'Connaissons-nous Botticelli?', *Gazette des Beaux-Arts*, ser. 6, vol. 4 (July 1930), pp. 80–99

MESNIL 1938
Jacques Mesnil, *Botticelli*, Paris 1938

MEYER 1890
Julius Meyer, 'Zur Geschichte der florentinischen Malerei des XV. Jahrhunderts. Sandro Botticelli in der zweiten Periode seiner Tätigkeit. Filippino Lippi, Raffaellino del Garbo, Piero di Cosimo', *Jahrbuch der Königlich Preußischen Kunstsammlungen*, vol. 11 (1890), pp. 3–35

MEYER AND BODE 1878
Julius Meyer and Wilhelm Bode, *Gemälde-Galerie. Beschreibendes Verzeichniss der während des Umbaues ausgestellten Gemälde*, Berlin 1878

MICHAUD 2000
Philippe-Alain Michaud, 'Ut Pictura Pellicola', in Marco Scotini (ed.), *Carlo Ludovico Ragghianti e il carattere cinematografico della visione*, exh. cat., Fondazione Ragghianti, Lucca 2000, pp. 179–84

MIDDLETON 1996
Robin Middleton, 'L'Hôtel Pourtalès-Gorgier', in *Félix Duban 1798–1870, Les couleurs de l'architecte*, ed. Sylvain Bellenger and Françoise Hamon, exh. cat., Château de Blois, Paris 1996, pp. 137–46

MILAN 2010–11
Andrea di Lorenzo (ed.), *Botticelli nelle collezioni lombarde*, exh. cat, Museo Poldi-Pezzoli, Milan 2010–11

MILLER 1992
Lillian B. Miller, 'Celebrating Botticelli: The Taste for the Italian Renaissance in the United States, 1870–1920', in Jaffe 1992, pp. 1–23

MIMITA LAMBERTI 1982
Maria Mimita Lamberti, 'La campagna romana nella pittura dell'Ottocento', in *AA. VV.*, Velletri 1982, pp. 104–5

MIRACCO 2006
Renato Miracco, *Giulio Aristide Sartorio, 1860–1932*, Florence 2006

MIRBEAU 1993a
Octave Mirbeau, 'Toujours des lys!', *Le Journal* (28 April 1895), reprinted in *Octave Mirbeau, Combats esthétiques, vol. 2, 1893–1914*, ed. Pierre Michel and Jean-François Nivat, Paris 1993, pp. 86–90

MIRBEAU 1993b
Octave Mirbeau, 'Botticelli proteste!', *Le Journal* (4 and 11 October 1896), reprinted in *Octave Mirbeau, Combats esthétiques, vol. 2, 1893–1914*, ed. Pierre Michel and Jean-François Nivat, Paris 1993, pp. 153–64

MIZIOLEK 1995
Jerzy Miziolek, 'The Lanckoroński Collection in Poland', *Antichità viva*, vol. 34 (1995), pp. 27–49

MOORE 1878
Charles Herbert Moore, *Catalogue, with Notes, of Studies and Fac-similes from Examples of the Works of Florence and Venice; and of Fac-similes and Original Works to be Used as Exercises in Drawing, Belonging to the Fine Arts Department of Harvard University*, Cambridge MA 1878

MOREAU 1974
Catalogue des peintures, dessins, cartons, aquarelles exposés dans les galeries du Musée Gustave Moreau, Paris 1974

MOREAU 2002
Gustave Moreau. Correspondance d'Italie, ed. Luisa Capodieci, Paris 2002

MORELLI 1880
Giovanni Morelli, *Die Werke Italienischer Meister in den Galerien von München, Dresden und Berlin: Ein kritischer Versuch*, Leipzig 1880

MORELLI 1883
Giovanni Morelli, *Italian Masters in German Galleries. A Critical Essay on the Italian Pictures in the Galleries of Munich – Dresden – Berlin, Translated by L.M. Richter*, London 1883

MORELLI 1890–3
Giovanni Morelli, *Kunstkritische Studien über Italienische Malerei*, 3 vols, Leipzig 1890–3

MORELLI 1892
Giovanni Morelli, *Italian Painters. Critical Studies of Their Works: The Borghese and Doria-Pamfili Galleries in Rome*, London 1892

MORI 2011
Gioia Mori (ed.), *Tamara de Lempicka: The Queen of Modern*, Milan and New York 2011

MORRIS AND HOPKINSON 1977
Edward Morris and Martin Hopkinson, *Foreign Catalogue: Walker Art Gallery*, Liverpool 1977

MOSCO 1982
Marilena Mosco, 'La collezione del cardinal Leopoldo (1613–1675)', in *La Galleria Palatina. Storia della quadreria granducale di Palazzo Pitti*, Florence 1982, pp. 37–41

MOWER 2005
Sarah Mower, *20 Years Dolce & Gabbana*, Milan 2005

MUELLER 1994
Roswitha Mueller, *Valie Export: Fragments of the Imagination*, Bloomington 1994

MÜLLER-WALDE 1897
Paul Müller-Walde, 'Beiträge zur Kenntnis des Leonardo da Vinci', *Jahrbuch der Königlich Preussischen Kunstsammlungen*, vol. 18 (1897), p. 165

MUNBY 1972
Alan Noel Latimer Munby, *Connoisseurs and Medieval Miniatures, 1750–1850*, Oxford 1972

MÜNDLER 1850
Otto Mündler, *Essai d'une analyse critique de la notice des tableaux italiens du Musée National du Louvre*, Paris 1850

MÜNTZ 1891
Eugène Müntz, *Histoire de l'art pendant la Renaissance. Vol. II: L'Italie, l'âge d'or*, Paris 1891

MURRAY'S HANDBOOK 1891
Murray's Handbook Advertiser, *Murray's Handbook for Travellers in Algeria and Tunis*, London 1891

MUSEO CAMPANA 1858
Cataloghi del Museo Campana. Classe VIII. Opere del Risorgimento della pittura in Italia dall'epoca delle scuole bizantine fino a Raffaello, Rome 1858

NATIONAL MUSEUM IN WARSAW 2001
National Museum in Warsaw. Guide: Galleries and Study Collections, ed. Dorota Folga-Januszewska and Katarzyna Murawska-Muthesius, Warsaw 2001

NELSON 2009
Jonathan Nelson, '"Botticelli" or "Filippino"? How to Define Authorship in a Renaissance Workshop', in Hatfield 2009, pp. 137–68

NELSON AND SHIFF 2003
Robert Nelson and Richard Shiff, *Critical Terms for Art History*, Chicago 2003

NESSELRATH 2003
Arnold Nesselrath, 'The Painters of Lorenzo the Magnificent in the Chapel of Pope Sixtus IV in Rome', in *The Fifteenth-Century Frescoes in the Sistine Chapel*, ed. Francesco Buranelli and Allen Duston, Vatican City State 2003

NETHERSOLE 2010
Scott Nethersole, 'Being Botticelli', www.nationalgallery.org.uk/paintings/research/being-botticelli (accessed 5 September 2014)

NEW YORK 1978
William Voelkle, *The Spanish Forger*, exh. cat, Pierpont Morgan Library, New York 1978

NEW YORK ET AL. 1997–9
Walter Hopps and Susan Davidson, *Robert Rauschenberg: A Retrospective*, exh. cat., Solomon R. Guggenheim Museum, New York et al. 1997–9

NEW YORK 1998–9
Stephen Wildman and John Christian, *Edward Burne-Jones: Victorian Artist-Dreamer*, exh. cat., Metropolitan Museum of Art, New York 1998–9

NEW YORK 2012–13
Eva Respini (ed.), *Cindy Sherman*, exh. cat., Museum of Modern Art, New York 2012–13

NICE 2005
Gilbert Perlein and Guy Scarpetta (eds), *Alain Jacquet: camouflages et trames*, exh. cat., Musée d'art Moderne et Contemporain, Nice 2005

NICHOLS 1998
Roger Nichols, *The Life of Debussy*, Cambridge 1998

NORTH 1997
Rachel North, 'The Holy Trinity with Saints John the Baptist, Mary Magdalen, Tobias and Raphael by Botticelli and Assistants: A Technical Examination for Attribution', *The Conservator*, vol. 21, no. 1 (1997), pp. 3–11

NUNN 2012
Pamela Gerrish Nunn, *A Pre-Raphaelite Journey: The Art of Eleanor Fortescue-Brickdale*, Liverpool 2012

OERTEL 1961
Robert Oertel, *Frühe Italienische Malerei in Altenburg*, Berlin 1961

OFFNER 1927
Richard Offner, *Italian Primitives at Yale University, Comments and Revisions*, New Haven 1927

OLIPHANT 1876
Margaret Oliphant, *The Makers of Florence: Dante, Giotto, Savonarola and their City*, London 1876

OLIVER 2010
William Oliver, 'David LaChapelle's Return to Fine Art', *The Art Newspaper* (3 May 2010)

O'MALLEY 2013a
Michelle O'Malley, *Painting under Pressure: Fame, Reputation and Demand in Renaissance Florence*, New Haven and London 2013

O'MALLEY 2013b
Michelle O'Malley, 'Quality Choices in the Production of Renaissance Art: Botticelli and Demand', *Renaissance Studies*, vol. 28, no. 1 (2013), pp. 4–32

O'NEILL 2010
Morna O'Neill, *Walter Crane: The Arts and Crafts, Painting, and Politics, 1875–1890*, New Haven and London 2010

OXFORD AND RAVENNA 2010
Colin Harrison and Christopher Newall (eds), *The Pre-Raphaelites and Italy*, exh. cat., Ashmolean Museum, Oxford; Museo d'Arte della Città di Ravenna 2010

PADOA RIZZO 2001
Anna Padoa Rizzo, 'Due tavole per le Convertite', in *Opere e giorni. Studi su mille anni di arte europea: dedicati a Max Seidel*, ed. Klaus Bergdolt and Giorgio Bonsanti, Venice 2001, pp. 355–62

PALICA 2009
Magdalena Palica, *Gustav Adolf von Ingenheim (1789–1855) – Kolekcjoner i Mecenas*, unpublished doctoral thesis, University of Wrocław 2009

PANOFSKY 1960
Erwin Panofsky, *Renaissance and Renascences in Western Art*, Stockholm 1960

PAOLINI 2002
Claudio Paolini, *Il mobile del Rinascimento. La collezione Herbert Percy Horne*, Florence 2002

PAPAPETROS 2014
Spyros Papapetros, 'Denkraum als Ornament: Warburg, Semper und der kosmische Schmuck', in *Warburgs Denkraum. Formen, Motive, Materialien*, ed. Martin Treml, Sabine Flach and Pablo Schneider, Munich 2014, pp. 91–119

PAPE 2008
Cora von Pape, *Kunstkleider: Die Präsenz des Körpers in textilen Kunstobjekten des 20. Jahrhunderts*, Bielefeld 2008

PARIS 1956
Michel Laclotte (ed.), *De Giotto à Bellini. Les primitifs italiens dans les musées de France*, exh. cat., Musée de l'Orangerie, Paris 1956

PARIS 1971–2
Gisela Bergsträsser, *Dessins du Musée de Darmstadt: Hessisches Landesmuseum*, exh. cat., Musée du Louvre, Paris 1971–2

PARIS 1993
Jean-Pierre Cuzin and Marie-Anne Dupuy (eds), *Copier Créer. De Turner à Picasso: 300 oeuvres inspirées par les maîtres du Louvre*, exh. cat., Musée du Louvre, Paris 1993

PARIS 1999–2000
Jean-Yves Tadié and Florence Callu (eds), *Marcel Proust, l'écriture et les arts*, exh. cat., Bibliothèque nationale de France, Paris 1999–2000

PARIS 2003–4
Daniel Arasse et al., *Botticelli: From Lorenzo the Magnificent to Savonarola / Botticelli. De Laurent le Magnifique à Savonarole*, exh. cat., Palais du Luxembourg, Paris 2003–4

PARIS 2004
Caroline Cros et al., *Orlan: Carnal Art*, exh. cat., Centre national de la photographie, Paris 2004

PARIS 2014–15a
Annie Le Brun (ed.), *Sade. Attaquer le soleil*, exh. cat. Musée d'Orsay, Paris 2014–15

PARIS 2014–15b
Laurence de Finance and Jean-Michel Leniaud (eds), *Viollet-le-Duc. Les visions d'un architecte*, exh. cat., Cité de l'architecture et du patrimoine, Paris 2014

PARRONCHI 1985
Alessandro Parronchi, *Botticelli fra Dante e Petrarca*, Florence 1985

PASSAVANT 1836
J.D. Passavant, *Tour of a German Artist in England: with notices of private galleries, and remarks on the state of art*, trans. Elizabeth Rigby, London 1836

PATCH 1770
Thomas Patch, *The Life of Masaccio / La vita di Masaccio*, Florence 1770

PATER 1870
Walter Pater, 'A Fragment on Sandro Botticelli', *Fortnightly Review*, vol. III (August 1870), pp. 155–60

PATER 1873
Walter Pater, *Studies in the History of the Renaissance*, London 1873

PATER 1912
Walter Pater, *The Renaissance: Studies in Art and Poetry*, London 1912

PATER 1986
Walter Pater, 'Sandro Botticelli', in *The Renaissance: Studies in Art and Poetry* (1870), ed. Adam Phillips, 4th ed., Oxford 1986

PAUL 2006
Barbara Paul, 'Ulrike Rosenbach: Reflexionen über die Geburt der Venus', in *Geschichte der bildenden Kunst in Deutschland, vol. 8: Vom Expressionismus bis heute*, ed. Barbara Lange, Darmstadt 2006, pp. 493–4, no. 129

PAUL 2012
Carole Paul (ed.), *The First Modern Museums of Art: The Birth of an Institution in 18th- and early 19th-century Europe*, Los Angeles 2012

PEACHAM 1906
Henry Peacham, *Peacham's Compleat Gentleman 1634*, introduction by G.S. Gordon, Oxford 1906

PERALDI AND NOVELLINI 1880
François Peraldi and Paul Novellini, *Notice des tableaux et des objets d'art exposées dans les galeries du musée et dans les salons de l'hôtel de ville d'Ajaccio*, Ajaccio 1880

PERALDI AND NOVELLINI 1892
François Peraldi and Paul Novellini, *Musée d'Ajaccio. Catalogue des tableaux et des statues*, Ajaccio 1892

PÉRIGNON 1826
Alexis Nicolas Pérignon, *Description des objets d'arts qui composent le cabinet de feu M. le Baron V. Denon ... tableaux, dessins et miniatures*, M. Masson St. Maurice, Paris 1826

PHILADELPHIA 2003–4
Dilys E. Blum, *Shocking! The Art and Fashion of Elsa Schiaparelli*, exh. cat., Philadelphia Museum of Art, Philadelphia 2003–4

PHILLIPS 1926
Duncan Phillips, *A Collection in the Making: A Survey of the Problems Involved in Collecting Pictures*, New York and Washington 1926

PICABIA 1978
Francis Picabia, 'Picabia contre Dada ou le retour de la raison', *Comœdia* (14 March 1927), reprinted in *Francis Picabia, Écrits, vol. 2, 1921–1953*, ed. Olivier Revault d'Allones and Dominique Bouissou, Paris 1978, pp. 185–7

PIERI 2007
Giuliana Pieri, *The Influence of Pre-Raphaelitism on Fin de siècle Italy: Art, Beauty and Culture*, London 2007

PIERRE 2002
Arnauld Pierre, *Francis Picabia. La peinture sans aura*, Paris 2002

PLAGENS 2007
Peter Plagens, 'Another Look at Clement Greenberg', *New England Review*, vol. 28, no. 1 (2007), pp. 51–7

PLAN-CATALOGUE 1882
Plan-catalogue complet du Musée du Louvre, Paris 1882

PLAZZOTTA 1999
Carol Plazzotta, *Kingdom Come: Botticelli's Mystic Nativity*, London 1999

PLOTINUS 1991
Plotinus, *The Enneads*, trans. Stephen MacKenna, London 1991

PLUNKETT 1900
George Noble Plunkett, *Sandro Botticelli*, London 1900

PODRO 1982
Michael Podro, *The Critical Historians of Art*, New Haven and London 1982

POLDI PEZZOLI [1989]
Botticelli e il ricamo del Museo Poldi Pezzoli: storia di un restauro, Cinisello Balsamo (Milan) n.d. [1989]

PONS 1989
Nicoletta Pons, *Botticelli, catalogo completo*, Milan 1989

PONS 2004
Nicoletta Pons, *Bartolomeo di Giovanni, Collaboratore di Ghirlandaio e Botticelli*, Florence 2004

POPE-HENNESSY 1964
John Pope-Hennessy, *Catalogue of Italian Sculpture in the Victoria and Albert Museum*, 3 vols, London 1964

POPHAM AND POUNCEY 1950
Arthur Ewart Popham and Philip Pouncey, *Italian Drawings in the Department of Prints and Drawings in the British Museum: The Fourteenth and Fifteenth Centuries*, 2 vols, London 1950

POST 1914
Chandler Post, 'A Neoplatonic Interpretation of the Chigi Madonna', *Art in America*, vol. 1 (1914), pp. 257–63

PRAGUE 2011
Thus Spoke – LaChapelle, with a text by Otto M. Urban, exh. cat., Galerie Rudolfinum, Prague 2011

PRATESI 1990
Mauro Pratesi, 'Firenze 1896. Festa dell'arte e dei Fiori', *Prospettiva*, vol. 57/60 (1989–90; Scritti d'arte in ricordo di Giovanni Previtali, vol. II), pp. 401–8

PRATESI AND UZZANI 1991
Mauro Pratesi and Giovanna Uzzani, *L'arte italiana nel Novecento: La Toscana*, Venice 1991

PRETI HAMARD 1999
Monica Preti Hamard, 'L'exposition des "écoles primitives" au Louvre', and 'Liste des oeuvres de l'exposition des "écoles primitives" en 1814', in *Dominique-Vivant Denon: l'œil de Napoléon*, exh. cat., Musée du Louvre, Paris 1999, pp. 226–43, 508–10

PRETTEJOHN 2007
Elizabeth Prettejohn, *Art for Art's Sake: Aestheticism in Victorian Painting*, New Haven and London 2007

PRETTEJOHN 2012
Elizabeth Prettejohn (ed.), *The Cambridge Companion to the Pre-Raphaelites*, Cambridge 2012

PREYER 1993
Brenda Preyer, *Il Palazzo Corsi-Horne. Dal Diario di Restauro di H.P. Horne*, Rome 1993

PREYER 1999
Brenda Preyer, 'Art, Architecture and Archives: The Case of Herbert Horne', in *Storia dell'arte e politica culturale intorno al 1900*, ed. Max Seidel, Venice 1999, pp. 281–96

PREYER 2000
Brenda Preyer, '"Art and Life" in the Scholarship and Palace of Herbert P. Horne', in *Gli Anglo-Americani a Firenze. Idea e costruzione del Rinascimento*, ed. Marcello Fantoni and Daniela Lamberini, Rome 2000

RACZYŃSKI 1847
Atanazy Raczyński, *Katalog der Raczyńskischen Bilder-Sammlung*, Berlin 1847

RACZYŃSKI 1853
Atanazy Raczyński, *Katalog der Raczyńskischen Bilder-Sammlung*, Berlin 1853

RAGGHIANTI 1952
Carlo L. Ragghianti, 'Critica d'arte e cinema' [1948], in *Cinema arte figurativa*, Turin 1952, p. 264

RAMPLEY 1997
Matthew Rampley, 'From Symbol to Allegory: Aby Warburg's Theory of Art', *The Art Bulletin*, vol. 79, no. 1 (March 1997), pp. 41–55

RANDOLPH 2002
Adrian W.B. Randolph, *Engaging Symbols: Gender, Politics, and Public Art in Fifteenth-Century Florence*, New Haven and London 2002

RAVE 1956
Paul Ortwin Rave, 'Botticellis Berliner Madonna der Sammlung Raczynski', in *Kunstgeschichtliche Studien für Hans Kauffmann*, ed. Wolfgang Braunfels, Berlin 1956, pp. 143–51

REGGIO EMILIA 2000–1
Mario Di Giampaolo (ed.), *Disegno antico. I disegni della collezione Villani donati ai Musei civici di Reggio Emilia*, exh. cat., Musei Civici, Reggio Emilia 2000–1

REGNAULT-DELALANDE
François Léandre Regnault-Delalande, *Catalogue de tableaux des Écoles D'Italie, de Flandres, de Holland et de France…, no. 12 rue Saint-Jacques, Paris,* Paris 1816

REHM 2009
Ulrich Rehm, *Botticelli. Der Maler und die Medici. Eine Biographie*, Stuttgart 2009

REPORT 1836
Report from the Select Committee on Arts and their Connexion with Manufactures: with the Minutes of Evidence Appendix and Index [of 1835], London 1836

RICHARDSON 1754
Jonathan Richardson, the senior and younger, *An Account of Statues, Bas-reliefs, Drawings and Pictures in Italy, France, &c. with remarks* [1st ed. 1722], London 1754

RICHTER 1949
Irma A. Richter, *Paragone: A Comparison of the Arts by Leonardo da Vinci*, London 1949

RICHTER 1898
Jean-Paul Richter, *Lectures on the National Gallery*, New York 1898

RIDOLFI 1952
Roberto Ridolfi, *Vita di Girolamo Savonarola*, 2 vols, Rome 1952

RIO 1836
Alexis-François Rio, *De la poésie Chrétienne dans son principe dans sa matière et dans ses formes*, Paris 1836

ROBERTS 2007
Rebecca Roberts (ed.), *MoMA: Highlights since 1980: 250 Works from The Museum of Modern Art New York*, New York 2007

ROBINSON 1876
John Charles Robinson, *Descriptive Catalogue of Drawings by the Old Masters: Forming the Collection of John Malcolm of Poltalloch, Esq.*, London 1876

ROECK 2009
Bernd Roeck, *Florence 1900: The Quest for Arcadia*, New Haven and London 2009

ROHLMANN 1996
Michael Rohlmann, 'Botticelli's "Primavera": zu Anlaß, Adressat und Funktion von mythologischen Gemälden im Florentiner Quattrocento', *Artibus et historiae*, vol. 33, no. 17 (1996), pp. 97–132

ROME 1933
Achille Bertini Calosso, *G.A. Sartorio*, exh. cat., Galleria Borghese, Rome 1933

ROME 1968
Jacques Foucart, *Ingres in Italia (1806–1824, 1835–1841)*, exh. cat., Villa Medici, Rome 1968

ROME 1985
Maurizio Fagiolo dell'Arco (ed.), *Antonio Donghi: Sessanta dipinti dal 1922 al 1961*, exh. cat., Palazzo Braschi, Rome 1985

ROME 1996–7
Geneviève Lacambre (ed.), *Gustave Moreau e l'Italia*, exh. cat., Villa Medici, Rome 1996–7

ROME 2006
Mauro Lucco and Giovanni Carlo Federico Villa (eds), *Antonello da Messina*, exh. cat., Scuderie del Quirinale, Rome 2006

ROS 1866
Lieut-Gen. Lord De Ros, *Memorials of the Tower of London*, London 1866

ROSCOE 1846a
William Roscoe, *Life of Lorenzo de' Medici*, London 1846

ROSCOE 1846b
William Roscoe, *The Life and Pontificate of Leo the Tenth*, 2 vols, London 1846

ROSE 2008
Carsten Rose, 'OZ Botticelli, Eins oder Drei', *Auto-Moto-Sport*, vol. 1 (2008)

ROSENBACH 1982
Ulrike Rosenbach, *Videokunst, Foto, Aktion, Performance, Feministische Kunst*, Cologne 1982

ROSENBERG 1960
Harold Rosenberg, *The Tradition of the New*, New York 1960

ROSENBERG 1965
Harold Rosenberg, *The Anxious Object, Art Today and its Audience*, London 1965

ROSINI 1839–7
Giovanni Rosini, *Storia della pittura italiana esposta coi monumenti*, 10 vols, Pisa 1839–7

ROSS 1909
Robert Ross, *Aubrey Beardsley*, London 1909

ROSSETTI 1911
Dante Gabriel Rossetti, *The Works of Dante Gabriel Rossetti*, ed. William M. Rossetti, London 1911; www.rossettiarchive.org

ROSSETTI 1895
William Michael Rossetti (ed.), *Dante Gabriel Rossetti: His Family Letters with a Memoir*, 2 vols, London 1895

ROSSETTI 1889
William Michael Rossetti, *Dante Gabriel Rossetti as Designer and Writer*, London 1889

ROTERMUND 2012
Meike Rotermund, *Metamorphosen in inneren Räumen. Video- und Performancearbeiten der Künstlerin Ulrike Rosenbach,* Göttingen 2012

RUBIN 2000
Patricia Rubin, 'Portrait of a Lady: Isabella Stewart Gardner, Bernard Berenson and the Market for Renaissance Art in America', *Apollo*, vol. CLII (September 2000), pp. 37–44

RUBIN 2007
Patricia Lee Rubin, *Images and Identity in Fifteenth-Century Florence*, New Haven and London 2007

RUSKIN 1875–7
John Ruskin, *Mornings in Florence: Being Simple Studies of Christian art, for English Travellers,* Orpington 1875–7

RUSKIN 1903–12
John Ruskin, *The Works of John Ruskin*, ed. Edward Tyas Cook and Alexander D.O. Wedderburn, 39 vols, London 1903–12

RUSSELL 1978
Francis Russell, 'Advice for a Young Traveller from Burne-Jones: Letters to Agnes Graham, 1876', *Apollo*, vol. CVIII, no. 202 (December 1978), pp. 424–7

SAINT LAURENT 2009
Collection Yves Saint Laurent et Pierre Bergé: la vente du siècle/ direction de l'ouvrage Christiane de Nicolay-Mazery, Paris 2009

SALVADORI 2005
Francesca Salvadori (ed.), *John Flaxman: The Illustrations for Dante's Divine Comedy*, London 2005

SAMUELS 1979
Ernest Samuels, *Bernard Berenson: The Making of a Connoisseur*, Cambridge and London 1979

SAMUELS 1987
Ernest Samuels, *Bernard Berenson: The Making of a Legend*, Cambridge and London 1987

SAN FRANCISCO AND NEW YORK 2012
Rineke Dijkstra: A Retrospective, exh. cat., San Francisco Museum of Modern Art; Solomon R. Guggenheim Museum, New York 2012

SANTI 1976
Bruno Santi (ed.), *Neri di Bicci, Le Ricordanze*, Pisa 1976

SARTORIO 1907
Giulio Aristide Sartorio, 'Le confessioni e le battaglie di un artista', *Il secolo XX* (August 1907), pp. 619–34

SAVONAROLA 2001
Gigliola Fragnito (ed.), *Girolamo Savonarola. Da Ferrara all'Europa*, Florence 2001

SAXL 1957
Fritz Saxl, 'Three "Florentines": Herbert Horne, Aby Warburg, Jacques Mesnil', in *Lectures: vol. I*, London 1957, pp. 331–4

SCARPETTA 2002
Guy Scarpetta, *Jacquet. Camouflages 1961–1964*, Paris 2002

SCHASLER 1855–6
Max Schasler, *Berlins Kunstschätze. Ein praktisches Handbuch zum Gebrauch bei der Besichtigung derselben*, 2 vols, Berlin 1855–6

SCHIFF 1973
Gert Schiff, *Johann Heinrich Füssli 1741–1825, Text und Oeuvrekatalog*, Zurich and Munich 1973

SCHMARSOW 1897
August Schmarsow, 'Meister des XIV. und XV. Jahrhunderts im Museum von Lindenau zu Altenburg', in *Festschrift zu Ehren des Kunsthistorischen Instituts in Florenz*, Leipzig 1897, pp. 143–96

SCHÖNBRUNNER AND MEDER 1896–1908
Josef Schönbrunner and Joseph Meder, *Handzeichnungen alter Meister aus der Albertina und anderen Sammlungen*, 12 vols, Vienna 1896–1908

SCHRÖTER 1997
Elisabeth Schröter, 'Die Maler Franz und Johannes Riepenhausen. Ihre Beschäftingung mit der Kunstgeschichte zu Zeiten Fiorillos, dargestellt an ihrer "Geschichte der Mahlerei in Italien" (1810). Mit einem Anhang unveröffentlichter Briefe zwischen 1805 und 1816', in *Johann Dominicus Fiorillo. Kunstgeschichte und die romantische Bewegung um 1800*, ed. Antje Middeldorf Kosegarten, Göttingen 1997, pp. 213–91

SCHULZE ALTCAPPENBERG 2000
Hein-Th. Schulze Altcappenberg, '"Per essere persona sofistica". Botticellis Bilderzyklus zur Göttlichen Komödie', in Berlin, Rome and London 2000–1, pp. 14–35

SCOTT 1871
William Bell Scott, 'Exhibition of Old Masters and Deceased British Artists', *The Academy* (15 January 1871), p. 90

SCREMIN 2010
Paola Scremin (ed.), *Parole dipinte: Il Cinema sull'arte di Luciano Emmer*, Bologna 2010

SÉCHERRE 2003
Hélène Sécherre, 'The Dubois and Fauchet Collections: The Connoisseurship of Italian Primitives in Paris at the time of the First Empire', *Apollo*, vol. CLVII, no. 496 (June 2003), pp. 21–31

SÉCHERRE 2005
Hélène Sécherre, 'Le marché des tableaux italiens a Paris sous la Restauration (1815–1830). Collectionneurs, marchands, spéculateurs', in *Collections et marché de l'art en France 1789–1848*, ed. Monica Preti-Hamard and Philippe Sénéchal, Rennes 2005, pp. 163–85

SECREST 2004
Meryle Secrest, *Duveen: A Life in Art*, Chicago 2004

SÉROUX D'AGINCOURT 1811–23
J.B.L.G. Séroux d'Agincourt, '*Histoire de l'art par les monumens, depuis sa décadence au IVe siècle jusqu'à son renouvellement au XVIe*, ed. Léon Dufourny, Toussaint Bernard Eméric-David and Laurent François Feuillet, 6 vols, Paris 1811–23

SEZNEC 1953
Jean Seznec, *The Survival of the Pagan Gods: The Mythological Tradition and its Place in Renaissance Humanism and Art*, New York 1953

SHANES 2010
Eric Shanes, *Pop Art*, New York 2010

SHANGHAI 2005
Yin Xin: Metamorphoses, exh. cat., Shanghai Art Museum, Shanghai 2005

SHAPIRO 1957
Meyer Shapiro, 'The Future Possibilities of the Arts', in *Meyer Shapiro, Worldview in Painting – Art and Society, Selected Papers*, New York 1999, pp. 192–9

SHEARMAN 1975
John Shearman, 'The Collections of the Younger Branch of the Medici Family', *The Burlington Magazine*, vol. CXVII, no. 862 (January 1975), pp. 12, 14–27

SHERMAN 1991
Cindy Sherman: History Portraits, with a text by Arthur C. Danto, New York 1991

SHERMAN 1993
Cindy Sherman: 1975–1993, with texts by Rosalind Krauss and Norman Bryson, New York 1993

SIMONSON 2013
Mary Simonson, *Body Knowledge: Performance, Intermediality and American Entertainment at the Turn of the Twentieth Century*, Oxford 2013

SIMPSON 1986
Colin Simpson, *Artful Partners: Bernard Berenson and Joseph Duveen*, New York 1986

SIRÉN 1916
Osvald Sirén, *A Descriptive Catalogue of the Pictures in the Jarves Collection belonging to Yale University*, New Haven 1916

LA SIZERANNE 1898
Robert de La Sizeranne, *English Contemporary Art*, trans. H.M. Poynter, London 1898 (first published in Paris 1895, as *La peinture anglaise contemporaine*)

SKUBISZEWSKA AND KUCZMAN 2010
Maria Skubiszewska and Kazimierz Kuczman, *Paintings from the Lanckoroński collection from the 14th through 16th centuries in the collections of the Wawel Royal Castle, Kracow*, Kracow 2010

SKWIRBLIES 2009
Robert Skwirblies, '"Ein Nationalgut, auf das jeder Einwohner stolz sein dürfte." Die Sammlung Solly als Grundlage de Berliner Gemäldegalerie' in *Jahrbuch der Berliner Museen*, 51 (2009), pp. 71–99

SMITH 1895
Charles Eastlake Smith (ed.), *Journals and Correspondence of Lady Eastlake*, 2 vols, London 1895

SMITH 2002
Elise Lawton Smith, *Evelyn Pickering De Morgan and the Allegorical Body*, London 2002

SMITH 2005
Graham Smith, 'Proust, Ruskin, and Botticelli', *Notes in the History of Art*, vol. 25, no. 1 (Autumn 2005), pp. 10–14

SMITH 1972
Robert Smith, 'Filippo Lippi and Ignazio Hugford', *The Burlington Magazine*, vol. CXIV, no. 829 (April 1972), p. 244

SOCIETY OF PAINTERS 1870
'Society of Painters in Water Colours: Sixty-Sixth Exhibition', *Art Journal* (1870), p. 173

SOZZANI 1999
Franca Sozzani, *Dolce & Gabbana*, London 1999

SPALLETTI 2008
Ettore Spalletti, 'Tommaso Puccini e il "nuovo ordine, e risalto maggiore" dato alla Galleria', in *La Galleria 'rinnovata' e 'accresciuta'. Gli Uffizi nella prima epoca lorenese*, ed. Miriam Fileti Mazza, Ettore Spaletti and Bruno M. Tomasello, Florence 2008, pp. 73–120

SPALLETTI 2010
Ettore Spalletti, *La Galleria di Pietro Leopoldo. Gli Uffizi al tempo di Giuseppe Pelli Bencivenni*, Florence 2010

STAPLEFORD 1995
Richard Stapleford, 'Vasari and Botticelli', *Mitteilungen des Kunsthistorischen Institutes in Florenz*, vol. 39, no. 2/3 (1995), pp. 397–408

STEBBINS ET AL. 2008
Theodore E. Stebbins Jr, Kimberly Orcutt and Virginia Anderson (eds), *American Paintings at Harvard, Volume Two: Paintings, Watercolors, Pastels and Stained Glass by Artists Born 1826–1856*, New Haven and London 2008

STEEGMAN 1947
John Steegman, 'Lord Lindsay's History of Christian Art', *Journal of the Warburg and Courtauld Institutes*, vol. 10 (1947), pp. 123–31

STENDAL 2001
Max Kunze, Beate Schroedter and Eva Hofstetter-Dolega (eds), *Zwischen Antike, Klassizismus und Romantik: die Künstlerfamilie Riepenhausen*, exh. cat., Winckelmann-Museum, Stendal 2001

STERN 2004
Radu Stern, *Against Fashion: Clothing as Art, 1850–1930*, Cambridge MA 2004

STOLTZ 2011
Barbara Stoltz, *Gesetz der Kunst, Ordo der Welt. Federico Zuccaros Dante-Zeichnungen*, Hildesheim 2011

STRACHEY AND SAMUELS 1983
Barbara Strachey and Jayne Samuels, *Mary Berenson: A Self-Portrait from her Letters and Diaries*, New York and London 1983

STREETER 1903
A. Streeter, *Botticelli*, London 1903

STREHLKE 1989
Carl B. Strehlke, 'Bernard and Mary Berenson, Herbert P. Horne and John G. Johnson', *Prospettiva*, vol. LVII–LX (1989), pp. 427–38

STRZYGOWSKI 1885–6
Josef Strzygowski, 'Neuentdeckte Handzeichnungen Botticellis zum Inferno', *Kunstchronik, Beiblatt zur Zeitschrift für Bildende Kunst und zum Kunstgewerbeblatt*, no. 28, vol. 21 (1885–6), pp. 465–72

STRZYGOWSKI 1887
Josef Strzygowski, *Die acht Handzeichnungen des Sandro Botticelli zu Dante's Göttlicher Komödie im Vatikan. Ein Supplement zu dem Codex im Kgl. Kupferstichkabinett zu Berlin*, 2 vols, facsimile, Berlin 1887

STURGIS 1998
Matthew Sturgis, *Aubrey Beardsley: A Biography*, London 1998

SURTEES 1971
Virginia Surtees, *The Paintings and Drawings of Dante Gabriel Rossetti (1828–1882): A Catalogue Raisonné*, 2 vols, Oxford 1971

SUTTON 1985
Denys Sutton, 'Letters from Herbert Horne to Roger Fry', *Apollo*, vol. 122 (August 1985), pp. 136–59

SWINBURNE 1868
Algernon Charles Swinburne, 'Notes on Designs of the Old Masters at Florence', *Fortnightly Review*, vol. IV (July 1868), pp. 16–40

SWINBURNE 1901
Algernon Charles Swinburne, 'Notes on Designs of the Old Masters at Florence' (1868), in *Essays and Studies, 1837–1909*, 5th ed., London 1901, pp. 314–57

SYLVESTER 1993
David Sylvester (ed.), *René Magritte: Catalogue Raisonné, vol. 3: Oil Paintings, Objects and Bronzes 1949–1967*, Antwerp and Basel 1993

SYMONDS 1899
John Addington Symonds, *Renaissance in Italy. Vol. III: The Fine Arts* (1877), London 1899

TEL AVIV 2014
Suzanne Landau (ed.), *Vik Muniz: Pictures of Anything*, exh. cat., Tel Aviv Museum of Art 2014

TERNOIS 1965
Daniel Ternois, *Peintures. Ingres et son temps. Inventaire des collections publiques française: Montauban*, Paris 1965

TERNOIS 1980
Daniel Ternois, *Ingres*, Paris 1980

THIÉBAUT 1987
Dominique Thiébaut, *Ajaccio. Musée Fesch. Les Primitifs italiens*, Paris 1987

TOKYO 1986
Tokyo Daigaku Hyakunenshi: Bukyokushi 1: Bunngakubu [100 Year History of the University of Tokyo: History of Departments 1: Faculty of Literature], Tokyo 1986

TORONTO 2010
Scotiabank CONTACT Photography Festival, exh. cat., CONTACT Gallery, Toronto 2010

TORRE DE' PASSERI 1990
Corrado Gizzi (ed.), *Botticelli e Dante*, exh. cat., Casa di Dante in Abruzzo, Torre de' Passeri 1990

TRNEK 1997
Renate Trnek, *Die Gemäldegalerie der Akademie der bildenden Künste in Wien. Die Sammlung im Überblick*, Vienna 1997

TURIN 1994–5
Rossanna Bossaglia, Ezio Godoli and Marco Rosci (eds), *Torino 1902. Le arti decorative internazionali del nuovo secolo*, exh. cat., Galleria Civica d'Arte Moderna, Turin 1994–5

TURNER 1996
Jane Turner (ed.), *The Dictionary of Art*, 34 vols, New York 1996

TURNER 2014
Nicholas Turner, 'Ottley, William Young', *Oxford Dictionary of National Biography*; http://www.oxforddnb.com/view/article/20941 (accessed 16 October 2014)

ULLRICH 2012
Wolfgang Ullrich, 'Zum wiedererwachten Interesse zeitgenössischer Künstler an Formen der Kopie', in Karlsruhe 2012, pp. 136–45

ULMANN 1893
Hermann Ulmann, *Sandro Botticelli*, Munich 1893

VALLANCE 1898
Aymer Vallance, 'The Invention of Aubrey Beardsley', *Magazine of Art*, vol. 21 (May 1898), pp. 362–9

VAN CLEAVE 1994
Claire Van Cleave, 'Tradition and Innovation in the Early History of Black Chalk Drawing', in *Florentine Drawing at the time of Lorenzo the Magnificent: Papers from a Colloquium held at the Villa Spelman, Florence, 1992*, ed. Elizabeth Cropper, Bologna 1994, pp. 231–43

VAN CLEAVE 2007
Claire Van Cleave, *Master Drawings of the Italian Renaissance*, London 2007

VASARI 1878
Giorgio Vasari, *Le opere di Giorgio Vasari*, ed. Gaetano Milanesi, Milan 1878

VASARI 1912–14
Giorgio Vasari, *Lives of the Most Eminent Painters, Sculptors and Architects*, trans. Gaston du C. de Vere, 10 vols, London 1912–14

VASARI 1971
Giorgio Vasari, *Le vite de' più eccellenti pittori, scultori e architettori, nelle redazioni del 1550 e 1568*, ed. Rosanna Bettarini and Paola Barocchi, 6 vols, Florence 1971

VASARI 1981
Giorgio Vasari, *Le opere di Giorgio Vasari, con nuove annotazioni e commenti di Gaetano Milanesi*, ed. Gaetano Milanesi, introduction by Paola Barocchi, 9 vols, Florence 1981

VASARI 1987
Giorgio Vasari, *Le vite de' più eccellenti pittori, scultori e architettori: nelle redazioni del 1550 e 1568*, ed. Rosanna Bettarini and Paola Barocchi, Florence 1987

VAUGHAN 1979
William Vaughan, *German Romanticism and English Art*, New Haven and London 1979

VENICE AND BASEL 2014
Andreas Beyer (ed.), *For Your Eyes Only. Eine Privatsammlung zwischen Manierismus und Surrealismus*, exh. cat., Peggy Guggenheim Collection, Venice; Kunstmuseum Basel 2014

VENTURI 1925
Adolfo Venturi, *Botticelli*, Rome 1925

VENTURI 1961
Lionello Venturi, *Botticelli*, London 1961

VENTURI 2010
Riccardo Venturi, '"Non può essere che così". Ragghianti e il modernismo di Mondrian', *Predella* (monographic issue edited by Emanuele Pellegrini 'Studi su Carlo Ludovico Ragghianti'), no. 2 (2010), pp. 331–46

VERTOVA 1948
Luisa Vertova, *Botticelli*, Paris 1948

VIENNA 1997
Split: Reality. Valie Export, exh. cat., Museum moderner Kunst Stiftung Ludwig Wien , Vienna 1997

VIENNA 2007–8
Agnes Husslein-Arco (ed.), *Wien–Paris. Van Gogh, Cézanne und Österreichs Moderne 1880–1960*, exh. cat., Galerie Belvedere, Vienna 2007–8

VIGNE 1995
Georges Vigne, *Dessins d'Ingres: Catalogue raisonné des dessins du Musée de Montauban*, Paris 1995

VILLARI 1859–61
Pasquale Villari, *La Storia di Girolamo Savonarola e de' suoi tempi*, 2 vols, Florence 1859–61

VILLIERS 2004
Caroline Villiers, 'La madonna botticelliana del visconte Lee di Fareham', in *Falsi d'autore: Icilio Federico Joni e la cultura del falso tra Otto e Novecento*, ed. Gianni Mazzoni, exh. cat., Complesso museale di Santa Maria della Scala, Siena 2004, pp. 47–58

VILLOT 1849
Frédéric Villot, *Notice des tableaux exposés dans les galeries du Musée National du Louvre, 1re partie: Ecoles d'Italie*, Paris 1849

VOGTHERR 1997
Christoph Martin Vogtherr, *Das Königliche Museum zu Berlin. Planungen und Konzeption des ersten Berliner Kunstmuseums* (supplement *Jahrbuch der Berliner Museen*, vol. 39), Berlin 1997

VOIGT 2014
'Alte Meister, von neuen geliebt. Interview mit Jorinde Voigt, aufgezeichnet von Boris Pofalla', *Monopol*, vol. 1 (2014), p. 32

VORRATSVERZEICHNIS 1886
Verzeichnis der im Vorrat der Galerie befindlichen sowie der an andere Museen abgegebenen Gemälde, Berlin 1886

WAAGEN 1830
G.F. Waagen, *Verzeichnis der Gemälde-Sammlung des Königlichen Museums zu Berlin*, Berlin 1830

WAAGEN 1839
G.F. Waagen, *Kunstwerke und Künstler in Paris*, Berlin 1839

WAAGEN 1854
G.F. Waagen, *Treasures of Art in Great Britain being an account of the chief collections of paintings, drawings, sculptures, illuminated mss., &c., &c.*, 3 vols, London 1854

WAAGEN 1857
G.F. Waagen, *Galleries and Cabinets of Art in Great Britain: being an account of more than forty collections of paintings, drawings, sculptures, mss., &c. &c. visited in 1854 and 1856…*, London 1857

WAGNER 1974
Hugo Wagner, *Kunstmuseum Bern. Italienische Malerei 13. bis 16. Jahrhundert*, Bern 1974

WAKEMAN 1973
Geoffrey Wakeman, *Victorian Book Illustration: The Technical Revolution*, Newton Abbot 1973

WALDMAN 2000
Louis A. Waldman, *Baccio Bandinelli and Art at the Medici Court: A Corpus of Early Modern Sources*, Philadelphia 2000

WALDMAN 2009
Louis A. Waldman, 'Botticelli and his Patrons: The Arte del Cambio, the Vespucci, and the Compagnia dello Spirito Santo in Montelupo', in Hatfield 2009, pp. 105–35

WARBURG 1893
Aby Warburg, *Sandro Botticellis "Geburt der Venus" und "Frühling": eine Untersuchung über die Vorstellungen von der Antike in der Italienischen Frührenaissance*, Hamburg and Leipzig 1893 (reprinted in Warburg 1932, pp. 1–57, addenda and corrigenda, pp. 307–28)

WARBURG 1898
Aby Warburg, 'Sandro Botticelli', *Das Museum* (1898), pp. 37–40 (reprinted in Warburg 1932, pp. 61–8)

WARBURG 1902a
Aby Warburg, *Bildniskunst und Florentinisches Bürgertum*, Leipzig 1902

WARBURG 1902b
Aby Warburg, 'Flandrische Kunst und florentinische Renaissance', *Jahrbuch der Königlich Preussischen Kunstsammlungen* (1902), pp. 247–66

WARBURG 1932
Aby Warburg, *Gesammelte Schriften*, ed. Gertrud Bing, 2 vols, Leipzig 1932

WARBURG 1998
Aby Warburg, *Die Erneuerung der heidnischen Antike*, ed. Horst Bredekamp and Michael Diers, *Gesammelte Schriften: Aby Warburg*, part 1, vol. 1, Berlin 1998

WARBURG 1999
Aby Warburg, *The Renewal of Pagan Antiquity: Contributions to the Cultural History of the European Renaissance*, trans. David Britt, ed. Kurt W. Forster, Los Angeles 1999

WARBURG 2010
Aby Warburg, *Werke in einem Band: auf der Grundlage der Manuskripte und Handexemplare*, ed. Martin Treml, Sigrid Weigel and Perdita Ladwig, Berlin 2010

WARD 2011–12
Henrietta Ward, '"The Rising Genius": Simeon Solomon's Unexplored Interpretation of Sandro Botticelli', *The British Art Journal*, vol. XII, no. 3 (Winter 2011–12), pp. 60–7

WARNER 1992
Malcolm Warner, 'The Pre-Raphaelites and the National Gallery', in *The Pre-Raphaelites in Context*, exh. cat., Henry E. Huntington Library and Art Gallery, San Marino 1992

WARSAW 2010–11
The Masters of Drawing: Drawings from the Barbara Piasecka Johnson Collection, exh. cat., The Royal Castle, Warsaw 2010–11

WASHINGTON 1979
David Alan Brown, *Berenson and the Connoisseurship of Italian Painting: A Handbook to the Exhibition*, exh. cat., National Gallery of Art, Washington DC, 1979

WASHINGTON 1991
Mary Yakush (ed.), *ROCI: Rauschenberg Overseas Culture Interchange*, exh. cat., National Gallery of Art, Washington DC 1991

WASHINGTON 2001–2
David Alan Brown (ed.),*Virtue and Beauty: Leonardo's 'Ginevra de' Benci' and Renaissance Portraits of Women*, exh. cat., National Gallery of Art, Washington DC, 2001–2

WATTS 1993
Barbara J. Watts, 'Dante's Role in the Nineteenth Century Rediscovery of Botticelli', *Italian Culture*, vol. XI (1993), pp. 59–76

WATSON 1940
F.J.B. Watson, 'Thomas Patch (1725–1782): Notes on his Life, together with a Catalogue of his Known Works', *The Walpole Society*, vol. 28 (1940), pp. 15–50

WATTS 1995
Barbara J. Watts, 'The Pre-Raphaelites and the International Competition for Sandro Botticelli's Dante Drawings Manuscript', in *Pre-Raphaelite Art in Its European Context*, ed. Susan P. Casteras and Alicia Craig Faxon, Madison and London 1995, pp. 81–99

WEINBERG 1987
Gail S. Weinberg, 'Ruskin, Pater and the Rediscovery of Botticelli', *The Burlington Magazine*, vol. CXXIX, no. 1006 (January 1987), pp. 25–7

WEINBERG 1995
Gail S. Weinberg, 'Aubrey Beardsley, the Last Pre-Raphaelite', in *Pre-Raphaelite Art in Its European Context*, ed. Susan P. Casteras and Alicia Craig Faxon, Madison and London 1995, pp. 210–33

WEINBERG 2004
Gail S. Weinberg, 'D.G. Rossetti's Ownership of Botticelli's "Smeralda Brandini"', *The Burlington Magazine*, vol. CXLVI, no. 1210 (January 2004), pp. 20–6

WEINSTEIN 1970
Donald Weinstein, *Savonarola and Florence*, Princeton 1970

WELLS 2004
Paul Wells, 'On Being an Impish God', in *Terry Gilliam: Interviews*, ed. David Sterritt and Lucille Rhodes, Jackson 2004, pp. 124–34

WESENBERG 1992
Angelika Wesenberg, 'Raczynski in Berlin', in *Sammlung Graf Raczynski. Malerei der Spätromantik aus dem Nationalmuseum Poznan*, ed. Konstanty Kalinowski and Christoph Heilmann, exh. cat., Munich, Berlin and Kiel 1992–3, pp. 70–84

WESTGARTH 2009
Mark Westgarth, 'A Biographical Dictionary of Nineteenth Century Antique and Curiosity Dealers', *Regional Furniture. The Journal of the Regional Furniture Society*, vol. XXIII (2009)

WHITE 1986
Palmer White, *Elsa Schiaparelli: Empress of Paris Fashion*, London 1986

WHITE 1853
Richard Grant White, *Companion to the Bryan Gallery of Christian Art*, New York 1853

WILDENSTEIN 1954
Georges Wildenstein, *Ingres*, London 1954

WILLARD 1902
Ashton Rollins Willard, *History of Modern Italian Art*, New York and Bombay, 2nd ed. 1902

WILSON 1996
Carolyn C. Wilson, *Italian Paintings, XIV–XVI Centuries in the Museum of Fine Arts, Houston*, Houston 1996

WIND 1958
Edgar Wind, *Pagan Mysteries in the Renaissance*, London 1958

WIND 1981
Edgar Wind, *Heidnische Mysterien in der Renaissance*, Frankfurt am Main 1981

WINIEWICZ-WOLSKA 2010
Joanna Winiewicz-Wolska, *Karol Lanckoroński i jego wiedeńskie zbiory*, 2 vols, Krakow 2010

WOLF 2013
Gerhard Wolf, 'Museumskulturen: Europäische Perspektiven um 1800', in *Die kaiserliche Gemäldegalerie in Wien und die Anfänge des öffentlichen Kunstmuseums*, ed. Gudrun Swoboda, 2 vols, 2013, vol. 2, pp. 317–35

WÖLFFLIN 1952
Heinrich Wölfflin, *Classic Art*, London (1898) 1952

WRIGHT AND SUOKKO 1986
Guy Wright and Glenn Suokko, 'Andy Warhol: An Artist and His Amiga', *AmigaWorld*, (January–February 1986), reprinted in *I'll be your Mirror: The Selected Andy Warhol Interviews 1962–1987*, ed. Kenneth Goldsmith, New York 2004, pp. 333–41

WUERTH 1928
Louis A. Wuerth, *Catalogue of the Etchings of Joseph Pennell*, Boston 1928

YASHIRO 1925
Yukio Yashiro, 'A Newly Discovered Botticelli', *The Burlington Magazine*, vol. XLVI, no. 265 (April 1925), pp. 156–63, 166–7

YASHIRO 1926
Yukio Yashiro, *Sandro Botticelli*, 3 vols, London 1926

YASHIRO 1929
Yukio Yashiro, *Sandro Botticelli and the Florentine Renaissance*, rev. ed., London and Boston 1929

YASHIRO 1972
Yukio Yashiro, *Watashi no bijutsu henreki* [My Art Pilgrimage], Tokyo 1972

YEIDE 2009
Nancy Yeide, *Beyond the Dreams of Avarice: The Hermann Goering Collection*, Dallas 2009

ZACCHIROLI 1783
Francesco Zacchiroli, *Description de la Galerie Royale de Florence*, 3 vols, Florence 1783

ZAMBRANO AND NELSON 2004
Patrizia Zambrano and Jonathan Katz Nelson, *Filippino Lippi*, Milan 2004

ZERI 1985
Federico Zeri, 'Questioni di Bottega del Botticelli', *Paragone*, nos 419, 421, 423 (January, March and May 1985), pp. 135–9

ZERI AND GARDNER 1971
Federico Zeri and Elizabeth E. Gardner, *Italian Paintings: A Catalogue of the Collection of the Metropolitan Museum of Art, Vol. 1: Florentine School*, New York 1971

ZERI AND ROSSI 1986
Federico Zeri and Francesco Rossi, *La raccolta Morelli nell'Accademia Carrara*, Bergamo 1986

ZERI ET AL. 1984
Federico Zeri et al, *Dipinti toscani e oggetti d'arte dalla collezione Vittorio Cini*, Vicenza 1984

ZÖLLNER 2005
Frank Zöllner, *Botticelli*, Munich, Berlin and London 2005

ZUCKER 2000
Mark J. Zucker, *Early Italian Masters: The Illustrated Bartsch, vol. 24: Commentary*, part 3, New York 2000

Index

Page numbers in *italic* refer to the illustrations

Picture credits

© ADAGP, Paris and DACS, London 2015: cats 10, 15, 29; © ADAGP, Paris and DACS, London / CNAP / 2015: cat. 24; Alinari Archives, Florence: fig. 30; Courtesy of Allinson Gallery, Inc.: cat. 56; © Amgueddfa Cymru – National Museum Wales: cat. 120; © Musée Anne-de-Beaujeu (Moulins, France), Jérome Mondière: fig. 44; Courtesy of the artist and Metro Pictures, New York: cat. 17; © Courtesy of the Artist and Nathalie Obadia Gallery, Paris / Brussels: cat. 4; © Courtesy of the Artist and Pace London: cat. 7; Les Arts décoratifs, Paris / Photo Les Arts décoratifs, Paris / Jean Tholance: cat. 35; © Ashmolean Museum, University of Oxford: cats 53, 63, 70, 72, 127; © The Barber Institute of Fine Arts, University of Birmingham: cat. 130; Courtesy of Anne Benoist d'Azy, France: fig. 58; Biblioteca Berenson, Villa I Tatti – The Harvard University Center for Italian Renaissance Studies, courtesy of the President and Fellows of Harvard College: fig. 55; Comune di Bergamo-Accademia Carrara: cats 133, 155; Kunstmuseum Bern, Legat Adolf von Sturler, Versailles: cats 115, 116; © BI ADAGP, Paris and DACS, London / Scala, Florence 2015: cat. 27; © 2015 Biblioteca Apostolica Vaticana: cats 147, 148, 149; Birmingham Museums and Art Gallery / Bridgeman Images: cat. 102; fig. 39; Booth-Clibborn Collection, London © Contemporary Editions Ltd, London: cats 95, 96; bpk / Kupferstichkabinett, Staatliche Museen zu Berlin / Philipp Allard: cats 150, 151, 152, 153; figs 23, 25; © Bradford Art Galleries and Museums, West Yorkshire, UK / Bridgeman Images: cat. 76; © The Trustees of the British Museum: cats 97, 138, 144, 145, 146, 165, 167; figs 42, 72; Galleria Palatina, Palazzo Pitti, Florence, Italy / Bridgeman Images: cat. 160; Brooklyn Museum of Art, New York, USA / Bridgeman Images: fig. 36; Courtesy Charim Galerie, Wien / Vienna: cat. 23; By permission of the Governing Body of Christ Church, Oxford: cat. 135; © 1989 Columbia Pictures Industries, Inc. All Rights Reserved. Courtesy of Columbia Pictures: fig. 2; © The Samuel Courtauld Trust, The Courtauld Gallery, London: cat. 43; fig. 7; © Salvador Dalí, Fundació Gala-Salvador Dalí, DACS, 2015: cat. 33; Hessisches Landesmuseum Darmstadt. Photo: Wolfgang Fuhrmannek: cats 84, 103; DEA / G. NIMATALLAH / De Agostini Picture Library / Getty Images: fig. 50; De Agostini Picture Library / Bridgeman Images: cat. 85; Photo © De Agostini / Getty Images: fig. 38; © The De Morgan Foundation: cats 52, 67, 79, 80; © Maggie Diaz Collection 2015: fig. 67; © Rineke Dijkstra. Courtesy of the artist and Marian Goodman Gallery: cat. 11; © Rineke Dijkstra. Photo © Tate, London 2015: cat. 12; © Courtesy of Dolce & Gabbana: cats 13, 14; © Courtesy Duhamel Fine Art, Paris: cat. 8; The Faringdon Collection Trust, Buscot Park, Oxfordshire: cat. 121; Courtesy of Film4: fig. 31; Ex S.S.P.S.A.E e per il Polo Museale della città di Firenze – Gabinetto Fotografico: figs 9, 16; © The Fitzwilliam Museum, Cambridge: cats 100, 104, 105, 122; Venezia, Fondazione Giorgio Cini, Matteo De Fina: cat. 168; Courtesy of Studio Philippe Formanoir – Paso Doble: cat. 28; Gemäldegalerie Berlin (Kriegsverlust) (Foto: Gemäldegalerie Staatliche Museen zu Berlin): cats 129, 134; figs 17, 18, 19, 20; Gemäldegalerie der Akademie der bildenden Künste Wien: cat. 124; Courtesy of Archivio Giorgini Firenze: fig. 59; Photo: Claudio Giusti Firenze, Courtesy of Moretti Fine Art: cat. 112; Collection of the Guild of St George, Museums Sheffield: cat. 78; © President and Fellows of Harvard College: cat. 77; Photo: Imaging Department © President and Fellows of Harvard College: cats 55, 71, 132; fig. 37; Photograph © The State Hermitage Museum / Vladimir Terebenin: cats 141, 142; © The Estate of Paul Himmel: cat. 30; © Photo: Houghton Library, Harvard University: figs 24, 26; Image © Museum of Fine Arts, Houston, Texas, USA / The Edith A. and Percy S. Straus Collection: cat. 159; © Isabella Stewart Gardner Museum, Boston, MA, USA / Bridgeman Images: fig. 56; Isabella Stewart Gardner Museum, Boston: cat. 109; Courtesy Comité Jacquet & Galerie GP & N Vallois, Paris: cats 25, 26; Simon James / FilmMagic / Getty Images: fig. 60; Collection of Valeri Jerlitsyn, London: cat. 31; © Michael Joaquin Grey: cat. 3; © David LaChapelle: cats 5, 6; Lady Gaga, ARTPOP album cover, 2013 Cover art © Jeff Koons: fig. 61; Distributed by LIMA Amsterdam: cat. 22; Image supplied courtesy of Lindenau-Museum Altenburg. Photography by Bernd Sinterhauf: cats 114, 161; © Susanna Mantovani / Galleria degli Uffizi, Florence, Italy. Su concessione del Ministero dei Beni e delle Attività Culturali e del Turismo: fig. 1; © Steven Meisel / By permission of Art + Commerce: fig. 62; © 2015. Image copyright The Metropolitan Museum of Art / Art Resource / Scala, Florence: cat. 137; Galleria d'Arte Moderna, Venice, Italy / Bridgeman Images: cat. 37; © Montauban, musée Ingres. Photo: Guy Roumagnac: cats 90, 91, 93; © Moretti Fine Art: cat. 119; © 2015. Digital image, The Museum of Modern Art, New York / Scala, Florence: fig. 65; © 2015. Digital image, The Museum of Modern Art, New York / Scala, Florence © 1998 Kate Rothko Prizel & Christopher Rothko / Artists Rights Society (ARS), New York and DACS, London: fig. 66; Musée Fabre de Montpellier Méditerranée Métropole – photograph by Frédéric Jaulmes: cat. 117; Museo Nacional del Prado © Photo MNP / Scala, Florence: fig. 34; Paris, Musée Jacquemart-André – Institut de France © Culturespaces – Musée Jacquemart-André: cat. 131; © Tomoko Nagao: cat. 1; Nationalgalerie, Staatliche Museen zu Berlin: fig. 46; © The National Gallery, London: cats 101, 118; figs 5, 6; National Gallery, London, UK / © Stefano Baldini / Bridgeman Images: fig. 35; National Gallery, London, UK / Bridgeman Images: figs 4, 33; Image courtesy of the National Gallery of Art, Washington: cat. 163; Rome, National Gallery of Modern and Contemporary Art. By permission of Ministero dei Beni delle Attività Culturali e del Turismo: cat. 49; Courtesy of the owner: fig. 32; Photo: Kira Perov, courtesy of Bill Viola Studio: cat. 9; Photograph and Digital Image © Philadelphia Museum of Art: cat. 34; figs 51, 52, 53, 54; PhotographerMoviestore Collection / REX: fig. 3; © Comité Picabia: cat. 38; fig. 69; © Museo Poldi Pezzoli, Milano: cat. 136; © Private Collection c/o Christie's Images Ltd., 2009: cat. 65; © Private Collection c/o Christie's Images Ltd., 2013: cat. 64; © Private Collection c/o Christie's Images Ltd., 2015: cat. 42; Private collection: cats 39, 50, 158, 166; Property of an American Private Collection: cat. 41; © Robert Rauschenberg Foundation / DACS, London / VAGA, New York 2015: cat. 16; Photo © RMN-Grand Palais / Agence Bulloz © ADAGP, Paris and DACS, London 2015: cat. 32; Photo © RMN-Grand Palais / Martine Beck-Coppola: cat. 128; Photo © RMN-Grand Palais / Gérard Blot: cat. 107; Photo © RMN-Grand Palais / Christian Jean: cat. 83; Photo © RMN-Grand Palais / Stéphane Maréchalle: cat. 86; Photo © RMN-Grand Palais / René-Gabriel Ojéda: cats 82, 89, 108, 123, 125, 139; Photo © RMN-Grand Palais (musée d'Orsay) / Hervé Lewandowski: cats 40, 66, 92; Photo © RMN-Grand Palais (musée du Louvre) / Daniel Arnaudet: cat. 110; Photo © RMN-Grand Palais (musée du Louvre) / Jean-Gilles Berizzi: fig. 14; Photo © RMN-Grand Palais (musée du Louvre) / Stéphane Maréchalle: cat. 51; Photo © RMN-Grand Palais (musée du Louvre) / Michel Urtado: fig. 45; Courtesy Galerie Rothamel: fig. 68; Royal Collection Trust © Her Majesty Queen Elizabeth II 2015: fig. 28; Ruskin Foundation (Ruskin Library, Lancaster University): cat. 69; © 2015. Photo Scala, Florence: cat. 140; © 2015. Photo Scala, Florence – courtesy of the Ministero Beni e Att. Culturali: cats 111, 164, 169; figs 8, 10; © 2015. Photo Scala Florence / Heritage Images: cat. 74; Eric Schaal © Fundació Gala-Salvador Dalí, Figueres, DACS 2015: fig. 64; © Peter Schälchli, Zürich: cat. 88; © Scottish National Gallery of Modern Art: cat. 36; © Staatliche Museen zu Berlin. Image: Jörg P. Anders: cats 47, 106, 113, 143, 154, 156, 170; © Städel Museum – U. Edelmann – ARTOTHEK: cats 126, 157; © Tate, London 2015: cats 68, 87; fig. 27; Galleria degli Uffizi, Florence, Italy / Bridgeman Images: fig. 15; Image © Victoria and Albert Museum, London: cats 2, 44, 45, 48, 54, 57, 58, 59, 60, 61, 62, 73, 81, 94, 98, 99, 162; figs 11, 13, 21, 29, 40, 41, 43, 47, 57, 70, 71; © The Wallace Collection, London: fig. 12; © 2015 The Andy Warhol Foundation for the Visual Arts, Inc. / Artists Rights Society (ARS), New York and DACS, London: cats 19, 21; Collection of The Andy Warhol Museum, Pittsburgh. Artists Rights Society (ARS), New York and DACS, London: cat. 16; Courtesy of the Warburg Institute: figs 48, 49; Courtesy of the Whitworth, The University of Manchester: cat. 75; Courtesy of Joel-Peter Witkin: cat. 18.

Acknowledgements

The authors should like to thank, above all, the lenders both private and institutional listed in this catalogue. For their support since the inception of the project, we are especially grateful to Michael Eissenhauer, Martin Roth, Christina Haak, Bernd Lindemann, Linda Lloyd Jones, Tim Reeves, Beth McKillop, Heike Kropff, Julius Bryant and Damien Whitmore.

For their contributions to this publication: Susanna Avery-Quash, Stephen Calloway, Caroline Campbell, Caroline Elam, Dagmar Korbacher, Antonio Natali, Susan Owens, Elizabeth Prettejohn, Ulrich Rehm, Sonnet Stanfill, Oliver Tostmann, Riccardo Venturi, Toshio Watanabe, Gerhard Wolf. We are much obliged to Tom Windross for editorial work, to Kate Bell for copy-editing the text, Philip Lewis for design, and Zara Anvari, Suzy Brogard, Fred Caws, Susanna Cordner, Clare Davis, Liz Edmunds, Catriona Gourlay, Paul Holberton and Caroline Waight for their work on the book, as well as Sigrid Wollmeiner, Kerstin Ludolph, Karen Angne, Barbara Delius and Lutz Stirl.

We are also grateful to Sarah Quantrill, Ross Head, Claire Everitt, Alexandra Kaspar, Eleanor Townsend and Stephanie Cripps at the V&A Exhibitions Department, to Annabel Judd and her colleagues in the Design Department, and to Technical services and the framing team at the V&A. At the Staatliche Museen zu Berlin we wish to thank, in the Exhibitions Department, Ramona Föllmer, Susanne Anger, Maren Eichhorn and Jörg Völlnagel, and in the Communications Department, Mechtild Kronenberg, Corinna Salmen-Mies, Manja Weinert, Marion Warther, Fabian Fröhlich, Friederike Foitzik and Bernd Rottenburg.

Many thanks are also due to the exhibition designers Hansjörg Hartung (for Berlin) as well as Tom Duncan and Margrit Barner from Duncan McCauley (for the London showing). Also, on behalf of the V&A, we thank Elizabeth Wells-Thulin and Eleanor Clarke at Focus Consultants, Sophie Lee and Susanna Haddon for copy-editing the exhibition text, and in Berlin, Mathias Illgen, Kathleen Raasch and Lisa Pepita Weiss from StanHema for the communications design.

For their contributions for the project, we are indebted to: Cristina Acidini, Brigitte Alasia, Derek and Jane Allinson, Bernhard Andergassen, Ursula Andress, Richard Armstrong, Yves Badetz, Nigel Baker, Francesca Baldassari, Maria Balshaw, Luca Massimo Barbero, Annamaria Bava, Martin Beisly, Lori Belilove, Gabriella Belli, Ines Bellin, John Berger, Heidi Blöcher, Dilys Blum, Matthias Bode, Thomas Bohl, Pilar Castillo, Charles Booth-Clibborn, Stephanie Brodel, David Brown, Peter Brown, Symon Brown, Monseigneur Jean-Louis Bruguès, Gabriele Caioni, Marina Calow, Beverley Calté, Thomas P. Campbell, Andrea Caravita, Kate Carreno, Marie-Sophie Carron de la Carrière, Matteo Ceriana, Hugo Chapman, Caterina Chiarelli, Keith Christiansen, Guy Cogeval, Caroline Collier, Sean Connery, Natalie Cothren, Philippe Costamagna, Jean Coulon, Rip Cronk, Charlotte Desaga, Florentine Dietrich, Rineke Dijkstra, Domenico Dolce, Harriet Drummond, Christine Exler, Valie EXPORT, Côme Fabre, Oliver Fairclough, Lord Faringdon, Konrad Feilchenfeldt, Gabriele Finaldi, Johanna Flaum, Martina Fleischer, Marie-Cécile Forest, Matthias Frehner, Martina Fusari, Stefano Gabbana, Olivier Gabet, Martin Gammon, Flavio Gianassi, Victor Gill, Terry Gilliam, Bruno Girveau, Daniel Godfrey, Barbara Gottschalk, Michael Joaquin Grey, Simon Groom, Mechthild Haas, Stefanie Hamm, Hans-Jürgen Harras, Babette Hartwieg, Anne Hawley, Bettina Held, Fabrice Hergott, Charly Herscovici, Uwe Heuer, Tessen von Heydebreck, Michel Hilaire, Lizzie Himmel, Monika Hoffmann, Max Hollein, Annett Hommen, Masayuki Inoue, Jill Iredale, Bobby Jablonski, Carol Jacobi, Valeri Jerlitsyn, Rebecca John, Alice Joubert, Theo Jülich, Nicola Kalinsky, Friedrich Kisters, Kurt Kladler, Tim Knox, Marion Kolanoski, Thomas Kren, Alexis Kugel, David LaChapelle, Mario Lamparelli, Bill Lasarow, Madalina Lazen, Thomas W. Lentz, Tania Lipowski, Claire Longworth, Marina Devovna Loshak, Neil MacGregor, Maria Vittoria Marini Clarelli, Jean-Luc Martinez, Marie Mayot, Ellen McAdam, Elizabeth McCall, Nina and Frank Moore, Fabrizio Moretti, Vik Muniz, Youssef Nabil, Christiane Naffah-Bayle, Tomoko Nagao, Antonio Natali, Julia M. Nauhaus, Cardinal Vincent Nichols, Jorge Nikaido, Fr John O'Leary, Caroline Oliphant, Reiner Opoku, ORLAN, David Packer, Valeria Paruzzo, Jeannette Pauly, Nicholas Penny, Kira Perov, Lerrj Piazza, Mikhail Piotrovsky, Earl Alexander Powell III, Frauke Probst, Louise Pullen, Adelheid Rasche, Joachim Rau, Yves Robert, Maria Cristina Rodeschini, Carlos Rogel, Isabel Rojas-Williams, Cristiana Romalli, Ulrike Rosenbach, Ramona Roth, Julie Rowlins, Timothy F. Rub, Francis Russell, Nicolas Sainte-Fare-Garnot, Christel Sanguinetti, Julia Scott, Peter Scheel, Christoph Schmidt, Barbara Schneider-Kempf, Frank Scholze,

Heinrich Schulze Altcappenberg, Nicholas Serota, Cindy Sherman, Eric Shiner, Frank Simonin, Jennifer Sliwka, Alison Smith, Gillian Smithson, Sonia Solicari, Carolin Stanneck, Ute Steigerwald, Axel Stein, Maria Stein, Volko Steinig, Sandra Stelzig, Kim Streets, Alexander Sturgis, Rodica Sybleyras, Angelo Tartuferi, Mandy Telle, Jacqueline Thalmann, Dominique Thiébaut, Carola Thielecke, Uma Thurman, Gary Tinterow, Georges-Philippe Vallois, Ernst Vegelin van Claerbergen, Florence Viguier, Giovanni F. Villa, Dominique Vingtain, Bill Viola, Roger Vlitos, Julie Waseige, Katharina Weick-Joch, Rainer Wendler, Julius White, Stephen Wildman, Joel-Peter Witkin, Moritz Wullen, Yin Xin, Annalisa Zanni, Irian Znork, Thomas Zuhr, and others who prefer to remain anonymous.

Finally, for their sound advice, expert insights and generous support, we thank: Glenn Adamson, Marta Ajmar, Zoe Allen, Anne Bancroft, Liz Barrett, Horst Bredekamp, Victoria Button, Olivia Colling, Roberto Contini, Louise Cooling, Katherine Coombs, Nicola Costaras, Alessandro Della Latta, Lara Flecker, Zoe Franklin, David Freedberg, Olivia Horsfall Turner, Stephan Kemperdick, Jenny Lister, Rainer Michaelis, Liz Miller, Roisin Morris, Raphaele Mouren, Tessa Murdoch, Christopher Newell, Catherine Nunn, François Quiviger, Clare Richardson, Sophie Robinson, Gill Saunders, Lucia Savi, Andreas Schalhorn, Claudia Wedepohl, Marta Weiss and Reinhild Weiss.

Research for this publication was carried out with the resources of the National Art Library and the Kunstbibliothek, Berlin.

Notes on the catalogue

CONTRIBUTORS

AD Ana Debenedetti
ME Mark Evans
SH Sabine Hoffmann
DK Dagmar Korbacher
MM Mary McMahon
GM Gabriel Montua
RR Ruben Rebmann
SW Stefan Weppelmann

As only two works by Botticelli are signed, and only a handful are documented, opinions vary widely over the nature and extent of his oeuvre. A principal theme of this exhibition is to show how understanding of Botticelli's artistic persona and his relationship to his workshop have shifted over the years. While the attributions and dating provided here express a current consensus, few are definitive.

Florentine paintings were traditionally painted in tempera on panel, mostly of poplar, or sometimes on cloth. Oil paint began to be used during the later fifteenth century, and recent technical analysis has shown that a number of works attributed to Botticelli and his workshop are actually in a mixed medium of tempera and oil. Some paintings were transferred by later restorers from panel to canvas. The technical data given here is based on published sources.

Exhibition organized by
Gemäldegalerie – Staatliche Museen zu Berlin
and the Victoria and Albert Museum, London

First published by V&A Publishing, 2016
Victoria and Albert Museum
South Kensington
London SW7 2RL
www.vandapublishing.com

Distributed in North America by Abrams,
an imprint of Abrams

Hardback edition
ISBN 978 1 85177 870 6

Library of Congress Control Number
2015948682

10 9 8 7 6 5 4 3 2 1
2020 2019 2018 2017 2016

MIX
Paper from responsible sources
FSC® C008047

A catalogue record for this book is
available from the British Library.

COPY-EDITOR Kate Bell
DESIGNER Philip Lewis
INDEX Hilary Bird
TRANSLATION – GERMAN Caroline Waight
TRANSLATION – ITALIAN Paul Holberton

New photography by
the V&A Photographic Studio

Printed in China

FRONT COVER
Cat. 20 (detail)
ANDY WARHOL (1928–1987)
Details of Renaissance Paintings (Sandro Botticelli, Birth of Venus, 1482), 1984

BACK COVER AND PAGES 246–7
Cat. 170 (detail)
SANDRO BOTTICELLI (c.1445–1510)
and workshop (?)
Venus, 1490s

FRONTISPIECE
Cat. 5 (detail)
DAVID LACHAPELLE (b.1963)
Rebirth of Venus, 2009

PAGE 7
Cat. 68 (detail)
WALTER CRANE (1845–1915)
The Renaissance of Venus, 1877

PAGES 20–1
Cat. 101 (detail)
SANDRO BOTTICELLI (c.1445–1510)
Mystic Nativity, 1501

PAGE 330
Cat. 31 (detail)
TAMARA DE LEMPICKA (1898–1980)
Trompe-l'oeil Painting with a Botticelli, 1946

V&A Publishing
Supporting the world's leading
museum of art and design,
the Victoria and Albert
Museum, London